# THE

# THEOLOGICAL WORKS

OF

## ISAAC BARROW, D.D.

𝕮𝖆𝖒𝖇𝖗𝖎𝖉𝖌𝖊:

Drawn by M. Noble.   Engraved by W. Holl.

## ISAAC BARROW.

*From a Statue in the Ante-Chapel of Trinity College; presented by the Most Noble the Marquess of Lansdowne, executed by Matthew Noble, Esq.*

# THE
# THEOLOGICAL WORKS

OF

## ISAAC BARROW, D.D.

MASTER OF TRINITY COLLEGE, CAMBRIDGE.

IN NINE VOLUMES.

Edited for the Syndics of the University Press

BY

## THE REV. ALEXANDER NAPIER, M.A.

TRINITY COLLEGE, CAMBRIDGE, VICAR OF HOLKHAM, NORFOLK.

VOLUME I.

CONTAINING

FIFTEEN SERMONS ON SEVERAL OCCASIONS.

CAMBRIDGE:
AT THE UNIVERSITY PRESS.
M.DCCC.LIX.

# CONTENTS OF VOLUME I.

## SERMONS ON SEVERAL OCCASIONS.

|  | PAGE |
|---|---|
| PREFACE | ix |
| LIFE | xxxvii |
| ADDITIONS TO LIFE | lvii |
| TILLOTSON'S PREFACE | lxxxi |
| THE DEDICATION | lxxxvii |

### SERMON I.

THE DUTY AND REWARD OF BOUNTY TO THE POOR.

PSALM CXII. 9.

*He hath dispersed, he hath given to the poor; his righteousness endureth for ever; his horn shall be exalted with honour* . 3—96

### SERMON II.

UPON THE PASSION OF OUR BLESSED SAVIOUR.

PHILIPPIANS II. 8.

*And being found in fashion as a man, he humbled himself, and became obedient unto death, even the death of the cross* 97—150

### SERMON III.
(COLLATED.)

THE PLEASANTNESS OF RELIGION.

PROVERBS III. 17.

*Her ways are ways of pleasantness, and all her paths are peace* 151—173

### SERMON IV.
(COLLATED.)

THE PROFITABLENESS OF GODLINESS.

1 TIMOTHY IV. 8.

*But godliness is profitable for all things* . . . . 174—201

## SERMON V.
(COLLATED.)

### THE PROFITABLENESS OF GODLINESS.

#### 1 TIMOTHY IV. 8.

*But godliness is profitable for all things* . . . . 202—233

## SERMON VI.
(COLLATED, WITH ADDITIONS FROM MS.)

### THE REWARD OF HONOURING GOD.

#### 1 SAMUEL II. 30.

*For them that honour me I will honour* . . . . 234—268

## SERMON VII.
(COLLATED.)

### UPRIGHT WALKING SURE WALKING.

#### PROVERBS X. 9.

*He that walketh uprightly, walketh surely* . . . 269—292

## SERMON VIII.
(COLLATED.)

### OF THE DUTY OF PRAYER.

#### 1 THESSALONIANS V. 17.

*Pray without ceasing* . . . . . . 293—312

## SERMON IX.
(COLLATED.)

### OF THE DUTY OF PRAYER.

#### 1 THESSALONIANS V. 17.

*Pray without ceasing* . . . . . . 313—337

## SERMON X.
(COLLATED, WITH ADDITIONS FROM MS.)

### OF THE DUTY OF THANKSGIVING.

#### EPHESIANS V. 20.

*Giving thanks always for all things unto God* . . 338—366

## Contents.

### SERMON XI.
(COLLATED, WITH ADDITIONS FROM MS.)
#### OF THE DUTY OF THANKSGIVING.
##### EPHESIANS v. 20.

*Giving thanks always for all things unto God* . . . 367—403

### SERMON XII.
(COLLATED.)
#### ON THE KING'S HAPPY RETURN.
##### 1 TIMOTHY II. 1, 2.

*I exhort therefore, that, first of all, supplications, prayers, intercessions, and giving of thanks, be made for all men: for kings, and for all that are in authority* . . 404—443

### SERMON XIII.
(COLLATED.)
#### ON THE GUNPOWDER TREASON.
##### PSALM LXIV. 9, 10.

*And all men shall fear, and shall declare the work of God; for they shall wisely consider of his doing. The righteous shall be glad in the Lord, and shall trust in him; and all the upright in heart shall glory* . . . . 444—484

### SERMON XIV.
(COLLATED.)
#### A CONSECRATION SERMON.
##### PSALM CXXXII. 16.

*I will also clothe her priests with salvation* . . . 485—525

### SERMON XV.
#### NOT TO OFFEND IN WORD, AN EVIDENCE OF A HIGH PITCH OF VIRTUE.
##### JAMES III. 2.

*If any man offend not in word, the same is a perfect man* . 526—551

# ERRATA.

Vol. I.  p. 157, line 26, *for* "only" *read* "wholly"
— p. 187, line 11, *for* "the *All*" *read* "*The All*"
— p. 211, (note) *for* "κατέρθωμα" *read* "κατόρθωμα"

Vol. II.  p. 71, line 30, *for* "discoast" *read* "discost"

Vol. V.  p. 236, line 5, *for* "conversation" *read* "conservation"
— p. 378, line 26, *for* "wills" *read* "evils"

Vol. VI.  p. 499, *for* "Lucentemque globum terræ" *read* "Lunæ"

Vol. VIII.  p. 254, the number "16" belongs to the paragraph beginning "Furthermore"
— p. 411, the number "10" belongs to the paragraph beginning "Ambiguity of words"
— p. 493, line 17, *for* "Marcian" *read* "Marcion"
— p. 548, line 7, *for* "subsisted" *read* "substituted"
— p. 639, line 5, *for* "policy" *read* "polity"
— p. 735, line 9, *for* "policy" *read* "polity"

# PREFACE.

OF all the great Theologians of the Church of England, among whom he has ever held one of the highest places of honour, Barrow had himself published the least. Celebrated both at home and abroad by his Mathematical Works and Discoveries, he had given to the world, at the time of his death, two Sermons only, both printed by special request; the Spital Sermon, preached and published in the year 1671; the Guildhall Sermon, preached in the year 1677, the last sheets of which were passing through the press during his fatal illness. His great fame as a Theologian rests on the works published at intervals after his death, under the careful editorship of Archbishop Tillotson, then Dean of Canterbury; who, amidst his many engagements, and at the height of his celebrity as the great preacher of the Age, could yet devote years of severe labour to examining, and arranging, and finally publishing, the body of works which Barrow had left in manuscript. In the strict sense of the term, Tillotson was not conjoined with Abraham Hill by Barrow himself in the literary executorship of his unpublished works, as his biographer Birch seems to have imagined, misled by the authority of Dr Walter Pope, who in all matters connected with Barrow is most inaccurate: for Barrow died intestate. That Barrow on his death-bed gave

Tillotson permission to publish the Treatise of the Pope's Supremacy, we learn from Tillotson's preface prefixed to the first publication of that work; but neither there nor elsewhere does he inform us, whether or to what extent he had been directly entrusted by Barrow himself with the discretionary publication of his manuscript works. Barrow's papers, after his death, naturally reverted to his father; by whom, as we may infer from Ward's account[a], "they were entrusted to the care of Dr John Tillotson, and Abraham Hill, Esq., with power to print such of them as they thought proper."

The editorial labours of Tillotson were continued during a period of nearly ten years; as the following chronological list of the several publications of the works will shew:

1. Sermons preached on several occasions. 8vo. London, 1678. (Sermons III.—XIV. of the present Edition.)
2. Several Sermons against Evil Speaking. 8vo. London, 1678. (Sermons XV.—XXIV. of this Edition.)
3. On the Love of God and our Neighbour, in several Sermons. 8vo. London, 1680. (Sermons XXV.—XXXII. of this Edition.)

These, in old advertisements and in the curious document, which will be mentioned further on, are termed, The First, Second and Third Volumes of Barrow's Sermons.

4. A Treatise of the Pope's Supremacy. To which is added a Discourse concerning the Unity of the Church. 4to. 1680.

[a] *Lives of the Gresham Professors*, p. 164.

In the same year the Discourse on the Unity of the Church was published separately.

5. A Brief Exposition of the Lord's Prayer, and the Decalogue. To which is added the Doctrine of the Sacraments. 8vo. London, 1682.
6. The preceding form the first folio volume of the first collected edition, published with a Preface by Tillotson, in the year 1683.

The Second Volume, containing the Sermons on the Creed, followed in the course of the same year. The Third Volume, containing Sermons preached on several occasions in the year 1686. The Fourth Volume, containing the Opuscula and Poemata, in the year 1687.

7. About three years after Tillotson's death, two small volumes were published by Brabazon Aylmer:

A Defence of the Blessed Trinity. London, 1697. (Printed in Vol. IV. of this Edition, p. 492, et seqq.)
A Brief Exposition of the Creed. London, 1697. (Printed in Vol. VII. of this Edition.)

The above, together with some additions, of which an account will be given, form the Theological Works of Barrow, as printed in this Edition; which have been thus conveniently divided:

I. Sermons preached on Several Occasions. Vol. I.—IV.
II. Sermons and Expositions on the Creed, the Lord's Prayer, the Decalogue, the Sacraments. Vol. V.—VII.
III. The Treatise of the Papal Supremacy, and the Discourse on the Unity of the Church. Vol. VIII.

IV. The Opuscula and Poemata. Vol. IX. pp. 1—574.
V. The Works attributed to Barrow. Vol. IX. pp. 576—726.

I. The first four Volumes contain sixty-five Sermons, preached on several occasions, and at several places.

It would be interesting to discover when and where these Sermons were preached; but except in a few instances, neither the date nor the place of their delivery can positively be ascertained. According to entries on the several MSS., three were preached at St Mary's, before the University, and at these dates:

Sermon III., June 30, 1661.
Sermon X., Jan. 17, 1662.
Sermon XI., July 19, 1663.

The latter was also preached, with a new heading, which is given Vol. I. p. 367 (note), at Gray's Inn, Jan. 16, 1664. Sermon III. was, according to Tillotson[b], the first sermon he ever preached. The same authority[c] informs us, that the Restoration Sermon, and the Gunpowder Plot Sermon, were preached in the year of his Vice-Chancellorship, 1675—1676; both, it is probable, before the University. Sermon VI. was preached, according to an entry on the MS. before the Court, Aug. 1670; and as we learn from Evelyn's *Diary*[d], Sermon XXVII. was also delivered to the Household, April,

---

[b] Preface to the first volume of the Collected Works.
[c] Ibid.
[d] See the extract, Vol. II. p. 192 of this Edition (note).

1675. The Sermon which, for distinction's sake, has been allowed to retain its first title, The Defence of the Blessed Trinity (Vol. IX. p. 492, et seqq.) was preached on Trinity Sunday, 1663. This is the sum of the positive information we possess, at present, on these two points. Internal evidence leads us to conclude, that the greater part of them were Academical Discourses, preached either before the University, or in the Chapel of Trinity College.

The first and second Sermons, the only Theological works published, as before remarked, during Barrow's life, are in this Edition printed *verbatim* from the original Editions, published the former in 1671, the latter in 1677.

Of all the remaining sixty-three discourses, manuscript copies are not found in the Trinity College Collection, which, as we may infer from the following fact, was probably incomplete when it passed by purchase into the possession of the College. The Sermon on the text Acts iii. 18 (Vol. IV. p. 371, et seqq.) is contained in Vol. 366 of the Lansdowne MSS. of the British Museum, with this short note on the fly-leaf:—*Brabazon Aylmer the Bookseller gave me this sermon. Febry.* 15, 1694. *Joh. Strype.* May it not thence be probably concluded, that Aylmer, to whom the copyright of the works belonged, was in the habit of giving single sermons to admirers of Barrow, or to the curious in the collection of manuscripts? and may not this instance account for the absence of several sermons from the Trinity College MSS?

It was necessary, therefore, to distinguish the Sermons collated with the MSS. from those which are printed as in Tillotson's Edition: and this, accordingly, has been done in the Table of Contents prefixed to each Volume.

The additions and changes, however, which are found in this Edition, derived from the collation of the old text with the MS. draughts, require more special notice.

1 The MSS. shew, that Tillotson, startled and offended by the strange words so frequently used by Barrow, was in the habit of substituting for them more simple expressions; and that occasionally he erased passages. For instance: in Sermon III. Vol. I. p. 14, "the best actions, if they swell in life," has been substituted for "the best actions, if they protuberate in life;" in Sermon XXXVI. Vol. II. p. 556, the passage "Those foul monsters, our sins, I say, did all stand before him in their own horrid shape and ugly aggravations, thirsting to suck his blood, and gaping to devour him," was erased by Tillotson. And throughout, "divert" is substituted for "avoce;" "satiety" for "fastidiousness;" "improve" for "meliorate;" "flattering" for "adulatorous;" "gain" for "acquist;" "thrust" for "extrude;" "without ceasing" for "indesinently;" "heedless" for "oscitant;" "such-like" for "semblable;" "forsake" for "derelinquish;" "invent" for "extund;" "rebuke" for "increpate;" "cast down" for "detruded," &c. The process of erasure has occasionally been so mischievously effective as to defy

all attempts at restoration; but in every case, where the words or phrases could be deciphered, they have been scrupulously restored. Nor has it been thought necessary to indicate in the text where in each case this has been done: the plan which the Editor imposed on himself being simply to print Barrow's Works as Barrow wrote them and left them.

2 But Tillotson permitted himself to take further liberties. In his Edition, several of the Sermons are subdivided by him differently from the manuscript copies, and differently therefore from the present Edition. Thus Sermons XL. Vol. III. p. 196, et seqq.; XLIII. Vol. III. p. 300, et seqq.; XLVII. Vol. III. p. 418, et seqq.; XLIX. Vol. III. p. 490, et seqq.; LI. Vol. IV. p. 80, et seqq.; LII. Vol. IV. p. 114, et seqq., were each divided into two sermons; the manuscripts of these Sermons clearly shewing the divisions made in Tillotson's handwriting, as directions to the printer. Again, Sermon L. Vol. IV. p. 1 et seqq. was divided into four; and Sermon XXXVII. Vol. III. p. 1 et seqq. into five Sermons; the division in each case being, as in the above, in Tillotson's handwriting. The length, indeed, of these discourses, as they are now printed,—the former extending to 79, the latter to 126 pages,—is excessive; beyond the measure even of that age, which was patient of long sermons. Whether when preached, they were preached at length, may well be doubted; but they are so written, and in accordance with the plan followed in this Edition, they are so printed. Of Sermon L. it may be noted, there are no less than three MS. draughts;

one the copy used by the printer, and two others, of which one is more sketchy than the other; but in none of these copies is there any indication of the threefold division adopted by Tillotson.

3 But besides these restorations, new matter will be found in this Edition, derived from second, third, or even fourth draughts of the same Sermon. In opposition to the express statement of his friend and biographer, Abraham Hill, "that subjects which he thought most important to be considered for his own use, he cast into the method of Sermons for the benefit of others, and herein was so exact as to write some of them four or five times over," Dugald Stewart has hazarded the opinion[e], that Barrow's sermons bear the internal marks of extreme rapidity of composition, that they are to be regarded as the almost extemporaneous effusions of his pen; and to this alleged rapidity of composition, the same author ascribes the hasty and not altogether consistent opinions which he finds expressed on some important topics. It would not be just to Barrow to allow this view to pass unnoticed and unrefuted, when the evidence is at hand to prove, that his Sermons, and all his Works, were not more the productions of his fertile genius than the results of extraordinary elaboration. The MSS. abundantly confirm Hill's account. Revision and correction of the minutest character are their great characteristics. His method of composition may, indeed, be easily traced, by the help of the manuscripts, in its several progres-

[e] Prelim. Disser. to the Encycl. Brit. Seventh Ed. p. 45.

Facsimile of Dr Isaac Barrow's Hand-writing.

This is that, which in some measure I shall endeavour to performe; but first it may be demanded, what this facetiousnesse or jocularity the thing we speake of is, what this facetiousnesse imports; to which question I might answer as Democritus did to him that asked for the definition of a man; 'tis that which we all see, and know; any one better apprehends what it is by acquaintance, then I can informe him by description; it is indeed a thing so versatile, and multiforme, appearing in so many shapes, so many postures, so many garbs, so variously apprehended by severall eys, and judgments, that it seemeth as hard to settle a cleare & certaine notion thereof, as to make a portraict of Proteus, or to define the figure of the fleeting aire; sometimes it lyeth in pat allusion to a knowne story, or in seasonable application of a triviall sayings sometime it playeth in words and phrases, taking advantage from the ambiguity of their sense, or the affinity of their sound; sometimes it is wrapped in a dresse of humorous expression; or lurketh under an odd similitude; sometimes it is lodged in a sly question, in a smart answer, in a quirkish reason, in a shrewd intimation, and appearing not obvious (all pausing expectation) sometimes it is couched in a bold scheme of speech, in a startling metaphor, in a tart irony, in a lusty hyperbola; in acute non-senses; sometimes a mimicall looke, or gesture passes for it; sometimes an affected simplicity, sometimes a presumptuous bluntnesse giveth it both; sometimes it lyeth only from a lucky hitting up on somewhat strange, sometimes from a crafty wresting of obvious matter to the purpose; often it consisteth in one knows not what, and springeth up one can hardly tell how; its ways are unaccomptable, & inexplicable, as answerable to the numberlesse roovings of fancy, and windings of language; it is in short, a manner of speaking, out of the simple & plaine way, which by a pretty surprizing oddnesse in conceit or expression, doth affect, and amuse the fancy exciting in it some wonder, and breeding some delight thereto.

sive stages. The subject chosen, he seems to have drawn up a scheme of his intended argument; this he unfolded at some length under several heads, leaving spaces for new matter; this again, after receiving the amplifications, was written out fully; and this fuller draught was replaced by another fuller still, into which additions and improvements, even to the most minute verbal corrections, were carefully introduced; nor even then does it appear that he thought, that his discourse or argument, after passing through these different states, could ever attain the state of finality. It may be doubted, on the unquestionable authority of these remarkable Manuscripts, whether any author ever elaborated his matter or his style in a higher degree than Barrow. Inconsistencies of opinion, if such there be, may not therefore be attributed to his rapidity of composition.

It is not however to be inferred, that there are several MS. copies of each Sermon. Of many there is but one MS. draught; this is the case with the following: Vol. I. Sermons III. IV. V. XII.; Vol. II. Sermons XXV. XXVII. XXVIII. XXIX.; Vol. III. Sermons XLIV. XLV.; Vol. IV. Sermons LVII. LVIII. LIX. LX. LXIV. Some of these, as the originals distinctly shew, are in an unfinished, almost fragmentary state; specially Sermons XXIX. LI. LII. LVI. LVIII.—LX. which may be regarded as specimens of Barrow's Sermons in their middle stage of progress, awaiting amplification and further revision.

There are two MSS. more or less full of each of the

following Sermons: Vol. I. Sermons VIII. IX. X. XI. XIII. XIV.; Vol. II. Sermons XXXIV. XXXV.; Vol. III. Sermons XXXVII. XXXIX. XL. XLI. XLII. XLIII. XLVII. XLIX.; Vol. IV. LII. From these second draughts interesting additions are given in this Edition; the Table of Contents of each volume indicating where this is the case. Particular attention is directed to the new matter added to Sermon XXXIX. Vol. III. on the text, 1 Thess. v. 16, *Rejoice evermore*, one of Barrow's noblest compositions; and also to a considerable portion of a second Sermon on the same text, in a more complete state than some of the Sermons before mentioned, which is also printed for the first time. Of the remarkable Sermon XVI. Vol. II. p. 1 et seqq. which contains the famous description of *facetiousness*, though the copy used by the printer is wanting, there are two other draughts in the Trinity College Collection: from one of which the accompanying facsimile has been made, which, it will be observed, is not exactly the same as in the printed text. The other less perfect copy, presenting this passage in another less advanced stage, is a striking specimen of the elaborate care bestowed by Barrow on his compositions.

There are three draughts, more or less complete, of the following: Vol. I. Sermon VI.; Vol. III. Sermons XLVI. XLVIII.; Vol. IV. Sermon L.; and of Sermon XXXVI. Vol. II. there are no less than four MS. copies: one in an early state, the other three full; one of them, indeed, even fuller than the copy used by the Printer, from which additions have been given.

## Preface. xix

This short account of the MSS. of several of the Sermons contained in these Volumes will be found, it is believed, both interesting and instructive in itself, and may be viewed as a corroboration of Abraham Hill's statement alluded to above. He speaks, indeed, of Sermons written *four* or *five* times over: which may be only a vague mode of saying, that of some Sermons several copies existed; but in one case at least, we see, four copies exist of one Sermon; and in all probability he was strictly correct when he speaks even of five casts of the same discourse. Neither also will it be considered strange, if the Trinity College Collection does not furnish this confirmation, when the risks and dangers to which all manuscripts are more or less subject, are remembered.

4   Sermon LXIV. Vol. IV. found by the late Dr Parkinson among the papers of Dr Byrom, while engaged in preparing them for publication in the Chetham Society's Works, and by him restored to Trinity College, is printed in this Edition for the first time. On the text Coloss. iii. 2, Barrow wrote two, if not more, Sermons; of which the first is the one thus recovered; and the second that entitled, "The Defence of the Blessed Trinity," not included in Tillotson's Edition, but first separately published in the year 1697, by Brabazon Aylmer, who prefixed to it a short notice[f].

---

[f] "THE BOOKSELLER'S ADVERTISEMENT.

"This excellent and seasonable Discourse in Defence of the Blessed Trinity, the original copy whereof was found in the late learned Arch-

II. The more doctrinal portion of Barrow's Theological Works, consisting of thirty-three Sermons on the Creed, a Brief Exposition of the Creed, the Lord's Prayer, the Decalogue, and the Doctrine of the Sacraments, is contained in Vols. v.—vii. of this Edition. The Expository Sermons on the Creed, formed the second volume of Tillotson's Edition, published in 1683; the brief Exposition of the Lord's Prayer, the Decalogue, the Sacraments, published at first in the year 1682, was also included in the first volume of the same edition: the Brief Exposition on the Creed, though undoubtedly among the MSS. committed to Tillotson's care, was not printed in his Edition, but published after his death in the year 1697, by Brabazon Aylmer, with a preface[g] vouching for the genuineness of the MS.

Of these the Exposition on the Creed was the earliest composition. By a statute of Trinity College[h], a Fellow, as a condition of his being appointed "College Preacher," was bound to observe a certain *Exercise*, which consisted in delivering discourses on the Creed, the Lord's Prayer, the Decalogue, the Sacraments, the

bishop Tillotson's study after his decease; and being among many other duplicate Manuscripts of the late learned Dr Isaac Barrow's Sermons, was most certainly overlooked by His Grace upon publishing his Works; which might very easily be in so great a number; for Dr Barrow usually writ them several times over before he thought them finished.

"This had his last hand, as may be presumed, being very fair and perfect, and every word of his own writing, which, lest any should doubt of, I have preserved the copy in my own hands, where any one that pleases may see it, and be satisfied.—B. AYLMER."

[g] Prefixed to Vol. vii. of this Edition.

[h] See Dr Whewell's *Observations*, Vol. ix. p. xxxviii.

Power of the Keys. Barrow was engaged in the year 1669, as we learn from a letter of his to Collins[i], in preparing for this Exercise; and this shorter Exposition of the Creed, the Lord's Prayer, &c. was, no doubt in due season, read from time to time in the Chapel of Trinity College. Of the existence of one, and the greater portion of this *Exercise*, consisting of the Exposition of the Creed, Tillotson, it would appear, must, at one period at least of his long editorial labours, have been ignorant; for in his short preface[j], prefixed to the separate publication (1682) of a portion of it, viz. the Exposition of the Lord's Prayer, the Decalogue, &c., he writes: "It were to be wished, the Creed had also been explained by him in the same manner; but that he hath handled in a larger way in a great many excellent Discourses, upon the several articles of it. These Discourses will make a considerable Treatise, which will in due time be made public."

The Discourses thus alluded to,—which are, for the most part, amplifications of the arguments of the Exposition—were accordingly published in the year 1683. But while preparing them for publication we must infer, that the Exposition of the Creed fell under his notice;

[i] "—— my business hath hindered me, which hath been imposed on me by the College; 'tis to make Theological Discourses (as our statutes order) upon the chief points of the Catechism (the Creed, Decalogue, Lord's Prayer, Sacraments, &c.), which out of term so takes up my thoughts that I cannot easily apply them to any other matter. For I have that imperfection, as not to be able to draw my thoughts easily from one subject to another."—*Correspondence of Scientific Men of the Seventeenth Century*, Vol. II. p. 71. Oxford, 1841.

[j] Prefixed to Vol. VII. of this Edition.

for in one or two cases, which will be mentioned, he has used portions of it in order to supplement and connect the series of these Expository Discourses.

Manuscripts of nearly all these Sermons are among the Trinity College Collection, with which the printed copies have been carefully collated. Collation shews, that fewer liberties have been taken with these Sermons, which upon the whole were printed as they were written. Duplicates and triplicates of the MSS. of this series occur also less seldom: of Sermons II. XVI. Vol. v., XVIII. XXVI. Vol. VI., there are two, and of Sermons III. Vol. v., XXX. XXXII. Vol. VI., there are three MS. copies, more or less complete.

In this Edition, Sermon I. slightly differs at the beginning and the end from the same sermon in Tillotson's Edition.

The Introduction of Sermon X. is partly by Tillotson; partly a portion of the shorter Exposition.

The Introduction of Sermon XII. is taken *verbatim* from the Exposition; the MS. begins with the words, "The Creation of the world."

Sermon XXVI. Vol. VI. forms two Sermons, viz. XXV. XXVI. in Tillotson's Edition; the second being augmented by a long extract from the shorter Exposition, viz. that portion of it, with slight verbal alterations, which treats of the words of the Creed *under Pontius Pilate*, Vol. VII. p. 226—231.

The part of the Exposition, on the *Descent into Hell*, Tillotson transformed into Sermon XXVIII. of his Edition, prefixing to it the text, Acts ii. 27. In the present, this will be found in its proper place as a constituent portion of the Exposition, Vol. VII. 274—291.

Sermon XXIII. on the text, *The word was made flesh*, is now for the first time printed, from the MS. in the Trinity College Collection. The substance, indeed, of one part of it is contained in the Sermon which follows: which was, perhaps, the reason why Tillotson thought fit to exclude it from his Edition: but the larger portion of it is both new and important, and of such excellence as to justify the publication of the whole Sermon, notwithstanding the evil of repetition, which is found too commonly, though from their posthumous character unavoidably, in the works of Barrow.

The Exposition of the Creed, as published by Brabazon Aylmer, of all the works of Barrow most needed an Editor's care and revision; the punctuation was so bad as very often to obscure the sense, and the misplacement of whole passages rendered the arguments incoherent. A careful collation with the original MS. has brought order and clearness into this Treatise. Repetitions almost without end will be discovered, when the Exposition is compared with the Expository Sermons; but the Editor did not consider himself endued with the power of suppression; his duty being to reproduce with fidelity whatever had undoubted claims to be regarded as the production of Barrow.

III. The treatise of the Pope's Supremacy, and the Discourse on the Unity of the Church, with a short Appendix, form the Eighth Volume.

"This excellent and elaborate Treatise of the Pope's Supremacy," says Tillotson, "the learned author gave me particular permission to publish; with this modest character of it, that he hoped it was indifferent perfect, though not altogether as he intended it, if God had granted him longer life."

The manuscript of this Work,—which imperfect as the author deemed it, has ever been regarded as a monumental work, and is still the unsurpassed treatise on the subject—is not in the Trinity College Collection: nor is it known to exist elsewhere. Portions, indeed, of the arguments, in various forms, are found scattered in *six* out of the fifteen volumes composing that Collection; but in no case are these fragments altogether the same with the printed text. In one of these Volumes (bearing the press mark R. 10. 16, of Trinity College Library) there are two early draughts of the Introduction; neither nearly so full as the Text: Volume R. 10. 23 presents two early draughts, one somewhat fuller than the other, of the matter of the first Five of the Seven Suppositions into which the Treatise is divided; in both cases cast in the form of a Sermon on the text, Matt. x. 2; and in another Volume (R. 10. 24) there is a yet earlier, very imperfect cast of the same portion, also in the form of a Sermon on that text; Volume R. 10. 19 contains a sketch corresponding to the review of the causes concurring and contributing to the growth of the Papal power, Vol. VII. pp. 400—27; Volume R. 10. 20 has a number of rough notes, many of them erased by Barrow himself; Volume R. 10. 22, containing the largest body of MSS., shews, indeed, abundant proofs of Barrow's care and industry in preparation; but furnishes no continuous portion of the Treatise as printed. The MSS. of this volume shew Supposition VI. cast differently from that form in which Tillotson found and printed it. This account of the MSS. is rendered necessary by the somewhat ambiguous notice prefixed to the Edition of this Treatise published in the year 1851, by the Society for Promoting Christian Knowledge, which seems to profess collation with the original MS.; and it will also serve, in some faint way, to exhibit the vast labour, which in this, as in all his other works, Barrow bestowed on his compositions.

In this Edition, therefore, the Treatise of the Papal Supremacy, and the Discourse on the Unity of the Church, of which no MS. in any form exists, are reproduced, as far as the text is concerned, from the first Edition; with one exception, that the paragraphs 1. 2, pp. 292—295, misplaced in former Editions, are here restored to their proper place, in accordance with the suggestion of the Rev. Frederic Field, late Fellow of Trinity College, Cambridge, adopted for the first time in the Edition, above mentioned, of the Christian Knowledge Society.

The Appendix entitled "Some Observations on the Synod and Canons of Sardica," &c., was first printed in the Edition just alluded to; but these do not form a substantive treatise on the subject, as its Editor seems to imagine; but are merely sections, numbered xv, xvi. xvii, of a draught of Supposition vi. cast in a different form from that of the printed text: and these numbers shew, that the observations extend to three different points—*the Synod of Sardica; the transactions at Sirmium, Ancyra, &c.; the passages concerning Pope Liberius.*

Special pains and labour have been bestowed in verifying the very numerous quotations of this important Volume. Every passage cited has been regarded as incorrect, till proved otherwise by comparison with the original. In many cases, both in the Treatise of the Pope's Supremacy and the Discourse on the Unity of the Church, the passages referred to are merely indicated by Barrow; in this Edition they are given at full length, in all cases where they do not exceed the due proportions of a note. Quotations from the Councils of the Church, and from Epistles of Popes, which abound throughout the volume, have been verified not only in the Collection of Councils used by Barrow—that of Severinus Binius, the best and fullest known in Barrow's age—but also in the latest and most authoritative, Cardinal Mansi's. So that the Notes, verified as they have been, will be found to present a body of original passages, from the most various and authentic sources, bearing on the subject of the Papal Supremacy.

Prefixed to the Volume is an Analytical Summary of the contents of the Treatise of the Papal Supremacy, which, the Editor believes, will render its full and varied matter more accessible and available to the student.

IV. The *Opuscula*, consisting for the most part of Academical Exercises, and the Latin Poems, are printed in Vol. IX. of the present Edition. The disorder which prevailed in the arrangement of its contents, as well as the abundance of false readings found throughout it, seem to justify the inference, that this volume had not the benefit of Tillotson's careful supervision. In the absence of positive information we are led to conjecture, that as his father's partiality may have prompted the publication of everything which came from the hand of his celebrated son, so his eye alone watched the sheets as they passed through the press[k].

In this Edition a new arrangement has been adopted. The *Opuscula* and *Poemata* have been, as far

---

[k] The following original letter of his Father, Thomas Barrow, accompanied in all probability a presentation-copy of the Fourth Volume to Dr Montague, the Master of Trinity College.

"To Dr Montague.

"Though under the infirmity of eighty and seven years, yet I have a memory ready to acknowledge your kindness to my son, the author. When he was, as it were, a child, exposed on the banks of the river Cam, Trinity College (Regia Proles) afforded him the love of a parent and the instruction of a tutor. Whom you received a distressed child, you returned a man accomplished with so great a share of that learning and merit, for which your Society is renowned, as fitted him for the honour of being Master of such a College. But so it pleased God that death seized him absent from his beloved seat. Wherefore give me leave to fancy this posthumous work as it were his ghost wandering towards the accustomed place, and, as far as he and I can, attending on his dear friends.

"I am, &c.
"T. BARROW."

Philosophical Papers collected by Abraham Hill, British Museum Cat. 2903, art. 31.

as possible, placed in chronological order; the grosser blunders and false readings have been amended; and short explanatory notes have been added where deemed necessary. These improvements are almost exclusively due to Dr Whewell, the Master of Trinity College, who has also enriched this Edition with *Observations on Barrow's Academical Times, as illustrated in his Latin Works*, which have been prefixed to the Volume which furnished the illustrations.

The second Epistle to the Master and Fellows of Trinity College, pp. 120—127, sent by Barrow from Constantinople, in the year 1658, was not included in the first Edition; but was first published in Ray's *Philosophical Letters*, edited by W. Derham, London, 1718.

Some pieces, thrown in, in the strangest manner, among the *Opuscula* in the first Edition, have been in this excluded, as having no claim to appear among Barrow's works; these are, *The Superstition of the Turks; An English and Italian Glossary of certain Turkish Terms; A series of Turkish Proverbs;* and *A true Relation of the Designs managed by the old Queen Wife of Sultan Ahmed, written by Albert Bohovius*.

V. The Ninth Volume also contains two Dissertations, and some Sermons and Fragments attributed to Barrow; which formed the volume edited (1834) by the Rev. J. P. Lee, formerly Fellow of Trinity College, Cambridge, now Bishop of Manchester: of these some account must be given.

The two Dissertations are in this Edition placed

first. The MS. of the First entitled, *Relating to the Dissenters,* is contained in the volume of the Trinity College MSS. with the class mark, R. 10. 19; and is undoubtedly in Barrow's handwriting. The very cast of the MS. vouches for its authenticity; the arguments are arranged under several heads, and spaces are left for new matter—Barrow's mode of composing, as evinced in many instances throughout the MSS. The sentiments and the style also bear the stamp of Barrow's mind and manner. This Dissertation may therefore be regarded as a genuine fragment.

The Second entitled, *Whether the Damned after the Last Judgment shall live in Everlasting Torments or be utterly destroyed?* found in the same MS. volume as the preceding, is also in Barrow's handwriting; but it is strange the Editor of that volume failed to perceive its true character—viz. that it is a transcript made by Barrow, who in his own hand has written on the fly-leaf, *Tract. Anon. de Pœnis Infernalibus.* Another copy of the same Essay, found among the papers of Ward, the author of the *Lives of the Gresham Professors,* preserved in the British Museum, seems to settle the question of its authorship. In the Ward MS. it is entitled, *Arcanum Theologicum. A sceptical Discourse concerning the torments of Hell, by N. N.* [Mr White-foot *of Norwich*]. With this transcript, Barrow's has been compared; and the variations of the former from the latter are given in the portions printed within brackets. The collation of these two MSS. shews also, that Barrow had not entirely transcribed the treatise; though the redundant leaves of his MS. seem to imply that he intended to complete it. It is curious, that Tillotson's name was also connected with this Dissertation in a manner which still further identifies it. As Dean of St Paul's he preached, as his biographer Birch relates, before their Majesties, a Sermon on the Eternity of Hell Torments[1], which gave rise to a great clamour against him. "Dr Hickes," the Non-juror, Birch relates, "discharges all the venom of his pen against this *wretched sermon*, as he styles it, calling out upon the Convocation to censure it,...and suggesting, that the reasoning of it was borrowed from a manuscript discourse upon the same subject, still extant, which Dr Hickes owns he had never seen, written *by an old sceptic of Norwich*[m],"—by whom, as Birch adds, was meant the Reverend John Whitefoot, Rector of Heigham near Norwich. There can be little doubt, that the treatise here alluded to by Dr Hickes in his coarse invective against Tillotson, is the one of which Barrow made a transcript, and which, for obvious reasons, was circulated only in MS. among the Theologians of that Age. The Latin Notes appended to the Dissertation are Barrow's, which, as they express his opinions on this doctrinal question, furnish its claim to a place among his Works.

Of the Sermons attributed on doubtful grounds to Barrow, the first four, published by the Bishop of

---

[1] This Sermon is found in Vol. I. p. 321 et seqq. of Birch's Edition. London, 1752.

[m] Tillotson's Works, Vol. I. p. lxv. (ed. 1752).

Manchester and republished here, are contained in a small volume, hitherto included among the collection of Barrow's MSS., belonging to Trinity College. The only external evidence on which these have been assigned to Barrow, is this note written on the fly-leaf: "*Dr Isaac Barrow's Sermons, preached in 1676; preached by him. These Sermons are not in print.*" Mr Joseph Netherclift, to whose judgment this volume was submitted, thus reports on the character of the MS.: This is a curious volume, chiefly written in a large, half-print, round text hand, in Roman capitals, shewing the study and attention of one who has devoted much time and care to the simple mechanical art of writing, perhaps a schoolmaster or a clerk; the work of a copyist, and not of Barrow[n]. It is, indeed, inconceivable that Barrow, whose own handwriting is a model of neatness and clearness, should either himself have adopted, or have employed another to adopt a character which would torture the strongest powers of vision to read continuously. But the Sermons themselves are the conclusive argument against their genuineness. It would scarcely be possible to find in the whole range of sermon-literature any productions more utterly unlike Barrow's than the four printed from this MS. volume. Let the second of these be compared with two on the same text, Vol. II. Sermons XXV. XXVI., which are undoubtedly genuine, and that comparison alone will leave hardly a doubt on the mind, that the same person who wrote the latter, could not

[n] Abridged from Mr Netherclift's *MS. Report.*

have written the former Sermon, which in argument is so incoherent, and in style so full of feeble conceits and affectations. Is it possible,—to take one passage, which may be regarded as a specimen of the average matter and style of these Discourses,—that Barrow could have written and spoken this mere rant?

"*It was the express declaration of our Lord in the penitent woman's case. 'Her sins which are many are forgiven, for she loved much.' She wrote her love there with tears; she wrote and blotted out, and dropped another tear and wrote again. Solicitous lest she had expressed her affection too well, she would express it worse. She wiped her tears again, as if at once she would be liberal and sparing too, seeming to fear lest, if her stock of tears were spent too soon, she should not weep enough. She would not wipe her eyes, she only wiped her Saviour's feet, as if her hairs recalled those waters to their fountain head, that they might bubble there a second time*[o]," &c.

The Editor cannot but express his conviction, that it would be not less than an affront to Barrow's name, to attribute to him compositions of the character of these four Sermons.

The remaining Sermons and Fragments, printed in that volume, are from MSS. belonging to the University Library, Cambridge; the volume forming part of the Library of Bishop Moor, purchased at his death, and presented to the University by George I. The external evidence for their genuineness is even of a

[o] Vol. IX. pp. 622, 623.

more slender character than that which could be claimed for the former: "*Hic liber, ut ex manu videtur, fuit viri illustrissimi Isaaci Barrow.*" The identity of the handwriting of this MS. volume with Barrow's is, then, the sole ground upon which it has been assigned to him. Mr Netherclift, to whom this volume also has been submitted, is of opinion, that it presents specimens of the handwriting of at least two different persons, but none of Barrow's[p]. Neither does the external evidence, somewhat shattered if not overthrown by this opinion, receive any support from the intrinsic ability and power of these Sermons and Fragments; which, if they be free from the extravagances which not seldom occur in the former, are yet uniformly dull and common-place, and present not a single passage bearing the impress of that full, vigorous, massive style, which at once identifies the prose of Barrow, amid the prose of all the great writers of the Language.

These, indeed, may seem sound arguments for the exclusion of these sermons, but it has been deemed expedient to publish them; and readers may determine, according to their own judgment, the question of their authenticity.

---

Much inquiry and research have added but little to what was already known of Barrow from the brief Memoir by his friend Abraham Hill, prefixed to the first Edition of the Works. Three original letters, and

[p] Substance of Mr Netherclift's *Report*.

a few particulars regarding Barrow from unpublished sources, were the discouraging results and rewards of years of laborious search. On such a foundation the Editor considered it useless to attempt to construct a life of Barrow on a more extended scale; he has, therefore, contented himself with reprinting Abraham Hill's sketch, with such slight additional materials as he has been able to collect.

The General Index will be found, it is hoped, both full and exact for all purposes of reference.

The pleasing task now remains to the Editor of thanking those persons, who have aided him in his labours.

And first and specially he offers his grateful thanks to the Master and Senior Fellows of Trinity College, who have entrusted him for so long a period with the interesting collection of the Barrow MSS.; feeling, as he does, that whatever of novelty, or interest, or completeness, may be found in the present, above any preceding Edition, is to be attributed to the free use he has thus been permitted to make of them. To Dr Whewell, the Master of the College, the Editor is under many obligations for his active sympathy and support throughout the progress of the Edition.

In the laborious task of verifying the quotations, abounding in Barrow's works, from books both rare and bulky, the Editor has received much welcome assistance; particularly from Dr Corrie, the Master of Jesus College, who, with unfailing courtesy and kindness, has on many occasions rendered him great service; and also from the following gentlemen, J. B. Mayor, Esq., Fellow of St John's College, Cambridge, the Rev. James Tillard, Rector of Conington, and the Rev. Canon Collyer, Rector of Warham.

In the Appendix (O) to the Life by Abraham Hill, a document of some interest—viz. the legal agreement between Thomas Barrow and Brabazon Aylmer, negotiating the sale of the copyright of a portion of Barrow's works—has been supplied by the Rev. Henry John Rose, late Fellow of St John's College, Cambridge, Rector of Houghton Conquest, who has most kindly copied it from a volume of literary curiosities bequeathed to the Parish by a former Rector, Dr Zachary Gray. An additional reason might be found, if needed, for its publication, in this curious fact in Literary History, which it brings to light; viz. that within fifteen years after the sale of the copyright of Milton's *Paradise Lost* to Samuel Symons, the printer, for the sum of five pounds, no less than four hundred and seventy pounds were given for the copyright of the first folio Volume of Tillotson's Edition of Barrow's Works.

His thanks are due to the Rev. Joseph Romilly, Registrar of the University, who very opportunely prevented him from reproducing in the additions to the Life, the letter published as Barrow's, in the *Cambridge Portfolio*, Vol. I. p. 71, by a person signing ακοη; which letter was written in the name of the Vice-Chancellor Dr Some and the Senate to Robert Hare, on the 1st of May, 1591, i.e. about forty years before Barrow was born.

For the original letter of Barrow to Sir Joseph Williamson, printed in Appendix (K) to the Life, he is indebted to the Rev. Joseph Edleston, Fellow of Trinity College.

The Editor also desires to thank C. H. Cooper, Esq. Town Clerk of Cambridge, for many hints and directions in conducting his researches.

Nor can he omit gratefully to mention the valuable aid and kind offices he has so frequently received from C. J. Clay, Esq. the Manager of the Pitt Press, who combines, as in days of old, the functions of a printer with the accomplishments of a scholar.

ALEXANDER NAPIER.

# SOME ACCOUNT
## OF
# THE LIFE
## OF
# DR. ISAAC BARROW:

TO THE

REV. DR TILLOTSON, DEAN OF CANTERBURY.

---

SIR,

THE affection of friends, or interest of the bookseller, has made it usual to prefix the Life of an Author before his works; and sometimes it is a care very necessary to give him a high and excellent character, the better to protect his writings against that censoriousness and misconstruction to which all are subject. What Dr Barrow has left, do as little as any need such an advantage, standing firm on their own worth; nay, his Works may supply the want of a history of his life, if the reader take along with him this general remark, that his Sermons were the counterpart of his actions; therein he has drawn the true picture of himself, so that in them *being dead he yet speaketh*, or rather, *is spoken of*[a]. Yet we the readers do gladly entertain any hopes of seeing his example added to his doctrine, and we think we express some kind of gratitude for your reviewing, digesting, and publishing his Sermons, if we desire from you his Life too. His Sermons have cost you so much pains, as would have produced many more of your own; if now his Life should ask a farther part of your time, it were still

---

[a] Heb. xi. 4. marg.

promoting the same ends, the doctor's honour, and the public good. What memorials I can recollect, I here present you, that when you have refined this ore, it may be admitted as my offering toward his statue. What may be said would have had a stronger impression upon our passions, when they were moved upon the first news of so great a loss; or perhaps it were best to forbear till the publication of all his Works, when the reader will be farther prepared to admire him. But I proceed in the order of time, that the other particulars occurring to your memory, or suggested by other friends, may more readily find their proper place, and so give the better lustre to one another: and this I think the fitter to be observed, because the harmonious, regular, constant tenor of his life is the most admirable thing in it. For though a life full of variety, and even of contrariety, were more easy to be writ, and to most more pleasant to be read, it less deserves to be imitated.

Dr Isaac Barrow was the son of Mr Thomas Barrow, (a citizen of London of good reputation[b] yet living, brother to Isaac Barrow, late Lord Bishop of St Asaph[c],) son of Isaac Barrow, Esq. of Spiny Abbey in Cambridgeshire, (where he was a justice of peace for forty years,) son of Philip Barrogh, who has in print a Method of Physic, and had a brother, Isaac Barrow, doctor of physic, a benefactor to Trinity College, and there tutor to Robert Cecil, Earl of Salisbury, and Lord Treasurer[d].

He was born in London, October, 1630[e]: his mother was Ann, daughter of William Buggin, of North Cray in Kent, Esquire; whose tenderness he did not long enjoy, she dying when he was about four years old.

[b] Appendix (A).   [c] Appendix (B).
[d] Appendix (C).   [e] Appendix (D).

His first schooling was at the Charter-house for two or three years, when his greatest recreation was in such sports as brought on fighting among the boys: in his aftertime a very great courage remained, whereof many instances might be set down; yet he had perfectly subdued all inclination to quarrelling, but a negligence of his clothes did always continue with him. For his book, he minded it not; and his father had little hope of success in the profession of a scholar, to which he had designed him. Nay, there was then so little appearance of that comfort which his father afterward received from him, that he often solemnly wished, that if it pleased God to take away any of his children, it might be his son Isaac: so vain a thing is man's judgment, and our providence unfit to guide our own affairs.

Removing thence to Felsted in Essex, he quickly made so great a progress in learning and all things praiseworthy, that his master appointed him a little tutor to the Lord Viscount Fairfax, of Emely, in Ireland. While he stayed here, he was admitted in Peter-house, his uncle the Bishop's college[f], but when he removed to (and was fit for) the University of Cambridge, Feb. 1645, he was planted in Trinity College. His condition was very low, his father having suffered much in his estate on account of adhering to the king's cause; and being gone away from London to Oxford, his chief support at first was from the liberality of the famous and reverend Dr Hammond, to whose memory he paid his thanks in an excellent Epitaph, (among his Poems[g],) wherein he describes the doctor and himself too; for the most, and most noble, parts of the character do exactly agree to them both. Being now, as it were, without relations, he abused not the opportunity to negligence in his studies,

---

[f] Appendix (E).     [g] Works, Vol. IX. p. 540.

or licentiousness in his manners, but seasoned his tender years with the principles and the exercise of diligence, learning, and piety, the best preparatives for the succeeding varieties of life.

The young man continued such a royalist, that he would never take the Covenant; yet carrying himself with fairness, candour, and prudence, he gained the good-will of the chief governors of the University. One day Dr Hill, Master of the College[h], laying his hand on his head, said, *Thou art a good lad; 'tis pity thou art a cavalier:* and when in an Oration on the Gunpowder-Treason[i] he had so celebrated the former times, as to reflect much on the present, some Fellows were provoked to mové for his expulsion; but the Master silenced them with this; *Barrow is a better man than any of us.* Afterward, when "*the Engagement*[k]" was imposed, he subscribed it; but upon second thoughts, repenting of what he had done, he went back to the Commissioners, and declared his dissatisfaction, and got his name rased out of the list.

For the juniors, he was always ready to give them his help, and very freely; though for all the exercises he made for them in verse and prose he never received any recompense but one pair of gloves.

While he was yet a young scholar, his judgment was too great to rest satisfied with the shallow and superficial Physiology then commonly taught and received in the universities, wherewith students of meaner abilities contentedly took up: but he applied himself to the reading and considering the writings of the Lord Verulam[l], Monsieur Descartes[m],

[h] Appendix (F).
[i] Vol. IX. pp. 48—78. See also Dr Whewell's *Notice*, &c. pp. viii—ix.
[k] Appendix (G).
[l] Cf. *Cartes. Hypoth. Works*, Vol. IX. pp. 86, 96, 97.
[m] Cf. Vol. IX. p. 81, et seqq.; p. 441, et seqq.

Galileo, and other the great wits of the last age, who seemed to offer something more solid and substantial.

When the time came that he could be chosen Fellow of his College, Ann. Dom. 1649[n], he obtained by his merit; nothing else could recommend him who was accounted of the contrary party. After his election, finding the times not favourable to men of his opinion in the affairs of Church and State, to qualify him (as he then thought) to do most good, he designed the profession of physic, and for some years bent his studies that way, and particularly made a great progress in the knowledge of Anatomy, Botanics, and Chymistry. But afterward, upon deliberation with himself, and conference with his uncle, the late Lord Bishop of St Asaph, thinking that profession not well consistent with the oath he had taken when admitted Fellow, to make Divinity the end of his studies, he quitted Medicine, and applied himself chiefly to what his oath seemed to oblige him.

He was upon all opportunities so open and communicative, that many of his friends in that College (for out of it he had few acquaintance) can, and I hope some one will, report frequent instances of his calm temper in a factious time, his large charity in a mean estate, his facetious talk upon fit occasions, his indefatigable industry in various studies, his clear judgment on all arguments, his steady virtue in all difficulties, which they must often have observed, and can better describe.

Of his way of discourse I shall here note one thing, that, when his opinion was demanded, he did usually speak to the importance as well as to the truth of the question: this was

---

[n] He was elected scholar in 1647, and took his degree of B.A. in 1649. In 1652 he commenced M.A., and on the 12th of June in the following year he was incorporated in that degree at Oxford. *Ward. Wood.*

an excellent advantage, and to be met with in few men's conversation.

Tractare res multi norunt, æstimare pauci. CARDAN.

While he read Scaliger on Eusebius, he perceived the dependence of Chronology on Astronomy, which put him on the study of Ptolemy's *Almagest;* and finding that book and all Astronomy to depend on Geometry, he applied himself to Euclid's *Elements*, not satisfied till he had laid firm foundations; and so he made his first entry into the Mathematics, having the learned Mr John Ray[o] then for his *socius studiorum*, and always for his esteemed friend: he proceeded to the demonstration of the other ancient Mathematicians, and published his *Euclid* in a less form and a clearer method than any one had done before him: at the end of his demonstration of *Apollonius* he has writ, *April 14. May 16. Intra hæc temporis intervalla peractum hoc opus.* To so much diligence nothing was impossible: and in all his studies his way was not to leave off his design till he brought it to effect; only in the Arabic language he made an essay for a little while, and then deserted it. In the same place having also writ, *Labore et constantia*, he adds, *bonæ si conjungantur humilitati et subministrent charitati.* With these speculations the largeness of his mind could join poetry, to which he was always addicted, and very much valued that part thereof which consists of description; but the hyperboles of some modern Poets he as much slighted: for our Plays, he was an enemy to them, as a principal cause of the debauchery of these times; (the other causes he thought to be the French education and the ill examples

---

[o] Ward corroborates this statement, on the authority of Dr Worthington's *Letter to Mr Hartlib*, Febr. 14, 1654, *MS. Mr Worthington's*. This letter does not appear to be included in *The Diary and Correspondence of Dr Worthington*, edited for the Chetham Society by James Crossley, Esq.

of great persons;) for satires, he writ none; his wit was pure and peaceable.

When Dr Duport resigned the chair of Greek professor, he recommended this his pupil for his successor, who justified his tutor's opinion by an excellent performance of the probation exercise; but being thought inclined to Arminianism, he obtained it not: however, he always acknowledged the favour which Dr Whichcote shewed him on that, as on all occasions. The partiality of others against him in that affair some thought might help forward his desire to see foreign countries. I make no doubt, but that he, who in lesser occurrences did very judiciously consider all circumstances, had on good grounds made this resolution, and wish we now knew them; for the reasons and counsels of action would take off from the dryness of this narration, and more strongly recommend him to imitation.

To provide for his voyage, Ann. Dom. 1654, he sold his books, and went first into France[p]: at Paris he found his father attending the English court, and out of his small *viaticum* made him a seasonable present. He gave his College an account of his voyage thither, which will be found among his Poems[q]; and some further observations in a letter[r], which will shew his piercing judgment in political affairs, when he applied his thoughts that way.

After some months he went to Italy, and made a stay at Florence; where he had the favour, and neglected not the advantage, to peruse many books in the great Duke's Library, and ten thousand of his Medals, and discourse thereon with Mr Fitton, the fame of whose extraordinary abilities in that sort of learning had caused the Duke to invite him to the charge of that great treasury of antiquity[s].

[p] Appendix (H).     [q] Vol. IX. pp. 444—457.
[r] Vol. IX. pp. 111—119.
[s] Dr Pope understood this passage as if the Grand Duke (at Mr Fitton's recom-

Florence was too dear a place for him to remain in long[t]: his desire was to visit Rome, rather than any other place; but the plague then raging there, he took ship at Livorn, (Nov. 1657) for Smyrna[u], where he made himself most welcome to Consul Bretton[x], and the merchants; and so at Constantinople to Sir Thomas Bendish, the English Ambassador, and Sir Jonathan Daws, from whose civility he received many favours; and there ever after continued between them an intimate friendship.

As he could presently learn to play at all games, so he could accommodate his discourse to all capacities, that it should be grateful and profitable; he could argue a point without arrogance or passion to convince the learned, and could talk pleasantly to the entertainment of easier minds, yet still maintaining his own character, which had some such authority as is insinuated in these words of Cicero to Atticus (Ep. xx. l. 14): *Non te Bruti nostri vulticulus ab ista oratione deterret?*

At Constantinople[y], the see of St Chrysostom, he read over all the works of that Father, whom he much preferred before any of the others, and remained in Turkey above a

---

mendation) had offered Barrow the keepership of his Medals;—not the only instance of his inaccuracy.—Pope's *Life of Seth Ward*, p. 134.

[t] Ward (*Lives of Gresham Professors*, p. 159), on the authority of a MS. letter of Worthington to Hartlib, of the date Aug. 5, 1656, states that at Florence he was generously aided with means to prosecute his travels by Mr James Stock, a young merchant of London, to whom he dedicated his edition of Euclid's *Data*, published 1657; and whose premature death he deplores in the letter written from Constantinople printed for the first time in the Appendix (I).

[u] The incidents of the voyage from Leghorn to Constantinople are described in the *Iter Maritimum* (Vol. IX. pp. 458—480), sent from Constantinople to the Master and Fellows of Trinity.

[x] An elegy on his death is found among the *Poemata*, Vol. IX. pp. 511—514.

[y] From Constantinople he wrote another letter to the Master and Fellows of Trinity, (Vol. IX. 120—127), which was first published in Ray's *Philosophical Letters*, edited by Derham, Lond. 1718, and in which he gives an account of the political state of Turkey. With this letter he sent also the Poem *De Religione Turcica* (pp. 481—510).

year[z]. Returning thence to Venice, as soon as he was landed, the ship took fire, and with all the goods was burnt, but none of the people had any harm. He came thence home[a] through Germany and Holland; and some part of these travels and observations are also related in his Poems.

The term of time was now somewhat past, before which all Fellows of Trinity College are by the oath obliged to take upon them priestly orders, or quit the College: he had no rest in his mind till he got himself ordained[b], notwithstanding the times were then very unsettled, the Church of England at a very low ebb, and circumstances much altered from what they were when he took the oath, wherewith others satisfied themselves in the neglect of orders.

When the Church and State flourished upon the King's restoration, his friends expected great things for him who had suffered and deserved so much: yet nothing came; so that he was sensible enough to say, (which he has not left among his Poems,)

> Te magis optavit rediturum, Carole, nemo,
> Et nemo sensit te rediisse minus.

1660, he was without a competitor chosen[c] to the Greek Professorship in Cambridge; of which I can only say, that some friend (to himself I mean) thought fit to borrow, and never to restore those Lectures[d].

---

[z] Appendix (I).     [a] In 1659.

[b] By Brownrigg bishop of Exeter, and Master of Catherine Hall, who, after being ejected from his see by the parliament, lived in retirement at Sunning in Berkshire.

[c] His Inaugural Oration as Greek Professor is in Vol. IX. pp. 137—154.

[d] Ward (*Lives of Gresham Professors*, p. 160) states, on the authority of a MS. letter of Worthington to Hartlib, of the date Oct. 21, 1661, that at first he chose Sophocles as the subject of his Lectures; but afterwards selected Aristotle's *Rhetoric*. This appears also by the *Oratio Sarcasmica*, Vol. IX. p. 155.

July 16, 1662[e], he was chosen to the Geometry Lecture at Gresham College, vacant by the death of Mr Laurence Rook. Dr Wilkins, who, while Trinity College had the happiness of his Mastership, throughly observed and much esteemed him, and was always zealous to promote worthy men and generous designs, did interpose vigorously for his assistance, well knowing that few others could fill the place of such a predecessor; he not only discharged the duty incumbent on him, but supplied the absence of his learned colleague, Dr Pope, Astronomy Professor; and among other of his Lectures were divers of the Projections of the Sphere; which he lent out also, and many other papers we hear no more of. He so well answered all expectation, and performed what Dr Wilkins had undertaken for him, that when (1663[f]) Mr Lucas founded a Mathematic Lecture at Cambridge, the same good and constant friend recommended him to the executors, Mr Raworth and Mr Buck, who very readily conferred on him that employment: and the better to secure the end of so noble and useful a foundation, he took care that himself and successors should be bound to leave yearly to the University ten written Lectures; and those of his which have been, and others yet to be printed, will best give an account how well he acquitted himself of that service[g]. But after that learned piece *Geometricæ Lectiones* had been some while in the world, he had heard only of two persons that had read it through; these

---

[e] His Inaugural Lecture is given Vol. IX. pp. 170—188.

[f] On the twentieth of May in this same year he was elected a fellow of the Royal Society, in the first choice made by the council after their charter.—Ward, *Lives*, p. 160.

[g] His Prefatory Oration, spoken in the Mathematical School, March 14, 1664, is still extant, and may be seen pp. 189—212. On the 20th of May of the same year he resigned his Gresham Professorship. Ward (p. 161) intimates, that about this time also, he held for a short time the care of the Cottonian Library; which he resigned, desiring to settle at Cambridge.

two were Monsieur Slusius of Liege, and Mr Gregory of Scotland, two that might be reckoned instead of thousands: yet the little relish that such things met with did help to loosen him from these speculations, and the more engage his inclination to the study of Morality and Divinity, which had always been so predominant, that when he commented on Archimedes, he could not forbear to prefer and admire much more Suarez for his book *De Legibus:* and before his *Apollonius* I find written this divine ejaculation:

Ὁ Θεὸς γεωμετρεῖ.

*Tu autem, Domine, quantus es geometra? quum enim hæc scientia nullos terminos habeat; cum in sempiternum novorum theorematum inventioni locus relinquatur, etiam penes humanum ingenium, tu uno hæc omnia intuitu perspecta habes, absque catena consequentiarum, absque tædio demonstrationum. Ad cætera pene nihil facere potest intellectus noster; et tanquam brutorum phantasia videtur non nisi incerta quædam somniare, unde in iis quot sunt homines tot existunt fere sententiæ: in his conspiratur ab omnibus, in his humanum ingenium se posse aliquid, imo ingens aliquid et mirificum visum est, ut nihil magis mirum; quod enim in cæteris pene ineptum in hoc efficax, sedulum, prosperum, &c. Te igitur vel ex hac re amare gaudeo, te suspicor, atque illum diem desiderare suspiriis fortibus, in quo purgata mente et claro oculo non hæc solum omnia absque hac successiva et laboriosa imaginandi cura, verum multo plura et majora ex tua bonitate et immensissima sanctissimaque benignitate conspicere et scire concedetur, &c.*

The last kindness and honour he did to his Mathematic Chair was to resign it (1669) to so worthy a friend and successor as Mr Isaac Newton, fixing his resolution to apply himself entirely to divinity; and he took a course very convenient for his public person as a preacher, and his private as a Christian; for those subjects which he thought most important to be considered for his own use, he cast into the method of sermons for the benefit of others, and herein was so exact, as to write some of them four or five times over[h]. And now he was only a fellow of Trinity College, till my Lord Bishop of St Asaph gave him a small sinecure in Wales, and the Right Reverend Seth, Lord Bishop of Salisbury (who very much valued his conversation), a Prebend in his church; the advantages of both which he bestowed in a way of charity, and parted with them as soon as he was made Master of his College (1672[i]), he and his relations being by that time out of a necessitous condition: the patent for his Mastership being so drawn for him, as it had been for some others, with permission to marry, he caused to be altered, thinking it not agreeable with the statutes, from which he desired no dispensation.

He had hitherto possessed but a scanty estate, which yet was made easy to him by a contented mind, and not made a trouble by envy at more plentiful fortunes: he could in patience possess his soul when he had little else; and now with the same decency and moderation could maintain his character under the temptations of prosperity.

When the King advanced him to this dignity, he was pleased to say, *he had given it to the best scholar in England:* his Majesty had several times done him the honour to discourse him, and this preferment was not at all obtained by faction or flattery; it was the King's own act, though his desert made those of the greatest power forward to contribute

---

[h] See Preface, pp. xvi—xviii.

[i] In 1670 he was created Doctor of Divinity by mandate. His patent of the mastership bears date February 13, 1672: and he was admitted the 27th of the same month.

to it, particularly Gilbert, Lord Archbishop of Canterbury, and the Duke of Buckingham, then Chancellor of Cambridge, and formerly a member of Trinity College.

It were a disrespect to his College to doubt that where he had spent so much time, and obliged so many persons, he should not be most welcome: they knew, as his power increased, the effects of his goodness would do so too; and the Senior Fellows so well understood and esteemed him, that with good-will and joy they received a Master much younger than any of themselves.

Besides the particular assistance he gave to many in their study, he concerned himself in everything that was for the interest of his College[k]. Upon the single affair of building their Library, he writ out quires of paper, chiefly to those who had been of the College, first to engage them, and then to give them thanks, which he never omitted. These letters he esteemed not enough to keep copies of[l]; but by the generous returns they brought in, they appeared to be of no small value: and those gentlemen that please to send back their letters will deserve to be accounted further benefactors to the Library. He had always been a constant and early man at the Chapel, and now continued to do the same; and was therein encouraged, not only by his own devotion, but by the efficacy his example had upon many others of his College.

In this place, seated to his ease and satisfaction, a station wherein of all others in the world he could have been most useful, and which he meant not to make use of as a step to ascend higher, he abated nothing of his studies; he yielded the day to his public business, and took from his morning sleep many hours, to increase his stock of Sermons, and write

[k] Appendix (K).      [l] Appendix (L).

his Treatise of the Pope's Supremacy. He understood Popery both at home and abroad; he had narrowly observed it militant in England, triumphant in Italy, disguised in France; and had earlier apprehensions than most others of the approaching danger, and would have appeared with the forwardest in a needful time: for his engagement in that case, and his place in your friendship, I would (with the leave of the most worthy Dean of St Paul's, his highly respected friend) call him another Dr Stillingfleet.

But so it pleased God, that being invited to preach the Passion-Sermon, April 13, 1677, at Guildhall Chapel, (and it was the second Sermon for which he received a pecuniary recompence,) he never preached but once more, falling sick of a fever: such a distemper he had once or twice before, otherwise of a constant health: this fatally prevailed against the skill and diligence of many physicians his good friends[m].

I think not myself competent to give an account of his life, much less of his sickness and death: if great grief had not forced silence, you, Sir, his dearest and most worthy friend, had perpetuated the remarkables of that sad scene, in a Funeral Sermon.

Our passions, which have hitherto been kept within the banks, should now be permitted to overflow, and they even expect to be moved by a breath of eloquence; but that is not my talent. In short, his death was suitable to his life; not this imperfect, slight life, as I relate it, but that admirable, heroic, divine life which he lived.

He died the 4th of May, 1677; and had it not been too inconvenient to carry him to Cambridge, then wit and eloquence had paid their tribute for the honour he has done them.

[m] Appendix (M).

Now he is laid in Westminster Abbey, with a monument erected by the contribution of his friends, a piece of gratitude not usual in this age, and a respect peculiar to him among all the glories of that Church. I wish they would (as I have adventured) bring in their symbols toward the history of his life: there are many which long before me had the advantage of his conversation, and could offer more judicious observations, and in a style fit to speak of Dr Barrow.

In the Epitaph[n], Dr Mapletoft[o], his much esteemed friend, doth truly describe him. His picture was never made from the life, and the effigies on his tomb doth little resemble him. He was in person of the lesser size, and lean; of extraordinary strength, of a fair and calm complexion, a thin skin, very sensible of the cold; his eyes grey, clear, and somewhat short-sighted; his hair of a light auburn, very fine and curling. He is well represented by the figure of Marcus Brutus on his denarii; and I will transfer hither what is said of that great man.

> Virtue was thy life's centre, and from thence
> Did silently and constantly dispense
> The gentle vigorous influence
> To all the wide and fair circumference.   COWLEY.

The estate he left was books; those he bought, so well chosen as to be sold for more than they cost; and those he made, whereof a catalogue is annexed[p]: and it were not improper to give a further account of his works than to name them: beside their number, variety, method, style, fulness, and usefulness, I might thence draw many proofs to confirm what I have before endeavoured to say to his advantage, and many more important reflections will be obvious to you, than to such a reader as I am. I will only take leave to say, that for his little piece of *The Unity of the Church*, he

[n] Printed at the conclusion of this Memoir.
[o] Appendix (N).        [p] Appendix (O).

has better deserved of the Church and Religion, than many who make a greater figure in Ecclesiastic History and Politics. But such remarks will be more fitly placed in what we expect from his learned friends of the University. And to them I must also refer for the observables at the taking his several Degrees, and discharging the office of Vice-Chancellor.

There are beside other particulars, which are grateful to talk over among friends, not so proper perhaps to appear in a public writing. For instance, one morning going out of a friend's house, before a huge and fierce mastiff was chained up, (as he used to be all day,) the dog flew at him; and he had that present courage to take the dog by the throat, and after much struggling bore him to the ground, and held him there, till the people could rise and part them, without any other hurt than the straining of his hands, which he felt some days after.

Some would excuse me for noting that he seemed intemperate in the love of fruit; but it was to him physic, as well as food; and he thought, that if fruit kill hundreds in autumn, it preserves thousands: and he was very free too in the use of tobacco, believing it did help to regulate his thinking.

I did at first mention the uniformity and constant tenor of his life, and proceeding on have noted several particulars of very different nature. I therefore explain myself thus; that he was always one by his exact conformity to the rule in a virtuous and prudent conversation; he steered by the same compass to the same port, when the storms forced him to shift his sails. His fortune did in some occasions partake of the unsettledness of the times wherein he lived; and to fit himself for the several works he was to do, he entered upon studies of several kinds, whereby he could not totally devote himself to one; which would have been more for the public benefit, according to his own opinion, which was, that general scholars did more please themselves, but they who prosecuted particular subjects did more service to others.

Being thus engaged with variety of men and studies, his mind became stored with a wonderful plenty of words wherewith to express himself; and it happened that sometime he let slip a word not commonly used, which upon reflection he would doubtless have altered, for it was not out of affectation.

But his life were a subject requiring other kind of discourses; and as he that acts another man, doth also act himself; so he that would give an account of the excellent qualities in Dr Barrow, would have a fair field wherein to display his own. Another Camerarius or Gassendus would make another Life of Melanchthon, or Piereskius. What I am doing will not prevent them; I shall be well satisfied with my unskilfulness, if I provoke them to take the argument into better hands[q].

All I have said, or can say, is far short of the idea which Dr Barrow's friends have formed of him, and that character under which he ought to appear to them who knew him not. Beside all the defects on my part, he had in himself this disadvantage of wanting foils to augment his lustre, and low places to give eminence to his heights; such virtues as his, contentment in all conditions, candour in doubtful cases, moderation among differing parties, knowledge without ostentation, are subjects fitter for praise than narrative.

If I could hear of an accusation, that I might vindicate our friend's fame, it would take off from the flatness of my expression; or a well-managed faction, under the name of zeal, for or against the Church, would shew well in story; but I have no shadows to set off my piece. I have laid together a

[q] Appendix (P).

few sticks for the funeral-fire, dry bones which can make but a skeleton, till some other hand lay on the flesh and sinews, and cause them to live and move. You will encourage others by pardoning me, which I promise myself from that goodness wherewith Dr Barrow and you have used to accept the small service with the great devotion of,

Sir,

Your obedient and humble servant,

A[BRAHAM] H[ILL].

LONDON, *April* 10, 1683.

# ISAACUS BARROW,

### S. T. P. REGI CAROLO II. A SACRIS.

Vir prope divinus, et vere magnus, si quid magni habent
Pietas, probitas, fides, summa eruditio, par modestia,
Mores sanctissimi undequaque, et suavissimi.
Geometriæ Professor Londini Greshamensis,
Græcæ Linguæ, et Matheseos apud Cantabrigienses suos,
Cathedras omnes, ecclesiam, gentem ornavit.
Collegium S. S. Trinitatis Præses illustravit,
Jactis bibliothecæ vere regiæ fundamentis auxit.
Opes, honores, et universum vitæ ambitum,
Ad majora natus, non contempsit, sed reliquit seculo.
Deum, quem a teneris coluit, cum primis imitatus est,
Paucissimis egendo, benefaciendo quam plurimis,
Etiam posteris, quibus vel mortuus concionari non desinit.
Cætera, et pene majora ex scriptis peti possunt.

Abi, Lector, et æmulare.

Obiit IV. die Maii, ann. Dom. MDCLXXVII.

Ætat. suæ XLVII.

Monumentum hoc Amici posuere.

# APPENDIX.

### (A.)

"His father's name was Thomas, a reputable citizen of London, and Linen-draper to King Charles the First, to whose interests he adhered, following him first to Oxford, and after his execrable murder, he went to his son Charles the Second, then in exile, there with great patience expecting the King's restoration, which at last happened, when 'twas almost despaired of. I remember Mr Abraham Cowley, who also was beyond sea with the King, told me, At our first coming into France, we expected every post would bring us news of our being recalled; but having been frustrated for so many years, we could not believe it when the happy news arrived."—*Pope's Life of Seth, Bishop of Salisbury*, p. 130.

In the year 1687, when the Fourth Volume of Barrow's Works was published, Thomas Barrow, his father, was then 87 years old; (see the original letter, General Preface, p. xxvii. (note)). How long after this he lived has not been ascertained.

### (B.)

"Isaac Barrow, Bishop of St Asaph, was educated at Peter-House, Cambridge, of which he was elected a Fellow. From his Fellowship he was however ejected by the Presbyterians, in the year 1643, the year of his nephew's entry as Pensioner of the College; and went to Oxford, the head-quarters of the royalist party, where he continued to remain till the surrender of the garrison to the forces of the Parliament. After which he shifted his residence from place to place, sharing the depressed condition of the Royalist Clergy, till the Restoration, when he was restored to his Fellowship at Peter-House, and also elected a Fellow of Eton. In the year 1663 he was made Bishop of Man; his consecration Sermon being preached in Henry the Seventh's Chapel, July 4, 1663, by his celebrated nephew. (Barrow's *Works*, Vol. I. Serm. XIV. pp. 484—525.) He died at Shrewsbury, June 24th, 1680, in the 67th year of his age; and on the first of July following was buried in the Cathedral of St Asaph. His epitaph, which is singular, occasioned some scandal. Over his grave was laid a large flat stone, and another over that supported by pedestals; on the last of which is the following inscription engraven: 'Exuviæ Isaaci Asaphensis Episcopi, in manum Domini depositæ, in spem lætæ resurrectionis per sola Christi merita. Obiit dictus reverendus Pater festo Divi Johannis Baptistæ, anno Domini 1680, ætatis 67, et translationis suæ undecimo.' On the lower stone which is even with the ground, is the following inscription, composed by the Bishop himself, and engraven on a brass plate fastened on the stone: *Exuviæ Isaaci Asaphensis Episcopi, in manum Domini depositæ, in spem lætæ resurrectionis per sola Christi merita. O vos transeuntes in Domum Domini, Domum orationis, orate pro conservo vestro, ut inveniat misericordiam in Die Domini.*" (Abridged from the *Biograph. Britann.*, Vol. I. pp. 628, 629. 2nd Edition, 1778).

## (C.)

## GENEALOGICAL TABLE OF THE BARROW FAMILY.

**HENRY BARROW.**

John Barrow, of ——, in the county of Suffolk. = Katherine, daughter of —— Mitson, of Linton, in Cambridgeshire.

Philip Barrow, of Gaseby, in Suffolk.

Isaac Barrow, M.D., a benefactor to Trinity College, in Cambridge, where he was sometime fellow. = Agnes, relict of George Cotton, of Benefield, in Essex, Esq., married anno 1570, and buried Jan. 7, 1589, at All-hallows, in Cambridge.

Isaac Barrow, baptised at Gaseby, anno 1563, was = Rebecca, daughter of Richard Yound, of Bartelinnsted, in Hertfordshire.
of Farnham, in Norfolk, anno 1609, afterwards Spinway Abbey, at Wickham, in Cambridgeshire, Esq. about forty years. J.P.

Thomas Barrow, citizen of London. = Anne, daughter of Will. Buggen, of North Cray, in Kent, married at St James', Clerkenwell, in County of Middlesex, May 29, 1628.

Isaac Barrow, D.D. Bishop of St Asaph.

ISAAC BARROW, D.D.

*From the Worthington MSS. in the Brit. Mus. 6209, fol. 92.*

### (D.)

"Mr Hill fixes Dr Barrow's birth in the month of October, A.D. 1630. But I hope he will not be offended if I dissent from him, both as to the year and month, and produce reason for so doing; 'tis this: I have often heard Dr Barrow say, that he was born on the 29th of February; and if he said true, it could not be either in October or in 1630, that not being a leap-year. I would not have asserted this, merely upon the credit of my memory, had it been any other day of any other month, it being told me so long since, had I not this remarkable circumstance to confirm it: he used to say, 'it is in one respect the best day in the year to be born upon, for it afforded me this advantage over my fellow-collegiates, who used to keep feasts on their birth-day; I was treated by them once every year, and I entertained them once in four years, when February had nine and twenty days.'"—*Pope's Life,* p. 129.

### (E.)

Hill's date is, however, more probably correct. In the Register of Peter-House he is thus entered as a pensioner: "Isaacus Barrow Londiniensis in Hospitii Suttononiani Schola educatus, annum agens decimum quartum examinatus et approbatus admissus est Pensionarius, ad primam mensam scholar. sub tutela M$^r$ Barrow, Dec. 15, 1643."

*Baker's MS. notes to Ward,* Brit. Mus. Cat. 6209, fol. 13.

This date of his admission is, as Ward[1] remarks, "wholly inconsistent with Dr Pope's account (of the date of his birth), the two nearest leap-years to 1630 being 1628 and 1632, which will fix his admission at Peter-House, either to the twelfth or sixteenth year of his age, whereas the words of the College Register are very express, *annum agens decimum quartum.*" Moreover, Barrow's epitaph, written during his father's life, and probably from information derived from him, tells us, he was in his 47th year, when he died in 1677.

### (F.)

"Dr Hill was appointed Master of the College during the Parliamentary visitation of the University at the end of the year 1643 by the Earl of Manchester. The test was *The Covenant.* Dr Comber, the Master, together with Dr Row, the Vice-Master, Herbert Thorn-

---

[1] *Lives of Gresham Professors,* p. 157.

dike, and John Sherman, two contributors to the Polyglott Bible, Cowley the poet, with others, refused, and were ejected."

*Memoir of Dr Duport*, Camb. Mus. Critic. Vol. II. p. 679.

(G.)

On the 2nd of January, 1649, an Act for subscribing the late Engagement was read a third time and past. The preamble runs to this effect:

"Whereas divers disaffected persons do, by sundry ways and means, oppose and endeavour to undermine the Peace of the Nation under this present Government; so that unless special care be taken a new War is likely to break forth. For the preventing thereof and also for the better uniting of this Nation, as well against all Invasions from abroad, as the common Enemy at home; and to the end that those who receive Benefit and Protection from this present Government, may give assurance of their living quietly and peaceably under the same, and that they will neither directly nor indirectly contrive or practice any Thing to the Disturbance thereof:"

Then it proceeds to enact, "That all men whatsoever, of the age of 18 years or upwards, shall take and subscribe the following Engagement: *I do declare and promise that I will be true and faithful to the Commonwealth of England, as it is now established, without a King or a House of Lords.*"

The subscriptions were to be taken before the Commissioners of the Great Seal, or Justices of the Peace for the County, City, or Town where the persons lived; their names and places of abode to be entered in a Book by the Justices of the Peace, to be by them certified to the respective Sheriffs, and delivered to the Clerk of the Parliament, whenever so required by the House or the Council of State.

The time for subscribing, originally fixed for 20th of February, was afterwards extended to the 10th of April following.

*Parl. Hist.* (old Ed.) Vol. XIX. 243.

This Act was repealed 1653 by an ordinance of Cromwell and his Council. See *Scobell's Collection of Acts and Ordinances*, p. 277.

(H.)

Some interesting particulars, never before published, regarding Barrow, at this period of his life, are found in letters from Dr Worthington to Mr Samuel Hartlib, *Brit. Mus. Cat.* 6209, fol. 92, 93.

14 *Febr.* 1654: "This afternoon I met with Mr Barrow, (it could not be sooner). He expressed himself obliged to you for the books you sent. I could not strictly tie him to any particular day of returning the Mathematical papers, because I would not have him straitened in his thoughts; but desired him to return them sometime next week. His book is in the stationer's hands, but I think the stationer is not able to print it. Something he gives Mr Barrow for the copy. For the gentleman is (as many scholars who tumble not in the world) not rich; but one of admirable parts, and had no body to instruct him in Mathematics, but *proprio Marte* he conquered all difficulties in the most crabbed authors. He is but a young man. He looks upon his performance upon Euclid as a small business to him. He knows Tacquet, &c. He is versed in Physick, an excellent Grecian. That which he would most direct himself to (if he had encouragement to subsist) is Natural Philosophy, and in that we are most at a loss. He is a free philosopher. He talks of travelling, and but that he is well-principled and fixed, the Jesuits would not stick at any thing to give (get?) a person of such accomplishments. He is a serious and modest person, not vain-glorious and supercilious. It is one of the greatest afflictions to my spirit, when I consider that there are such accomplished persons here and there in the world, and yet because they could not be base or servile, nor scramble for the things of the world, are too often without those helps, which might enable them to do good, as to the advancement of knowledge, &c. There are divers rich men, to whom to part with £20 or £40 a year would not be more hurtful than a flea-bite, that yet cannot be possessed with any noble thoughts. I have sometimes thought, that God would not honour some men because of their wickedness (though speciously covered) to be instrumental to so high and noble ends with their wealth. That persons of true worth and such as might be eminently serviceable, should want what may in a modest way encourage them, is to me an affliction, and makes me the more sensible of the vanity and slightness of the world."

*Eidem.* 2 *March*, 1654.

"Mr Barrow is preparing for his travels. He thinks of beginning his long journey this month. He is therefore straitened in time as to the account and perusal of Mercator's paper. He would do nothing slightly. He hath scarce time to publish something which he intends to add upon Euclid, which he is now upon, and would despatch. I wish he could be encouraged to stay."

# Appendix.　　　　　　　　　　　　　lxiii

### (I.)

Letter of Barrow to Mr THOMAS HILL, of London, written from Constantinople. (Brit. Mus. Letters belonging to the Hill Family. *Add. Cat.* 5488, fol. 125.)

*Pera of Constantinople,*
*December* 17, 1658.

SIR,

Receiving your very kind lines, I find myself overcharged with courtesy by a gentleman, whom I had not formerly the happiness to know, but now think myself familiarly acquainted with, at least with the better part of him, his soule, by that glimpse of goodness and ingenuity, which you have been pleased to discover unto me; and in all reason I am the more to esteem your kindness, by how much I am conscious how small invitation my desert could afford it, for as to the merits you are pleased to acknowledge, I have so little right to them, that I am far from pretending any. However I gladly and thankfully embrace your tender of friendship, which I shall esteem as a great honour, and being otherwise unable shall correspond in hearty affection and due observance; as in the same to your brother, if that gentleman please also to condescend to so mean an acquaintance.

The news of Mr Stock's death must of necessity be very ungrateful to me, being thereby deprived of a friend to whom I was infinitely obliged, to manifest my thankful respects to whom I should have been desirous of long life, though I had otherwise hated it; beside that it hath plunged me into some straits and quite splitt (*sic*) all my desires of future travel, whereof his assistance would have been the main support. For the medails you have bought I am glad they are fallen into such hands, not despairing hereafter by your favour to obtaine a sight of them, and so renew that little knowledge in them, which that worthy gentleman Mr Fitton was pleased to impart; in which I have made no progresse here, not meeting with any matter to exercise upon, nor indeed much enquiring after any, my slender accommodation not enabling me to purchase any curiosities, had they presented themselves. Mr Fitton's paper *Of the value and rarity of medails*, I should have been glad, if I could have communicated to you; but I find myself robbed of them by a presumptuous negligence; for thinking, that Mr Catcher (Batcher?) had with others his books and papers, left that with me, upon search I found my hope disappointed, and that unhappy Fate had with him ravished it also from me, wherein I accompted to have lost a treasure. I should advise you to pursue your designed acquisition of it, thinking it worth your enjoying, and wish you success therein. I hope I may now be untacked from this place to which by a fatal chain I seem to have been tyed (as Prometheus to his rock), and that this day (if the Winds and Turks give leave) I shall take my passage in the *Rose and Crown* bound for Venice, but touching at Smyrna. From Venice my intention is, after very small stay, to haste through Germany and Holland into England, so that I doubt, whether I shall see and salute you in Italy, though I should be very desirous of that content, that I might have opportunity more fully to express my sense of your kindness, to receive your commands, and know if in any thing I could be subservient to your virtuous inclinations. In the meanwhile be pleased to accept of the hearty thanks and earnest good wishes of

Your most humble Servant

Isaac Barrow.

Be pleased to present my humble service to Dr Duncan, Dr Kirton, Mr Beale.

I should be glad to hear of any circumstances or particularities concerning Mr Stock's death.

*Endorsed*, Isaac Barrow, *Constantinople, Dec.*

Received March 1658.

### (K.)

His firmness in supporting the interests of the College is shewn by the letter (now first published), replying to an application for dispensing with certain statutes, probably exemption from taking orders, (State Paper Office, Domestic 1674. N°. 102).

To the Right Hon. Sir Joseph Williamson, Principal Secretary of State at Whitehall.

Right Hon$^{ble}$.

I should be heartily glad of opportunity to serve you in anything, and even ambitious to deserve your favour; I have also much respect and kindnesse for Mr Aston, and should be ready to doe him any good that I could; but I am so unhappy, that in the busynesse about which you did me the honour to write unto me, I am not capable to yeeld any furtherance, it being, as I apprehend, inconsistent with my obligations: nor can I thinke this course adviseable for Mr Aston to take, upon divers accompts; I doe not see how he can well seeke, accept, or make use of a dispensation in this case, it seeming expressely repugnant to severall clauses in the oath which he tooke when he was admitted to be Fellow: upon which if he will seriously reflect, it is likely he will not satisfy himself to accept such a dispensation, and certainly others will be dissatisfyed in his doing it. The thing itselfe will be distastfull, as anything can be, to the College, nor I am confident will the Senior Fellows passe it without an addresse to prevent its effect, by reason of the pernicious consequence thereof; it being visible, that there will never want divers young men (if not most) who will be very urgent and make great friends to follow such an example; which would tend not only to the destroying succession, but to the subversion of the maine designe of our foundation, which is to breed Divines: and probably to a greater inconveniense, obvious enough, than any of these: whence never hitherto, as I conceive, any such thing hath been attempted, at least with successe. Indeed a Fellowship with us is now so poore, that I cannot thinke it worth holding by an ingenuous person upon terms lyable to so much scruple, to so much clamour and obloquy, to the inducing so much prejudice on a society, the welfare whereof he is obliged to tender. This is my sense, expressed with that freedome, which I hope your goodnesse will pardon to, Right Hon.,

Your devoted servant,<br>
ISAAC BARROW.

*Trin. Coll., Dec.* 3, 1674.

(L.)

The following Letter to a person unknown, the only one of those alluded to by Abraham Hill, which the Editor has succeeded in recovering, is printed in Hartshorne's *Book-Rarities of the University of Cambridge*, p. 274. It were, indeed, greatly to be wished that the statement of the Author of that volume was correct—"that the numerous letters of Barrow, written on this occasion, and displaying a wonderful fertility of invention in varying the manner of address to the persons whom he solicited, were preserved."

" SIR,

"We presume both humbly and earnestly to recommend unto you, the great enterprise of a new and magnificent Library, proportioned to the grandeur of the Founder, and not inferior to any other buildings of the College; to which we, of the present Society, were obliged by the great munificence and favour of the Right Reverend father in God, John, late Lord Bishop of Lichfield and Coventry, our most worthy benefactor, who hath given us (by the building of the new Hostell) fifty pounds a year for ever, to be expended in buying books, which our present Library (being already filled, and overburdened with those we have) can neither contain nor support. Now, Sir, that relation you have to our College, of which you were sometime a worthy member, the candour of your nature, and that great esteeme you have alwayes held for learning, do encourage us to this address; especially considering, that the benefit and convenience of this building, will not only redound to us, but will also add great ornament to the whole University, some honour to the Nation, and may be very advantageous and useful, to such of your own posterity, who shall come to this place, where you had some part of your happy education. We have been able by our own private contribution, and by the assistance of many noble benefactors and friends, to erect and cover this building. And, though it be a structure of vast expense, even of twelve or fourteen thousand pounds; yet by God's permission, we have a fair prospect of finishing it, and of joining the south side of Neville's Court unto it, to make up the Square; if generous persons inclined to pious and laudable works (amongst whom we are ambitious to place yourself) will afford us their aid and assistance. We, therefore, most earnestly beg your favour, and supply in this great concern; being very desirous to have your name in the catalogue of our Benefactors, which lest we should seem to doubt of, we add no more, but only wish you all happinesse, and remain,

"Sir,

"Your most humble servants,

"The Master and Senior Fellows

"Of Trinity College in Cambridge."

Harleian MSS. Brit. Mus. 7001.

The circumstances attending the building of the Library are thus described in the *Lives of the Norths*, Vol. III. pp. 364—366. Lond. 1826:

"When the doctor (Dr North) entered upon the Mastership of Trinity College, the building of the Great Library, begun by his immediate predecessor Dr Barrow, was advanced about three quarters of the height of the outward wall; and the doctor most heartily and diligently applied his best forces towards carrying it on; besides his own contributions, most of his friends and relations, upon his encouragement, became benefactors; the particulars whereof will appear in the accounts of this noble structure. The tradition of this undertaking runs thus. They say that Dr Barrow pressed the heads of the university to build a theatre; it being a profanation and scandal that the speeches should be had in the university Church, and that also be deformed with scaffolds, and defiled with rude crowds and outcries. This matter was formally considered at a council of the heads; and arguments of difficulty, and want of supplies, went strong against it. Dr Barrow assured them that if they made a sorry building, they might fail of contributions; but if they made it very magnificent and stately, and at least, exceeding that at Oxford, all gentlemen of their interest would generously contribute; it being what they desired, and little less than required of them; and money would not be wanted as the buildings went up, and occasion called for it. But sage caution prevailed, and the matter, at that time, was wholly laid aside. Dr Barrow was piqued at this pusillanimity, and declared that he would go straight to his college, and lay out the foundations of a building to enlarge his back court, and close it with a stately library, which should be more magnificent and costly than what he had proposed to them, and doubted not but, upon the interest of his college, in a short time to bring it to perfection. And he was as good as his word; for that very afternoon he, with his gardeners and servants, staked out the very foundation upon which the building now stands; and Dr North saw the finishing of it, except the classes, which were forward, but not done, in his time; and divers benefactions came in upon that account; wherewith, and the liberal supply from the college, the whole is rendered complete; and the admirable disposition and proportion on the inside is such as touches the very soul of any one who first sees it."

See also the account of the building of Trinity Library in the Memoir of Dr James Duport.—*Cam. Mus. Crit.* Vol. II. p. 696; and Barrow's *V. C. Speech*, Vol. IX. p. 222, and the *Notice of his Life*, p. xlii.

(M.)

"The good Dr Barrow ended his days in London, in a prebend's house that had a little stair to it out of the cloisters, which made him call it a man's nest, and I presume it is so called at this day. The master's disease was a high fever. It had been his custom, contracted when (upon the fund of a travelling fellowship) he was at Constantinople, in all his maladies, to cure himself with opium; and being very ill (probably) he augmented his dose, and so inflamed his fever, and at the same time obstructed the crisis: for he was as a man knocked down, and had the eyes of one distracted. Our doctor (the Hon. and Rev. Dr John North) seeing him so, was struck with horror; for he, that knew him so well in his best health, could best distinguish; and when he left him, he concluded he should see him no more alive; and so it proved."

*Lives of the Norths* (1826), Vol. III. pp. 319, 320.

Pope (*Life of Seth Ward*, p. 166) gives this account of his illness.

"Some few days after he came again to Knightsbridge, and sate down to dinner, but I observed he did not eat: whereupon I asked him, how it was with him: he answered, that he had a slight indisposition hanging upon him, with which he had struggled two or three days, and that he hoped by fasting and *opium* to get it off, as he had removed another, and more dangerous sickness, at Constantinople some years before."

And this of the place of his death, differing from North's statement, which is most probably correct, Dr Walter Pope not being addicted to accuracy.

"He died *May* 4, *Anno Dom.* 1677, in the 47th year of his age, in mean lodgings, at a Sadler's near Charing-Cross, an old, low, ill-built house, which he had used for several years: For though his condition was much bettered by his obtaining the Mastership of Trinity College, yet that had no bad influence upon his morals, he still continued the same humble person, and could not be prevailed upon to take more reputable lodgings." Pope, *Life of Seth Ward*, p. 167. See the *Notice of his Life*, Vol. IX.

### (N.)

Among a number of letters from eminent men to Dr Mapletoft published from the papers in the possession of his grandson, Mr Mapletoft, "an eminent surgeon at Chertsey," in the *European Magazine* (1789), Vol. XIV., XV., are the following from Barrow to Mapletoft:

# *Appendix.*

### I.

SIR,

I hope you are not so much mistaken as to suppose you left in my custody that parcell of bookes which I bought of you, and for which I pay'd sixe pounds to Mr. Pulleyn, according to your order (the chiefe of which were Curio his dictionary, a Plato, an imperfect Plutarch of Stephens' print). Of any other bookes of your's left with me I have neither knowledge, memory, nor footstep, excepting that I doubt of three small bookes, which are a Virgil and a Horace with Indexes, and a Greeke testament, Gr. and Lat. in octavo (with some notes of Beza); all which being out of keltred, I did cause to be rebinded; and the latter did give away to a friend, who beginninge to study Greeke, desired such a one: the two former I have reason to thinke that I payed for, but being not thoroughly sure, I had rather wrong myselfe than you, and therefore, if you thinke good, shall be ready to make them good to you, altho' I confesse I am not willing to part with the bookes themselves. The other I find not in the catalogue of my bookes, and therefore believe that either you left it with me, or that it was overseen when you removed your hampires and things from my chamber, and I shall make it good to you in specie or value, as you shall choose, although when I disposed of it I did not esteeme it worth consideration. I am certaine you left no other booke in my custody. I have parted with few bookes, though I have been so unwise as to purchase very many; and therefore if ever I had any of your bookes I am confident it is with me still, and if your memory doe suggest any that you doubt of, I will search for it; but I am well assured there never was any such. There are but few remaining here, I take it, of your old acquaintance; those that are, Mr Hawkins especially, and Mr Pulleyn, receive kindly and returne your salutes. So doth

Your assured friend and humble servant,
ISAAC BARROW.

TRIN. COLL. 11 *March*, 64.

### II.

HON. AND DEARE SIR,

Mr Eusden intends, God willing, for London in the coach next Wednesday; will present himselfe to you, and obey your directions. He shall have recommendations from our Master to the Bishop of London for receiving orders immediately. He is satisfied with the conditions you propound, and will performe what shall be required of him. I am very confident you shall find him so in all respects to answer your desires, that you shall not have cause to repent of the obligation you have putt upon him and me. Please to forward the enclosed, and to present my hearty love and service to Mr Pomeroy; it was my unhappinesse not to see him at London. Thanking you (more than I can expresse) for all your kindnesse,

       I am, most affectionately
         and obligedly your's,
           IS. BARROW.

TRIN. COLL. *March* 12, 69.

Mr Eusden desired me to present his humble service to you.

### III.

DEARE DOCT<sup>R</sup>,

> "Grates persolvere dignas
> Non opis est nostræ, Doctor; nec quicquid ubique est
> Gentis Dardaniæ."

You have driven me to my snipps, being *de proprio* insolvent of fit expression. In sooth I never find any regrett for my being a poore meane fellow, but when upon such occasions I consider myselfe to be hopelesse of getting opportunity to shew my willingnesse to be thankfull for such courtesyes. I could now even wish myselfe an Arch-Bishop, yea, almost a Pope, that I might have preferments for you to dispose of to your friends, beside that I might be able to keepe a company of crazy knaves, and allow good fees for them. My comfort is yet, although you can receive none from me, yet that you will have some requitall in the satisfaction of having obliged your friends, this good college, that worthy wag whom I doubt not but you will find in respects correspondent to your best expectations, and to the character thought due to his deserts from

      Your ever most affectionate friend
        and thankful servant,
          IS. BARROW.

I shall offer (though I know nothing) upon a kind of intimation in your's to wish you much joy; for surely you could not leave such a Lord but for a very good Lady.

TRIN. COLL. *Jun.* 23, 1669.

### IV.

DEAR DOCTOR,

  I should have satisfyed myselfe with an — or all conveyance of my devoirs to you by some of our tribe of Gad, but that I have an earnest sute to you, which cannot be well prosecuted otherwise then by the penn, and with which I dare not trust any scholer errant of them all: in few, 'tis this; that you would use your best endeavours (which, *ni fallor*, will be very powerfull) towards excusing me to the gentle Bellerophon of these, for not attending on him to Oxford; whither a fond desire of seeing a certain Doctor hath drawne him (I think that Doctor be a conjuror) after a laudable resolution he had taken of staying at home with me and following his studyes. I will not furnish you with rational weapons wherewith to worke this feat of absolution, as not pretending to the wisdome of doing all things with good reason; only I advise you to employ thereon this one to my seeming, plausible discourse, that I must surely have some great reason, or (which is tantamount) a very strong humour on my side, since the instigation of a person (of your acquaintance) to whom you know I beare a great respect, and to whom I am much obliged, could not stirr me (though I must confess to you it did somewhat stagger me): you may also, if you please, tell him that I designe to compensate for this neglect by some signall demonstration, if industry can find out or good fortune shall offer an opportunity. But I forgot where you are, and how this, that, and t'other gentleman are lugging you hither and thither. I pray comply with them all as you can; only first let your sweet hands be kissed by

Your most affectionate
and obliged servant,
ISAAC BARROW.

Much gratulation and service to your Reverend à sacris Dr Blomer.

TRIN. COLL. *July* 6, 1669.

V.

DEARE SIR,

I did, upon my returne hither from the waters in Oxfordshire, find your very obliging letter (for which I thanke you) together with my papers; and since you invite me to trouble you, I will not, having a fitt occasion, be so rude as to wave your curtesy. Needing mony here, and having a small sume, about 8 or 9 pounds due to me from a pupill, brother to the gentleman to whom the enclosed is directed, and who I suppose will pay it if you please to ask for it and receive it, I request of you that favour, and that you receiving it will cause it to be returned to me hither, supposing you know how to do it. Mr Richards promised me to pay it to Dr. Tillotson: if he should have done so, I request you to ask that good Doctor for it, unto whom (by the way) having commended the trouble of obstetricating to my Spittal Sermon, I have requested him to present 4 to you for your self and friends. I shall, God willing, about the end of this month (if our master the King doe not ramble another way) come to serve him and thanke you. In the meane time, I am

      Your most obliged and
        affectionate servant,
          ISAAC BARROW.

My service I pray to Mr Firman and all our friends, particularly to Dr Blomer and his lady, who I hope is well.

SARUM, *July* 1, 1671.

## VI.

DEARE SIR,

 I doe heartily bid you welcome home, and receive your kind salutations most thankfully; but your project concerning Mr Davies I cannot admitt. Trinity College is, God be thanked, in peace, (I wish all Christendome were so well) and it is my duty, if I can, to keep uproars thence. I do wish Mr Davyes heartily well, and would doe him any good I could; but this I conceive neither faisible nor fitting. We shall discourse more of it when I come. I have severely admonished T. H. for his clownish poltronry in not daring to encountre the gentle Monsieur that saluted him from Blois. Pardon my grave avocations that I deferr saying more till I shall be so happy to see you. In the meane time (with my best wishes and services to you, your good madam Comfortable, the good Doctor, and all our friends) I am,    Deare Sir,
    Your most affectionate friend
      and obliged servant,
        IS. BARROW.

TRIN. COLL. *July* 19, 1673.

## VII.

DEARE SIR,

 Could I be assured of so good successe, I should willingly undergoe many a rapp; and saying no more, I heartily thank you for straining so farr to shew your kindnesse to the College, taking it for a great obligation to myselfe. I doe also thank you for your good offices to Sir John Holman, whose favourable answer will much encourage our businesse; for indeed we doe need some positive declarers *per verba de præsenti*, to suppresse the infidelity and timorousnesse of some, even among us, who feare that after we have begunn we shall be deserted. Our design is indeed great, but no greater then the

place doth require, and then we may well accomplish, if we doe not faile of that assistance, which, upon a very reasonable and moderate computation, we may hope. I have forborn answering to your case about practise, because Mr Crouch hath been every day expected to come hither; but hearing now that it will be a weeke before he cometh, I shall tell you what I think, according to the best information and judgment I can make. We do here generally concurr in opinion that every Doctor of Physick, by taking his degree, hath a license to practise every where in the kingdome; that this hath ever been a privilege of the University; and that whoever attempteth to infringe this privilege doth violate his obligations and oaths to the University. Besides oure custome and possession of this right, we have this evident proofe that the University hath ever exercised a power of licensing sufficient persons to practise universally, according to the forme which I send you inclosed; which licence no Doctor of Physick taketh, because his taking the degree doth involve it. And whereas in this Parliament the College (or some of them) did putt in to get an Act for appropriating practise to themselves, the University privilege being objected against them, they were forced to desist: their seeking of an Act did argue their want of present right; and their disappointment, that they had small colour for it. Wherefore if they intend (by application to his Majesty, or otherwise) to endeavour any thing in prejudice to our privilege, you may be assured that I shall do my best to defend it, and I doubt not to find a concurrence of the whole University in opposing them; wherein we may be confident of our Chancellour's helpe, whom we have found ready upon all occasions to protect our rights. I have no more to say at present, but that I am
Your most affectionate friend
and servant,
ISAAC BARROW.

TRIN. COLL. *Feb.* 8, 1675.


(O.)

Of the Theological Works a full account has been given in the General Preface. His published Mathematical Works are these:

1. Euclidis Elementa. 8vo. Cantab. 1655 et sæpius.
2. Euclidis Data. 8vo. Cantab. 1657. This was subjoined to the *Elements* in some following Editions.

3 Lectiones Opticæ, XVIII. 4to. Lond. 1669.
4 Lectiones Geometricæ, XIII. 4to. Lond. 1670.
5 Archimedis Opera, Apollonii Conicorum Libri IV., Theodosii Sphærica, methodo nova illustrata et succinte demonstrata. 4to. Lond. 1675.

After his death, these were published:

1 Lectio, in qua Theoremata Archimedis de Sphæra et Cylindro, per methodum indivisibilium investigata ac breviter demonstrata, exhibentur. 12mo. Lond. 1678.
2 Mathematicæ Lectiones, habitæ in Scholis publicis Academiæ Cantabrigiensis. An. Dom. 1664—6. 8vo. Lond. 1683.

From Ward's *Lives of Gresham Professors*, p. 165: where also a list is given of his unpublished Mathematical Works.

---

## COPY OF THE AGREEMENT BETWEEN THOMAS BARROW AND BRABAZON AYLMER.

KNOW all men by these Presents that I Thomas Barrow Sen$^r$ of the Citty of Westminster Gentleman: Administrator to the Late Reverend and Learned D$^r$ Isaac Barrow Master of Trinity Colledge in Cambridge dec$^d$ my beloved Son. For and in Consideration of the sum of ffour hundred pounds of lawful mony of England to me in hand paid By Brabazon Aylmer Cittizen and Stationer of London before the sealing and delivery hereof, the receipt whereof I do hereby acknowledge. Have granted bargain'd, sold, assigned, and set over, and by these presents do grant, bargain, sell, assign, and set over unto the said Brabazon Aylmer, his Executors Administrators and Assigns: The several Bookes and Coppys of Bookes, Sermons, or Discourses hereunder writ: with all the prefaces Epistles Titles Tables, &c. writ or preached by the said D$^r$ Isaac Barrow dec$^d$ and since his death published by the Reverend D$^r$ Tillotson Dean of Canterbury, as follows, viz.

1 Inprimis. A Sermon of Bounty to the Poor: preached at the Spittal in Easter week Ano Domi 1671. By the said D$^r$ Isaac Barrow.

2 Item. A Sermon on the Passion of our blessed Saviour: preached at Guild-hall Chappel on Good ffriday the 13$^{th}$ day of April 1677. By D$^r$ Isaac Barrow.

3 Item. A Vollum, containing Twelve Sermons; preached upon several occasions. By the said D$^r$ Isaac Barrow; comonly called the first vol: and printed first in the year 1678.

4 Item. A Vollum containing Te Sermons Entituled Severall Sermons against Evil-speaking. By Dr Isaac Barrow; comonly called the Second Volum: and printed first in the year 1678.

5 Item. A vollum containing Eight Sermons; comonly called the third Volum and entituled Of the Love of God and our neighbour in several Sermons: By the said D$^r$ Isaac Barrow: and printed first in the year 1680.

6 Item. And also a Larg Booke in Quarto entituled: A treatise of the Popes Supremacy. To which is added a Discourse concerning the Unity of the Church. By the said D$^r$ Isaac Barrow. And printed first in the year 1680.

To have and to hold the said Coppys, Bookes, Sermons, or Discourses Unto him the said Brabazon Aylmer his Execut$^{rs}$ Administrat$^{rs}$ and Assignes to his and their own proper use and behoofe for ever.

And I the said Thomas Barrow do hereby covenant promise and grant to and with the said Brabazon Aylmer his execut$^{rs}$ Administrat$^{rs}$ and Assignes by these presents that I the said Thomas Barrow now have in myselfe good right, full power and lawful authority; to grant bargain and sell the said Bookes and Coppys to him the said Brabazon Aylmer, in maner aforesaid.

And I do hereby desire and authorize the Master and Wardens of the Company of Staconers London to permit and suffer the said Bookes or Coppys &c. to be entered in their Register to him the said Brabazon Aylmer as his own proper Bookes & Coppys. Wittness my hand and seale the ... fourth day of April Ano Domi one thousand six hundred and eighty one (1681).

THOMAS BARROW.

*Wittness,*
—— HARUEY,
MARY POWELL (Servant to —— HARVEY).

N. B. The whole of the above in the original is on one page, on the back of which is written the following:

I do hereby acknowledge to have Rec$^d$ of Brabazon Aylmer the sum off seaventy pounds; being in full payment for another Booke of D$^r$ Isaac Barrows Intitled A Briefe Exposition of the Lords Prayer And the Decalogue; to which is added the Doctrine of the Sacraments in 8$^{vo}$: } £70

Wittness my hand this 13$^{th}$ day of October 1681.

THOMAS BARROW.

*Wittness,*
   WALTER JURIN.
   WILLIAM WILKINS.

### (P.)

Abraham Hill's wish was never gratified. No *Camerarius* or *Gassendus* among Barrow's friends arose to write his biography. A very insufficient substitute appeared in the person of Dr Walter Pope, who devoted a portion of the volume containing his *Life of Seth Ward, Bishop of Salisbury* (Lond. 1697), to notices of Barrow and other distinguished men of that age. From these the following are reproduced,—with the caution, that absolute veracity seems not to have adorned their Author's character.

#### I.

"As soon as Dr Ward was made Bishop of Exeter, he procured for his old friend Dr Wilkins, the rectory of St Laurence-Jewry, who was then destitute of any place, the reason whereof I have given before: he being minister there, and forced by some indisposition to keep his chamber, desired Dr Barrow to give him a Sermon the next Sunday, which he readily consented to do. Accordingly, at the time appointed, he came, with an aspect pale and meagre, and unpromising, slovenly and carelessly dressed, his collar unbuttoned, his hair uncombed, &c. Thus accoutred, he mounts the pulpit, begins his prayer, which, whether he did read or not, I cannot positively assert, or deny: immediately all the congregation was in an uproar, as if the church were falling, and they scampering to save their lives, each shifting for himself with great precipitation; there was such a noise of pattens of serving-maids, and ordinary women, and of unlocking of pews, and cracking of seats, caused by the younger sort hastily climbing over them, that I confess, I thought all the congregation were mad: but the good Doctor seeming not to take notice of this disturbance proceeds, names his text, and preached his Sermon, to two or three gathered, or rather left together, of which number, as it fortunately happened, Mr Baxter, that eminent Non-conformist was one, who afterwards gave Dr Wilkins a visit, and commended the Sermon to that degree, that he said, he never heard a better Discourse. There was also amongst those who stayed out the Sermon, a certain young man, who thus accosted Dr Barrow as he came down from the pulpit: 'Sir, be not dismayed, for I assure you, 'twas a good Sermon.' By his age and dress he seemed to be an apprentice, or, at the best, a foreman of a shop, but we never heard more of him. I asked the Doctor what he thought, when he saw the congregation running away from him? 'I thought,' said he, 'they did not like me, or my Sermon, and I have no reason to be angry with them for that.' 'But what was your opinion,' said I, ' of the apprentice?' 'I take him,' replied he, ' to be a very civil person, and if I could meet with him I'd present him with a bottle of wine.' There were then in that parish a company of formal, grave, and wealthy citizens, who having been many years under famous ministers, as Dr Wilkins, Bishop Ward, Bishop Reynolds, Mr Vines, &c. had a great opinion of their skill in divinity, and their ability to judge of the goodness and badness of Sermons. Many of these came in a body to Dr Wilkins, to expostulate with him, why he suffered such an ignorant, scandalous fellow, meaning Dr Barrow, to have the use of his pulpit. I cannot precisely tell whether it was the same day, or some time after in that week, but I am certain it happened to be when Mr Baxter was with Dr Wilkins. They came, as I said before, in full cry, saying, they wondered he should permit such a man to preach before them, who looked like a starved cavalier, who had been long sequestered, and out of his living for delinquency, and came up to London to beg, now the King was restored; and much more to this purpose. He let them run their selves out of breath, when they had done speaking, and expected an humble submissive answer, he replied to them in this manner: 'The person you thus despise, I assure you, is a pious man, an eminent scholar, and an excellent preacher: for the truth of the last, I appeal to Mr Baxter here present, who heard the Sermon you so vilify: I am sure you believe Mr Baxter is a competent judge, and will pronounce according to truth;' then turning to him, 'Pray, Sir,' said he, 'do me the favour to declare your opinion concerning the Sermon now in controversy, which you heard at our church the last Sunday.' Then did Mr Baxter very candidly give the Sermon the praise it deserved, nay more, he said, 'That Dr Barrow preached so well, that he could willingly have been his auditor all day long.' When they heard Mr Baxter give him this high encomium, they were pricked in their hearts, and all of them became ashamed, confounded, and speechless; for, though they had a good opinion of their selves, yet they durst not pretend to be equal to Mr Baxter; but at length, after some pause, they all, one after another, confessed, they did not hear one word of the Sermon, but were carried to mislike it by his unpromising garb and mien, the reading of his prayer, and the going away of the congregation; for they would not by any means have it thought, if they had heard the Sermon, they should not have concurred with the judgment of Mr Baxter. After their shame was a little over, they earnestly desired Dr Wilkins to procure Dr Barrow to preach again, engaging their selves to make him amends, by bringing to his Sermon their wives and children, man-servants and maid-servants, in a word, their whole families, and to enjoin them not to leave the church till the blessing was pronounced. Dr Wilkins promised them to use his utmost endeavour for their satisfaction, and accordingly solicited Dr Barrow to appear once more upon that stage, but all in vain, for he would not by any persuasions be prevailed upon to comply with the request of such conceited, hypocritical coxcombs."

## II.

"He had one fault more, if it deserves that name, he was generally too long in his Sermons; and now I have spoken as ill of him as the worst of his enemies could, if ever he had any: he did not consider, that men cannot be attentive to any discourse of above an hour's duration, and hardly so long, and that therefore even in plays, which are discourses made for diversion, and more agreeable to mankind, there are frequent pauses and music betwixt the acts, that the spectators may rise from their seats and refresh their weary bodies and minds. But he thought he had not said enough, if he omitted anything that belonged to the subject of his Discourse, so that his Sermons seemed rather complete Treatises, than Orations, designed to be spoke in an hour; hereof I will give you two or three instances. He was once requested by the Bishop of Rochester then, and now Dean of Westminster, to preach at the Abbey, and withal desired not to be long, for that auditory loved short Sermons, and were used to them. He replied, 'My Lord, I will shew you my Sermon;' and pulling it out of his pocket, puts it into the Bishop's hands. The text was in the tenth chapter of the Proverbs, the latter end of the eighteenth verse, the words these; *He that uttereth slander is a liar*. The Sermon was accordingly divided into two parts, one treated of slander, the other of lies[1]. The Dean desired him to content himself with preaching only the first part, to which he consented, not without some reluctancy, and in speaking that only it took up an hour and a half. This Discourse is since published in two Sermons, as it was preached. Another time, upon the same person's invitation, he preached at the Abbey on a holiday: here I must inform the reader, that it is a custom for the servants of the church upon all holidays, Sundays excepted, betwixt the Sermon and Evening Prayers, to shew the tombs and effigies of the Kings and Queens in wax, to the meaner sort of people, who then flock thither from all the corners of the town, and pay their twopence to see 'The play of the dead volks,' as I have heard a Devonshire clown not improperly call it. These perceiving Dr Barrow in the pulpit after the hour was past, and fearing to lose that time in *hearing*, which they thought they could more profitably employ in *receiving*,—these, I say, became impatient, and caused the organ to be struck up against him, and would not give over playing till they had blowed him down. But the Sermon of the greatest length was that concerning Charity, before the Lord Mayor and Aldermen at the Spittle; in speaking which, he spent three hours and a half. Being asked, after he came down from the pulpit, whether he was not tired; 'Yes, indeed,' said he, 'I began to be weary with standing so long[2].'"

### III.

"All the while he continued with the Bishop of Salisbury I was his bedfellow, and a witness of his indefatigable study; at that time he applied himself wholly to divinity, having given a divorce to mathematics and poetry, and the rest of the Belles Lettres, wherein he was profoundly versed, making it his chief, if not only business, to

---

[1] As usual, Pope is inaccurate. He does not give even the text correctly; nor is he right about the division of the subject-matter of the Sermon: the first (Vol. II. pp. 102—127) treats of slander and its various manifestations; the second (pp. 128—146) of the folly of slander. Nor, if the Sermons as printed be the Sermons that were preached, is it credible, that the first of less than twenty-four pages took an hour and a half to deliver. Both of these are discourses of moderate length even according to modern notions.

[2] Here, again, another opportunity presents itself of testing the truthfulness of Pope's stories. The Spital Sermon, exclusive of notes, occupies about ninety pages of this Edition; an amount of matter which might well be delivered within three hours and a half. But it is evident Barrow did not preach all he had written; for in the formal request to publish it (see Vol. I. p. 2), he is asked to print his Sermon, *with what farther he had prepared to deliver at that time.*

write in defence of the Church of England, and compose Sermons, whereof he had great store, and, I need not say, very good.

"We were once going from Salisbury to London, he in the coach with the Bishop, and I on horseback; as he was entering the coach I perceived his pockets strutting out near half a foot, and said to him, 'What have you got in your pockets?' He replied, 'Sermons.' 'Sermons,' said I, 'give them me, my boy shall carry them in his portmanteau, and ease you of that luggage.' 'But,' said he, 'suppose your boy should be robbed:' 'That's pleasant,' said I, 'do you think there are parsons padding upon the road for Sermons?' 'Why, what have you,' said he, 'it may be five or six guineas, I hold my Sermons at a greater rate, they cost me much pain and time.' 'Well then,' said I, 'if you'll insure my five or six guineas against lay-padders, I'll secure your bundle of Sermons against ecclesiastical highwaymen.' This was agreed; he emptied his pockets, and filled my portmanteau with divinity, and we had the good fortune to come safe to our journey's end without meeting either sort of the padders forementioned, and to bring both our treasures to London.

"He was of a healthy constitution, used no exercise or physic, besides smoking tobacco, in which he was not sparing, saying, it was an *instar omnium*, or *panfarmacon*: he was unmercifully cruel to a lean carcase, not allowing it sufficient meat or sleep: during the winter months, and some part of the rest, he rose always before it was light, being never without a tinder-box and other proper utensils for that purpose; I have frequently known him, after his first sleep, rise, light, and, after burning out his candle, return to bed before day. I say, I have known him do this; I report it not upon hearsay, but experience, having been, as I said before, his bedfellow whilst he lived with the Bishop of Salisbury."

### IV.

"He was careless of his cloaths, even to a fault; I remember he once made me a visit, and I perceiving his band sat very awkwardly, and asked him, 'What makes your band sit so?' 'I have,' said he, 'no buttons upon my collar.' 'Come,' said I, 'put on my nightgown, here's a tailor at hand,' for by chance my tailor was then with me, 'who will presently set all things right.' With much ado I prevailed with him; the buttons were supplied, the gown made clean, the hands and face washed, and the clothes and hat brushed; in a word, at his departure, he did not seem the same man who came in just before."

# THE

# PUBLISHER TO THE READER.

THE Author of the following Sermons was so publicly known, and so highly esteemed by all learned and good men, that nothing either needs or can be said more to his advantage. Not but that I think it very fit, that the picture of this truly great man should be drawn at full length, for the knowledge and imitation of posterity; and it will, I hope, be done hereafter by some more skilful hand: however, I shall not within the narrow limits of a Preface, so much as attempt the character of him; of whom, either not a little, or nothing at all ought to be said.

And the Sermons themselves do as little need commendation as the Author; their own excellency and eloquence will praise them best. I shall therefore only advertise the reader of some few things concerning them.

The design of the five first is, to recommend religion to our esteem and practice, from the consideration of the manifold excellencies and advantages of it. The four next do treat of the two great duties of religion, and parts of divine worship, prayer and thanksgiving; and contain likewise a very powerful persuasive to the practice of them. The three following were preached upon three solemn occasions: the first of them upon the 29th of May, 1676, the anniversary of His Majesty's happy restoration: the second upon the fifth of November, 1675, in commemoration of our great deliverance from the Powder Treason, both in the year of his Vice-Chancellorship: the third at the consecration of the Bishop of Man, (afterwards Lord Bishop of St Asaph) his uncle; in which he pleads for the due respect and revenue of the Clergy with so much modesty, and yet with so great force of reason and eloquence, that the whole profession may justly think themselves for ever indebted to him.

Some of these twelve Sermons were the very first that he made; by which we may judge with what preparation and furniture he entered upon this sacred employment. The first of them was preached at St Mary's in Cambridge, June 30, 1661, and was, I think, the first that he ever preached. Those two excellent Sermons of thanksgiving were, as I am informed, the next. The fourth in order was the first that he preached before the King's Majesty. In the placing of them as they now stand, I had very little regard to the order of time, but rather to some small reason taken from the subject matter of them, not worth the mentioning; any reason almost being good enough in a matter so indifferent, and where none is necessary.

The next ten Sermons are thought fit to be put together, because of their affinity to one another, all of them relating to the same argument, and tending to reform the several vices of the tongue. The last two of them indeed against pragmaticalness and meddling in the affairs of others, do not so properly belong to this subject; but considering that this vice is chiefly managed by the tongue, and is almost ever attended with some irregularity and indiscretion of speech, they are not altogether so foreign and unsuitable to it. And never were discourses of this kind more necessary than in this wicked and perverse generation; wherein the vices here reprehended are so very rife, and out of the abundant impiety of men's hearts there proceeds so much evil speaking of all kinds, in atheistical discourses, and blasphemous raillery, and profane swearing; and when censoriousness, detraction and slander are scarce accounted faults, even with those who would seem to be most strict in other parts and duties of Religion.

The author of them, as he was exemplary in all manner of conversation, so especially in this part of it, being of all men I ever had the happiness to know, the clearest of this common guilt, and most free from offending in word; coming as near as is possible for human frailty to do, to the perfect idea of St James his perfect man. So that in these excellent Discourses of his he hath only transcribed his own practice. All the rules which he hath given he most religiously observed himself, and was very uneasy when at any time he saw them transgressed by others in his company.

There is one thing in them needs excuse, namely, that several things which are more briefly and summarily said in the first of these Sermons about evil speaking are repeated in some of the following Discourses: which because it could not well be avoided, but either by wholly leaving out the first Sermon, or very much mangling some of the rest, will, it is hoped, for that reason be easily pardoned.

The eight following Sermons are likewise sorted together, because they explain and enforce the two great commandments of the law, the love of God, and of our neighbour.

The two next were published by himself, and only those two. The first of them, about the Duty and Reward of Bounty to the Poor, was preached at the Spital, and published at the desire of the Lord Mayor and Court of Aldermen. This was received with universal approbation; and perhaps there is nothing extant in Divinity more perfect in its kind: it seems to have exhausted the whole argument, and to have left no consideration belonging to it untouched. The other, on the Passion of our blessed Saviour, was the last he preached, but one; and, I think, the occasion of his death, by a cold he then got, which, in all probability, was the cause of the fever of which he died, to our unspeakable loss. This he sent to the press himself, but did not live to see it published.

The next part of this Volume is a brief Explication of the Lord's Prayer, the Decalogue, and the Doctrine of the Sacraments. It were to be wished that the

Creed also had been explained by him in the same manner; but that he hath handled in a larger way, in a great many excellent Sermons upon the several articles of it, wherein he hath not only explained and confirmed the great doctrines of our religion, but likewise shewn what influence every article of our faith ought to have upon our practice. Which Discourses make the second Volume of his works.

The last part of this first Volume is his learned Treatise of the Pope's Supremacy, to which, because there is prefixed a Preface giving a short account, I need not here to say anything farther of it.

Besides these, the Author hath left many other excellent Sermons, upon several important and useful subjects in Divinity: besides a great many learned Lectures and Treatises in the Mathematics; and divers excellent Orations and Poems, all in Latin. All which may, God willing, in convenient time be communicated to the public, to the great advantage and furtherance of religion and learning.

In the mean time, I heartily recommend these Sermons which are already published to thy serious perusal; and shall only say this of them, that as they want no other kind of excellency, so particularly they are animated throughout with so genuine a spirit of true piety and goodness, that he must either be a perfectly good, or prodigiously bad man, that can read them over without being the better for them.

JOHN TILLOTSON.

TO THE RIGHT HONOURABLE

## HENEAGE,

EARL OF NOTTINGHAM,

LORD HIGH CHANCELLOR OF ENGLAND,

AND

ONE OF HIS MAJESTY'S MOST HONOURABLE PRIVY-COUNCIL.

---

My Lord,

I TAKE the boldness to present your Lordship with some of the fruits of my deceased son's studies in Divinity. And since it hath pleased God, to my unspeakable grief and loss, to deprive me of so great a blessing and comfort of my old age; it is no small mitigation of my sorrow, that whilst he lived he was not unprofitable to the world; and that, now he is dead, he hath left those monuments of his piety and learning behind him, which, I am told, are generally thought not unworthy to be imparted to the public.

If these Sermons be such, I have no cause to doubt but they will easily obtain your Lordship's patronage, who are so known a favourer of all that is virtuous and worthy, especially of Religion and the ministers of it; of which I had particular experience upon the death of my good son, when your Lordship was pleased, with so much humanity and condescension, to send to comfort me under that sad loss, and to express your own resentment of it.

But whatever these Sermons be, since I have no other way to acknowledge my great obligations to your Lordship upon all occasions, I hope your Lordship will please favourably to accept of this, how small soever, yet sincere testimony of my dutiful respects and gratitude. I am,

My Lord,
Your Lordship's most obliged
and most obedient servant,
THOMAS BARROW.

# THE DUTY AND REWARD OF BOUNTY TO THE POOR:

## IN A SERMON

PREACHED AT

## THE SPITTAL

UPON WEDNESDAY IN EASTER WEEK,
ANNO DOM. M.DC.LXXI.

---

TO THE RIGHT HONOURABLE

SIR RICHARD FORD,

LORD MAYOR OF LONDON,

AND THE COURT OF ALDERMEN.

Right Hon[ble],

As out of grateful respect, I did (although otherwise indisposed for such employments) endeavour to discharge that service, which you vouchsafed to call me unto, in conceiving and uttering these meditations; so now in publishing them, I do purely submit to your commands, meaning therein to approve myself,

Right Hon[ble],

Your most obedient Servant,

*Isaac Barrow.*

## FORD, MAYOR.

Martis secundo die Maii 1671. Annoq; Domini Regis CAROLI Secundi Angliæ, &c. vicesimo tertio.

*This Court doth desire Dr BARROW to print his Sermon, preached at the Spittal on Wednesday in Easter Week last, with what farther he had prepared to deliver at that time.*

AVERY.

---

## IMPRIMATUR.

Sam. Parker, R$^{mo}$ in Christo Patri ac Domino D$^{no}$ Gilberto Archiep. Cantuar. a Sac. Dom.

**Jul. 3, 1671.**

# SERMON I.

## THE DUTY AND REWARD OF BOUNTY TO THE POOR.

PSALM CXII. 9.

*He hath dispersed, he hath given to the poor; his righteousness endureth for ever; his horn shall be exalted with honour.*

AS this whole Psalm appears to have a double intent; one to describe the proper actions and affections of a truly religious or pious man; (of a man *Who feareth the Lord, and delighteth greatly in his commandments;*) the other to declare the happiness of such a man's state, consequent upon those his affections and actions, whether in way of natural result, or of gracious recompense from God: so doth this verse particularly contain both a good part of a pious man's character, and some considerable instances of his felicity. The first words (*He hath dispersed, he hath given to the poor*) express part of his character; the latter (*His righteousness endureth for ever, his horn shall be exalted with honour*) assign instances of his felicity. So that our text hath two parts, one affording us good information concerning our duty, the other yielding great encouragement to the performance thereof; for we are obliged to follow the pious man's practice, and so doing we shall assuredly partake of his condition. These parts we shall in order prosecute, endeavouring (by God's assistance) somewhat to illustrate the words themselves, to confirm the truths couched in them, and to inculcate the duties which they imply.

For the first part, *He hath dispersed, he hath given to the poor;* these words in general do import the liberal bounty and mercy which a pious man is wont to exercise; doing which doth in good part constitute him pious, and signally declareth him such; is a necessary ingredient of his piety, and a conspicuous mark thereof. But particularly they insinuate some things concerning the nature, the matter, the manner, and the object of those acts.

*He hath dispersed, he hath given.* Those words being put indefinitely, or without determining what is dispersed and given by him, may be supposed to imply a kind of universality in the matter of his beneficence; that he bestoweth whatever he hath within compass of his possession, or his power; his Τὰ ὑπάρχοντα, (the things which he hath,) and his Τὰ ἐνόντα, (the things which he may,) according to the prescriptions of our Lord in the Gospel. Every thing, I say, which he hath in substance, or can do by his endeavour, that may conduce to the support of the life, or the health, or the welfare in any kind of his neighbour, to the succour or relief of his indigency, to the removal or easement of his affliction, he may well here be understood to disperse and give. Feeding the hungry, clothing the naked, visiting the sick, entertaining the stranger, ransoming the captive, easing the oppressed, comforting the sorrowful, assisting the weak, instructing

Luke xii. 33; xi. 41.

or advising the ignorant, together with all such kinds or instances of beneficence, may be conceived either meant directly as the matter of the good man's dispersing and giving, or by just analogy of reason reducible thereto: substantial alms, as the most sensible and obvious matter of bounty, was (it is probable) especially intended, but thence no manner of expressing it is to be excluded; for the same reasons which oblige us, the same affections which dispose us to bestow our money, or deal our bread, will equally bind and move us to contribute our endeavour and advice, for the sustenance and comfort of our poor neighbour. Answerably our discourse will more expressly regard the principal matter, liberal communication of our goods; but it may be referred to all sorts of beneficence.

Further, the word *dispersed* intimateth the nature of his bounty, in exclusion of practices different from it. He *disperseth*, and is therefore not tenacious, doth not hoard up his goods, or keep them close to himself, for the gratifying his covetous humour, or nourishing his pride, or pampering his sensuality; but sendeth them abroad for the use and benefit of others. He *disperseth* his goods, and therefore doth not fling them away altogether, as if he were angry with them, or weary of them, as if he loathed or despised them; but fairly and softly with good consideration he disposeth of them here and there, as reason and need do require. He *disperseth* them *to the poor*, not dissipateth them among vain or lewd persons in wanton or wicked profusions, in riotous excesses, in idle divertisements, in expensive curiosities, in hazardous gamings, in any such courses which swallow whole all that a man hath, or do so cripple him, that he becomes unable to disperse any thing: our good man is to be understood wisely provident, honestly industrious, and soberly frugal, that he may have wherewith to be just first, and then liberal[a].

His *dispersing* also (or *scattering*, so the Hebrew[b] word here used is otherwise rendered: *There is*, saith the Wise Man, *that scattereth, and yet increaseth*: where we may remark, that this word singly by itself, without any adjunct matter to limit or interpret it, is used to signify this kind of practice. This his *dispersing*, I say, also) denotes the extent of the pious man's bounty, that it is very large and diffusive, and in a manner unrestrained; that it reacheth to many places, and is withheld from no persons within the verge of his power and opportunity to do good. This practice commonly by a like phrase (unto which perhaps this word refers) is termed *sowing*: *He*, saith St Paul, *which soweth sparingly shall also reap sparingly; and he which soweth bountifully shall also reap bountifully.* Now, he that soweth, having chosen a good soil, and a fit season, doth not regard one particular spot, but throweth all about so much as his hand can hold, so far as the strength of his arm doth carry. It is likewise called *watering*: (*He that watereth*, saith Solomon, *shall be watered himself*:) which expression also seemeth to import a plentiful and promiscuous effusion of good dropping in showers upon dry and parched places; that is, upon persons dry for want, or parched with

---

[a] Οὐ γὰρ οἷόν τε χρήματ' ἔχειν μὴ ἐπιμελούμενον, ὅπως ἔχῃ.—Arist. Eth. iv. 1. [21.]

[b] פִּזֵּר

affliction. So the good man doth not plant his bounty in one small hole, or spout it on one narrow spot, but with an open hand disseminates it, with an impartial regard distils it all about. He stints it not to his own family or relations; to his neighbours, or friends, or benefactors; to those of his own sect and opinion, or of his humour and disposition; to such as serve him, or oblige him, or please him; whom some private interest ties, or some particular affection endears him to; but scatters it indifferently and unconfinedly toward all men that need it[c]; toward mere strangers, yea, toward known enemies; toward such who never did him any good, or can ever be able to do any; yea, even toward them who have done evil to him, and may be presumed ready to do more. Nothing in his neighbour but absence of need, nothing in himself but defect of ability, doth curb or limit his beneficence. In that Προθυμία, (that proclivity and promptitude of mind,) which St Paul speaketh of, he doth good everywhere: wherever a man is, there is room for his wishing well, and doing good, if he can[d]: he observes that rule of the Apostle, *As we have opportunity, let us do good unto all men.* So the pious man hath *dispersed.* It follows,

*He hath given to the poor.* These words denote the freeness of his bounty, and determine the principal object thereof: he not only lendeth (though he also doth that upon reasonable occasion; for, *A*

2 Cor. viii. 12.

Gal. vi. 10.
2 Cor. ix. 13.

Ps. cxii. 5.

[c] Ἐὰν ἴδῃς τινὰ κακῶς πάσχοντα, μηδὲν περιεργάζου λοιπόν· ἔχει τὸ δικαίωμα τῆς βοηθείας, τὸ κακῶς παθεῖν αὐτόν.—Τοῦ Θεοῦ ἐστι, κἂν Ἕλλην ᾖ, κἂν Ἰουδαῖος.—Chrys. in Heb. Orat. x. [Opp. Tom. IV. p. 489.]

[d] Ubicunque homo est, ibi beneficio locus est.—Sen. de Vit. B. cap. xxiv. [2.]

good man, as it is said before in this Psalm, *sheweth mercy, and lendeth;* and otherwhere, *The righteous is ever merciful, and lendeth;* he, I say, not only sometimes willingly lendeth) to those who in time may repay, or requite him; but he freely giveth to the poor, that is, to those from whom he can expect no retribution back. He doth not (as good and pious, he doth not) present the rich: to do so is but a cleanly way of begging, or a subtle kind of trade[e]; it is hardly courtesy; it is surely no bounty; for such persons (if they are not very sordid or very careless, and such men are not usually much troubled with presents) will, it is likely overdo him, or at least will be even with him in kindness. In doing this, there is little virtue; for it there will be small reward. For, *If you do good to them who do good to you,* (or whom you conceive able and disposed to requite you,) Ποία χάρις, *what thanks* are due to you? *For that,* saith our Saviour, *even sinners* (even men notoriously bad) *do the same: And if you lend to them from whom you hope to receive, what thanks have you? For sinners even lend to sinners, to receive as much again.* All men commonly, the bad no less than the good, are apt to be superfluously kind in heaping favours on those whom fortune befriends, and whose condition requires not their courtesy[f]; every one almost is ready to adopt himself into the kindred, or to screw himself into the friendship of the wealthy and

SERM. I.

Ps. xxxvii. 26.

Luke vi. 33, 34.

---

[e] Qui diviti donat, petit. "He that giveth to the rich shall surely come to want."—Prov. xxii. 16.

[f] Ὅταν δ' ὁ δαίμων εὖ διδῷ, τί δεῖ φίλων;
Ἀρκεῖ γὰρ αὐτὸς ὁ Θεὸς ὠφελεῖν θέλων.—
Eurip. Orest. [667.]

prosperous[g]: but where kindred is of use, there it is seldom found; it is commonly so deaf, as not to hear when it is called; so blind, as not to discern its proper object and natural season, (*The time of adversity, for which a brother is born.*) Men disclaim alliance with the needy, and shun his acquaintance; so the Wise Man observed, *All the brethren of the poor do hate him; how much more do his friends go far from him?* Thus it is in vulgar practice[h]: but the pious man is more judicious, more just, and more generous in the placing of his favours; he is courteous to purpose, he is good to those who need. He, as such, doth not make large entertainments *for his friends, his brethren, his kindred, his rich neighbours;* but observes that precept of our Lord, *When thou makest a feast, call the poor, the maimed, the lame, the blind, and thou shalt be blessed: for they cannot recompense thee; thou shalt be recompensed at the resurrection of the just.* Thus the pious man giveth, that is, with a free heart and pure intention bestoweth his goods on the indigent, without designing any benefit, or hoping for any requital to himself; except from God, in conscience, respect, and love to whom he doeth it.

SERM. I.

Prov. xvii. 17.

Prov. xix. 7, 4.

Luke xiv. 12, 13, 14.

It may be also material to observe the form of speech here used in reference to the time: *He hath dispersed, and he hath given;* or, *He doth disperse, he doth give;* (for in the Hebrew language the past and present times are not distin-

---

[g] Τῶν εὐτυχούντων πάντες εἰσὶ συγγενεῖς.—[Menand. Sentent. sing. 510. (Ed. Meineke.)]

[h] Εὖ πρᾶσσε· τὰ φίλων δ' οὐδὲν, ἤν τις δυστυχῇ.—
Eurip. [Phœn. 403.]

guished:) which manner of speaking may seem to intimate the reality, or the certainty, and the constancy of his practice in this kind; for what is past or present, we are infallibly secure of; and in morals, what one is said to have done, or to do, is always understood according to habit or custom. It is not, *He will disperse, he will give;* that were no fit description of a good man; to pretend to, would be no argument of piety; those words might import uncertainty, and delay in his practice. He that saith, *I will give,* may be fallacious in his professions, may be inconsistent with his resolutions, may wilfully or negligently let slip the due season of performing it. Our good man is not a *Doson,* or *Will-give,* (like that king of Macedon, who got that name from often signifying an intention of giving, but never giving in effect[1];) he not only purposes well, and promises fairly for the future, but he hath effectually done it, and perseveres doing it upon every fit occasion. He puts not his neighbour into tedious expectations, nor puts him off with frivolous excuses, saying to him, as it is in the Proverbs, *Go, and come again, and to-morrow I will give,* when he hath it by him: he bids him not have patience, or says unto him, *Depart in peace,* when his need is urgent, and his pain impatient, when hunger or cold do then pinch him, when sickness incessantly vexeth him, when present straits and burdens oppress him; but he affordeth a ready, quick, and seasonable relief.

*He hath dispersed,* and *given,* while he lives,

---

[1] Ἐπεκλήθη δὲ Δώσων, ὡς ἐπαγγελτικὸς μὲν, οὐ τελεσιουργὸς δὲ τῶν ὑποσχέσεων.—Plut. in Paulo Æmil. [Opp. Tom. IV. p. 471. Ed. Steph.]

not reserving the disposal of all at once upon his death, or by his last will; that unwilling will, whereby men would seem to give somewhat, when they can keep nothing; drawing to themselves those commendations and thanks, which are only due to their mortality: whenas were they immortal, they would never be liberal: No; it is, *He hath freely dispersed;* not an inevitable necessity will extort it from him; it cannot be said of him, that he never does well, but when he dies[k]; so he hath done it really and surely.

He also doth it constantly, through all the course of his life, whenever good opportunity presents itself. He doth it not by fits, or by accident, according to unstable causes or circumstances moving him, (when bodily temper or humour inclineth him, when a sad object makes vehement impression on him, when shame obligeth him to comply with the practice of others, when he may thereby promote some design, or procure some glory to himself,) but his practice is constant and uniform, being drawn from steady principles, and guided by certain rules, proceeding from reverence to God, and good-will toward man, following the clear dictates and immutable laws of conscience. Thus hath the pious man *dispersed*, and *given to the poor:* and let thus much suffice for explicatory reflection upon the first words.

The main drift and purport of which is, to represent the liberal exercising of bounty and mercy to be the necessary duty, the ordinary practice, and the proper character of a truly pious man; so that

[k] Avarus, nisi cum moritur, nil recte facit.
[Publ. Syrus, Sentent (Poet. Scen. Latin. Vol. vi. p. 227. Ed. Bothe.)]

performing such acts is a good sign of true piety; and omitting them is a certain argument of ungodliness. For the demonstration of which points, and for exciting us to a practice answerable, I shall propound several considerations, whereby the plain reasonableness, the great weight, the high worth and excellency of this duty, together with its strict connection with other principal duties of piety, will appear. And first, I will shew with what advantage the holy scripture represents it to us, or presses it upon us.

I. Head of discourse.

1 We may consider, that there is no sort of duties which God hath more expressly commanded, or more earnestly inculcated, than these of bounty and mercy toward our brethren: whence evidently the great moment of them, and their high value in God's esteem may be inferred. Even in the ancient law, we may observe very careful provisions made for engaging men to works of this kind, and the performance of them is with huge life and urgency prescribed: *Thou shalt not harden thy heart, nor shut thine hand from thy poor brother.—Thou shalt open thy hand wide unto thy brother, unto thy poor, and to thy needy in the land.* So did Moses, in God's name, with language very significant and emphatical, enjoin to the children of Israel. The holy prophets also do commonly with an especial heat and vigour press these duties, most smartly reproving the transgression or neglect of them; especially when they reclaim men from their wicked courses, urging them seriously to return unto God and goodness, they propose this practice as a singular instance most expressive of their conversion, most apt to appease God's

Deut. xv. 7, 11.

wrath, most effectual to the recovery of his favour. *Wash you*, saith God in Isaiah, *make you clean; put away the evil of your doings from before mine eyes; cease to do evil, learn to do well.* So in general he exhorts to repentance: then immediately he subjoins these choice instances thereof: *Seek judgment, relieve the oppressed, judge the fatherless, plead for the widow.—Come now*, then he adds, *let us reason together: though your sins be as scarlet, they shall be as white as snow; though they be red like crimson, they shall be as wool.* When Daniel would prescribe to king Nebuchadnezzar the best way of amendment, and the surest means of averting God's judgments impendent on him, he thus speaks: *Wherefore, O king, let my counsel be acceptable unto thee; break off thy sins by righteousness, and thine iniquities by shewing mercy to the poor*[1]. This he culled out as of all pious acts chiefly grateful to God, and clearly testifying repentance; and, *So very impious a person was alms able to justify*, says the Father thereupon[m]. So also when God himself would declare what those acts are which render penitential devotions most agreeable to him, and most effectual, he thus expresseth his mind: *Is not this the fast which I have chosen? To loose the bands of wickedness, to undo the heavy burdens, to let the oppressed go free, and that ye break every yoke? Is it not to deal thy bread to the hungry, and that thou bring the poor that are cast out to thine house? when thou*

---

[1] Τὰς ἁμαρτίας σου ἐν ἐλεημοσύναις λύτρωσαι: so the LXX. render those words, reading, it seems, פרק for פרת

[m] Ναβουχοδονόσορ, τὸν τοιοῦτον ἀσεβῆ, ἴσχυσεν ἡ ἐλεημοσύνη δικαιῶσαι.—Athan. ad Antioch. Quæst. LXXXVIII. [Opp. Tom. II. p. 288 E.]

*seest the naked, that thou cover him; and that thou hide not thyself from thine own flesh?* Of so great consideration and moment was this sort of duties, even under that old dispensation of weakness, servility, and fear; so much tenderness of compassion and benignity did God exact even from that hard-hearted and worldly people, who were so little capable of the best rules, and had encouragements, in comparison, so mean toward performances of this nature. The same we may well conceive, under the more perfect discipline of universal amity, of ingenuity, of spiritual grace and goodness, in a higher strain, with more force and greater obligation to be imposed on us, who have so much stronger engagements, and immensely greater encouragements to them. And so indeed it is: for those precepts delivered by our Lord, *Sell all that you have, and give alms; If thou wilt be perfect, sell all that thou hast, and give to the poor; Give to every man that asketh thee; Treasure not up to yourselves treasures upon the earth,* do indeed sound high, but are not insignificant or impertinent. They cannot signify or design less, than that we should be always, in affection and disposition of mind, ready to part with anything we have for the succour of our poor brethren; that to the utmost of our ability (according to moral estimation prudently rated) upon all occasions we should really express that disposition in our practice; that we are exceedingly obliged to the continual exercise of these duties in a very eminent degree. These indeed were the duties which our Lord, as he did frequently in his discourse commend and prescribe, so he did most signally exemplify in his practice;

his whole life being in effect but one continual act of most liberal bounty and mercy toward mankind; in charity to whom he outdid his own severest rules, being content never to possess any wealth, never to enjoy any ease in this world. And therein (both as to doctrine and practice) did the holy apostles closely follow their Master: *As poor, yet enriching many; as having nothing, yet possessing all things.* So they throughly in deeds practised these duties, which in words they taught and earnestly pressed; admonishing their converts to *Distribute to the necessities of the saints*, to *Do good to all men*; *To do good, and to communicate not to forget*; to *Shew mercy with cheerfulness*, to *Put on bowels of mercy*; to *Be kind and tender-hearted one toward another*; to *Abound in the grace of liberality.* Such are their directions and injunctions to all Christian people; so did they preach themselves, and so they enjoined others to preach. *Charge the rich in this world,* saith St Paul to his scholar Timothy, *that they do good, that they be rich in good works, ready to distribute, willing to communicate*; and, *These things,* saith he likewise, advising Bishop Titus, *I will that thou affirm constantly, that they which believe in God may be careful to maintain good works*; what *good works* he meaneth, the reason adjoined doth shew; *For these things,* saith he, *are good and profitable unto men.*

2 It is indeed observable, that as in every kind that which is most excellent doth commonly assume to itself the name of the whole kind; so among the parts of righteousness (which word is used to comprehend all virtue and goodness) this of exercising bounty and mercy is peculiarly called

SERM. I.

2 Cor. vi. 10.

Rom. xii. 13.
Gal. vi. 10.
Heb. xiii. 16.
Coloss. iii. 12.
Eph. iv. 32.
2 Cor. viii. 7.

1 Tim. vi. 17, 18.

Tit. iii. 8.

*Righteousness*; so that *Righteousness* and *Mercifulness* (or *Almsdeeds*,) the righteous and bountiful person, are in scripture expression ordinarily confounded, as it were, or undistinguishably put one for the other; it being often, when commendations are given to righteousness, and rewards promised to righteous persons, hard to discern, whether the general observance of God's law, or the special practice of these duties, are concerned in them. Likewise works of this nature are in way of peculiar excellency termed *Good works*; and to perform them is usually styled, *To do good*, and *To do well*; (Ἀγαθὸν ἐργάζεσθαι, Καλὸν ποιεῖν, Ἀγαθοεργεῖν, Ἀγαθοποιεῖν, Εὐποιεῖν, Εὐεργετεῖν, are words applied to this purpose;) which manners of expression do argue the eminent dignity of these performances.

Acts ix. 36.
1 Tim. v. 10; vi. 18.
Tit. iii. 8, 14.
2 Cor. ix. 8.
Gal. vi. 9.
Ib. 10.
Luke vi. 35.
Heb. xiii. 16.
Acts x. 38.

3 We may also consequently mark, that in those places of scripture where the divine law is abridged, and religion summed up into a few particulars of main importance, these duties constantly make a part: so when the prophet Micah briefly reckons up those things which are best in the law, and chiefly required by God, the whole catalogue of them consisting but of three particulars, *mercy* comes in for one; *He hath shewed thee, O man*, saith he, *what is good: and what doth the Lord require of thee, but to do justly, and to love mercy, and to walk humbly with thy God?* Likewise of those (Βαρύτερα τοῦ νόμου, those) more substantial and *Weighty things of God's law* the neglect of which our Saviour objecteth as an argument of impiety, and a cause of woe, to those pretending zealots, this is one: *Woe unto you, Scribes and Pharisees, hypocrites; for ye pay tithe of mint and*

Mic. vi. 8.

Matt. xxiii. 23.

*cummin, and have omitted the weightier matters of the law, judgment, mercy, and faith.* The sum of St John the Baptist's instruction of the people is by St Luke reduced to this point; *The people asked him, saying, What shall we do?* He answering saith unto them, *He that hath two coats, let him impart to him that hath none; and he that hath meat, let him do likewise.* St James's system of religion is this: *Pure and undefiled religion before God and the Father is this; to visit the fatherless and widow in their affliction,* (that is, to comfort and relieve all distressed and helpless persons,) *and to keep himself unspotted from the world.* St Paul seems to be yet more compendious and close: *Bear ye,* saith he, *one another's burdens, and so fulfil the law of Christ.* Yea, God himself compriseth all the substantial part of religion herein, when, comparing it with the circumstantial part, he saith, *I will have mercy, and not sacrifice.*

SERM. I.

Luke iii. 10, 11.

Jam. i. 27.

Gal. vi. 2.

Hos. vi. 6.

4 It is in like manner considerable, that in the general descriptions of piety and goodness, the practice of these duties is specified as a grand ingredient of them. In this Psalm, where such a description is intended, it is almost the only particular instance; and it is not only mentioned, but reiterated in divers forms of expression. In the 37th Psalm it is affirmed and repeated, that *The righteous sheweth mercy; he sheweth mercy, and giveth; he sheweth mercy, and lendeth.* In the Proverbs[n] it is a commendation of the virtuous woman, *Whose price is far above rubies,* that *She stretcheth out her hand to the poor, yea, stretcheth*

Ps. xxxvii. 21, 26.

Prov. xxxi. 10, 20.

---

[n] "The righteous giveth, and spareth not."—Prov. xxi. 26.

*forth both her hands to the needy.* And in Ezekiel, (which is especially remarkable,) the 18th chapter, where the principal things constituting a pious man are more than once professedly enumerated, this among a very few other particulars is expressed, and taketh up much room in the account; of such a person (who *Shall surely live, and not die,* that is, who certainly shall abide in God's favour, and enjoy the happy consequences thereof) it is supposed, that he *Neither hath oppressed any, nor hath withholden the pledge, nor hath spoiled by violence; but hath given his bread to the hungry, and hath covered the naked with a garment, and hath taken off his hand from the poor.*

5 Also in the particular histories of good men, this sort of practice is specially taken notice of, and expressed in their characters. In the story of our father Abraham, his benignity to strangers, and hospitableness, is remarkable among all his deeds of goodness, being propounded to us as a pattern and encouragement to the like practice. In this the conscience of Job did solace itself, as in a solid assurance of his integrity: *I delivered the poor that cried, and the fatherless, and him that had none to help him. The blessing of him that was ready to perish came upon me, and I caused the widow's heart to sing. I was eyes to the blind, and feet I was to the lame; I was a father to the poor. Did not I weep for him that was in trouble? Was not my soul grieved for the poor?* Hence also did the good publican recommend himself to the favour and approbation of our Saviour, saying, *Behold, Lord, half of my goods I give to the poor:* hence did *salvation come to* his *house:* hence he is

proclaimed, *a son of Abraham.* Of Dorcas, that good woman, who was so gracious and precious among the disciples, this is the commendation and character; *She was full of good works and alms-deeds, which she did;* such practice made her capable of that favour, so great and extraordinary, the being restored to life; at least in St Chrysostom's judgment: *The force of her alms,* saith he, *did conquer the tyranny of death*[o]. Cornelius also, that excellent person, who was, though a Gentile, so acceptable to God, and had so extraordinary graces conferred on him, is thus represented; *He was a devout man, and one that feared God, with all his house; who gave much alms to the people, and prayed to God alway.* We may add, that to be hospitable (one branch of these duties, and inferring the rest) is reckoned a qualification of those who are to be the guides and patterns of goodness unto others. And particularly, one fit to be promoted to a widow's office in the church is thus described; *Well reported of for good works; if she have brought up children; if she have lodged strangers; if she have washed the saints' feet; if she have relieved the afflicted; if she have diligently followed every good work.*

SERM. I.

Acts ix. 36.

Acts x. 2.

1 Tim. iii. 2.
Tit. i. 8.

1 Tim. v. 10.

6 So near to the heart of piety doth the holy scripture lay the practice of these duties: and no wonder; for it often expressly declares charity to be the fulfilling of God's law, as the best expression of all our duty toward God, of faith in him, love and reverence of him, and as either formally containing, or naturally producing all our duty toward

Gal. v. 14.
Rom. xiii. 9, 10.
1 Tim. i. 5.
Matt. vii. 12.

---

[o] Ἡ τῆς ἐλεημοσύνης δύναμις ἐνίκησε καὶ τούτου (θανάτου sc.) τὴν τυραννίδα.—Chrys. in Gen. Orat. LV. [Opp. Tom. I. p. 431.]

our neighbour. And of charity, works of bounty and mercy are both the chief instances and the plainest signs: for whereas all charity doth consist either in mental desire, or in verbal signification, or in effectual performance of good to our neighbour; this last is the end, the completion, and the assurance of the rest[p]. Good-will is indeed the root of charity; but that lies under ground, and out of sight; nor can we conclude its being or life without visible fruits of beneficence. Good words are at best but fair leaves thereof, such as may, and too often do, proceed from a weak and barren disposition of mind. But these *Good works* are *real fruits* (so St Paul calls them; *Let ours also,* saith he, *learn to maintain good works for necessary uses, that they be not unfruitful,*) which declare a true life, and a good strength of charity in the bearer of them: by them, Τὸ τῆς ὑμετέρας ἀγάπης γνήσιον, *The sincerity* (or genuineness) *of our charity is proved.* For as no man ever doth impress a false stamp on the finest metal; so costly charity is seldom counterfeit. It is to decline spending their goods or their pains, that men forge and feign; pretending to make up in wishing well, the defect of doing so, and paying words instead of things: but he that freely imparts what he hath, or can do for his neighbour's good, needs no other argument to evince that he loves in good earnest, nor can indeed well use any other; for words, if actions are wanting, seem abusive; and if actions are present, they are superfluous. Wherefore St John thus advises; *My little children, let us not love in word,*

---

[p] Ἐπίτασις ἀγάπης ὁ ἔλεος.—Greg. Nyss. in Matt. v. 7. [De Beatit. Orat. v. Opp. Tom. I. p. 803 A.]

*or in tongue,* ('Αλλ' ἔργῳ καὶ ἀληθείᾳ,) *but in work and in truth.* To love in *work*, and to love in *truth*, he signifies to be the same thing; and to pretend love in speech, without practising it in deed, he implies not allowable. And St James in way of comparison says, that as faith without works is dead, so love without beneficence is useless. For, *If a brother or sister be naked, and destitute of daily food, and one of you say unto him, Depart in peace, be you warmed and filled, notwithstanding ye give them not those things which are needful to the body, what doth it profit? Even so faith without works is dead.* Cold wishes of good, working no real benefit to our neighbour, and a faint assent unto truth, producing no constant obedience to God, are things near of kin, and of like value; both of little worth or use. Charity then being the main point of religion, mercy and bounty being the chief parts of charity, well may these duties be placed in so high a rank, according to the divine heraldry of scripture.

SERM. I.

Jam. ii. 15, 16, 17.

7 To enforce which observations, and that we may be further certified about the weight and worth of these duties, we may consider, that to the observance of them most ample and excellent rewards are assigned; that, in return for what we bestow on our poor brethren, God hath promised all sorts of the best mercies and blessings to us. The best of all good things, (that which in David's opinion was better than life itself,) the fountain of all blessings, (God's love and favour, or mercy,) is procured thereby, or is annexed to it. For, *God loveth a cheerful giver,* saith St Paul; and, *The merciful shall obtain mercy,* saith our Saviour: and, *Mercy*

Ps. lxiii. 3.

2 Cor. ix. 7.
Matt. v. 7.
Jam. ii. 13.

*rejoiceth against judgment,* (or boasteth, and triumpheth over it; Κατακαυχᾶται ἔλεος κρίσεως: that is, it appeaseth God's wrath, and prevents our condemnation and punishment,) saith St James; God will not continue displeased with him, nor will withhold his mercy from him, who is kind and merciful to his neighbour. It is true, if rightly understood, what the Hebrew Wise Man saith, *Water will quench a flaming fire, and alms maketh an atonement for sins.* For this practice hath the nature and name of a sacrifice, and is declared as such both in excellency and efficacy to surpass all other sacrifices; to be most acceptable to God, most available for expiation of guilt, most effectual in obtaining mercy and favour[q]. Other sacrifices performed in obedience to God's appointment (on virtue of our Lord's perfect obedience, and with regard to his pure sacrifice of himself) did in their way propitiate God, and atone sin: but this hath an intrinsic worth, and a natural aptitude to those purposes. Other obligations did signify a willingness to render a due homage to God: this really and immediately performs it. They were shadows or images well resembling that duty, (parting with anything we have for the sake of God, and for purchasing his favour,) whereof this is the body and substance. This is therefore preferred as in itself excelling the rest, and more estimable in God's sight; so that in comparison or competition therewith, the other seem to be slighted and rejected. *I will,* saith God, *have mercy, and*

---

[q] Si nudum vestias, teipsum induis justitiam.—Ambr. Offic. I. 11. [Opp. Tom. II. col. 11 F.] Hier. in Psalm. cxxxiii. [Opp. Tom. II. col. 475.] Chrys. Opp. Tom. V. Orat. LV. [p. 374.]

*not sacrifice:* and, *Will the Lord be pleased with thousands of rams, or with ten thousands of rivers of oil?* Will he? that is, he will not be pleased with such sacrifices, if they be abstracted from the more delightful sacrifices of bounty and mercy. God never made an exception against these, or derogated from them in any case: they absolutely and perpetually are, as St Paul speaketh, *Odours of a sweet smell, sacrifices acceptable and well-pleasing to God.* And the apostle to the Hebrews seconds him: *To do good,* saith he, *and to communicate, forget not; for with such sacrifices God is well pleased.* By these, all other works and all enjoyments are sanctified: for, *Give alms,* saith our Lord, *of what ye have; and, behold, all things are pure unto you.* Such charitable persons are therefore frequently pronounced blessed, that is, in effect instated in a confluence of all good things. *Blessed is he that considereth the poor,* says the Psalmist; and, *He that hath a bountiful eye is blessed,* saith Solomon; and, *He that hath mercy on the poor, happy is he,* saith the Wise Man again; and, *Blessed are the merciful,* saith our Lord himself. So in gross and generally. Particularly also, and in retail, the greatest blessings are expressly allotted to this practice; prosperity in all our affairs is promised thereto. *Thou,* saith Moses, *shalt surely give thy poor brother, and thine heart shall not be grieved that thou givest unto him; because that for this thing the Lord thy God shall bless thee in all thy works, and in all that thou puttest thine hand unto.* Stability in a good condition is ordinarily consequent thereon: so the prophet Daniel implies, when, advising king Nebuchadnezzar to these

SERM. I.

Mic. vi. 7.

Phil. iv. 18.

Heb. xiii. 16.

Luke xi. 41.

Ps. xli. 1.

Prov. xxii. 9.
Prov. xiv. 21.

Matt. v. 7.

Deut. xv. 10.

works, he adds, *If it may be a lengthening of thy tranquillity.* Deliverance from evil incumbent, protection in imminent danger, and support in afflictions, are the sure rewards thereof; so the Psalmist assures us: *Blessed,* saith he, *is he that considereth the poor: the Lord will deliver him in time of trouble. The Lord will preserve him and keep him alive, and he shall be blessed upon earth; and thou wilt not deliver him unto the will of his enemies. The Lord will strengthen him upon the bed of languishing; thou wilt make all his bed in his sickness.* Security from all want is likewise a recompense proper thereto: for, *He that giveth to the poor shall not lack,* saith the Wise Man. *If thou draw out thy soul to the hungry, and satisfy the afflicted soul, then shall thy light arise in obscurity, &c.* Thriving in wealth and estate is another special reward: for, *The liberal soul shall be made fat;* the same author gives us his word for it. Even of the good things here below, to those who for his sake in this or any other way do *Let go houses or lands,* our Lord promiseth the return of *a hundredfold,* either in kind or in value. So great encouragements are annexed to this practice even in relation to the concernments of this transitory life: but to them beside God hath destinated rewards incomparably more considerable and precious, spiritual and eternal rewards, treasures of heavenly wealth, crowns of endless glory, the perfection of joy and bliss to be dispensed *At the resurrection of the just. He that for my sake hath left houses or lands, shall receive a hundredfold now at this time,* (or in this present life,) *and in the world to come shall inherit everlasting life;* so infallible truth hath assured us.

They who perform these duties are said to *Make themselves bags which wax not old, a treasure that faileth not in the heavens;* to *Make themselves friends of the unrighteous mammon, who, when they fail,* (when they depart, and leave their earthly wealth,) *will receive them into everlasting habitations;* to *Lay up in store for themselves a good foundation against the time to come, that they may lay hold on eternal life.* Such rewards are promised to the observers.

SERM. I.

Luke xii. 33; xvi. 9.

1 Tim. vi. 19.

8 And correspondently grievous punishments are designed and denounced to the transgressors of these duties; the worst of miseries is their portion and doom: they, for being such, do forfeit God's love and favour; they lose his blessing and protection; they can have no sure possession, nor any comfortable enjoyment of their estate; for *He,* saith St James, *shall have judgment without mercy, who sheweth no mercy.* And of such a person it is said in Job, *That which he laboureth for he shall restore, and shall not swallow it down: according to his substance shall the restitution be, and he shall not rejoice therein; because he hath oppressed and forsaken the poor.* (Not only because he hath unjustly oppressed, but because he hath uncharitably forsaken the poor.) If by the divine forbearance such persons do seem to enjoy a fair *Portion in this life,* (*Prospering in the world, and increasing in riches,*) they will find a sad reckoning behind in the other world: this will be the result of that audit; *Woe be unto you, rich men, for ye have received your consolation;* (such rich men are meant, who have got, or kept, or used their wealth basely; who have detained all the consolation it

Jam. ii. 13.

Job xx. 18, 19.

Ps. xvii. 14; lxxiii. 12.

Luke vi. 24.

yields to themselves, and imparted none to others;) and, *Remember, son, thou didst receive thy good things in this life;* (so didst receive them, as to swallow them, and spend them here, without any provision or regard for the future in the use of them;) and, *Cast that unprofitable servant* (who made no good use of his talent) *into utter darkness.* Such will be the fate of *Every one that treasures up to himself, and is not rich unto God;* not rich in piety and charity, not rich in performing for God's sake works of bounty and mercy.

9 It is indeed most considerable, that at the final reckoning, when all men's actions shall be strictly scanned, and justly sentenced according to their true desert, a special regard will be had to the discharge or neglect of these duties. It is the bountiful and merciful persons, who have relieved Christ in his poor members and brethren, who in that day will appear to be the sheep at the right hand, and shall hear the good Shepherd's voice uttering those joyful words, *Come, ye blessed of my Father, enter into the kingdom prepared for you from the foundation of the world: for I was an hungred, and ye gave me meat; I was thirsty, and ye gave me drink; I was a stranger, and ye took me in; I was naked, and ye clothed me; I was sick, and ye visited me; I was in prison, and ye came unto me.* He doth not say, because you have made goodly professions, because you have been orthodox in your opinions, because you have frequented religious exercises, (have prayed often and long, have kept many fasts, and heard many sermons,) because you have been staunch in your conversations, because you have been punctual in

your dealings, because you have maintained a specious guise of piety, sobriety, and justice; (although, indeed, he that will come off well at that great trial, must be responsible, and able to yield a good account in respect to all those particulars;) but because you have been charitably benign and helpful to persons in need and distress, therefore blessed are you, therefore enter into the kingdom of glorious bliss prepared for such persons. This proceeding more than intimates, that, in the judgment of our Lord, no sort of virtue or good practice is to be preferred before that of charitable bounty; or rather that, in his esteem, none is equal thereto: so that if the question were put to him, which is one of them to Antiochus, (in Athanasius's works,) which is the most eminent virtue[r]? our Lord would resolve it no otherwise than is done by that father, affirming, that mercifulness is the queen of virtues; for that, at the final account, the examination chiefly proceeds upon that; it is made the special touchstone of piety, and the peculiar ground of happiness. On the other side, those who have been deficient in these performances (uncharitable and unmerciful persons) will at the last trial appear to be the wretched goats on the left hand, unto whom this uncomfortable speech shall by the great Judge be pronounced; *Depart from me, ye cursed, into everlasting fire, prepared for the devil and his angels: for I was hungry, and ye gave me no meat; I was thirsty, and ye gave me no drink; I was a stranger, and ye took me not in; naked, and ye clothed me not; sick and in prison, and ye visited me not.* It is not, we may see, for having

Matt. xxv. 41, 42, 43.

[r Quæst. cxx. Inter Athan. Opp. Tom. II. p. 297 B.]

done that which in this world is called rapine or wrong, for having pillaged or cozened their neighbour, for having committed adultery or murder, or any other thing prohibited, that these unhappy men are said to be formally impeached, and finally condemned to that miserable doom; but for having been unkind and unmerciful to their poor brethren[s]: this at that high tribunal will pass for a most enormous crime, for the capital offence; for this it is that they shall be cursed, and cast down into a wretched consortship with those malicious and merciless fiends, unto whose disposition they did so nearly approach.

Thus it appears how mighty a stress God in the holy scripture doth lay upon these duties, so peremptorily commanding them, so vehemently pressing them, so highly commending them, so graciously by promises alluring us to the performance, so dreadfully by threatenings deterring us from the neglect of them. What an affront then will it be to God's authority, what a distrust to his word, what a contempt of his power, his justice, his wisdom, what a despite to his goodness and mercy, if, notwithstanding all these declarations of his will and purposes, we shall presume to be uncharitable in this kind! There are also considerations, (very many, very clear, and very strong,) which discover the great reasonableness and equity of these laws, with our indispensable obligation to obey them; the which indeed with greater force

---

[s] Οὐχ ὅτι διηρπάκασιν, οὐδ' ὅτι σεσυλήκασιν, ἢ μεμοιχεύκασιν, ἢ ἄλλο τι τῶν ἀπηγορευμένων πεποιήκασιν, ταύτην τὴν τάξιν κατακριθέντες, ἀλλ' ὅτι μὴ Χριστὸν διὰ τῶν δεομένων τεθεραπεύκασιν.—Greg. Naz. Orat. [xiv. Opp. Tom. i. p. 285 c.]

do exact these duties from us, and do more earnestly plead in the poor man's behalf, than he can beg or cry. If we either look up unto God, or down upon our poor neighbour, if we reflect upon ourselves, or consider our wealth itself, every where we may discern various reasons obliging us, and various motives inducing us to the practice of these duties.

SERM. I.

In regard to God,

1 We may consider, that, by exercising of bounty and mercy, we are kind and courteous to God himself; by neglecting those duties, we are unkind and rude to him : for that, what of good or evil is by us done to the poor, God interprets and accepts as done to himself. The poor have a peculiar relation to God; he openly and frequently professeth himself their especial friend, patron, and protector; he is much concerned in, and particularly chargeth his providence with their support. In effect therefore they shall surely be provided for, one way or the other ; (*The poor shall eat and be satisfied: God will save the afflicted people: The Lord preserveth the strangers, he relieveth the fatherless and widow. When the poor and needy seek water, and there is none, and their tongue faileth for thirst, I the Lord will hear them, I the God of Israel will not forsake them:*) but out of goodness to us, he chooseth, (if it may be, we freely concurring therein,) and best liketh, that it should be done by our hands; this conducing no less to our benefit, than to theirs ; we thereby having opportunity to shew our respect to himself, and to lay an engagement on him to do us good. God therefore lendeth the poor man his own name, and

II. Head of discourse.

Ps.xxii.26; xviii.27; cxlvi.9.

Isai.xli.17.

SERM. alloweth him to crave our succour for his sake.
I.
(When the poor man asketh us in God's name, or
for God's sake, he doth not usurp or forge, he hath
good authority, and a true ground for doing so:)
God gives him credit from himself unto us for what
he wants, and bids us charge what he receiveth
on his own account; permitting us to reckon him
obliged thereby, and to write him our debtor; engaging his own word and reputation duly to repay,
Prov. xix. fully to satisfy us. *He that hath pity on the poor
17. *lendeth to the Lord; and that which he hath given
will he pay him again*, saith the Wise Man: and,
Matt. xxv. *Inasmuch as ye have done it to the least of my bre-
40, 45. thren, ye have done it unto me*, saith our Saviour:
Heb. vi. 10. and, *God is not unrighteous to forget your work and
labour of love, which ye have shewed toward his
name, in that ye have ministered to the saints, and
do minister*, saith the apostle. What therefore we
give to the poor, God accepteth as an expression
of kindness to himself, being given to one of his
friends and clients, in respect to him; he regards
it as a testimony of friendly confidence in him, signifying that we have a good opinion of him, that
we take him for able and willing to requite a good
turn, that we dare take his word, and think our
goods safe enough in his custody. But if we stop
our ears, or shut our hands from the poor, God
interprets it as a harsh repulse, and an heinous
affront put upon himself: we doing it to one who
bears his name, and wears his livery, (for the poor
man's rags are badges of his relation unto God,)
he thereby judges, that we have little good-will,
little respect, little compassion toward himself:
since we vouchsafe not to grant him so mean a

favour, since we refuse at his request, and (as it were) in his need, to accommodate him with a small sum, he justly reputes it as an argument of unkindly diffidence in him, that we have sorry thoughts of him, deeming him no good correspondent, little valuing his word, suspecting his goodness, his truth, or his sufficiency.

2  We by practising those duties are just, by omitting them are very unjust toward God. For our goods, our wealth, and our estate are indeed none of them simply or properly our own, so that we have an absolute property in them, or an entire disposal of them: no, we are utterly incapable of such a right unto them, or power over them: God necessarily is the true and absolute proprietary of them. They are called the gifts of God: but we must not understand that God, by giving them to us, hath parted with his own right to them: they are deposited with us in trust, not alienated from him; they are committed to us as stewards, not transferred upon us as masters: they are so ours, that we have no authority to use them according to our will or fancy, but are obliged to manage them according to God's direction and order. He, by right immutable, is Lord paramount of all his creation; every thing unalienably belongs to him upon many accounts. He out of nothing made all things at first, and to every creature through each moment a new being is conferred by his preservative influence: originally therefore he is Lord of all things, and continually a new title of dominion over every thing springeth up unto him: it is his always, because he always maketh it. We ourselves are naturally mere slaves and vassals to him:

SERM. I.

Eccles. v. 19; vi. 2.

SERM. I.

as we can never be our own, (masters of ourselves, of our lives, of our liberties,) so cannot we ever properly be owners of any thing; there are no possible means by which we can acquire any absolute title to the least mite; the principal right to what we seem to get, according to all law and reason, accrueth to our master. All things about us, by which we live, with which we work and trade, the earth which supports and feeds us, and furnisheth us with all commodities, the air we breathe, the sun and stars which cherish our life, are all of them his, his productions and his possessions, subsisting by his pleasure, subject to his disposal. How then can any thing be ours? How can we say, with the foolish churl Nabal, *Shall I take my bread, and my water, and my flesh, and give it?* Thine? O inconsiderate man! How camest thou by it? How dost thou hold it? Didst thou make it? Or dost thou preserve it? Canst thou claim any thing by nature[t]? No; thou broughtest nothing with thee into the world; thou didst not bring thyself hither. Canst thou challenge any thing to thyself from chance? No, for there is no such thing as chance, all things being guided and governed by God's providence. Dost thou conceive thy industry can entitle thee to any thing? Thou art mistaken; for all the wit and strength thou appliest, the head thou contrivest with, and the hands thou workest with, are God's; all the success thou findest did wholly depend on him, was

Ps. xxiv. 1;
l. 12;
lxxxix. 11;
xcv. 5.

1 Sam. xxv. 11.

---

[t] Sed ais, Quid injustum est, si cum aliena non invadam, propria diligentius servo? O impudens dictum, propria dicis? quæ? ex quibus reconditis in hunc mundum detulisti?—Ambros. [Serm. LXIV. Dom. viii. post Pent. Opp. Tom. v. fol. 92 L. Ed. Paris. 1632.]

altogether derived from him; all thy projects were vain, all thy labours would be fruitless, did not he assist and bless thee. Thou dost vainly and falsely *Lift up thine heart, and forget the Lord thy God, whenas thy herds and flocks multiply, and thy silver and gold is multiplied, and all that thou hast is multiplied; if thou sayest in thy heart, My power, and the might of my hand, hath gotten me this wealth. But thou must remember the Lord thy God, for it is he that giveth thee power to get wealth.* [——*Who am I*, saith David, *and what is my people, that we should be able to offer so willingly after this sort? For all things come of thee; and of thine own have we given thee.*] Since then upon all scores every thing we have doth appertain to God, he may without any injury recall or resume whatever he pleaseth; and while he letteth any thing abide with us, we cannot justly use it otherwise than he hath appointed, we cannot duly apply it otherwise than to his interest and service[u]. God then having enjoined, that after we have satisfied our necessities, and supplied our reasonable occasions, we should employ the rest to the relief of our poor neighbours; that *If we have two coats,* (one more than we need,) *we should impart one to him that hath none; if we have meat* abundant, that we *likewise* communicate to him that wants it:

SERM. I.

Deut. viii. 13, 14, 17, 18.

1 Chron. xxix. 14.

Luke iii. 11.

[u] Aliena rapere convincitur, qui ultra necessaria sibi retinere probatur.—Hieron.

Quicquid enim nobis Deus plusquam opus est dederit, non nobis specialiter dedit, sed per nos aliis erogandum transmisit; si non dederimus, res alienas invasimus.—Aug. [Serm. CLXXVIII. Opp. Tom. v. col. 461 F.]

Terra communiter omnibus hominibus data est, proprium nemo dicat quod commune; plus quam sufficeret, sumptum et violenter obtentum est.—Ambros. [ubi supra. fol. 92 M.]

SERM. I.

God, by the poor man's voice, (or by his need and misery,) demanding his own from us, we are very unjust if we presume to withhold it; doubly unjust we are, both toward God and toward our neighbour: we are unfaithful stewards, misapplying the goods of our Master, and crossing his order[x]: we are wrongful usurpers, detaining from our neighbour that which God hath allotted him; we are in the court of conscience; we shall appear at the bar of God's judgment no better than robbers, (under vizards of legal right and possession,) spoiling our poor brother of his goods; his, I say, by the very same title as any thing can be ours, by the free donation of God, fully and frequently expressed, as we have seen, in his holy word. (He cannot take it away by violence or surreption against our will, but we are bound willingly to yield it up to him; to do that, were disorder in him; to refuse this, is wrong in us.) 'Tis the hungry man's bread which we hoard up in our barns, 'tis his meat on which we glut, and his drink which we guzzle[y]: 'tis the naked man's apparel which we shut up in our presses, or which we exorbitantly ruffle and flaunt in: 'tis the needy person's gold and silver which we closely hide in our chests, or spend idly, or put out to useless use. We are in thus holding, or thus spending, truly Πλεονέκται, not only covetous, but wrongful, or havers of more than our own, against the will of the right owners; plainly vio-

[x] Σὺ δὲ οὐκ ἀποστερητὴς, ἃ πρὸς οἰκονομίαν ἐδέξω, ταῦτα ἴδια σεαυτοῦ ποιούμενος;—Bas. M. [Hom. in Luc. XII. 18. Opp. Tom. II. p. 50 B.]

[y] Nostrum est (pauperes clamant) quod effunditis; nobis crudeliter subtrahitur, quod inaniter expenditis.—Bern. Ep. XLII. [(De Offic. Episc.) Opp. Tom. I. col. 470 B.]

lating that precept of Solomon; *Withhold not good from them to whom it is due, when it is in the power of thy hand to do it.* If we are ambitious of having a property in somewhat, or affect to call any thing our own, 'tis only by nobly giving that we can accomplish our desire; that will certainly appropriate our goods to our use and benefit: but from basely keeping, or vainly embezzling them, they become not our possession and enjoyment, but our theft and our bane[z]. (These things, spoken after the holy fathers, wise instructors in matters of piety, are to be understood with reasonable temperament, and practised with honest prudence. I cannot stand to discuss cases, and remove scruples; a pious charity will easily discern its due limits and measures, both declining perplexity, and not evading duty. The sum is, that justice towards God and man obligeth us not to suffer our poor brother to perish, or pine away for want, when we surfeit and swim in plenty, or not to see him lack necessaries, when we are well able to relieve him.)

3 Shewing bounty and mercy are the most proper and the principal expressions of our gratitude unto God; so that in omitting them, we are not only very unjust, but highly ingrateful. Innumerable are the benefits, favours, and mercies, (both common and private,) which God hath bestowed on us, and doth continually bestow: he incessantly showers down blessings on our heads; *He daily loadeth us with his benefits;* he perpetually *Crowneth us with lovingkindness and tender*

SERM. I.

Prov. iii. 27.

Ps. lxviii. 19; ciii. 4.

---

[z] Omne igitur quod male possidetur, alienum est: male autem possidet, qui male utitur.—August. [Ep. CLIII. ad Maced. Opp. Tom. II. col. 534 E.]

*mercies:* all that we are, all that we have, all that we can hope for of good, is alone from his free bounty: our beings and lives, with all the conveniences and comforts of them, we entirely owe to him as to our Maker, our Preserver, our constant Benefactor: all the excellent privileges we enjoy, and all the glorious hopes we have as Christians, we also stand indebted for purely to his undeserved mercy and grace. And, *What shall we render unto the Lord for all his benefits toward us?* Shall we render him nothing? Shall we refuse him anything? Shall we boggle at making returns so inconsiderable, in regard to what he hath done for us? What is a little gold, or silver, or brass perhaps, which our poor neighbour craveth of us, in comparison to our life, our health, our reason; to all accommodations of our body, and all endowments of our mind? What are all the goods in the world to the love and favour of God, to the pardon of our sins, to the gifts of God's Spirit, to the dignity of being the children of God and heirs of salvation; to the being freed from extreme miseries, and made capable of eternal felicity? And doth not this unexpressible goodness, do not all these inestimable benefits require some correspondent thankfulness? Are we not obliged, shall we not be willing to exhibit some real testimony thereof? And what other can we exhibit beside this? We cannot directly or immediately requite God, for he cannot so receive anything from us; he is not capable of being himself enriched or exalted, of being anywise pleasured or bettered by us, who is in himself infinitely sufficient, glorious, joyful, and happy: *Our goodness extends not to him; A man cannot be profitable to his Maker.* All that we can do in this kind is thus indirectly, in the persons of his poor relations, to gratify him, imparting at his desire, and for his sake, somewhat of what he hath bestowed on us upon them. Such a thankful return we owe unto God, not only for what he hath given us, but even for the capacity of giving to others; for that we are in the number of those who can afford relief, and who need not to demand it[a]. Our very wealth and prosperous state should not seem to us so contemptible things, that we should be unwilling to render somewhat back in grateful resentment for them: the very act of giving is itself no mean benefit; (having so much of honour in it, so much of pleasure going with it, so much of reward following it;) we receive far more than we return in giving; for which therefore it is fit that we should return our gratitude, and consequently that we should perform these duties. For indeed without this practice, no other expression of gratitude can be true in itself, or can be acceptable to God. We may seem abundantly to thank him in words; but a sparing hand gives the lie to the fullest mouth:

[a] Δός τι τῷ Θεῷ χαριστήριον, ὅτι τῶν εὖ ποιεῖν δυναμένων ἐγένου, ἀλλ' οὐ τῶν εὖ παθεῖν δεομένων.—Greg. Naz. [Orat. XIV. Opp. Tom. I. p. 276 A.]

—Τὸν φιλάνθρωπον ὑμνῆσαι δεσπότην, ὅτι τοῖς ἀλλοτρίοις ἡμᾶς σωφρονίζει παθήμασι, καὶ οὐκ ἡμᾶς εἰς ἑτέρων παρέπεμψεν οἰκίας, ἀλλ' εἰς τὰς ἡμετέρας ἄλλους ἤγαγε θύρας.—Theodor. Ep. XXX. [Opp. Tom. III. p. 920 C.]

Εἰ μὴ νομίζεις λαμβάνειν μᾶλλον, ἢ διδόναι, μὴ παράσχῃς.— Chrys. Orat. LIV. [Opp. Tom. V. p. 365.]

Neque enim homo Deo præstat beneficium in his quæ dederit, sed Deus in his homini quæ acceperit.—Salvian. [adv. Avar. Lib. I. p. 234. Ed. Baluz.]

we may spare our breath, if we keep back our substance; for all our praising God for his goodness, and blessing him with our lips, if we will do nothing for him, if we will not part with anything for his sake, appears mere compliment; is, in truth, plain mockery, and vile hypocrisy.

4 Yea, which we may further consider, all our devotion, severed from a disposition of practising these duties, is no less such; cannot have any true worth in it, shall not yield any good effect from it. Our prayers, if we are uncharitably disposed, what are they other than demonstrations of egregious impudence and folly? For how can we with any face presume to ask anything from God, when we deny him requesting a small matter from us? How can we with any reason expect any mercy from him, when we vouchsafe not to shew any mercy for his sake? Can we imagine that God will hearken unto, or mind our petitions, when we are deaf to his entreaties, and regardless of his desires? No; *Whoso stoppeth his ears at the cry of the poor, he also shall cry himself, but shall not be heard.* 'Tis his declaration to such bold and unreasonable petitioners, *When you spread forth your hands, I will not hear you; when you make many prayers, I will not hear.* No importunity, no frequency of prayers will move God in such a case; the needy man's cries and complaints will drown their noise; his sighs and groans will obstruct their passage, and stop the ears of God against them. Likewise all our semblances of repentance, all our corporal abstinences and austerities, if a kind and merciful disposition are wanting, what are they truly but presumptuous dallyings, or impertinent triflings

with God? For do we not grossly collude with sin, when we restrain the sensual appetites of the body, but foment the soul's more unreasonable desires; when we curb our wanton flesh, and give licence to a base spirit[b]? Do we not palpably baffle, when in respect to God we pretend to deny ourselves, yet upon urgent occasion allow him nothing? Do we not strangely prevaricate, when we would seem to appease God's anger, and purchase his favour by our submissions, yet refuse to do that which he declares most pleasing to him, and most necessary to those purposes? It is an ordinary thing for men thus to serve God, and thus to delude themselves: *I have known many,* saith St Basil, *who have fasted, and prayed, and groaned, and expressed all kind of costless piety, who yet would not part with one doit to the afflicted*[c]. Such a cheap and easy piety, which costs us little or nothing, can surely not be worth much; and we must not conceit, that the all-wise God (*The God of knowledge, by whom actions are weighed,* as Anna sang, and who *Weigheth the spirits* also, as the Wise Man saith) will be cheated therewith, or take it for more than its just value. No; he hath expressly signified, that he hath *Not chosen* such services, nor doth take any pleasure in them: he hath called them *Vain and impertinent oblations;* not *Sweet* or *acceptable,* but *abominable* and *troublesome* to him, such as he *cannot away with,* and *is weary to bear.* 'Tis religious liberality that doth prove us

SERM. I.

2 Sam. xxiv. 24.

1 Sam. ii. 3.

Prov. xvi. 2.

Isai. lviii. 5, 6; i. 13, 14.
Mic. vi. 6, 7.
Jer. vi. 20.

[b] Τί δὲ κέρδος, σωφροσύνη μετὰ ἀπανθρωπίας; &c.—Chrys. Or. LV. [Opp. Tom. v. p. 373.]

[c] Οἶδα πολλοὺς νηστεύοντας, προσευχομένους, στενάζοντας, πᾶσαν τὴν ἀδάπανον εὐλάβειαν ἐνδεικνυμένους, ὀβολὸν δὲ ἕνα μὴ προϊεμένους τοῖς θλιβομένοις.—Bas. M. [Hom. in Div. Opp. Tom. II. p. 54 c.]

to be serious and earnest in other religious performances; which assures that we value matters of piety at a considerable rate; which gives a substance and solidity to our devotions; which sanctifies our fasts, and verifies our penances; which renders our praises real, and our prayers effectual; so that these being combined, we may reasonably expect acceptance and recompense; and in effect to hear that from God, which by him was returned to good Cornelius, *Thy prayers and thine alms are come up for a memorial before God.*

Acts x. 4.

5 The conscionable practice of these duties doth plainly spring from those good dispositions of mind regarding God, which are the original grounds and fountains of all true piety; and the neglect of them issueth from those vicious dispositions which have a peculiar inconsistency with piety, being destructive thereof in the very foundation and root. Faith in God is the fundamental grace upon which piety is grounded; love and fear of God are the radical principles from which it grows: all which as the charitable man discovers in his practice, so they are apparently banished from the heart of the illiberal and unmerciful person.

As for faith, the good man, in shewing bounty, exerciseth the chief act thereof; he freely parteth with his goods, because he trusteth on God's providence more than them, and believeth God more ready to help him, than any creature can do, in his need; because he is persuaded that God is most good and benign, so as never to suffer him to be oppressed with want; because he taketh God to be just and faithful, who, having charged him *To care for nothing,* but *To cast his care and burden upon*

Matt. vi. 25.
Phil. iv. 6.

*the Lord*, having promised to *care for him*, to *Sustain him, Never to leave or forsake him*, having also engaged himself to repay and recompense him for what he giveth to his poor neighbour, will not fail to make good his word; because he thinks God abundantly solvent, and himself never the poorer for laying out in his behalf; because, in short, he is content to live in a dependance upon God, and at his disposal. It is mentioned by the apostle to the Hebrews, as a special instance of a resolute and constant faith in the first Christians, that *They took joyfully the spoiling of their goods, knowing in themselves that they had in heaven a better and an enduring substance*. He that not forcibly by the violent rapacity of others, but voluntarily by his own free resignation for the service of God delivereth them up with the same alacrity, opinion, and hope, thereby demonstrates the same faith. But the gripple wretch, who will bestow nothing on his poor brother for God's sake, is evidently an infidel, having none at all, or very heathenish conceits of God[d]. He must be either a mere atheist, disbelieving the existence of God; or an epicurean, in his heart denying God's providence over human affairs; (for did he conceive God to have any regard unto, or any influence over what passes here, how could he be afraid of wanting upon this score? how could he repose any confidence in these possessions? how could he think himself secure in such a neglect or defiance of God?) or he must be exceedingly profane, entertaining most dishonour-

SERM. I.

1 Pet. v. 7.
Ps. lv. 22.
Heb. xiii. 5.

Heb. x. 34.

---

[d] Ὁ γὰρ τοιοῦτος οὐ τῷ Θεῷ πεπίστευκεν, ἀλλὰ τῷ ἑαυτοῦ χρυσίῳ, Θεὸν τοῦτο ἡγούμενος, καὶ ἐπ᾽ αὐτῷ πεποιθώς.—Const. Apost. IV. 4. [Cotel. Pat. Apost. Tom. I. p. 293.]

able and injurious apprehensions of God. He cannot but imagine God very unkind, not only in neglecting men that want his help, but in making them to suffer for spending upon his account; very unjust, in not repaying what he borrows; very unfaithful, in breaking his word; very deceitful, in gulling us of our things by fair promises of restitution and requital: or he must apprehend God forgetful of what we do, and himself says; or that he is needy and impotent, not having wherewith to make satisfaction, not being able to make good what he pretends. He must in his conceit debase God even beneath the vilest creatures, thinking a senseless lump of clay more apt in his need to help him, than God can be with all his power and care; supposing his money safer in his own coffers than in God's hands, and that iron bars will guard it more surely than divine protection; esteeming his neighbour's bond for much better security than God's word, and that a mortal man is far more able or more true than the eternal God. He certainly cannot think one word true that God says, being loath to trust him for a penny, for a piece of bread, or for an old garment. All God's promises of recompense, and threatenings of punishment, he takes for idle fictions: heaven and hell are but Utopias in his conceit; the joys of one, offered to the charitable person, are but pleasant fancies; the torments of the other, denounced to the uncharitable, but fearful dreams. All other things are but names; money and lands are the only real things unto him; all the happiness he can conceive or wish is contained in bags and barns; these are the sole points of his faith, and objects of his confidence. *He makes gold his hope, and saith to the fine gold, Thou art my confidence. He rejoices because his wealth is great, and because his hand hath gotten much,* as Job speaketh, disclaiming that practice in himself, and tacitly charging it on the persons we speak of. He doth, in fine, affect a total independency upon God, and cares to have no dealing with him; he would trust to himself, and live on his own estate: so gross infidelity and horrible profaneness of mind lie couched under this sort of vices.

As for the love of God, the liberal man declares it, in that for God's sake he is willing to part with anything, that he values God's love and favour above all other goods; that he deems himself rich and happy enough in the enjoyment of God. But, *Who hath this world's goods, and seeth his brother have need, and shutteth up his bowels from him, how dwelleth the love of God in him?* saith St John: that is, it is impossible he should love God; 'tis a vain conceit to think he does; 'tis a frivolous thing for him to pretend it. For how possibly can he bear in his heart any affection to God, who will not for his sake, and at his instance, part with a little worthless trash and dirty pelf? who prizes so inconsiderable matters beyond God's favour and friendship? who prefers the keeping of his wealth before the enjoyment of God; and chooses rather certainly to quit his whole interest in God, than to adventure a small parcel of his estate with God? His practice indeed sufficiently discovers, that his hard and stupid heart is uncapable of any love, except of a corrupt, inordinate, and fond love, or dotage toward himself, since so present and sensible objects cannot affect him. *He that loveth not his brother, whom he hath seen, how can he love God, whom he hath not seen?*

And as to the fear and reverence of God, the liberal man expresses it in submission to God's commands, although with his own present seeming diminution and loss; in preferring the discharging of his conscience before the retaining his money; in casting overboard his temporal goods, that he may secure his spiritual and eternal concernments. He can say (his practice attesting to his profession) with David, *I love thy commandments above gold;* and, *The law of thy mouth is dearer to me than thousands of gold and silver:* he shews that he is *A man of truth, fearing God, and hating covetousness;* which dispositions, as having much affinity and connection, are well joined together by Jethro. But the uncharitable man can have little fear of God before his eyes: since the commands of God have no efficacy on his conscience; since he dreads not the effects of divine power and justice, provoked by his disobedience; since he deems an imaginary danger of want from giving, worse than a certain commission of sin in withholding; and is more afraid of penury here, than of damnation hereafter.

The truth is, the covetous or illiberal man is therefore uncapable of being truly pious, because his heart is possessed with vain devotion toward somewhat beside God, which in effect is his sole divinity; he is justly styled an idolater, for that he directs and employs the chief affections of his mind upon an idol of clay, which he loves with all his heart and all his soul, which he entirely confides in, which he esteems and worships above all things. It is Mammon, which of all the competitors and antagonists of God, invading God's right, and usurping his place, is (as our Lord intimates) the most dangerous, and desperately repugnant: where he becomes predominant, true religion is quite excluded; *Ye cannot serve God and mammon.* Other vicious inclinations combat reason, and often baffle it, but seldom so vanquish it, as that a man doth approve or applaud himself in his miscarriages: but the covetous humour seizeth on our reason itself, and seateth itself therein; inducing it to favour and countenance what is done amiss. The voluptuous man is swayed by the violence of his appetite; but the covetous is seduced by the dictate of his judgment: he therefore scrapes and hoards, and lets go nothing, because he esteems wealth the best thing in the world, and then judges himself most wise, when he is most base. *Labour not to be rich; cease from thine own wisdom,* saith Solomon; intimating the judgment such persons are wont to make of their riches: whence, of all dispositions opposite to piety, this is the most pernicious. But further,

6 Let us consider, that nothing is more conformable to God's nature, or renders us more like to him, than beneficence and mercy; and that consequently nothing can be more grateful to him: that nothing is more disagreeable and contrary to the essential disposition of God, than illiberality and unmercifulness; and therefore that nothing can be more distasteful to him. What is any being in the world, but an efflux of his bounty, and an argument of his liberality? Look everywhere about

SERM. I.

<small>Exod. xxxiv. 6.
Joel ii. 13.
Mic. vii. 18.
Isai. xxx. 18.
Rom. xv. 5, 33.
Eph. ii. 4.
2 Cor. xiii. 11; i. 3.
James v. 11.
1 Pet. v. 10.
Luke vi. 35.
Ps. cxlv. 9.</small>

nature, and consider the whole tenor of providence, survey all the works, and scan all the actions of God, you will find them all conspiring in attestation to those sweet characters and elogies which the holy scripture ascribeth to God, representing him to be *Merciful and gracious, longsuffering, and abundant in goodness;* to be *Sorry for evil,* (incident to, or inflicted upon any creature,) to *Delight in mercy,* to *Wait that he may be gracious;* styling him the *God of love, of peace, of hope, of patience, of all grace, and of all consolation, the Father of pities, rich in mercy, and full of bowels;* affirming of him, and by manifold evidences demonstrating, that he is *Benign even unto the ungrateful and evil;* that *He is good to all, and his tender mercies are over all his works.* Nature, I say, providence, and revelation, do all concur in testifying this, that there is nothing in God so peculiarly admirable, nothing, as it were, so godlike, that is, so highly venerable and amiable, as to do good and shew mercy[e]. We therefore by liberal communication to the needy do most approach to the nature of God, and most exactly imitate his practice; acquiring to ourselves thereby somewhat of divinity, and becoming little gods to our neighbour[f]. *Nothing,* saith St Chrysostom, *maketh us so near equal to God as beneficence*[g]: and, *Be,* saith St Gregory Nazianzen, *a god to the unfortunate, imitating the*

---

[e] Θεοῦ πολλῶν ὄντων ἐφ' οἷς θαυμάζεται, οὐδὲν οὕτως ὡς τὸ πάντας εὐεργετεῖν, ἰδιώτατον.—Greg. Naz. Orat. [XXXII. Tom. I. Opp. p. 596 E.]

[f] Deus est mortali juvare mortalem.—Plin. Hist. Nat. II. [5. 4.]

[g] Οὐδὲν γὰρ ἡμᾶς ἴσους Θεῷ ποιεῖ, ὡς τὸ εὐεργετεῖν.—Chrys. in Matt. Hom. XXXV. [Opp. Tom. II. p. 243.]

*mercy of God; for a man hath nothing of God so much as to do good*[h]. That such hath always been the common apprehension of men, the practice of all times sheweth, in that men have been ever apt to place their benefactors among their gods, deferring that love and veneration unto them in degree, which in perfection do appertain to the supreme Benefactor[i]. *Be merciful, as your heavenly Father is merciful;* so our Saviour proposeth God's mercy to us, both as a pattern directing, and as an argument inducing us to mercifulness: implying it also to be a good sign, declaring us the children of God, the genuine offspring of the all-good and all-merciful Father; yea, that it even renders and constitutes us such, (we thereby coming most truly to represent, and most nearly to resemble him). Our Lord further teaches us, saying, *Love your enemies, bless them that curse you, do good to those that hate you......that ye may be the sons of your Father which is in heaven.* And they who thus are God's children must consequently be very dear to him, and most gracious in his sight; he cannot but greatly like and love himself (the best of himself) in them; he cannot but cherish and treat them well, who are the fairest and truest images of himself; no spectacle can be so pleasant to him, as to see us in our practice to act himself, doing good

Luke vi. 35, 36.

Matt. v. 44, 45.

[h] Γένου τῷ ἀτυχοῦντι Θεός, τὸν ἔλεον τοῦ Θεοῦ μιμησάμενος. Οὐδὲν γὰρ οὕτως, ὡς τὸ εὖ ποιεῖν, ἄνθρωπος ἔχει Θεοῦ.—Greg. Naz. [Orat. xiv. Opp. Tom. i. p. 276 B.]

[i] Hic est vetustissimus referendi bene merentibus gratiam mos, ut tales numinibus adscribantur [ascribant].—Plin. Nat. Hist. ii. 7. [ii. 5. 5.]

Suscepit vita hominum, consuetudoque communis, ut beneficiis excellentes viros in cœlum fama ac voluntate tollerent.—Cic. de Nat. Deor. ii. [24, 62.]

SERM. I.

Col. iii. 12, 13.

Eph. v. 1, 2.

to one another; *As the elect of God, holy and beloved, putting on bowels of mercies and kindness, humbleness of mind, meekness, longsuffering; forbearing one another, and forgiving one another, even as Christ forgave us; Being followers of God as dear children, and walking in love, even as Christ also loved us.* But on the other side, there is not in nature anything so remotely distant from God, or so extremely opposite to him, as a greedy and griping niggard: hell is scarce so contrary to heaven, as such a man's disposition to the nature of God: for 'tis goodness which sits gloriously triumphant at the top of heaven; and uncharitableness lieth miserably grovelling under the bottom of hell: heaven descends from the one, as its principal cause; hell is built on the other, as its main foundation: as the one approximates the blessed angels to God, and beatifies them; so the other removeth the cursed fiends to such a distance from God and happiness: not to wish, not to do any good, is that which renders them both so bad and so wretched; and whoever in his conditions is so like to them, and in his practice so agrees with them, cannot but also be very odious to God, and extremely unhappy. God cannot but abhor so base a degeneration from his likeness in those who by nature are his children, and should be further such according to his gracious design; neither can anything more offend his eyes, than seeing them to use one another unkindly. So that if obtaining the certain favour of the great God, with all the benefits attending it, seem considerable to us; or if we think it advisable to shun his displeasure, with its sad effects; it concerns us to practise these duties. So I conclude that sort of considerations, enforcing these duties, which more immediately regard God.

SERM. I.

Further, before we deny our relief to our poor neighbour, let us with the eyes of our mind look on him, and attentively consider who he is, what he is in himself, and what he is in relation unto us. *The righteous considereth the cause of the poor; but the wicked regardeth not to know it. Blessed is he that considereth the poor.*

III. Head of discourse.

Prov. xxix. 7.

Ps. xli. 1.

1 He whose need craves our bounty, whose misery demands our mercy, what is he? He is not truly so mean and sorry a thing, as the disguise of misfortune, under which he appears, doth represent him. He who looks so deformedly and dismally, who to outward sight is so ill bestead, and so pitifully accoutred, hath latent in him much of admirable beauty and glory. He within himself containeth a nature very excellent; an immortal soul, and an intelligent mind, by which he nearly resembleth God himself, and is comparable to angels: he invisibly is owner of endowments, rendering him capable of the greatest and best things. What are money and lands? What are silk and fine linen? What are horses and hounds, in comparison to reason, to wisdom, to virtue, to religion, which he hath, or (in despite of all misfortune) he may have if he please? He whom you behold so dejectedly sneaking, in so despicable a garb, so destitute of all convenience and comfort, (lying in the dust, naked, or clad with rags, meagre with hunger or pain,) he comes of a most high and heavenly extraction: he was born a prince, the son of the greatest King eternal; he can truly call the sovereign Lord of all the world

his father, having derived his soul from the mouth, having had his body formed by the hands of God himself. (In this, *The rich and poor,* as the Wise Man saith, *do meet together; the Lord is the maker of them all.*) That same forlorn wretch, whom we are so apt to despise and trample upon, was framed and constituted lord of the visible world; had all the goodly brightnesses of heaven, and all the costly furnitures of earth created to serve him. (*Thou madest him,* saith the Psalmist of man, *to have dominion over the works of thine hands; thou hast put all things under his feet.*) Yea, he was made an inhabitant of paradise, and possessor of felicities superlative; had immortal life and endless joy in his hand, did enjoy the entire favour and friendship of the Most High. Such in worth of nature and nobleness of birth he is, as a man; and highly more considerable he is, as a Christian. For, as vile and contemptible as he looks, God hath so regarded and prized him, as for his sake to descend from heaven, to clothe himself with flesh, to assume the form of a servant; for his good to undertake and undergo the greatest inconveniences, infirmities, wants, and disgraces, the most grievous troubles and most sharp pains incident to mortal nature. God hath adopted him to be his child; the Son of God hath deigned to call him brother: he is a member of Christ, a temple of the Holy Ghost, a free denizen of the heavenly city, an heir of salvation, and candidate of eternal glory. The greatest and richest personage is not capable of better privileges than God hath granted him, or of higher preferments than God hath designed him to. He equally with the mightiest prince is the object of

God's especial providence and grace, of his continual regard and care, of his fatherly love and affection; who, as good Elihu saith, *Accepteth not the persons of princes, nor regardeth the rich more than the poor; for they are all the work of his hands.* In fine, this poor creature whom thou seest is a man, and a Christian, thine equal, whoever thou art, in nature, and thy peer in condition[k]: I say not, in the uncertain and unstable gifts of fortune, not in this worldly state, which is very inconsiderable; but in gifts vastly more precious, in title to an estate infinitely more rich and excellent. Yea, if thou art vain and proud, be sober and humble; he is thy better, in true dignity much to be preferred before thee, far in real wealth surpassing thee: for, *Better is the poor that walketh in his uprightness, than he that is perverse in his ways, though he be rich.*

2 That distinction which thou standest upon, and which seemeth so vast between thy poor neighbour and thee, what is it? whence did it come? whither tends it? It is not anywise natural, or according to primitive design: for as all men are in faculties and endowments of nature equal, so

SERM. I.

Job xxxiv. 19.

Ecclus. x. 24. Prov. xxviii. 6.

---

[k] Ἐννόησον, ὅτι ὁμοίως σοι ἐλεύθερός ἐστι, καὶ τῆς αὐτῆς σοι κοινωνεῖ εὐγενείας, καὶ πάντα σοι κοινὰ κέκτηται.—Chrys. in Heb. Orat. XI. [Opp. Tom. IV. p. 493.]

Οἱ τοίνυν ἐν τοῖς πνευματικοῖς τοσαύτην ἔχοντες ἰσοτιμίαν, πόθεν μέγα φρονεῖτε; ὅτι ὁ δεῖνα πλούσιος, καὶ ὁ δεῖνα ἰσχυρός;—Id. in Eph. iv. 4. [Opp. Tom. III. p. 818.]

Cf. in Joh. Hom. XV. Tom. II. p. 615. [Εἰ γὰρ καὶ μὴ συγγενὴς μηδὲ φίλος ἐστὶν, ἀλλ᾽ ἄνθρωπός ἐστι τῆς αὐτῆς σοι μετέχων φύσεως, τὸν αὐτὸν ἔχων δεσπότην, ὁμόδουλος καὶ ὁμόσκηνος..... Εἰ δὲ καὶ τῆς πίστεως μετέχει τῆς αὐτῆς, ἰδού σοι καὶ μέλος γέγονε.]

Τοιαύτη γὰρ ἡ τοῦ Πνεύματος χάρις· ὁμοτίμους ποιεῖ τοὺς ὁμόφρονας.—Greg. Naz [Orat. XXXIV. Opp. Tom. I. p. 622 A.]

SERM. I.

were they all originally equal in condition, all wealthy and happy, all constituted in a most prosperous and plentiful estate; all things at first were promiscuously exposed to the use and enjoyment of all, every one from the common stock assuming as his own what he needed. Inequality and private interest in things (together with sicknesses and pains, together with all other infelicities and inconveniences) were the by-blows of our fall[l]: sin introduced these degrees and distances; it devised the names of rich and poor; it begot these ingrossings and inclosures of things; it forged those two small pestilent words, *Meum* and *Tuum,* which have engendered so much strife among men, and created so much mischief in the world: these preternatural distinctions were, I say, brooded by our fault, and are in great part fostered and maintained thereby; for were we generally so good, so just, so charitable as we should be, they could hardly subsist, especially in that measure they do[m]. God indeed (for

[l] Πενία καὶ πλοῦτος, ἐλευθερία τε, ἣν φαμὲν, καὶ δουλεία, καὶ τὰ τοιαῦτα τῶν ὀνομάτων, ὕστερον ἐπεισῆλθον τῷ γένει τῶν ἀνθρώπων, ὥσπερ ἀρρωστήματα κοινά τινα τῇ κακίᾳ συνεισπέσοντα, κἀκείνης ὄντα ἐπινοήματα.—Greg. Naz. [Orat. XIV. Opp. Tom. I. p. 275 B.]

[m] Τὸ γὰρ ἐμὸν, καὶ τὸ σὸν, τοῦτο τὸ ψυχρὸν ῥῆμα, καὶ μυρίους πολέμους εἰς τὴν οἰκουμένην εἰσαγαγὸν, &c.—Chrys. Orat. LIV. [Opp. Tom. V. p. 364.] et in Act. ii. 47. [Tom. IV. p. 648.]

Natura omnia omnibus in commune profudit. Sic enim Deus generari jussit omnia, ut pastus omnibus communis esset, et terra foret omnium quædam communis possessio. Natura igitur jus commune generavit, usurpatio jus fecit privatum.—Amb. Offic. I. 28. [Opp. Tom. II. col. 35 E.]

Καὶ γὰρ εἰ μετὰ ἀκριβείας τοῦτο ἐφυλάττετο, οὐ δοῦλος, οὐκ ἐλεύθερος ἦν, οὐκ ἄρχων, οὐκ ἀρχόμενος, οὐ πλούσιος, οὐ πένης, οὐ μικρὸς, οὐ μέγας, οὐ διάβολος ἂν ἐγνώσθη ποτέ.—Chrys. in 1 Cor. Orat. XXXII. [Opp. Tom. III. p. 455.]

Ὥσπερ ἂν εἴ τις ἐν θεάτρῳ θεὰν καταλαβὼν, εἶτα ἐξείργοι τοὺς ἐπεισιόντας, ἴδιον ἑαυτοῦ κρίνων τὸ κοινῶς πᾶσι κατὰ τὴν χρῆσιν προκείμενον·

promoting some good ends, and for prevention of some mischiefs, apt to spring from our ill-nature in this our lapsed state; particularly to prevent the strife and disorder which scrambling would cause among men, presuming on equal right and parity of force) doth suffer them in some manner to continue, and enjoins us a contented submission to them: but we mistake, if we think that natural equality and community are in effect quite taken away; or that all the world is so cantonized among some few, that the rest have no share therein. No; every man hath still a competent patrimony due to him, and a sufficient provision made for his tolerable subsistence. God hath brought no man hither to be necessarily starved, or pinched with extreme want; but hath assigned to every one a child's portion, in some fair way to be obtained by him, either by legal right, or by humble request, which according to conscience ought to have effect[n]. No man therefore is allowed to detain, or to destroy superfluously what another man apparently wants: but is obliged to impart it to him; so that rich men are indeed but the treasurers, the stewards, the caterers of God for the rest of men, having a strict charge to *Dispense unto every one his meat in due season*, and no just privilege to withhold it from any: the honour of distribution is conferred on them, as a reward of their fidelity and care; the right of enjoyment is reserved to the poor, as a

Matt. xxiv. 45. Luke xii. 42.

τοιοῦτοί εἰσι καὶ οἱ πλούσιοι. τὰ γὰρ κοινὰ προκατάσχοντες, ἴδια ποιοῦνται διὰ τὴν πρόληψιν.—Basil. M. [Hom. in Luc. xii. 18. Opp. Tom. II. p. 49 E.]

[n] Incassum se innocentes putant, qui commune Dei munus sibi privatum vindicant.—Greg. M. [Pastor. Curæ, Pars III. Admon. 22. Opp. Tom. II. col. 66 E.]

provision for their necessity. Thus hath God wisely projected, that all his children should both effectually and quietly be provided for, and that none of them should be oppressed with penury; so that, as St Paul hath it, *One man's abundance shall supply another man's want, that there may be an equality:* for since no man can enjoy more than he needs, and every man should have so much as he needs, there can be really no great inequality among men; the distinction will scarce remain otherwhere than in fancy. What the philosopher said of himself, *What I have is so mine, that it is every man's*[o], is according to the practice of each man, who is truly and in due measure charitable; whereby that seemingly enormous discrimination among men is well moderated[p], and the equity of divine Providence is vindicated. But he that ravenously grasps for more than he can well use, and gripes it fast into his clutches, so that the needy in their distress cannot come by it, doth pervert that equity which God hath established in things, defeats his good intention, (so far as he can,) and brings a scandal on his providence: and so doing is highly both injurious and impious.

3 It was also (which we should consider) even one main end of this difference among us, permitted and ordered by God's providence, that as some men's industry and patience might be exercised by their poverty, so other men by their wealth should have ability of practising justice and charity; that

---

[o] Ego sic omnia habeo, ut omnium sint.—Demetrius apud Sen. de Ben. VII. 10. [5.]

[p] Ὁ ἀγαπῶν τὸν πλησίον ὡς ἑαυτὸν, οὐδὲν περισσότερον κέκτηται τοῦ πλησίον.—Basil. M. [Hom. in Div. Opp. Tom. II. p. 52 B.]

so both rich and poor might thence become capable of recompences, suitable to the worth of such virtuous performances. *Why art thou rich,* saith St Basil, *and he poor? Surely for this; that thou mayest attain the reward of benignity, and faithful dispensation; and that he may be honoured with the great prize of patience*[q]. God in making thee rich, would have thee to be a double benefactor, not only to thy poor neighbour, but also to thyself, whilst thou bestowest relief on him, purchasing a reward to thyself. God also by this order of things designs, that a charitable intercourse should be maintained among men, mutually pleasant and beneficial; the rich kindly obliging the poor, and the poor gratefully serving the rich. Wherefore by neglecting these duties we unadvisedly cross the good purpose of God toward us, depriving ourselves of the chief advantages our wealth may afford.

4 We should also do well to consider, that a poor man, even as such, is not to be disregarded, and that poverty itself is no such contemptible thing as we may be prone to imagine. There are considerations, which may qualify poverty even to dispute the place with wealth, and to claim precedence to it. If the world vulgarly doth account and call the rich man happy, a better Author hath pronounced the poor man such: *Blessed are the* Luke vi. 20.

[q] Διατί σὺ μὲν πλουτεῖς, ἐκεῖνος δὲ πένεται; ἢ πάντως, ἵνα καὶ σὺ χρηστότητος καὶ πιστῆς οἰκονομίας μισθὸν ὑποδέξῃ, κἀκεῖνος τοῖς μεγάλοις ἄθλοις τῆς ὑπομονῆς τιμηθῇ.—[Hom. in Luc. xii. 18. Opp. Tom. II. p. 50 A.]

Πλοῦτον καὶ πενίαν τοῖς ἀνθρώποις διένειμεν ὁ τῶν ὅλων δημιουργός τε καὶ πρύτανις, οὐκ ἀδίκῳ ψήφῳ χρησάμενος, ἀλλ' ἀφορμὴν ὠφελείας τοῖς πλουσίοις παρέχων, τῶν πενήτων τὴν ἔνδειαν.—Theodor. Ep. XXIII. [Opp. Tom. III. p. 917 B.]

poor, doth march in the van of the beatitudes; and a reason goeth along therewith, which asserteth its right to the place, *for theirs is the kingdom of heaven;* for that they are not only in an equal capacity as men, but in a nearer disposition as poor, to the acquisition of that blissful state; for that poverty (the mistress of sobriety and honest industry, the mother of humility and patience, the nurse of all virtue) renders men more willing to go, and more expedite in the way toward heaven: by it also we conform to the Son of God himself, the heir of eternal majesty, the Saviour of the world, *Who for our sake became poor,* (Δι' ἡμᾶς ἐπτώχευσε, for our sake became a beggar,) *that we through his poverty* (or beggary) *might become rich:* he willingly chose, he especially dignified and sanctified that depth of poverty, which we so proudly slight and loathe. The greatest princes and potentates in the world, the most wealthy and haughty of us all, but for one poor beggar had been irrecoverably miserable; to poverty it is, that every one of us doth owe all the possibility there is, all the hopes we can have of our salvation; and shall we then ingratefully requite it with scorn, or with pitiless neglect[r]? Shall we presume, in the person of any poor man, to abhor or contemn the very poor, but most holy and most happy JESUS, our Lord and Redeemer? No; if we will do poverty right, we must rather for his dear sake and memory defer an especial respect and veneration thereto.

5 Thus a due reflection on the poor man himself, his nature and state, will induce us to succour.

[r] Dedignatur aliquis paupertatem, cujus tam claræ imagines sunt?—Sen. Consol ad Helv. [XII. 5.]

But let us also consider him as related unto ourselves: every such person is our near kinsman, is our brother, is by indissoluble bands of cognation in blood, and agreement in nature, knit and united to us. We are all but several streams issuing from one source, several twigs sprouting from one stock; *One blood*, derived through several channels; one substance, by miraculous efficacy of the divine benediction multiplied or dilated unto several times and places. We are all fashioned according to the same original idea, resembling God our common Father; we are all endowed with the same faculties, inclinations, and affections; we all conspire in the same essential ingredients of our constitution, and in the more notable adjuncts thereof; it is only some inconsiderable accidents (such as age, place, figure, stature, colour, garb) which diversify and distinguish us; in which, according to successions of time and chance, we commonly no less differ from ourselves, than we do at present from them: so that in effect and reasonable esteem, every man is not only our brother, but (as Aristotle[a] saith of a friend) Ἄλλος αὐτός, *Another one's self;* is not only our most lively image, but in a manner our very substance; another ourself under a small variation of present circumstances: the most of distinction between us and our poor neighbour consists in exterior show, in moveable attire, in casual appendages to the nature of man; so that really when we use him well, we are kind to ourselves; when we yield him courteous regard, we bear respect to our own nature; when we feed and comfort him, we do sus-

SERM. I.

Acts xvii. 26.

[a] [Eth. ix. 4. 5.]

tain and cherish a member of our own body[t]. But when we are cruel or harsh to him, we abuse ourselves; when we scorn him, we lay disparagement and disgrace on mankind itself; when we withhold succour or sustenance from him, we do, as the prophet speaketh, *Hide ourselves from our own flesh;* we starve a part of our own body, and wither a branch of our stock; immoderate selfishness so blindeth us, that we oversee and forget ourselves: it is in this, as it is in other good senses, true what the Wise Man saith, *The merciful man doeth good to his own soul; but he that is cruel troubleth his own flesh.*

6 Further, as the poor man is so nearly allied to us by society of common nature, so is he more strictly joined to us by the bands of spiritual consanguinity. All Christians (high and low, rich and poor) are children of the same heavenly Father, spring from the same incorruptible seed, are regenerated to the same lively hope, are coheirs of the same heavenly inheritance; are all members of one body[u], (*Members,* saith St Paul, *one of another,*) and animated by one holy Spirit: which relation, as it is the most noble and most close that can be, so it should breed the greatest endearments, and should express itself in correspondent

---

[t] Nemo est in genere humano, cui non dilectio, etsi non pro mutua caritate, pro ipsa tamen communis naturæ societate debeatur.—Aug. [Ep. cxxx. (ad Probam.) Opp. Tom. II. col. 387 c.]

Οἰκεῖον ἅπας ἄνθρωπος ἀνθρώπῳ καὶ φίλον.—Arist. [Eth. VIII. i. 3.]

Ἐν ἀλλοτρίοις πάθεσι θεραπευτέον, ἀδελφοί, τὸ συγγενὲς, καὶ ὁμόδουλον.—Greg. Naz. [Orat. XIV. Opp. Tom. I. p. 262 B.]

Nihil est enim unum uni tam simile, tam par, quam omnes inter nosmetipsos sumus.—Cic. de Leg. [I. 10. 29.]

[u] Gal. iii. 28. Πάντες γὰρ ὑμεῖς εἷς ἐστε ἐν Χριστῷ Ἰησοῦ. *Are all one.*—Cf. Chrys. in Joh. Hom. xv. [Opp. Tom. II. p. 615.]

effects; it should render us full of affection and sympathy one toward another; it should make us to tender the needs, and feel the sufferings of any Christian as our own; it should dispose us freely to communicate whatever we have, how precious soever, to any of our brethren[x]; this holy friendship should establish a charitable equality and community among us, both in point of honour and of estate: for since all things considerable are common unto us, since we are all purchased and purified by the same precious blood, since we all partake of the same precious faith, of the same high calling, of the same honourable privileges, of the same glorious promises and hopes; since we all have the same Lord and Saviour; why should these secular trifles be so private and particular among us? Why should not so huge a parity in those only valuable things not wholly (I say, not in worldly state or outward appearance, such as the preservation of order in secular affairs requireth, but) in our opinion and affection extinguish that slight distinction of rich and poor, in concernments temporal? How can we slight so noble, so great a personage as a Christian, for wanting a little dross? How can we deem ourselves much his superior, upon so petty an advantage, for having that, which is not worth speaking or thinking of, in comparison to what he enjoyeth? Our Lord himself is not ashamed to call the least among us his brother and his friend: and shall we then disdain to yield to such an one the regard and treat-

Heb. ii. 11.
Matt. xxv. 40.
John xv. 14.

[x] Φίλων γὰρ οὐδὲν ἴδιον, οἵτινες φίλοι
'Ορθῶς πεφύκασ', ἀλλὰ κοινὰ χρήματα.—
Eurip. Androm. [376.]

ment suitable to such a quality? Shall we not honour any brother of our Lord? Shall we not be civil and kind to any friend of his? If we do not, how can we pretend to bear any true respect or affection unto himself? It is his express precept, that the greatest among us should, in imitation of his most humble and charitable self, be ready to serve the meanest; and that we should *In honour prefer one another*, and *In lowliness of mind esteem others better than ourselves*, are apostolical rules, extending indifferently to rich and poor, which are plainly violated by disregarding the poor. Yea, this relation should, according to St John's doctrine, dispose us not only freely to impart these temporal goods, but even, if occasion be, willingly to expose our very lives for our brethren: *Hereby*, saith he, *we perceive the love of God, because he laid down his life for us; and we ought to lay down our lives for our brethren.* How greatly then are they deficient from their duty, how little in truth are they Christians, who are unwilling to part with the very superfluities and excrements of their fortune for the relief of a poor Christian! Thus considering our brother, may breed in us charitable dispositions toward him, and induce us to the practice of these duties.

Moreover, if we reflect upon ourselves, and consider either our nature, or our state here, we cannot but observe many strong engagements to the same practice.

1 The very constitution, frame, and temper of our nature directeth and inclineth us thereto; whence, by observing those duties, we observe our own nature, we improve it, we advance it to the

best perfection it is capable of; by neglecting them, we thwart, we impair, we debase the same—*Hæc nostri pars optima sensus*[y]; the best of our natural inclinations (those sacred relics of God's image originally stamped on our minds) do sensibly prompt, and vehemently urge us to mercy and pity: the very same bowels, which in our own want do by a lively sense of pain inform us thereof, and instigate us to provide for its relief, do also grievously resent the distresses of another, admonishing us thereby, and provoking us to yield him succour[z]. Such is the natural sympathy between men, (discernible in all, but appearing most vigorous in the best natures,) that we cannot see, cannot hear of, yea, can hardly imagine the calamities of other men, without being somewhat disturbed and afflicted ourselves. As also nature, to the acts requisite toward preservation of our life, hath annexed a sensible pleasure, forcibly enticing us to the performance of them: so hath she made the communication of benefits to others to be accompanied with a very delicious relish upon the mind of him that practises it; nothing indeed carrying with it a more pure and savoury delight than beneficence. A man may be virtuously voluptuous, and a laudable epicure by doing much good; for to receive good, even in the judgment of Epicurus himself, (the great patron of pleasure,) is nowise so plea-

[y] Juv. Sat. xv. [133.]
[z]     Mutuus ut nos
Affectus petere auxilium et præstare juberet.—
                                [Id. ibid. 149.]
Φιλόπτωχον καὶ συμπαθὲς τὸ τῶν ἀνθρώπων γένος.—Arch. ad Mon. 852.

sant as to do it[a]: God and nature therefore within us do solicit the poor man's case: even our own ease and satisfaction demand from us compassion and kindness towards him; by exercising them we hearken to nature's wise disciplines, and comply with her kindly instincts: we cherish good humour, and sweeten our complexion; so ennobling our minds, we become not only more like to God, but more perfectly men: by the contrary practice we rebel against the laws, and pervert the due course of our nature; we do weaken, corrupt, and stifle that which is best in us; we harden and stupify our souls; so monstrously degenerating from the perfection of our kind, and becoming rather like savage beasts than sociable men; yea, somewhat worse perhaps than many beasts; for commonly brutes will combine to the succour of one another, they will defend and help those of the same kind.

2 And if the sensitive part within us doth suggest so much, the rational dictates more unto us: that heavenly faculty, having capacities so wide, and so mighty energies, was surely not created to serve mean or narrow designs; it was not given us to scrape eternally in earth, or to amass heaps of clay for private enjoyment; for the service of one puisne creature, for the sustenance and satisfaction of a single carcass: it is much below an intelligent person to weary himself with servile toils, and distract his mind with ignoble cares, for concernments so low and scanty: but to regard and pursue the common good of men; to dispense,

[a] Ἐπίκουρος τοῦ εὖ πάσχειν, τὸ εὖ ποιεῖν, οὐ μόνον κάλλιον ἀλλὰ καὶ ἥδιον εἶναί φησι.—Plut. de Philos. conv. cum Princ. [Opp. Tom. III. p. 1393. Ed. Steph.]

advise, and aid, where need requires; to diffuse its virtue all about in beneficial effects; these are operations worthy of reason, these are employments congruous to the native excellency of that divine power implanted in us; such performances declare indeed what a man is, whence he sprang, and whither he tends.

3 Further, examining ourselves, we may also observe, that we are in reality, what our poor neighbour appears to be, in many respects no less indigent and impotent than he: we no less, yea far more, for our subsistence depend upon the arbitrary power of another, than he seemeth to rely upon ours. We as defectible creatures do continually want support; we as grievous sinners do always need mercy; every moment we are contracting huge debts, far beyond our ability to discharge; debts of gratitude for benefits received, debts of guilt for offences committed; we therefore perpetually stand obliged to be craving for mercy and relief at the gates of heaven. We all, from prince to peasant, live merely upon alms, and are most really in condition beggars: *To pray always*, is a duty incumbent on us from the condition of our nature, as well as by the command of God. Such a likeness in state should therefore dispose us to succour our fellows, and, Δανείζειν Θεῷ τὸν ἔλεον, ἐλέου χρῄζοντας, *To lend mercy to God, who need mercy from him*, as the good father[b] speaketh. We should, as the apostle advises and argues, *Remember them that are in bonds, as bound with them; and them which suffer adversity, as being ourselves also in the body;* as being companions in necessity,

Luke xviii. 1.

Heb. xiii. 3.

---

[b] Greg. Naz. [Orat. XLIII. Opp. Tom. I. p. 818 D.]

or subject to the like distress. If we daily receive mercy and relief, yet, unmindful of our obligation to God, refuse them to others, shall we not deserve to hear that dreadful exprobration, *O thou wicked servant, I forgave thee all that debt, because thou desiredst me: shouldest not thou also have had compassion on thy fellow-servant, even as I had pity on thee?*

4 The great incertainty and instability of our condition doth also require our consideration. We, that now flourish in a fair and full estate[c], may soon be in the case of that poor creature, who now sues for our relief; we, that this day enjoy the wealth of Job, may the morrow need his patience: there are Sabeans, which may come, and drive away our cattle; there are tempests which may arise, and smite down our houses; there is a fire of God, which may fall from heaven, and consume our substance; a messenger of all these mischiefs may, for all we know, be presently at our doors; it happened so to a better man than we, as unexpectedly, and with as small ground to fear it, as it can arrive to us: all our weal is surrounded with dangers, and exposed to casualties innumerable: violence may snatch it from us, treachery may cheat us of it; mischance may seize thereon, a secret moth may devour it; the wisdom of Providence for our trial, or its justice for our punishment, may bereave us thereof; its own light and fluid nature (if no other accountable causes were apparent) might easily serve to waft it from us;

[c] Ὅμως δ' ἔνεστι τοῖσιν εὖ σκοπουμένοις
Ταρβεῖν τὸν εὖ πράσσοντα, μὴ σφαλῇ ποτε.—
Soph. Trachin. [296.]

for *Riches*, saith the Wise Man, *make themselves wings*, (they, it seems, do need no help for that,) *and fly away like as an eagle toward heaven;* that is, of their own accord they do so swiftly convey themselves away, out of our sight, and beyond our reach; they are but wind: *What profit*, says the Preacher, *hath he that laboureth for the wind?* For wind; that is, for a thing which can nowise be fixed or settled in one corner; which, therefore, it is a vanity to conceive that we can surely appropriate, or long retain. How then can we think to stand firm upon a place so slippery? how can we build any confidence on a bottom so loose and brittle? how can we suffer our minds to be swelled up like bubbles with vain conceit, by the breath of such things, more fleeting and vertiginous than any air? against the precepts of the wisest and best men: *If riches increase*, saith the Psalmist, *set not your heart on them: Wilt thou set thine eyes upon that which is not?* saith the Wise Man: (that is, wilt thou regard that which is so transitory and evanid, that it hardly may be deemed real; which we can scarce look on, before it is gone?) And, *Charge them*, saith St Paul, *that are rich in this world, that they be not high-minded, nor trust in uncertain riches:* ('Επὶ πλούτου ἀδηλότητι, in the obscurity, or inevidence of riches; things, which we can never plainly discern how long we shall keep them, how much we can enjoy them:) what should make us unwilling, with certain advantages to ourselves, freely to let that go, which presently without our leave may forsake us? How can we reasonably judge our case much different from that of the poorest body, whenas in a trice we may perhaps change places and persons; when, the scene turning, he may be advanced unto our wealth, we may be depressed into his want[d]? Since every age yieldeth instances of some Crœsus, some Polycrates, some Pompey, some Job, some Nebuchodonosor, who within a small compass of time doth appear to all men the object both of admiration and pity, is to the less wise the mark both of envy and scorn[e]; seeing every day presenteth unexpected vicissitudes, the sea of human affairs continually ebbing and flowing, now rolling on this, now on the other shore, its restless waves of profit and credit; since especially there is a God, who arbitrarily disposeth things, and with a turn of his hand changeth the state of men; who, as the scripture saith, *Maketh rich and poor, bringeth low and lifteth up; Poureth contempt upon princes; Raiseth the poor out of the dust, and lifteth the beggar from the dunghill, to set them among princes, and to make them inherit the throne of glory:* seeing, I say, apparently, such is the condition of things here, that we may soon need his pity and help, who now requesteth ours, why should we not be very ready to afford them to him? Why should we not gladly embrace our opportunity, and use our turn well; becoming aforehand with others, and preventing their reciprocal contempt or neglect of us hereafter: *Cast thy bread upon the waters; for thou shalt find it after many days. Give a portion to seven, and*

1 Sam. ii. 7.
Job xii. 21.
Ps. cvii. 40, 41.
cxiii. 7, 8.

Eccles. xi. 1, 2.

---

[d] Καὶ γὰρ ἐσχάτης ἀνοίας ἂν εἴη, ὧν καὶ ἄκοντες ἐξίστασθαι μέλλομεν ἑτέροις, τούτων μὴ μεταδοῦναι ἑκόντας τοῖς δεομένοις.—Chrys. Orat. LV. [Opp. Tom. v. p. 374.]

[e] Sejanus—quo die illum Senatus deduxerat, populus in frusta divisit.—Sen. de Tranq. [cap. xi. 9.]

*also unto eight; for thou knowest not what evil shall be upon the earth:* that is, considering the inconstancy and uncertainty of affairs here, and what adversity may befall thee, be liberal upon all occasions, and thou shalt (even a good while after) find returns of thy liberality upon thee: so the Wise Man advises, and so wisdom certainly dictates that we should do.

5 And equity doth exact no less: for were any of us in the needy man's plight, (as easily we may be reduced thereto,) we should believe our case deserved commiseration; we should importunately demand relief; we should be grievously displeased at a repulse; we should apprehend ourselves very hardly dealt with, and sadly we should complain of inhumanity and cruelty, if succour were refused to us. In all equity therefore we should be apt to minister the same to others; for nothing can be more unreasonable or unjust, than to require or expect that from another, which in a like case we are unwilling to render unto him[f]: it is a plain deviation from that fundamental rule, which is the base of all justice, and virtually the sum, as our Saviour telleth us, of whatever is prescribed us: *All things whatsoever ye would that men should do to you, do ye even so to them; for this is the Law and the Prophets.* I add, that upon these considerations, by unmerciful dealing, we put ourselves into a very bad and ticklish condition, wholly depending upon the constancy of that which is most inconstant; so that if our fortune do fail, we can neither reasonably hope for, nor justly pre-

[f] Beneficium dare qui nescit, injuste petit.—
 [Publ. Syrus. (Poet. Scen. Latin Vol. VI. p. 288. Ed. Bothe.)]

tend to, any relief or comfort from others: *He that doeth good turns is mindful of that which may come hereafter; and when he falleth, he shall find a stay.*

6  We should also remember concerning ourselves, that we are mortal and frail. Were we immortal, or could we probably retain our possessions for ever in our hands; yea, could we foresee some definite space of time, considerably long, in which we might assuredly enjoy our stores, it might seem somewhat excusable to scrape hard, and to hold fast; to do so might look like rational providence: but since *Riches are not for ever, nor doth the crown endure to all generations,* as the Wise Man speaketh; since they must infallibly be soon left, and there is no certainty of keeping them for any time, it is very unaccountable why we should so greedily seek them, and hug them so fondly. *The rich man,* saith St James, *as the flower of the grass, shall pass away;* it is his special doom *to fade away* suddenly; it is obvious why in many respects he is somewhat more than others obnoxious to the fatal stroke, and upon special accounts of justice he may be further more exposed thereto: considering the case of the rich fool in the Gospel, we may easily discern them: we should reckon, that it may happen to us as it did there to him; that after we have reared great barns, and *Stored up much goods for many years,* our *soul this very night* may be *required of us:* however, if it be uncertain when, it is most certain, that after a very short time our thread will be spun out; then shall we be rifled, and quite stript of all; becoming stark-naked, as when we came into the world: we shall not carry with us one grain of our glistering metals, or one

rag of our gaudy stuff; our stately houses, our fine gardens, and our spacious walks, must all be exchanged for a close hole under ground; we must for ever bid farewell to our pomps and magnificences, to our feasts and jollities, to our sports and pastimes; not one of all our numerous and splendid retinue, no companion of our pleasure, no admirer of our fortune, no flatterer of our vices, can wait upon us; desolate and unattended we must go down to the chambers of darkness: then shall we find that to die rich, as men are wont improperly to speak, is really to die most poor; that to have carefully kept our money, is to have lost it utterly; that by leaving much, we do indeed leave worse than nothing: to have been wealthy, if we have been illiberal and unmerciful, will be no advantage or satisfaction to us after we are gone hence; yea, it will be the cause of huge damage and bitter regret unto us. All our treasures will not procure us any favour, or purchase one advocate for us in that impartial world; yea, it shall be they, which will there prosecute us with clamorous accusations, will bear sore testimony against us, (*The rust of them*, saith St James, *shall be a witness against us*, signifying our unjust or uncharitable detention of them,) will obtain a most heavy sentence upon us; they will render our audit more difficult, and inflame our reckoning; they will aggravate the guilt of our sins with imputations of unfaithfulness and ingratitude; so with their load they will press us deeper into perdition: to omit, that having so ill managed them, we shall leave them behind us as marks of obloquy, and monuments of infamy upon our memories; for ordinarily of such a rich person

SERM. I.

Isai. xiv. 11.

James v. 3.
Luke xvi. 25.
vi. 24.
xii. 21.
Matt. xxv. 30.
James v. 5.

1 Tim. vi. 9.

SERM. I.

Job xxvii. 19, 23.

it is true, that Job says of him, *Men shall clap their hands at him, and shall hiss him out of his place;* like one who departs from off this stage, after having very ill acted his part. Is it not, therefore, infinitely better to prevent this being necessarily and unprofitably deprived of our goods, by seasonably disposing them so as may conduce to our benefit, and our comfort, and our honour[g]; being very indifferent and unconcerned in our affection toward them; modest and humble in our conceits about them; moderate and sober in our enjoyments of them; contented upon any reasonable occasion to lose or leave them; and especially most ready to dispense them in that best way, which God hath prescribed, according to the exigencies of humanity and charity? By thus ordering our riches, we shall render them benefits and blessings to us; we shall by them procure sure friendship and favour, great worship and respect in the other world; having so lived, (in the exercise of bounty and mercy,) we shall truly die rich, and in effect carry all our goods along with us, or rather we have thereby sent them before us; having, like wise merchants, transmitted and drawn them by a most safe conveyance into our country and home; where infallibly we shall find them, and with everlasting content enjoy them. So considering ourselves, and our state, will dispose us to the practice of these duties.

Luke xvi. 9.

V. Head of discourse.

Furthermore, if we contemplate our wealth

[g] Τῆς γὰρ ἐσχάτης ἀνοίας ἐστὶν ἀφεῖναί τι τῶν ἡμετέρων ἀναπομεῖναι ἐνταῦθα, ἡμῶν μικρὸν ὕστερον μελλόντων ἐντεῦθεν ἀποδημεῖν. Καὶ γὰρ ὅπερ ἀπολειφθῇ ζημία γίνεται. Πάντα τοίνυν ἐκεῖ προπεμπέσθω, ἔνθα καὶ ἡμεῖς διαπαντὸς διατρίβειν μέλλομεν λοιπόν.—Chrys. Or. LV. Opp. Tom. V. [p. 365.]

itself, we may therein descry great motives to bounty.

SERM. I.

1 Thus to employ our riches is really the best use they are capable of; not only the most innocent, most worthy, most plausible, but the most safe, most pleasant, most advantageous, and consequently in all respects most prudent way of disposing them. To keep them close without using or enjoying them at all, is a most sottish extravagance, or a strange kind of madness; a man thence affecting to be rich quite impoverisheth himself, dispossesseth himself of all, and alienateth from himself his estate[h]: his gold is no more his than when it was in the Indies, or lay hid in the mines; his corn is no more his than if it stood growing in Arabia or China; he is no more owner of his lands than he is master of Jerusalem, or Grand Cairo: for what difference is there, whether distance of place, or baseness of mind, sever things from him? whether his own heart, or another man's hand, detain them from his use? whether he hath them not at all, or hath them to no purpose? whether one is a beggar out of necessity or by choice? is pressed to want or a volunteer thereto? Such an one may fancy himself rich, and others as wise as himself may repute him so: but so distracted persons to themselves, and to one another, do seem great princes, and style themselves such; with as much reason almost he might pretend to be wise, or to be good. Riches are,

[h] Σκορπιζόμενος ὁ πλοῦτος, καθ' ὃν ὁ Κύριος ὑποτίθεται τρόπον, πέφυκε παραμένειν· συνεχόμενος δὲ ἀλλοτριοῦσθαι.—Basil. M. [Hom. in Div. Opp. Tom. II. p. 53 A.]

Tam deest avaro, quod habet, quam quod non habet.—
[Publ. Syrus. (Poet. Scen. Lat. Vol. VI. p. 257. Ed. Bothe.)]

SERM. I.

Prov. xiii. 7.

Eccles. v. 11.

Χρήματα, things, whose nature consists in usefulness[1]; abstract that, they become nothing, things of no consideration or value; he that hath them is no more concerned in them than he that hath them not: it is the art and skill to use affluence of things wisely and nobly, which makes it wealth, and constitutes him rich that hath it; otherwise the chests may be crammed, and the barns stuffed full, while the man is miserably poor and beggarly[k]: it is in this sense true, which the Wise Man says, *There is that maketh himself rich, yet hath nothing.* But the very having riches (will such a man say) is matter of reputation; men do esteem and honour him that hath them. True, if he knows how, and hath the mind to use them well: otherwise all the credit they yield consists in making their master ridiculous to wise men, and infamous among all men. But, putting case that any should be so foolish as to respect us merely for seeming rich, why should we accommodate our practice to their vain opinion, or be base ourselves, because others are not wise? But, however, (may he say again,) it is a pleasant thing to see them; a heap of gold is the most lovely spectacle that one can behold; it does a man's heart good to view an abundance of good things about him. For this plea, indeed, he hath a good author: this, it should seem, was all the benefit the Wise Man observed in them accruing to such persons: *What good, saith he, is there to the owners thereof, saving the*

[1] Καὶ γὰρ χρήματα διὰ τοῦτο λέγεται, οὐχ ἵνα κατορύξωμεν, ἀλλ' ἵνα εἰς δέον αὐτοῖς χρησώμεθα.—Chrys. in Matt. Hom. XLIX. [Opp. Tom. II. p. 316.]

[k] Desunt inopiæ multa, avaritiæ omnia.—
[Publ. Syrus. apud] Sen. Epist. CVIII. [9.]

*beholding of them with their eyes?* But if this be all they are good for, it is, one would think, a very slim benefit they afford, little able to balance the pain and care requisite to the acquist and custody of them; a benefit indeed not proper to the possessor; for any one may look on them as well as he, or on the like; any one at pleasure may enjoy better sights; all the riches and ornaments of nature, the glorious splendours of heaven, and the sweet beauties of the field, are exposed to common view; the choicest magnificences and gallantries of the world do studiously present themselves to every man's eye; these in part every man truly may appropriate to himself; and by imagination any man can as well take all that he sees for his own, as the tenacious miser doth fancy his dear pelf to be his.

But mine heir (perhaps he will further say) will thank me, will praise me, will bless me for my great care and providence. If he doth, what is that to thee? Nothing of that will concern thee, or can reach thee; thou shalt not hear what he says, or feel any good from what he does: and most probably thou art mistaken in thy opinion concerning him; as thou *Knowest not who* he shall be, *that shall gather all thou heapest up*, or *Shall rule over all thy labour*, (*whether he shall be a wise man or a fool*, a kinsman or a stranger, a friend or a foe,) so thou canst as little guess what he will think or say: if he hath wit, he may sweetly laugh at thee for thy fond wisdom; if he hath none, his commendations will little adorn thy memory; he will to thy disgrace spend what thou leavest, as vainly as thou didst get or keep it. But (this to be sure he will in the end say for himself) money is a good reserve against necessary occasions, or bad times that may come; against a time of old age, of sickness, of adversity; it is the surest friend a man can have in such cases, which, when all fails, will be ready to help him: *The rich man's wealth is his strong city:* the Wise Man, he thinks, never spake more wisely; he therefore will not dismantle this fortress, but will keep it well stored, letting therefore his wealth lie dead and useless by him. But (to let pass now the profane infidelity of this plea, excluding all hope in God, and substituting our providence in the room of his) what a folly is it thus to anticipate evil, and to create to ourselves a present adversity from a suspicion of one future; to pinch ourselves now, lest we should suffer hereafter; to pine to-day, because we can imagine it possible that we may starve to-morrow; to forego certain occasions of enjoying our goods, for that perchance the like occasions may happen one day, we know not when; not to use things now, when reason bids us, because they may be useful at another time! Not considering also, that many intervenient accidents, more probably than a moderate and handsome use of our wealth, may crop the excrescences thereof.

2 But setting aside these absurd excuses of penuriousness, we may consider, that, secluding the good use of them in beneficence, riches are very impertinent, very cumbersome, very dangerous, very mischievous things; either superfluous toys, or troublesome clogs, or treacherous snares, or rather all these in combination, productive of trouble, sorrow, and sin. A small pittance will

and must suffice, to all reasonable purposes, to satisfy our necessities, to procure conveniences, to yield innocent delight and ease: our nature doth not require, nor can bear much: (*Take heed and beware of covetousness,* saith our Lord; *for a man's life consisteth not in the abundance of the things which he possesseth;* that is, a man may live well without it:) all the rest, setting beneficence apart, can only serve vanity or vice, will make us really fools and slaves[1]. (*They that will be rich,* saith the apostle, *fall into temptation and a snare, and into many foolish and hurtful lusts, which drown men in destruction and perdition.*) They puff up our minds with vain and false conceits; making us, as if we were in a dream or phrensy, to take ourselves for other persons, more great, more wise, more good, more happy than we are; for constantly, as the Wise Man observed, *The rich man is wise in his own conceit; Great men are not always wise.* And Agur thus intimates in his prayer, *Remove far from me vanity and lies; give me neither poverty nor riches.* They render us insensible and forgetful of God, of ourselves, of piety and virtue, of all that is good and worthy of us; (*Lest I be full,* said that good man again, assigning a reason why he deprecated being rich, *and deny thee, and say, Who is the Lord?*) they swallow up our thoughts, our affections, our endeavours, our time and leisure, possessing our hearts with a doting love unto them, (excluding other good affections,) distracting our minds with anxious

SERM. I.

Luke xii. 15.
1 Tim. vi. 8.

1 Tim. vi. 9.

Prov. xxviii. 11.
Job xxxii. 9.
Prov. xxx. 8.

Prov. xxx. 9.

Matt. vi. 24.
Ecclus. xxxi. 1.
Matt. xiii. 22.

---

[1] Corporis exigua desideria sunt; frigus submovere vult, alimentis famem ac sitim extinguere; quicquid extra concupiscitur, vitiis, non usibus, laboratur.—Sen. Consol. ad Helv. [cap. IX. 9.]

cares about them, (choking other good thoughts,) encumbering all our life with business about them, (inconsistent with due attention to our other more weighty and necessary concernments,) filling our heads with suspicions and fears, piercing our hearts with troubles and sorrows; they immerse our souls in all the follies of pride, in all the filths of luxury, in all the mischiefs emergent from sloth and stupidity; they are *The root of all evils* unto us, and the greatest obstructions of our true happiness, rendering salvation almost impossible, and heaven in a manner inaccessible to us: so that to be rich (if severed from a sober mind, and a free heart) is a great disease, and the source of many grievous distempers both of body and mind; from which we cannot well otherwise secure or rescue ourselves, than by liberally spending them in works of bounty and mercy; so shall we ease ourselves of the burdens[m], so shall we elude the temptations, so shall we abandon the vices, and so shall we escape all the sad mischiefs incident to them: thus to use wealth shall turn it into a convenience, and an ornament of our lives, into a considerable blessing, and a ground of much comfort to us. Excluding this use of wealth, or abstracting a capacity of doing good therewith, nothing is more pitiful and despicable than it; it is but like the load or the trappings of an ass: a wise man on that condition would not choose it, or endure to be pestered with it; but would serve it as those philosophers did, who flung it away, that it might not disturb their contemplations: 'tis the power it affords of benefit-

---

[m] Ἀποφόρτισαί τι τῆς νηὸς, ἵνα πλέῃς κουφότερος.—Greg. Naz. [Orat. XXXVI. Opp. Tom. I. p. 642 E.]

ing men, which only can season and ingratiate it SERM.
to the relish of such a person: otherwise it is evi- I.
dently true, which the Wise Man affirms, *Better is* Prov. xv.
*a little with the fear of the Lord, than great treasure,* 16.
*and trouble therewith.*

3 Again; we may consider, that to dispense our wealth liberally is the best way to preserve it, and to continue masters thereof; what we give is not thrown away, but saved from danger[n]: while we detain it at home (as it seems to us) it really is abroad, and at adventures; it is out at sea, sailing perilously in storms, near rocks and shelves, amongst pirates; nor can it ever be safe, till it is brought into this port, or ensured this way: when we have bestowed it on the poor, then we have lodged it in unquestionable safety; in a place where no rapine, no deceit, no mishap, no corruption can ever by any means come at it[o]. All our doors and bars, all our forces and guards, all the circumspection and vigilancy we can use, are no defence or security at all in comparison to this disposal thereof: the poor man's stomach is a granary for our corn, which never can be exhausted; the poor man's back is a wardrobe for our clothes, which never can be pillaged; the

---

[n] Μὴ δὴ νόμιζε τὴν ἐλεημοσύνην ἀνάλωμα εἶναι, ἀλλὰ πρόσοδον, μηδὲ δαπάνην, ἀλλὰ πραγματείαν. Μείζω γὰρ λαμβάνεις, ἢ δίδως. &c.— Chrys. Orat. XXXIII. Opp. Tom. v. p. 208.

[o] Μὴ τοίνυν φειδώμεθα χρημάτων, μᾶλλον δὲ φειδώμεθα τῶν χρημάτων. Ὁ γὰρ φειδόμενος τῶν ὄντων, εἰς τὰς τῶν πενήτων χεῖρας, αὐτὰ ἐναποτίθεται, εἰς τὸν ἄσυλον θησαυρὸν, καὶ λῃσταῖς καὶ οἰκέταις καὶ συκοφάνταις κακούργοις καὶ πάσαις ἐφόδοις ἀνάλωτον.—Id. Orat. LV. [Opp. Tom. v. p. 373.]

Multi sancti et sanctæ omni modo caventes, ipsas velut matres deliciarum divitias dispergendo pauperibus abjecerunt, et tali modo in cœlestibus thesauris tutius condiderunt.—Aug. [Ep. CXXX. (ad Probam.) Opp. Tom. II. col. 385 E.]

poor man's pocket is a bank for our money, which never can disappoint or deceive us: all the rich traders in the world may decay and break; but the poor man can never fail, except God himself turn bankrupt; for what we give to the poor, we deliver and intrust in his hands, out of which no force can wring it, no craft can filch it; it is laid up in heaven, whither no thief can climb, where no moth or rust do abide. In despite of all the fortune, of all the might, of all the malice in the world, the liberal man will ever be rich: for God's providence is his estate; God's wisdom and power are his defence; God's love and favour are his reward; God's word is his assurance; who hath said it, that *He which giveth to the poor shall not lack:* no vicissitude therefore of things can surprise him, or find him unfurnished; no disaster can impoverish him; no adversity can overwhelm him; he hath a certain reserve against all times and occasions: he that *Deviseth liberal things, by liberal things shall he stand*, saith the prophet. But, on the other hand, being niggardly is the likeliest course we can take to lose our wealth and estate; we thereby expose them to danger, and leave them defenceless; we subject them to the envious eye, to the slanderous tongue, to the ravenous and insidious hand; we deprive them of divine protection, which if it be away, *The watchman waketh but in vain:* we provoke God irrecoverably to take it from us, as he did the talent from that unprofitable servant, who did not use it well. We do indeed thereby yield God just cause of war and enmity against us; which being, *Omnia dat qui justa negat;* we do forfeit all to divine justice, by denying that portion which belongs to him, and which he claims. Can we hope to live in quiet possession of any thing, if we refuse to pay our due tributes and taxes imposed upon us by our almighty Sovereign; if we live in such rebellion against his authority, such violation of his right, such diffidence to his word? No: *He that trusteth in his riches shall fall; but the righteous shall flourish as a branch:* such is the difference between the covetous and the liberal, in point of security and success concerning their estate.

Prov. xi. 28.

Even according to the human and ordinary way of esteeming things, (abstracting from the special providence of God,) the liberal person hath, in consequence of his bounty, more real security for his wealth, than this world hath any other: he thereby gets an interest in the gratitude and affection of those whom he obligeth, together with the goodwill and respect of all men, who are spectators of his virtuous and generous dealing: the hearts and memories of men are repositories to him of a treasure, which nothing can extort from him, or defraud him of. If any mischance should arrive, or any want come near him, all men would be ready to commiserate him, every man would hasten to his succour. As when a haughty, a greedy, or a gripple man do fall into calamity or disgrace, scarce any one regardeth or pitieth him[p]: fortune, deserting such a person, carries all with it, few or none stick to him; his most zealous flatterers are commonly the first that forsake him; contempt and neglect are the only adherents to his condition;

---

[p]  Miraris, cum tu argento post omnia ponas,
    Si nemo præstet, quem non merearis, amorem?—
                                Hor. Sat. I. i. [86.]

that of the Wise Man appears verified, *He that hideth his eyes from the poor shall have many a curse.* So the courteous and bountiful person, when fortune seems to frown on him, hath a sure refuge in the good-will and esteem of men; all men, upon the accounts of honour and honesty, take themselves to be concerned in his case, and engaged to favour him; even those, who before were strangers, become then his friends, and in effect discover their affection to him; it, in the common judgment of people, appears an indignity and a disgrace to mankind, that such a man should want or suffer.

4 Nay further, we may consider, that exercising bounty is the most advantageous method of improving and increasing an estate; but that being tenacious and illiberal doth tend to the diminution and decay thereof. The way to obtain a great increase is, to sow much: he that sows little, how can he expect a good crop? It is as true in spiritual husbandry, as in the other; that *What a man soweth, that he shall reap,* both in kind and according to proportion: so that great husbandman St Paul assureth us, *He that soweth sparingly shall reap sparingly; but he that soweth bountifully shall also reap bountifully:* and Solomon means the same, when he saith, *To him that soweth righteousness shall be a sure reward.* The way to gain abundantly is, you know well, to trade boldly; he that will not adventure any thing considerable, how can he think of a large return? *Honour the Lord with thy substance, so shall thy barns be filled with plenty, and thy presses shall burst out with new wine.* 'Tis so likewise in the evangelical negotia-

tions; if we put out much upon score of conscience or charity, we shall be sure to profit much. Liberality is the most beneficial traffic that can be; it is bringing our wares to the best market; it is letting out our money into the best hands; we thereby lend our money to God, who repays with vast usury; an hundred to one is the rate he allows at present, and above a hundred millions to one he will render hereafter; so that if you will be merchants this way, you shall be sure to thrive, you cannot fail to grow rich most easily and speedily: *The liberal soul, shall be made fat, and he that watereth shall be watered himself:* this is that which St Paul again argues upon, when, commending the Philippians' free kindness toward him, he says, *Not because I desire a gift, but I desire fruit that may abound to your account.* Bounty yields Καρπὸν πλεονάζοντα, a fruit that multiplies, and abundantly turns to good account; it indeed procuring God's benediction, the fountain of all desirable plenty and prosperity; for *The blessing of the Lord, it maketh rich, and he addeth no sorrow with it.* It is therefore the greatest want of policy, the worst ill-husbandry and unthriftiness that can be, to be sparing this way; he that useth it cannot be thriving; he must spend upon the main stock, and may be sure to get nothing considerable. God ordinarily so proceeds, as to recompense and retaliate men in the same kind, wherein they endeavour to please him, or presume to offend him; so that for them who freely offer him their goods, he in regard thereto will prosper their dealings, and bless their estates: (*For this very thing the Lord thy God shall bless thee in all thy works,*

SERM. I.

Prov. xi. 25.

Phil. iv. 17.

Prov. x. 22.

Deut. xv. 18.

*and in all that thou puttest thine hand unto,* says Moses:) but they who will not lay out any thing for him, he will not concern himself in their success otherwise than to cross it, or, which is worse, to curse it; for if he seem to favour them for a time with some prosperity in their affairs, their condition is much worse thereby, their account will be more grievous, and their fate more disastrous in the end.

*Ps. lxxiii. 17.*

5 Further, the contributing part of our goods to the poor will qualify us to enjoy the rest with satisfaction and comfort. The oblation of these first-fruits, as it will sanctify the whole lump of our estate, so it will sweeten it; having offered this well-pleasing sacrifice of piety, having discharged this debt of justice, having paid this tribute of gratitude, our hearts being at rest, and our conscience well satisfied, we shall, like those good people in the Acts, *Eat our meat with gladness and singleness of heart;* to see the poor man by our means accommodated, eased, and refreshed, will give a delicious relish to all our enjoyments. But withholding his portion from the poor, as it will pollute and profane all our estate, so it will render the fruition thereof sour or unsavoury to us: for can we with any content taste our dainties, or view our plenties, while the poor man stands in sight pining with hunger[q]? Can we without regret see our walls clothed with tapestry, our horses decked with golden trappings, our attendants strutting in

*Acts ii. 46.*

---

[q] Ἐγγὺς ὁ πένης, τῇ νόσῳ βοήθησον· εἰς τοῦτον ἀπέρευξαί τι τῶν περιττῶν. Τί καὶ σὺ κάμνεις ἀπεπτῶν, καὶ οὗτος πεινῶν; καὶ σὺ κραιπαλῶν, καὶ οὗτος ὑδεριῶν; καὶ σὺ κόρῳ κόρον βαρύνων, καὶ οὗτος περιτρεπόμενος νόσῳ;—Greg. Naz. [Orat. xxxvi. Opp. Tom. I. p. 643 A.]

wanton gaiety, while our honest poor brother appears half naked, and trembling with cold? Can we carry on one finger enough to furnish ten poor people with necessaries, and have the heart within us, without shame and displeasure, to see them want? No; the sense of our impiety and ingratitude toward God, of our inhumanity and unworthiness toward our neighbour, will not fail (if ever we considerately reflect on our behaviour) to sting us with cruel remorse and self-condemnation; the clamours of want and misery surrounding us will pierce our ears, and wound our hearts; the frequent objects of pity and mercy, do what we can to banish them from our prospect or regard, will so assail, and so pursue us, as to disturb the freedom of our enjoyments, to quash the briskness of our mirth, to allay the sweetness of our pleasure; yea, rather, if stupidity and obduration have not seized on us, to imbitter all unto us; we shall feel that true, which Zophar speaks of the cruel and covetous oppressor, *Surely he shall not feel quietness in his belly—he shall not rejoice in his substance—in the fulness of his sufficiency he shall be in straits.* Job xx. 18, 20, 22.

6 I shall touch but one consideration more, persuasive of this practice; it is this: The peculiar nature of our religion specially requires it, and the honour thereof exacts it from us; nothing better suits Christianity, nothing more graces it, than liberality; nothing is more inconsistent therewith, or more disparageth it, than being miserable and sordid. A Christian niggard is the veriest nonsense that can be; for what is a Christian? what, but a man, who adores God alone, who loves God above all things, who reposes all his trust and con-

fidence in God? What is he, but one who undertaketh to imitate the most good and bountiful God; to follow, as the best pattern of his practice, the most benign and charitable JESUS, the Son of God; to obey the laws of God, and his Christ, the sum and substance of which is charity; half whose religion doth consist in loving his neighbour as himself? What is he, further, but one who hath renounced this world, with all the vain pomps and pleasures of it; who professes himself in disposition and affection of mind to forsake all things for Christ's sake; who pretends little to value, affect, or care for any thing under heaven; having all his main concernments and treasures, his heart, his hopes, and his happiness, in another world? Such is a Christian. And what is a niggard? All things quite contrary: one, whose practice manifestly shews him to worship another thing beside and before God; to love Mammon above God, and more to confide in it, than in him; one who bears small good-will, kindness, or pity toward his brother; who is little affected or concerned with things future or celestial; whose mind and heart are riveted to this world; whose hopes and happinesses are settled here below; whose soul is deeply immersed and buried in earth; one who, according to constant habit, notoriously breaketh the two great heads of Christian duty, *Loving God with all his heart, and his neighbour as himself;* it is therefore, by comparing those things, very plain, that we pretend to reconcile gross contradictions and inconsistencies, if we profess ourselves to be Christians, and are illiberal. It is indeed the special grace and glory of our religion, that it consisteth not in barren speculations, or empty formalities, or forward professions; not in fancying curiously, or speaking zealously, or looking demurely; but in really producing sensible fruits of goodness; in doing, as St Paul signifies, *Things good and profitable unto men,* such as those chiefly are, of which we speak. The most gracious wisdom of God hath so modelled our religion, that according to it piety and charity are the same thing; that we can never express ourselves more dutiful toward him, or better please him, or more truly glorify him, than when we are kind and good to our poor brother. We grossly mistake, if we take giving of alms to be a Jewish or Popish practice, suitable to children and dullards in religion, beneath so refined, so improved, so loftily spiritual gallants as we: No, 'tis a duty most properly and most highly Christian, as none more, a most goodly fruit of grace, and a most faithful mark thereof: *By the experiment of this ministration, we,* as St Paul saith, *glorify God for our professed subjection unto the Gospel of Christ, and for our liberal distribution unto our brethren and unto all men:* without it our faith is dead and senseless, our high attainments are fond presumptions, our fine notions and delicate spiritualities are in truth but silly dreams, the issues of a proud and ignorant fancy: he that appears hard-hearted and close-fisted towards his needy brother, let him think or call himself what he pleaseth, he plainly is no Christian, but a blemish, a reproach, and a scandal to that honourable name.

SERM. I.

Tit. iii. 8.

2 Cor. ix. 13.

7 To all these considerations and reasons inducing to the practice of this kind of charity, I

might subjoin examples, and set before you the fairest copies that can be imagined thereof. We have for it the pattern of God himself, who is infinitely munificent and merciful; *From whom every good and perfect gift descendeth; Who giveth life, and breath, and all things unto all; Who giveth liberally, and upbraideth not.* We have the example of the Son of God, who out of pure charity did freely part with the riches and glories of eternity, voluntarily embracing extreme poverty and want for our sake, that we who were poor might be enriched, we that were miserable might become happy; who *Went about doing good,* spent all his life in painful dispensation of beneficence, and relieving the needs of men in every kind. We have the blessed patriarchs to follow, who at God's pleasure and call did readily leave their country, their friends, their goods, and all they had. We have the practice of the holy apostles, who freely *Let go all to follow their Lord;* who cheerfully sustained all sorts of losses, disgraces, and pains, for promoting the honour of God, and procuring good unto men: we have to move and encourage us hereto the first and best Christians, most full of grace and holy zeal, who *So many as were possessors of lands and houses, did sell them,* and did impart the price of them to the community, *so that there was none poor among them,* and that *distribution was made to every one as he had need.* We have all the saints and eminent servants of God in all times, who have been high and wonderful in the performance of these duties. I could tell you of the blessed martyr St Cyprian, who was liberal by wholesale, bestowing all at once a fair estate on God and the poor[r]; of the renowned bishop St Basil, who constantly waited on the sick, and kissed their sores[s]; of the most pious confessor St Martin, who having but one coat left, and seeing a poor man that wanted clothes, tore it in two pieces, and gave one to that poor man[t]: and many like instances out of authentic history might be produced, apt to provoke our imitation. I might also, to beget emulation and shame in us, represent exemplary practices of humanity and charity even in Jews, Mahometans, and pagans, (such as in these cold days might pass for more than ordinary among us;) but I shall only propound one present and sensible example; that of this noble city, whose public bounty and charity in all kinds (in education of orphans, in curing the diseased both in body and mind, in provision for the poor, in relieving all sorts of necessities and miseries) let me earnestly entreat and exhort us all for God's sake, as we are able, by our private charity to imitate, to encourage, and to assist; let us do this so much the more willingly and freely, as the sad circumstances of things, by God's judgments brought upon us, do plainly require, that the public charity itself (lying under so great impediments,

SERM. I.

[r] Pontius in vit. Cypr. [Distractis rebus suis ad indigentiam pauperum sustentandam, tota prædia pretio dispensans, duo bona simul junxit, &c.—Inter Opp. Cypr. col. cxxxvi.]

[s] Greg. Naz. [Διὰ τοῦτο, οὐδὲ τοῖς χείλεσιν ἀπηξίου τιμᾶν τὴν νόσον.—Orat. XLIII. Opp. Tom. I. p. 818 D.]

[t] Sulp. Sever. [de Vit. B. Mart. cap. iii. p. 303. Obvium habet in porta Ambianensium civitatis pauperem nudum..... nihil præter chlamyden qua indutus erat, habebat..... Arrepto itaque ferro, quo accinctus erat, mediam dividit, partemque ejus pauperi tribuit, reliqua rursus induitur.]

SERM. I.

discouragements, and distresses) should be supported, supplied, and relieved by particular liberality. No words that I can devise will be so apt to affect and move you, as the case itself, if you please to consider it: hear it therefore speaking, and, I pray, with a pious and charitable disposition of mind attend thereto:

*A true report,* &c.

For this excellent pattern of pious bounty and mercy, let us heartily thank Almighty God; let us humbly implore God's blessing on the future management of it; let us pay due respects to the worthy promoters thereof, and pray for rewards upon them, answerable to their charitable care and industry employed therein; let us also according to our ability perform our duty in following and furthering it: for encouragement to which practice, give me leave briefly to reflect upon the latter part of my text; which represents some instances of the felicity proper to a bountiful person, or some rewards peculiar to the exercising the duties of bounty and mercy.

The first is, *His righteousness endureth for ever.* These words are capable of various senses, or of divers respects; they may import, that the fame and remembrance of his bounty is very durable, or that the effects thereof do lastingly continue, or that eternal rewards are designed thereto; they may respect the bountiful man himself, or his posterity here; they may simply relate to an endurance in God's regard and care; or they may with that also comprehend a continuance in the good memory and honourable mention of men. Now in truth, according to all these interpretations, the bountiful man's righteousness doth endure for ever, that is, very lastingly, (or so long as the special nature of the case doth bear,) in any sense; or for an absolute perpetuity in some sense: the words in their plenitude do naturally and without straining involve so many truths; none of which therefore we think fit to exclude, but shall briefly touch them all.

1 As for future reputation and fame, (which, that it in part is intended here, that which precedes, *The righteous shall be had in everlasting remembrance*, doth argue,) it is evident that it peculiarly attends upon this practice: the bountiful person is especially that *Just* man, whose *memory is blessed*, (is Μετ' ἐγκωμίων, as the Greek renders it; that is, is prosecuted with commendations and praises). No spices can so embalm a man, no monument can so preserve his name and memory, as works of beneficence; no other fame is comparably so precious, or truly glorious, as that which grows from thence: the renown of power and prowess, of wit or learning, of any wisdom or skill, may dwell in the fancies of men with some admiration; but the remembrance of bounty reigns in their hearts with cordial esteem and affection; there erecting immoveable trophies over death and oblivion, and thence spreading itself through the tongues of men with sincere and sprightly commendations. The bountiful man's very dust is fragrant, and his grave venerable; his name is never mentioned without respect; his actions have always these best echoes, with innumerable iterations resounding after them: *His goods shall be established, and the congregation shall declare his*

Ps. cxii. 6.

Prov. x. 7.

Ecclus. xxxi. 11.

*alms.* This was a true friend to mankind; this was a real benefactor to the world; this was a man good in earnest, and pious to good purpose.

2 The effects of his righteousness are likewise very durable: when he is departed hence, and in person is no more seen, he remains visible and sensible in the footsteps and fruits of his goodness; the poor still beholds him present in the subsistence of himself and his family; the sick man feels him in the refreshment which he yet enjoys by his provision; he supervives in the heart of the afflicted which still resents the comfort, and rejoices in the ease, which he procured him; all the world derives benefit from him by the edification it receiveth from his example; religion obtaineth profit and ornament, God himself enjoyeth glory and praise from his righteousness.

3 *His righteousness* also *endureth* in respect to his posterity. It is an usual plea for tenacity and parsimony, that care must be had of posterity, that enough must be provided and laid up for the family: but in truth this is a very absurd excuse; and doing according thereto is a very preposterous method of proceeding toward that end; it is really the greatest improvidence in that respect, and the truest neglect that can be of our children: for so doing, together with a seeming estate, we entail a real curse upon them: we divest them of God's protection and benediction, (the only sure preservatives of an estate;) we leave them heirs of nothing so much as of punishments due to our ingratitude, our infidelity, our impiety and injustice both toward God and man: whereas by liberally bestowing on the poor, we demise unto them God's

blessing, which is the best inheritance; we recommend them to God's special care, which is the best tuition; we leave them God's protection and providence, which are a wealth indefectible and inexhaustible; we constitute God their guardian, who will most faithfully manage, and most wisely improve their substance, both that which we leave to them, and that which we gave for them to the poor; we thereby in good part entitle them to the rewards appropriate to our pious charity, our faith, our gratitude, our self-denial, our justice, to whatever of good is virtually contained in our acts of bounty; to omit the honour and good-will of men, which constantly adhere to the bountiful man's house and family. *A good man leaveth an inheritance to his children's children.* It is therefore expressly mentioned in Scripture as a recompense peculiar to this virtue, that security from want and all happiness do attend the posterity of the bountiful person: *He is ever merciful and lendeth, and his seed is blessed*, saith David of him generally: and David also particularly observed, that in all the course of his long life he could find no exception to the rule: *I have been young, and now am old; yet have I not seen the righteous forsaken, nor his seed begging their bread.*

4 *His righteousness* also *endureth for ever* in the perpetual favour of God, and in the eternal rewards which God will confer upon him, who, out of conscience and reverence toward God, out of good-will and kindness toward his brother, hath dispersed, and given to the poor. *God will not*, as the apostle saith, *be unjust to forget his labour of charity in ministering* to his poor brother: from the seed

SERM. I.

Prov. xiii. 22.

Ps. xxxvii. 26.

Ps. xxxvii. 25.

Heb. vi. 10.

which he hath sown to the Spirit, he shall assuredly reap a most plentiful crop of blessings spiritual; he shall effectually enjoy *The good foundation* that he hath *stored up:* for the goods he hath sold and delivered, he shall *bona fide* receive his bargain, the *Hidden treasure* and *Precious pearl* of eternal life; for this best improvement of his talent of worldly riches, he shall hear the *Euge bone serve, Well done, good and faithful servant, enter into thy master's joy:* he shall at last find God infinitely more bountiful to him, than he hath been unto the poor.

Thus when all the flashes of sensual pleasure are quite extinct; when all the flowers of secular glory are withered away; when all earthly treasures are buried in darkness; when this world and all the fashion of it are utterly vanished and gone, the bountiful man's state will still be firm and flourishing, and *His righteousness shall endure for ever.*

It follows, *His horn shall be exalted with honour.* A horn is an emblem of power; for in it the beasts' strength, offensive and defensive, doth consist; and of plenty, for it hath within it a capacity apt to contain what is put into it; and of sanctity, for that in it was put the holy oil, with which kings were consecrated; and of dignity, both in consequence upon the reasons mentioned, (as denoting might, and influence, and sacredness accompanying sovereign dignity,) and because also it is an especial beauty and ornament to the creature which hath it; so that this expression (*His horn shall be exalted with honour*) may be supposed to import, that an abundance of high and holy, of firm and solid honour shall attend upon the bountiful person. And that so it truly shall, may from many considerations appear.

1 Honour is inseparably annexed thereto, as its natural companion and shadow. God hath impressed upon all virtue a majesty and a beauty, which do command respect, and with a kindly violence extort veneration from men: such is the natural constitution of our souls, that as our sense necessarily liketh what is fair and sweet, so our mind unavoidably will esteem what is virtuous and worthy; all good actions as such are honourable: but of all virtues, beneficence doth with most unquestionable right claim honour, and with irresistible force procures it; as it is indeed the most divine of virtues, so men are most apt to venerate them, whom they observe eminently to practise it. Other virtues men see, and approve as goodly to the sight; but this they taste and feel; this by most sensible experience they find to be pleasant and profitable, and cannot therefore but highly prize it[u]. They, who *Do their alms before men*, although out of an unworthy vain-glorious design, *have* yet, as our Saviour intimates, *their reward;* they fail not to get honour thereby; and even so have no bad pennyworth: for, in the Wise Man's judgment, *A good name is rather to be chosen than great riches;* they receive at least fine air, for gross earth; and things very spiritual, for things most material; they obtain that which every man doth naturally desire and prize, for that which only fashion in some places endeareth and commendeth: they get the end for the means; for scarce any man seeketh

---

[u] Φιλοῦνται δὲ σχεδὸν μάλιστα οἱ ἐλευθέριοι τῶν ἀπ' ἀρετῆς· ὠφέλιμοι γάρ, τοῦτο δ' ἐν τῇ δόσει.—Arist. [Eth. IV. 1, 11.]

wealth for itself, but either for honour[x], or for virtue's sake, that he may live creditably, or may do good therewith: necessity is served with a little, pleasure may be satisfied with a competence; abundance is required only to support honour or promote good; and honour by a natural connection adhereth to bounty. *He that followeth after righteousness and mercy findeth life, righteousness, and honour.*

<small>Prov. xxi. 21.</small>

2 But further, an accession of honour, according to gracious promise, (grounded upon somewhat of special reason, of equity and decency in the thing itself,) is due from God unto the bountiful person, and is by special providence surely conferred on him. There is no kind of piety, or instance of obedience, whereby God himself is more signally honoured, than by this. These are chiefly those *Good works,* the which *men seeing,* are apt to *glorify our Father which is in heaven; Being filled with the fruits of righteousness, which are by Christ Jesus to the glory and praise of God.* To these fruits that is most applicable which our Lord saith, *Hereby is my Father glorified, if ye bear much fruit;* for as *He that oppresseth the poor reproacheth his Maker;* so *he honoureth him, that hath mercy on the poor.* The comfortable experience of good in this sort of actions will most readily dispose men to admire and commend the excellency, the wisdom, the goodness of the divine laws, will therefore procure God hearty praise and thanks for them: for, as St Paul teacheth us, *The administration of this service not only supplieth the want of the saints, but is abundant also by many thanksgivings unto*

<small>Matt. v. 16.
Phil. i. 11.
John xv. 8.
Prov. xiv. 31.
2 Cor. ix. 12, 13.</small>

---

[x] Αἱ γὰρ δυναστεῖαι καὶ ὁ πλοῦτος διὰ τὴν τιμήν ἐστιν αἱρετά.—Id. [Ibid. IV. 3, 18.]

*God; whilst by experiment of this ministration, they glorify God for your professed subjection unto the Gospel of Christ, and for your liberal distribution unto them, and unto all men.* Since then God is so peculiarly honoured by this practice, it is but equal and fit that God should remunerate it with honour: God's noble goodness will not let him seem defective in any sort of beneficial correspondence toward us; we shall never be able to yield him any kind of good thing in duty, which he will not be more apt to render us in grace; they who, as Solomon speaketh, *Honour God with their substance,* shall by God certainly be honoured with his blessing: reason intimates so much, and we beside have God's express word for it: *Them,* saith he, *who honour me, I will honour.* He that absolutely and independently is the fountain of all honour, *From whom,* as good king David saith, *riches and honour cometh,* for that *he reigneth over all,* he will assuredly prefer and dignify those who have been at special care and cost to advance his honour. He that hath the *Hearts of all men in his hands,* and *Fashioneth them* as he pleaseth, will raise the bountiful man in the judgments and affections of men. He that ordereth all the events of things, and disposeth success as he thinks fit, will cause the bountiful person's enterprizes to prosper, and come off with credit. He will not suffer the reputation of so real an honourer of himself to be extremely slurred by disaster, to be blasted by slander, to be supplanted by envy or malice; but will *Bring forth his righteousness as the light, and his judgment as the noon-day.*

3 God will thus exalt the bountiful man's horn

*Prov. iii. 9.*

*1 Sam. ii. 30.*

*1 Chron. xxix. 12.*

*Prov. xxi. 1.*
*Ps. xxxiii. 15.*

*Ps. xxxvi. 6.*

even here in this world, and to an infinitely higher pitch he will advance it in the future state: he shall there be set at the right hand, in a most honourable place and rank, among the chief friends and favourites of the heavenly King, in happy consortship with the holy angels and blessed saints: where, in recompense of his pious bounty, he shall, from the bountiful hands of his most gracious Lord, receive *An incorruptible crown of righteousness*, and *An unfading crown of glory*. The which God of his infinite mercy grant unto us all, through Jesus Christ our Lord; to whom for ever be all praise. Amen.

*Now the God of peace, that brought again from the dead our Lord Jesus, that great Shepherd of the sheep, through the blood of the everlasting covenant, make us perfect in every good work to do his will, working in us that which is well-pleasing in his sight, through Jesus Christ; to whom be glory for ever and ever. Amen.*

# A SERMON

## UPON

# THE PASSION

## OF

# OUR BLESSED SAVIOUR:

### PREACHED AT

# GUILDHALL CHAPEL,

### ON GOOD FRIDAY, THE 13th DAY OF APRIL,

### ANNO DOM. M.DC.LXXVII.

Sacramentum salutis humanæ non licet tacere, etiam si nequeat explicari.—P. Leo. I. *Serm. de Pass.* 7.

## DAVIES, Mayor.

Martis xxiv die Aprilis, 1677, Annóque Regis Caroli Secundi Angliæ, &c. vicesimo nono.

*This Court doth earnestly desire* Dr Barrow *to print his Sermon, preached at the* Guildhall Chapel, *on* Good Friday *last, before the Mayor and Aldermen of this City.*

WAGSTAFFE.

# SERMON II.

## UPON THE PASSION OF OUR BLESSED SAVIOUR.

### PHIL. II. 8.

*And being found in fashion as a man, he humbled himself, and became obedient unto death, even the death of the cross.*

WHEN, in consequence of the original apostasy from God, which did banish us from paradise, and by continued rebellions against him, inevitable to our corrupt and impotent nature, mankind had forfeited the amity of God[a], (the chief of all goods, the fountain of all happiness,) and had incurred his displeasure; (the greatest of all evils, the foundation of all misery:) *John iii. 36. Col. iii. 6.*

When poor man having deserted his natural Lord and Protector, *Other lords had got dominion over him*, so that he was captivated by the foul, malicious, cruel spirits, and enslaved to his own vain mind, to vile lusts, to wild passions[b]: *Isai. xxvi. 13.*

When, according to an eternal rule of justice, that sin deserveth punishment, and by an express law, wherein death was enacted to the transgressors of God's command, the root of our stock, and consequently all its branches, stood adjudged to utter destruction[c]: *Gen. iv. 7; ii. 17.*

---

[a] Cyril. c. Jul. VIII. [Opp. Tom. VI. p. 278 A, B. IX. p. 303 B.]
[b] Iren. iii. 33, 34; iii. 8.
[c] Iren. v. 16.

When, according to St Paul's expressions, *All the world was become guilty before God*, Ὑπόδικος τῷ Θεῷ, (or subjected to God's judgment:) *All men* (Jews and Gentiles) *were under sin, under condemnation, under the curse; All men were concluded into disobedience*, Εἰς ἀπείθειαν, and *shut up together* (as close prisoners) *under sin; All men had sinned, and come short of the glory of God: Death had passed over all, because all had sinned:*

When for us, being plunged into so wretched a condition, no visible remedy did appear, no possible redress could be obtained here below: for what means could we have of recovering God's favour, who were apt perpetually to contract new debts and guilts, but not able to discharge any old scores? What capacity of mind or will had we to entertain mercy, who were no less stubbornly perverse and obdurate in our crimes, than ignorant or infirm? How could we be reconciled unto Heaven, who had an innate antipathy to God and goodness? [*Sin*, according to our natural state, and secluding evangelical grace, *reigning in our mortal bodies, No good thing dwelling in us;* there being a predominant *Law in our members, warring against the law of our mind, and bringing us into captivity to the law of sin;* a main ingredient of our *Old man* being a *carnal mind,* which is *enmity to God,* and *cannot submit*, Οὐχ ὑποτάσσεται, *to his law;* we being *Alienated from the life of God by the blindness of our hearts, and enemies in our minds by wicked works:*] How could we revive to any good hope, who were *Dead in trespasses and sins,* God having withdrawn his quickening Spirit? How at least could we for one moment stand upright in God's

sight, upon the natural terms, excluding all sin, SERM. II.
and exacting perfect obedience?

When this, I say, was our forlorn and desperate case, then Almighty God, out of his infinite goodness, was pleased to look upon us (as he sometime did upon Jerusalem, *Lying polluted in her blood*) with an eye of pity and mercy, so as graciously to design a redemption for us out of all that woful distress: and no sooner by his incomprehensible wisdom did he foresee we should lose ourselves, than by his immense grace he did conclude to restore us.

<small>Eph. ii. 5.
Rom. vi.
11, 13.
Ps. cxliii.
2.
Exod.
xxxiv. 7.
Ezek. xvi.
6.</small>

But how could this happy design well be compassed? How, in consistence with the glory, with the justice, with the truth of God, could such enemies be reconciled, such offenders be pardoned, such wretches be saved? Would the omnipotent Majesty so affronted, deign to treat with his rebels immediately, without an intercessor or advocate? Would the sovereign Governor of the world suffer thus notoriously his right to be violated, his authority to be slighted, his honour to be trampled on, without some notable vindication or satisfaction? Would the great Patron of justice relax the terms of it, or ever permit a gross breach thereof to pass with impunity? Would the immutable God of truth expose his veracity or his constancy to suspicion, by so reversing that peremptory sentence of death upon sinners, that it should not in a sort eminently be accomplished[d]? Would the most righteous and most Holy God let slip an

<small>Eph. i. 4, 9, 11, &
iii. 11.
2 Tim. i. 9.
1 Pet. i.
20.
Rev. xiii.
8.
Rom. xvi.
25.
Tit. i. 2.

Gen. ii. 17.</small>

---

[d] Athan. de Incarn. [Θανάτου γὰρ ἦν χρεία, καὶ θάνατον ὑπὲρ πάντων ἔδει γενέσθαι, ἵνα τὸ παρὰ πάντων ὀφειλόμενον γένηται.—Opp. Tom. I. p. 64 F.]

SERM. II.

opportunity so advantageous for demonstrating his perfect love of innocence, and abhorrence of iniquity? Could we therefore well be cleared from our guilt without an expiation, or reinstated in freedom without a ransom, or exempted from condemnation without some punishment?

No: God was so pleased to prosecute his designs of goodness and mercy, as thereby nowise to impair or obscure, but rather to advance and illustrate the glories of his sovereign dignity, of his severe justice, of his immaculate holiness, of his unchangeable steadiness in word and purpose. He accordingly would be sued to for peace and mercy: nor would he grant them absolutely, without due compensations for the wrongs he had sustained; yet so, that his goodness did find us a Mediator, and furnish us with means to satisfy him. He would not condescend to a simple remission of our debts; yet so, that, saving his right and honour, he did stoop lower for an effectual abolition of them. He would make good his word, not to let our trespasses go unpunished; yet so, that by our punishment we might receive advantage. He would manifest his detestation of wickedness in a way more illustrious than if he had persecuted it down to hell, and irreversibly doomed it to endless torment.

But how might these things be effected? Where was there a Mediator proper and worthy to intercede for us? Who could presume to solicit and plead in our behalf? Who should dare to put himself between God and us, or offer to screen mankind from the divine wrath and vengeance? Who had so great an interest in the court of heaven, as to ingratiate such a brood of apostate enemies thereto? Who could assume the confidence to propose terms of reconciliation, or to agitate a new Covenant, wherewith God might be satisfied, and whereby we might be saved? Where, in heaven or earth, could there be found a priest fit to atone for sins so vastly numerous, so extremely heinous? And whence should a sacrifice be taken, of value sufficient to expiate for so manifold enormities, committed against the infinite Majesty of Heaven? Who could *Find out the everlasting redemption*[e] of innumerable souls, or lay down a competent ransom for them all? Not to say, could also purchase for them eternal life and bliss?

SERM. II.

These are questions which would puzzle all the wit of man, yea, would gravel all the wisdom of angels to resolve: for plain it is, that no creature on earth, none in heaven, could well undertake or perform this work.

Where on earth, among the degenerate sons of Adam, could be found *Such an high priest as became us, holy, harmless undefiled, separate from sinners?* and how could a man, however innocent and pure as a seraphim, so perform his duty, as to do more than merit or satisfy for himself? How many lives could the life of one man serve to ransom; seeing that it is asserted of the greatest and richest among men, that *None of them can by any means redeem his brother, or give to God a ransom for him.*

Heb. vii. 26.

Ps. xlix. 7.

And how could available help in this case be expected from any of the angelical host; seeing (beside their being in nature different from us,

---

e Αἰωνίαν λύτρωσιν εὑράμενος.—Heb. ix. 12.

SERM. II.

and thence improper to merit or satisfy for us; beside their comparative meanness, and infinite distance from the majesty of God) they are but our fellow-servants, and have obligations to discharge for themselves, and cannot be solvent for more than for their own debts of gratitude and service to their infinitely-bountiful Creator; they also themselves needing a Saviour, to preserve them by his grace in their happy state?

Indeed, no creature might aspire to so august an honour, none could achieve so marvellous a work, as to redeem from infinite guilt and misery the noblest part of all the visible creation: none could presume to invade that high prerogative of God, or attempt to infringe the truth of that reiterated proclamation, *I, even I, am the Lord, and beside me there is no Saviour.*

Isai. xliii. 11; xlv. 21.
Hos. xiii. 4.

Wherefore, seeing that a supereminent dignity of person was required in our Mediator, and that an immense value was to be presented for our ransom; seeing that *God saw there was no man, and wondered* (or took special notice[f]) *that there was no intercessor;* it must be *his arm* alone that could *bring salvation;* none beside God himself could intermeddle therein.

Isai. lix. 16.

But how could God undertake the business? Could he become a suitor or intercessor to his offended self? Could he present a sacrifice, or disburse a satisfaction to his own justice? Could God alone contract and stipulate with God in our behalf? No; surely man also must concur in the transaction: some amends must issue from him, somewhat must be paid out of our stock: human

[f] Κατενόησε. LXX.

will and consent must be interposed, to ratify a firm covenant with us, inducing obligation on our part. It was decent and expedient, that as man, by wilful transgression and presumptuous self-pleasing, had so highly offended, injured, and dishonoured his Maker; so man also, by willing obedience, and patient submission to God's pleasure, should greatly content, right, and glorify him.

Here then did lie the stress; this was the knot, which only Divine wisdom could loose. And so indeed it did in the most effectual and admirable way: for in correspondence to all the exigencies of the case, (that God and man both might act their parts in saving us,) the blessed eternal Word, the only Son of God, by the good-will of his Father, did vouchsafe to intercede for us, and to undertake our redemption[g]; in order thereto voluntarily being sent down from heaven, assuming human flesh, subjecting himself to all the infirmities of our frail nature, and to the worst inconveniences of our low condition; therein meriting God's favour to us, by a perfect obedience to the law, and satisfying God's justice by a most patient endurance of pains in our behalf; in completion of all, willingly laying down his life for the ransom of our souls, and pouring forth his blood in sacrifice for our sins.

This is that great and wonderful *Mystery of godliness,* (or of our holy religion,) the which St Paul here doth express, in these words concerning our blessed Saviour; *Who being in the form of God, thought it no robbery to be equal with God;*

Eph. i. 8, 9.
Luke i. 78.
Eph. i. 5.
Tit. iii. 4.
Rom. v. 8.
Gal. iv. 4.
John vi. 38.
Heb. x. 7.
John i. 14.
Heb. v. 2; iv. 15.
Eph. i. 6.
1 Tim. ii. 6.
Tit. ii. 14.
Heb. ix. 15; ii. 9.
Col. i. 22.

1 Tim. iii. 16.

Phil. ii. 6, 7, 8.

[g] Constit. Apost. VIII. 12. [Cotel. Pat. Apost. Tom. I. p. 402.]

SERM. II.

*but made himself of no reputation, and took upon him the form of a servant, and was made in the likeness of men: and being found in fashion as a man, he humbled himself, and became obedient unto death, even the death of the cross.*

In which words are contained divers points very observable. But seeing the time will not allow me to treat on them in any measure as they deserve, I shall (waving all the rest) insist but upon one particular, couched in the last words, *Even the death of the cross,* Θανάτου δὲ σταυροῦ; which by a special emphasis do excite us to consider the manner of that holy passion which we now commemorate; the contemplation whereof, as it is most seasonable, so it is ever very profitable.

Now then in this kind of passion we may consider divers notable adjuncts; namely these: 1 Its being in appearance criminal. 2 Its being most bitter and painful. 3 Its being most ignominious and shameful. 4 Its peculiar advantageousness to the designs of our Lord in suffering. 5 Its practical efficacy.

I. We may consider our Lord's suffering as criminal; or as in semblance being an execution of justice upon him. *He*, as the prophet foretold of him, *was numbered among the transgressors;* and God, saith St Paul, *Made him sin for us, who knew no sin:* that is, God ordered him to be treated as a most sinful or criminous person, who in himself was perfectly innocent, and void of the least inclination to offend.

Isai. liii. 12.

2 Cor. v. 21.

John v. 18; x. 30, &c.; vii. 12.

So in effect it was, that he was impeached of the highest crimes; as a violator of the divine laws in divers instances; as a designer to subvert their religion and temple; as an impostor, deluding and seducing the people; as a blasphemer, assuming to himself the properties and prerogatives of God; as a seditious and rebellious person, *Perverting the nation*, inhibiting payments of tribute to Cæsar, usurping royal authority, and styling himself *Christ a king*: in a word, as a malefactor, or one guilty of enormous offences[h]; so his persecutors avowed to Pilate, *If*, said they, *he were not a malefactor*, Κακοποιός, *we would not have delivered him up unto thee*. As such he was represented and arraigned; as such, although by a sentence wrested by malicious importunity, against the will and conscience of the judge, he was condemned, and accordingly suffered death.

SERM. II.

Matt. xxvi. 61; xxvii. 40.

Luke xxiii. 2.

Matt. xxvii. 63.

John xviii. 30.

Now whereas any death or passion of our Lord, as being in itself immensely valuable, and most precious in the sight of God, might have been sufficient toward the accomplishment of his general designs, (the appeasing God's wrath, the satisfaction of divine justice, the expiation of our guilt;) it may be inquired, why God should thus expose him, or why he should choose to suffer under this odious and ugly character[i]? Which inquiry is the more considerable, because it is especially this circumstance which crosseth the fleshly sense and worldly prejudices of men, so as to have rendered the gospel offensive to the superstitious Jews, and despicable to conceited Gentiles. For so Tryphon in Justin Martyr[k], although from conviction by testi-

[h] Constit. Apost. v. 14. [Cotel. Pat. Apost. Tom. I. p. 317.]
[i] Cur si Deus fuit, et mori voluit, non saltem honesto aliquo mortis genere affectus est? &c.—Lact. Instit. IV. 26.
[k] Just. M. Dial. cum Tryph. [p. 197 A, B.] [Εἰ δὲ καὶ ἀτίμως οὕτως

monies of scripture, he did admit the Messias was to suffer hardly, yet that it should be in this accursed manner, he could not digest. So the great adversaries of Christianity (Celsus[l], Porphyry[m], Julian[n]) did with most contempt urge this exception against it. So St Paul did observe, that *Christ crucified was unto the Jews a stumblingblock, and unto the Greeks foolishness.* Wherefore, to avoid those scandals, and that we may better admire the wisdom of God in this dispensation, it may be fit to assign some reasons intimated in holy scripture, or bearing conformity to its doctrine, why it was thus ordered. Such are these.

1 As our Saviour freely did undertake a life of greatest meanness and hardship, so upon the like accounts he might be pleased to undergo a death most loathsome and uncomfortable. There is nothing to man's nature (especially to the best natures, in which modesty and ingenuity do survive) more

σταυρωθῆναι τὸν Χριστὸν, ἀποροῦμεν· ἐπικατάρατος γὰρ ὁ σταυρούμενος ἐν τῷ νόμῳ λέγεται εἶναι. ὥστε πρὸς τοῦτο ἀκμὴν δυσπείστως ἔχω. παθητὸν μὲν τὸν Χριστὸν ὅτι αἱ γραφαὶ κηρύσσουσι, φανερόν ἐστιν· εἰ δὲ διὰ τοῦ ἐν τῷ νόμῳ κεκατηραμένου πάθους, βουλόμεθα μαθεῖν, εἰ ἔχεις καὶ περὶ τούτου ἀποδεῖξαι.]

[l] Orig. con. Cels. II. p. 83. [Πῶς δ' οὐκ ἄντικρυς ψεῦδος τὸ ὑπὸ τοῦ παρὰ τῷ Κέλσῳ Ἰουδαίου λεγόμενον, ὅτι, "Μηδένα πείσας μέχρι ἔζη, ὅτι (ὅγε) μηδὲ τοὺς ἑαυτοῦ μαθητὰς, ἐκολάσθη καὶ τοιαῦτα ὑπέμεινε;"] VII. p. 368. [Τὸν δὲ βίῳ μὲν ἐπιρρητοτάτῳ, θανάτῳ δὲ οἰκτίστῳ χρησάμενον, Θεὸν τίθεσθε.]

[m] Aug. de Civ. Dei, x. 28. [Opp. Tom. VII. col. 263 c.] [Hunc autem Christum esse non credis; contemnis enim eum propter corpus ex femina acceptum, et propter crucis opprobrium.]

[n] Cyril. c. Jul. VI. Opp. Tom. VI. p. 194 c. [Εἶτα ὦ δυστυχεῖς ἄνθρωποι—τὸ τοῦ σταυροῦ προσκυνεῖτε ξύλον, εἰκόνας αὐτοῦ σκιαγραφοῦντες ἐν τῷ μετώπῳ καὶ πρὸ τῶν οἰκημάτων ἐγγράφοντες, ἆρα ἀξίως ἄν τις συνετωτέρους ὑμῶν μισήσειεν, ἢ τοὺς ἀφρονεστέρους ἐλεήσειεν, οἱ κατακολουθοῦντες ὑμῖν εἰς τοῦτο ἦλθον ὀλέθρου, ὥστε τοὺς αἰωνίους ἀφέντες θεοὺς ἐπὶ τῶν Ἰουδαίων μεταβῆναι νεκρόν.]

abominable than such a death. God for good purposes hath planted in our constitution a quick sense of disgrace; and, of all disgraces, that which proceedeth from an imputation of crimes is most pungent; and being conscious of our innocence doth heighten the smart; and to reflect upon ourselves dying under it, leaving the world with an indelible stain upon our name and memory, is yet more grievous. Even to languish by degrees, enduring the torments of a long, however sharp disease, would to an honest mind seem more eligible, than in this manner, being reputed and handled as a villain, to find a quick and easy despatch.

Of which human resentment may we not observe a touch in that expostulation, *Be ye come out, as against a thief, with swords and staves?* If as a man he did not like to be prosecuted as a thief; yet willingly did he choose it, as he did other most distasteful things pertaining to our nature, (*The likeness of man,*) and incident to that low condition, (*The form of a servant,*) into which he did put himself: such as were, to endure penury, and to fare hardly, to be slighted, envied, hated, reproached through all his course of life.

It is well said by a pagan philosopher, that, *No man doth express such a respect and devotion to virtue, as doth he who forfeiteth the repute of being a good man, that he may not lose the conscience of being such*°. This our Lord willingly made his case, being content not only to expose his life, but to prostitute his fame, for the interests of goodness.

---

° Nemo mihi videtur pluris æstimare virtutem, nemo illi magis esse devotus, quam qui boni viri famam perdidit, ne conscientiam perderet.—Sen. Ep. LXXXI. [19.]

Had he died otherwise, he might have seemed to purchase our welfare at a somewhat easier rate; he had not been so complete a sufferer; he had not tasted the worst that man is liable to endure: there had been a comfort in seeming innocent, detracting from the perfection of his sufferance.

Whereas therefore he often was in hazard of death, both from the clandestine machinations and the outrageous violences of those who maligned him, he did industriously shun a death so plausible, and honourable, if I may so speak; it being not so disgraceful to fall by private malice, or by sudden rage, as by the solemn deliberate proceeding of men in public authority and principal credit.

John v. 18; viii. 37, 40, 59; vii. 1, 19, 25; x. 32, 39.

Accordingly this kind of death did not fall upon him by surprise or by chance; but he did *From the beginning* foresee it; he plainly with satisfaction did aim at it: he, as it is related in the Gospels, did shew his disciples, that it was incumbent on him by God's appointment and his own choice; that *He ought*, it is said, *to suffer many things, to be rejected by the chief priests, elders, and scribes, to be vilified by them, to be delivered up to the Gentiles, to be mocked, and scourged, and crucified,* as a flagitious slave. Thus would our blessed Saviour in conformity to the rest of his voluntary afflictions, and for a consummation of them, not only suffer in his body by sore wounds and bruises, and in his soul by doleful agonies, but in his name also and reputation by the foulest scandals; undergoing as well all the infamy as the infirmity which did belong to us, or might befall us: thus meaning by all means throughly to express his charity, and exercise his compassion towards us; thus advancing his merit,

John vi. 64.

Matt. xvi. 21.
Luke ix. 22; xviii. 32, 33.
Mark ix. 31.

and discharging the utmost satisfaction in our behalf.

2 Death passing on him as a malefactor by public sentence, did best suit to the nature of his undertaking, was most congruous to his intent, did most aptly represent what he was doing, and imply the reason of his performance. For we all are guilty in a most high degree, and in a manner very notorious: the foulest shame, together with the sharpest pain, is due to us for affronting our glorious Maker; we deserve an open condemnation and exemplary punishment: wherefore he, undertaking in our stead to bear all, and fully to satisfy for us, was pleased to undergo the like judgment and usage; being termed, being treated as we should have been, in quality of an heinous malefactor, as we in truth are. What we had really acted in dishonouring and usurping upon God, in disordering the world, in perverting others, that was imputed to him; and the punishment due to that guilt was inflicted on him. *All we like sheep have gone astray; we have turned every one to his own way; and the Lord hath laid on him the iniquities of us all.* He therefore did not only sustain an equivalent pain for us, but in a sort did bear an equal blame with us, before God and man.

3 Seeing, *By the determinate counsel of God*, it was appointed that our Lord should die for us, and that not in a natural, but violent way, so as perfectly to satisfy God's justice, to vindicate his honour, to evidence both his indignation against sin, and willingness to be appeased; it was most fit that affair should be transacted in a way, wherein God's right is most nearly concerned, and his providence most

Isai. liii. 6.

Acts ii. 23.

plainly discernible; wherein it should be most apparent that God did exact and inflict the punishment, that our Lord did freely yield to it, and submissively undergo it, upon those very accounts. All *Judgment*, as Moses of old did say, *is God's*, or is administered by authority derived from him, in his name, for his interest; all magistrates being his officers and instruments, whereby he governeth and ordereth the world, his natural kingdom: whence that which is acted in way of formal judgment by persons in authority, God himself may be deemed in a more special and immediate manner to execute it, as being done by his commission, in his stead, on his behalf, with his peculiar superintendence. It was therefore in our Lord a signal act of deference to God's authority and justice, becoming the person sustained by him of our Mediator and Proxy, to undergo such a judgment, and such a punishment; whereby he received a doom as it were from God's own mouth, uttered by his ministers, and bare the stroke of justice from God's hand, represented by his instruments. Whence very seasonably and patiently did he reply to Pilate, *Thou hadst no power over me*, Κατ' ἐμοῦ, (or *against me*) *except it were given thee from above*: implying that it was in regard to the originally supreme authority of God his father, and to his particular appointment upon this occasion, that our Saviour did then frankly subject himself to those inferior powers, as to the proper ministers of divine justice. Had he suffered in any other way, by the private malice or passion of men, God's special providence in that case had been less visible, and our Lord's obedience not so remarkable. And if he must die by public hands, it must be as a criminal, under a pretence of guilt and demerit; there must be a formal process, how full soever of mockery and outrage; there must be testimonies produced, how void soever of truth or probability; there must be a sentence pronounced, although most corrupt and injurious: for no man is in this way prosecuted, without colour of desert: otherwise it would cease to be public authority, and become lawless violence; the prosecutor then would put off the face of a magistrate, and appear as a cut-throat or a robber.

SERM. II.

4  In fine, our Saviour hardly with such advantage, in any other way, could have displayed all kinds of virtue and goodness, to the honour of God, to the edification of men, to the furtherance of our salvation.

The judgment-hall, with all the passages leading him thither, and thence to execution, attended with guards of soldiers, amidst the crowds and clamours of people, were as so many theatres, on which he had opportune convenience, in the full eye of the world, to act divers parts of sublimest virtue: to express his insuperable constancy, in attesting truth, and maintaining a good conscience; his meekness, in calmly bearing the greatest wrongs; his patience, in contentedly enduring the saddest adversities; his entire resignation to the will and providence of God; his peaceable submission to the law and power of man; his admirable charity, in pitying, in excusing, in obliging those by his good wishes, and earnest prayers for their pardon, who in a manner so injurious, so despiteful, so cruel, did persecute him, yea, in gladly suffering all this from their hands for their salvation; his unshakeable faith in God, and unal-

John xviii. 37.
1 Tim. vi. 13.

terable love toward him, under so fierce a trial, so dreadful a temptation. All these excellent virtues and graces, by the matter being thus ordered, in a degree most eminent, and in a manner very conspicuous, were demonstrated to the praise of God's name, and the commendation of his truth; for the settlement of our faith and hope, for an instruction and an encouragement to us of good practice in those highest instances of virtue.

It is a passable notion among the most eminent pagan sages, that no very exemplary virtue can well appear otherwise than in notable misfortune[p]. Whence it is said in Plato, that to approve a man heartily righteous, *He must be scourged, tortured, bound, have his two eyes burnt out, and in the close, having suffered all evils, must be impaled*, or crucified[q]. And, *It was*, saith Seneca, *the cup of poison which made Socrates a great man*, and *which out of prison did transfer him to heaven*[r]; or did procure to him that lofty esteem, affording him opportunity to signalize his constancy, his equanimity, his unconcernedness for this world and life. And, *The virtue*, saith he again, *and the innocence of Rutilius would have lain hid, if it had not* (by condemnation and exile) *received injury; while it was violated, it*

[p] Magnum exemplum, nisi mala fortuna, non invenit.—Sen. de Prov. [cap. iii. 5.]

[q] Ὁ δίκαιος μαστιγώσεται, στρεβλώσεται, δεδήσεται, ἐκκαυθήσεται τὼφθαλμώ, τελευτῶν πάντα κακὰ παθὼν ἀνασκινδυλευθήσεται.—Plat. de Rep. II. [361 E.]

[r] Cicuta magnum Socratem confecit.—Sen. Ep. XIII. [14.]

Calix venenatus, qui Socratem transtulit e carcere in coelum.—Id. Ep. LXVII. [9.]

Æqualis fuit in tanta inæqualitate fortunæ. &c.—Id. Ep. CIV. [28.]

*brightly shone forth*[s]. And he that said this of others, was himself in nothing so illustrious, as in handsomely entertaining that death to which he was by the bloody tyrant adjudged. And generally, the most honourable persons in the judgment of posterity for gallant worth, to this very end (as such philosophers teach) were by divine Providence delivered up to suffer opprobrious condemnations and punishments, by the ingrateful malignity of their times[t]. So that the Greeks, in consistence with their own wisdom and experience, could not reasonably scorn that cross which our good Lord (did not only, as did their best worthies, by forcible accidental constraint undergo, but) advisedly by free choice did undertake, to recommend the most excellent virtues to imitation, and to promote the most noble designs that could be, by its influence.

So great reason there was that our Lord should thus suffer as a criminal.

II. We may consider that in that kind his suffering was most bitter and painful. Easily we may imagine what acerbity of pain must be endured by our Lord in his tender limbs being stretched forth, racked, and tentered, and continuing for a good time in such a posture; by the *Piercing his hands and his feet*, parts very nervous and exquisitely sensible, with sharp nails, (so that, as it is said of Joseph, *The iron entered into his soul*;) by abiding exposed to the injuries of the sun scorching, the wind beating, the weather searching his

Ps. xxii. 16.

Ps. cv. 18.

---

[s] Rutilii innocentia ac virtus lateret, nisi accepisset injuriam; dum violatur, effulsit.—Id. Ep. LXXIX. [12.]

[t] Sen. de Prov. cap. II. III. &c. Plut. de Stoic. Contr. [Opp. Tom. III. p. 1931. Ed. Steph.]

grievous wounds and sores. Such a pain it was; and that no stupifying, no transient pain, but one both very acute and lingering: for we see, that he together with his fellow-sufferers had both presence of mind and time to discourse. Even six long hours did he remain under such torture, sustaining in each moment of them beyond the pangs of an ordinary death. But as the case was so hard and sad, so the reason of it was great, and the fruit answerably good. Our Saviour did embrace such a passion, that, in being thus content to endure the most intolerable smarts for us, he might demonstrate the vehemence of his love; that he might signify the heinousness of our sins, which deserved that from such a person so heavy a punishment should be exacted; that he might appear to yield a valuable compensation for those pains which we should have suffered; that he throughly might exemplify the hardest duties of obedience and patience.

III. This manner of suffering was (as most sharp and afflictive, so) most vile and shameful; being proper to the basest condition of the worst men, and unworthy of a freeman, however nocent and guilty[u]. It was *Servile supplicium*, a punishment never by the Romans, under whose law our Lord suffered, legally inflicted upon freemen, but upon slaves only; that is, upon people scarcely regarded as men, having in a sort forfeited or lost themselves. And among the Jews that execution which most approached thereto, and in part agreed with it, (for their law did not allow any so inhu-

[u] Quod etiam homine libero, quamvis nocente, videatur indignum.—Lact. Instit. iv. 26.

man punishment,) hanging up the dead bodies of some that had been put to death, was held most infamous and execrable: for, *Cursed*, said the law, *is every one that hangeth upon a tree;* cursed, that is, devoted to reproach and malediction[x]; *Accursed by God*, saith the Hebrew, that is, seeming to be rejected by God, and by his special order exposed to affliction.

SERM. II.

Deut. xxi. 23.
Gal. iii. 13.

Indeed, according to the course of things, to be set on high, and for continuance of time to be objected to the view of all that pass by, in that calamitous posture, doth infuse bad suspicion, doth provoke censure, doth invite contempt and scorn, doth naturally draw forth language of derision, despite, and detestation; especially from the inconsiderate, hardhearted, and rude vulgar, which commonly doth think, speak, and deal according to event and appearance: (—*Sequitur fortunam, ut semper, et odit damnatos*[y]—) whence Θεατρίζεσθαι, *To be made a gazing-stock*, or an object of reproach to the multitude, is by the apostle mentioned as an aggravation of the hardships endured by the primitive Christians. And thus in extremity did it befall our Lord: for we read[z], that the people did in that condition mock, jeer, and revile him, drawing up their noses, abusing him by scurrilous gestures, letting out their virulent and wanton tongues against him; so as to verify that prediction, *I am a reproach of men, and despised of the people. All they that see me laugh me to scorn:*

Heb. x. 33.

Ps. xxii. 6, 7, 8.

[x] Τοῦτο γὰρ μόνον τῆς τελευτῆς τὸ εἶδος ὑπὸ ἀρὰν ἔκειτο.—Chrys. Or. LXI. Opp. Tom. VI. [p. 631.]

[y] [Juv. Sat. x. 73.]

[z] Luke xxiii. 35, 36. Ἐξεμυκτήριζον, Ἐνέπαιζον. Matt. xxvii. 39. Ἐβλασφήμουν.

SERM. II.

*they shoot out the lip, they shake the head, saying, He trusted in the Lord: let him deliver him, seeing he delighted in him.*

Matt. ix. 33; xii. 23; xxi. 9.

The same persons who formerly had admired his glorious works, who had been ravished with his excellent discourses, who had followed and favoured him so earnestly, who had blessed and magnified him, (*For he,* saith St Luke, *taught in the synagogues, being glorified by all,*) even those very persons did then behold him with pitiless contempt and despite. In correspondence to that prophecy, *They look and stare upon me,* Ἐιστήκει ὁ λαὸς θεωρῶν, *The people stood gazing* on him, in a most scornful manner, venting contemptuous and spiteful reproaches; as we see reported in the evangelical story.

Luke iv. 15.

Ps. xxii. 17.
Luke xxiii. 35.

Heb. xii. 2.

Thus did our blessed Saviour *Endure the cross, despising the shame. Despising the shame,* that is, not simply disregarding it, or (with a stoical haughtiness, with a cynical immodesty, with a stupid carelessness) slighting it as no evil; but not eschewing it, or not rating it for so great an evil, that to decline it he would neglect the prosecution of his great and glorious designs.

Heb. xi. 36.

There is innate to man an aversation and abhorrency from disgraceful abuse, no less strong than are the like antipathies to pain: whence *Cruel mockings and scourgings* are coupled as ingredients of the sore persecutions sustained by God's faithful martyrs. And generally men with more readiness will embrace, with more contentedness will endure the cruelty of the latter, than of the former; pain not so smartly affecting the lower sense, as being insolently contemned doth grate upon the fancy, and wound even the mind itself. For, *The wounds of infamy do*, as the Wise Man telleth us, *go down into the innermost parts of the belly*, reaching the very heart, and touching the soul to the quick.

SERM. II.

Prov. xviii. 8; xii. 18.

We therefore need not doubt, but that our Saviour as a man, endowed with human passions, was sensible of this natural evil; and that such indignities did add somewhat of loathsomeness to his cup of affliction; especially considering that his great charity disposed him to grieve, observing men to act so indecently, so unworthily, so unjustly toward him: yet in consideration of the glory that would thence accrue to God, of the benefit that would redound to us, of the *Joy that was set before him*, when *He should see of the travail of his soul, and be satisfied*, he most willingly did accept, and most gladly did comport with it. *He became a curse for us*, exposed to malediction and reviling; *He endured the contradiction*, or obliquy, *of sinful men: He was despised, rejected, and disesteemed of men:* he in common apprehension was deserted by God, according to that of the prophet, *We did esteem him stricken, smitten of God, and afflicted;* himself even seeming to concur in that opinion. So was *He made a curse for us*, that *we*, as the apostle teacheth, might *be redeemed from the curse of the law;* that is, that we might be freed from the exemplary punishment due to our transgressions of the law, with the displeasure of God appearing therein, and the disgrace before the world attending it. He chose thus to *Make himself of no reputation*, vouchsafing to be dealt with as a wretched slave, and a wicked miscreant, that we might be exempted, not only from the torment,

Heb. xii. 2.
Isai. liii. 11.
Gal. iii. 13.
Heb. xii. 3.
Isai. liii. 3.
Isai. liii. 4.
Gal. iii. 13.
Phil. ii. 7.

SERM. II.

but also from the ignominy which we had merited: that together with our life, our safety, our liberty, we might even recover that honour which we had forfeited and embezzled.

But lest any should be tempted not sufficiently to value these sufferances of our Lord, as not so rare, but that other men have tasted the like; lest any should presume to compare them with afflictions incident to other persons, as Celsus did compare them with those of Anaxarchus and Epictetus[a]; it is requisite to consider some remarkable particulars about them.

We may then consider, that not only the infinite dignity of his person, and the perfect innocency of his life, did enhance the price of his sufferings; but some endowments peculiar to him, and some circumstances adhering to his design, did much augment their force.

He was not only, according to the frame and temper of human nature, sensibly touched with the pain, the shame, the whole combination of disasters apparently waiting on his passion; as God (when he did insert sense and passion into our nature, ordering objects to affect them) did intend we should be, and as other men in like circumstances would have been; but in many respects beyond that ordinary rate: so that no man, we may suppose, could have felt such grief from them as he did, no man ever hath been sensible of anything

[a] Orig. con. Cels. VII. pp. 367, 368. [Ἀνάξαρχον γοῦν, ὃς εἰς ὅλμον ἐμβληθεὶς, καὶ παρανομώτατα συντριβόμενος, εὖ μάλα κατεφρόνει τῆς κολάσεως, λέγων, Πτίσσε, πτίσσε τὸν Ἀναξάρχου θύλακον, αὐτὸν γὰρ οὐ πτίσσεις. . . . . Οὐκοῦν Ἐπίκτητον; ὃς, τοῦ δεσπότου στρεβλοῦντος αὐτοῦ τὸ σκέλος, ὑπομειδιῶν ἀνεκπλήκτως ἔλεγε, Κατάσσεις· καὶ κατάξαντος, Οὐκ ἔλεγον, εἶπεν, ὅτι κατάσσεις;]

comparable to what he did endure; that passage being truly applicable to him, *Behold, and see if there be any sorrow like to my sorrow, which is done unto me, wherewith the Lord hath afflicted me in the day of his fierce anger;* as that unparalleled *Sweating out great lumps of blood* may argue; and as the terms expressing his resentments do intimate. For, in respect of present evils, he said of himself, *My soul is exceeding sorrowful to death;* he is said Ἀδημονεῖν, to be in great anguish and anxiety, to be in *An agony* or pang of sorrow. In regard to mischiefs which he saw coming on, he is said to be *Disturbed in spirit*, and to be *Sore amazed*, or dismayed at them. To such an exceeding height did the sense of incumbent evils, and the prospect of impendent calamities, the apprehension of his case, together with a reflection on our condition, screw up his affections.

*SERM. II.*

Lam. i. 12.

Luke xxii. 44.

Matt. xxvi. 37, 38.

John xiii. 21; xii. 27. Mark xiv. 33.

And no wonder that such a burden, even the weight of all the sins (the numberless most heinous sins and abominations) that ever were committed by mankind, by appropriation of them to himself, lying on his shoulders, he should feel it heavy, or seem to crouch and groan under it; that in the mystical Psalm, applied by the apostle to him, he should cry out, *Innumerable evils have compassed me about; mine iniquities have taken hold upon me, so that I am not able to look up; they are more than the hairs of my head, and my heart faileth me.* The sight of God's indignation, so dreadfully flaming out against sin, might well astonish and terrify him: to stand, as it were, before the mouth of hell belching fire and brimstone in his face; to lie down in the hottest furnace of divine ven-

Heb. x. 5.

Ps. xl. 12.

geance; to quench with his own heart-blood the wrath of heaven, and the infernal fire, (as he did in regard to those who will not rekindle them to themselves,) might well in the heart of a man beget unconceivable and unexpressible pressures of affliction. When such a Father (so infinitely good and kind to him, whom he so dearly and perfectly loved) did hide his face from him, did frown on him, how could he otherwise than be mightily troubled? Is it strange that so hearty a love, so tender a pity, contemplating our sinfulness, and experimenting our wretchedness, should be deeply touched? To see, I say, so plainly, to feel so throughly the horrible blindness, the folly, the infidelity, the imbecility, the ingratitude, the incorrigibility, the strange perverseness, perfidiousness, malice, and cruelty of mankind in so many instances, (in the treason of Judas, in the denial of Peter, in the desertion of all the apostles, in the spite and rage of the persecutors, in the falsehood of the witnesses, in the abuses of the people, in the compliance of Pilate, in a general conspiracy of friends and foes to sin,) all these surrounding him, all invading him, all discharging themselves upon him; would it not astone a mind so pure? would it not wound a heart so tender and full of charity?

Surely, any of those persons who fondly do pretend unto, or vainly do glory in, a sullen apathy, or a stubborn contempt of the evils incident to our nature and state, would in such a case have been utterly dejected: the most resolved philosopher would have been dashed into confusion at the sight, would have been crushed into desperation under the sense of those evils which did assault him.

With the greatness of the causes, the goodness of his constitution did conspire to increase his sufferings. For surely, as his complexion was most pure and delicate, his spirit most vivid and apprehensive, his affections most pliant and tractable; so accordingly would the impressions upon him be most sensible, and consequently the pains which he felt (in body or soul) most afflictive.

That we in like cases are not alike moved, that we do not tremble at the apprehensions of God's displeasure, that we are not affrighted with the sense of our sins, that we do not with sad horror resent our danger and our misery, doth arise from that we have very glimmering and faint conceptions of those matters; or that they do not in so clear and lively a manner strike our fancy; (not appearing in their true nature and proper shape, so heinous and so hideous as they really are in themselves and in their consequences;) or because we have but weak persuasions about them; or because we do but slightly consider them; or from that our hearts are very hard and callous, our affections very cold and dull, so that nothing of this nature (nothing beside gross material affairs) can mollify or melt them; or for that we have in us small love to God, and a slender regard to our own welfare; in fine, for that in spiritual matters we are neither so wise, so sober, so serious, nor so good or ingenuous, in any reasonable measure, as we should be. But our Saviour, in all those respects, was otherwise disposed. He most evidently discerned the wrath of God, the grievousness of sin, the wretchedness of man, most truly, most fully, most strongly represented to his mind: he most firmly believed, yea most certainly knew, whatever God's law had declared about them: he did exactly consider and weigh them: his heart was most soft and sensible, his affections were most quick and excitable by their due objects: he was full of dutiful love to God, and most ardently desirous of our good, bearing a more than fraternal good-will towards us. Whence it is not so marvellous that as a man, as a transcendently wise and good man, he was so vehemently affected by those occurrences, that his imagination was so troubled, and his passions so stirred by them; so that he thence did suffer in a manner and to a degree unconceivable; according to that ejaculation in the Greek liturgies, Διὰ τῶν ἀγνώστων σου παθημάτων ἐλέησον ἡμᾶς, Χριστὲ, *By thy unknown sufferings, O Christ, have mercy on us.* But further,

IV. We may consider, that this way of suffering had in it some particular advantages, conducing to the accomplishment of our Lord's principal designs.

Its being very notorious, and lasting a competent time, were good advantages. For if he had been privately made away, or suddenly despatched, no such great notice would have been taken of it, nor would the matter of fact have been so fully proved, to the confirmation of our faith, and conviction of infidelity; nor had that his excellent deportment under such bitter affliction (his most divine patience, meekness, and charity) so illustriously shone forth. Wherefore, to prevent all exceptions, and excuses of unbelief, (together with other collateral good purposes,) divine Providence did so manage the business, that as the course of his life, so also the manner of his death, should be most conspicuously remarkable. *I spake freely to the world, and in secret have I done nothing,* said he of himself; and, *These things,* said St Paul to king Agrippa, *were not done in a corner.* Such were the proceedings of his life, not close or clancular, but frank and open; not presently hushed up, but leisurely carried on in the face of the world, that men might have the advantage to observe and examine them. And as he lived, so he died, most publicly and visibly; the world being witness of his death, and so prepared to believe his resurrection, and thence disposed to embrace his doctrine; according to what he did foretell, *I, being lifted up from the earth, shall draw all men to me:* for he drew all men, by so obvious a death, to take notice of it; he drew all well-disposed persons, from the wondrous consequences of it, to believe on him. And, *As,* said he again, *Moses did exalt the serpent in the wilderness, so must the Son of man be exalted.* As the elevation of that mysterious serpent did render it visible[b], and did attract the eyes of people toward it; whereby, God's power invisibly accompanying that sacramental performance, they were cured of those mortiferous stings which they had received: so our Lord, being mounted on the cross, allured the eyes of men to behold him, and their hearts to close with him; whereby, the heavenly virtue of God's Spirit cooperating, they became saved from those destructive sins, which from the Devil's serpentine instigations they had incurred.

SERM. II.

John xviii. 20.

Acts xxvi. 26.

John xii. 32.

John iii. 14.

[b] Iren. IV. 5.

SERM. II.

Another advantage of this kind of suffering was, that by it the nature of that kingdom, which he did intend to erect, was evidently signified: that it was not such as the carnal people did expect, an external, earthly, temporal kingdom, consisting in domination over the bodies and estates of men, dignified by outward wealth and splendour, managed by worldly power and policy, promoted by forcible compulsion and terror of arms, affording the advantages of safety, quiet, and prosperity here; but a kingdom purely spiritual, celestial, eternal; consisting in the governance of men's hearts and minds; adorned with the endowments of wisdom and virtue; administered by the conduct and grace of God's holy Spirit; upheld and propagated by meek instruction, by virtuous example, by hearty devotion, and humble patience; rewarding its loyal subjects with spiritual joys and consolations now, with heavenly rest and bliss hereafter. No other kingdom could he presume to design, who submitted to this dolorous and disgraceful way of suffering; no other exploits could he pretend to achieve by expiring on a cross; no other way could he rule, who gave himself to be managed by the will of his adversaries; no other benefits would this forlorn case allow him to dispense. So that well might he then assert, *My kingdom is not of this world;* when he was going in this signal way to demonstrate that important truth.

John xviii. 36.

Luke ii. 35.

It was also a most convenient touchstone to prove the genuine disposition and worth of men; so as to discriminate those wise, sober, ingenuous, sincere, generous souls, who could discern true goodness through so dark a cloud, who could love it though so ill-favouredly disfigured, who could embrace and avow it notwithstanding so terrible disadvantages; it served, I say, to distinguish those *Blessed* ones, who *would not be offended in him*, or by *The scandal of the cross* be discouraged from adhering to him, from the crew of blind, vain, perverse, haughty people, who, being scandalized at his adversity, would contemn and reject him.

SERM. II.

Matt. xi. 6.
Gal. v. 11.
1 Pet. ii. 7, 8.
1 Cor. i. 23.

Another considerable advantage was this, that by it God's special providence was discovered, and his glory illustrated in the propagation of the gospel[c]. For how could it be, that a person of so low parentage, of so mean garb, of so poor condition, who underwent so lamentable and despicable a kind of death, falling under the pride and spite of his enemies, so easily should gain so general an opinion in the world (even among the best, the wisest, the greatest persons) of being *The Lord of life and glory?* How, I say, could it happen, that such a miracle could be effected without God's aid and special concurrence? That king Herod, who from a long reign in flourishing state, with prosperous success in his enterprises, did attain the name of Great; or that Vespasian, who triumphantly did ascend the imperial throne, should either of them, by a few admirers of worldly vanity, seriously be held, or in flattery be called the Messias, is not so strange: but that one who was trampled on so miserably, and treated as a wretched caitiff, should instantly conquer innumerable hearts, and, from such a depth of extreme adversity, should be advanced to the sublimest

1 Cor. ii. 8.
James ii. 1.

[c] Chrys. Orat. LXI. Opp. Tom. VI. [p. 632.]

pitch of glory; that *The stone which the builders with so much scorn did refuse, should become the head-stone of the corner; this* (with good assurance we may say) *was the Lord's doing, and it is marvellous in our eyes.*

Hereby indeed *The excellency of divine power and wisdom* was much glorified; by so impotent, so improbable, so implausible means accomplishing so great effects; subduing the world to obedience of God, not by the active valour of an illustrious hero, but through the patient submission of a poor, abused, and oppressed person; restoring mankind to life and happiness by the sorrowful death of a crucified Saviour.

V. Lastly, the consideration of our Lord's suffering in this manner is very useful in application to our practice: no point is more fruitful of wholesome instruction, none is more forcible to kindle devout affections, none can afford more efficacious inducements and incentives to a pious life. For what virtue will not a serious meditation on the cross be apt to breed and to cherish? To what duty will it not engage and excite us?

1 Are we not hence infinitely obliged, with most humble affection and hearty gratitude, to adore each Person of the blessed Trinity?

That God the Father should design such a redemption for us; *Not sparing his own Son,* (the *Son of his love,* dear to him as himself,) but *delivering him up for us,* to be thus dealt with for our sake: that God would endure to see his Son in so pitiful a condition, to hear him groaning under so grievous pressures, to let him be so horribly abused; and that for us, who deserved nothing from him, who had demerited so much against him; for us, who were no friends to him, (for *Even when we were enemies, we were reconciled to God by the death of his Son;*) who were not any ways commendable for goodness or righteousness: (for *Christ did suffer for sinners, the just for the unjust;* and *God commended his love to us, that while we were sinful, Christ died for us:*) that God thus should *Love us, sending his Son to be a propitiation for our sins,* in so dismal a way of suffering, how stupendous is that goodness! how vast an obligation doth it lay upon us to reciprocal affection! If we do owe all to God, as our Maker, from whose undeserved bounty we did receive all that we have; how much further do we stand indebted to him as the author of our redemption, from whose ill-deserved mercy we receive a new being, and better state; and that in a way far more obliging! For God created us with a word, without more cost or trouble: but to redeem us stood him in huge expenses and pains; no less than the debasing of his only Son to our frailty, the exposing him to more than our misery, the withdrawing his face and restraining his bowels from his best beloved. If a Jew then were commanded by law, if a Gentile were obliged by nature, to *Love God with all his heart and all his soul;* what affection doth a Christian, under the law and duty of grace, owe unto him? By what computation can we reckon that debt? What faculties have we sufficient to discharge it? What finite heart can hold an affection commensurate to such an obligation?

And how can it otherwise than inflame our heart with love toward the blessed Son of God, our

SERM.
II.

Eph. iii.
19; v. 2, 25.
Gal. ii. 20.
Apoc. i. 5.

John xv. 13.

Saviour, to consider that, merely out of charitable pity toward us, he purposely came down from heaven, and took our flesh upon him, that he might therein undergo those extreme acerbities of pain, and those most ugly indignities of shame for us? *Greater love*, said he, *hath no man than this, that a man lay down his life for his friends*. But that God should lay down his life, should pour forth his blood, should be aspersed with the worst crimes, and clothed with foulest shame, should be executed on a cross as a malefactor and a slave, for his enemies and rebellious traitors, what imagination can devise any expression of charity or friendship comparable to this? Wherefore if love naturally be productive of love, if friendship justly meriteth a correspondence in good-will, what effect should the consideration of so ineffable a love, of so unparalleled friendship, have upon us?

How can any serious reflection on this event fail to work hearty gratitude in us toward our good Lord? For put case, any person for our sake (that he might rescue us from the greatest mischiefs, and purchase for us the highest benefits) willingly should deprive himself of all his estate, (and that a very large one,) of his honour, (and that a very high one,) of his ease and pleasure, (and those the most perfect and assured that could be;) that he should expose himself to the greatest hazards, should endure the sorest pains and most disgraceful ignominies; should prostitute his life, and in most hideous manner lose it, merely for our sake: should we not then apprehend and confess ourselves monstrously ingrateful, if we did not most deeply resent such kindness; if upon all occasions we did not express our thankfulness for it; if we did not ever readily yield all the acknowledgment and all the requital we were able? The case in regard to our blessed Saviour is like in kind; but in degree, whatever we can suppose doth infinitely fall below the performances of him for us, who stooped from the top of heaven, who laid aside the majesty and the felicity of God, for the infamies and the dolours of a cross, that he might redeem us from the torments of hell, and instate us in the joys of paradise. So that our obligations of gratitude to him are unexpressibly great; and we cannot with any face deny ourselves to be most basely unworthy, if the effects in our heart and life be not answerable.

SERM.
II.

Nor should we forget, that also upon this account we do owe great love and thanks to God the Holy Ghost, who, as he did originally conspire in the wonderful project of our redemption, as he did executively by miraculous operation conduct our Saviour into his fleshly tabernacle, as he did by unmeasurable communications of divine virtue assist his humanity through all the course of his life; so in this juncture he did inspire him with charity more than human, and did support him to undergo those pressures with invincible patience; and so did sanctify all this sacerdotal performance, that our Lord, as the apostle doth affirm, *Did through the eternal Spirit offer himself without spot to God.*

John iii. 34.

Heb. ix. 14.

2 What surer ground can there be of faith in God, what stronger encouragement of hope, than is suggested by this consideration? For if God steadfastly did hold his purpose, and faithfully did accomplish his word in an instance so distasteful to his own heart and bowels; how can we ever suspect

1 Pet. i. 20.
Eph. i. 4.
Luke i. 70.

his constancy and fidelity in any case? how can we distrust the completion of any divine promise?

*If God spared not his own Son, but delivered him up for us,* to the suffering of so contumelious affliction; how can we any ways be diffident of his bounty, or despair of his mercy? *how,* as the apostle doth argue, *shall he not also with him freely give us all things?*

If ever we be tempted to doubt of God's goodness, will not this experiment thereof convince and satisfy us? For what higher kindness could God express, what lower condescension could he vouchsafe, by what pledge could he more clearly or surely testify his willingness and his delight to do us good, than by thus ordering his dearest Son to undergo such miseries for us?

If the greatness of our sins discourageth us from entertaining comfortable hopes of mercy[d], will it not rear our hearts, to consider that such a punishment hath been inflicted to expiate them, which might content the most rigorous severity; that such a price is laid down to *Redeem us from the curse,* which richly may suffice to discharge it; that such a sacrifice hath been offered, which God hath avowed for most available, and acceptable to himself? So that now what can justice exact more from us? What have we further to do, than with a penitent and thankful heart to embrace the mercy purchased for us? *Who is he that condemneth,* seeing *Christ hath died,* and *Hath his own self borne our sins in his own body on the tree?* Whatever the wounds of our conscience be, is not *The blood of the cross,* tem-

---

[d] Quis de se desperet, pro quo tam humilis esse voluit Filius Dei?—Aug. de Ag. Chr. cap. xi. [Opp. Tom. VI. col. 251 B.]

pered with our hearty repentance, and applied by a lively faith, a sovereign balsam, of virtue sufficient to cure them? And may we not *By his stripes be healed?* Have we not abundant reason, with the holy apostle, to *Joy in God through our Lord Jesus Christ; by whom we have received the atonement?* Is it not to depreciate the worth, to disparage the efficacy of our Lord's passion, any ways to despair of mercy, or to be disconsolate for guilt; as if the cross were not enough worthy to compensate for our unworthiness, or our Saviour's patience could not balance our disobedience?

*SERM. II.*

1 Pet. ii. 24.

Rom. v. 11.

3 It indeed may yield great joy and sprightly consolation to us, to contemplate our Lord upon the cross, exercising his immense charity toward us, transacting all the work of our redemption, defeating all the enemies, and evacuating all the obstacles of our salvation.

May we not delectably consider him as there stretching forth his arms of kindness[e], with them to embrace the world, and to receive all mankind under the wings of his protection? as there spreading out his hands, with them earnestly inviting and entreating us to accept the overtures of grace, procured by him for us?

Isai. lxv. 2.

Is it not sweet and satisfactory, to view our great High Priest on that high altar offering up his own pure flesh, and pouring out his precious blood, as an universal, complete sacrifice, propitiatory for the sins of mankind[f]?

Lev. ix. 22.

Is it not a goodly object to behold humility

---

[e] Extendit ergo in passione manus suas, &c.—Lact. Instit. IV. 26.

[f] Chrys. Orat. LXXXII. Opp. Tom. v. [p. 563.]

SERM. II.

and patience so gloriously rearing themselves above all worldly, all infernal pride and insolence; by the cross ascending unto the celestial throne of dignity and majesty superlative?

Is it not pleasant to contemplate our Lord there standing erect, not only as a resolute sufferer, but as a noble conqueror, where *Having spoiled principalities and powers, he made a solemn show, triumphing over them?* Did ever any conqueror, loftily seated in his triumphal chariot, yield a spectacle so gallant and magnificent? Was ever tree adorned with trophies so pompous and splendid?

Col. ii. 15.

To the exterior view and carnal sense of men, our Lord was then indeed exposed to scorn and shame; but to spiritual and sincere discerning, all his and our enemies did there hang up as objects of contempt, utterly overthrown and undone.

Matt. xii. 29.
Luke xi. 21, 22.
Heb. ii. 14.

There the Devil, that *Strong* and sturdy *one*, Ὁ ἰσχυρός, did hang up bound in chains, disarmed and rifled, quite baffled and confounded, mankind being rescued from his tyrannic power.

There the world, with its vain pomps, its counterfeit beauties, its bewitching pleasures, its fondly admired excellencies, did hang up, all defaced and disparaged; as it appeared to St Paul: for *God*, saith he, *forbid that I should glory, save in the cross of Christ, by which the world is crucified to me, and I unto the world.*

Gal. vi. 14.

Gal. ii. 20;
v. 24.
Col. iii. 5.
Rom. viii. 13.
Rom. vi. 6.

There, in a most lively representation, and most admirable pattern, was exhibited, *the Mortification of our flesh, with its affections and lusts;* and our *Old man was crucified, that the body of sin might be destroyed.*

1 Pet. ii. 24.

There our sins, being, as St Peter telleth us,

*Carried up by him unto the gibbet*, did hang as marks of his victorious prowess, as malefactors by him *Condemned in the flesh*, as objects of our horror and hatred. [SERM. II.] [Rom. viii. 3.]

There death itself hung gasping, with its sting pulled out, and all its terrors quelled; his death having prevented ours, and induced immortality. [1 Cor. xv. 54, 55. 2 Tim. i. 10. Heb. ii. 14.]

There all wrath, *Enmity*, strife, (the banes of comfortable life,) did hang *abolished in his flesh*, and *slain upon the cross, by the blood whereof he made peace, and reconciled all things in heaven and earth*. [Eph. ii. 15, 16. Col. i. 20.]

There manifold yokes of bondage, instruments of vexation, and principles of variance, even all *The handwriting of ordinannces that was against us*, did hang up, *cancelled* and *nailed to the cross*. [Col. ii. 14.]

So much sweet comfort by special consideration may be extracted from this event, which in appearance was most doleful, but in effect the most happy that ever by Providence was dispensed to the world. Further,

4 This consideration is most useful to render us very humble and sensible of our weakness, our vileness, our wretchedness. For how low was that our fall, from which we could not be raised without such a depression of God's only Son! How great is that impotency, which did need such a succour to relieve it! How abominable must be that iniquity, which might not be expiated without so costly a sacrifice! How deplorable is that misery, which could not be removed without commutation of so strange a suffering! Would the Son of God have so *Emptied*, (Ἑαυτὸν ἐκένωσε), and [Phil. ii. 7.]

abased himself for nothing? Would he have endured such pains and ignominies for a trifle? No, surely; if our guilt had been slight, if our case had been tolerable, the divine wisdom would have chosen a more cheap and easy remedy for us.

Is it not madness for us to be conceited of any worth in ourselves, to confide in any merit of our works, to glory in any thing belonging to us, to fancy ourselves brave, fine, happy persons, worthy of great respect and esteem; whenas our unworthiness, our demerit, our forlorn estate did extort from the most gracious God a displeasure needing such a reconciliation, did impose upon the most glorious Son of God a necessity to undergo such a punishment in our behalf?

How can we reasonably pretend to any honour, or justly assume any regard to ourselves, whenas the firstborn of heaven, *The Lord of glory*, partaker of divine majesty, was fain to *Make himself of no reputation*, to put himself into *the garb of a servant*, and, under the imputation of a malefactor, to bear such disgrace and infamy in our room, in lieu of the confusion due to us?

What more palpable confutation can there be of human vanity and arrogance, of all lofty *Imaginations,* all presumptuous confidences, all turgid humours, all fond self-pleasings and self-admirings, than is that tragical cross, wherein, as in a glass, our foul deformity, our pitiful meanness, our helpless infirmity, our sad wofulness are so plainly represented?

Well surely may we say with St Austin, *Let man now at length blush to be proud, for whom God is made so humble*[g]. [And since, as he doth add, *This great disease of soul did bring down the almighty Physician from heaven, did humble him to the form of a servant, did subject him to contumelies, did suspend him on a cross, that this tumour by virtue of so great a medicine might be cured*[h];] may not he well be presumed incurable, who is not cured of his pride by this medicine[i]; in whom neither the reason of the case, nor the force of such an example, can work humility?

5 But further, while this contemplation doth breed sober humility, it also should preserve us from base abjectness of mind; for it doth evidently demonstrate, that, according to God's infallible judgment, we are very considerable; that our souls are capable of high regard; that it is a great pity we should be lost and abandoned to ruin. For surely, had not God much esteemed and respected us, he would not for our sakes have so debased himself, or deigned to endure so much for our recovery; divine justice would not have exacted or accepted such a ransom for our souls, had they been of little worth. We should not therefore slight ourselves, nor demean ourselves like sorry, contemptible wretches, as if we deserved no consideration, no pity from ourselves; as if we thought our souls not worth saving, which yet our Lord

Acts xiii. 46.

---

[g] Jam tandem erubescat homo esse superbus, propter quem factus est humilis Deus.—Aug. in Ps. xviii. [Opp. Tom. IV. col. 87 E.]

[h] Iste ingens morbus omnipotentem Medicum de coelo deduxit, usque ad formam servi humiliavit, contumeliis egit, ligno suspendit, ut per salutem tantæ medicinæ curetur hic tumor.—Ibid.

[i] Quæ superbia sanari potest, si humilitate Filii Dei non sanatur?—Id. de Agone Chr. cap. xi. [Opp. Tom. VI. col. 251 E.]

thought good to purchase at so dear a rate[k]. By so despising or disregarding ourselves, do we not condemn the sentiments, do we not vilify the sufferings of our Lord; so with a pitiful meanness of spirit joining the most unworthy injustice and ingratitude? Again,

6 How can we reflect upon this event without extreme displeasure against, and hearty detestation of our sins? those sins which indeed did bring such tortures and such disgraces upon our blessed Redeemer? Judas, the wretch who betrayed him; the Jewish priests who did accuse and prosecute him; the wicked rout which did abusively insult over him; those cruel hands that smote him; those pitiless hearts that scorned him; those poisonous tongues that mocked him and reviled him; all those who were the instruments and abettors of his affliction, how do we loathe and abhor them! how do we detest their names and execrate their memories! But how much greater reason have we to abominate our sins, which were the true, the principal actors of all that woful tragedy! *He was delivered for our offences;* they were indeed the traitors, which by the hands of Judas delivered him up. *He that knew no sin, was made sin for us;* that is, was accused, was condemned, was executed as a sinner for us. It was therefore we, who by our sins did impeach him; the spiteful priests were but our advocates: we by them did adjudge

---

[k] Aut vero pro minimo habet Deus hominem, propter quem mori voluit Unicum suum?—Id. in Psal. cxlviii. [Opp. Tom. IV. col. 1676 F.]

Si vobis ex terrena fragilitate viles estis, ex pretio vestro vos æstimate.—Id.

and sentence him; Pilate was but drawn in against his will and conscience to be our spokesman in that behalf: we by them did inflict that horrid punishment on him; the Roman executioners were but our representatives therein. *He became a* Serm. II. *curse for us;* that is, all the mockery, derision, and contumely he endured, did proceed from us; the silly people were but properties acting our parts. Our sins were they that cried out, *Crucifige, (Crucify him, crucify him,)* with clamours more loud and more importunate than did all the Jewish rabble; it was they, which by the borrowed throats of that base people did so outrageously persecute him. *He was wounded for our transgressions, and bruised for our iniquities:* it was they, which by the hands of the fierce soldiers, and of the rude populace, as by senseless engines, did buffet and scourge him; they by the nails and thorns did pierce his flesh and rend his sacred body. Upon them, therefore, it is most just and fit that we should turn our hatred, that we should discharge our indignation.

Gal. iii. 13.

Luke xxiii. 21.
John xix. 6, 15.

Isai. liii. 5.

7 And what in reason can be more powerful toward working penitential sorrow and remorse, than reflection upon such horrible effects, proceeding from our sins? How can we forbear earnestly to grieve, considering ourselves by them to have been the perfidious betrayers, the unjust slanderers, the cruel persecutors and barbarous murderers of a person so innocent and lovely, so good and benign, so great and glorious; of God's own dear Son, of our best friend, of our most gracious Redeemer?

8 If ingenuity will not operate so far, and

SERM. II.

Ps. cxix. 120.

hereby melt us into contrition; yet surely this consideration must needs affect us with a religious fear. For can we otherwise than tremble to think upon the heinous guilt of our sins, upon the dreadful fierceness of God's wrath against them, upon the impartial severity of divine judgment for them, all so manifestly discovered, all so livelily set forth in this dismal spectacle? If the view of an ordinary execution is apt to beget in us some terror, some dread of the law, some reverence toward authority; what awful impressions should this singular example of divine justice work upon us!

How greatly we should be moved thereby, what affections it should raise in us, we may even learn from the most inanimate creatures: for the whole world did seem affected thereat with horror and confusion; the frame of things was discomposed and disturbed; all nature did feel a kind of compassion and compunction for it. The sun (as from aversion and shame) did hide his face, leaving the world covered for three hours with mournful blackness; the bowels of the earth did yearn and quake; the rocks did split; the veil of the temple was rent; the graves did open themselves, and the dead bodies were roused up. And can we then (who are the most concerned in the event) be more stupid than the earth, more obdurate than rocks, more drowsy than interred carcases, the most insensible and immoveable things in nature? But further,

9 How can the meditation on this event do otherwise than hugely deter us from all wilful disobedience and commission of sin? For how thereby can we violate such engagements, and thwart such

an example of obedience? How thereby can we abuse so wonderful goodness, and disoblige so transcendent charity? How thereby can we reject that gentle dominion over us, which our Redeemer did so dearly purchase, or renounce *The Lord that bought us* at so high a rate? With what heart can we bring upon the stage, and act over that direful tragedy, renewing all that pain and all that disgrace to our Saviour: as the apostle teacheth that we do by apostasy, *Crucifying to ourselves the Son of God afresh, and putting him to an open shame?* Can we without horror *Tread under foot the Son of God, and count the blood of the covenant an unholy thing;* (as the same divine apostle saith[1] all wilful transgressors do;) vilifying that most sacred and precious blood[m], so freely shed for the demonstration of God's mercy, and ratification of his gracious intentions toward us, as a thing of no special worth or consideration; despising all his so kind and painful endeavours for our salvation; defeating his most charitable purposes and earnest desires for our welfare; rendering all his so bitter and loathsome sufferings in regard to us utterly vain and fruitless, yea indeed very hurtful and pernicious? For if the cross do not save us from our sins, it will much aggravate their guilt, and augment their punishment; bringing a severer condemnation and a sadder ruin on us. Again,

10 This consideration affordeth very strong engagements to the practice of charity towards our neighbour. For what heart can be so hard, that the blood of the cross cannot mollify into a chari-

SERM. II.

Tit. ii. 14.
1 Pet. i. 18, 19.
Rom. xiv. 9.
2 Cor. v. 15.
2 Pet. ii. 1.
1 Cor. vi. 20.
Heb. vi. 6.

Heb. x. 29.

---

[1] Ἑκουσίως ἁμαρτανόντων ἡμῶν.—Heb. x. 26.
[m] Κοινὸν ἡγησάμενος.—v. 29.

table and compassionate sense? Can we forbear to love those, toward whom our Saviour did bear so tender affection, for whom he was pleased to sustain so woful tortures and indignities? Shall we not, in obedience to his most urgent commands, in conformity to his most notable example, in grateful return to him for his benefits, who thus did gladly suffer for us, discharge this most sweet and easy duty towards his beloved friends? Shall we not be willing, by parting with a little superfluous stuff for the relief of our poor brother, to requite and gratify him, who, to succour us in our distress, most bountifully did part with his wealth, with his glory, with his pleasure, with his life itself? Shall we not meekly comport with an infirmity, not bear a petty neglect, not forgive a small injury to our brother, whenas our Lord did for us and from us bear a cross, to procure remission for our innumerable most heinous affronts and offences against Almighty God? Can a heart void of mercy and pity, with any reason or modesty pretend to the mercies and compassions of the cross? Can we hope that God for Christ's sake will pardon us, if we for Christ's sake will not forgive our neighbour?

Can we hear our Lord saying to us, *This is my command, that ye love one another, as I have loved you;* and, *Hereby shall all men know that ye are my disciples, if ye love one another?* Can we hear St Paul exhorting, *Walk in love, as Christ also hath loved us, and hath given himself for us, an offering and a sacrifice to God for a sweetsmelling savour;* and, *We that are strong ought to bear the infirmities of the weak—For even Christ pleased not himself, but, as it is written, The reproaches of them that reproached thee fell on me?* Can we attend to St John's arguing, *Beloved, if God so loved us, then ought we also to love one another. Hereby we perceive the love of God, because he laid down his life for us: wherefore we ought to lay down our lives for the brethren?*

Can we, I say, consider such precepts, and such discourses, without effectually being disposed to comply with them for the sake of our crucified Saviour? all whose life was nothing else but one continual recommendation and enforcement of this duty; but his death especially was a pattern most obliging, most incentive thereto. This use of the point is the more to be regarded, because the apostle doth apply it hereto, our text coming in upon that occasion; for having pathetically exhorted the Philippians to all kinds of charity and humble condescension, he subjoineth, *Let this mind be in you, which was in Christ Jesus; who being in the form of God, &c.*

11   But furthermore, what can be more operative than this point toward breeding a disregard of this world, with all its deceitful vanities and mischievous delights; toward reconciling our minds to the worst condition into which it can bring us; toward supporting our hearts under the heaviest pressures of affliction which it can lay upon us? For can we reasonably expect, can we eagerly affect, can we ardently desire great prosperity, whenas the Son of God, our Lord and Master, did only taste such adversity? How can we refuse, in submission to God's pleasure, contentedly to

SERM. II.

1 John iv. 11; iii. 16.

Phil. ii. 5, 6.

bear a slight grievance, whenas our Saviour gladly did bear a cross, infinitely more distasteful to carnal will and sense than any that can befall us? Who now can admire those splendid trifles, which our Lord never did regard in his life, and which at his death only did serve to mock and abuse him? Who can relish those sordid pleasures, of which he living did not vouchsafe to taste, and the contraries whereof he dying chose to feel in all extremity? Who can disdain or despise a state of sorrow and disgrace, which he, by voluntary susception of it, hath so dignified and graced; by which we so near resemble and become conformable to him; by which we concur and partake with him; yea, by which in some cases we may promote, and after a sort complete his designs, *Filling up*, as St Paul speaketh, *that which is behind of the afflictions of Christ in our flesh?*

Rom. viii. 17.
Phil. iii. 10.
Apoc. i. 9.
1 Pet. iv. 13.
Col. i. 24.

Who now can hugely prefer being esteemed, approved, favoured, commended by men, before infamy, reproach, derision, and persecution from them; especially when these do follow conscientious adherence to righteousness? Who can be very ambitious of worldly honour and repute, covetous of wealth[n], or greedy of pleasure, who doth observe the Son of God choosing rather to hang upon a cross, than to sit upon a throne; inviting the clamours of scorn and spite, rather than acclamations of blessing and praise; divesting himself of all secular power, pomp, plenty, conveniences, and solaces; embracing the garb of a slave, and the

[n] Cogitemus crucem ejus, et divitias lutum putabimus.—Hier. ad Nepot. [Ep. xxxiv. Opp. Tom. iv. p. ii. p. 263.]

repute of a malefactor, before the dignity and respect of a prince, which were his due, which he most easily could have obtained?

SERM. II.

Can we imagine it a very happy thing to be high and prosperous in this world, to swim in affluence and pleasure? Can we take it for a misery to be mean and low, to conflict with some wants and straits here; seeing the Fountain of all happiness did himself purposely condescend to so forlorn a state, and was pleased to become so deep a sufferer[o]? If with devout eyes of our mind we do behold our Lord hanging naked upon a gibbet, besmeared all over with streams of his own blood, groaning under smart anguish of pain, encompassed with all sorts of disgraceful abuses, *Yielding* (as it was foretold of him) *his back to the smiters, and his cheeks to them who plucked off the hair, hiding not his face from shame and spitting;* will not the imagination of such a spectacle dim the lustre of all earthly grandeurs and beauties, damp the sense of all carnal delights and satisfactions, quash all that extravagant glee which we can find in any wild frolics or riotous merriments? Will it not stain all our pride, and check our wantonness? Will it not dispose our minds to be sober, placing our happiness in things of another nature, seeking our content in matters of higher importance; preferring obedience to the will of God before compliance with the fancies and desires of men; according to that precept of St Peter, *Forasmuch then as Christ hath suffered for us in the flesh, arm yourselves likewise*

Isai. l. 6.

1 Pet. iv. 1, 2.

[o] Quis beatam vitam esse arbitretur in iis, quæ contemnenda esse docuit Filius Dei?—Aug. de Ag. Chr. cap. xi. [Opp. Tom. vi. col. 252 B.]

SERM. II.

*with the same mind—so as no longer to live the remaining time in the flesh to the lusts of men, but to the will of God?*

12 This indeed will instruct and incline us cheerfully to submit unto God's will, and gladly to accept from his hand whatever he disposeth, however grievous and afflictive to our natural will; this point suggesting great commendation of afflictions, and strong consolation under them. For if such hardship was to our Lord himself a school of duty, Heb. v. 8. *He,* as the apostle saith, *learning obedience from what he suffered;* if it was to him a fit mean of perfection, as the apostle doth again imply when he Heb. ii. 10. saith, *That it became God to perfect the Captain of our salvation by suffering;* if it was an attractive of the divine favour even to him, as those words John x. 17. import, *Therefore the Father loveth me, because I lay down my life;* if it was to him a step toward Luke xxiv. 26. glory, according to that saying, *Was not Christ to suffer, and so to enter into his glory?* yea, if it was a ground of conferring on him a sublime pitch of Phil. ii. 9. dignity above all creatures, *God for this obedience having exalted him, and given him a name above* Heb. ii. 9. *all names; We seeing Jesus—for the suffering of death, crowned with glory and honour;* the heavenly society in the Revelations with one voice crying Rev. v. 12. 9. out, *Worthy is the Lamb that was slain (Who redeemed us to God by his blood) to receive power, and riches, and wisdom, and strength, and honour, and glory, and blessing:* if affliction did minister such advantages to him; and if by our conformity to him in undergoing it, (with like equanimity, humility, and patience,) it may afford the like to us; what reason is there that we should anywise be

discomposed at it, or disconsolate under it? Much greater reason, surely, there is, that, with St Paul and all the holy apostles, we should rejoice, boast, and exult in our tribulations; far more cause we have with them to esteem it a favour, a privilege, an ornament, a felicity to us, than to be displeased and discontented therewith.

*Rom. v. 3. Col. i. 24. Matt. v. 12. Luke vi. 23. Phil. i. 29. Acts v. 41. James i. 2. Heb. x. 34. 1 Pet. i. 7. Heb. xii. 2. 1 Cor. i. 4. 1 Thess. iii. 3. Rom. viii. 29. Acts xiv. 22. 2 Tim. iii. 12. Matt. x. 38; xvi. 24. Luke xiv. 27; ix. 23.*

To do thus is a duty incumbent on us as Christians. For, *He,* saith our Master, *that doth not take up his cross, and follow me, is not worthy of me: He that doth not carry his cross, and go after me, cannot be my disciple.* He that doth not willingly take the cross, when it is presented to him by God's hand; he that doth not contentedly bear it, when it is by Providence imposed on him, is nowise worthy of the honour to wait on Christ; he is not capable to be reckoned among the disciples of our heavenly Master[p]. He is not worthy of Christ, as not having the courage, the constancy, the sincerity of a Christian; or of one pretending to such great benefits, such high privileges, such excellent rewards, as Christ our Lord and Saviour doth propose. He cannot be Christ's disciple shewing such an incapacity to learn those needful lessons of humility and patience, dictated by him; declaring such an indisposition to transcribe those copies of submission to the divine will, self-denial, and self-resignation, so fairly set him by the instruction and example of Christ: for, *Christ,* saith St Peter, *Suffered for us, leaving us an example,* Ὑπολιμπάνων ὑπογραμμὸν, *that we should follow his steps.*

*1 Pet. ii. 21.*

[p] Greg. Naz. [Τέλος συσταυρώθητι, συννεκρώθητι, συντάφηθι προθύμως, ἵνα καὶ συναναστῇς, καὶ συνδοξασθῇς, καὶ συμβασιλεύσῃς, &c.—Orat. XXXVIII. Opp. Tom. I. p. 675 c.]

SERM. II.

13 The willing susception and the cheerful sustenance of the cross, is indeed the express condition, and the peculiar character of our Christianity; in signification whereof, it hath been from most ancient times a constant usage to mark those who enter into it with the figure of it. The cross, as the instrument by which our peace with God was wrought, as the stage whereon our Lord did act the last part of his marvellous obedience, consummating our redemption, as the field wherein the Captain of our salvation did achieve his noble victories, and erect his glorious trophies[q] over all the enemies thereof, was well assumed to be the badge of our profession, the ensign of our spiritual warfare, the pledge of our constant adherence to our crucified Saviour; in relation to whom our chief hope is grounded, our great joy and sole glory doth consist: for, *God forbid*, saith St Paul, *that I should glory, save in the cross of Christ.*

Gal. vi. 14.

1 Cor. i. 23.

14 Let it be, *To the Jews a scandal*, (or offensive to their fancy, prepossessed with expectations of a Messias flourishing in secular pomp and prosperity;) let it be *folly to the Greeks*, (or seem absurd to men puffed up and corrupted in mind with fleshly notions and maxims of worldly craft, disposing them to value nothing which is not grateful to present sense or fancy,) that God should put his own most beloved Son into so very sad and despicable a condition[r]; that salvation from death and misery should

---

[q] Τὸ τρόπαιον τοῦ σταυροῦ.—Const. Apost. VIII. 12. [Cotel. Pat. Apost. Tom. I. p. 399.]

[r] Orig. con. Cels. II. p. 79. [Καὶ οἴεταί γε κρατύνειν τὸ ἔγκλημα· ἐπεὶ λόγον ἐπαγγελόμενοι υἱὸν εἶναι τοῦ Θεοῦ, ἀποδείκνυμεν οὐ λόγον καθαρὸν καὶ ἅγιον, ἀλλὰ ἄνθρωπον ἀτιμότατα ἀπαχθέντα καὶ ἀποτυμπανισθέντα.]

be procured by so miserable a death; that eternal joy, glory, and happiness should issue from these fountains of sorrow and shame; that a person in external semblance devoted to so opprobrious usage, should be the Lord and Redeemer of mankind, the King and Judge of all the world: let, I say, this doctrine be scandalous and distasteful to some persons tainted with prejudice; let it be strange and incredible to others blinded with self-conceit; let all the inconsiderate, all the proud, all the profane part of mankind openly with their mouth, or closely in heart, slight and reject it: yet to us it must appear grateful and joyous; to us it is Πιστὸς λόγος, *A faithful* and most credible *proposition worthy of all acceptation, that Jesus Christ came into the world to save sinners*, in this way of suffering for them: to us, who discern by a clearer light, and are endowed with a purer sense, kindled by the divine Spirit; from whence we may with comfortable satisfaction of mind apprehend and taste, that God could not in a higher measure or fitter manner, illustrate his glorious attributes of goodness and justice, his infinite grace and mercy toward his poor creatures, his holy displeasure against wickedness, his impartial severity in punishing iniquity and impiety, or in vindicating his own sacred honour and authority, than by thus ordering his only Son, clothed with our nature, to suffer for us; that also true virtue and goodness could not otherwise be taught, be exemplified, be commended and impressed with greater advantage.

Since thereby indeed a charity and humanity so unparalleled, (far transcending theirs who have been celebrated for devoting their lives out of love to

SERM. II.

1 Tim. i. 15.
2 Tim. ii. 11.

their country, or kindness to their friends,) a meekness so incomparable, a resolution so invincible, a patience so heroical, were manifested for the instruction and direction of men; since never were the vices and the vanities of the world (so prejudicial to the welfare of mankind) so remarkably discountenanced; since never any suffering could pretend to so worthy and beneficial effects, the expiation of the whole world's sins, and reconciliation of mankind to God, the which no other performance, no other sacrifice did ever aim to procure; since, in fine, no virtue had ever so glorious rewards, as sovereign dignity to him that exercised it, and eternal happiness to those that imitate it; since, I say, there be such excellent uses and fruits of the cross borne by our Saviour; we can have no reason to be offended at it, or ashamed of it; but with all reason heartily should approve and humbly adore the deep wisdom of God, together with all other his glorious attributes displayed therein. To whom therefore, as is most due, let us devoutly render all glory and praise. And,

*Unto him that loved us, and washed us from our sins in his blood, and hath made us kings and priests unto God and his Father; to him be glory and dominion for ever and ever. Blessing, and honour, and glory, and power, be unto him that sitteth upon the throne, and unto the Lamb for ever and ever. Amen.*

# SERMON III.[a]

## THE PLEASANTNESS OF RELIGION.

PROV. III. 17.

*Her ways are ways of pleasantness, and all her paths are peace.*

THE meaning of these words seems plain and obvious, and to need little explication. *Her ways*, that is, the ways of wisdom. What this wisdom is, I shall not undertake accurately to describe (in an audience so well acquainted with it). Briefly, I understand by it, an habitual skill or faculty of judging aright about matters of practice, and choosing according to that right judgment, and conforming the actions to such good choice. *Ways* and *Paths* in Scripture-dialect are the courses and manners of action. For *doing* there is commonly called *walking*; and the methods of doing are the *Ways* in which we walk. By *Pleasantness* may be meant the joy and delight accompanying, and by *Peace* the content and satisfaction ensuing such a course of actions. So that in short, the sense of these words seems simply to be this; that a course of life directed by wisdom and good judgment is delightful in the practice, and brings content after it. The truth of which proposition it shall be my

[a] St Mary's, June 30, 1661.

SERM.
III.
endeavour at this time to confirm by divers reasons, and illustrate by several instances.

I. Then, wisdom of itself is delectable and satisfactory, as it implies a revelation of truth, and a detection of error to us[b]. It is like light, pleasant to behold, casting a sprightly lustre, and diffusing a benign influence all about; presenting a goodly prospect of things to the eyes of our mind; displaying objects in their due shapes, postures, magnitudes, and colours; quickening our spirits with a comfortable warmth, and disposing our minds to a cheerful activity; dispelling the darkness of ignorance, scattering the mists of doubt, driving away the spectres of delusive fancy; mitigating the cold of sullen melancholy; discovering obstacles, securing progress, and making the passages of life clear, open, and pleasant. We are all naturally endowed with a strong appetite to know, to see, to pursue truth; and with a bashful abhorrency of being deceived, and entangled in mistake. And as success in inquiry after truth affords matter of joy and triumph; so being conscious of aberration and miscarriage therein, is attended with shame and sorrow. These desires wisdom in the most perfect manner satisfies, not by entertaining us with dry, empty, fruitless theories, upon mean and vulgar subjects; but by enriching our minds with excellent and useful knowledge, directed to the noblest objects and serviceable to the highest ends. Nor in its own nature only, but,

II. Much more in its worthy consequences is wisdom exceedingly pleasant and peaceable: in

[b] Nihil est ei (menti hominis) veritatis luce dulcius.—Cic. Acad. [IV. 10.]

general, by disposing us to acquire and to enjoy all the good, delight, and happiness we are capable of; and by freeing us from all the inconveniences, mischiefs, and infelicities our condition is subject to. For whatever good from clear understanding, deliberate advice, sagacious foresight, stable resolution, dexterous managery and address, right intention, and orderly proceeding, doth naturally result, wisdom confers: whatever evil blind ignorance, false presumption, unwary credulity, precipitate rashness, unsteady purpose, ill contrivance, backwardness, inability, unwieldiness and confusion of thought, beget, wisdom prevents. From a thousand snares and treacherous allurements, from innumerable rocks and dangerous surprises, from exceedingly many needless encumbrances and vexatious toils of fruitless endeavour, she redeems and secures us. More particularly,

III. Wisdom assures us we take the best course, and proceed as we ought. For by the same means we judge aright, and reflecting upon that judgment are assured we do so: as the same arguments by which we demonstrate a theorem convince us we have demonstrated it, and the same light by which we see an object makes us know we see it. And this assurance in the progress of the action exceedingly pleases, and in the sequel of it infinitely contents us. He that judges amiss, not perceiving clearly the rectitude of his process, proceeds usually with a dubious solicitude; and at length, discovering his error, condemns his own choice, and receives no other satisfaction but of repentance. Like a traveller, who, being uncertain whether he goes in the right way, wanders in continual perplexity, till he be informed, and then too late understanding his mistake, with regret seeks to recover himself into it. But he that knows his way, and is satisfied that it is the true one, makes on merrily and carelessly, not doubting he shall in good time arrive to his designed journey's end. Two troublesome mischiefs therefore wisdom frees us from, the company of anxious doubt in our actions, and the consequence of bitter repentance: for no man can doubt of what he is sure, nor repent of what he knows good.

IV. Wisdom begets in us a hope of success in our actions, and is usually attended therewith. Now what is more delicious than hope? what more satisfactory than success? That is like the pursuit of a flying enemy, this like gathering the spoil; that like viewing the ripe corn, this like the joy of harvest itself. And he that aims at a good end, and knows he uses proper means to attain it, why should he despair of success, since effects naturally follow their causes, and the Divine Providence is wont to afford its concourse to such proceedings? Beside that such well-grounded hope confirms resolution, and quickens activity, which mainly conduce to the prosperous issue of designs. Further,

V. Wisdom prevents discouragement from the possibility of ill success, yea, and makes disappointment itself tolerable. For if either the foresight of a possible miscarriage should discourage us from adventuring on action, or inculpable frustration were intolerable, we should with no heart apply ourselves to any thing; there being no designs in this world, though founded upon the most sound advice, and prosecuted by the most diligent endeavour, which may not be defeated, as depending upon divers causes above our power, and circumstances beyond our prospect. The inconstant opinions, uncertain resolutions, mutable affections, and fallacious pretences of men, upon which the accomplishment of most projects rely, may easily deceive and disappoint us. The imperceptible course of nature exerting itself in sudden tempests, diseases, and unlucky casualties, may surprise us, and give an end to our business and lives together. However, the irresistible power of the Divine Providence, guided by the unsearchable counsel of his will, we can never be assured that it will not interpose and impede the effects of our endeavours. Yet notwithstanding, when we act prudently, we have no reason to be disheartened; because, having good intentions, and using fit means, and having done our best, as no deserved blame, so no considerable damage can arrive to us: and though we find Almighty God hath crossed us, yet we are sure he is not displeased with us. Which consideration, wherewith wisdom furnishes us, will make the worst success not only tolerable, but comfortable to us. For hence we have reason to hope, that the All-wise Goodness reserves a better reward for us, and will sometime recompense not only the good purposes we unhappily pursued, but also the unexpected disappointment we patiently endured; and that however we shall be no losers in the end. Which discourse is mainly fortified by considering how the best and wisest attempts have oft miscarried. We see Moses, authorized by God's command, directed by his counsel, and conducted by his hand, intended to bring the Israelites into the land of Canaan: yet, by the unreasonable incredulity and stubborn perverseness of that people, he had his purpose frustrated. The holy prophets afterward earnestly endeavoured to contain the same people within compass of obedience to the divine commands, and to reduce them from their idolatrous and wicked courses; yet without correspondent effect. Our Saviour, by the example of his holy life, careful instruction, and vehement exhortations, assayed to procure a belief of and submission to his most excellent doctrine; yet how few believed his report, and complied with his discipline! Yea, Almighty God himself often complains, how in a manner his designs were defeated, his desires thwarted, his offers refused, his counsels rejected, his expectations deceived. *Wherefore,* (saith he concerning his vineyard,) *when I looked it should bring forth grapes, brought it forth wild grapes?* And again, *I have spread out my hands all the day to a rebellious people.* And again, *I have even sent unto you all my prophets, daily rising up early, and sending them: yet they hearkened not unto me.* Wherefore there is no good cause we should be disheartened, or vexed, when success is wanting to well-advised purposes. It is foolish and ill-grounded intentions, and practices unwarrantable by good reason, that make the undertakers solicitous of success, and being defeated leave them disconsolate. Yea further,

VI. Wisdom makes all the troubles, griefs, and pains incident to life, whether casual adversities, or natural afflictions, easy and supportable; by rightly valuing the importance, and moderating the influence of them. It suffers not busy fancy to alter

## The Pleasantness of Religion. 157

the nature, amplify the degree, or extend the duration of them, by representing them more sad, heavy, and remediless than they truly are. It allows them no force beyond what naturally and necessarily they have, nor contributes nourishment to their increase. It keeps them at a due distance, not permitting them to encroach upon the soul, or to propagate their influence beyond their proper sphere. It will not let external mischances, as poverty and disgrace, to produce an inward sense which is beyond their natural efficacy: nor corporeal affections of sickness and pain to disturb the mind, with which they have nothing to do. The region of these malignant distempers being at most but the habit of the body, wisdom by effectual antidotes repels them from the heart, and inward parts of the soul. If any thing, sin, and our unworthy miscarriages toward God, should vex and discompose us: yet this trouble wisdom, by representing the divine goodness, and his tender mercies in our ever-blessed Redeemer, doth perfectly allay. And as for all other adversities, it abates their noxious power, by shewing us they are either merely imaginary, or very short and temporary; that they admit of remedy, or at most do not exclude comfort, not only hindering the operations of the mind, nor extinguishing its joys; that they may have a profitable use, and pleasant end; and, however, neither imply bad conscience, nor induce obligation to punishment. For,

VII. Wisdom hath always a good conscience attending it, that purest delight and richest cordial of the soul; that brazen wall, and impregnable fortress against both external assaults and internal

SERM. III.

SERM. III.

Prov. xv. 15.

Prov. iii. 24.

commotions; that *Continual feast*, whereon the mind, destitute of all other repast, with a never languishing appetite may entertain itself; that faithful witness, and impartial judge, whoever accuses, always acquitting the innocent soul; that certain friend, in no strait failing, in no adversity deserting; that sure refuge in all storms of fortune, and persecutions of disgrace; which, as Solomon here notes, renders a man's *Sleep sweet*, and undisturbed with fearful phantasms, his heart light, and his steps secure; and, if anything, can make the Stoical paradox good, and cause the wise man to smile in extremity of torment; arming his mind with an invincible courage, and infusing a due confidence into it, whereby he bears up cheerfully against malicious reproach, undauntedly sustains adversity, and triumphs over bad fortune. And this invaluable treasure the wise man is only capable of possessing; who certainly knows and heartily approves the grounds upon which he proceeds; whenas the fool, building his choice upon blind chance, or violent passion, or giddy fancy, or uncertain example, not upon the steady warrant of good reason, cannot avoid being perplexed with suspicion of mistake, and so necessarily is deprived of the comfort of a good conscience.

VIII. Wisdom confers a facility, expert readiness, and dexterity in action; which is a very pleasant and commodious quality, and exceedingly sweetens activity. To do things with difficulty, struggling, and immoderate contention, disheartens a man, quells his courage, blunts the edge of his resolution, renders him sluggish and averse from business, though apprehended never so necessary, and of great moment. These obstructions wisdom removes, facilitating operations by directing the attention to ends possible and attainable, by suggesting fit means and instruments to work by, by contriving right methods and courses of process; the mind by it being stored with variety of good principles, sure rules, and happy expedients, reposed in the memory, and ready upon all occasions to be produced, and employed in practice.

IX. Wisdom begets a sound, healthful, and harmonious complexion of the soul, disposing us with judgment to distinguish, and with pleasure to relish savoury and wholesome things, but to nauseate and reject such as are ingrateful and noxious to us; thereby capacifying us to enjoy pleasantly and innocently all those good things the divine goodness hath provided for and consigned to us; whence to the soul proceeds all that comfort, joy, and vigour, which results to the body from a good constitution and perfect health.

X. Wisdom acquaints us with ourselves, our own temper and constitution, our propensions and passions, our habitudes and capacities; a thing not only of mighty advantage, but of infinite pleasure and content to us. No man in the world less knows a fool than himself; nay, he is more than ignorant, for he constantly errs in the point, taking himself for, and demeaning himself as toward another, a better, a wiser, an abler man than he is. He hath wonderful conceits of his own qualities and faculties; he affects commendations incompetent to him; he soars at employment surpassing his ability to manage. No comedy can represent a mistake more odd and ridiculous than his: for he

SERM. III.

wanders, and stares, and hunts after, but never can find nor discern himself; but always encounters with a false shadow instead thereof, which he passionately hugs and admires. But a wise man, by constant observation, and impartial reflection upon himself, grows very familiar with himself: he perceives his own inclinations, which, if bad, he strives to alter and correct; if good, he cherishes and corroborates them: he apprehends the matters he is fitting for, and capable to manage, neither too mean and unworthy of him, nor too high and difficult for him; and those applying his care to, he transacts easily, cheerfully, and successfully. So being neither puffed up with vain and overweening opinion, nor dejected with heartless diffidence of himself; neither admiring, nor despising; neither irksomely hating, nor fondly loving himself; he continues in good humour, maintains a sure friendship and fair correspondence with himself, and rejoices in the retirement and private conversation with his own thoughts: whence flows a pleasure and satisfaction unexpressible.

XI. Wisdom procures and preserves a constant favour and fair respect of men, purchases a good name, and upholds reputation in the world: which things are naturally desirable, commodious for life, encouragements to good, and preventive of many inconveniences. The composed frame of mind, uniform and comely demeanour, compliant and inoffensive conversation, fair and punctual dealing, considerate motions, and dexterous addresses of wise men, naturally beget esteem and affection in those that observe them. Neither than these things is there anything more commendable

## The Pleasantness of Religion. 161

to human regard. As symmetry and harmony to the animal senses, so delectable is an even temper of soul and orderly tenour of actions to rational apprehensions. Folly is freakish and humorous, impertinent and obstreperous, inconstant and inconsistent, peevish and exceptious; and consequently fastidious to society, and productive of aversation and disrespect. But the wise man is stable in his ways, consonant to himself, suiting his actions to his words, and those to his principles, and all to the rule of right reason; so that you may know where to find him, and how to deal with him, and may easily please him, which makes his acquaintance acceptable, and his person valuable: beside that real worth of itself commands respect, and extorts veneration from men, and usually prosperity waits upon his well-advised attempts, which exceedingly adorn and advance the credit of the undertaker; however, if he fail sometime, his usual deportment salves his repute, and easily makes it credible it was no fault of his, but of his fortune. If a fool prosper, the honour is attributed to propitious chance; if he miscarry, to his own ill management: but the entire glory of happy undertakings crowns the head of wisdom; while the disgrace of unlucky events falls otherwhere. His light, like that of the sun, cannot totally be eclipsed; it may be dimmed, but never extinguished, and always maintains a day, though overclouded with misfortune. Who less esteems the famous African captain for being overthrown in that last fatal battle, wherein he is said to have shewn the best skill, and yet endured the worst of success? Who contemns Cato, and other the grave citizens of Rome, for embracing the just, but improsperous cause of the commonwealth? A wise man's circumstances may vary and fluctuate like the floods about a rock; but he persists unmovably the same, and his reputation unshaken: for he can always render a good account of his actions, and by reasonable apology elude the assaults of reproach.

XII. Wisdom instructs us to examine, compare, and rightly to value the objects that court our affections, and challenge our care; and thereby regulates our passions, and moderates our endeavours, which begets a pleasant serenity and peaceable tranquillity of mind. For when, being deluded with false shows, and relying upon ill-grounded presumptions, we highly esteem, passionately affect, and eagerly pursue things of little worth in themselves or concernment to us, as we unhandsomely prostitute our affections, and prodigally mispend our time, and vainly lose our labour; so the event not answering our expectation, our minds thereby are confounded, disturbed, and distempered. But when, guided by right reason, we conceive great esteem of, and zealously are enamoured with, and vigorously strive to attain things of excellent worth, and weighty consequence; the conscience of having well placed our affections, and well employed our pains, and the experience of fruits corresponding to our hopes, ravishes our mind with unexpressible content. And so it is: present appearance and vulgar conceit ordinarily impose upon our fancies, disguising things with a deceitful varnish, and representing those that are vainest with the greatest advantage; whilst the noblest objects, being of a more subtle and spiritual nature, like fairest jewels enclosed in a homely casket, avoid the notice of gross sense, and pass undiscerned by us. But the light of wisdom, as it unmasks specious imposture, and bereaves it of its false colours; so it penetrates into the retirements of true excellency, and reveals its genuine lustre. For example, corporeal pleasure, which so powerfully allures and enchants us, wisdom declares that it is but a present, momentary, and transient satisfaction of brutish sense, dimming the light, sullying the beauty, impairing the vigour, and restraining the activity of the mind; avocing from better operations, and indisposing it to enjoy purer delights; leaving no comfortable relish or gladsome memory behind it, but often followed with bitterness, regret, and disgrace. That the profit the world so greedily gapes after is but a possession of trifles, not valuable in themselves, nor rendering the masters of them so; accidentally obtained, and promiscuously enjoyed by all sorts, but commonly by the worst of men; difficultly acquired, and easily lost; however, to be used but for a very short time, and then to be resigned into uncertain hands. That the honour men so dote upon is ordinarily but the difference of a few petty circumstances, a peculiar name or title, a determinate place, a distinguishing ensign; things of only imaginary excellence, derived from chance, and conferring no advantage, except from some little influence they have upon the arbitrary opinion and fickle humour of the people; complacence in which is vain, and reliance upon it dangerous. That power and dominion, which men so impatiently struggle for, are but necessary evils introduced to restrain the bad tempers of men; most

SERM. III.

evil to them that enjoy them; requiring tedious attendance, distracting care, and vexatious toil; attended with frequent disappointment, opprobrious censure, and dangerous envy; having such real burdens, and slavish encumbrances, sweetened only by superficial pomps, strained obsequiousness, some petty privileges and exemptions scarce worth the mentioning. That wit and parts, of which men make such ostentation, are but natural endowments, commendable only in order to use, apt to engender pride and vanity, and hugely dangerous, if abused or misemployed. What should I mention beauty, that fading toy; or bodily strength and activity, qualities so palpably inconsiderable? Upon these and such like flattering objects, so adored by vulgar opinion, wisdom exercising severe and impartial judgment, and perceiving in them no intrinsic excellence, no solid content springing from them, no perfection thence accruing to the mind, no high reward allotted to them, no security to the future condition, no durable advantages proceeding from them; it concludes they deserve not any high opinion of the mind, not any vehement passion of the soul, nor any laborious care to be employed on them, and moderates our affections toward them: it frees us from anxious desire of them; from being transported with excessive joy in the acquisition of them; from being overwhelmed with disconsolate sorrow at the missing of them, or parting with them; from repining and envying at those who have better success than ourselves in the procuring them; from immoderate toil in getting, and care in preserving them: and so delivering us from all these unquiet anxieties of thought, tumultuous perturbations of passion, and tedious vexations of body, it maintains our minds in a cheerful calm, quiet indifferency, and comfortable liberty. On the other side, things of real worth and high concernment, that produce great satisfaction to the mind, and are mainly conducible to our happiness, such as are a right understanding and strong sense of our obligations to Almighty God, and relations to men, a sound temper and complexion of mind, a virtuous disposition, a capacity to discharge the duties of our places, a due qualification to enjoy the happiness of the other world; these and such like things, by discovering their nature, and the effects resulting from them, it engages us highly to esteem, ardently to affect, and industriously to pursue; so preventing the inconveniences that follow the want of them, and conveying the benefits arising from the possession of them.

XIII. Wisdom distinguishes the circumstances, limits the measures, determines the modes, appoints the fit seasons of action; so preserving decorum, and order the parent of peace, and preventing confusion, the mother of iniquity, strife, and disquiet. It is in the business of human life as in a building; a due proportion of bulk, a fit situation of place, a correspondency of shape, and suitableness of colour, is to be observed between the parts thereof: a defect in any of which requisites, though the materials hap to be choice and excellent, makes the whole fabric deformed and ugly to judicious apprehension. The best actions, if they protuberate in life, and exceed their due measure, if they be unskilfully misplaced, if in uncouth manner performed, they lose their quality, and turn both to the disgrace and disadvantage of life. It is commendable to pray; but they that would always be performing that duty, by their absurd devotion procured to themselves the title of heretics: and they that will stand praying in places of public concourse, deserved our Saviour's reprehensions; and those men who, against the custom and ordinary use, would needs pray with their faces covered, you know St Paul insinuates of them, that they were fond and contentious persons. Friendly admonition is very laudable, and of rare use; but being upon all occasions immoderately used, or in public society so as to encroach upon modesty, or endamage reputation; or when the person admonished is otherwise employed, and attent upon his business; or being delivered in an imperiously insulting way, or in harsh and opprobrious language; it becomes unsavoury and odious, and both in show and effect resembles a froward, malicious exceptiousness. It were infinite to compute in how many instances want of due order, measure, and manner, do spoil and incommodate action. It is wisdom that applies remedy to these mischiefs. Things must be compared to, and arbitrated by, her standard, or else they will contain something of monstrous enormity; either strutting in unwieldy bulk, or sinking in defective scantness. If she do not fashion and model circumstances, they will sit ugly on the things that wear them; if she do not temper the colours, and describe the lineaments, the draught of practice will be but rude and imperfect, and little resemble the true patterns of duty; but if she interpose, and perform her part, all things will appear conformable, neat, and delicate.

XIV. Wisdom discovers our relations, duties, and concernments, in respect of men, with the natural grounds of them; thereby both qualifying and inclining us to the discharge of them: whence exceeding convenience, pleasure and content ensues. By it we understand we are parts and members of the great body, the universe; and are therefore concerned in the good management of it, and are thereby obliged to procure its order and peace, and by no irregular undertaking to disturb or discompose it; which makes us honest and peaceable men: that we proceed from the same primitive stock, are children of the same father, and partake of the same blood with all men; are endowed with like faculties of mind, passions of soul, shape of body, and sense of things: that we have equally implanted in our original constitution inclinations to love, pity, gratitude, sociableness, quiet, joy, reputation: that we have an indispensable need and impatient desire of company, assistance, comfort, and relief; that therefore it is according to the design of nature, and agreeable to reason, that to those, to whom our natural condition by so many bands of cognation, similitude, and mutual necessitude hath knit and conjoined us, we should bear a kind respect and tender affection; should cheerfully concur in undergoing the common burdens: should heartily wish and industriously promote their good, assist them in accomplishing their reasonable desires, thankfully requite the courtesies received from them, congratulate and rejoice with them in their prosperity, comfort them in their distresses, and, as we are able, relieve them; however, tenderly compassionate their disappointments, miseries, and sor-

SERM. III.

SERM. III.

rows. This renders us kind and courteous neighbours, sweet and grateful companions. It represents unto us the dreadful effects and insupportable mischiefs arising from breach of faith, contravening the obligations of solemn pacts, infringing public laws, deviating from the received rules of equity, violating promises, and interrupting good correspondence among men; by which considerations it engages us to be good citizens, obedient subjects, just dealers, and faithful friends. It minds us of the blindness, impotence, and levity, the proneness to mistake and misbehaviour that human nature necessarily is subject to; deserving rather our commiseration, than anger or hatred, which prompts us to bear the infirmities of our brethren, to be gentle in censure, to be insensible of petty affronts, to pardon injuries, to be patient, exorable, and reconcileable to those that give us greatest cause of offence. It teaches us, the good may, but the evil of our neighbour can in no wise advantage us; that from the suffering of any man, simply considered, no benefit can accrue, nor natural satisfaction arise, to us; and that therefore it is a vain, base, brutish, and unreasonable, thing, for any cause whatsoever, to desire or delight in the grief, pain, or misery of our neighbour, to hate or envy him, or insult over him, or devise mischief to him, or prosecute revenge upon him; which makes us civil, noble, and placable enemies, or rather no enemies at all. So that wisdom is in effect the genuine parent of all moral and political virtue, justice, and honesty; as Solomon says in her person, *I lead in the way of righteousness, and in the midst of the paths of judgment.* And how sweet these are in the practice, how com-

Prov. viii. 20.

fortable in the consequences, the testimony of continual experience, and the unanimous consent of all wise men sufficiently declare. But further,

SERM. III.

XV. The principal advantage of wisdom is, its acquainting us with the nature and reason of true Religion, and affording convictive arguments to persuade to the practice of it; which is accompanied with the purest delight, and attended with the most solid content imaginable. I say, the nature of Religion, wherein it consists, and what it requires; the mistake of which produceth daily so many mischiefs and inconveniences in the world, and exposes so good a name to so much reproach. It sheweth it consisteth not in fair professions and glorious pretences, but in real practice; not in a pertinacious adherence to any sect or party, but in a sincere love of goodness, and dislike of naughtiness, wherever discovering itself; not in vain ostentations and flourishes of outward performance, but in an inward good complexion of mind, exerting itself in works of true devotion and charity; not in a nice orthodoxy, or politic subjection of our judgments to the peremptory dictates of men, but in a sincere love of truth, in a hearty approbation of, and compliance with, the doctrines fundamentally good, and necessary to be believed; not in harsh censuring and virulently inveighing against others, but in careful amending our own ways; not in a peevish crossness and obstinate repugnancy to received laws and customs, but in a quiet and peaceable submission to the express laws of God, and lawful commands of man; not in a furious zeal for or against trivial circumstances, but in a conscionable practising the substantial parts of religion; not in a frequent talking or contentious disputing about it, but in a ready observance of the unquestionable rules and prescripts of it: in a word, that Religion consists in nothing else but doing what becomes our relation to God, in a conformity or similitude to his nature, and in a willing obedience to his holy will: to which by potent incentives it allures and persuades us; by representing to us his transcendently glorious attributes, conspicuously displayed in the frame, order, and government of the world: that wonderful power, which erected this great and goodly fabric; incomprehensible wisdom, which preserves it in a constant harmony; that immense goodness, which hath so carefully provided for the various necessities, delights, and comforts of its innumerable inhabitants. I say, by representing those infinitely glorious perfections, it engages us with highest respect to esteem, reverence, and honour him. Also, by minding us of our manifold obligations to him, our receiving being, life, reason, sense, all the faculties, powers, excellencies, privileges, and commodities of our natures from him; of his tender care and loving providence continually supporting and protecting us; of his liberal beneficence, patient indulgence, and earnest desire of our good and happiness, by manifold expressions evidently manifested toward us; it inflames us with ardent love, and obliges us to officious gratitude toward him. Also, by declaring the necessary and irreconcileable contrariety of his nature to all impurity and perverseness, his peerless majesty, his irresistible power, and his all-seeing knowledge, it begets an awful dread and a devout fear of him. By discovering him from his infinite benignity willing, and from his unlimited power, only able to supply our needs, relieve us in distresses, protect us from dangers, and confer any valuable benefit upon us, it engenders faith, and encourages us to rely upon him. By revealing to us his supereminent sovereignty, uncontrollable dominion, and unquestionable authority over us; together with the admirable excellency, wisdom, and equity of his laws, so just and reasonable in themselves, so suitable to our nature, so conducible to our good, so easy and practicable, so sweet and comfortable; it powerfully inclines, and by a gentle force, as it were, constrains us to obedience. By such efficacious inducements wisdom urges us to all duties of Religion, and withal surely directs us (as I before said) wherein it consists; teaching us to have right and worthy apprehensions of the divine nature, to which our devotion, if true and good, must be suited and conformed: and so it frees us, as from irreligion and profane neglect of God, so from fond superstitions, the sources of so much evil to mankind. For he that wisely hath considered the wisdom, goodness, and power of God, cannot imagine God can with a regardless eye overlook his presumptuous contempts of his laws, or endure him to proceed in an outrageous defiance of Heaven, to continue hurting himself, or injuring his neighbour; nor can admit unreasonable terrors, or entertain suspicious conceits of God, as of an imperious master, or implacable tyrant over him, exacting impossible performances from, or delighting in the fatal miseries of his creatures; nor can suppose him pleased with hypocritical shows, and greatly taken with superficial courtships of ceremonious address; or that he can in any wise favour our fiery zeals, fierce passions, or unjust partialities about matter of opinion and ceremony; or can do otherwise than detest all factious, harsh, uncharitable, and revengeful proceedings, of what nature, or upon what ground soever; or that he can be so inconsistent with himself, as to approve any thing but what is like himself, that is, righteousness, sincerity, and beneficence.

Lastly, Wisdom attracts the favour of God, purchaseth a glorious reward, and secureth perpetual felicity to us. *For God loveth none but him that dwelleth with wisdom.* And, *Glorious is the fruit of good labours: and the root of wisdom shall never fall away.* And, *Happy is the man that findeth wisdom:* and, *Whoso findeth* her, *findeth life, and shall obtain favour of the Lord.* These are the words of wise Solomon in the book of Wisdom, and in the Proverbs. God loveth her, as most agreeable to his nature; as resembling him; as an offspring, beam, and efflux of that wisdom which founded the earth, and established the heavens; as that which begetteth honour, love, and obedience to his commands, and truly glorifies him; and as that which promotes the good of his creatures, which he earnestly desires. And the paths she leads in are such as directly tend to the promised inheritance of joy and bliss.

Thus have I simply and plainly presented you with part of what my meditation suggested upon this subject: it remains that we endeavour to obtain this excellent endowment of soul, by the faithful exercise of our reason, careful observation of things, diligent study of the divine law, watchful reflection upon ourselves, virtuous and religious practice; but especially, by imploring the divine influence, the original spring of light, and fountain of all true knowledge, following St James's advice: *If any man lack wisdom, let him ask it of God, who giveth freely.* Therefore, O everlasting Wisdom, the Maker, Redeemer, and Governor of all things, let some comfortable beams from thy great body of heavenly light descend upon us, to illuminate our dark minds, and quicken our dead hearts; to inflame us with ardent love unto thee, and to direct our steps in obedience to thy laws, through the gloomy shades of this world, into that region of eternal light and bliss, where thou reignest in perfect glory and majesty, one God ever blessed, world without end. Amen.

SERM. III.

James i. 5.

# SERMON IV.

## THE PROFITABLENESS OF GODLINESS.

---

### 1 Tim. IV. 8.

*—— But godliness is profitable for all things.*

SERM. IV.

HOW generally men, with most unanimous consent, are devoted to profit, as to the immediate scope of their designs, and subject of their doings, if with the slightest attention we view what is acted upon this theatre of human affairs, we cannot but discern. All that we see men so very serious and industrious about, which we call business; that which they trudge for in the streets, which they work or wait for in the shops, which they meet and crowd for at the exchange[a], which they sue for in the hall, and solicit for at the court, which they plough and dig for, which they march and fight for in the field, which they travel for at land, and sail for (among rocks and storms) upon the sea, which they plod for in the closet, and dispute for in the schools, (yea, may we not add, which they frequently pray for and preach for in the church?) what is it but profit? Is it not this apparently, for which men so eagerly contest and quarrel, so bitterly envy and emulate, so fiercely clamour and inveigh, so cunningly supplant and undermine one another; which stuffeth their hearts with mutual

Prov. xiv. 23.

---

[a] Φεῦ, ὡς μέγα δύνασθον πανταχοῦ τὼ δύ' ὀβολώ.—
Aristoph. [Ran. 141.]

hatred and spite, which tippeth their tongues with slander and reproach, which often embrueth their hands with blood and slaughter; for which they expose their lives and limbs to danger, for which they undergo grievous toils and drudgeries, for which they distract their mind with cares, and pierce their heart with sorrows; to which they sacrifice their present ease and content, yea, to which commonly they prostitute their honour and conscience? This, if you mark it, is the great mistress, which is with so passionate rivality every where wooed and courted; this is the common mark, which all eyes aim, and all endeavours strike at; this the hire which men demand for all their pains, the prize they hope for all their combats, the harvest they seek from all the year's assiduous labour. This is the bait, by which you may inveigle most men any whither; and the most certain sign, by which you may prognosticate what any man will do: for mark where his profit is, there will he be. This some professedly and with open face, others slily and under thin veils of pretence; (under guise of friendship, of love to public good, of loyalty, of religious zeal;) some directly and in a plain track, others obliquely and by subtle trains; some by sordid and base means, others in ways more cleanly and plausible; some gravely and modestly, others wildly and furiously; all (very few excepted) in one manner or another, do clearly in most of their proceedings level and drive at[b].

[b]   Prima fere vota, et cunctis notissima templis
     Divitiæ, crescent ut opes, &c.—
                    Juv. Sat. x. [23.]
Omnes ad affectum atque appetitum utilitatis suæ naturæ ipsius

This practice then being so general, and seeing that men are reasonable creatures, that it is so cannot surely proceed from mere brutishness or dotage; there must be some fair colour or semblance of reason, which draweth men into, and carrieth them forward in this way. The reason indeed is obvious and evident enough; the very name of profit implieth it, signifying that which is useful, or conducible to purposes really or seemingly good. The gain of money, or of somewhat equivalent thereto, is therefore specially termed profit, because it readily supplieth necessity, furnisheth convenience, feedeth pleasure, satisfieth fancy and curiosity, promoteth ease and liberty, supporteth honour and dignity, procureth power, dependencies, and friendships, rendereth a man somebody considerable in the world; in fine, enableth to do good, or to perform works of beneficence and charity. Profit is therefore so much affected and pursued, because it is, or doth seem, apt to procure or promote some good desirable to us.

If therefore a project should be proposed to us very feasible, and probable to succeed, in pursuance whereof assuredly we might obtain great profit; methinks, in consistence with ourselves, and conformably to our usual manner of acting, we should be very ready to embrace and execute it. Such a project it is, which in my text, by a very trusty voucher and skilful judge of such things, and one who had himself fully experimented it, is proposed; which in itself is very practicable, so that any of us may, if we have a mind to it and will be at the

magisterio atque impulsione ducuntur.—Salv. ad Eccl. Cath. II. (adv. Avar. II. p. 253. Ed. Baluz.)

pains, throughly compass and carry it on: which will exceedingly turn to account, and bring in gains unto us unspeakably vast; in comparison whereto all other designs, which men with so much care and toil do pursue, are very unprofitable or detrimental, yielding but shadows of profit, or bringing real damage to us.

It is briefly this, to be religious or pious; that is, in our minds steadfastly to believe on God, (such as nature in some measure, and revelation more clearly, declareth him,) in our hearts earnestly to love and reverence him, through all our practice sincerely and diligently to observe his laws. This is it which St Paul affirmeth to be *profitable for all things*, and which it is my intent, by God's help, to recommend unto you as such; demonstrating it really to be so, by representing some of those numberless benefits and advantages which accrue from it, extending to all conditions and capacities of men, to all states, all seasons, and in effect to all affairs of life.

It hath been ever a main obstruction to the practice of piety, that it hath been taken for no friend, or rather for an enemy, to profit; as both unprofitable and prejudicial to its followers: and many semblances there are countenancing that opinion. For religion seemeth to smother or to slacken the industry and alacrity of men in following profit, many ways: by charging them to be content with a little, and careful for nothing; by diverting their affections and cares from worldly affairs to matters of another nature, place, and time, prescribing in the first place to seek things spiritual, heavenly, and future; by disparaging all secular wealth, as a thing, in comparison to virtue and spiritual goods, very mean and inconsiderable; by checking greedy desires and aspiring thoughts after it; by debarring the most ready ways of getting it, (violence, exaction, fraud, and flattery,) yea, straitening the best ways, eager care and diligence; by commending strict justice in all cases, and always taking part with conscience when it clasheth with interest; by paring away the largest uses of wealth, in the prohibition of its free enjoyment to pride or pleasure; by enjoining liberal communication thereof in ways of charity and mercy; by engaging men to expose their goods sometimes to imminent hazard, sometimes to certain loss; obliging them to forsake all things, and to embrace poverty for its sake.

It favoureth this conceit, to observe, that often bad men by impious courses do appear to thrive and prosper; while good men seem for their goodness to suffer, or to be no wise visibly better for it, enduring much hardship and distress.

It furthereth the prejudice, that some persons, void of true piety, or imperfectly good, (some dabblers in religion,) do not from their lame, slight, and superficial performances, feel satisfactory returns, such as they did presume to find; and thence, to the defamation of piety, are apt to say, with those men in the prophet, *It is vain to serve God: and what profit is it that we have kept his ordinance, and that we have walked mournfully before the Lord of hosts?* Yea, that sometimes very pious men, being out of humour, and somewhat discomposed by the urgent pressures of affliction, the disappointments and crosses incident to all men here in this region of trouble, are apt to complain and express themselves dissatisfied, saying with Job, *It profiteth a man nothing that he should delight himself with God. What advantage will it be unto me, and what profit shall I have, if I be cleansed from my sin?* or with David, *Verily I have cleansed my heart in vain, and washed my hands in innocency: for all the day long I have been plagued, and chastened every morning.*

To these considerations, disadvantageous in this respect to piety, may be added, that the constant and certain profits emergent from it (although incomparably more substantial, and to the mind more sensible than any other) are not yet so gross and palpable, that men, who from being immersed in earth and flesh are blind in error, dull of apprehension, vain and inconsiderate in their judgments, tainted and vitiated in their palates, can discern their worth, or relish their sweetness. Hence it is that so many follow the judgment and practice of those in Job, *Who say unto God, Depart from us; for we desire not the knowledge of thy ways. What is the Almighty, that we should serve him? and what profit should we have, if we pray unto him?*

For voiding which prejudices, and the recommendation of St Paul's project, I shall, as I said, propose some of those innumerable advantages, by considering which the immense profitableness of piety will appear. And first, I shall mention those considerations which more plainly do import universality; then shall touch some benefits thereof, seeming more particular, yet in effect vastly large, and of a very diffusive influence.

SERM. IV.

I. First then, we may consider that piety is exceeding useful for all sorts of men, in all capacities, all states, all relations; fitting and disposing them to manage all their respective concernments, to discharge all their peculiar duties, in a proper, just, and decent manner.

Eph. vi. 9.
Col. iv. 1.

It rendereth all superiors equal and moderate in their administrations; mild, courteous, and affable in their converse; benign and condescensive in all their demeanour toward their inferiors.

Eph. vi. 5.

Correspondently it disposeth inferiors to be sincere and faithful, modest, loving, respectful, diligent, apt willingly to yield due subjection and service.

Col. iii. 22.
1 Pet. ii. 18.

It inclineth princes to be just, gentle, benign, careful for their subjects' good, apt to administer justice uprightly, to protect right, to encourage virtue, to check wickedness.

Rom. xiii. 1.
Tit. iii. 1.
1 Pet. ii. 13.
1 Pet. iv. 9.
Phil. ii. 14.

Answerably it rendereth subjects loyal, submissive, obedient, quiet, and peaceable, ready to yield due honour, to pay the tributes and bear the burdens imposed, to discharge all duties, and observe all laws prescribed by their governors, conscionably, patiently, cheerfully, without reluctancy, grudging, or murmuring.

Eph. vi. 4.
Col. iii. 21.
1 Tim. v. 8.
Eph. vi. 1.
Col. iii. 20.

It maketh parents loving, gentle, provident for their children's good education, and comfortable subsistence; children again, dutiful, respectful, grateful, apt to requite their parents.

Eph. v. 25.
Col. iii. 19.
1 Pet. iii. 7.
Eph. v. 22.
Col. iii. 18.

Husbands from it become affectionate and compliant to their wives; wives submissive and obedient to their husbands.

Tit. ii. 5.
1 Pet. iii. 5.

It disposeth friends to be friends indeed, full of cordial affection and good-will, entirely faithful, firmly constant, industriously careful and active in performing all good offices mutually.

It engageth men to be diligent in their calling, faithful to their trusts, contented and peaceable in their station, and thereby serviceable to public good.

It rendereth all men just and punctual in their dealing, orderly and quiet in their behaviour, courteous and complaisant in their conversation, friendly and charitable upon all occasions, apt to assist, to relieve, to comfort one another.

*Gal. vi. 2, 10. Phil. iv. 8. 1 Thess. iii. 12. 2 Cor. ix. 13.*

It tieth all relations more fastly and strongly, assureth and augmenteth all endearments, enforceth and establisheth all obligations by the firm bands of conscience; set aside which, no engagement can hold sure against temptations of interest or pleasure. Much difference there is between performing these duties out of natural temper, fear of punishment, hope of temporal reward, selfish design, regard to credit, or other the like principles, and the discharging them out of religious conscience: this alone will keep men tight, uniform, resolute, and stable; whereas all other principles are loose and slippery, will soon be shaken and falter.

In consequence to those practices springing from it, piety removeth oppression, violence, faction, disorders, and murmurings, out of the state; schisms and scandals out of the church; pride and haughtiness, sloth and luxury, detraction and sycophantry, out of the court; corruption and partiality out of judicatures; clamours and tumults out of the street; brawlings, grudges, and jealousies out of families; extortion and cozenage out of trade; strifes, emulations, slanderous backbitings, bitter and foul language out of conversation: in all places, in all societies it produceth, it advanceth, it establisheth, order, peace, safety, prosperity, all that is good, all that is lovely or handsome, all that is convenient or pleasant for human society and common life. It is that which, as the Wise Man saith, *Exalteth a nation;* it is that which *Establisheth a throne.*

It is indeed the best prop and guard that can be of government, and of the commonweal: for it settleth the body politic in a sound constitution of health, it firmly cementeth the parts thereof; it putteth all things into a right order and steady course. It procureth mutual respect and affection between governors and subjects, whence ariseth safety, ease, and pleasure to both. It rendereth men truly good, (that is, just and honest, sober and considerate, modest and peaceable,) and thence apt, without any constraint or stir, to yield every one their due; not affected to needless change, nor disposed to raise any disturbance. It putteth men in good humour, and keepeth them in it; whence things pass smoothly and pleasantly. It cherisheth worth, and encourageth industry; whence virtue flourisheth, and wealth is increased; whence the occasions and means of disorder are stopped, the pretences for sedition and faction are cut off. In fine, it certainly procureth the benediction of God, the source of all welfare and prosperity; whence, *When it goeth well with the righteous, the city rejoiceth;* and, *When the righteous are in authority, the people rejoice,* saith the great politician Solomon.

It is therefore the concernment of all men, who as the Psalmist speaketh, *Desire to live well, and would fain see good days;* it is the special interest of great persons, (of the magistracy, the nobility, the gentry, of all persons that have any considerable interest in the world,) who would safely and sweetly enjoy their dignity, power, or wealth, by all means to protect and promote piety, as the best instrument of their security, and undisturbedly enjoying the accommodations of their state. 'Tis in all respects their best wisdom and policy; that which will as well preserve their outward state here, as satisfy their consciences within, and save their souls hereafter. All the Machiavelian arts and tricks, all the sleights and fetches of worldly craft, do signify nothing in comparison to this one plain and easy way of securing and furthering their interests.

If then it be a gross absurdity to desire the fruits, and not to take care of the root, not to cultivate the stock, whence they sprout; if every prince gladly would have his subjects loyal and obedient, every master would have his servants honest, diligent, and observant, every parent would have his children officious and grateful, every man would have his friend faithful and kind, every one would have those just and sincere with whom he doth negotiate or converse; if any one would choose to be related to such, and would esteem their relation a happiness; then consequently should every man in reason strive to further piety, from whence alone those good dispositions and practices do proceed.

II. Piety doth fit a man for all conditions, qualifying him to pass through them all with the best advantage, wisely, cheerfully, and safely; so as to incur no considerable harm or detriment by them.

Is a man prosperous, high, or wealthy in condition? Piety guardeth him from all the mischiefs incident to that state, and disposeth him to enjoy the best advantages thereof. It keepeth him from being swelled and puffed up with vain conceit, from being transported with fond complacence or confidence therein; minding him, that it is purely the gift of God, that it absolutely dependeth on his disposal, so that it may soon be taken from him; and that he cannot otherwise than by humility, by gratitude, by the good use of it, be secure to retain it; minding him also, that he shall assuredly be forced to render a strict account concerning the good management thereof. It preserveth him from being perverted or corrupted with the temptations to which that condition is most liable; from luxury, from sloth, from stupidity, from forgetfulness of God, and of himself; maintaining among the floods of plenty a sober and steady mind. It fenceth him from insolence, and fastuous contempt of others; rendereth him civil, condescensive, kind and helpful to those who are in a meaner state. It instructeth and inciteth him to apply his wealth and power to the best uses, to the service of God, to the benefit of his neighbour, for his own best reputation, and most solid comfort. It is the right ballast of prosperity, the only antidote for all the inconveniences of wealth; that which secureth, sweeteneth, and sanctifieth all other goods: without it all apparent goods are very noxious, or extremely dangerous; riches, power, honour, ease, pleasure, are so many poisons, or so many snares, without it. Again, is a man poor and low in the world? Piety doth improve and sweeten even that state: it keepeth his spirits up above dejection, desperation, and disconsolateness; it freeth him from all grievous solicitude and anxiety; shewing him, that although he seemeth to have little, yet he may be assured to want nothing, he having a certain succour and never-failing supply from God's good providence; that, notwithstanding the present straitness of his condition, or scantness of outward things, he hath a title to goods infinitely more precious and more considerable. A pious man cannot but apprehend himself like the child of a most wealthy, kind, and careful father, who, although he hath yet nothing in his own possession, or passing under his name, yet is assured that he can never come into any want of what is needful to him: the Lord of all things (who hath all things in heaven and earth at his disposal, who is infinitely tender of his children's good, who doth incessantly watch over them) being his gracious Father, how can he fear to be left destitute, or not to be competently provided for, as is truly best for him?

SERM.
IV.

This is the difference between a pious and an impious man. Is the pious man in need? he hath then an invisible refuge to fly to, an invisible store to furnish him; he hath somewhat beyond all present things to hope in, to comfort himself with: whereas the impious person hath nothing beside present appearances to support or solace himself by; the which failing, down he sinketh into dejection and despair. Is the good man in affliction? he knoweth that it cometh not on him without God's wise appointment, nor without good intention toward him, for probation, exercise, and improvement of his virtues, or for wholesome correction of his bad dispositions; that it is only physic

SERM. IV.

and discipline to him, which shall have a comfortable issue; that it shall last no longer than it is expedient for him that it should: wherefore he patiently submitteth to it, and undergoeth it cheerfully, with the same mind wherewith a patient swalloweth down an unsavoury potion, which he presumeth will conduce to his health[c]. Never, indeed, hath any man enjoyed more real content, or hath been more truly satisfied, than good men have been in a seeming depth of adversity[d]. What men ever upon earth have been more sorely afflicted, have underwent greater losses, disgraces, labours, troubles, distresses in any kind, than did the holy apostles? Yet did they most heartily rejoice, exult, and triumph in them all. Such a wondrous virtue hath piety to change all things into matter of consolation and joy. No condition in effect can be evil or sad to a pious man: his very sorrows are pleasant, his infirmities are wholesome, his wants enrich him, his disgraces adorn him, his burdens ease him; his duties are privileges, his falls are the grounds of advancement, his very sins (as breeding contrition, humility, circumspection, and vigilance) do better and profit him: whereas impiety doth spoil every condition, doth corrupt and embase all good things, doth embitter all the conveniences and comforts of life.

[c] Scimus enim amicos Dei ab amantissimo ac misericordissimo Patre Deo mala ista poenalia recipere, et hæc non ut poenam, seu vindictam iracundiæ, sed magis ut correctiones et medicamenta stultitiæ, et adjumenta virtutis, ut malleationes sive fabricationes, et tunsiones, sive ablutiones, et candidationes.—Guil. Par. de Sacram. [Opp. Tom. I. p. 414 E.]

[d] Ἐκείνους μὲν γὰρ ἐπεκούφιζεν ἡ χαρὰ τῆς μαρτυρίας, καὶ ἡ ἐλπὶς τῶν ἐπηγγελμένων, καὶ ἡ πρὸς τὸν Χριστὸν ἀγάπη, καὶ τὸ πνεῦμα τὸ πατρικόν.—Euseb. Eccl. Hist. v. 1. Mart. Lugd. [Tom. I. p. 204.]

III. Piety doth virtually comprise within it all other profits, serving all the designs of them all: whatever kind of desirable good we can hope to find from any other profit, we may be assured to enjoy from it.

He that hath it is *ipso facto* vastly rich, is entitled to immense treasures of most precious wealth; in comparison whereto all the gold and all the jewels in the world are mere baubles. He hath interest in God, and can call him his, who is the *All*, and in regard to whom all things existent are less than nothing. The infinite power and wisdom of God belong to him, to be ever, upon all fit occasions, employed for his benefit. All the inestimable treasures of heaven (a place infinitely more rich than the Indies) are his, after this moment of life, to have and to hold for ever: so that great reason had the Wise Man to say, that *In the house of the righteous is much treasure*. Piety therefore is profitable, as immediately instating in wealth: and whereas the desired fruits of profit are chiefly these, honour, power, pleasure, safety, liberty, ease, opportunity of getting knowledge, means of benefiting others; all these, we shall see, do abundantly accrue from piety, and in truth only from it. Prov. xv. 6.

The pious man is in truth most honourable. *Inter homines pro summo est optimus*, saith Seneca[e]: whom Solomon translateth thus; *The righteous is more excellent than his neighbour*. He is dignified by the most illustrious titles, a son of God, a friend and favourite to the sovereign King of the world, Prov. xii. 26.

[e] Ep. xc. [4.]
Κατ' ἀλήθειαν δ' ὁ ἀγαθὸς μόνος τιμητέος.—Arist. Eth. [IV. 3. 20.]

SERM. IV.

an heir of heaven, a denizen of the Jerusalem above: titles far surpassing all those which worldly state doth assume. He is approved by the best and most infallible judgments, wherein true honour resideth. He is respected by God himself, by the holy angels, by the blessed saints, by all good and all wise persons; yea, commonly, by all men: for the effects of genuine piety are so venerable and amiable, that scarce any man can do otherwise than in his heart much esteem him that worketh them.

Prov. xii. 8.

The pious man is also the most potent man: he hath a kind of omnipotency, because he can do whatever he will, that is, what he ought to do[f]; and because the Divine Power is ever ready to assist him in his pious enterprises, so that *He can do all things by Christ that strengtheneth him.* He is able to combat and vanquish him that is Ὁ ἰσχυρός, *The stout and mighty one;* to wage war with happy success *Against principalities and powers.* He conquereth and commandeth himself, which is the bravest victory and noblest empire[g]: he quelleth fleshly lusts, subdueth inordinate passions, and repelleth strong temptations. He, *By his faith, overcometh the world* with a conquest far more glorious than ever any Alexander or Cæsar could do. He, in fine, doth perform the most worthy exploits, and deserveth the most honourable triumphs that man can do.

Phil. iv. 13.

Matt. xii. 29.
Luke xi. 21.
Eph. vi. 12.
Prov. xvi. 32; xxv. 28.
1 John v. 4.

[f] Tantum enim quantum vult potest, qui se, nisi quod debet, non putat posse.—Sen. Ep. xc. [4.]

[g] Id. de Ben. v. 7.[3.] [Quem magis admiraberis, quam qui imperat sibi, quam qui se habet in potestate? Gentes facilius est barbaras, impatientesque alieni arbitrii, regere, quam animum suum continere, et tradere sibi.]

## The Profitableness of Godliness. 189

The pious man also doth enjoy the only true pleasures; hearty, pure, solid, durable pleasures; such pleasures as those of which the divine Psalmist singeth: *In thy presence is fulness of joy; at thy right hand there are pleasures for evermore.* That *All joy in believing,* that *Gaiety of hope,* that incessant *Rejoicing in the Lord,* and *Greatly delighting in his law,* that continual feast of a good conscience, that *Serving the Lord with gladness,* that *Exceeding gladness with God's countenance,* that *Comfort of the Holy Spirit,* that *Joy unspeakable and full of glory;* the satisfaction resulting from the contemplation of heavenly truth, from the sense of God's favour, and the pardon of his sins, from the influence of God's grace, from the hopes and anticipation of everlasting bliss; these are pleasures indeed, in comparison whereto all other pleasures are no more than brutish sensualities, sordid impurities, superficial touches, transient flashes of delight: such as should be insipid and unsavoury to a rational appetite; such as are tinctured with sourness and bitterness, have painful remorses or qualms consequent[h]. All the pious man's performances of duty and of devotion are full of pure satisfaction and delight here, they shall be rewarded with perfect and endless joy hereafter.

As for safety, the pious man hath it most absolute and sure; he being guarded by Almighty power and wisdom; *Resting under the shadow of*

SERM. IV.

Ps. xvi. 11.

Rom. xv. 13.
Heb. iii. 6.
Phil. iv. 4.
Ps. xliii. 4;
cxii. 1; i. 2;
cxix. 16, 24, 47, 70, 77, 92, 111;
c. 2; xxi. 6; xciv. 19;
Isai. xxix. 19.
John xvi. 20, &c.
1 Pet. i. 8.
Rom. xiv. 17.

Ps. xvii. 8; xxxvi. 7;

[h] Quid enim jucundius, quam Dei Patris et Domini reconciliatio, quam veritatis revelatio, quam errorum recognitio, quam tantorum retro criminum venia? quæ major voluptas, quam fastidium ipsius voluptatis, quam seculi totius contemptus, quam vera libertas, quam conscientia integra, quam vita sufficiens, quam mortis timor nullus?—Tert. de Spectac. cap. xxix. [Opp. p. 84 c.]

SERM. IV.

Ps. lvii. 1; lx. 4; xci. 4; xxxvii. 24; cxix. 117; xxxvii. 23, 31; cxix. 133; lxvi. 9; cxix. 45.

*God's wings; God Upholding him with his hand, Ordering his steps, so that none of them shall slide, Holding his soul in life, and suffering not his feet to be moved;* he being, by the grace and mercy of God, secured from the assaults and impressions of all enemies, from sin and guilt, from the Devil, world, and flesh, from death and hell, which are our most formidable, and in effect only dangerous enemies.

As for liberty, the pious man most entirely and truly doth enjoy that; he alone is free from captivity to that cruel tyrant Satan, from the miserable slavery to sin, from the grievous dominion of lust and passion. He can do what he pleaseth, having a mind to do only what is good and fit. The law he observeth is worthily called *The perfect law of liberty;* the Lord he serveth pretendeth only to command freemen[i] and friends: *Ye are my friends,* said he, *if ye do whatever I command you;* and, *If the Son set you free, then are ye free indeed.*

James i. 25.

John xv. 14; viii. 36.

And for ease, it is he only that knoweth it; having his mind exempted from the distraction of care, from disorder of passion, from anguish of conscience, from the drudgeries and troubles of the world, from the vexations and disquiets which sin produceth. He findeth it made good to him, which our Lord inviting him did promise, *Come unto me all ye that labour and are heavy laden, and I will give you rest:* he feeleth the truth of those divine assertions, *Thou wilt keep him in perfect peace, whose mind is stayed on thee;* and, *Great*

Matt. xi. 28.

Isai. xxvi. 3.
Ps. cxix. 165.

---

[i] Οὐ γάρ ἐστιν, οὐκ ἔστιν ἐλεύθερος, ἀλλ' ἢ μόνος ὁ Χριστῷ ζῶν.—Chrys. ad Theod. [Orat. I. Opp. Tom. VI. p. 59.]

*peace have they which love thy law, and nothing shall offend them.*

SERM. IV.

As for knowledge, the pious man alone doth attain it considerably, so as to become truly wise and learned to purpose. *Evil men,* saith the Wise Man himself, who knew well, *understand not judgment: but they that seek the Lord understand all things.* It is the pious man that employeth his mind upon the most proper and worthy objects, that knoweth things which certainly best deserve to be known, that hath his soul enriched with the choicest notions; he skilleth to aim at the best ends, and to compass them by the fittest means; he can assign to each thing its due worth and value; he can prosecute things by the best methods, and order his affairs in the best manner: so that he is sure not to be defeated or disappointed in his endeavours, nor to mispend his care and pains, without answerable fruit. He hath the best master to instruct him in his studies, and the best rules to direct him in his proceedings: he cannot be mistaken, seeing in his judgment and choice of things he conspireth with infallible wisdom. Therefore Ὁ εὐσεβῶν ἄκρως φιλοσοφεῖ, *The pious man is the exquisite philosopher*[k]. *The fear of the Lord, that is wisdom; and to depart from evil is understanding. The fear of the Lord* (as is said again and again in scripture) *is the head* (or *top*) *of wisdom. A good understanding have all they that keep his commandments.*

Prov. xxviii. 5.

Job xxviii. 28.
Prov. ix. 10; i. 7.
Ps. cxi. 10; cxix. 34, 99, 104, 130.

Further: the pious man is enabled and disposed (hath the power and the heart) most to benefit and

---

[k] Herm. Trismeg. [Stob. Eclog. Lib. I. cap. xxxv. § 1. Tom. I. p. 273. Ed. Gaisford.]

oblige others. He doth it by his succour and assistance, by his instruction and advice, which he is ever ready to yield to any man upon fit occasion: he doth it by the direction and encouragement of his good example: he doth it by his constant and earnest prayers for all men: he doth it by drawing down blessings from heaven on the place where he resideth. He is upon all accounts the most true, the most common benefactor to mankind; all his neighbours, his country, the world are in some way or other obliged to him: at least, he doth all the good he can, and in wish doth benefit all men.

Thus all the fruits and consequences of profit, the which engage men so eagerly to pursue it, do in the best kind and highest degree result from piety, and indeed only from it. All the philosophical bravados concerning a wise man being only rich, only honourable, only happy, only above fortune, are verified in the pious man: to him alone, as such, with a sure foundation, without vanity, with evident reason, those aphorisms may be applied. They are paradoxes and fictions abstracting from religion, or considering men only under the light and power of nature: but supposing our religion true, a good Christian soberly, without arrogance, in proportion and according to the measure of his piety, may assume them to himself, as the holy apostle did: *I possess all things, I can do all things*, he may in a sort say after St Paul.

As for all other profits, secluding it, they are but imaginary and counterfeit, mere shadows and illusions, yielding only painted shows instead of substantial fruit[1].

[1] Sen. Ep. LIX.

## The Profitableness of Godliness. 193

If from bare worldly wealth (that which usurpeth the name of profit here) a man seeketh honour, he is deluded, for he is not thereby truly honourable; he is but a shining earth-worm, a well-trapped ass, a gaudy statue, a theatrical grandee; with God, who judgeth most rightly, he is mean and despicable: no intelligent person can inwardly respect him. Even here, in this world of fallacy and dotage, the wisest and soberest men, whose judgment usually doth sway that of others, cannot but contemn him, as master of no real good, nor fit for any good purpose; as seeing that in the end he will prove most beggarly and wretched.

If a man affecteth power thence, he is grievously mistaken: for, instead thereof, he proveth exceedingly feeble and impotent, able to perform nothing worthy a man, subject to fond humours and passions, servant to divers lusts and pleasures, *Captivated by the Devil at his pleasure*, overborne by temptation, hurried by the stream of the world, and liable to the strokes of fortune.

2 Tim. ii. 26.

If he propoundeth to himself thence the enjoyment of pleasure, he will also much fail therein: for in lieu thereof he shall find care and trouble, surfeiting and disease, wearisome fastidiousness and bitter regret; being void of all true delight in his mind, satisfaction in his conscience; nothing here being able to furnish solid and stable pleasure.

If he fancieth safety, he deludeth himself: for how can he be safe, who is destitute of God's protection and succour; who is the object of divine wrath and vengeance; who is assailed by many fierce and powerful enemies; whom the roaring lion is ready to devour; whom death and *Sudden*

1 Thess. v. 3.
Prov. x. 29.

*destruction* are coming to seize upon; whom guilt threateneth, and hell gapeth for; who without any guard or fence standeth exposed to such imminent, such horrid and ghastly dangers?

If he thirst for liberty, he will be frustrated: for he can be no otherwise than a slave, while he continueth impious; *Servus tot dominorum, quot vitiorum*[m], *A slave to so many masters as he keepeth vices:* a slave to himself and his own lusts: carrying about with him the fetters of unsatiable desire, being hampered with inconsistent and irregular affections.

Ease he cannot obtain, being oppressed with unwieldy burdens of sin, of care, of trouble; being tossed with restless agitations of lust and passion; being *Like the troubled sea, which cannot rest, whose waters cast up mire and dirt.*

If he meaneth to get wisdom, he is out: for wisdom and impiety are incompatible things. All his knowledge is vain, all his speculations are no better than dreams, seeing he erreth in the main point, and is not *Wise to salvation.*

He is, in fine, extremely mistaken, and in all his projects will be lamentably disappointed, whoever fancieth any true profit without piety: he never can attain to be so much as wealthy; but drudge and plod what he can, must be a beggar, and a forlorn wretch. For how can he be any wise rich, who doth want all the best things, the only valuable things in the world, which any man may have, which any good man doth possess? How can he be rich, who is destitute of the most needful accommodations of life; who constantly feedeth on the

---

[m] **Aug.** [de Civ. Dei, IV. 3. Opp. Tom. VII. col. 90 F.]

coarsest and most sordid fare, (the dust of pelf, the dung of sensuality;) who hath no faithful or constant friends, (nothing earthly can be such;) who is master of nothing but dirt, or chaff, or smoke? Whereas also riches do consist, not in what one enjoyeth at present, (for that can be little,) but in a presumed ability to enjoy afterward what he may come to need or desire; or in well-grounded hopes that he shall never fall into want or distress. How can that man be rich, who hath not any confidence in God, any interest in him, any reason to expect his blessing? yea, who hath much ground to fear the displeasure of him, in whose hand all things are, and who arbitrarily disposeth of all? Piety therefore is the only profitable thing, according to just esteem. *She is more precious than rubies, and all the things we can desire are not to be compared to her.* Upon this account it is most true, what the Psalmist affirmeth, *A little that the righteous hath is better than great riches of the ungodly.*

Prov. iii. 15.

Ps. xxxvii. 16.

IV. That commendation is not to be omitted, which is nearest at hand, and suggested by St Paul himself to back this assertion concerning the universal profitableness of piety; *For,* saith he, *it hath the promise of the life that now is, and of that which is to come:* that is, God hath promised to reward it with blessings appertaining to this mortal life, and with those which concern the future eternal state.

As for the blessings of this life, although God hath not promised to load the godly man with affluence of worldly things, not to put him into a splendid and pompous garb, not to dispense to him that which may serve for pampering the flesh, or gratifying wanton fancy, not to exempt him from all the inconveniences to which human nature and this worldly state are subject; yet hath he promised to furnish him with whatever is needful or convenient for him, in due measure and season, the which he doth best understand. There is no good thing which a man naturally desireth, or reasonably can wish for, which is not in express terms proposed as a reward, or a result of piety.

In general, it is declared, that *Blessings are upon the head of the just;* that, *No good thing God will withhold from them that walk uprightly;* that, *whatever otherwise doth fall out, It assuredly shall be well with them that fear God;* that, *Blessed is every one that feareth the Lord, that walketh in his ways:— happy shalt thou be, and it shall be well with thee;* that, *There shall no evil happen to the just;* that, *All things work together for good to them that love God.*

Particularly, there are promised to the pious man,

A supply of all wants. *The Lord will not suffer the soul of the righteous to famish. The righteous eateth to the satisfying of his soul. There is no want to them that fear God. The young lions do lack, and suffer hunger; but they that seek the Lord shall not want any good thing.*

A protection in all dangers. *The eye of the Lord is upon them that fear him, upon them that hope in his mercy; to deliver their soul from death, and to keep them alive in famine. There shall no evil befall thee, neither shall any plague come nigh thy dwelling: He shall give his angels charge over thee, to keep thee in all thy ways.*

Guidance in all his undertakings and proceedings. *The steps of a good man are ordered by the Lord——none of his steps shall slide.——In all thy ways acknowledge him, and he shall direct thy paths.* SERM. IV.<br>Ps. xxxvii. 23, &c.<br>Prov. iii. 6.<br>Prov. xi. 3, 5; xvi. 3.

Success and prosperity in his designs. *Commit thy way unto the Lord; trust also in him, and he shall bring it to pass.——Whatsoever he doeth, it shall prosper.——Thou shalt decree a thing, and it shall be established; and the light shall shine upon thy ways. The Lord shall command a blessing upon thee in thy storehouses, and in all that thou settest thine hand unto. Thine expectation shall not be cut off.* Ps. xxxvii. 5.<br>Ps. i. 3.<br>Job xxii. 28.<br>Deut. xxviii. 8.<br>Prov. xxiii. 18.

Comfortable enjoying the fruits of his industry. *Thou shalt eat the labour of thine hands.* Ps. cxxviii. 2.

Satisfaction of all reasonable desires. *The desire of the righteous shall be granted. Delight thyself in the Lord, and he shall give thee the desires of thine heart. He will fulfil the desire of them that fear him: he will hear their cry, and will save them.* Prov. x. 24.<br>Ps. xxxvii. 4.<br>cxlv. 19.

Firm peace and quiet. *The work of righteousness shall be peace; and the effect of righteousness, quietness and assurance for ever. Great peace have they which love thy law. The fruit of righteousness is sowed in peace.* Isai. xxxii. 17.<br>Ps. cxix. 165.<br>James iii. 18.

Joy and alacrity. *Light is sown for the righteous, and gladness for the upright in heart. In the transgression of an evil man there is a snare: but the righteous doth sing and rejoice.* Ps. xcvii. 11.<br>Prov. xxix. 6.

Support and comfort in afflictions. *He healeth the broken in heart, and bindeth up their wounds. Be of good courage, and he shall strengthen your heart, all ye that hope in the Lord.* Ps. cxlvii. 3.<br>Ps. xxxi. 24; xxvii. 14.

Deliverance from trouble. *Many are the afflic-* Ps. xxxiv. 19, 20.

tions of the righteous, but the Lord delivereth him out of them all. He keepeth all his bones, not one of them is broken.

Preservation and recovery from mishaps or miscarriages. *Though he fall, he shall not be utterly cast down: for the Lord upholdeth him with his hand.*

Preferment of all sorts, to honour and dignity, to wealth and prosperity. *Wait upon the Lord, and keep his way; and he shall exalt thee to inherit the land. By humility and fear of the Lord are riches and honour. Blessed is the man that feareth the Lord——wealth and riches are in his house. The upright shall have good things in possession. If they obey and serve him, they shall spend their days in prosperity, and their years in pleasure. The tabernacle of the righteous shall flourish.*

Long life. *The fear of the Lord prolongeth days. By me thy days shall be multiplied, and the years of thy life shall be increased. Let thine heart keep my commandments: for length of days, and long life, and peace, shall they add unto thee.*

A good name enduring after death. *The memory of the just is blessed.*

Blessings entailed on posterity. *His seed shall be mighty upon earth; the generation of the upright shall be blessed. The root of the righteous shall not be moved.*

Thus is a liberal dispensation even of temporal goods annexed by God's infallible word unto the practice of piety. It is indeed more frequently, abundantly, and explicitly promised unto God's ancient people, as being a conditional ingredient of the covenant made with them, exhibited in that as a recompense of their external performance of religious works prescribed in their law. The Gospel doth not so clearly propound it, or so much insist upon it, as not principally belonging to the evangelical covenant, the which, in reward to the performance of its conditions by us, peculiarly doth offer blessings spiritual, and relating to the future state; as also scarce deserving to be mentioned in comparison to those superior blessings. Yet as the celestial benefits, although not openly tendered in the Jewish law, were yet mystically couched therein, and closely designed for the spiritual and hearty practisers of religion; so is the collation of temporal accommodations to be understood to belong to all pious Christians: there is a codicil, as it were, annexed to the New Testament, in which God signifieth his intention to furnish his children with all that is needful or convenient for them. His providence hath not ceased to watch over us, his bounty doth not fail toward us even in this respect; his care will not be wanting to feed us and clothe us comfortably, to protect us from evil, to prosper our good undertakings. Hence doth he command us to care for nothing, but *To cast our care upon him, to recommend our business to him, because he careth for us; He will never forsake us;* he will hear our prayers, and help us. Hence we are enjoined *Not to trust in uncertain riches, but in the living God, who giveth us richly all things to enjoy.* Hence it is said, that *The divine power hath given us all things pertaining unto life and godliness, through the knowledge of him that hath called us to glory and virtue.* Hence it is promised by our Lord, that if we *Seek*

SERM. IV.

2 Cor. iv. 17.
Rom. viii. 18.

1 Pet. v. 7.
Phil. iv. 6.
Heb. xiii. 5.
Matt. vi. 25.
1 Tim. vi. 17.
2 Pet. i. 3.
Matt. vi. 33.

*first the kingdom of God, all things shall be added to us.* Hence it is inferred, as consequential to the nature of the evangelical dispensation, that we cannot want any good thing; *He,* saith St Paul, *that spared not his own Son, but delivered him up for us all, how shall he not with him also freely give us all things?* In fine, hence it is proposed as notorious, that nothing is permitted to fall out otherwise than as conduceth to our good. *We know,* saith St Paul, *that all things work together for good unto those that love God:* nor *Will God,* in any case, *suffer us to be tempted,* by any want or pressure, *beyond what we are able to bear.* Thus is piety evidently profitable, as having the promises of this life, or exhibiting all temporal blessings desirable to the practisers thereof.

But infinitely more profitable it is, as having the promises of the future life, or as procuring a title to those incomparably more excellent blessings of the other world; those indefectible treasures, that *Incorruptible, undefiled, and never-fading inheritance, reserved in heaven for us;* that *Exceeding weight of glory;* those ineffable joys of paradise, that lightsome countenance and beatifying presence of God; that unconceivably and unexpressibly joyful, glorious, perfect, and endless bliss; briefly, all that is comprised and intimated in those words of the apostle, *Eye hath not seen, nor ear heard, neither have entered into the heart of man the things which God hath prepared for them that love him.* Infinitely profitable surely must that be, which procureth those things for us: and in these respects great reason had St Paul to say, that *Godliness is profitable for all things.*

But further to evidence and recommend this point, I might propound certain peculiar advantages arising from piety, which have a very general influence upon our lives, and do afford unto them exceeding benefit: but this I must, in regard to the time and your patience, at present forbear.

# SERMON V.

## THE PROFITABLENESS OF GODLINESS.

1 TIM. IV. 8.

——*But godliness is profitable for all things.*

IN discoursing formerly upon these words, I did propound divers general considerations, serving to confirm and recommend this assertion of St Paul. I shall now insist upon some others more particular, which yet seem much conducible to the same purpose, declaring the vast utility of religion or piety.

I. We may consider, that religion doth prescribe the truest and best rules of action; thence enlightening our mind, and rectifying our practice in all matters and upon all occasions, so that, whatever is performed according to it is done well and wisely, with a comely grace in regard to others, with a cheerful satisfaction in our own mind, with the best assurance, that things are here capable of, to find happy success and beneficial fruit.

Of all things in the world there is nothing more generally profitable than light: by it we converse with the world, and have all things set before us; by it we truly and easily discern things in their right magnitude, shape, and colour; by it we guide our steps safely in prosecution of what is good, and shunning what is noxious; by it our spirits are comfortably warmed and cheered, our life consequently, our health, our vigour, and activity are preserved. The like benefits doth religion, which is the light of our soul, yield to it. Pious men are *Children of the light;* pious works are works of light *Shining before men.* God's word (or true religion) *is a lamp unto our feet, and a light unto our path;* enabling us to perceive things, and judge rightly of them; teaching us to walk straightly and surely, without erring or stumbling; qualifying us to embrace what is useful, and to avoid hurtful things; preserving our spiritual life, and disposing us to act well with a vigorous alacrity: without it a man is stark blind, and utterly benighted, gropeth in doubt, wandereth in mistake, trippeth upon all occasions, and often falleth into mischief. *The path of the just,* saith the Wise Man, *is as the shining light. The way of the wicked is as darkness, they know not at what they stumble. Righteousness keepeth him that is upright in the way; but wickedness overthroweth the sinner.*

Luke xvi. 8.
Eph. v. 8.
1 Thess. v. 5.
John xii. 36.
Matt. v. 16.
Eph. v. 11.
Psal. cxix. 105.

Isai. lix. 10.
Job v. 14.
Deut. xxviii. 29.
Prov. iv. 18, 19.

Prov. xiii. 6; xi. 3, 5.

Again: it is a fair ornament of a man, and a grand convenience both to himself, and to others with whom he converseth or dealeth, to act regularly, uniformly, and consistently; freeing a man's self from distraction and irresolution in his mind, from change and confusion in his proceedings; securing others from delusion and disappointment in their transactions with him. Even a bad rule constantly observed is therefore better than none[a]: order and perseverance in any way seemeth more convenient than roving and tossing about in uncertainties. But, secluding a regard to the precepts of religion, there can hardly be any sure or settled

[a] Viâ eunti aliquid extremum est; error immensus est.—Sen. Ep. xvi. [8.]

SERM. V.

James i. 8.

rule, which firmly can engage a man to, or effectually restrain a man from any thing.

There is scarce in nature any thing so wild, so untractable, so unintelligible, as a man who hath no bridle of conscience to guide or check him. A profane man is like a ship, without anchor to stay him, or rudder to steer him, or compass to guide him; so that he is tossed with any wind, and driven with any wave, none knoweth whither; whither bodily temper doth sway him, or passion doth hurry him, or interest doth pull him, or example leadeth him, or company inveigleth and haleth him, or humour transporteth him; whither any such variable and unaccountable causes determine him, or divers of them together distract him: whence he so rambleth and hovereth, that he can seldom himself tell what in any case he should do, nor can another guess it; so that you cannot at any time know where to find him, or how to deal with him: you cannot with reason ever rely upon him, so *Unstable he is in all his ways.* He is in effect a mere child, all humour and giddiness, somewhat worse than a beast, which, following the instinct of its nature, is constant and regular, and thence tractable; or at least so untractable, that no man will be deceived in meddling with him. Nothing therefore can be more unmanly than such a person, nothing can be more unpleasant than to have to do with him[b].

But a pious man, being steadily governed by conscience, and a regard to certain principles, doth both understand himself and is intelligible to others:

[b] Nihil est enim tam occupatum, tam multiforme, tot ac tam variis affectibus concisum atque laceratum, quam mala mens.—Quint. XII. 1. [7.]

he presently descrieth what in any case he is to do, and can render an account of his acting: you may know him clearly, and assuredly tell what he will do, and may therefore fully confide in him[c].

SERM. V.

What therefore law and government are to the public, things necessary to preserve the world in order, peace, and safety, (that men may know what to do, and distinguish what is their own,) that is piety to each man's private state, and to ordinary conversation: it freeth a man's own life from disorder and distraction; it prompteth men how to behave themselves toward one another with security and confidence.

This it doth by confining our practice within settled bounds: but this advantage appeareth greater, considering that the rules which it prescribeth are the best that can be. Such they must needs be, as proceeding from infallible wisdom and immense goodness; being indeed no other than laws, which the all-wise and most gracious Lord and Maker of the world, out of tender kindness to his subjects and creatures, with especial regard to our welfare, hath been pleased to enact and declare. What of old he said to the Israelites concerning their laws, may with greater advantage be applied to those which should regulate our lives: *And now, Israel, what doth the Lord thy God require of thee, but to fear the Lord thy God, to walk in all his ways, and to love him, and to serve the Lord thy God with all thy heart, and with all thy*

Deut. x. 12, 13.

---

[c] Ἔστι δ' ἡ τοιαύτη ὁμόνοια ἐν τοῖς ἐπιεικέσιν· οὗτοι γὰρ καὶ ἑαυτοῖς ὁμονοοῦσι καὶ ἀλλήλοις, ἐπὶ τῶν αὐτῶν ὄντες, ὡς εἰπεῖν· τῶν τοιούτων γὰρ μένει τὰ βουλήματα, καὶ οὐ μεταρρεῖ, ὥσπερ Εὔριπος.—Arist. Eth. IX. 6. [3.]

SERM. V.

soul; *to keep the commandments of the Lord, and his statutes, which I command thee this day for thy good?* (*For thy good;* that was the design of their being commanded; thereto the observance of them did tend.) And that commendation, which by the Levites in Nehemiah is given to that, doth more clearly and fully agree to the Christian (general and perfect) institution; *Thou camest down from mount Sinai, and spakest with them from heaven, and gavest them right judgments, and true laws, good statutes and commandments.* And, *The law*, saith the apostle Paul, *is holy; the commandment is holy, just, and good:* as such it is recommended to us by its Author, so we Christians are by many great arguments assured that it is, and that it is such even our natural reason dictateth; so (as to the chief instances thereof) the most wise and sober men always have acknowledged, so the general consent doth avow, and so even common experience doth attest. For, heartily to love and reverence the Maker of all things, who by every thing apparent before us demonstrateth himself incomprehensibly powerful, wise, and good, to be kind and charitable to our neighbours, to be just and faithful in our dealings, to be sober and modest in our minds, to be meek and gentle in our demeanours, to be staunch and temperate in our enjoyments, and the like principal rules of duty, are such, that the common reason of men and continual experience do approve them as hugely conducible to the public good of men, and to each man's private welfare. So notoriously beneficial they appear, that for the justification of them we might appeal even to the judgment and conscience

Neh. ix. 13.

Rom. vii. 12.

of those persons, who are most concerned to derogate from them. For hardly can any man be so senseless, or so lewd, as seriously to disapprove or condemn them, as inwardly to blame or slight those who truly act according to them. The will of men sometimes may be so depraved, that dissolute persons wantonly and heedlessly may scoff at and seem to disparage goodness; that good men by very bad men for doing well may be envied and hated: (their being so treated is commonly an argument of the goodness of their persons and of their ways:) but the understanding of men can hardly be so corrupted, that piety, charity, justice, temperance, meekness, can in good earnest considerately by any man be disallowed, or that persons apparently practising them can be despised; but rather, in spite of all contrary prejudice and disaffections, such things and such persons cannot but in judgment and heart be esteemed by all men. The lustre of them by a natural and necessary efficacy (like that of heaven's glorious light) dazzleth the sight and charmeth the spirits of all men living; the beauty of them irresistibly conquereth and commandeth in the apprehensions of men: the more they are observed, the more useful and needful they appear for the good of men; all the fruits which grow from the observance of them being to all men's taste very pleasant, to all men's experience very wholesome. Indeed, all the good, whereby common life is adorned, is sweetened, is rendered pleasant and desirable, doth spring thence; all the mischiefs which infest particular men, and which disturb the world, palpably do arise from the transgression or neglect thereof.

If we look on a person sticking to those rules,

SERM. V.

we shall perceive him to have a cheerful mind and composed passions, to be at peace within, and satisfied with himself; to live in comely order, in good repute, in fair correspondence, and firm concord with his neighbours. If we mark what preserveth the body sound and lusty, what keepeth the mind vigorous and brisk, what saveth and improveth the estate, what upholdeth the good name, what guardeth and graceth a man's whole life; it is nothing else but proceeding in our demeanour and dealings according to the honest and wise rules of piety. If we view a place where these commonly in good measure are observed, we shall discern, that peace and prosperity do flourish there; that all things proceed on sweetly and fairly; that men generally drive on conversation and commerce together contentedly, delightfully, advantageously, yielding friendly advice and aid mutually, striving to render one another happy; that few clamours or complaints are heard there, few contentions or stirs do appear, few disasters or tragedies do occur; that such a place hath indeed much of the face, much of the substance of paradise.

But if you mind a person who neglecteth them, you will find his mind galled with sore remorse, racked with anxious fears and doubts, agitated with storms of passion and lust, living in disorder and disgrace, jarring with others, and no less dissatisfied with himself. If you observe what doth impair the health, doth weaken and fret the mind, doth waste the estate, doth blemish the reputation, doth expose the whole life to danger and trouble; what is it but thwarting these good rules? If you consider a place where these are much neglected, it will appear like a wilderness of savage beasts, or a sty of foul swine, or a hell of cursed fiends; full of roaring and tearing, of factions and feuds, of distractions and confusions, of pitiful objects, of doleful moans, of tragical events. Men are there wallowing in filth, wildly revelling, bickering and squabbling, defaming, circumventing, disturbing and vexing one another; as if they affected nothing more than to render one another as miserable as they can. It is from lust and luxury, from ambition and avarice, from envy and spite, and the like dispositions, which religion chiefly doth interdict, that all such horrid mischiefs do spring.

In fine, the precepts of Religion are no other, than such as physicians would prescribe for the health of our bodies, as politicians would avow needful for the peace of the state, as Epicurean philosophers do recommend for the tranquillity of our mind, and pleasure of our lives; such as common reason dictateth, and daily trial sheweth conducible to our welfare in all respects: which consequently, were there no law exacting them of us, we should in wisdom choose to observe, and voluntarily impose on ourselves, confessing them to be fit matters of law, as most advantageous and requisite to the good (general and particular) of mankind. So that what Plutarch reporteth Solon to have said, that *He had so squared his laws to the citizens, that all of them might clearly perceive, that to observe them was more for their benefit and interest than to violate them*[d], is far more true concerning the divine laws.

[d] Plut. in Sol. [Καὶ τοὺς νόμους αὐτὸς οὕτως ἁρμόζεται τοῖς πολίταις, ὥστε πᾶσι τοῦ παρανομεῖν βέλτιον ἐπιδεῖξαι τὸ δικαιοπραγεῖν.—Opp. Tom. I. p. 322. Ed. Reisk.]

SERM. V.

II. We may consider more particularly, that piety yieldeth to the practiser all kind of interior content, peace, and joy; freeth him from all kinds of dissatisfaction, regret, and disquiet; which is an inestimably great advantage: for certainly the happiness and misery of men are wholly or chiefly seated and founded in the mind. If that is in a good state of health, rest, and cheerfulness, whatever the person's outward condition or circumstances be, he cannot be wretched: if that be distempered or disturbed, he cannot be happy. For what if a man seem very poor; if he be abundantly satisfied in his own possessions and enjoyments? What if he tasteth not the pleasures of sense; if he enjoyeth purer and sweeter delights of mind? What if tempests of fortune surround him; if his mind be calm and serene? What if he have few or no friends; if he yet be throughly in peace and amity with himself, and can delightfully converse with his own thoughts? What if men slight, censure, or revile him; if he doth value his own state, doth approve his own actions, doth acquit himself of blame in his own conscience? Such external contingencies can surely no more prejudice a man's real happiness, than winds blustering abroad can harm or trouble him that abideth in a good room within doors, than storms and fluctuations at sea can molest him who standeth firm upon the shore. On the other hand, the greatest affluence of seeming goods will avail nothing, if real content of mind be wanting. For what will the highest eminence of outward state import to him that is dejected in his own conceit? What if the world court and bless him, or if all people do admire and applaud him; if he be dis-

*The Profitableness of Godliness.* 211

pleased with, if he condemneth, if he despiseth himself? What if the weather look fair and bright without, if storms rage in his breast, if black clouds do overcast his soul? What if he do abound with friends, and enjoy peace abroad; if he find distraction at home, and is at cruel variance with himself? How can a man enjoy any satisfaction, or relish any pleasure, while sore remorse doth sting him, or solicitous doubts and fears do rack him[e]?

SERM. V.

Now that from the practice of religion, and from it alone, such inward content and pleasure do spring; that it only ministereth reason of content, and disposeth the mind to enjoy it; that it extirpateth the grounds and roots of discontent; that it is the only mother of true, sober alacrity and tranquillity of mind, will, upon considering things, be manifest.

There is no other thing here in this world that can yield any solid or stable content to our mind. For all present enjoyments are transient and evanid; and of any future thing, in this kingdom of change and contingency, there can be no assurance. There is nothing below large enough to fill our vast capacities, or to satiate our boundless desires, or to appease our squeamish delicacy. There is nothing whose sweetness we do not presently exhaust and suck dry; whereof thence we do not soon grow weary, quite loathing, or faintly liking it. There is not any thing which is not slippery and fleeting; so that we can for a long time hope to possess it,

Prov. xxvii. 24.

Prov. xxvii. 20.

[e] Εὐθυμίαν γὰρ καὶ χαρὰν οὐκ ἀρχῆς μέγεθος, οὐ χρημάτων πλῆθος, οὐ δυναστείας ὄγκος, οὐκ ἰσχὺς σώματος, οὐ πολυτέλεια τραπέζης, οὐχ ἱματίων κόσμος, οὐκ ἄλλο τι τῶν ἀνθρωπίνων ποιεῖν εἴωθεν, ἀλλ' ἢ κατέρθωμα μόνον πνευματικὸν, καὶ συνειδὸς ἀγαθόν.—Chrys. in Rom. Hom. I. [Opp. Tom. III. p. 9.]

SERM. V.

or for any time can enjoy it, without restless care in keeping it, and anxious fear of losing it. Nothing there is, in the pursuance, the custody, the defence and maintenance whereof we are not liable to disappointments, and crosses. Nothing consequently there is productive of any sound content to the fastidious, impatient, greedy, and restless heart of man. The greatest confluence of present, corporeal, secular things (of all the health, the riches, the dignity, the power, the friendships and dependencies, the wit, the learning and wisdom, the reputation and renown in this world) will not afford much of it: which yet is but an imaginary supposition; for in effect hardly do all such accommodations of life concur in any state. There is ever some dead fly in our box, which marreth our ointment; some adherent inconvenience, which soureth the gust of our enjoyments: there is always some good thing absent, which we do want or long for; some ill thing present, or in prospect, which we abhor, would avoid, do fear may come. If therefore we would find content, we must not seek it here; we must want it, or have it from another world: it must come hither from heaven, and thence only piety can fetch it down. This, instead of these unsatisfying, uncertain, and unstable things, supplieth us with goods adequate to our most outstretched wishes, infallibly sure, incessantly durable; *An indefectible treasure,* Θησαυρὸν ἀνέκλειπτον, *An incorruptible inheritance,* Κληρονομίαν ἄφθαρτον, *An unshakable kingdom,* Βασιλείαν ἀσάλευτον, a perfect and endless joy, capable to replenish the vastest heart: which he that hath a good title to, or a confident hope of, how can he be otherwise than extremely

Eccles. x. 1.

Luke xii. 33.
1 Pet. i. 4.
Heb. xii. 28.

pleased, than fully content? It assureth the favour and friendship of God, of him that is absolute Lord and disposer of all things: the which he that hath, and confideth in, what can he want or wish more? what can he fear? what can annoy or dismay him? what can hap to him worthy to be deemed evil or sad? What is poverty to him, for whom God is concerned to provide? What is disgrace to him, that hath the regard and approbation of God? What is danger to him, whom God continually protecteth? What can any distress work on him, whom God doth comfort, and will relieve? What is any thing to him, who is sensible that all things are purposely disposed to him by that wisdom which perfectly knoweth what is best; by that goodness which entirely loveth him? In fine, he that is conscious to himself of being well-affected in mind, and acting the best way, who is satisfied in the state of his soul, secure from God's displeasure, and hopeful of his favour, what can make any grievous impression on him? What other affections than such as are most grateful and pleasant can lodge in his soul? Joy and peace have natural seeds in such a mind, and necessarily must spring up there; in proportion, I mean, and according to the degrees of piety resident therein.

The Epicureans did conceit and boast, that having by their atheistical explications of natural effects, and common events here, discarded the belief and dread of religion, they had laid a strong foundation for tranquillity of mind, had driven away all the causes of grief and fear, so that nothing then remained troublesome or terrible unto us; and consequently, what, said they, could forbid, but that we should be entirely contented, glad and happy? —*Nos exæquat victoria cœlo*[f]; no God then surely could be more happy than we. But their attempt in many respects was vain and lame. They presumed of a victory which it is impossible to obtain: and supposing they had got it, their triumph would not have been so glorious, their success would not have been so great, as they pretended. For seeing no Epicurean discourse can baffle the potent arguments which persuade Religion; (those arguments, which the visible constitution of nature, the current tradition of all ages, the general consent of men, the pregnant attestations of history and experience concerning supernatural and miraculous events, do afford;) since the being and providence of God have proofs so clear and valid, that no subtlety of man can so far evade them, as not to be shaken with them, as wholly to be freed from doubt and suspicion of their truth; since there can be no means of evincing the negative part in those questions to be true or probable; it is impossible that any considering man, in this cause against religion, should suppose himself to have acquired an absolute and secure victory, or that he should reap substantial fruit of comfort thence. It cannot be that any man should enjoy any perfect quiet, without acting so as to get some good hope of avoiding those dreadful mischiefs, which religion threateneth to the transgressors of its precepts. Were there indeed but reason enough to stir, if not to stagger, an infidel; were it somewhat dubious whether, yea, were it great odds that there are not reserved any punishments for impiety, as indeed there is, if not the perfectest

[f] [Lucret. I. 80.]

assurance imaginable, yet vast advantage on the contrary side; were there but any small reason for a judgment to come, as there are apparently very many and great ones; had most men conspired in denying Providence, as ever generally they have consented in avowing it; were there a pretence of miracles for establishing the mortality and impunity of souls, as there have been numberless strongly testified by good witnesses and great events, to confirm the opposite doctrines; did most wise and sober men judge in favour of irreligion, as commonly they ever did and still do otherwise; yet wisdom would require that men should choose to be pious, since otherwise no man can be throughly secure. It is a wildness, not to dread the least possibility of incurring such horrible mischiefs: any hazard of such importance cannot but startle a man in his wits. To be in the least obnoxious to eternal torments, if men would think upon it as men, (that is, as rational and provident creatures,) could not but disturb them. And indeed so it is in experience; for whatever they say, or seem, all atheists and profane men are inwardly suspicious and fearful; they care not to die, and would gladly escape the trial of what shall follow death. But let us grant or imagine the Epicurean successful as he could wish in this enterprize of subduing religion: yet except therewith he can also trample down reason, new mould human nature, subjugate all natural appetites and passions, alter the state of things here, and transform the world, he will yet in the greatest part fail of his conceited advantages; very short he will fall of triumphing in a contented and quiet mind. That which accrueth thence will at most be no more than

SERM. V.

some negative content, or a partial indolency, arising from his being rescued from some particular cares and fears; which exceedeth not the tranquillity of a beast, or the stupidity of one that is out of his senses: that is all he can claim, which yet is more than he can ever compass. For he cannot be as a beast, or a mere sot, if he would: reason, reflecting on present evils, and boding others future, will afflict him; his own unsatiable desires, unavoidable fears, and untameable passions, will disquiet him. Were the other world quite out of his faith, or his thought, yet this world would yield trouble sufficient to render him void of any steady rest or solid joy. All men ever have, and ever will complain, that the burdens, crosses, satieties of this life, do much surpass the conveniences and comforts of it. So that, were no other to be expected or feared, this of itself would become grievous and nauseous[g]; we should soon have enough or too much of it, without a support and supply from otherwhere. In the largest affluence of things, in the deepest calm of our state, we are apt to nauseate, and are weary even of our prosperity itself; the which indeed commonly hath ingredients not only somewhat unsavoury, but very bitter and loathsome. We may add, that had those profane attempters quite banished religion, they with it must have driven away all the benefits and comforts of it: which, even supposing them but imaginary, are yet the greatest which common life doth need or can desire: with it they would send packing justice, fidelity, charity, sobriety, and all solid virtue, things which cannot

[g] Ut vera tibi similitudine id de quo queror exprimam, non tempestate vexor, sed nauseâ.—Sen. de Tranq. An. I. [12.]

firmly subsist without conscience: which being gone, human life would be the most disorderly, most unsafe, most wretched and contemptible thing that can be; nothing but insipid and flashy sensualities would be left behind to comfort a man with; and those hardly any man (by reason of competitions and contentions for them, nowise restrainable) could enjoy quietly or safely. It is therefore piety alone, which, by raising hopes of blessings and joys incomparably superior to any here that cannot be taken from us, can lay any ground of true content, of substantial and positive content; such as consisteth not only in removing the objects and causes of vexatious passions, but in employing the most pleasant affections (love, hope, joy) with a delightful complacence upon their proper and most noble objects. *The kingdom of God* (and that only, no other kingdom hath that privilege) *consisteth in righteousness* (first, then in) *peace and spiritual joy.* No philosopher, with truth and reason, can make that overture to us which our Lord doth; *Come unto me all ye that are weary and heavy laden, and ye shall find rest to your souls.* Out of Religion, there can be no aphorism pretended, like to that of the prophet, *Thou shalt keep him in perfect peace whose mind is stayed on thee.*

Rom. xiv. 17.

Matt. xi. 28.

Isai. xxvi. 3.

If indeed we distinctly survey all the grounds and sources of content, it will appear that Religion only can afford it.

Doth it result from a well governing and ordering our passions? Then it is plain, that only a pious man is capable thereof; for piety only can effect that: it alone, with the powerful aid of Divine grace, doth guide our passions by exact rules, doth set them upon worthy objects, doth temper and tune them in just harmony, doth seasonably curb and check them, doth rightly correct and reform them.

This no bare reason (which naturally is so dim and so feeble in man) can achieve: much less can unreasonableness do it, which is ever prevalent in irreligious persons. Their passions do ever run wildly and at random, in no good pace, within no good compass, toward the meanest and basest objects; whence they can have no rest or quiet in their minds[h]. As they are constantly offending, so will they ever be punishing themselves, with intestine broils and conflicts, with dissatisfactions and regrets[i]. Hence, *There is no peace to the wicked. He is like the troubled sea, which cannot rest.* God (as St Austin speaketh) *hath said it, and so it is, every inordinate mind is a punishment to itself*[k].

Doth content spring from a hearty approbation of, or a complacence in a man's own actions[l]; from reflection that he constantly doth act according to reason and wisdom, to justice and duty? Then can the pious man alone pretend to it, who knoweth that he walketh *Inoffensively toward God and man;* that he consulteth his own best interest and welfare; that assuredly no bad consequence can

[h] Mala mens—cum insidiatur, spe, curis, labore distringitur; et jam cum sceleris compos fuerit, solicitudine, pœnitentia, pœnarum omnium exspectatione torquetur.—Quint. XII. 1. [7.]

[i] Nec ulla major pœna nequitiæ est, quam quod sibi ac suis displicet.—Sen. Ep. XLII. [2.]

Τιμωρία ἀδικίας ἀκόλουθος.—Plat. de Leg. v. [728 c.]

[k] Jussisti enim, et sic est, ut pœna sua sibi sit omnis inordinatus animus.—Conf. [Lib. I. cap. xii. Opp. Tom. I. col. 77 A.]

[l] Nisi sapienti sua non placent: omnis stultitia laborat fastidio sui —Sen. Ep. IX. [19.]

*The Profitableness of Godliness.*

attend his unblameable behaviour; that most wise men have declared their approbation of his proceedings; that if he prove in his chief design mistaken, yet no mischief can thence befall him; yea, that he is not thereby quite disappointed, seeing even much present satisfaction and convenience do arise up to him from his practice.

Doth content grow from a sound and healthful constitution of soul? It is the pious man alone that hath that, whose mind is clear from distempers of vice and passion. The impious man is infirm, out of order, full of disease and pain, according to the prophet's description of him;—*The whole head is sick, and the whole heart faint: from the sole of the foot even unto the head there is no soundness in it; but wounds, and bruises, and putrifying sores.*

Doth content arise specially from good success in our attempts, or from prosperous events befalling us? Then it is the pious man who is most capable thereof: for he only is secure, that what seemeth good and prosperous is really such to him, as meant for his good by the Divine goodness, as tending thereto by the guidance of infallible wisdom. As he only hath ground to hope for success, because he confideth in God, because he dutifully seeketh God's help, because God is favourably disposed toward him, because God ordereth his steps, because God is by promise engaged to bless him, because he is conscious of intentions to render God thanks and praise for it, to employ his success to God's honour and service: so he only can be satisfied with the appearance of success, being able with assurance to say after St Paul, *We know*

SERM. V.

Isai. i. 5, 6.

Ps. xxxvii. 23.

Rom. viii. 28.

SERM. V.

*that to those who love God all things co-operate for good.*

Is security from danger, from trouble, from want, from all evil, a source or matter of content? It certainly doth attend the pious man; God being his especial protector, his comforter, his purveyor. *There shall no evil befall the just: There shall no plague come near his dwelling. God keepeth all his bones, not one of them is broken. He delivereth the righteous out of their troubles. The desire of the righteous shall be granted. There is no want to them that fear God.* So do the holy oracles assure us.

Prov. xii. 21.
Ps. xci. 10; xxxiv. 20, 17.
Prov. x. 24.
Ps. xxxiv. 9.

Doth contentedness spring from sufficiency, real or apprehended? This appertaineth peculiarly to the pious man: for, having God, the master of all, for his portion, he hath the richest estate that can be; he hath all that he can desire, he cannot but take himself to have enough. Hence *Godliness with contentedness* (Μετ' αὐταρκείας, *with sufficiency*) *is*, as St Paul saith, Πορισμὸς μέγας, *the great way of gaining.* He saith it not, as supposing godliness and contentedness to be separable; but rather, as implying godliness therefore to be most gainful, because sufficiency and contentedness do ever attend it. In fine, if that saying of Seneca be true, that, *If to any man the things he possesseth do not seem most ample, although he be master of the whole world, he is yet miserable*[m]; then assuredly the pious man only can be happy; for to him alone his possessions can seem the largest and best, such as there can be no possible accession to, or amend-

Ps. lxxiii. 26.
1 Tim. vi. 6.

---

[m] Si cui sua non videntur amplissima, licet totius mundi dominus sit, tamen miser est.—Sen. Ep. ix. [18.]

ment of. For nothing can be greater or better than God, in whom he hath a steadfast propriety, whose infinite power and wisdom are engaged to do him the utmost good that he is capable of. And further,

III. Seeing we have mentioned happiness, or the *Summum bonum*, the utmost scope of human desire, we do add, that piety doth surely confer it. Happiness, whatever it be, hath certainly an essential coherence with piety. These are reciprocal propositions, both of them infallibly true, He that is pious is happy; and, He that is happy is pious. No man doth undertake or prosecute any thing, which he doth not apprehend in some order or degree, conducing to that which all men under a confused notion regard and tend to, which they call happiness, the highest good, the chiefest desirable thing. But in their judgments about this thing, or the means of attaining it, as men dissent much; so of necessity most of them must be mistaken. Most, indeed, do aim and shoot at a mere shadow of profit, or at that which is very little considerable, and in comparison nothing at all; which little conduceth to the perfection of their nature, or the satisfaction of their desire. If they miss the mark, they are disappointed; if they hit it, they are no less, and in effect hit nothing. But whatever this grand matter is, in whatever it consisteth, however it be procured; be it the possession and fruition of some special choice goods, or an aggregation and affluence of all goods; piety surely is the main ingredient and principal cause thereof. All other goods without it are insignificant and unuseful thereto; and it cannot be wanting where piety

SERM. V.

is. Be a man never so rich, so powerful, so learned and knowing, so prosperous in his affairs, so honourable in the opinions and affections of men: yet nowise happy can he be, if he is not pious; being he wanteth the best goods, and is subject to the worst evils; being he wanteth the love and favour of God, he wanteth peace and satisfaction of conscience, he wanteth a right enjoyment of present things, he wanteth security concerning his final welfare. Be he never so poor, so low in the eyes of men, so forlorn and destitute of worldly conveniences; yet if he be pious, he cannot be wretched: for he hath an interest in goods incomparably most precious, and is safe from all considerable evils; he hath a free resort to the inexhaustible fountain of all happiness, he hath a right to immense and endless felicity, the which eminently containeth all the goods we are capable of; he is possessed thereof in hope and certain reversion, there is but a moment to pass before his complete fruition of it. The want of all other petty things no more can maim the integrity of his felicity, than cutting the hair, or paring the nails, do mutilate a man: all other things are but superfluities or excrescences in regard to the constitution of happiness. Whatever happeneth, that will assuredly be true, which is so much inculcated in holy scripture. *Blessed is every one that feareth the Lord, that walketh in his ways; happy shall he be, and it shall be well with him.* Piety is indeed fraught with beatitudes, every part thereof yieldeth peculiar blessedness. To the love of God, to charity toward our neighbour, to purity of heart, to meekness, to humility, to patience, to mercifulness, to peaceableness, beatitude is ascribed

Ps. cxxviii. 1, 2; cxii. 1.

Matt. v. 3—12.

by our Lord, the great Judge and dispenser of it. Each religious performance hath happy fruits growing from it, and blissful rewards assigned thereto. All pious dispositions are fountains of pleasant streams, which by their confluence do make up a full sea of felicity.

IV. It is a peculiar advantage of piety, that it furnisheth employment fit for us, worthy of us, hugely grateful and highly beneficial to us. Man is a very busy and active creature, which cannot live and do nothing, whose thoughts are in restless motion, whose desires are ever stretching at somewhat, who perpetually will be working either good or evil to himself: wherefore greatly profitable must that thing be, which determineth him to act well, to spend his care and pain on that which is truly advantageous to him; and that is Religion only. It alone fasteneth our thoughts, affections, and endeavours upon occupations worthy the dignity of our nature, suiting the excellency of our natural capacities and endowments, tending to the perfection and advancement of our reason, to the enriching and ennobling of our souls. Secluding that, we have nothing in the world to study, to affect, to pursue, not very mean and below us, not very base and misbecoming us, as men of reason and judgment. What have we to do but to eat, drink, like horses or like swine; but to sport and play, like children or apes; but to bicker and scuffle about trifles and impertinences, like idiots? what, but to scrape or scramble for useless pelf; to hunt after empty shows and shadows of honour, or the vain fancies and dreams of men? what, but to wallow or bask in sordid pleasures, the which

SERM. V.

soon degenerate into remorse and bitterness? To which sort of employments were a man confined, what a pitiful thing would he be, and how inconsiderable were his life! Were a man designed only, like a fly, to buz about here for a time, sucking in the air, and licking the dew, then soon to vanish back into nothing, or to be transformed into worms; how sorry and despicable a thing were he! And such without Religion we should be. But it supplieth us with business of a most worthy nature and lofty importance; it setteth us upon doing things great and noble as can be; it engageth us to free our minds from all fond conceits, and cleanse our hearts from all corrupt affections; to curb our brutish appetites, to tame our wild passions, to correct our perverse inclinations, to conform the dispositions of our soul and the actions of our life to the eternal laws of righteousness and goodness: it putteth us upon the imitation of God, and aiming at the resemblance of his perfections; upon obtaining a friendship and maintaining a correspondence with the High and Holy One; upon fitting our minds for conversation and society with the wisest and purest spirits above; upon providing for an immortal state, upon the acquist of joy and glory everlasting. It employeth us in the divinest actions, of promoting virtue, of performing beneficence, of serving the public, and doing good to all: the being exercised in which things doth indeed render a man highly considerable, and his life excellently valuable.

It is an employment most proper to us as reasonable men. For what more proper entertainments can our mind have, than to be purifying and beautifying itself, to be keeping itself and its subordinate faculties in order, to be attending upon the management of thoughts, of passions, of words, of actions depending upon its governance?

It is an employment most beneficial to us: in pursuing which we greatly better ourselves, and meliorate our condition; we benefit and oblige others; we procure sound reputation and steady friendships; we decline many irksome mischiefs and annoyances; *We do* not, like those in the prophet, *spend our labour for that which satisfieth not, nor spend our money for that which is not bread:* for both temporal prosperity and eternal felicity are the wages of the labour which we take herein. [Isai. lv. 2.]

It is an employment most constant, never allowing sloth or listlessness to creep in, incessantly busying all our faculties with earnest contention; according to that profession of St Paul, declaring the nature thereof, *Herein always do I exercise myself, to have a conscience void of offence toward God and toward man.* Whence it is called a *Fight*, and a *Race*, implying the continual earnestness of attention and activity, which is to be spent thereon. [Acts xxiv. 16.] [1 Tim. vi. 12. Heb. xii. 1.]

It is withal a sweet and grateful business: for it is a pious man's character, that *He delighteth greatly in God's commandments;* that *The commandments are not grievous to him;* that it is *His meat and drink to do God's will;* that *God's words* (or precepts) *are sweeter than honey to his taste;* that *The ways of religious wisdom are ways of pleasantness, and all her paths are peace.* Whereas all other employments are wearisome, and soon become loathsome; this, the further we proceed in [Ps. cxii. 1.] [1 John v. 3.] [John iv. 34.] [Ps. cxix. 103.] [Prov. iii. 17.]

SERM.
V.

it, the more pleasant and satisfactory it groweth[n]. There is perpetual matter of victory over bad inclinations pestering us within, and strong temptations assailing us without: which to combat hath much delight: to master, breedeth unexpressible content. The sense also of God's love, the influences of his grace and comfort communicated in the performances of devotion and all duty, the satisfaction of good conscience, the assured hope of reward, the foretastes of future bliss, do season and sweeten all the labours taken, and all the difficulties undergone therein.

In fine, the bare light of nature hath discerned, that were it not for such matters as these to spend a man's care and pains upon, this would be a lamentable world to live in. There was, for instance, an emperor great and mighty as ever did wield sceptre upon earth, whose excellent virtue, coupled with wisdom, (inferior, perhaps, to none that any man ever without special inspiration hath been endowed with,) did qualify him with most advantage to examine and rightly to judge of things here; who, notwithstanding all the conveniences which his royal estate and well settled prosperity might afford, (the which surely he had fully tasted and tried,) did yet thus express his thoughts: Τί μοι ζῆν ἐν κόσμῳ κενῷ Θεῶν, ἢ προνοίας κενῷ; *What doth it concern me to live in a world void of God, or void of Providence*[o]*?* To govern the greatest empire that ever was, in the deepest

[n] Non potest cuiquam semper idem placere, nisi rectum.—Sen. Ep. xx. [5.]

Dedit enim hoc providentia hominibus munus, ut honesta magis juvarent.—Quint. I. 12. [19.]

[o] M. Ant. II. § 11. Cf. VI. § 10.

calm; to enjoy the largest affluences of wealth, of splendour, of respect, of pleasure; to be loved, to be dreaded, to be served, to be adored by so many nations; to have the whole civil word obsequious to his will and nod; all these things seemed vain and idle, not worthy of a man's regard, affection, or choice, in case there were no God to worship, no providence to observe, no piety to be exercised. So little worth the while, common sense hath adjudged it to live without religion.

V. It is a considerable benefit of piety, that it affordeth the best friendships and sweetest society. Man is framed for society, and cannot live well without it[p]; many of his faculties would be useless, many of his appetites would rest unsatisfied in solitude. To have a friend wise and able, honest and good, unto whom upon all occasions we may have recourse for advice, for assistance, for consolation, is a great convenience of life[q]: and this benefit we owe to religion, which supplieth us with various friendships of the best kind, most beneficial and most sweet unto us.

It maketh God our friend, a friend infinitely better than all friends, most affectionate and kind, most faithful and sure, most able, most willing, and ever most ready to perform all friendly offices, to yield advice in all our doubts, succour in all our needs, comfort in all our troubles, satisfaction to all our desires. Unto him it ministereth a free address upon all occasions; with him it alloweth us

Prov. xii. 2.
Ps. xxxiv. 15; xxxiii.

[p] Nullius boni sino socio jucunda possessio est.—Sen. Ep. vi. [4.]

[q] Nam ut aliarum rerum nobis innata dulcedo est, sic amicitiæ.—Id. Ep. ix. [14.]

continually a most sweet and pleasant intercourse. The pious man hath always the all-wise God to counsel him, to guide his actions and order his steps; he hath the Almighty to protect, support, and relieve him; he hath the immense goodness to commiserate and comfort him; unto him he is not only encouraged, but obliged to resort in need: upon him he may, he ought to discharge all his cares and burdens.

It consequently doth engage all creatures in the world to be our friends, or instruments of good to us, according to their several capacities, by the direction and disposal of God. All the servants of our great Friend will, in compliance to him, be serviceable to us, *Thou shalt be in league with the stones of the field, and the beasts of the field shall be at peace with thee:* so Job's friend promiseth him upon condition of piety. And God himself confirmeth that promise; *In that day,* saith he in the prophet, *will I make a covenant for them with the beasts of the field, and with the fowls of heaven, and with the creeping things of the ground.* And again, *When thou passest through the waters, I will be with thee; and through the rivers, they shall not overflow thee: when thou walkest through the fire, thou shalt not be burnt; neither shall the flame kindle upon thee.* And, *The sun shall not smite thee by day, nor the moon by night. Thou shalt tread upon the lion and adder, the young lion and the dragon shalt thou trample under foot. They shall take up scorpions; and if they drink any deadly thing, it shall not hurt them:* (so our Lord promised to his disciples.) Not only the heavens shall dispense their kindly influences, and the earth yield her plentiful stores, and all the elements discharge their natural and ordinary good offices; nor only the tame and sociable creatures shall upon this condition faithfully serve us; but even the most wild, most fierce, most ravenous, most venomous creatures shall, if there be need, prove friendly and helpful, or at least harmless to us: as were the ravens to Elias, the lions to Daniel, the viper to St Paul, the fire to the three children.

SERM. V.

1 Kings xvii. 6.

But especially piety doth procure the friendship of the good angels, that puissant host of glorious and happy spirits: they all do tenderly love the pious person; they are ever ready to serve and do him good, to protect him from danger, to aid him in his undertakings, to rescue him from mischiefs. What an honour, what a blessing is this, to have such an innumerable company of noble friends (the courtiers and favourites of heaven) deeply concerned and constantly vigilant for our welfare!

Ps. xxxiv. 7; xci. 11. Heb. i. 14.

It also engageth the blessed saints in glory, *The spirits of just men perfected, the church of the first-born*, to bear dearest affection to us, to further our prosperity with their good wishes and earnest prayers, mightily prevalent with God.

Heb. xii. 23.

It rendereth all sorts of men our friends. To good men it uniteth us in holy communion; the communion of brotherly charity and hearty goodwill, attended with all the good offices they are able to perform: to other men it reconcileth and endeareth us; for that innocent and inoffensive, courteous and benign, charitable and beneficent demeanour, (such as piety doth require and produce,) are apt to conciliate respect and affection from the worst men.

SERM. V.

For, *Vincit malos pertinax bonitas*[r]; men hardly can persist enemies to him whom they perceive to be their friend: and such the pious man in disposition of mind, and in effect when occasion serveth, is toward all men[s]; being sensible of his obligation to love all men, and, *As he hath opportunity, to do good to all men.* It assureth and more strictly endeareth our friends to us. For, as it maketh us hearty, faithful, constant friends to others; so it reciprocally tieth others to us in the like sincerity and fastness of good-will[t].

Gal. vi. 10.

Prov. xvi. 7.

It reconcileth enemies. For, *When a man's ways do please the Lord, he maketh his enemies to be at peace with him.* It hath a natural efficacy to that purpose, and Divine blessing promoteth it.

By it all conversation becometh tolerable, grateful, and useful. For a pious man is not easily disturbed with any crossness or perverseness, any infirmity or impertinency of those he converseth with: he can bear the weaknesses and the failings of his company; he can by wholesome reflections upon all occurrences advantage and please himself[u].

In fine, piety rendereth a man a true friend and a good companion to himself[x]; satisfied in himself,

---

[r] Sen. de Benef. VII. [31.]

[s] Qui sibi amicus est, scito hunc amicum omnibus esse.—Sen. Ep. VI. [6.]

[t] Ὁμοίως δὲ καὶ ἡδεῖς· καὶ γὰρ ἁπλῶς οἱ ἀγαθοὶ ἡδεῖς καὶ ἀλλήλοις.— Arist. Eth. VIII. [3. 6.]

[u] Συνδιάγειν τε ὁ τοιοῦτος ἑαυτῷ βούλεται· ἡδέως γὰρ αὐτὸ ποιεῖ· τῶν τε γὰρ πεπραγμένων ἐπιτερπεῖς αἱ μνῆμαι, καὶ τῶν μελλόντων ἐλπίδες ἀγαθαί.—Id. Eth. IX. [4. 5.]

[x] Quæris quid profecerim? amicus esse mihi cœpi.—Sen. Ep. VI. [6.]

able to converse freely and pleasantly with his own thoughts. It is for the want of pious inclinations and dispositions, that solitude (a thing which sometimes cannot be avoided, which often should be embraced) is to most men so irksome and tedious, that men do carefully shun themselves, and fly from their own thoughts; that they decline all converse with their own souls, and hardly dare look upon their own hearts and consciences: whence they become aliens from home, wholly unacquainted with themselves, most ignorant of their own nearest concernments, no faithful friends or pleasant companions to themselves; so for refuge and ease they unseasonably run into idle or lewd conversation, where they disorder and defile themselves[y]. But the pious man is, like Scipio, *Never less alone, than when alone*[z]: his solitude and retirement is not only tolerable, but commonly the most grateful and fruitful part of his life: he can ever with much pleasure, and more advantage, converse with himself[a]; digesting and marshalling his

[y] Nemo est, cui non satius sit cum quolibet esse, quam secum.—Sen. Ep. [xxiv. 7.]

Ἔνιοι τὸν ἴδιον βίον, ὡς ἀτερπέστατον θέαμα, προσιδεῖν οὐχ ὑπομένουσιν, &c.—Plut. περὶ Πολυπρ. Opp. Tom. ii. p. 916. Ed. Steph.

Ζητοῦσιν οἱ μοχθηροὶ μεθ' ὧν συνδιημερεύσουσι, ἑαυτοὺς δὲ φεύγουσιν.—Arist. Eth. ix. 4. [9.]

[z] [Scipionem—dicere solitum, scripsit Cato nunquam se—minus solum quam cum solus esset.—Cic. de Off. iii. 1. 1. Rep. i. 17. 27.]

[a] Acquiescit sibi, cogitationibus suis traditus.—Sen. Ep. ix. [13.]

Sapiens autem nunquam solus esse potest: habet secum omnes qui sunt, qui unquam fuerunt boni, et animum liberum quocunque vult transfert. Quod corpore non potest, cogitatione complectitur. Et si hominum inopia fuerit, loquitur cum Deo. Nunquam minus

thoughts, his affections, his purposes into good order; searching and discussing his heart, reflecting on his past ways, enforcing his former good resolutions, and framing new ones; inquiring after edifying truths; stretching his meditations toward the best and sublimest objects, raising his hopes and warming his affections towards spiritual and heavenly things; asking himself pertinent questions, and resolving incident doubts concerning his practice: in fine, conversing with his best friend in devotion; with admiration and love contemplating the divine perfections displayed in the works of nature, of providence, of grace; praising God for his excellent benefits and mercies; confessing his defects and offences; deprecating wrath and imploring pardon, with grace and ability to amend; praying for the supply of all his wants. All which performances yield both unconceivable benefit and unexpressible comfort. So that solitude (that which is to common nature so offensive, to corrupt nature so abominable) is to the pious man extremely commodious and comfortable: which is a great advantage peculiar to piety, and the last which I shall mention.

So many, and many more than I can express, vastly great and precious advantages do accrue from piety; so that well may we conclude with St Paul, that *Godliness is profitable for all things.*

It remaineth that, if we be wise, we should, if we yet have it not ingraffed in us, labour to ac-

solus erit, quam cum solus fuerit.—Hier. adv. Jovin. Lib. I. [Opp. Tom. IV. pars ii. col. 190.]

quire it; if we have it, that we should endeavour to improve it, by constant exercise, to the praise of God, the good of our neighbour, and our own comfort. Which that we may effectually perform, Almighty God in mercy vouchsafe, by his grace, through Jesus Christ our Lord; to whom for ever be all glory and praise. Amen.

# SERMON VI.[a]

## THE REWARD OF HONOURING GOD.

---

1 Sam. II. 30.

*For them that honour me I will honour.*

SERM. VI.

THE words are in the strictest sense the word of God, uttered immediately by God himself; and may thence command from us an especial attention and regard. The history of that which occasioned them is, I presume, well known; neither shall I make any descant or reflection thereon; but take the words separately, as a proposition of itself, affording a complete instruction and ample matter of discourse. And as such, they plainly imply two things: a duty required of us to honour God; and a reward proffered to us, upon performance of that duty, being honoured by God. It is natural for us, before we are willing to undertake any work, to consider the reward or benefit accruing from it; and it is necessary, before we can perform any duty, to understand the nature thereof. To this our method of action I shall suit the method of my discourse; first endeavouring to estimate the reward, then to explain the duty. Afterward I mean to shew briefly why in reason the duty is enjoined; how in effect the reward is conferred.

I. The reward may be considered either abso-

[a Ad Aulam. Aug. 1670. MS.]

lutely, (as what it is in itself;) or relatively, (as to its rise, and whence it comes).

1 For itself, it is honour; a thing, if valued according to the rate it bears in the common market, of highest price among all the objects of human desire; the chief reward which the greatest actions and which the best actions do pretend unto, or are capable of; that which usually bears most sway in the hearts, and hath strongest influence upon the lives of men; the desire of obtaining and maintaining which doth commonly overbear other most potent inclinations. The love of pleasure stoops thereto: for men, to get or keep reputation, will decline the most pleasant enjoyments, will embrace the hardest pains. Yea, it often prevails over the love of life itself, which men do not only frequently expose to danger, but sometimes devote to certain loss, for its sake\*. If we observe what is done in the world, we may discern it to be the source of most undertakings therein: that it not only moveth the wheels of public action, (that not only for it great princes contend, great armies march, great battles are fought;) but that from it most private business derives its life and vigour:

---

\* Even the sex which naturally is so tender and timorous hath afforded many instances, that life may be less dear than honour. What Cicero[1] somewhere professes to be his may seem to be the general sense of men, that nothing in life is desirable without it. MS.

[1] Denique, cum omnia semper ad dignitatem retulissem, nec sine ea quidquam expetendum esse homini in vita putassem, mortem, quam etiam virgines Athenis, regis, opinor, Erecthei filiæ, pro patria contempsisse dicuntur, ego, vir consularis, tantis rebus gestis, timerem?—Orat. pro Sext. [xxi. 48.]

SERM. VI.

that for honour especially the soldier undergoes hardship, toil, and hazard; the scholar plods and beats his brains; the merchant runs about so busily, and adventures so far; yea, that for its sake the meanest labourer and artificer doth spend his sweat, and stretch his sinews\*. The principal drift of all this care and industry (the great reason of all this scuffling for power, this searching for knowledge, this scraping and scrambling for wealth)

---

\* Riches themselves (procuring which may seem the immediate cause of all that care and industry employed in several ways) men chiefly (as Aristotle well observes) do seek for honour's sake that they may live in reputation; for necessity is served with a little, pleasure may be satisfied from a competence, abundance is required only to support honour; take away credit from wealth, there will be no such scraping and scrambling for it; there was not so in Rome, when poor Fabricius, Curius and Quintius were capable of being consuls and dictators there: nor in Sparta for many hundred years, where the citizens (as Plutarch tells us) enjoyed much of ease and leisure to attend nobler employments, because riches were not there at all invidious, or honourable. Yea, we daily see men to contemn or neglect riches, who can hope to procure respect some other way: by getting knowledge, or any other creditable endowments: the care and pains men expend upon which do commonly grow from this same root: for take away esteem from knowledge, curiosity will soon languish and study expire. This is the reason Plato assigns, why the sciences did not flourish in Greece, in his times, because no city did then honour them; and why in the ancienter times of the Roman state, picture, music, poetry, with other ingenious arts, were altogether unknown, Cicero could not give a better account, than because honour, which feedeth arts, and glory, which kindleth studies, were wanting. MS.

## The Reward of honouring God. 237

doth seem to be, that men would live in some credit, would raise themselves above contempt[b].

SERM. VI.

In such request, of such force, doth honour appear to be. If we examine why, we may find more than mere fashion (or mutual imitation and consent) to ground the experiment upon. There is one obvious reason why no mean regard should be had thereto: its great convenience and usefulness: for that a man cannot himself live safely, quietly, or pleasantly, without some competent measure thereof; cannot well serve the public, perform offices of duty to his relations, of kindness to his friends, of charity to his neighbours, but under its protection, and with its aid: it being an engine very requisite for the managing any business, for the compassing any design, at least sweetly and smoothly; it procuring to us many furtherances in our proceedings, removing divers obstacles out of our way, guarding a man's person from offences, adding weight to his words, putting an edge upon his endeavours: for every one allows a favourable ear to his discourse, lends an assisting hand to his attempts, grants a ready credence to his testimony,

[b] Ἴδοις δ' ἂν καὶ τῶν ἰδιωτῶν τοὺς ἐπιεικεστάτους ὑπὲρ ἄλλου μὲν οὐδενὸς ἂν τὸ ζῆν ἀντικαταλλαξαμένους, ὑπὲρ δὲ τοῦ τυχεῖν καλῆς δόξης, ἀποθνήσκειν ἐθέλοντας.—Isocr. Orat. ad Philip. [§ 135.]

Mors tum æquissimo animo oppetitur, cum suis se laudibus vita occidens consolari potest.—Cic. Tusc. Quæst. [I. 45. 109.]

Laudis avidi pecuniæ liberales erant, gloriam ingentem divitias honestas volebant; hanc ardentissimo dilexerunt, propter hanc vivere voluerunt, pro hac et mori non dubitaverunt. Cæteras cupiditates hujus unius ingenti cupiditate presserunt.—Aug. de Civ. Dei, v. 12. [Opp. Tom. VII. col. 126 F.]

Αἱ γὰρ δυναστεῖαι καὶ ὁ πλοῦτος διὰ τὴν τιμήν ἐστιν αἱρετά.—Arist. Eth. IV. 3. [18.]

Honos alit artes, omnesque incenduntur ad studia gloria, &c.—Cic. Tusc. Quæst. I. [2. 4.]

and makes a fair construction of his doings, whom he esteems and respects\*. So is honour plainly valuable among the *Bona utilia*, as no small accommodation of life; and as such, reason approves it to our judgment<sup>c</sup>.

But, searching further, we shall find the appetite of honour to have a deeper ground, and that it is rooted even in our nature itself. For we may descry it budding forth in men's first infancy, (before the use of reason or speech;) even little children being ambitious to be made much of<sup>d</sup>, maintaining

---

<sup>c</sup> Vide Hier. [Paulin.] Ep. ad Celant.

Conscientia tibi, fama proximo tuo. Qui fidens conscientiæ suæ negligit famam suam, crudelis est.—Aug. [Serm. CCCLV. Opp. Tom. v. col. 1380 B.]

Galen. ['Ο γάρ τοι τῶν πολλῶν ἀνθρώπων ἔπαινος εἰς μὲν χρείας τινὰς ἐπιτήδειον ὄργανον ἐνίοτε γίγνεται.—De Method. Med. VII. 1. Opp. Tom. x. p. 457. Ed. Kühn.]

Nec vero negligenda fama est; nec mediocre telum ad res gerendas existimare oportet benevolentiam civium.—Cic. de Amic. [XVII. 61.]

Vide Chrys. Tom. VI. Orat. XVII.

<sup>d</sup> Vidi ego et expertus sum zelantem parvulum, &c.—Aug. [Conf. I. 7. Opp. Tom. I. col. 73 D.]

---

\* What hath been said of war (*Fama constant bella*) may be said of all business, the success thereof much depends upon credit; 'tis not he that is really stronger, or wiser, or better, but he that is so reputed, who commonly in the conduct of affairs hath the advantage. St Augustine observing this, how necessary reputation is, that a man may be able to do any good, or considerably to benefit others, says this: Seeing our fame is as necessary in respect to our neighbour, as our conscience is for ourselves, he, that confiding in his conscience, doth neglect his reputation, is uncharitable and cruel. MS.

*The Reward of honouring God.* 239

among themselves petty emulations and competitions, as it were about punctilios of honour. We may observe it growing with age, waxing bigger and stronger together with the increase of wit and knowledge, of civil culture and experience; that the maturest age doth most resent and relish it; that it prevails most in civilized nations; that men of the best parts, of the highest improvements, of the weightiest employments, do most zealously affect it and stand upon it; that they who most struggle with it do most feel its might, how difficult it is to resist and restrain it, how impossible it is to stifle or extinguish it. For the philosopher with all his reasons and considerations cannot dispute it down, or persuade it away; the anchoret cannot with all his austerities starve it, or by his retirement shun it: no affliction, no poverty, no wretchedness of condition, can totally suppress it. It is a spirit that not only haunts our courts and palaces, but frequents our schools and cloisters, yea, creeps into cottages, into hospitals, into prisons, and even dogs men into deserts and solitudes[e]; so close it sticks to our nature. Plato saith, it is the last coat which a wise man doth put off. But I question whether he could shew us that wise man who had done it, or could tell us where he dwelt, except perhaps in his own Utopian republic. For they who most pretend to have done it (who in their discourse most vilify honour; who talk like Chrysippus[f], that a wise man for reputation sake will not so much as stretch out

SERM. VI.

[e] In solitudine cito subrepit superbia.—Hier. [ad Rusticum Mon. Ep. xcv. Opp. Tom. iv. p. ii. p. 773.]

[f] Cic. de Fin. [iii. 17.] [De bona autem fama . . . . Chrysippus et Diogenes, detracta utilitate, ne digitum quidem, ejus causa, porrigendum esse dicebant.]

SERM. VI.

his finger; or like Seneca[g], that we should do every thing purely for conscience sake, without any regard to men's opinion; who make harangues and write volumes against glory) do yet appear by their practice, sometimes by so doing, to aim at it: even as men do usually complain of and eagerly quarrel with that which they most affect and woo. Chrysippus wrote, as we are told, above 700 books[h], most of them concerning logical quirks, and such as one can hardly imagine what other drift he could have in composing them, besides ostentation of his subtilty and sharpness of wit. Seneca, if history do not wrong him, and the face of his actions do not misrepresent him, was not in his heart exempt from a spice of ambition. Yea, that excellent emperor M. Aurelius, who would often speak like a Stoic, could not but commonly act like a man, more by his practice commending honour, than he disparaged it in his words. For story represents him very careful and jealous of his credit, very diligent to preserve it and to repair it[i]. Tertullian calls such philosophers *Negotiatores famæ*[k], *Merchants for fame*: and it is perchance some part of their cunning in their trade, which makes them strive to beat down

[g] Nihil opinionis causa, omnia conscientiæ faciam.—De Vit. B. [xx. 3.]

Nihil sit illi cum ambitione famaque: sibi placeat. Hoc ante omnia sibi quisque persuadeat, Me justum esse gratis oportet—Id. Ep. cxiii. [24.]

Id. de Ira, iii. [41. 2.]

[h] Diog. Laert. [in Chrys. vii. 7. 3. Τὸν ἀριθμὸν γὰρ ὑπὲρ πέντε καὶ ἑπτακόσιά ἐστιν.]

[i] Erat famæ suæ curiosissimus.

Male loquentium dictis, vel literis vel sermone respondebat.—Capitolinus [Hist. Aug. Script. p. 31 A., p. 32 A.]

[k] Tertull. Apol. [cap. xlvi. Opp. p. 36 c.]

the price of this commodity, that they may more easily engross it to themselves. However, experience proves that such words are but words, (words spoken out of affectation and pretence, rather than in good earnest and according to truth:) that endeavours to banish or to extirpate this desire are but fond and fruitless attempts. The reason why is clear: for it is as if one should dispute against eating and drinking, or should labour to free himself from hunger and thirst: the appetite of honour being indeed, as that of food, innate unto us, so as not to be quenched or smothered, except by some violent distemper or indisposition of mind[1]; even by the wise Author of our nature originally implanted therein for very good ends and uses, respecting both the private and public benefit of men; as an engagement to virtue, and a restraint from vice; as an excitement of industry, an incentive of courage, a support of constancy in the prosecution of worthy enterprises; as a serviceable instrument for the constitution, conservation, and improvement of human society*. For did not some

[1] Sed nimirum, ut quidam, morbo aliquo et sensus stupore, suavitatem cibi non sentiunt: sic libidinosi, avari, facinorosi, veræ laudis gustum non habent.—Cic. Philipp. [II. 45.]

* For as men are made naturally to approve, and commend acts of justice, of goodness, of sobriety; to esteem and respect persons, whom they observe disposed to perform them; so by a desire to obtain such approbation and esteem are men prompted and instigated to perform such acts, to acquire such dispositions. As general respect doth commonly attend those who are useful to society, or capable of being so, (by their endowments of mind, or other accessory enablements: by their skilfulness, their courage, their

love of honour glow in men's breasts, were that noble spark quite extinct, few men probably would study for honourable qualities, or perform laudable deeds; there would be nothing to keep some men within bounds of modesty and decency, to deter them from doing odious and ugly things; men, not caring what

---

wealth,) so by the love of such respect men are rendered industrious in procuring to themselves such qualities and capacities. And because honour is nowhere to be obtained, but in society; and it is chiefly got by actions beneficial thereto, by an inclination thereto men are driven to embrace society, and induced to endeavour its welfare. So that in effect were this instinct wanting, few would do laudable deeds, or study for honourable qualities; most men would perhaps, if not altogether shun society, yet at least decline the cares and burdens necessary toward the promoting its good: for the sustaining which the chief recompense is usually this of honour; common life would want most of its ornaments, much of its convenience; a barbarous sloth, a brutish stupidity would overspread the world; there being nothing to inflame men's desire of worthy things, nothing to whet their courage in prosecution of them; nothing to support their constancy in the encountering difficulties and dangers incident to gallant enterprises, nothing of that kind (nothing noble or brave) would be achieved or attempted. There would be then no such virtue as modesty, to keep men within bounds of honesty and decency, to restrain men from doing odious and ugly things. The best examples would become idle shows, looked upon unconcernedly without any influence or effect. The judgments of wise and good men about what is just and fit to be done would pass for empty speculations; men not caring what others think of them, would not regard what they do themselves; that would happen in extremity, which experience shews us to be now in degree, that the most shameless men do the most shameful things. MS.

others thought of them, would not regard what they did themselves[m]; a barbarous sloth or brutish stupidity would overspread the world, withdrawing from common life most of its ornaments, much of its convenience; men generally would, if not altogether, shun society, yet at least decline the cares and burdens requisite to the promoting its welfare, for the sustaining which usually the chief encouragement, the main recompense, is this of honour. That men therefore have so tender and delicate a sense of their reputation (so that touching it is like pricking a nerve, as soon felt, and as smartly offensive) is an excellent provision in nature; in regard whereto honour may pass among the *Bona naturalia*, as a good necessary for the satisfaction of nature, and for securing the accomplishment of its best designs.

A moderate regard to honour is also commendable as an instance of humanity or good-will to men, yea, as an argument of humility, or a sober conceit of ourselves. For to desire another man's esteem, and consequently his love, (which in some kind or degree is an inseparable companion of esteem,) doth imply somewhat of reciprocal esteem and affection toward him; and to prize the judgment of other men concerning us, doth signify that we are not oversatisfied with our own.

We might for its further commendation allege the authority of the more cool and candid sort of philosophers, (such as grounded their judgment of things upon notions agreeable to common sense and experience; who adapted their rules of prac-

---

[m] Αἰδὼς δ' οἰχομένη, πάντων γενέτειρα κακίστων.—Greg. Naz. [Carm. ad Olymp. Opp. Tom. II. p. 1066.]

tice to the nature of man, such as they found it in the world, not such as they framed it in their own fancies,) who have ranked honour among the principal of things desirable, and adorned it with fairest elogies; terming it a divine thing[n], the best of exterior goods[o], the most honest fruit and most ample reward of true virtue; adjudging, that to neglect the opinions of men (especially of persons worthy and laudable) is a sign of stupid baseness, that to contemn them is an effect of unreasonable haughtiness[p]; representing the love of honour (rightly grounded and duly moderated) not only as the parent and guardian (as productive and preservative) of other virtues, but as a virtue itself, of no small magnitude and lustre in the constellation of virtues, the virtue of generosity[q]. A virtue, which, next to the spirit of true Religion, (next to a hearty reverence toward the supreme, blessed goodness, and that holy charity toward men which springeth thence,) doth lift a man up nearest to heaven; doth raise his mind above the sordid desires, the sorry cares, the fond humours, the perverse and froward passions, with which men commonly are possessed and acted: that virtue,

[n] Θεῖον γὰρ ἀγαθόν που τιμή.—Plat. [de Leg. v. 727 A.]

Καλὸν ταῖς πολλαῖς πόλεσι τὸ παρακέλευμά ἐστι, προτιμᾶν τὴν εὐδοξίαν πρὸς τῶν πολλῶν.—Id. [de Leg. XII. 950 c.]

[o] Τοιοῦτον δ' ἡ τιμή· μέγιστον γὰρ δὴ τοῦτο τῶν ἐκτὸς ἀγαθῶν.—Arist. Eth. IV. 3. [10.]

[p] Nam negligere, quid de se quisque sentiat, non solum arrogantis, sed etiam omnino dissoluti.—Cic. de Offic. I. [28. 99.]

[q] Levis est animi, lucem splendoremque fugientis, justam gloriam, qui est fructus veræ virtutis honestissimus, repudiare.—Id. in Pis. [XXIV. 57.]

Sed tamen, ex omnibus præmiis virtutis, si esset habenda ratio præmiorum, amplissimum esse præmium gloriam.—Id. pro Mil. [XXXV. 97.]

which inflames a man with courage, so that he dares perform what reason and duty require of him, that he disdains to do what is bad or base; which inspires him with sincerity, that he values his honesty before all other interests and respects, that he abhors to wrong or deceive, to flatter or abuse any man, that he cannot endure to seem otherwise than he is, to speak otherwise than he means, to act otherwise than he promises and professes; which endows him with courtesy, that he is ready to yield every man his due respect, to afford any man what help and succour he is able; that virtue, which renders a man upright in all his dealings, and correspondent to all his obligations; a loyal subject to his prince, and a true lover of his country, a candid judge of persons and things, an earnest favourer of whatever is good and commendable, a faithful and hearty friend, a beneficial and useful neighbour, a grateful resenter and requiter of courtesies, hospitable to the stranger, bountiful to the poor, kind and good to all the world: that virtue, in fine, which constitutes a man of honour, who surely is the best man next to a man of conscience. Thus may honour be valued from natural light, and according to common sense[r].

But beyond all this, the holy scripture (that most certain standard by which we may examine and determine the true worth of things) doth not teach us to slight honour, but rather in its fit order and just measure to love and prize it. It indeed

---

[r] Trahimur omnes laudis studio; et optimus quisque maxime gloria ducitur.—Cic. pro Arch. [XI. 26.]

Οἱ χαρίεντες καὶ πρακτικοὶ, plausible and active men do, saith Aristotle, place happiness in honour.—Eth. [I. 3, 4.]

instructs us to ground it well, (not upon bad qualities or wicked deeds, that is villainous madness; not upon things of a mean and indifferent nature, that is vanity; not upon counterfeit shows and pretences, that is hypocrisy; but upon real worth and goodness, that may consist with modesty and sobriety:) it enjoins us not to be immoderate in our desires thereof, or complacences therein, not to be irregular in the pursuit or acquist of it; (to be so is pride and ambition;) but to affect it calmly, to purchase it fairly: it directs us not to make a regard thereto our chief principle, not to propound it as our main end of action: it charges us to bear contentedly the want or loss thereof, (as of other temporal goods;) yea, in some cases, for conscience sake, or for God's service, (that is, for a good incomparably better than it,) it obliges us willingly to prostitute and sacrifice it, choosing rather to be infamous than impious[a], (to be in disgrace with men, rather than in disfavour with God:) it, in fine, commands us to seek and embrace it only in subordination and with final reference to God's honour. Which distinctions and cautions being provided, honour is represented in holy scripture as a thing considerably good, which may be regarded without blame, which sometimes in duty must be regarded. It is there preferred before other good things, in themselves not despicable. For, *A good name is better than precious ointment;* yea, *A good name is rather to be chosen than great riches,* saith the Wise Man. It is called a gift of God: for, *There is a man,* saith the preacher, *to*

Eccles. vii. 1.
Prov. xxii. 1.
Eccles. vi. 2.

[a] Non vis esse justus sine gloria? at mehercule sæpe justus esse debebis cum infamia.—Sen. Epist. cxiii. [25.]

*whom God hath given riches and honour.* Yea, not only a simple gift, but a blessing, conferred in kindness, as a reward and encouragement of goodness: for, *By humility and the fear of the Lord,* saith he again, *are riches and honour.* Whence it is to be acknowledged as an especial benefit, and a fit ground of thanksgiving; as is practised by the Psalmist in his royal hymn: *Honour,* saith he, *and majesty hast thou laid upon him.* Wisdom also is described unto us bearing *in her left hand riches and honour:* and wisdom surely will not take into any hand of hers, or hold therein, what is worth nothing. No: we are therefore moved to procure her, because, *Exalting her, she shall promote us.—She shall give unto our head an ornament of grace, a crown of glory shall she deliver to us.* We are also enjoined to render honour as the best expression of good-will and gratitude toward them who best deserve in themselves, or most deserve of us; to our prince, to our parents, to our priests, especially to such of them as govern and teach well, to all good men, (*Have such in reputation,* says the apostle). And were not honour a good thing, such injunctions would be unreasonable. Yea, because we are obliged to bear good-will toward all men, St Peter bids us to *Honour all men.* From hence also, that we are especially bound to render honour unto God himself, we may well infer with Aristotle, that *Honour is the best thing in our power to offer*[t]. To these considerations may be added, that we are commanded to walk Εὐσχημόνως, (*Decently,* or speciously, which implies a regard to men's opinion;) to *Provide*

SERM. VI.

Prov. xxii. 4.

Ps. xxi. 5.
Prov. iii. 16.

Prov. iv. 8, 9.

1 Pet. ii. 17.
1 Tim. v. 17.
Phil. ii. 29.

1 Pet. ii. 17.

Rom. xiii. 13.
Rom. xii. 17.

[t] Eth. IV. 3. [10.]

*things honest in the sight of all men*, (Καλὰ, that is, not only things good in substance, but goodly in appearance;) to *Have our conversation honest before the Gentiles*, (Καλὴν again, that is, fair, or comely, and plausible, such as may commend us and our profession to the judgment of them who observe us.) St Paul also exhorts us to *Mind*, not only *what things are true, are just, are pure;* but also Ὅσα σεμνά, (*Whatever things are venerable*, or apt to beget respect,) Ὅσα προσφιλῆ, (*Whatever things are lovely*, or gracious in men's eyes and esteem,) Ὅσα εὔφημα, (*Whatever things are well reported, or well reputed of*). He requires us not only, *If there be any virtue*, (any thing very good in itself,) but, *If there be any praise*, (any thing much approved in common esteem,) that we should *Mind such things*. Lastly, the blessed state hereafter (the highest instance of divine bounty, the complete reward of goodness) is represented and recommended to us as a state of honour and glory; to be ambitious whereof is the character of a good man. *To every man*, saith St Paul, *shall God render according to his works: to them, who by patient continuance in well doing seek for glory, and honour, and immortality, eternal life.*

Such is the reward propounded to us in itself; no vile or contemptible thing, but upon various accounts much valuable; that which the common apprehensions of men, plain dictates of reason, a predominant instinct of nature, the judgments of very wise men, and divine attestation itself, conspire to commend unto us as very considerable and precious. Such a reward our text prescribes us the certain, the only way of attaining.

## *The Reward of honouring God.* 249

2 Such a benefit is here tendered to us (that which yet more highly commends it, and exceedingly enhances its worth) by God himself: *I,* saith he, *will honour.* It is sanctified by coming from his holy hand; it is dignified by following his most wise and just disposal; it is fortified and assured by depending on his unquestionable word, and uncontrollable power: who, as he is the prime author of all good, so he is in especial manner the sovereign dispenser of honour. The king, we say, is the fountain of honour. What any king, as the representative and delegate of God, is in his particular kingdom, that is Almighty God absolutely and independently in all the world. *Both riches and honour,* said good king David, *come of thee, for thou rulest over all: in thine hand is power and might; in thine hand it is to make great, and to give strength unto all.* He whose grants are in effect only sure and valid, whose favours only do in the end turn to good account, he freely offers us most desirable preferment; he doth himself graciously hold forth most authentic patents, by virtue of which we may all become right honourable, and persons of quality indeed; having not only the names and titles, the outward ensigns and badges of dignity, (such as earthly princes confer,) but the substantial reality, the assured enjoyment thereof. (For man can only impose law upon tongues and gestures; God alone commandeth and inclineth hearts, wherein honour chiefly resideth.) He offers it, I say, most freely indeed, yet not absolutely: he doth not go to sell it for a price, yet he propounds it under a condition; as a most just and equal, so a very gentle and easy condition. It is but an

SERM. VI.

1 Chron. xxix. 12.

exchange of honour for honour; of honour from God, which is a free gift, for honour from us, which is a just duty; of honour from him our sovereign Lord, for honour from us his poor vassals; of honour from the most high Majesty of heaven, for honour from us vile worms creeping upon the earth. Such an overture one would think it not unreasonable to accept, but impossible to refuse. For can any man dare not to honour invincible power, infallible wisdom, inflexible justice? Will any man forbear to honour immense goodness and bounty? Yes, it seems there are men so mad as to reject so fair an offer; so bad as to neglect so equal a duty. Let us therefore consider what it is that is here required of us, or wherein this honouring of God consists, that we may thereby discern when we perform this duty, when we are deficient therein.

II. There are several ways of honouring God, or several parts and degrees of this duty; all which we may refer to two sorts, conceiving the duty as a compound, made up of two main ingredients, (correspondent to those two parts in which they reside, and of which our nature consists; which distinction St Paul suggesteth, when he saith, *Glorify God in your body, and in your spirit, which are God's*) one of them being, as it were, the form and soul, the other as the matter and body of the duty.

1 The soul of that honour which is required of us toward God, is that internal esteem and reverence which we should bear in our hearts towards him; importing that we have impressed upon our minds such conceptions about him as are worthy

of him, suitable to the perfection of his nature, to the eminency of his state, to the just quality of his works and actions: that we apprehend him to be, what he really is, in his nature, superlatively good, wise, powerful, holy, and just: that we ascribe unto him the production and conservation of all beings, together with an entire superintendency over, and absolute disposal of, all events: that we conceive ourselves obliged to submit unto, and acquiesce in, all his dispensations of providence, as most wise and most righteous; to rely upon the declarations of his mind, (whether in way of assertion or promise,) as infallibly true and certain. In such acts of mind the honouring of God doth primarily consist. In acts, I say: not in speculative opinions concerning the divine excellencies, (such as all men have, who are not downright atheists or infidels, floating in the fancy, or dormant in the mind;) but in continually present, lively, effectual acts of apprehension and judgment, sinking down into the heart and affections, and quickening them to a congruous, real performance. Such an apprehension of God's power, as shall make us to dread his irresistible hand, shall cause us to despair of prospering in bad courses, shall dispose us to confide in him, as able to perform whatever he wills us to expect from him: such an opinion of his wisdom, as shall keep us from questioning whether that is best which God declares to be so; as shall hinder us from presuming (in compliance with our own shallow reason or vain fancy) to do any thing against God's judgment and advice: such a conceit of God's justice, as shall render us careful to perform what his law promises to reward, and fearful to commit what it threatens to punish: such a persuasion concerning God's goodness, as shall kindle in us an hearty affection toward him, shall make us very sensible of his bounty, and ready to yield returns of duty and gratitude unto him; as shall preserve us from being distrustful of his providence, or doubtful in our need and distress of finding relief from him: such a vigorous and fruitful esteem of God in all respects, as shall produce in us dispositions of mind, and actions of life, agreeable to our various relations and obligations to him; becoming us as his creatures and children, as his subjects and servants. This is indeed the soul of the duty, which being absent, all exterior (how specious soever) either professions or performances, are but as pictures, having in them somewhat of resemblance in shape and colour, nothing of life: yea rather, as carcases, not only dead and senseless, but rotten and filthy in God's sight. *This people,* saith God, *do honour me with their lips, but their heart is far from me.* Such honour is indeed no honour at all, but impudent abuse and profane mockery: for what can be more abominably vain, than for a man to court and cajole him, who knows his whole heart, who sees that he either minds not, or means not what he says? It behoves us therefore by all proper means, by contemplating the works and actions of God, (his admirable works of nature, the wise proceedings of his providence, the glorious dispensations of his grace,) by meditating on his word, by praying for his grace, by observing his law and will, to raise up in our hearts, to foment and cherish this internal reverence, which is the true spring of all piety, the principle which forms and actuates that other sort, coming next to be touched on, being the body of our due honour to God; concurring in its order to the integrity thereof, as without which the interior part would be a kind of ghost, too thin in substance, too remote from sense, too destitute of good fruit and use.

2 This bodily part consists in outward expressions and performances, whereby we declare our esteem and reverence of God, and produce or promote the like in others. For our thus honouring God respects those two ends and effects, the uttering our own, the exciting in others a reverence toward him. And it we may first view in the general or gross bulk thereof; then survey its principal members.

First, in general, God is honoured by a willing and careful practice of all piety and virtue for conscience sake, or in avowed obedience to his holy will. This is the most natural expression of our reverence toward him, and the most effectual way of promoting the same in others. A subject cannot better demonstrate the reverence he bears toward his prince, than by (with a cheerful diligence) observing his laws; for by so doing he declares that he acknowledgeth the authority, and revereth the majesty, which enacted them; that he approves the wisdom which devised them, and the goodness which designed them for public benefit; that he dreads his prince's power, which can maintain them, and his justice, which will vindicate them; that he relies upon his fidelity, in making good what of protection or of recompense he propounds to the observers of them. No less pregnant a signification of our reverence toward God do we yield in our gladly and strictly obeying his laws; thereby evidencing our submission to God's sovereign authority, our esteem of his wisdom and goodness, our awful regard to his power and justice, our confidence in him, and dependance upon his word. As also the practice of wholesome laws, visibly producing good fruits, (peace and prosperity in the commonwealth,) doth conciliate respect unto the prince, he thereby appearing wise and good, able to discern, and willing to choose what confers to public benefit: so actions conformable to the divine law, being (by God's wise and gracious disposal) both in themselves comely and lovely, and in effect, as St Paul saith, *Good and profitable to men*, conducing indeed not only to private, but also to public welfare, to the rendering human society comfortable, to the settling and securing common tranquillity, the performance of them must needs bring great commendation to the author and ordainer of them. By observing them we shall, as St Peter speaks, *Set forth the virtues of him that called us* to such a practice. The light and lustre of good works, done in regard to divine command, will cause men to see clearly the excellencies of our most wise and gracious Lord; will consequently induce and excite them *To glorify our Father which is in heaven. In this*, saith our Saviour, *is my Father glorified, if you bear much fruit*. The goodliness to the sight, the pleasantness to the taste, which is ever perceptible in those fruits which genuine piety beareth, the beauty men see in a calm mind and a sober conversation, the sweetness they taste from works of justice and charity, will

*The Reward of honouring God.* 255

certainly produce veneration to the doctrine which teacheth such things, and to the authority which enjoins them. It is an aggravation of impiety, often insisted upon in scripture, that it slurs, as it were, and defames God, brings reproach and obloquy upon him, causes his name to be profaned, to be cursed, to be blasphemed; and it is answerably a commendation of piety, that by the practice thereof we (not only procure many great advantages to ourselves, many blessings and comforts here, all joys and felicities hereafter: but do also thereby) beget esteem to God himself, and sanctify his ever-blessed name; cause him to be regarded and reverenced, his name to be praised and blessed among men. It is by exemplary piety, by *Providing things honest in the sight of all men*, by doing things honourable and laudable, (such are all things which God hath been pleased to command us,) that we shall be sure to fulfil that precept of St Paul, of *Doing all things to the glory of God;* which is the body of that duty we speak of.

SERM. VI.

Rom. ii. 23, 24.
Tit. ii. 5.
2 Sam. xii. 14.
Isai. lii. 5.
Ezek. xxxvi. 20.

Eph. iv. 1.
Phil. i. 27.
Col. i. 10.
1 Thess. ii. 12.
Rom. xii. 17.

1 Cor. x. 31.

Secondly, But there are, deserving a particular inspection, some members thereof, which in a peculiar and eminent manner do constitute this honour; some acts which more signally conduce to the illustration of God's glory. Such are,

1 The frequent and constant performance (in a serious and reverent manner) of all religious duties or devotions immediately addressed to God, or conversant about him: that which the Psalmist styles, *Giving the Lord the honour due to his name, worshipping the Lord in the beauty of holiness.*

Ps. xxix. 2.

2 Using all things peculiarly related unto God,

his holy name, his holy word, his holy places, (*The places where his honour dwelleth,*) his holy times, (religious fasts and festivities,) with especial respect.

<small>Ps. xxvi. 8. Isai. lviii. 13.</small>

3 Yielding due observance to the deputies and ministers of God (both civil and ecclesiastical) as such, or because of their relation to God: the doing of which God declares that he interprets and accepts as done unto himself.

<small>Rom. xiii. 4. Mal. ii. 7. 1 Sam. viii. 7. Matt. x. 40. John xiii. 20. 2 Cor. ix. 13.</small>

4 Freely spending what God hath given us (out of respect unto him) in works of piety, charity, and mercy; that which the Wise Man calls *Honouring the Lord with our substance.*

<small>Prov. iii. 9; xiv. 31.</small>

5 All penitential acts, by which we submit unto God, and humble ourselves before him. As Achan, by confessing of his sin, is said to *Give glory to the Lord God of Israel.*

<small>Josh. vii. 18, 19. Apoc. xvi. 9.</small>

6 Cheerful undergoing afflictions, losses, disgraces, for the profession of God's truth, or for obedience to God's commands. (As St Peter is said by his death, suffered upon such accounts, to glorify God.)

<small>John xxi. 19.</small>

These signal instances of this duty (represented as such in holy scripture) for brevity's sake I pass over; craving leave only to consider one, most pertinent to our present business, and indeed a very comprehensive one; which is this:

7 We shall especially honour God, by discharging faithfully those offices which God hath intrusted us with; by improving diligently those talents which God hath committed to us; by using carefully those means and opportunities, which God hath vouchsafed us, of doing him service and promoting his glory. Thus he to whom God hath

*The Reward of honouring God.*

given wealth, if he expend it (not to the nourishment of pride and luxury, not only to the gratifying his own pleasure or humour, but) to the furtherance of God's honour, or to the succour of his indigent neighbour, (in any pious or charitable way,) he doth thereby in especial manner honour God. He also on whom God hath bestowed wit and parts, if he employ them (not so much in contriving projects to advance his own petty interests, or in procuring vain applause to himself, as) in advantageously setting forth God's praise, handsomely recommending goodness, dexterously engaging men in ways of virtue, (doing which things is true wit and excellent policy indeed,) he doth thereby remarkably honour God. He likewise that hath honour conferred upon him, if he subordinate it to God's honour, if he use his own credit as an instrument of bringing credit to goodness, thereby adorning and illustrating piety, he by so doing doth eminently practise this duty. The like may be said of any other good quality, any capacity or advantage of doing good; by the right use thereof we honour God: for that men, beholding the worth of such good gifts, and feeling the benefit emergent from them, will be apt to bless the donor of them; as did they in the Gospel, who, seeing our Saviour cure the paralytic man, did presently *Glorify God, who had given such power unto men.* But especially they to whom power and authority is committed, as they have the chief capacity, so they are under an especial obligation thus to honour God: they are particularly concerned to hear and observe that royal proclamation, *Give unto the Lord, O ye mighty, give unto the Lord glory and strength;*

SERM. VI.

Matt. ix. 8.

Ps. xxix. 1, 2.

SERM. VI.

Dan. iv. 34.

*give unto the Lord the honour due unto his name.* When such persons (like king Nebuchadnezzar[u] returned to his right senses) do seriously acknowledge their power and eminency derived from God alone; when they profess subjection unto him, and express it in their practice, not only driving others by their power, but drawing them by their example, to piety and goodness; when they cause God's name to be duly worshipped, and his laws to be strictly observed; when they favour and encourage virtue, discourage and chastise wickedness; when they take care that justice be impartially administered, innocence protected, necessity relieved, all iniquity and oppression, all violence and disorder, yea, so much as may be, all affliction and wretchedness be prevented or removed; when they by all means strive to promote both the service of God and the happiness of men (*Dispensing equally and benignly to the family over which their Lord hath set them, their meat in due season;* providing that men under them *May live a peaceable and quiet life, in all godliness and honesty;* doing which is the business allotted to them, the interest, as it were, of God, which he declares himself concernedly to tender, and by their ministry to prosecute;) when they carefully do such things, then do they indeed approve themselves worthy honourers of their high Master and heavenly King; then do they truly act God's part, and represent his person decently. When the actions of these visible gods are so divinely good and beneficial, men will be easily induced, yea, can hardly forbear to reverence and

Matt. xxiv. 45.
Luke xii. 42.

1 Tim. ii. 2.

---

[u] "I blessed the most High, and praised and honoured him," &c.—Dan. iv. 34.

magnify the invisible founder of their authority. By so doing, as they will set before men's eyes the best pattern of loyalty; as they will impress upon men's hearts the strongest argument for obedience and respect toward themselves: as they shall both more plainly inform and more effectually persuade people to the performance of their duty unto them, than by all the law and all the force in the world; as they will thereby consequently best secure and maintain their own honour, and their own welfare, (for men will never be heartily loyal and submissive to authority till they become really good; nor will they ever be very good till they see their leaders such:) so they will together greatly advance the praise and glory of him in whose name they rule, to whose favour they owe their power and dignity; *In whose hand,* as the prophet saith, *is their breath, and whose are all their ways.* For all men will be ready most awfully to dread him, unto whom they see princes themselves humbly to stoop and bow; no man will be ashamed or unwilling to serve him, whom he shall observe that his lords and governors do concern themselves to worship: the world cannot but have a good opinion of him, a participation of whose power and majesty yields such excellent fruits; it will not fail to adore him, whose shadows and images are so venerable. It is a most notorious thing, both to reason and in experience, what extreme advantage great persons have, especially by the influence of their practice, to bring God himself, as it were, into credit: how much it is in their power easily to render piety a thing in fashion and request. For in what they do, they never are alone, or are ill attended: whither they go they carry the

SERM. VI.

Dan. v. 23.

world along with them: they lead crowds of people after them, as well when they go in the right way, as when they run astray. The custom of living well, no less than other modes and garbs, will be soon conveyed and propagated from the Court; the city and country will readily draw good manners thence, (good manners truly so called, not only superficial forms of civility, but real practices of goodness). For the main body of men goeth not *Qua eundum, sed qua itur,* not according to rules and reasons, but after examples and authorities; especially of great persons, who are like stars, shining in high and conspicuous places, by which men steer their course: their actions are to be reckoned not as single or solitary ones, but are, like their persons, of a public and representative nature, involving the practice of others, who are by them awed, or shamed into compliance. Their good example especially hath this advantage, that men can find no excuse, can have no pretence why they should not follow it. Piety is not only beautified, but fortified by their dignity; it not only shines in them with a clearer lustre, but with a mightier force and influence: a word, a look (the least intimation) from them will do more good, than others' best eloquence, clearest reason, most earnest endeavours. For it is in them, if they would apply themselves to it, as the wisest prince implies, to scatter iniquity with their eyes. A smile of theirs were able to enliven virtue, and diffuse it all about; a frown might suffice to mortify and dissipate wickedness. Such apparently is their power of honouring God; and in proportion thereto surely great is their obligation to do it: of them peculiarly God expects it, and all equity exacts it.

What the meaner rank of servants (who are employed in baser drudgeries, whose fare is more coarse, whose wages are more scant, who stand at greater distance from their lord, and receive no such ample or express marks of his favour, what these) do is of some consequence indeed, but doth not import so much to the master's reputation; their good word concerning him, their good carriage toward him doth not credit him so much. But those whom he employs in matters of highest trust and importance to his affairs, whom he places in the nearest degree to himself, (seats even in his own throne, upon his own tribunal,) whom he feeds plentifully and daintily, maintains in a handsome garb, allows largely, as their deportment doth much reflect on their lord's esteem, as they are highly capable of advancing his repute; so all the rules of ingenuity and gratitude, all the laws of justice and equity do oblige them earnestly to endeavour it. And it is indeed no less their concernment to do so. For if there be disorders, prejudicial to the master's honour and interest, frequently committed in the family, it is those servants must be responsible: if due order be there kept to his glory and advantage, they shall chiefly be commended, and peculiarly hear the *Euge, bone serve.* They must be loaded with other men's faults, or crowned for other men's virtues, as their behaviour hath respectively contributed to them. Those universal rules of equity, proposed in the Gospel, will, in God's reckoning with and requiting men, be punctually observed: *To whomsoever much is given, of him much shall be required;* answerable to the improvement of what is delivered in trust shall the acceptance be.

SERM. VI.

Matt. xxv. 23.

Luke xii. 48.

SERM. VI.

I have insisted somewhat more largely on this point, because our text hath a particular aspect thereon; the words being uttered upon occasion of Eli, then judge in Israel, his not using authority to these purposes; his forbearing to redress a grievous abuse, committed by his own sons, to the disservice and dishonour of God. Whence to persons of his rank is this law especially directed; upon them is this duty chiefly incumbent: on them assuredly, (as sure as God is true,) if they will observe the duty, the reward shall be conferred. God will certainly not only preserve the honour they have already, but will accumulate more honours on them.

These are general truths; the particular application of them is ours. God, I pray, vouchsafe his grace and blessing, that it may be made to our benefit and comfort.

III. I should now shew why the duty is required of us, or how reasonable it is. I must not (and the matter is so palpable that I need not) spend many words on that. God surely doth not exact honour from us because he needs it, because he is the better for it, because he, for itself, delights therein. For (beside that he cannot want any thing without himself, that he cannot any wise need mortal breath to praise him[x], or hands of flesh to serve him, who hath millions of better creatures than we absolutely at his devotion, and can with a word create millions of millions more, fitter than we to honour him) the best estimation

[x] Ἀκήρατος γὰρ αὐτοῦ ἡ οὐσία καὶ ἀνενδεὴς οὖσα, οὐδενὸς ἑτέρου προσδεῖται· οἱ δὲ αἰνοῦντες αὐτὸν λαμπρότεροι γίνονται.—Chrys. in Psal. cxliv. [Opp. Tom. I. p. 885.] et vide in Psal. ciii.

we can have of him is much below him; the best expression we can make is very unworthy of him. He is infinitely excellent, beyond what we can imagine or declare: *His name is exalted above all blessing and praise; His glory is above the earth and heaven.* So that all our endeavours to honour him are, in comparison to what is due, but defects, and in a manner disparagements to him. It is only then (which should affect our ingenuity to consider) his pure goodness that moves him, for our benefit and advantage, to demand it of us.

SERM. VI.

Neh. ix. 5.
Ps. cxlviii. 13.
Ecclus. xliii. 30.

1 For that to honour God is the most proper work of reason; that for which primarily we were designed and framed; (for as other things were made to afford the matter and occasion, so man was designed to exercise the act of glorifying God;) whence the performance thereof doth preserve and perfect our nature[y]; to neglect it being unnatural and monstrous.

2 For that also it is a most pleasant duty. He is not a man, (hath lost all natural ingenuity and humanity,) who doth not delight to make some returns thither, where he hath found much good-will, whence he hath felt great kindness. Since then all the good we have, we have received from God's favour, it cannot but be very pleasant to render somewhat of requital, as it were, unto him; and we can render no other but this. We cannot make God more rich, more joyful, more happy than he is: all that we can do is, to express our reverence toward him.

3 For that likewise our honouring God dis-

[y] Sen. Ep. LXXVI. [17.] [Virum bonum, concedas necesse est, summæ pietatis erga deos esse.]

poses us to the imitation of him, (for what we do reverence we would resemble,) that is, to the doing those things wherein our chief perfection and happiness consists, whence our best content and joy doth spring.

4 In fine, for that the practice of this duty is most profitable and beneficial to us; unto it by an eternal rule of justice our final welfare and prosperity being annexed: whence God hath declared it to be the way and condition of our attaining that thing which we so like and prize, honour to ourselves; the which by promise he hath engaged himself to confer on those who honour him. And,

IV. This promise he makes good several ways: some of them I shall briefly suggest.

1 The honouring God is of itself an honourable thing; the employment which ennobles heaven itself, wherein the highest angels do rejoice and glory. It is the greatest honour of a servant to bring credit to his master, of a subject to spread his prince's renown, and (upon grounds vastly more obliging) of a creature to glorify his Maker: that we may do so is an honour we should be glad, may be proud of.

2 By honouring God we are immediately instated in great honour; we enter into most noble relations, acquire most illustrious titles, enjoy most glorious privileges; we become the friends and favourites of heaven, are adopted into God's family, and are styled his children; do obtain a free access unto him, a sure protection under him, a ready assistance from him in all our needs. And what honour can exceed, can equal this?

3 God hath so ordered it, that honour is natu-

rally consequent upon the honouring him. God hath made goodness a noble and a stately thing; hath impressed upon it that beauty and majesty which commands an universal love and veneration, which strikes presently both a kindly and an awful respect into the minds of all men. *The righteous is* (not only in himself, but in common esteem) *more excellent than his neighbour.* Power may be dreaded, riches may be courted, wit and knowledge may be admired; but only goodness is truly esteemed and honoured[z]. Not only men of goodness and discretion, but even the vulgar sort of men (yea, as Plato hath well observed, the worst men) do pass this judgment, do prefer true goodness above all things[a].

SERM. VI.

Prov. xii. 26.

4 God, by his extraordinary providence, as there is reason and occasion, doth interpose, so as to procure honour to them, to maintain and further their reputation, who honour him. *God fashioneth the hearts of men: The hearts of the greatest men are in his hand; he turneth them as the rivers of waters, whithersoever he will:* he consequently raiseth or depresseth us, as he pleases, in the judgments and affections of men. *When a man's ways please the Lord, he maketh even his enemies to be at peace with him,* saith the Wise Man;

Ps. xxxiii. 15.
Prov. xxi. 1.

Prov. xvi. 7.

[z] Γενοῦ τοῦ πλησίον τιμιώτερος, ἐκ τοῦ φανῆναι χρηστότερος, &c.—Greg. Naz. [Orat. xxiv. Tom. i. p. 276 B.]

Is gloria maxime excellat, qui virtute plurimum præstet.—Cic. [pro Planc. xxv.]

Κατ' ἀλήθειαν δ' ὁ ἀγαθὸς μόνος τιμητέος.—Arist. Eth. iv. 3. [20.]

Adeo gratiosa virtus est, ut insitum sit etiam malis probare meliora.—Sen. de Benef. iv. 17. [2.]

[a] Θεῖόν δέ τι καὶ εὔστοχον ἔνεστι καὶ τοῖσι κακοῖς, ὥστε πάμπολλοι καὶ τῶν σφόδρα κακῶν εὖ τοῖς λόγοις καὶ ταῖς δόξαις διαιροῦνται τοὺς ἀμείνους τῶν ἀνθρώπων, καὶ τοὺς χείρονας.—Plat. [de Leg. xii. 950 B.]

that is, he disposeth the most averse minds to love and honour him. No envy can supplant, no slander can deface the credit of such a person; since God hath taken it into his charge and care, since he hath said it, that *He will bring forth his righteousness as the light, and his judgment as the noonday.* God also by secret methods, and undiscernible trains, ordereth all events, managing our thoughts and designs, our enterprises and actions so, that the result of them shall be matter of benefit, comfort, and reputation, or of disaster, regret, and disgrace, as he thinks good. Victory and success he absolutely disposeth of, and consequently of the honour that follows them; and they do usually attend the honours of God: for, as it is in the Psalm, *A good success have they who keep his commandments.* Many are the instances of persons, (such as Abraham, Joseph, Moses, David, Job, and Daniel,) who, for their signal honouring of God, from a base and obscure, or from an afflicted and forlorn condition, have, in ways strange and wonderful, been advanced to eminent dignity, have been rendered most illustrious, by the providence of him, *Who raiseth the poor out of the dust, and lifteth the beggar out of the dunghill, to set them among princes, and to make them inherit the throne of glory.* He doth it in an evident manner, and eminent degree, to some; he doth it in a convenient way, and competent measure, to all that honour him.

5 Whereas men are naturally inclined to bear much regard to the judgment of posterity concerning them[b], are desirous to leave a good name be-

---

[b] Cic. Tusc. I. [14. 31.]

hind them, and to have their memory retained in esteem[c]; God so disposes things, that *The memory of the just shall be blessed;* that *His righteousness shall be had in everlasting remembrance;* that *His light shall rejoice,* (or burn clearly and pleasantly, even when his life is put out here). No spices can so embalm a man, no monument can so preserve his name and memory, as a pious conversation, whereby God hath been honoured, and men benefited. The fame of such a person is, in the best judgments, far more precious and truly glorious, than is the fame of those who have excelled in any other deeds or qualities. For what sober man doth not in his thoughts afford a more high and hearty respect to those poor fishermen, who by their heroical activity and patience did honour God in the propagation of his heavenly truth, than to all those Hectors in chivalry, those conquerors and achievers of mighty exploits, (those Alexanders and Cæsars) who have been renowned for doing things which seemed great, rather than for performing what was truly good? To the honour of those excellent poor men, conspicuous monuments have been erected everywhere; anniversary memorials of their names and virtues are celebrated; they are never mentioned or thought of without respect; their commendations are interwoven with the praises of their great Lord and Maker, whom they honoured[d].

SERM. VI.

Prov. x. 7.
Ps. cxii. 6.
Prov. xiii. 9.

[c] Ἀνάγκη γὰρ, ὡς ἔοικε, μέλειν ἡμῖν καὶ τοῦ ἔπειτα χρόνου, ἐπειδὴ καὶ τυγχάνουσι κατά τινα φύσιν οἱ μὲν ἀνδραποδωδέστατοι οὐδὲν φροντίζοντες αὐτοῦ, οἱ δ᾽ ἐπιεικέστατοι πᾶν ποιοῦντες, ὅπως ἂν εἰς τὸν ἔπειτα χρόνον εὖ ἀκούσωσιν.—Plat. Epist. II. [311 c.]

[d] Τῶν δὲ δούλων τοῦ Χριστοῦ καὶ τὰ σήματα λαμπρὰ, τὴν βασιλικωτάτην καταλαβόντα πόλιν· καὶ ἡμέραι καταφανεῖς, ἑορτὴν τῇ οἰκουμένῃ ποιοῦσαι, &c.—Chrys. in 2 Cor. [Hom. XXVI. Opp. Tom. III. p. 687.]

6 Lastly, to those who honour God here, God hath reserved an honour infinitely great and excellent, in comparison whereto all honours here are but dreams, the loudest acclamations of mortal men are but empty sounds, the brightest glories of this world are but duskish and fleeting shadows; an honour most solid, most durable; *An eternal weight of glory.* They shall, in the face of all the world, be approved by the most righteous Judge's unquestionable sentence; they shall be esteemed in the unanimous opinion of angels and saints; they shall be applauded by the general voice and attestation of heaven; they shall then be seated upon unmovable thrones, their heads encircled with unfading crowns, their faces shining with rays of unconceivable glory and majesty. The less of honour they have received here, in this transitory moment of life, the more thereof they shall enjoy in that future eternal state; where, with him who, through the whole course of his life, sought not his own honour, but the honour of him that sent him; *Who, for the suffering of death, was crowned with glory and honour; Who, for the joy that was set before him, endured the cross, despising the shame, and is set at the right hand of God;* with those who consecrated all their endeavours, and who sacrificed their lives to the promoting of God's honour, they shall possess everlasting glory. Which, together with them, God Almighty of his infinite mercy grant unto us all, through Jesus Christ our Lord; to whom, with God the Father, and God the Holy Ghost, be for ever all honour and praise. Amen.

# SERMON VII.

## UPRIGHT WALKING SURE WALKING.

### Prov. X. 9.

*He that walketh uprightly walketh surely.*

THE world is much addicted to the politics; the heads of men are very busy in contrivance, and their mouths are full of talk about the ways of consulting our safety, and securing our interests. May we not therefore presume, that an infallible maxim of policy, proposing the most expedite and certain method of security in all our transactions, will be entertained with acceptance? Such an one the greatest politician and wisest man for business (if we may take God's own word for it) that ever was or will be, doth here suggest to us. For the practice couched in our text he otherwhere voucheth for a point of policy, telling us, that *A man of understanding walketh uprightly:* and here he recommendeth it as a method of security, *He that walketh uprightly walketh surely.*

Treating upon which aphorism, I shall, by God's help, endeavour, first, in way of explication, briefly to describe the practice itself; then, in way of proof, by some considerations to declare, that security doth attend it.

For explication. *To walk* (as well in the style of holy scripture, as in other writings, and even in common speech) doth signify our usual course of dealing, or the constant tenor of our practice.

*Uprightly*, according to the original[a], might be rendered, in perfection, or with integrity: and by the Greek translators in several places is supposed chiefly to denote sincerity and purity of intention.

In effect, the phrase, *He that walketh uprightly*, doth import, one who is constantly disposed in his designs and dealings to bear a principal regard to the rules of his duty, and the dictates of his conscience: who in every case emergent is ready to perform that, which upon good deliberation doth appear most just and fit, in conformity to God's law[b] and sound reason, without being swayed by any appetite, any passion, any sinister respect to his own private interest of profit, credit, or pleasure, to the commission of any unlawful, irregular, unworthy, or base act; who generally doth act out of good principles; (namely, reverence to God, charity to men, sober regard to his own true welfare;) who doth aim at good ends, that is, at God's honour, public benefit, his own salvation, other good things subordinate to those, or well consistent with them; who doth prosecute his designs by lawful means, in fair ways, such as honest providence and industry, veracity and fidelity, dependance upon God's help, and prayer for his blessing: in short, one who never advisedly doth undertake any bad thing, nor any good thing to ill purposes; nor doth use any foul means to compass his intents.

---

[a] בְּתֹם.

[b] "He that walketh in his uprightness, feareth the Lord."—Prov. xiv. 2.

Now, that such an one doth ever proceed with much security, from the following considerations may appear.

I. An upright walker is secure of easily finding his way. For it commonly requireth no reach of wit or depth of judgment, no laborious diligence of inquiry, no curious intentness of observation, no solicitous care, or plodding study, to discern in any case what is just; we need not much trouble our heads about it, for we can hardly be to seek for it. If we will but open our eyes, it lieth in view before us, being the plain, straight, obvious road, which common reason prompteth, or which ordinary instruction pointeth out to us: so that usually that direction of Solomon is sufficient, *Let thine eyes look right on, and let thine eyelids look straight before thee.—Turn not to the right hand, nor to the left.* Prov. iv. 25, 27; xvii. 24.

The ways of iniquity and vanity, (if we may call them ways, which indeed are but exorbitances and seductions from the way,) ill designs and bad means of executing designs, are very unintelligible, very obscure, abstruse, and intricate; being infinitely various, and utterly uncertain: so that out of them to pick and fix on this or that may puzzle our heads, and perplex our hearts; as to pursue any of them may involve us in great difficulty and trouble. But the ways of truth, of right, of virtue, are so very simple and uniform, so fixed and permanent, so clear and notorious, that we can hardly miss them, or (except wilfully) swerve from them. For they by divine wisdom were chalked out, not only for ingenious and subtle persons, (men of great parts, of refined wits, of long experience,) but rather for the vulgar community of men, the great body of God's subjects consisting in persons of meanest capacity and smallest improvement: being designed to *Make wise the simple,* to *Give the young man knowledge and discretion:* to direct all sorts of people in their duty, toward their happiness; according to that in the prophet, *A high way*[c] *shall be there, and it shall be called, The way of holiness—the wayfaring men, though fools, shall not err therein.*

They are in very legible characters graven by the finger of God upon our hearts and consciences, so that by any considerate reflection inwards we may easily read them; or they are extant in God's word, there written as with a sunbeam, so perspicuously expressed, so frequently inculcated, that without gross negligence or strange dulness we cannot but descry them. For who with half an eye may not see, that the practice of pious love and reverence toward God, of entire justice and charity toward our neighbour, of sober temperance and purity toward ourselves, is approved by reason, is prescribed by God to us?

Hence in the holy scriptures, as bad ways are called dark, crooked, rough, slippery ways; so the good ways are said to be clear, plain, direct, even ways: *The path of the just,* say they, *is as a shining light. All the words of my mouth are plain to him that understandeth*[d], (or, *that considereth* them.) *My foot standeth in an even place. The law of his God is in his heart: and none of his steps shall slide.*

[c] Ὁδὸς καθαρά.—LXX.
[d] Πάντα ἐνώπια τοῖς συνιοῦσι.—LXX.

*Upright walking sure walking.*

Hence it is affirmed, that an upright man doth hardly need any conduct beside his own honesty. For, *The integrity*, saith Solomon, *of the upright shall guide them;* and, *The righteousness of the perfect shall direct his way.*

But in case such an one should ever be at a stand or at a loss, in doubt of his course, he hath always at hand a most sure guide to conduct or direct him. It is but asking the way of him, or saying, with the Psalmist, *Shew me thy ways, O Lord, teach me thy paths; Teach me to do thy will,* and, *Lead me in the way everlasting; O let me not wander from thy commandments:* and then *His ears,* as the prophet saith, *shall hear a word behind him, saying, This is the way, walk ye in it;* then the words of the Psalmist shall be verified, *What man is he that feareth the Lord? Him shall he teach in the way that he shall choose. The meek will he guide in judgment, and the meek he will teach his way.*

Hence is the upright man happily secured from tiring pains in the search, from racking anxieties in the choice, from grating scruples and galling regrets in the pursuit of his way.

II. The upright walker doth tread upon firm ground. He doth build his practice, not upon the perilous bogs, the treacherous quagmires, the devouring quicksands of uncouth, bold, impious, paradoxes, (such as have been vented by Epicurus, by Machiavel, by others more lately, whose infamous names are too well known, as the effects of their pestilent notions are too much felt;) but upon solid, safe, approved, and well-tried principles; viz. these, and the like coherent with them: That there

SERM. VII.

Deut. v. 32; xxviii. 14.
Prov. iv. 18; viii. 8, 9.
Ps. xxxvii. 31; xxvi. 1; xvii. 5; xviii. 36.
Prov. xi. 3, 5.

Ps. xxv. 4; xvi. 11; xvii. 5; cxliii. 10; cxxxix. 24; cxix. 10, 27, 33, 35, &c.
Isai. xxx. 21.
Ps. xxv. 9, 12; xxxvii. 23.

Prov. xii. 5.

SERM. VII.

is an eternal God, incomprehensibly powerful, wise, just, and good; who is always present with us, and ever intent upon us; viewing not only all our external actions, (open and secret,) but our inmost cogitations, desires, and intentions, by the which our actions chiefly are to be estimated: that he, as governor of the world, and judge of men, doth concern himself in all human affairs, disposing and managing all events according to his righteous pleasure; exacting punctual obedience to his laws, and dispensing recompenses answerable thereto; with impartial justice rewarding each man according to the purposes of his heart and the practices of his life: that all our good and happiness doth absolutely depend on God's favour; so that to please him can only be true wisdom, and to offend him the greatest folly: that virtue is incomparably the best endowment whereof we are capable, and sin the worst mischief to which we are liable: that no worldly good or evil is considerable in comparison with goods or evils spiritual: that nothing can be really profitable or advantageous to us, which doth not consist with our duty to God, doth not somewise conduce to our spiritual interest and eternal welfare; yea, that every thing not serviceable to those purposes is either a frivolous trifle, or a dangerous snare, or a notable damage, or a woeful bane to us: that content of mind, springing from innocence of life, from the faithful discharge of our duty, from satisfaction of conscience, from a good hope in regard to God and our future state, is in our esteem and choice much to be preferred before all the delights which any temporal possession or fruition can afford; and, that a bad mind is the sorest adversity which can befall us. Such are the grounds of upright practice, more firm than any rock, more unshakeable than the foundations of heaven and earth; the which are assured by the sacred oracles, and attested by many remarkable providences; have ever been avowed by the wiser sort, and admitted by the general consent of men, as for their truth, most agreeable to reason, and for their usefulness, approved by constant experience; the belief of them having apparently most wholesome influence upon all the concerns of life, both public and private; indeed, being absolutely needful for upholding government, and preserving human society; no obligation, no faith or confidence between men, no friendship or peace being able to subsist without it. Whence the practice built on such foundations must be very secure. And if God shall not cease to be, if he will not let go the reins, if his word cannot deceive, if the wisest men are not infatuated, if the common sense of mankind do not prove extravagant, if the main props of life and pillars of society do not fail; he that walketh uprightly doth proceed on sure grounds.

III. The upright person doth walk steadily, maintaining his principal resolutions, and holding his main course, through all occasions, without flinching or wavering, or desultory inconsistence and fickleness; his integrity being an excellent ballast, holding him tight and well poised in his deportment; so that waves of temptation dashing on him do not make him roll in uncertainty, or topple over into unworthy practices.

Lust, passion, humour, interest, are things very mutable, as depending upon temper of body, casualties of time, the winds and tides of this vertiginous world: whence he that is guided or moved by them must needs be many minded and *Unstable in all his ways*; will *Reel to and fro like a drunken man, and be at his wit's end;* never enjoying any settled rest of mind, or observing a smooth tenor of action. But a good conscience is very stable, and persisteth unvaried through all circumstances of time, in all vicissitudes of fortune. For it steereth by immoveable pole-stars, the inviolable rules of duty; it aimeth at marks which no force can stir out of their place; its objects of mind and affection are not transitory; its hopes and confidences are fixed on the *Rock of ages*. Whence an upright person in all cases, and all conditions, (prosperous or adverse,) is the same man, and goeth the same way[e]. Contingences of affairs do not unhinge his mind from its good purposes, or divert his foot from the right course. Let the weather be fair or foul, let the world smile or frown, let him get or lose by it, let him be favoured or crossed, commended or reproached, (*By honour and dishonour, by evil report and good report,*) he will do what his duty requireth: the external state of things must not alter the moral reason of things with him. This is that which the Psalmist observeth of him: *He shall not be afraid of evil tidings, for his heart standeth fast, and believeth in the Lord. His heart is stablished, and will not shrink.* And this the Wise Man promiseth to him; *Commit thy works unto the Lord, and thy thoughts shall be established.*

[e] Justum ac tenacem propositi virum.—
Hor. [Carm. III. 3. 1.]

Hence a man is secured from diffidence in himself, and distraction in his mind, from frequently being off the hooks, from leading an unequal life, clashing with itself, from deluding and disappointing those with whom he converseth or dealeth, and consequently from the inconveniences issuing thence.

IV. The way of uprightness is the surest for despatch, and the shortest cut toward the execution or attainment of any good purpose; securing a man from irksome expectations and tedious delays, the which, as the Wise Man saith, do *Make the heart sick*. Prov. xiii. 12.

It in scripture is called *The straight and the plain way*. And as in geometry, of all lines or surfaces contained within the same bounds, the straight line and the plain surface are the shortest; so it is also in morality: by the right line of justice, upon the plain ground of virtue, a man soonest will arrive to any well-chosen end. Luke iii. 5.

In this way there are no bewildering intrigues and mazes, no crooked windings and turnings, no occasions forcing men to dance hither and thither, to skip backward and forward, to do and undo; which courses do protract business, and commonly do hinder from ever despatching it. But a man acting justly and fairly doth continually proceed on in the direct open road, without retreat, excursion, or deflection; *Not turning aside* (as the phrase is in holy writ) *to the right hand or to the left*. Prov. iv. 27. Deut. v. 32; xxviii. 14.

To clamber over fences of duty, to break through hedges of right, to trespass upon hallowed enclosures, may seem the most short and compendious

SERM. VII.

ways of getting thither where one would be: but doth not a man venture breaking his neck, or scratching his face, incurring mischief and trouble thereby? Is he not liable to the fate to which the Preacher doometh him, *He that diggeth a pit shall fall into it: and whoso breaketh a hedge, a serpent shall bite him?* For instance, to grow rich, fraud, extortion, corruption, oppression, overreaching and supplanting may seem the readiest and most expedite ways; but in truth they are the furthest ways about, or rather no ways at all: for that which is got by those means is not our own: nor is the possession of it truly wealth, but usurpation, or detention of spoil and rapine, which we ought to disgorge. And however to the getting it there are often mighty difficulties occurring from men, there are commonly insuperable obstacles interposed by God; who hath expressly condemned and cursed those ways, declaring, that *Wealth gotten by vanity* (or cozenage) *shall be diminished;* that *He that oppresseth to increase his riches, shall surely come to want;* that *He, who* (thus) *hasteth to be rich, hath an evil eye, and considereth not that poverty shall come upon him;* that *As the partridge sitteth on eggs, and hatcheth them not: so he that getteth riches and not by right, shall leave them in the midst of his days, and at his end shall be a fool.* Whereas the plain way of honest, harmless industry, (joined with a pious regard to him who is the dispenser of all good things,) how slow soever it may seem, is the most speedy, because the only safe way to thrive; having, beside all secondary advantages, the security of those oracles; *The hand of the diligent shall make rich: He that gathereth by labour*

Eccles. x. 8.

Prov. xiii. 11;
xxii. 16;
xxviii. 22,
20; xxi. 6.

Jer. xvii. 11.

Prov. x. 4;
xxviii. 19;
xiii. 11;
xxii. 4.

*shall increase: By humility and the fear of the Lord are riches, and honour, and life.*

V. The way of uprightness is in itself very safe, free of danger, tending to no mischief; according to those sayings of the Wise Man; *There shall no evil happen to the just: In the way of righteousness is life; and in the path thereof there is no death.*

He who designeth only that which is just and reasonable, who innocently and fairly prosecuteth his intent, can run no great hazard, cannot fall into any extreme disaster, cannot irrecoverably sink into miserable disappointment.

He probably will not receive much harm from men, or trouble from the world: for, as he meaneth innocently, as he dealeth inoffensively, (not violently assailing, nor fraudulently circumventing, not any wise injuriously or maliciously abusing any man,) as he doth yield no just provocation or urgent temptation to oppose him; so is he not very likely to meet with obstructions or crosses thwarting his designs. He can hardly raise up adversaries; at least such as will prove very formidable, or very fierce and implacable toward him.

He may be sure that few wise men, and no good men, will trouble him; but that such rather will afford their countenance and furtherance to his undertakings.

But assuredly he shall have the favourable protection of Almighty God, who throughly knowing his heart, and observing the righteousness of his intentions and proceedings, will not suffer him to incur any notable, destructive, remediless calamity.

His prayer, dictated by good conscience, *Let inte-*

*grity and uprightness preserve me,* will certainly be heard; God having passed his word for it in numberless places of scripture; particularly in those remarkable words of Isaiah: *He that walketh righteously, and speaketh uprightly; he that despiseth the gain of oppressions, that shaketh his hands from holding of bribes, that stoppeth his ears from hearing of blood, and shutteth his eyes from seeing evil; he shall dwell on high: his place of defence shall be the munitions of rocks; his bread shall be given him, his water shall be sure.* That is, a man who is constantly upright in his dealings shall by the divine Providence be infallibly and impregnably preserved from any grievous mischief, from any sore want, from any extreme distress.

The way of uprightness is ever guarded with angels ready to promote the affairs of the honest person, or at least to protect him from evil. He may hopefully say to himself, as Abraham did to his servant, *The Lord, before whom I walk, will send his angel with thee, and prosper thy way:* or he confidently may apply to himself that of the Psalmist, *He shall give his angels charge over thee, to keep thee in all thy ways. They shall bear thee up in their hands, lest thou dash thy foot against a stone.*

However, the sequel will be tolerable: whatever the success of his undertaking be, it can be no ruin, no slur, no heart-breaking to him. His conscience is safe, his credit is entire, his hopes are good; he is perfectly secure from being tainted with foul guilt, from being exposed to due reproach, from being stung with vexatious remorse, from being plunged into a gulf of desperation or disconsolateness. For,

VI. The way of uprightness is fair and pleasant. He that walketh in it hath good weather, and a clear sky about him; a hopeful confidence and a cheerful satisfaction do ever wait upon him. *It is joy*, as the Wise Man saith, *to the just to do judgment.* [Prov. xxi. 15.]

Being conscious to himself of an honest meaning, and a due course of prosecuting it, he feeleth no check or struggling of mind, no regret or sting of heart; being throughly satisfied and pleased with what he is about, his judgment approving, and his will acquiescing in his procedure, as worthy of himself, agreeable to reason, and conformable to his duty.

He therefore briskly moveth forward with alacrity and courage; there being within him nothing to control or countermand him, to pull him back, to make him halt, to distract or disturb him.

Nor hardly can any thing abroad dismay or discourage him. For he may reasonably hope for the good-will of men, and cannot hugely dread their opposition. He may strongly presume upon the propitious aspect and favourable succour of Heaven, which always smileth and casteth benign influences on honest undertakings. [Prov. xi. 20.]

He that hath chosen a good way may with assurance commend his way to God's providence; he may depend upon God for his concurrent benediction; he, with an humble boldness, may address prayers to God for his protection and aid. He, so doing, hath interest in divers clear declarations and express promises of good success; such as those; *Commit thy way unto the Lord, trust also in him, and he shall bring it to pass. The Lord is nigh* [Jer. xxxii. 19. Prov. xxiv. 14. Heb. iv. 16. Ps. xxxvii. 5; lv. 22. Prov. xvi. 3. Ecclus. ii. 10.]

*unto all that call upon him in truth: he will fulfil the desire of them that fear him; he will hear their cry, and will save them.*

He may dare to refer his case to the severest examination, saying with Job, *Let me be weighed in an even balance, that God may know mine integrity;* and with the Psalmist, *Judge me, O Lord, according to my righteousness, and according to mine integrity that is in me.*

He with an humble confidence can appeal to God, borrowing the words of Hezekiah, *I beseech thee, O Lord, remember how I have walked before thee in truth and with a perfect heart, and have done that which is good in thy sight.*

Hence, *The hope of the righteous,* as the Wise Man telleth us, *is gladness.* He, considering the goodness, the justice, the fidelity of God, whereof his integrity doth render him capable and a proper object, cannot but conceive a comfortable hope of a good issue.

And obtaining success, he doth not only enjoy the material pleasure thereof, but the formal satisfaction that it is indeed good success, or a blessing indulged to him by special favour of God; enabling him to say with the Psalmist, *The Lord rewarded me according to my righteousness; according to the cleanness of my hands hath he recompensed me. For I have kept the ways of the Lord, and have not wickedly departed from my God.*

However, an upright dealer hath this comfortable reserve, that whatever doth befall him, however the business goeth, he shall not condemn and punish himself with remorse; he shall not want a consolation able to support and to erect his mind. He shall triumph, if not in the felicity of his success, yet in the integrity of his heart, and the innocence of his deportment; even as blessed Job did under all the pressures of his adversity: for, *Till I die*, said he, *I will not remove my integrity from me. My righteousness I hold fast, and will not let it go: my heart shall not reproach me so long as I live.*

SERM. VII.

Job xxvii. 5, 6.

So true it is upon all accounts, that, according to that assertion in the Psalm, *Light is sown for the righteous, and joyful gladness for the upright in heart.*

Ps. xcvii. 11.

VII. He that walketh uprightly is secure as to his honour and credit. He is sure not to come off disgracefully, either at home in his own apprehensions, or abroad in the estimations of men. He doth not blush at what he is doing, nor doth reproach himself for what he hath done. No blemish or blame can stick upon his proceeding.

By pure integrity, a man first maintaineth a due respect and esteem for himself, then preserveth an entire reputation with others: he reflecteth on his own heart with complacence, and looketh upon the world with confidence. He hath no fear of being detected, or care to smother his intents. He is content that his thoughts should be sounded, and his actions sifted to the bottom. He could even wish that his breast had windows, that his heart were transparent, that all the world might see through him, and descry the clearness of his intentions. The more curiously his ways are marked, the more exactly his dealings are scanned, the more throughly his designs are penetrated and

SERM. VII.
known; the greater approbation he is sure to receive.

The issue of things assuredly will be creditable to him; and when the daylight hath scattered all mists, hath cleared all misprisions and mistakes, his reputation will shine most brightly: the event declaring, that he had no corrupt ends; the course of his proceedings being justified by the very light of things.

God himself will be concerned to vindicate his reputation, not suffering him to be considerably defamed; according to that promise, *He shall bring forth thy righteousness as the light, and thy judgment as the noon-day.* That in Job will be made good to him, *Then shalt thou lift up thy face without spot:* and he may confidently aver with the Psalmist, *Then shall I not be ashamed, when I have respect to all thy commandments.*

Ps. xxxvii. 6, 19; xxxiv. 5.

Job xi. 15.

Ps. cxix. 6, 39, 46.

If he findeth good success, it will not be invidious, appearing well deserved, and fairly procured: it will be truly honourable, as a fruit and recompense of virtue, as a mark and pledge of the divine favour toward him.

If he seemeth disappointed, yet he will not be disparaged: wise and candid men will excuse him; good men will patronise his cause; no man of sense and ingenuity will insult on his misfortune. *He shall not*, as the Psalmist assureth, *be ashamed in an evil time.* Yea, often his repute from under a cloud will shine, if not with so glaring splendour, yet with a pleasant lustre; uprightness disposing him to bear adverse events with a graceful decency.

Ps. xxxvii. 19.

VIII. The particular methods of acting which uprightness disposeth to observe, do yield great security from troubles and crosses in their transactions.

What is the conduct of the upright man? He is clear, frank, candid, harmless, consistent in all his behaviour, his discourse, his dealing. His heart commonly may be seen in his face, his mind doth ever suit with his speech, his deeds have a just correspondence with his professions; he never faileth to perform what he doth promise, and to satisfy the expectations which he hath raised.

He doth not wrap himself in clouds, that none may see where he is, or know how to find him; may discern what he is about, or whither he tendeth.

He disguiseth not his intents with fallacious pretences of conscience, of public good, of special friendship and respect.

He doth use no disingenuous, spiteful, unjust tricks or sleights, to serve the present turn.

He layeth no baits or snares to *Catch men*, alluring them into mischief or inconvenience.

As he doth not affect any poor base ends, so he will not defile his fair intentions by sordid means of compassing them; such as are illusive simulations, and subdolous artifices, treacherous collusions, sly insinuations and sycophantic detractions, versatile whifflings and dodgings, adulatorous colloguings and glozings, servile crouchings and fawnings, and the like.

He hath little of the serpent, (none of its lurking insidiousness, of its surprising violence, of its rancorous venom, of its keen mordacity,) but

SERM. VII.

Prov. xiii. 5.
Ps. xxxiv. 13; xv. 2.

Jer. v. 26.
Ps. lxiv. 5;
lvi. 6; ix. 15; vii. 15;
x. 2; lvii. 6; xxxv. 7;
cxl. 5.
Prov. xxvi. 27.
Eccles. x. 8.
Ps. x. 7;
lv. 21; lxiv. 6; x. 9, 10;
lvi. 5.
Rom. xvi. 18.
Ecclus. xix. 26.
2 Sam. xv. 5.
Prov. xi. 9;
xxvi. 25.

much of the dove, (all its simplicity, its gentleness, its fidelity, its innocence,) in his conversation and commerce.

His wisdom is ever tempered with sincerity, and seasoned with humanity, with meekness, with charity; being *The wisdom which is from above, first pure, then peaceable, gentle, easy to be entreated, full of good fruits, without partiality, and without hypocrisy.*

He sometime may prudently reserve his mind, not venting it by foolish loquacity: but his words do never clash with his meaning, so as to deceive or disappoint any man.

He may warily prevent harm and decline perils: but it is without hurtful countermining, or deriving mischief on his neighbour.

He may discreetly pick out seasons, and embrace opportunities of righting or benefiting himself: but he never will seek or lay hold of advantages to prejudice others.

He sometimes may repress insurrections of anger or disgust: but he never doth allow them to bake into rancour or malice.

He may be apt to use courteous, affable, obliging demeanour, serving to breed friendships, and to stifle enmities: but he never thereby meaneth to gull, inveigle, and entrap men; or to procure instruments and aids of any perverse design.

He is no enemy to himself, but (according to the obligations of reason and conscience) he hath always a regard to the good of others; nor is ever so selfish, as to be unjust or uncharitabe to any man.

The principal engines he doth employ for achieving his enterprises are, a careful and cautious providence in contriving, a sedulous and steady diligence in acting, a circumspect heedfulness not to provoke any man by offensive carriage, by injury, by discourtesy, to obstruct him, but rather by kind demonstrations and real beneficence to engage men to further him in his proceedings: but especially his main instrument, wherein he most confideth, is devout supplication to God for his succour and blessing.

Now is not this conduct the most secure that can be? doth it not afford many great commodities and advantages? doth it not exempt from manifold fears, and cares, and crosses, and slaveries?

It cannot but derive blessings from the God of truth, the great friend of simplicity and sincerity, the hater of falsehood and guile.

And humanly regarding things, he that useth these methods, doth from them obtain many conveniences. He doth not lie under perpetual constraint, engaged to keep a constant guard upon himself, to watch his memory, to curb his tongue, to manage his very looks and gestures, lest they betray his intentions, and disclose his plots. He is not at the trouble of stopping holes, of mending flaws, of patching up repugnances in his actions, that his mind do not break through them. He is not afraid of the disappointment and shame which attend the detection of unworthy designs. He is not at pains to obviate the jealousies, the surmises, the diffidences, the counterplots, the preventive oppositions and assaults, which gloomy closeness and crafty dissimulation ever do raise against the practisers of them. In fine, men do not shun the conversation and the commerce of an upright person, but gladly do consort and deal with him; do seek his acquaintance and alliance: they are not apt to distrust him, to suspect him, to be shy and reserved in their intercourse with him; but readily do place an entire confidence in him, and use a clear frankness toward him. No man doth fear him as dangerous, or will cross him as an adversary. Whence as he seldom hath cause to fear, or occasion to contest with others; so he doth undisturbedly enjoy the benefits of society with great safety, ease, and comfort.

IX. Lastly, an upright walker hath perfect security, as to the final result of affairs, that he shall not be quite baffled in his expectations and desires. And if prosperity doth consist in a satisfaction of mind concerning events, he cannot fail of most prosperous success. *Whatsoever he doeth,* saith the Psalmist of him, *it shall prosper.* How is that? Doth he, if he warreth, always get the victory? is he perpetually, when he tradeth, a considerable gainer? will he certainly, after sowing, reap a plentiful crop? Probably yes; and perhaps no. Yet assuredly he shall prosper, in the true notion of prosperity, explained by those divine sayings: *Mark the perfect man, and behold the upright; for the end of that man is peace. The work of righteousness shall be peace, and the effect of righteousness quietness and assurance for ever. Surely I know it shall be well with them that fear God.*

He cannot be much defeated in his purposes: for, as to his general, principal, absolute designs, (that is, his design of pleasing God, and procuring his favour; his design of satisfying himself, and discharging his conscience; his design of promoting his own spiritual interest, and saving his soul; his design of doing good, of exercising charity to his neighbour, of serving the public, of obliging the world by virtuous example, and by real beneficence,) these he cannot fail throughly to accomplish; nothing can obstruct him in the prosecution, nothing can debar him from the execution of these undertakings; in spite of all the world, by the succour of that divine grace which ever doth favour and further such designs, he most happily will achieve them. And for other inferior designs, he can hardly be crossed in regard to them: for it is an essential part of integrity, not otherwise to affect or aim at private, secular interests, than under condition, and with a reservation, if it be God's pleasure, if it seem good to divine wisdom. He knoweth that his pains employed on any honest purpose, in a fair way, (be it to procure some worldly advantage for himself, for his relations, or for his friend,) are not lost, if they have the fruit of submission to God's will, and acquiescence in the event disposed by him. He is assured that it is good luck to have his project blasted, and that missing is better than getting, when by sovereign wisdom it is so determined. He therefore could not so fix his heart, or engage his affection in any such concern, that his mind is surprised, or his passions discomposed by a seeming adverseness of events to his endeavours. So that in effect he can have no bad success. For how can that occurrence be deemed bad, which plain reason dictateth in certain judgment to be most expedient for him;

about which he ever was very indifferent, and with which at present he is not heartily displeased? How can it be taken for disappointment and misfortune, which one was prepared to embrace with satisfaction and complacence?

Yea, to a person so disposed, that success which seemeth most adverse, justly may be reputed the best and most happy, as promoting ends incomparably more excellent than any worldly acquist: as producing fruits exceedingly more wholesome and more savoury than any temporal commodity; as exercising and improving the divinest virtues, (humility, patience, meekness, moderation, contentedness,) a grain whereof is worth all the wealth, all the preferment, all that is desirable in the world.

Wherefore let the worst that can arrive, (or that which human blindness and fondness do count the worst,) yet upright persons do not come off ill, or so (matters being rightly stated) as to be losers upon the foot of the account.

If this do not satisfy grosser apprehensions, we may add, that even in these meaner concerns Almighty God is pleased commonly to reward and encourage upright persons by the best success. For he hath, as it were, a natural inclination to gratify those who desire to please him; and, as the Psalmist expresseth it, *Hath pleasure in the prosperity of his servants.* He may seem concerned in honour to countenance those who have regard to his will, and who repose confidence in his aid; discriminating them from such as presume to act against or without him, in defiance to his will, with no deference to his providence. As they do render him his due respect, by submitting to his authority, and avowing his power; so he will acknowledge them by signally favouring their concerns. Even his truth and fidelity are engaged in their behalf; seeing he very often hath declared and promised, that in all matters, and upon all occasions, he will be ready to bless them.

SERM. VII.

Deut. xxviii. 2; xxx. 9.
Ps. cxxviii. 1, 2; xci. 1; xxxiv. 9, 10; lxxxiv. 11.
Matt. vi. 33.
Eccles. viii. 5.
Prov. xxviii. 10, 20; x. 6.

X. To conclude; It is an infinite advantage of upright dealing, that at the last issue, when all things shall be most accurately tried and impartially decided, a man is assured to be fully justified in it, and plentifully rewarded for it. As then all the deceits, which now pass under specious masks, shall be laid bare; all varnish of pretence shall be wiped off; all perverse intrigues shall be unravelled; all wicked and base intentions shall be quite stripped of the veils which now enfold them; all shrewd contrivers and engineers of mischief, all practisers of unjust and malicious guile, shall be exposed to shame, *Shall lie down in sorrow:* so then *The righteous man shall stand in great boldness;* his case will be rightly stated, and fully cleared from slanderous aspersions, from odious surmises, from unlucky prejudices and mistakes: what he hath done shall be approved; what he hath suffered shall be repaired. So that it then evidently will appear, that upright simplicity is the deepest wisdom, and perverse craft the merest shallowness; that he, who is true and just to others, is most faithful and friendly to himself; that whoever doth abuse his neighbour, is his own greatest cheater and foe. For, *In the day when God shall judge the secrets of men by Jesus Christ, Every man's*

Isai. l. 11.

Wisd. v. 1.

Rom. ii. 16.
1 Cor. iii. 13; iv. 5.

*work shall be made manifest. The Lord will bring to light the hidden things of darkness, and will make manifest the counsels of the hearts; and then shall every man have praise of God.* Unto which our upright Judge, *The King eternal, immortal, invisible, the only wise God, be honour and glory for ever and ever. Amen.*

# SERMON VIII.

## OF THE DUTY OF PRAYER.

1 Thess. V. 17.

*Pray without ceasing.*

IT is the manner of St Paul in his Epistles, after that he hath discussed some main points of doctrine or discipline, (which occasion required that he should clear and settle,) to propose several good advices and rules, in the observance whereof the life of Christian practice doth consist. So that he thereby hath furnished us with so rich a variety of moral and spiritual precepts, concerning special matters, subordinate to the general laws of piety and virtue; that out of them might well be compiled a body of ethics, or system of precepts *De officiis*, in truth and in completeness far excelling those which any philosophy hath been able to devise or deliver. These he rangeth not in any formal method, nor linketh together with strict connection, but freely scattereth them, so as from his mind (as out of a fertile soil, impregnated with all seeds of wisdom and goodness) they did aptly spring up, or as they were suggested by that holy Spirit which continually guided and governed him.

Among divers such delivered here, this is one, which shall be the subject of my present discourse;

the which, having no other plain coherence (except by affinity of matter) with the rest enclosing it, I shall consider absolutely by itself, endeavouring somewhat to explain it, and to urge its practice.

*Pray without ceasing.* For understanding these words, let us first consider what is meant by the act enjoined, *Praying;* then, what the qualification or circumstance adjoined, *Without ceasing,* doth import.

1 The word prayer doth, in its usual latitude of acception, comprehend all sorts of devotion, or all that part of religious practice, wherein we do immediately address ourselves to God, having by speech (oral or mental) a kind of intercourse and conversation with him. So it includeth that praise which we should yield to God, implying our due esteem of his most excellent perfections, most glorious works, most just and wise dispensations of providence and grace; that thanksgiving whereby we should express an affectionate resentment of our obligation to him for the numberless great benefits we receive from him; that acknowledgment of our entire dependence upon him, or our total subjection to his power and pleasure; together with that profession of faith in him, and avowing of service to him, which we do owe as his natural creatures and subjects; that humble confession of our infirmity, our vileness, our guilt, our misery, (joined with deprecation of wrath and vengeance,) which is due from us as wretched men and grievous sinners; that petition of things needful or convenient for us, (of supply in our wants, of succour and comfort in our distresses, of direction and

## The Duty of Prayer.

assistance in our undertakings, of mercy and pardon for our offences,) which our natural state (our poor, weak, sad, and sinful state) doth engage us to seek; that intercession for others, which general charity or special relation do require from us, as concerned or obliged to desire and promote their good. All these religious performances, prayer, in its larger notion, doth comprise; according whereto in common use the whole body of divine service, containing all such acts, is termed prayer; and temples, consecrated to the performance of all holy duties, are styled houses of prayer; and that brief directory, or pregnant form of all devotion, which our Lord dictated, is called his prayer; and in numberless places of scripture it is so taken.

SERM. VIII.

In a stricter sense, it doth only signify one particular act among those, the petition of things needful or useful for us.

But according to the former more comprehensive meaning, I choose to understand it here; both because it is most commonly so used, (then, especially, when no distinctive limitation is annexed, or the nature of the subject-matter doth not restrain it,) and because general reasons do equally oblige to performance of all these duties in the manner here prescribed: nor is there any ground to exclude any part of devotion from continual use; we being obliged no less incessantly to praise God for his excellencies, and thank him for his benefits, to avow his sovereign majesty and authority, to confess our infirmities and miscarriages, than to beg help and mercy from God. All devotion therefore, all sorts of proper and due address to God, (that Πᾶσα προσευχή, *All prayer and suppli-*

Eph. vi. 18.

*cation*, which St Paul otherwhere speaketh of) are here enjoined, according to the manner adjoined, *Without ceasing*, Ἀδιαλείπτως, that is, indesinently, or continually.

2 For the meaning of which expression, we must suppose, that it must not be understood as if we were obliged in every instant or singular point of time actually to apply our minds to this practice: for to do thus is in itself impossible, and therefore can be no matter of duty; it is inconsistent with other duties, and therefore must not be practised; yea, will not consist with itself; for, that we may pray, we must live; that we may live, we must eat; that we may eat, we must work; and must therefore attend other matters: so that actual devotion neither must nor can swallow up all our time and care. The deliberate operations of our mind are sometimes interrupted by sleep, sometimes will be taken up in satisfying our natural appetites, sometimes must be spent in attendance upon other reasonable employments commanded or allowed by God; whence there can be no obligation to this practice according to that unlimited interpretation. This precept therefore (as divers others of a like general purport and expression) must be understood not in a natural, but moral sense, according as the exigence of things permitteth, or as the reason of the case requireth; so far as it is conveniently practicable, or as it is reasonably compatible with other duties and needs. But we must not so restrain it as to wrong it, by pinching it within too narrow bounds[a]. How then it may be

[a] Adoro scripturæ plenitudinem.—Tertull. [adv. Hermog. cap. xxii. Opp. p. 241 D.]

*The Duty of Prayer.* 297

understood, and how far it should extend, we shall SERM. VIII.
endeavour to declare, by propounding divers senses
whereof it is capable, grounded upon plain testimonies of scripture, and enforcible by good reason; according to which senses we shall together press the observance thereof.

I. First then, *Praying incessantly* may import the maintaining in our souls a ready disposition or habitual inclination to devotion; that which in scripture is termed *The spirit of supplication.* This Zech. xii. 10.
in moral esteem, and according to current language derived thence, amounteth to a continual practice; a man being reckoned and said to do that, to which he is ever prompt and propense: as it is said of the righteous man, that *He is ever merciful,* Ps. xxxvii. 26.
*and lendeth,* because he is constantly disposed to supply his neighbour with needful relief; although he doth not ever actually dispense alms, or furnish his neighbour with supplies for his necessity. The words may signify this; they do at least by consequence imply so much: for if we do not in this, we can hardly perform the duty in any sense; without a good temper fitting, and a good appetite prompting to devotion, we scarce can or will ever apply ourselves thereto. If there be not in our heart a root of devotion, whence should it spring? how can it live or thrive? If the organs of prayer are out of kelter, or out of tune, how can we pray? If we be not *Accincti,* have not the loins of our 1 Pet. i. 13.
mind girt, and our feet shod in preparation to the Luke xii. 35.
service, when shall we set forward thereto? *My* Eph. vi. 14. Ps. cviii. 1.
*heart,* said David, *is fixed, I will sing and give* 2 Chron. xxx. 19.
*praise: fixed,* that is, readily prepared, and steadily Ezra vii. 10.
inclined to devotion. So should ours constantly

be. As a true friend is ever ready to entertain his friend with a frank courtesy and complacency; as he ever is apt upon occasion for advice and assistance to have recourse to him: so should we be always disposed cheerfully and decently to converse with God, when he freely cometh to us, or we have need to apply ourselves to him. If there be (from stupidity of mind, from coldness of affection, from sluggishness of spirit, from worldly distraction) any indisposition or averseness thereto, we should, by serious consideration and industrious care, labour to remove them; rousing our spirits, and kindling in our affections some fervency of desire toward spiritual things; otherwise we shall be apt to shun, or to slip the opportunities inviting to devotion; our hearts will be so resty or listless, that hardly we shall be induced to perform it, when it is most necessary or useful for us.

II. *Praying incessantly* may denote a vigilant attendance (with earnest regard, and firm purpose) employed upon devotion: such attendance as men usually bestow on their affairs, whereof, although the actual prosecution sometime doth stick, yet the design continually proceedeth; the mind ever so directing its eye toward them, as quickly to espy, and readily to snatch any advantages of promoting them. This is a kind of continuance in practice, and is commonly so termed: as we say, that such a one is building a house, is writing a book, is occupying such land, although he be at present sleeping, or eating, or following any other business; because his main design never sleepeth, and his purpose resteth uninterrupted. This is that which is so often enjoined under the phrase of watching about prayer. *Watch ye therefore, and pray always,* saith our Lord. *Continue in prayer, and watch in the same,* saith St Paul. *Be ye sober, and watch unto prayer,* saith St Peter. Which expressions import a most constant and careful attendance upon this duty: that we do not make it a Πάρεργον, or by-business in our life, (a matter of small consideration or indifference, of curiosity, of chance,) to be transacted drowsily or faintly, with a desultorious and slight endeavour, by fits, as the humour taketh us; but that, accounting it a business of the choicest nature and weightiest moment, we do adhere thereto with unmoveable purpose, regard it with undistracted attention, pursue it with unwearied diligence, being always upon the guard, wakeful and expedite, intent upon and apt to close with any occasion suggesting matter thereof. That we should do thus, reason also doth oblige: for that, as in truth no business doth better deserve our utmost resolution and care; so none doth more need them; nature being so backward, and occasion so slippery, that if we do not ever mind it, we shall seldom practise it.

III. *Praying incessantly* may signify, that we do actually embrace all fit seasons and emergent occasions of devotion. This, in moral computation, doth pass for continual performance: as a tree is said to bear that fruit, which it produceth in the season; and a man is accounted to work in that trade, which he exerciseth whenever he is called thereto. This sense is, in several precepts parallel to that in hand, plainly expressed. *Pray,* saith St Paul, *with all prayer and supplication,* Ἐν παντὶ καιρῷ; and, *Watch,* saith our Lord, Ἐν παντὶ καιρῷ δεόμενοι, *praying in every season,* or upon every opportunity. Devotion, indeed, is rarely unseasonable or impertinent: we may offer it Εὐκαίρως, ἀκαίρως, *In season, and out of season;* that is, not only taking opportunities presented for it, or urgently requiring it, but catching at them, and creating them to ourselves, when there is no such apparent and pressing need of it. But there are some special occasions, which more importunately and indispensably do exact it: some seasons there are, (either ministered by extrinsical accidents, or springing from internal dispositions,) when, without both great blame and much damage to ourselves, we cannot neglect it: times there be most proper and acceptable, when we do especially need to pray, and when we are likely to speed well therein. *Every one,* saith the Psalmist, *that is godly will pray unto thee in a time when thou mayest be found:* and, *My prayer,* saith he again, *is unto thee in an acceptable time.*

Thus, when we have received any singular blessing or notable favour from God, when prosperous success hath attended our honest enterprises, when we have been happily rescued from imminent dangers, when we have been supported in difficulties, or relieved in wants and straits; then is it seasonable to render sacrifices of thanksgiving and praise to the God of victory, help, and mercy; to admire and celebrate him, who is our *Strength, and* our *deliverer,* our *faithful refuge in trouble,* our *fortress, and the rock of* our *salvation.* To omit this piece of devotion then is vile ingratitude, or stupid negligence and sloth.

When any rare object or remarkable occurrence

*The Duty of Prayer.* 301

doth, upon this theatre of the world, present itself SERM. VIII.
to our view, in surveying the glorious works of
nature, or the strange events of Providence; then
is a proper occasion suggested to send up hymns of
praise to the power, the wisdom, the goodness of
the world's great Creator and Governor.

When we undertake any business of special moment and difficulty, then it is expedient (wisdom prompting it) to sue for God's aid, to commit our affairs into his hand, to recommend our endeavours to the blessing of him, by whose guidance all things are ordered, without whose concourse nothing can be effected, upon whose arbitrary disposal all success dependeth.

The beginning of any design or business (although ordinary, if considerable) is a proper season of prayer unto him, to whose bounty and favour we owe our ability to act, support in our proceedings, any comfortable issue of what we do: (for *All our sufficiency is of him: Without him we can do nothing.*) Whence we can never apply ourselves to any business or work, not go to eat, to sleep, to travel, to trade, to study, with any true content, any reasonable security, any satisfactory hope, if we do not first humbly implore the favourable protection, guidance, and assistance of God[b].

2 Cor. iii. 5.
John xv. 5.

When we do fall into doubts, or darknesses, (in the course either of our spiritual or secular affairs,) not knowing what course to steer, or which way to turn ourselves; (a case which, to so blind and silly creatures as we are, must often happen;) then doth the time bid us to consult the great oracle of truth, *The mighty Counsellor, The Father of lights,* seek-

Isai. ix. 6.
James i. 17.

[b] Δεῖ πάσης πράξεως προηγεῖσθαι προσευχήν.—Marc. Erem.

ing resolution and satisfaction, light and wisdom from him; saying with the Psalmist, *Shew me thy ways, O Lord, lead me in thy truth, and teach me; for thou art the God of my salvation: Order my steps in thy word, and let not any iniquity have dominion over me;* following the advice of St James, *If any man lack wisdom, let him ask of God, that giveth to all men liberally, and upbraideth not; and it shall be given him.*

When any storm of danger blustereth about us, perilously threatening, or furiously assailing us with mischief, (so that hardly by our own strength or wit we can hope to evade,) then with the wings of ardent devotion we should fly unto God for shelter and for relief.

When any anxious care distracteth, or any heavy burden presseth our minds, we should by prayer ease ourselves of them, and discharge them upon God, committing the matter of them to his care and providence; according to that direction of St Paul, *Be careful for nothing: but in every thing by prayer and supplication with thanksgiving let your requests be made known to God.*

When we do lie under any irksome trouble or sore distress, (of want, pain, disgrace,) then, for succour and support, for ease and comfort, we should have recourse to *The Father of pities, and God of all consolation; Who is nigh to all that call upon him, will also hear their cry, and will save them;* who, when *The righteous cry, doth hear them, and delivereth them out of all their troubles;* who is so often styled *The hiding-place from troubles, the help and strength, the shield and buckler, the rock, the fortress, the high tower, the horn of salvation*, to all good and distressed people. To him we should in such a condition have recourse, imitating the pious Psalmist, whose practice was this: *In the day of my trouble I sought the Lord: I poured out my complaint before him, I shewed before him my trouble: I called unto the Lord in my distress: the Lord answered me, and set me in a large place.*

SERM. VIII.

Ps. lxxvii. 2; xviii. 6; cxlii. 2; cxviii. 5.

When any strong temptation doth invade us, with which by our own strength we cannot grapple, but are like to sink and falter under it; then is it opportune and needful that we should seek to God for a supply of spiritual forces, and the succour of his almighty grace, as St Paul did: when *There was given to him a thorn in the flesh, a messenger of Satan to buffet him;* then *He besought the Lord thrice that it might depart from him:* and he had this return from God, *My grace is sufficient for thee.*

2 Cor. xii. 7, 8, 9.

When also (from ignorance or mistake, from inadvertency, negligence, or rashness, from weakness, from wantonness, from presumption) we have transgressed our duty, and incurred sinful guilt; then, (for avoiding the consequent danger and vengeance, for unloading our consciences of the burden and discomfort thereof,) with humble confession in our mouths, and serious contrition in our hearts, we should apply ourselves to the God of mercy, deprecating his wrath, and imploring pardon from him; remembering that promise of St John, *If we confess our sins, he is faithful and just to forgive us our sins, and to cleanse us from all iniquity;* and that declaration of the Wise Man, *He that*

1 John i. 9.

Prov. xxviii. 13.

*covereth his sins shall not prosper, but he that confesseth and forsaketh them shall have mercy.*

In these and the like cases God by our necessities doth invite and summon us to come unto him; and no less foolish than impious we are, if we do then slink away, or fly from him. Then we should (as the apostle to the Hebrews exhorteth) *Come boldly unto the throne of grace, that we may obtain mercy, and find grace to help in time of need,* (or, for seasonable relief[c].)

And beside those outwardly prompting and urging us, there be other opportunities, springing from within us, which we are no less obliged and concerned to embrace. When God by his gentle whispers calleth us, or by his soft impulses draweth us into his presence; we should then take heed of stopping our ears, or turning our hearts from him, refusing to hearken or to comply. We must not any wise quench or damp any sparks of devout affection kindled in us by the divine Spirit; we must not repel or resist any of his kindly suggestions or motions.

Whenever we find ourselves well affected to, or well framed for devotion; that we have a lively sense of, and a coming appetite to spiritual things; that our spirits are brisk and pure, our fancy calm and clear, our hearts tender and supple, our affections warm and nimble; then a fair season offereth itself; and when the iron is so hot, we should strike.

If at any time we feel any forward inclinations or good dispositions to the practice of this duty, we should never check or curb them, but rather

[c] Εἰς εὔκαιρον βοήθειαν.

should promote and advance them; pushing ourselves forward in this hopeful career; letting out the stream of our affections into this right channel, that it may run freely therein, that it may overflow and diffuse itself in exuberance of devotion.

Further,

IV. *Praying incessantly* may signify, that we should with assiduous urgency drive on the intent of our prayers, never quitting it, or desisting, till our requests are granted, or our desires are accomplished. Thus doing we may be said to pray continually: as he that goeth forward in his journey, (although he sometime doth bait, sometime doth rest and repose himself,) is said yet to be in travel; or as he that doth not wave the prosecution of his cause, (although some demurs intervene,) is deemed still to be in suit. This is that which our Lord did in the Gospel prescribe and persuade, where it is recorded of him, that *He spake a parable unto them, that men ought always to pray, and not to faint.* That praying always the ensuing discourse sheweth to import restless importunity, and perseverance in prayer: the same which so often is commended to us by the phrases of Μὴ ἐκκακεῖν, *Not to faint or falter*; Μὴ παύεσθαι, *Not to cease, or give over*; Προσκαρτερεῖν, *To continue instant, or hold out stoutly*; Ἀγωνίζεσθαι, *To strive earnestly, or contest and struggle in prayers*; Προσμένειν ταῖς δεήσεσι, *To abide at supplications*; Ἀγρυπνεῖν ἐν πάσῃ προσκαρτερήσει, *To watch with all perseverance.* That which also is implied by those terms, which in scriptural style do commonly express devotion: by *Seeking God;* which implieth, that God doth

Luke xviii. 1.

Col. i. 9.
Eph. i. 16.
Rom. xii. 12.
Col. iv. 2, 12.
Eph. vi. 18.
Ps. x. 4; xi. 10; xiv. 2; xxiv. 6; lxiii. 1; lxix. 6, 32; lxx. 4; lxxxiii. 16.
Job viii. 5.
Deut. iv. 29.

SERM. VIII.

Prov. viii. 17.
Ps. lxxvii. 6; cxxiii. 2; lxix. 3; cxxx. 5; xxxvii. 7; xxv. 5; xxvii. 14; xxxvii. 34; xxv. 21; lii. 9; lix. 9; cxlv. 15.
Isai. viii. 17; xl. 31; xlix. 23.
Hos. xii. 6.
Lam. iii. 25, 26.
Prov. xx. 22.
Ps. cxxiii. 2.
Luke xii. 36.
Matt. vii. 7.

not presently, upon any slight address, discover himself in beneficial effects answerable to our desires, but after a careful and painful continuance in our applications to him: by *Waiting upon God;* which signifieth, that if God do not presently appear granting our requests, we should patiently stay, expecting till he be pleased to do it in his own best time, according to that in the Psalm, *Our eyes wait upon the Lord our God, until he have mercy upon us:* by *Knocking;* which intimateth, that the door of grace doth not ever stand open, or that we can have an effectual access to God, until he, warned, and as it were excited, by our earnest importunity, pleaseth to listen, to disclose himself, to come forth unto us.

And this practice reason also doth enforce. For there are some good things absolutely necessary for our spiritual life and welfare, (such as are freedom from bad inclinations, disorderly affections, vicious habits, and noxious errors[d]; the sanctifying presence and influence of God's holy Sprit, with the blessed graces and sweet fruits thereof; growth in virtue, delight in spiritual things, the sense of God's love and favour, with the like,) which good reason engageth us perseveringly to seek, as never to rest or be satisfied till we have acquired them in perfect degree; since we cannot ever do well without them, or ever get enough of them. In begging other inferior things, it may become us to be reserved, indifferent, and modest; but about these matters (wherein all our felicity is extremely concerned) it were a folly to be slack or

[d] Vid. Chrys. ad Theod. II. Opp. Tom. VI.

# The Duty of Prayer. 307

timorous[e]: as we cannot be said immoderately to desire them, so we cannot be supposed immodestly to seek them there, where only they can be found, in God's presence and hand. The case doth bear, yea, doth require, that we should be eager and hot, resolute and stiff, free and bold, yea, in a manner peremptory and impudent solicitors with God for them. So our Saviour intimateth, where comparing the manner of God's proceeding with that of men, he representeth one friend yielding needful succour to another, not barely upon the score of friendship, but Διὰ τὴν ἀναίδειαν, *For his impu-* Luke xi. 8. *dence;* that is, for his confident and continued urgency, admitting no refusal or excuse. So doth God, in such cases, allow and oblige us to deal with him, being instant and pertinacious in our requests, *Giving him no rest;* (as the phrase is in Isai. lxii. 7. the prophet;) not enduring to be put off, or brooking any repulse; never being discouraged, or cast into despair, by any delay or semblance of neglect. We may wrestle with God, like Jacob, and with Jacob may say, *I will not let thee go, except thou bless* Gen. xxxii. *me.* Thus God suffereth himself to be prevailed upon, 26. and is willingly overcome: thus Omnipotence may be mastered, and a happy victory may be gained over invincibility itself. Heaven sometime may be forced by storm; (or by the assaults of extremely fervent prayer;) it assuredly will yield to a long siege. God will not ever hold out against the attempts of an obstinate suppliant. So *The king-* Matt. xi. *dom of heaven suffereth violence, and the violent* 12. *take it by force.* We read in St John's Gospel of John v. 5.

SERM.
VIII.

[e] Αἰδὼς δ' οὐκ ἀγαθὴ κεχρημένῳ ἀνδρὶ προΐκτῃ.
[Hom. Od. XVII. 347.]

SERM. VIII.

a man, that, being thirty-eight years diseased, did wait at the pool of Bethesda seeking relief: him our Lord pitied and helped, crowning his patience with miraculous relief, and proposing it for an example to us of perseverance[f]. It is said of the patriarch Isaac, that *He entreated the Lord for his wife, because she was barren; and the Lord was entreated of him, and Rebecca his wife conceived.* Whereupon St Chrysostom doth observe, that he had persevered twenty years in that petition[g].

Gen. xxv. 21.

Of good success to this practice we have many assurances in holy scripture. *The Lord is good unto them that wait for him, to the soul that seeketh him*[h]. *Blessed are 'all they that wait for him. None that wait on him shall be ashamed. They that wait upon the Lord shall renew their strength; they shall mount up with wings as eagles; they shall run, and not be weary; they shall walk, and not faint.* So hath God assured by his word, and engaged himself by promise, that he will yield unto constant and patient devotion; so that it shall never want good success.

Lam. iii. 25.
Isai. xxx. 18; xlix. 23.
Ps. xxv. 3; xxxvii. 9.
Isai. xl. 31.
1 Chron. xxviii. 9.
Ezra viii. 22.
Amos v. 4.
2 Chron. xv. 12.
Ps. ix. 10; xxiv. 6; lxix. 6; lxx. 4; cxix. 2; x. 4.

Without this practice we cannot indeed hope to obtain those precious things; they will not come at an easy rate, or be given for a song; a lazy wish or two cannot fetch them down from heaven. God will not bestow them at first asking, or deal them out in one lump: but it is upon assiduous soliciting, and by gradual communication, that he dispenseth them. So his wise good-will, for many

[f] Vid. Chrys. Orat. xl. Opp. Tom. v. [p. 266.] et in Joh. Hom. xxxvi. Tom. ii. [p. 700.]

[g] Vid. Orat. lxviii. Tom. vi. [p. 701.]

[h] "*Seeking God*, the periphrasis of a religious man."—Ps. xiv. 2.

special reasons, disposeth him to proceed: that we may (as it becometh and behoveth us) abide under a continual sense of our natural impotency and penury: of our dependance upon God, and obligation to him for the free collation of those best gifts: that by some difficulty of procuring them we may be minded of their worth, and induced the more to prize them: that by earnestly seeking them we may improve our spiritual appetites, and excite holy affections: that by much conversing with heaven our minds may be raised above earthly things, and our hearts purified from sordid desires: that we may have a constant employment answerable to the best capacities of our souls, worthy our care and pain, yielding most solid profit and pure delight unto us: that, in fine, by our greater endeavour in religious practice we may obtain a more ample reward thereof.

For the same reason indeed that we pray at all, we should pray thus with continued instance. We do not pray to instruct or advise God; not to tell him news, or inform him of our wants: (*He knows them*, as our Saviour telleth us, *before we ask:*) nor do we pray by dint of argument to persuade God, and bring him to our bent; nor that by fair speech we may cajole him or move his affections toward us by pathetical orations: not for any such purpose are we obliged to pray. But for that it becometh and behoveth us so to do, because it is a proper instrument of bettering, ennobling, and perfecting our souls; because it breedeth most holy affections, and pure satisfactions, and worthy resolutions, because it fitteth us for the enjoyment of happiness, and leadeth us thither: for such ends devotion is

SERM. VIII.

Matt. vi. 8.

SERM. VIII.

prescribed; and constant perseverance therein being needful to those purposes, (praying by fits and starts not sufficing to accomplish them,) therefore such perseverance is required of us. Further,

V. *Praying incessantly* may import, that we do with all our occupations and all occurrences interlace devout ejaculations of prayer and praise; lifting up our hearts to God, and breathing forth expressions of devotion, suitable to the objects and occasions which present themselves. This, as it nearly doth approach to the punctual accomplishment of what our text prescribeth, so it seemeth required by St Paul, when he biddeth us *Pray always* Ἐν πνεύματι, *in spirit*, and to sing Ἐν τῇ καρδίᾳ, *in the heart*: that is, with very frequent elevations of spirit in holy thoughts and desires toward heaven; with opportune resentments of heart, directing thanks and praise to God. We cannot ever be framing or venting long prayers with our lips, but almost ever our mind can throw pious glances, our heart may dart good wishes upwards; so that hardly any moment (any considerable space of time) shall pass without some lightsome flashes of devotion[l]. As bodily respiration, without intermission or impediment, doth concur with all our actions; so may that breathing of soul, which preserveth our spiritual life, and ventilateth that holy flame within us, well conspire with all other occupations[k]. For devotion is of a nature so spiritual,

Eph. vi. 18; v. 19. Col. iii. 16.

---

[l] Sed non satis perspiciunt, quantum natura humani ingenii valeat: quæ ita est agilis et velox, sic in omnem partem, ut ita dixerim, spectat, ut ne possit quidem aliquid agere tantum unum: in plura vero, non eodem die modo, sed eodem temporis momento, vim suam impendat.—Quint. I. 12. [2.]

[k] Μνημονευτέον γὰρ Θεοῦ μᾶλλον ἢ ἀναπνευστέον· καὶ, εἰ οἷόν τε

## The Duty of Prayer. 311

so subtle, and penetrant, that no matter can exclude or obstruct it. Our minds are so exceedingly nimble and active, that no business can hold pace with them, or exhaust their attention and activity. We can never be so fully possessed by any employment, but that divers vacuities of time do intercur, wherein our thoughts and affections will be diverted to other matters. As a covetous man, whatever beside he is doing, will be carking about his bags and treasures; an ambitious man will be devising on his plots and projects; a voluptuous man will have his mind in his dishes; a lascivious man will be doting on his amours; a studious man will be musing on his notions; every man, according to his particular inclination, will lard his business and besprinkle all his actions with cares and wishes tending to the enjoyment of what he most esteemeth and affecteth: so may a good Christian, through all his undertakings, wind in devout reflections and pious motions of soul toward the chief object of his mind and affection[1]. Most businesses have wide gaps, all have some chinks, at which devotion may slip in. Be we never so urgently set or closely intent upon any work, (be we feeding, be we travelling, be we trading, be we studying,) nothing yet can forbid, but that we may together wedge in a thought concerning God's goodness, and bolt forth a word of praise for it; but that we may reflect on our sins, and spend a penitential sigh on them; but that we may descry our need of God's help, and despatch a brief peti-

SERM. VIII.

τοῦτο εἰπεῖν, μηδὲ ἄλλο τι ἢ τοῦτο πρακτέον.—Greg. Naz. [Orat. XXVII. Opp. Tom. I. p. 490 B.]

[1] Vid. Chrys. Orat. v. in Annam. Opp. Tom. v. [pp. 77, 78.]

SERM. VIII.

tion for it: a *God be praised,* a *Lord have mercy,* a *God bless,* or *God help me,* will nowise interrupt or disturb our proceedings<sup>m</sup>. As worldly cares and desires do often intrude and creep into our devotions, distracting and defiling them; so may spiritual thoughts and holy affections insinuate themselves into, and hallow our secular transactions. This practice is very possible, and it is no less expedient: for that if our employments be not thus seasoned, they can have no true life or savour in them; they will in themselves be dead and putrid, they will be foul and noisome, or at least flat and insipid unto us.

There are some other good meanings of this precept, according to which, holy scripture (backed with good reason) obligeth us to observe it: but those, (together with the general inducements to the practice of this duty,) that I may not further now trespass on your patience, I shall reserve to another opportunity.

---

[m] Εἰπὲ κατὰ διάνοιαν, Ἐλέησόν με, ὁ Θεὸς, καὶ ἀπήρτισταί σου ἡ εὐχή.—Chrys. [ubi supra, p. 77.]

# SERMON IX.

## OF THE DUTY OF PRAYER.

1 THESS. V. 17.

*Pray without ceasing.*

WHAT the prayer here enjoined by St Paul doth import, and how by it universally all sorts of devotion should be understood, we did formerly discourse. How also according to divers senses (grounded in holy scripture, and enforced by good reason) we may perform this duty incessantly, we did then declare; five such senses we did mention and prosecute: I shall now add two or three more, and press them.

VI. *Praying* then *incessantly* may imply, that we do appoint certain times conveniently distant for the practice of devotion, and carefully observe them. To keep the Jews in a constant exercise of divine worship, God did constitute a sacrifice, which was called *Tamidh*, (Ἡ διαπαντὸς θυσία,) *The continual sacrifice.* And as at that sacrifice, being constantly offered at set times, was thence denominated continual; so may we, by punctually observing fit returns of devotion, be said to pray incessantly.

Dan. viii. 11.
Heb. xiii. 15.
Neh. x. 33.

And great reason there is that we should do so. For we know that all persons, who would not lead a loose and slattering life, but design with good assurance and advantage to prosecute an orderly course of action, are wont to distribute their time into several parcels; assigning some part thereof to the necessary refection of their bodies, some to the convenient relaxation of their minds, some to the despatch of their ordinary affairs, some also to familiar conversation and interchanging good offices with their friends[a]; considering, that otherwise they shall be uncertain and *Unstable in all their ways.* And in this distribution of time devotion surely should not lack its share: it rather justly claimeth the choicest portion to be allotted thereto, as being incomparably the noblest part of our duty, and mainest concernment of our lives. The feeding our souls and nourishing our spiritual life, the refreshing our spirits with those no less pleasant than wholesome exercises, the driving on our correspondence and commerce with heaven, the improving our friendship and interest with God, are affairs which above all others do best deserve, and most need being secured. They must not therefore be left at random, to be done by the by, as it hitteth by chance, or as the fancy taketh us. If we do not depute vacant seasons, and fix periodical returns for devotion, engaging ourselves by firm resolution, and inuring our minds by constant usage to the strict observance of them, secluding from them, as from sacred enclosures, all other businesses; we shall often be dangerously tempted to neglect it, we shall be commonly listless to it, prone to defer it, easily seduced from it by the en-

---

[a] Cur ipsi aliquid forensibus negotiis, aliquid desideriis amicorum, aliquid rationibus domesticis, aliquid curæ corporis, nonnihil voluptatibus quotidie damus?—Quint. I. 12. [7.]

croachment of other affairs, or enticement of other pleasures. It is requisite that our souls also (no less than our bodies) should have their meals, settled at such intervals as the maintenance of their life, their health, their strength and vigour do require; that they may not perish or languish for want of timely repasts; that a good appetite may duly spring up, prompting and instigating to them; that a sound temper and robust constitution of soul may be preserved by them.

Prayers are the bulwarks of piety and good conscience, the which ought to be placed so as to flank and relieve one another, together with the interjacent spaces of our life; that the enemy (*The sin which doth so easily beset us*) may not come on between, or at any time assault us, without a force sufficiently near to reach and repel him.

In determining these seasons and measures of time according to just proportion, honest prudence (weighing the several conditions, capacities, and circumstances of each person) must arbitrate. For some difference is to be made between a merchant and a monk, between those who follow a court, and those who reside in a cloister or a college. Some men having great encumbrances of business and duty by necessity imposed on them, which consume much of their time, and engage their thoughts; of them in reason, neither so frequent recourses to, nor so long durances in prayer can be demanded, as from those who enjoy more abundant leisure, and freer scope of thoughts. But some fit times all may and must allow, which no avocation of business, no distraction of care should purloin from them.

SERM. IX.

Ps. xcii. 1, 2; lv. 17.

Certain seasons and periods of this kind nature itself (in correspondence to her unalterable revolutions) doth seem to define and prescribe: those which the royal prophet recommendeth, when he saith, *It is a good thing to give thanks unto the Lord, and to sing praises unto thy name, O thou most high: to shew forth thy lovingkindness every morning and thy faithfulness every night.* Every day we do recover and receive a new life from God; every morning we do commence business, or revive it; from our bed of rest and security we then issue forth, exposing ourselves to the cares and toils, to the dangers, troubles, and temptations of the world: then especially therefore it is reasonable, that we should sacrifice thanks to the gracious preserver of our life, and the faithful restorer of its supports and comforts; that we should crave his direction and help in the pursuit of our honest undertakings; that to his protection from sin and mischief we should recommend ourselves and our affairs; that, by offering up to him the first-fruits of our diurnal labours, we should consecrate and consign them all to his blessing; that, as we are then wont to salute all the world, so then chiefly with humble obeisance we should accost him, who is ever present with us and continually watchful over us. Then also peculiarly devotion is most seasonable, because then our minds being less prepossessed and pestered with other cares, our fancies becoming lively and gay, our memories fresh and prompt, our spirits copious and brisk, we are better disposed for it.

Every night also reason calleth for these duties; requiring that we should close our business and

## The Duty of Prayer. 317

wind up all our cares in devotion; that we should SERM. then bless God for his gracious preservation of us IX. from the manifold hazards and the sins to which we stood obnoxious; that we should implore his mercy for the manifold neglects and transgressions of our duty, which through the day past we have incurred; that our minds being then so tired with study and care, our spirits so wasted with labour and toil, that we cannot any longer sustain ourselves, but do of our own accord sink down into a posture of death, we should, as dying men, resign our souls into God's hand, depositing ourselves and our concernments into his custody, who alone *Doth* Ps. cxxi. 4. *never sleep nor slumber;* praying that he would guard us from all the dangers and disturbances incident to us in that state of forgetfulness, and *interregnum* of our reason; that he would grant us a happy resurrection in safety and health, with a good and cheerful mind, enabling us thereafter comfortably to enjoy ourselves, and delightfully to serve him.

Thus if we do constantly bound and circumscribe our days, dedicating those most remarkable breaks of time unto God's service, since beginning and end do comprehend the whole, seeing, in the computation and style of Moses, *Evening and* Gen. i. *Morning* do constitute a day, we may with some good congruity be said to pray incessantly.

Especially if, at the middle distance between those extremes, we are wont to interpose somewhat of devotion. For as then usually our spirits, being somewhat shattered and spent, do need a recruit, enabling us to pass through the residue of the day with its incumbent business; so then it would do well, and may be requisite, in a meal of devotion to refresh our souls with spiritual sustenance, drawn from the never-failing storehouse of divine grace; which may so fortify us, that with due vigour and alacrity we may perform the ensuing duties to God's honour and our own comfort. Thus to practise was the resolution of the Psalmist, that great master of devotion; *Evening*, said he, *and morning, and at noon, will I pray, and cry aloud.* And this was the custom of the noble Daniel, from which no occasion could divert, no hazard could deter him: *He kneeled*, saith the story, *upon his knees three times a day, and prayed, and gave thanks before his God.*

These are times which it is necessary, or very expedient, that all men (even persons of highest rank, and greatest employment) should observe. These even of old were the practices of religious persons, not expressly prescribed by God's law, but assumed by themselves; good reason suggesting them to the first practisers, and the consenting example of pious men afterward enforcing them.

God indeed did himself in his law, or by his prophets, appoint public and solemn celebrations of worship to himself, in sacrifices (involving prayer and accompanied therewith) constantly to be offered every morning and evening: religious princes also did institute services of thanksgiving and praise to be performed at those times: but there doth not appear any direct institution of private devotion, or its circumstances; but the practice thereof seemeth originally to have been purely voluntary, managed and measured according to the reason, by the choice of each person; yet so, that the prac-

*The Duty of Prayer.* 319

tice of eminently good men leading, and others following, it grew into a kind of common law, or standing rule, (seeming to carry an obligation with it,) to observe the times specified.

SERM.
IX.

Besides those three times, there were further other middle times observed by devout people, who had leisure and disposition of mind thereto; once between morning and noon, and once between noon and evening were sequestered to that purpose: whence in the Acts the ninth hour of the day (that is, the middle interval between noon and evening) is called *The hour of prayer*. Yea, some did impose on themselves the observation of two other times, one between evening and midnight, the other between midnight and morn. To which practice those places in the Psalms do seem to allude; *My mouth shall praise thee with joyful lips, when I remember thee on my bed, and meditate on thee in the night-watches. I prevented the dawning of the morning, and cried: Mine eyes prevent the night-watches, that I may meditate on thy word.* And plainly the whole number of those times which the Psalmist observed is expressed in those words: *Seven times a day will I praise thee, because of thy righteous judgments.* Which examples whoever shall choose to follow, (in any measure,) he shall do wisely and commendably; he shall certainly have no cause to repent; he will find it richly worth his while; great benefit and comfort will thence accrue unto him.

Acts iii. 1.

Ps. lxiii. 5, 6.

Ps. cxix. 147, 148.

Ps. cxix. 164.

If indeed Jews were so liberal in assigning, so punctual in affording such portions of time for yielding praise, and offering supplications unto God; how much more free and ready, more careful

SERM. IX.

and diligent, should we be in this way of practice! we who have a religion so far more spiritual, and exempt from corporeal encumbrances; precepts so much more express and clear; so much higher obligations and stronger encouragements to this duty; whom God in especial manner so graciously doth invite, so powerfully doth attract unto himself. But further,

VII. More especially this precept may be supposed to exact from us a compliance in carefully observing the times of devotion ordained by public authority, or settled by general custom. This in a popular and legal sense is doing a thing indesinently, when we perform it so often as is required by law or custom. So the apostle to the Hebrews saith of the priests, that *They went always into the tabernacle, accomplishing the service of God: Always,* that is, at all the solemn times appointed. And thus of the apostles it is affirmed by St Luke, that *They were continually in the temple, blessing and praising God;* that is, they constantly resorted thither at the stated times of concourse for prayer. This good reason also plainly doth enjoin: for that the neglecting it is not only a disorderly behaviour in a matter of high consequence; a criminal disregard and disobedience to authority; a scandalous contempt of our neighbours, from whose laudable fashion we discost; a wrongful deserting the public, to whose good, mainly promoted by the public worship of God, we do owe the contribution of our endeavour; but a heinous affront to Almighty God, who thereby is plainly dishonoured, and in a manner openly disavowed; a huge prejudice to religion, the credit and power whereof, without

Lev. xix. 30; xxvi. 2.

Heb. ix. 6.

Luke xxiv. 53.

## The Duty of Prayer.

visible profession, exemplary compliance, mutual consent and encouragement, cannot be upheld. Were there times by law or custom defined, (as in some places indeed there are,) when all men should be required in person solemnly to attend on their prince, for professing their allegiance, or deferring any homage to him; would not those, who should wilfully refuse or decline appearance, be justly chargeable as guilty of dishonouring and wronging him? would not their such defailance pass for sufficient proof that they do not acknowledge him, that at least they do not much regard or value him? So, by not joining at stated times in celebration of divine worship, we may be well conceived wholly to disclaim God, or greatly to disesteem him; to slight religion, as a thing insignificant and unprofitable. Do we not indeed thereby more than intimate, that we little believe God to be our sovereign Lord and Governor; that we stand in no great awe or dread of him; that we are not much sensible of his benefits and mercies; that we repose small trust or hope in him; that we do not take ourselves much to want his protection, his guidance, his assistance, his favour and mercy? Are we not in effect like to those in Job, who *Say unto God, Depart from us; for we desire not the knowledge of thy ways? What is the Almighty, that we should serve him? or what profit shall we have, if we pray unto him?* Thus the standers-by commonly (some so as to be much offended at, others so as to be corrupted by our bad example) will interpret this neglect: and so assuredly God himself will take it from us, and accordingly deal with us. As he claimeth this public attendance

SERM. IX.

Job xxi. 14, 15.

SERM. IX.

Ps. xxix. 1, 2; lxvi. 2.

on him for his due: (*Give*, proclaimeth he by the mouth of one of his great heralds, *Give unto the Lord, O ye mighty, give unto the Lord glory and strength: Give unto the Lord the glory due to his name: worship the Lord in the beauty of holiness:*) so if we to his wrong and disgrace refuse to yield it, we shall certainly find answerable resentment and recompense from him: that as we are careless to serve him, so he will be unmindful to bless us; as we are backward to avow and glorify him, so he will not be forward to own and grace us; as we do so *Deny him before men*, so *he will deny us before them also.* What other measure indeed can we imagine or expect to receive? Will God, think we, be so partial and fond to us, so disregardful and injurious toward himself, that he will vouchsafe to appear in favour to us, when we deign not to appear in respect to him? that he will openly tender our repute, when we apparently disregard his honour? that he will employ his wisdom, or exert his power, in our behalf, when we scarce will think a thought, or stir a step, for his service? Can we hope that he will freely dispense prosperous success to our enterprises, when we either care not or scorn to implore his help? that he will reach forth undeserved blessings to us, when we subtract due praises from him? that he will any wise shew himself bountiful and merciful toward us, when we so palpably are injust and ingrateful toward him? No, *Surely he scorneth the scorners;* and, *Whosoever despiseth him shall be lightly esteemed;* so he expressly hath threatened; and seeing he is both infallibly true and invincibly able, we may reasonably presume that he will accomplish his word.

Matt. x. 33. Luke ix. 26; xii. 9. 2 Tim. ii. 12.

Prov. iii. 34. 1 Sam. ii. 30.

*The Duty of Prayer.*

VIII. Lastly, *Praying incessantly* may import at large a frequency in devotion. This the words at least do exact or necessarily imply, however expounded. For doing incessantly cannot imply less than doing frequently: in no tolerable sense can we be said to do that continually, which we do seldom: but it is an ordinary scheme of speech to say, that a man doth that always, which he is wont to do, and performeth often. As of the pious soldier Cornelius it is said, that *He gave much alms to the people, and prayed to God always*; and of Anna the prophetess, that *She departed not from the temple, but served God with prayers and fastings night and day*; that is, she frequently resorted to the temple, and served God with an assiduous constancy. As the words may bear and do involve this sense, so doth the reason of the case enforce it: for very just, very fit, very needful it is to practise thus. There is ever at hand abundant reason for, and apposite matter of, devotion; therefore no large space of time should pass without it: there be perpetually depending many causes thereof; whence there is not to be allowed any long vacation from it. As every moment we from God's mercy and bounty partake great favours; so should we often render thanks and praise for them: for perpetually to receive courtesies, and rarely to return acknowledgments, is notorious ingratitude and iniquity. We frequently (and in a manner continually) do fall into sins; often therefore we are obliged to confess sins, we are concerned to deprecate wrath, and beg mercy; otherwise we must long crouch under the sore burden of guilt, the sad dread of punishment, the

SERM. IX.

Acts x. 2.

Luke ii. 37.

bitter pangs of remorse, or the desperate hazard of stupid obduration. Whatever we design or undertake, toward the good management and happy success thereof, we (being ignorant and impotent creatures) do need the guidance, the assistance, and the blessing of God; so often therefore it is requisite that we should be seeking and suing for them: if not, we do not only transgress our duties, but fondly neglect or foully betray our own concernments. The causes therefore of devotion being so constant, the effects in some correspondence should be frequent.

Such frequency is indeed necessary for the breeding, the nourishment, the growth and improvement of all piety. Devotion is that holy and heavenly fire, which darteth into our minds the light of spiritual knowledge, which kindleth in our hearts the warmth of holy desires: if therefore we do continue long absent from it, a night of darkness will overspread our minds, a deadening coldness will seize upon our affections. It is the best food of our souls, which preserveth their life and health, which repaireth their strength and vigour, which rendereth them lusty and active: if we therefore long abstain from it, we shall starve or pine away; we shall be faint and feeble in all religious performances; we shall have none at all, or a very languid and meagre piety.

To maintain in us a constant and steady disposition to obedience, to correct our perverse inclinations, to curb our unruly passions, to strengthen us against temptations, to comfort us in anxieties and distresses, we do need continual supplies of grace from God; the which ordinarily are commu-

### The Duty of Prayer. 325

nicated in devotion, as the channel which conveyeth, or the instrument which helpeth to procure it, or the condition upon which it is granted. Faith, hope, love, spiritual comfort, and joy, all divine graces are chiefly elicited, expressed, exercised therein and thereby: it is therefore needful that it should frequently be used; seeing otherwise we shall be in danger to fail in discharging our chief duties, and to want the best graces.

It is frequency of devotion also, which maintaineth that friendship with God which is the soul of piety. As familiar conversation (wherein men do express their minds and affections mutually) breedeth acquaintance, and cherisheth good-will of men to one another; but long forbearance thereof dissolveth or slakeneth the bonds of amity, breaking their intimacy, and cooling their kindness: so is it in respect to God; it is frequent converse with him which begetteth a particular acquaintance with him, a mindful regard of him, a hearty liking to him, a delightful taste of his goodness, and consequently a sincere and solid good-will toward him; but intermission thereof produceth estrangement or enmity toward him. If we seldom come at God, we shall little know him, not much care for him, scarce remember him, rest insensible of his love, and regardless of his favour; a coldness, a shyness, a distaste, an antipathy toward him will by degrees creep upon us. Abstinence from his company and presence will cast us into conversations destructive or prejudicial to our friendship with him; wherein soon we shall contract familiarity and friendship with his enemies, (the world and the flesh,) which are inconsistent with love to him, which will dispose us to forget him, or to dislike and loathe him.

It is, in fine, the frequency of devotion which alone can secure any practice thereof, at least any practice thereof duly qualified: so hearty, so easy, so sweet and delightful as it should be. We have all a natural averseness or indisposition thereto, as requiring an abstraction of thoughts and affections from sensible things, and a fastening them upon objects purely spiritual; a rearing our heavy spirits above their common pitch; a staying and settling our roving fancies; a composing our vain hearts in a sober and steady frame, agreeable to devotion: to effect which things is a matter of no small difficulty and pain; which therefore, without much use and exercise, cannot be accomplished; but with it, may; so that by frequent practice, the bent of our heart being turned, the strangeness of the thing ceasing, the difficulty of the work being surmounted, we shall obtain a good propension to the duty, and a great satisfaction therein.

This will render the way into God's presence smooth and passable; removing, as all other obstacles, so particularly those of fear and doubt in respect to God, which may deter or discourage us from approaching to him. God being most holy and pure, most great and glorious, we, sensible of our corruption and vileness, may be fearful and shy of coming near unto him. But when, coming into his presence, we do find that *Such as his majesty is, such is his mercy;* when we do *Taste and see that the Lord is good;* when by experience we feel, that *In his presence there is fulness of joy;* being *Abundantly satisfied with the fatness of his house;* having our souls there *Satisfied as with marrow and fatness;* finding, that *A day in his courts is better than a thousand* spent otherwhere; perceiving that he biddeth us welcome, that he treateth us kindly, that he sendeth us away refreshed with sweetest comforts, and rewarded with most excellent benefits; this will not only reconcile our hearts to devotion, but draw us into a cordial liking and earnest desire thereof; such as the Psalmist expresseth, when he saith, *My soul longeth, yea, even fainteth, for the courts of the Lord: my heart and my flesh crieth out for the living God.* This will engage us into strong resolutions of constantly practising it; such as the same holy person again declareth in these words; *I love the Lord, because he hath heard my voice and my supplications; because he hath inclined his ear unto me, therefore will I call upon him as long as I live.* Hence, instead of a suspicious estrangedness, a servile dread, or an hostile disaffection toward God, there will spring up an humble confidence, a kindly reverence, a hearty love toward him; which will upon all occasions drive us to him, hoping for his friendly succour, longing after his kind embraces. So will the frequency of devotion render it facile and pleasant. Whereas, on the contrary, disuse thereof will make it at any time hard and irksome; strengthening and increasing our natural averseness thereto: performing it seldom, we shall never perform it well, with that attention, that affection, that promptitude, that willingness and alacrity, which are due thereto.

According to so many senses, in so many respects, may we, and should we observe this precept. From thus praying continually there can be no good exception or just excuse. The most common pleas that will be alleged for the omission thereof are two; one drawn from external avocations, the other from internal indispositions obstructing it: both of which are so far from being good, that, being scanned, they will soon appear serving rather to aggravate than to excuse or abate the neglect.

I. I cannot, saith one, now attend to prayers, because I am not at liberty, or at leisure, being urgently called away, and otherwise engaged by important affairs. How much a flam this apology is we shall presently descry, by asking a few questions about it.

1 Do we take devotion itself to be no business, or a business of no consideration? Do we conceit, when we pay God his debts, or discharge our duties toward him, when we crave his aid or mercy, when we solicit the main concerns of our soul, (yea, of our body also and its estate,) that we are idle or misemployed; that we lavish our time, or lose our pains?

2 What other affairs can we have of greater moment or necessity than this? Can there be any obligation more indispensable than is that of yielding due respect and service to our Maker, our great Patron, our most liberal Benefactor? Can there be any interest more close or weighty than this, of providing for our soul's eternal health and happiness? Is not this indeed the grand work, *The only necessary matter*, in comparison whereto

all other occupations are mere trifling, or unprofitable fiddling about nothing[b]? What will all other business signify, what will come of it, if this be neglected? Busy we may be, we may plod, we may drudge eternally; but all to no end. All our care is in effect improvidence, all our industry may be well reckoned idleness, if God be not served, if our souls are not secured.

SERM. IX.

3 If we survey and prize all worldly businesses, which among them will appear so importunate as to demand, so greedy as to devour, so worthy at least as to deserve all our time, that we cannot spare a few minutes for maintaining our most pleasant intercourse, and most gainful commerce with heaven? What are the great businesses of the world? what but scraping and scrambling for pelf, contriving and compassing designs of ambition, courting the favour and respect of men, making provision for carnal pleasure, gratifying fond curiosity or vain humour? And do any of these deserve to be put into the scale against, shall all of them together be able to sway down our spiritual employments? Shall these images, these shadows of business, supplant or crowd our devotion; that which procureth wealth inestimably precious, pleasure infinitely satisfactory, honour incomparably noble above all this world can afford? If the expense of time be, as the philosopher[c] said, Πολυτελέστατον ἀνάλωμα, *The most precious expense* that can be; how can it better be laid out than upon

[b] Αἱ τέχναι τῶν πιστῶν ἐπέργιά εἰσιν· ἔργον δὲ ἡ θεοσέβεια.—Const. Apost. II. 61. [Cot. Pat. Apost. Tom. I. p. 269.]

[c] Theophr. [Συνεχές τε ἔλεγε πολυτελὲς ἀνάλωμα εἶναι τὸν χρόνον.—Diog. Laert. (Vit. Theoph.) v. 2. 10.]

the worthiest things, such as devotion alone can afford the purchase and possession of? True virtue, sound wisdom, a quiet conscience, and steady tranquillity of mind, the love and favour of God, a title unto endless joy and bliss, are purely the gifts of Heaven; and thence they will not descend of themselves, but prayer must fetch them down. If nothing then in the world be comparable to those things, how can any time be so well spent as in prayer, which acquireth them; which also best secureth whatever we have, and is the readiest way to procure whatever we want?

4 Should we not further, honestly comparing things, easily discern, that it is no such indispensable business, but rather indeed some base dotage on lucre, some inveigling bait of pleasure, some bewitching transport of fancy, that crosseth our devotion? Is it not often a complimental visit, an appointment to tattle or to tipple, a match for sport, a wild ramble in vice or folly, that so deeply engageth us to put off our duty?

5 Yea, is it not commonly sloth rather than activity, an averseness from this, rather than an inclination to any other employment, which diverteth us from our prayers? Is not, I say, the true reason why we pray so seldom, not because we are very busy, but because we are extremely idle; so idle, that we cannot willingly take the pains to unscrew our affections from sensible things, to reduce our wandering thoughts, to compose our hearts into a right frame, to bend our untoward inclinations to a compliance with our duty? Is it not because we do not feel that savour and satisfaction in these, which we do in other trivial and worth-

less employments, nor will be at the trouble to work such dispositions in our souls? Do we not betake ourselves to other conversations and commerces merely for refuge, shunning this intercourse with God and with ourselves? These, I fear, are oftener the real causes of our neglecting devotion, than any such mighty avocations which we pretend.

SERM. IX.

6 But were there indeed not only a counterfeit or imaginary, but a real competition between devotion and other lawful business, which, in reason, should carry it? in conscience, which of the two should be forborne or suspended? Is it not evidently better, that the pursuit of our temporal interests, whatever they be, should be a littlec hecked, than that our affairs of everlasting consequence should be quite laid aside? that we should venture a small impairing of our estate, than surely endamage our souls; that we hazard to disappoint or displease a man, than dare to affront and offend the Almighty God?

7 Were it not strangely absurd and unhandsome to say, I cannot wait on God, because I must speak with a friend; I cannot go to church, although God calleth me thither, because I must haste to market; I cannot stand to pray, because I am to receive money, or to make up a bargain; I cannot discharge my duty to God, because a greater obligation than that doth lie upon me? How unconceivable an honour, how unvaluable a benefit is it, that the incomprehensibly great and glorious majesty of heaven doth vouchsafe us the liberty to approach so near unto him, to converse so freely with him, to demand and derive from his

hand the supply of all our needs, and satisfaction of all our reasonable desires! and is it then just or seemly, by such comparisons to disparage his favour, by such pretences to baffle with his goodness?

Put the case, our prince should call for us to speak with him about matters nearly touching his service and our welfare; would it be according unto duty, discretion, or decency, to reply, that we are at present busy, and have no leisure, and must therefore hold ourselves excused; but that if he will stay a while, at another time, when we have less to do, we shall be perhaps disposed to wait upon him? The case is propounded by our Lord in that parable, wherein God is represented as a great man, that had prepared a feast, and invited many guests thereto; but they excused themselves: *One said, that he had purchased land, and must needs go out to see it; another had bought five yoke of oxen, and must go to prove them; another had married a wife, and therefore could not come.* These indeed were affairs considerable, as this world hath any; but yet the excuses did not satisfy[d]: for, notwithstanding, the great person was angry, and took the neglect in huge disdain.

Matt. xxii. 2, &c.
Luke xiv. 16, &c.

8 Moreover, if we reflect what vast portions of time we squander away upon our petty matters, upon voluptuous enjoyments, upon fruitless pastimes, upon impertinent talk; how can we satisfy ourselves in not allotting competent time for God's service, our own salvation, and the future everlasting state? Doth not he, who, with the con-

---

[d] Ἔπειτα ὅτι σκῆψις ταῦτα καὶ πρόφασις, &c.—Chrys. in Joh. Hom. XI. [Opp. Tom. II. p. 597.]

tinuance of our life, bestoweth on us all our time, deserve that a pittance of it should be reserved for himself? Can all the world duly claim so great an allowance thereof. May not our soul (which is far our noblest part, which indeed is all ourselves) justly challenge a good share of our time to be expended on it? or shall this mortal husk engross it all? Must eternity, which comprehendeth all time, have no time belonging to it, or allotted for its concernments?

SERM. IX.

9 Again, is it not great imprudence so to lay our business, that any other matter shall thwart or thrust out devotion? Easily with a little providence may things be so ordered, that it, without interfering or justling, may well consist with all other both needful business and convenient divertisement; so that it shall neither obstruct them, nor they extrude it: and are we not very culpable, if we do not use so much providence[e]?

10 In truth, attending upon devotion can be no obstacle, but will be great furtherance to all other good business. It is the most sure, most pleasant, most advantageous and compendious way of transacting affairs, to mix prayers and praises with them; it is the best oil that can be, to make the wheels of action go on smoothly and speedily: it not only sanctifieth our undertakings, but much promoteth and exceedingly sweeteneth the management of them. For the conscience of having rendered unto God his due respect and service, of having intrusted our affairs to his care, of having

[e] Πρῶτον μὲν, αὐτὸ τοῦτο ἔγκλημα οὐ μικρὸν, τὸ κυκλοῦσθαι τοσούτων πραγμάτων πλήθει, καὶ τοῖς βιωτικοῖς οὕτω προσηλῶσθαι διὰ παντὸς, ὡς μηδὲ μικρὰν εἰς τὰ πάντων ἀναγκαιότερα ἄγειν σχολήν.—[Id. ibid.]

consequently engaged his protection and assistance for us, will dispose us to do things with a courageous alacrity and comfortable satisfaction; will fill us with a good hope of prospering; will prepare us however to be satisfied with the event, whatever it shall be; will in effect procure a blessing and happy success, such as we may truly rejoice and triumph in, as conferred by God in favour to us. Whereas neglecting these duties, we can have no solid content or savoury complacence in any thing we undertake: reflecting on such misbehaviour (if we be not downright infidels, or obdurate reprobates in impiety) will quash or damp our courage: having thence forfeited all pretence to God's succour, and provoked him to cross us, we must needs suspect disappointment: as we have no reasonable ground to hope for success; so we cannot, if success arriveth, be heartily satisfied therein, or take it for a blessing.

He therefore that is such a niggard of his time, that he grudgeth to withhold any part thereof from his worldly occasions, deeming all time cast away that is laid out in waiting upon God, is really most unthrifty and prodigal thereof: by not sparing a little, he wasteth all his time to no purpose; by so eagerly pursuing, he effectually setteth back his designs; by preposterously affecting to despatch his affairs, he rendereth them endless, or which is the same, altogether unprofitable.

In fine, we may be sure that no time is spent even so prudently and politicly, with so great advantage and so real fruit to ourselves, as that which is employed upon devotion. In sacrificing his time, his pains, his substance, any thing he

## The Duty of Prayer. 335

hath or can do, to God's service, no man can be a loser.

SERM. IX.

We have also many examples plainly demonstrating the consistency of this practice with all other business. Who ever had more or greater affairs to manage, and who ever managed them with greater success, than David; upon whom did lie the burden of a royal estate, and the care over a most populous nation; the which *He fed with a faithful and true heart, and ruled prudently with all his power;* who waged great wars, vanquished mighty enemies, achieved many glorious exploits, underwent many grievous troubles? Yet could not such engagements distract or depress his mind from a constant attendance on devotion. *I will bless the Lord at all times; his praise shall be continually in my mouth. My mouth shall shew forth thy righteousness and thy salvation all the day. I will abide in thy tabernacle for ever.* So he declareth his resolution and his practice. Who is more pressingly employed than was Daniel, first president over so vast a kingdom, chief minister of state to the greatest monarch on earth? yet constantly *Thrice a day did he pray and give thanks unto his God.* Who can be more entangled in varieties and intricacies of care, of pains, of trouble, than was he that prescribeth unto us this rule of praying continually? Upon him did lie *The care of all the churches; Night and day with labour and toil did he work* for the sustenance of his life, *that he might not* (to the disparagement of the Gospel) *burden any man;* perpetually he was engaged in all sorts of labour and travail, ever conflicting with perils, with wants, with inconveniences numberless:

Ps. lxxviii. 72.

Ps. xxxiv. 1; lxxi. 6; cxlv. 2; xxxv. 28; lxi. 4.

Dan. vi. 10.

2 Cor. xi. 28.
2 Thess. iii. 8.

SERM. IX.

yet did he exactly conform his practice to his rule, being no less indefatigable and incessant in his devotion than he was in his business. Who ever managed a greater empire than Constantine? Yet *Every day*, as Eusebius reporteth, *at stated times, shutting himself up, he alone privately did converse with his God*[f]. The most pious men indeed have never been idle or careless men, but always most busy and active, most industrious in their callings, most provident for their families, most officious toward their friends, most ready to serve their country, most abundant in all good works; yet have they always been most constant in devotion. So that experience clearly doth evidence, how reconcileable much devotion is to much business; and that consequently the prosecution of the one cannot well palliate the neglect of the other.

II. No better can any man ward himself from blame, by imputing the neglect of devotion to some indisposition within him thereto. For this is only to cover one fault with another, or to lay on a patch more ugly than the sore. It is, in effect, to say we may sin, because we have a mind to it, or care not to do otherwise. Our indisposition itself is criminal; and, as signifying somewhat habitual or settled, is worse than a single omission: it ought therefore to be corrected and cured; and the way to do it is, by setting presently upon the practice of the duty, and persisting resolutely therein: otherwise how is it possible that it should ever be removed? The longer we forbear it, the

---

[f] Καιροῖς ἑκάστης ἡμέρας τακτοῖς ἑαυτὸν ἐγκλείων, μόνος μόνῳ τῷ αὐτῷ προσωμίλει Θεῷ.—Euseb. de Vita Const. IV. 22. [Tom. I. p. 637.]

more seldom we perform it, the stronger surely will our indisposition grow, and the more difficult it will be to remove it. But if (with any degree of seriousness and good intention) we come indisposed to prayer, we may thereby be formed into better disposition, and by continual attendance thereon, we shall (God's grace cooperating, which never is wanting to serious and honest intentions) grow toward a perfect fitness for it: prayer by degrees will become natural and delightful to us.

# SERMON X.[a]

## OF THE DUTY OF THANKSGIVING.

---

EPHES. V. 20.

*Giving thanks always for all things unto God.*

THESE words, although (as the very syntax doth immediately discover) they bear a relation to, and have a fit coherence with, those that precede, may yet, (especially considering St Paul's style and manner of expression[*] in the preceptive

[a] [St Mary's, Aug. 17, 1662. MS.]

---

[*] It is the usual manner of St Paul, (who, out of a good heart inflamed with devout piety towards God, and cordial charity to men, is wont to pour forth abundance of excellent precepts and seasonable admonitions) by a special artifice so to order his discourses, that those duties, which have a near affinity between themselves, springing from the same root, grounded on the same reason, or tending to the same end, may not be dissevered from each other by becoming the matter of different exhortations; but coupled rather and connected together by a common relation to some one more general or more principal duty, wherein they are included, or upon which by some causality or consequence they depend; which general or principal duties expressing in the imperative mood, the others he subjoins as accessories to them, and parts of their train by means of participles, or of adjectives equivalent. I shall not need to spend time in exemplifying that, which to him, who with competent

## The Duty of Thanksgiving.

and exhortative part of his Epistles,) without any violence or prejudice on either hand, be severed from the context, and considered distinctly by themselves. And (to avoid encumbrance by further comparison) so taking them we may observe, that every single word among them carries with it something of notable emphasis and especial significancy. The first *Giving thanks* expresses the substance of a duty, to which we are exhorted. The next (I mean, in order of construction) *to God*, denotes the object or term to which it is directed. The following *always* determines the main circum-

SERM. X.

---

attention peruses the original scripture is every where observable; especially in that rich treasury of wholesome advices, the 12th chapter of the Epistle to the Romans: where often what is in the Greek couched in participles and adjectives is by our translators understood and rendered imperatively; and what there is introduced in way of relative dependence, is interpreted as spoken absolutely and distinctly. In such manner here the particular and consequent duties of praising and thanking God for his mercies and benefits are annexed (by this form of syntax) to that original and most comprehensive duty of being replenished with the Divine Spirit, from which as all other gracious dispositions, so more especially this of devout gratitude to God, doth immediately result and is derived. Although therefore as to the form and manner of speech, these words do not precisely constitute an entire sentence of themselves, and do manifestly contain a respect to those, which precede in the next verse save one, *Be filled with the Spirit;* yet considering St Paul's way of expressing his mind and the nature of the matter it-itself, (designing to avoid encumbrance in our discourse) we need not scruple to take them as an absolutely distinct exhortation and to pronounce them thus: *Give thanks always for all things unto God.* MS.

stance of this and all other duties, the time of performance. The last *for all things*, declares the adequate matter of the duty, and how far it should extend. These particulars I shall consider severally, and in order.

I. First then, concerning the duty itself, *To give thanks*, or rather, *to be thankful;* (for Εὐχαριστεῖν doth not only signify *Gratias agere, reddere, dicere,* to *give, render,* or *declare thanks,* but also *Gratias habere, grate affectum esse, to be thankfully disposed,* to entertain a grateful affection, sense, or memory: in which more comprehensive notion I mean to consider it, as including the whole duty or virtue of gratitude due to Almighty God for all his benefits, favours, and mercies ;) I say, concerning this duty itself, (abstractedly considered,) as it involves a respect to benefits or good things received; so in its employment about them it imports, requires, or supposes these following particulars.

1 It implies a right apprehension of, and consequently a considerate attention unto, benefits conferred. For he that is either wholly ignorant of his obligations, or mistakes them, or passes them over with a slight and superficial view, can nowise be grateful. *Whoso is wise, and will observe these things, even they shall understand the lovingkindness of the Lord. Men shall fear, and shall declare the work of God; for they shall wisely consider of his doings. The works of the Lord are great, sought out of all that have pleasure therein. O taste* (first, and then) *see that the Lord is good.*

This is the method that great master of thanksgiving prescribes; first experimental notice, then wise consideration, then grateful sense, then public acknowledgment. And those we find both by him and by the prophet Isaias (in the very same words) reprehended as wickedly ingrateful persons, who *Regarded not the work of the Lord, nor considered the operation of his hands.* 'Tis part therefore of this duty incumbent on us, to take notice of diligently, and carefully to consider, the divine benefits; not to let them pass undiscerned and unregarded by us, as persons either wofully blind, or stupidly drowsy, or totally unconcerned.

<sup>Ps. xxviii. 5.</sup>
<sup>Isai. v. 12.</sup>

'Tis a general fault, that the most common and frequent, the most obvious and conspicuous favours of God, (like the ordinary phenomena of nature, which, as Aristotle observes, though in themselves most admirable, are yet least admired,) the constant rising of the sun upon us, the descent of fruitful showers, the recourse of temperate seasons, the continuance of our life, the enjoyment of health, the providential dispensation of wealth, and competent means of livelihood, the daily protection from incident dangers, the helps of improving knowledge, obtaining virtue, becoming happy, and such like most excellent benefits, we commonly little mind or regard, and consequently seldom return the thanks due for them. Possibly some rare accidents of providence, some extraordinary judgment, some miraculous deliverance, may rouse and awaken our attention: (as it is said of the Israelites, *When he slew them, then they sought him—and remembered that God was their rock, and the high God their Redeemer:*) but such advertency is not the effect so much of gratitude, as of curiosity or of necessity: the notable rarity

Ps. lxxviii. 34, 35.

SERM. X.

invites, or some powerful impulse commands our notice. But the truly grateful industriously design, and are studious to know, throughly their obligations, that they may be able to render answerable returns for them.

2 This duty requires a faithful retention of benefits in memory[b], and consequently frequent reflections upon them. For he that is no longer affected with a benefit than it incurs the sense, and suffers not itself to be disregarded, is far from being grateful; nay, if we believe the philosopher, is ingrateful in the worst kind and highest degree. For, *Ingratus est*, saith he, *qui beneficium accepisse se negat, quod accepit; ingratus est, qui dissimulat; ingratus, qui non reddit: ingratissimus omnium, qui oblitus est. He that falsely denies the reception of a benefit, and he that dissembles it, and he that doth not repay it, is ingrateful; but most ingrateful of all is he that forgets it*[c]. It is a sign the benefit made no deep impression on his mind, since it left no discernible footstep there; that he hardly ever thought of making recompense, since he hath suffered himself to become altogether uncapable of doing it: neither is there any hope of his amending the past neglect; no shame, no repentance, no fair occasion can redeem him from ingratitude, in whom the very remembrance of his obligation is extinguished.

If to be sensible of a present good turn deserved the title of gratitude, all men certainly would be grateful: the Jews questionless were so.

[b] Ἀχάριστος, ὅστις εὖ παθὼν ἀμνημονεῖ.
[Menand. Sentent. sing. 10. Ed. Meincke.]
[c] Sen. de Benef. III. [1. 2.]

*The Duty of Thanksgiving.* 343

When Almighty God, by his wonderful power in extraordinary ways, delivered them from the tyranny and oppression of their prevalent enemies; when he caused streams to gush forth from the bowels of a hard rock to refresh their thirst; when bread descended from heaven in showers, and the winds were winged with flesh, to satisfy their greedy desires; then surely they were not altogether unsensible of the divine goodness; then could they acknowledge his power, and be forward enough to engage themselves in promises of correspondent observance toward him for the future. But the mischief was, immediately after, as the Psalmist complains, *They forgat his works, and the wonders he had shewed them: They remembered not his hand, nor the day when he delivered them from the enemy. They refused to obey, neither were mindful of the wonders that God did among them,* as Nehemiah confesses in their behalf. *Of the rock that begat them they were unmindful, and forgot the God that formed them,* as it is in Deuteronomy. They distrusted his promises, repined at his dealings, disobeyed his laws, and treacherously apostatised from his covenant. Such were the fruits of their ingrateful forgetfulness; which therefore that people is so often charged with, and so sharply reproved for by the prophets.

On the contrary, we find that great pattern of gratitude, the royal prophet David, continually revolving in his thoughts, imprinting upon his fancy, studying and meditating upon, recollecting and renewing in his memory, the results of divine favour. *I will remember,* saith he, *thy wonders of old; I will meditate of all thy works, and talk of*

SERM.
X.

Ps. lxxviii. 11, 42.

Neh. ix. 17.

Deut. xxxii. 18.

Ps. lxxvii. 11, 12; cxliii. 5;

*thy doings:* and, *I remember the days of old; I will meditate on all thy works; I muse on the works of thy hands:* and, *Bless the Lord, O my soul, and forget not all his benefits:* and, *My mouth shall praise thee with joyful lips, when I remember thee upon my bed, and meditate on thee in the night-watches, because thou hast been my help.* No place unfit, it seems, no time unseasonable for the practice of this duty; not the place designed for rest, not the time due to sleep, but, as David thought, more due to a wakeful contemplation of the divine goodness. Whose vigilant gratitude we should strive to imitate, devoting our most solitary and retired, our most sad and serious thoughts (not the studies only of our closet, but the consultations also of our pillow) to the preservation of those blessed ideas; that neither length of time may deface them in our fancy, nor other care extrude them thence.

It was a satirical answer, (that of Aristotle,) and highly opprobrious to mankind; who, being asked, Τί τάχιστον γηράσκει; *What doth the soonest grow old?* replied, Χάρις, *Thanks*[d]: and so was that adagial verse, Ἅμ' ἠλέηται καὶ τέθνηκεν ἡ χάρις. *No sooner the courtesy born, than the resentment thereof dead*[e]. Such reproachful aphorisms we should labour to confute, especially as they are applicable to the divine favours, by so maintaining and cherishing our thanks for them, that they neither decay with age, nor prematurely die, nor be buried in oblivion; but may resemble the pictures

---

[d] [Ἐρωτηθεὶς τί γηράσκει ταχύ, Χάρις, ἔφη.—Diog. Laert. (Vit. Arist.) v. 1. 11.]

[e] [Menand. Epig. p. 299. Ed. Meineke.]

and poetical descriptions of the Graces, those goodly daughters of heaven, smiling always with a never-fading serenity of countenance, and flourishing in an immortal youth.

SERM.
X.

The middle, we may observe, and the safest, and the fairest, and the most conspicuous places in cities are usually deputed for the erections of statues and monuments dedicated to the memory of worthy men, who have nobly deserved of their countries. In like manner should we in the heart and centre of our soul, in the best and highest apartments thereof, in the places most exposed to ordinary observation, and most secure from the invasions of worldly care, erect lively representations of, and lasting memorials unto, the divine bounty; constantly attending to which we may be disposed to gratitude. Not one blessing, not the least favourable passage of providence ought to perish with us, though long since passed, and removed out of the sphere of present sense.

We must not in our old age forget who formed us in the womb, who brought us into the light, who suckled our infancy, who educated our childhood, who governed our youth, who conducted our manhood through the manifold hazards, troubles, and disasters of life. Nor in our prosperity, our affluence of good things, our possession of Canaan, should we be unmindful of him who relieved us in our straits, who supplied our wants, sustained our adversity, who redeemed us from Egypt, and led us through the wilderness. A succession of new and fresh benefits should not (as among some savages, the manner is for the young to make away

Ps. lxxi. 6.

Deut. vi. 12; viii. 11.

the old) supplant and expunge ancient ones, but make them rather more dear and venerable to us. Time should not weaken or diminish, but rather confirm and radicate in us the remembrance of God's goodness; to render it, as it doth gold and wine, more precious and more strong. We have usually a memory more than enough tenacious of injuries and ill turns done to us: let it never be said, to the disgrace of that noble faculty, that we can hardly forget the discourtesies of man, but not easily remember the favours of God. But further,

3 This duty implies a due esteem and valuation of benefits; that the nature and quality, the measure and quantity, the circumstances and consequences of them be well expended; else the gratitude is like to be none, or very defective. For we commensurate our thankfulness, not so much to the intrinsic excellency of things, as to our peculiar estimations of them. A cynic perhaps would not return more thanks for a diamond than for a pebble; nor more gratefully receive a talent of gold than an ounce of copper; because he equally values, or rather alike contemns both.

Wherefore we find (our never-to-be-forgotten) example, the devout thanksgiver, David, continually declaring the great price he set upon the divine favours; admiring and displaying their transcendent perfections, their wonderful greatness, their boundless extension, their excessive multitude, their endless duration, their advantageous circumstances, (the excellent needfulness, convenience, and seasonableness of them; together with the admirable freeness, wisdom, and power of the Benefactor, shining forth in and by them.) *I will praise thee, O Lord, saith he, among the people, I will sing unto thee among the nations: for thy mercy is great unto the heavens, and thy faithfulness reacheth unto the clouds.* And, *Remember the marvellous works that he hath done, his wonders, and the judgments of his mouth. He is the Lord our God, his judgments are in all the earth.* And again, *Thy mercy, O Lord, is in the heavens, thy faithfulness reacheth unto the clouds. Thy righteousness is like the great mountains; thy judgments are a great deep: O Lord, thou preservest man and beast. How excellent is thy lovingkindness, O God!* and, *How precious are thy thoughts unto me, O Lord! O how great is the sum of them! If I should count them, they are more in number than the sand.* And again, *His work is honourable and glorious, his righteousness endureth for ever:* and, *The Lord is good to all, and his tender mercies are over all his works:* and, *Blessed be the Lord, who daily loadeth us with his benefits.*

SERM. X.

Ps. cviii. 3, 4.

Ps. cv. 5, 7.

Ps. xxxvi. 5, 6, 7.

Ps. cxxxix. 17, 18.

Ps. cxi. 3.
Ps. cxlv. 9.

Ps. lxviii. 19.

In such manner ought we diligently to survey and judiciously to estimate the effects of divine beneficence, examining every part, and descanting upon every circumstance thereof: like those that contemplate some rare beauty, or some excellent picture; some commending the exact proportions, some the graceful features, some the lively colours discernible therein. There is not the least of the divine favours, which, if we consider the condescensive tenderness, the clear intention, the undeserved frankness, the cheerful debonairity expressed therein, hath not dimensions larger than our comprehension, colours too fair, and lineaments too comely for our weak sight thoroughly to discern; requiring therefore our highest esteem and our utmost thanks.

'Tis perhaps somewhat dangerous to affix a determinate value upon any of God's benefits: (for to value them seems to undervalue them, they being really inestimable:) what then is it to extenuate, to vilify, to despise the greatest? We should esteem them, as we measure the heavens with our eye, as we compute the sands upon the shore, as we would prize inexhaustible mines of gold, and treasures of pearl; that is, by confessing heartily their worth surpasses the strength of our imagination to conceive, and of our speech to utter; that they are immense, innumerable, unconceivable, and unexpressible. But still,

4 *Giving thanks* imports, that benefits be received with a willing mind, a hearty sense, a vehement affection. The forementioned particulars are indeed necessary properties, inseparable concomitants, or prerequisite conditions to: but a cheerful and cordial acceptance of benefits is the form, as it were, and soul, the life and spirit, the principal and most essential ingredient of this duty.

It was not altogether unreasonable, though it went for a paradox, that dictate of the Stoics, that *Sufficit animus animo,* and, that *Qui libenter accipit beneficium, reddidit*[f]: that he, who with a willing and well-affected mind receives a courtesy, hath fully discharged the duty of gratitude; that other endeavours of return and compensation are

[f] [Sen. de Ben. II. 31.]

*The Duty of Thanksgiving.* 349

rather handsome accessions to it, than indispensably requisite to the completion thereof. For as in the collation, it is not the gold or the silver, the food or the apparel, in which the benefit consists, but the will and benevolent intention of him that bestows them; so reciprocally it is the good acceptance, the sensibleness of, and acquiescence in the benefactor's goodness, that constitutes the gratitude; which who affords, though he be never capable of yielding other satisfaction, *Voluntate voluntati satisfecit;* and, *Regum æquabat opes animis*[g]——. It is ingenuity that constitutes (respectively) both a bountiful giver and a thankful receiver. A truly noble benefactor purely aimeth at, not any material reward or advantage to himself; (it were trading this, not beneficence;) but the good, profit, and content of him, to whom he dispenseth his favour: of which being assured, he rests satisfied, and accounts himself royally recompensed[h].

SERM. X.

Such a benefactor is Almighty God, and such a tribute he requires of us; a ready embracement of, and a joyful complacency in his kindness; even such as he expressed, who said, *Because thy lovingkindness is better than life, my lips shall praise thee:*

Ps. lxiii. 3; civ. 33; lxxi. 22; lxiii. 5; ix. 1, 2.

[g] [Virg. Georg. iv. 132.]

[h] Quoties quod proposuit quis consequitur, capit operis sui fructum. Qui beneficium dat, quid proponit? prodesse ei cui dat, et voluptati sibi esse. Si quod voluit, effecit, pervenitque ad me munus ejus, ac mutuo gaudio affecit, tulit quod petiit. Non enim sibi invicem aliquid reddi voluit; aut non fuit beneficium sed negotiatio ... Habet quod voluit, si bene acceptum est. Sed speravit emolumentum aliquod: non fuit hoc beneficium, cujus proprium est, nihil de reditu cogitare.—Senec. [De Benef. ii. 31.]

Nec est dubium, quin is, qui liberalis benignusve dicitur, officium, non fructum, sequatur.—Cic. de Leg. i. [18. 48.]

and, *My soul shall be filled as with marrow and fatness, and my mouth shall praise thee with joyful lips:* and, *I will praise thee with my whole heart; I will be glad and rejoice in thee:* and, *Bless the Lord, O my soul; and all that is within me, praise his holy name.*

*Ps. ciii. 1.*

No holocaust is so acceptable to God, as a heart inflamed with a sense of his goodness. He loves not only Ἱλαρὸν δότην, (*A merry giver*), but Ἱλαρὸν δέκτην (*A cheerful receiver*) also. He would have us, as to desire his favour with a greedy appetite, so to taste it with a savoury relish. He designs not only to fill our mouths with food, but our hearts also with gladness.

*2 Cor. ix. 7.*

*Acts xiv. 17.*

We must not seem to grudge or repine, to murmur or disdain, that we are necessitated to be beholden to him; lest it happen to us as it did to them of whom it is said, *While the meat was yet in their mouths, the wrath of God came upon them, and slew the fattest of them.* Yea, 'tis our duty not to be contented only, but to be delighted, to be transported, to be ravished with the emanations of his love: to entertain them with such a disposition of mind, as the dry and parched ground imbibes the soft dew and gentle showers; as the chill and darksome air admits the benign influences of heavenly light; as the thirsty soul takes in the sweet and cooling stream. He that with a sullen look, a dead heart, a faint sense, a cold hand, embraces the gifts of heaven, is really unthankful, though with deluges of wine and oil he makes the altars to overflow, and clouds the sky with the steam of his sacrifices. But yet further,

*Ps. lxxviii. 30, 31.*

5 This duty requires due acknowledgment of

## The Duty of Thanksgiving. 351

our obligation, significations of our notice, declarations of our esteem and good acceptance of favours conferred. It is the worst and most detestable of ingratitudes, that which proceeds from pride and scorn: and such is he guilty of, who is either unwilling or ashamed to confess himself obliged; who purposely dissembles a benefit, or disavows the benefactor; who refuses to render those most manifestly due, and most easily discharged, those neither toilsome nor expensive oblations of praise and acknowledgment[1]. This part of our duty requires, that we offer to God, not costly hecatombs, but *The calves only of our lips;* (as the prophet Hosea speaks;) not the fruit of our lands, but Καρπὸν χειλέων only, (as the apostle to the Hebrews styles it,) *The fruit of our lips, confessing to his name;* that we employ some few blasts of the breath he gave us on the celebration of his goodness, and advancement of his repute. *I will praise the name of God with a song, and will magnify him with thanksgiving. This shall please the Lord better than an ox or bullock that hath horns and hoofs,* saith David.

SERM. X.

Hos. xiv. 2.

Heb. xiii. 15.

Ps. lxix. 30, 31.

And surely it is the least homage we in gratitude owe and can pay to Almighty God, to avow our dependence upon and obligation to him for the good things we enjoy, to acknowledge that his favours do deserve thanks, to publish to the world our experience of his goodness, to proclaim solemnly with the voice of thanksgiving his most deserved

---

[1] Οὐδὲ γὰρ βαρύ τι καὶ ἐπαχθὲς ἐπιζητεῖ παρ' ἡμῶν, ἀλλ' ἢ τὸ ὁμολογεῖν μόνον τὰς τοσαύτας εὐεργεσίας, καὶ τὰς ὑπὲρ τούτων αὐτῷ εὐχαριστίας ἀναφέρειν.—Chrys. [in Gen. Orat. IX. Opp. Tom. I. p. 54.]

praise; resembling him who abounds in such expressions as these: *I will sing of the mercies of the Lord for ever; with my mouth will I make known his faithfulness to all generations. I will publish with the voice of thanksgiving, and tell of all his wondrous works. I will speak of the glorious honour of thy majesty, and of thy wondrous works. I have not hid thy righteousness in my heart, I have declared thy faithfulness and thy salvation: I have not concealed thy lovingkindness and thy truth from the great congregation*[k].

Thus if a grateful affection live in our hearts, it will respire through our mouths, and discover itself in the motion of our lips. There will be a conspiracy and faithful correspondence between our mind and our tongue: if the one be sensible, the other will not be silent; as if the spring works, the wheels will turn about, and the bell not fail to speak. Neither shall we content ourselves in lonesome tunes, and private soliloquies, to whisper out the divine praises; but shall loudly excite and provoke others to a melodious consonance with us. We shall, with the sweet singer of Israel, cite and invoke heaven and earth; the celestial choir of angels; the several estates and generations of men, the numberless company of all the creatures, to assist and join in concert with us, in celebrating the worthy deeds, and magnifying the glorious name of our most mighty Creator, of our most bountiful Benefactor.

Gratitude is of a fruitful and diffusive nature, of a free and communicative disposition, of an open

---

[k] Vid. Ps. lxvi. 5: 'O come hither, and behold the works of God,' &c.

*The Duty of Thanksgiving.*

SERM. X.

and sociable temper: it will be imparting, discovering, and propagating itself: it affects light, company, and liberty; it cannot endure to be smothered in privacy and obscurity. Its best instrument therefore is speech, that most natural, proper, and easy mean of conversation, of signifying our conceptions, of conveying, and as it were transfunding our thoughts and our passions into each other[1]. This therefore glory of ours, and best organ that we have, (as the Psalmist seems to call it,) our tongue, we should in all reason devote to the honour, and consecrate to the praise of him who made it, and who conserves it still in tune.

Ps. lvii. 8.

And, the further to provoke us, we may consider, that it hath been the manner prompted by nature, and authorized by general practice, for men of all nations, and all times, and all ways, by composed hymns and panegyrical elogies, to express their gratitude for the gifts of nature, and for the benefits indulged by Providence; in their public sacrifices and solemn festivities extolling the excellent qualities of their imaginary deities, and reciting the famous achievements of their heroes and supposed benefactors: to whose favourable help and blessing, in their conceit, they owed the fruits of the earth, the comforts of life, the defence and patronage of their countries: being indeed mistaken in the object, but not transgressing in the substance of the duty; paying a due debt, though to false creditors. And I wish we were as ready to imitate them in the one, as we are, perhaps, prone to blame

[1] Ψυχὴ γὰρ, οἶμαι, ψυχῇ, καὶ πνεῦμα πνεύματι συναπτόμενα, κατὰ τὴν τοῦ λόγου σπορὰν, &c.—Clem. Alex. Strom. I. [Opp. Tom. I. p. 317.]

them for the other. For, certainly, acknowledgments of the divine goodness, and solemn testifications of our thankful sense thereof, (whatever the abused world may now imagine,) was always, is now, and ever will be the principal and most noble part of all religion immediately addressed to God. But moreover,

<small>1 Sam. xii. 24.</small>

6 This duty requires endeavours of real compensation, and a satisfactory requital of benefits, according to the ability and opportunity of the receiver: that we do not only verbally *Dicere*, and *Agnoscere;* but really *Agere,* and *Referre gratias:* that to him, who hath by his beneficence obliged us, we minister reciprocal assistance, comfort, and relief, if he need them, and be capable to receive them: however, by evident testimonies to discover our ready disposition to make such real returns; and withal, to suit our actions to his good liking, and in our carriage to comply with his reasonable desires. For,

<small>Heb. vi. 7, 8.</small>

*As the earth which drinketh the rain often coming upon it, and,* having been by great labour tilled and manured with expense, *yieldeth* yet no *meet herbage* Βοτάνην εὔθετον, or *fruit agreeable to the expectation of him that dresseth it,* but is either wholly barren, or *produceth* only *thorns and briers, is* (as the apostle to the Hebrews tells us) *to be reprobated, and nigh unto cursing;* that is, deserves no further care or culture to be employed on it, and is to be reputed desperately worthless: so is he, (that we may apply an apodosis to the apostle's comparison,) who, daily partaking the influences of divine providence and bounty, affords no answerable return, to be accounted execrably unthankful, and unworthy of any further favour to be shewed toward him.

'Tis true, our *Righteousness* (or beneficence, so the word there signifies) *doth not extend unto God:* his benefits exceed all possibility of any proportionable requital: he doth not need, nor can ever immediately receive any advantage from us: we cannot enrich him with our gifts, who by unquestionable right, and in unalterable possession, is Lord and Master of all things that do actually or can possibly exist; nor advance him by our weak commendations, who already enjoyeth the supreme pitch of glory; nor any way contribute to his in itself complete and indefectible beatitude. Yet we may by apposite significations declare our willingness to serve and exalt him: we may by our obsequious demeanour highly please and content him: we may, by our charity and benignity to those whose good he tenders, yield (though not an adequate, yet) an acceptable return to his benefits. *What shall I render unto the Lord for all his benefits?* saith David, in way of counsel and deliberation: and thereupon resolves, *I will take the cup of salvation, and call upon the name of the Lord: I will pay my vows unto the Lord.* Seasonable benedictions, officious addresses, and faithful performances of vows, he intimates to bear some shadow at least, some resemblance of compensation. And so did his wise son likewise, when he thus advised, *Honour the Lord with thy substance, and with the first-fruits of thy increase.*

Almighty God, though he really doth, and cannot otherwise do, yet will not seem to bestow his favours altogether gratis, but to expect some competent return, some small use and income from them. He will assert his rightful title, and be acknowledged the chief proprietary, by signal expressions of our fealty, and the payment of some, though inconsiderable, quit-rent, for our possessions derived from him: he will rather himself be seemingly indigent, than permit us to be really ingrateful. For knowing well, that our performance of duty and respect toward him greatly conduceth to our comfort and happiness[m], he requireth of us such demonstrations of them, as we conveniently are able to exhibit; he appoints services expressive of thankfulness, exacts tributes and customs, demands loans and benevolences, encourages and accepts free-will offerings from us. *Thou shalt not appear empty before the Lord*, was a statute to the Jews, qualified and moderated by certain measures: the first-fruits of their lands, the first-born of their cattle and of themselves, the tenths of their annual increase, and a certain allotment from the spoils acquired in wars, did God challenge to himself, as fitting recompenses due for his bounty to and care over them.

Neither did the Gentiles conceive themselves exempted from the like obligation. For the Ἀκροθίνια, the top or chief of their corn-heaps, they were wont to consecrate unto him who had blessed their fields with increase; and the Ἀκρόλεια, the first and best of the prey, they dedicated to the adornment of his temple by whose favourable disposal they had obtained the victory. Neither would they sooner begin their meal, and partake of their necessary

---

[m] Ἀκήρατος γὰρ αὐτοῦ ἡ οὐσία καὶ ἀνενδεὴς οὖσα, οὐδενὸς ἑτέρου προσδεῖται· οἱ δὲ αἰνοῦντες αὐτὸν, αὐτοὶ λαμπρότεροι γίνονται.—Chrys. in Ps. cxliv. [Opp. Tom. i. p. 885.]

*The Duty of Thanksgiving.*

refreshment, than, by pouring forth their gratulatory libation, they had performed some homage to heaven for it.

SERM. X.

Οὐδέ τις ἔτλη
Πρὶν πιέειν, πρὶν λεῖψαι ὑπερμενέϊ Κρονίωνι[n],

was the custom, it seems, in Homer's time. I shall not insist upon their Ἀναθήματα, their anniversary or their casual sacrifices; but only observe, (what, if seasonable, might by many sufficient testimonies be evinced,) that those men (at least the most intelligent of them) were not so senseless as to imagine, that the gods, to whom they performed those services, and devoted those oblations, did any wise need, or were truly benefited by them[o]; but that they esteemed it a comely thing, by the most significant means they could invent, to declare their grateful sense of the divine goodness and indulgence toward them.

And though we are, perhaps, disobliged now from the circumstantial manner, yet are we no wise freed from (but rather more strongly engaged to) the substantial performance of this sort of gratitude. We are to offer still, not dead bulls and goats, but, as St Paul saith, *Our own bodies, living sacrifices, holy and acceptable to God.* We are excused from material, but are yet bound to yield Πνευματικὰς θυσίας, *Spiritual sacrifices* unto God, as St Peter tells us. We must burn incense still, that of fervent devotion; and send up continually to heaven Θυσίαν αἰνέσεως, that *Thank-offering of praise*, which the apostle to the Hebrews mentions. We must con-

Rom. xii. 1.

1 Pet. ii. 5.

Heb. xiii. 15.

---

[n] Hom. Il. [VII. 480.]

[o] Οὐ γὰρ, οἶμαι, τοιοῦτόν ἐστι τὸ τῶν θεῶν, ὥστε ὑπὸ δώρων παράγεσθαι οἷον κακὸν τοκιστήν· &c.—Plat. Alcib. II. [149 E.]

secrate the first-born of our souls, (pure and holy thoughts,) and the first-fruits of our strength, (our most active endeavours,) to God's service. We must slay our impure desires, mortify our corrupt affections, and abandon our selfish respects for his sake. We must give him our hearts, and present our wills entirely to his disposal. We must vow to him, and pay the daily oblation of sincere obedience[p]. We must officiously attend his pleasure, and labour to content him by an innocent and unblemished conversation. With these things Almighty God is effectually gratified; he approves of and accepts these, as real testimonies of our thankfulness, and competent returns of his benefits.

Especially our charity and beneficence, our exhibiting love and respect to good men, (his faithful servants and near relations,) our affording help and succour to persons in need and distress, he accounts a suitable retaliation of his kindness, acknowledges to be an obligation laid upon himself, and hath by settled rules and indispensable promises obliged himself to requite them. For, *He that hath pity on the poor, lendeth unto the Lord; and that which he hath given, he will pay him again:* and, *God is not unrighteous, to forget your work and labour of love, which ye have shewed toward his name, in that ye have ministered to the saints, and do minister:* and, *To do good and to communicate, forget not; for with such sacrifices God is well pleased:* and, *I desire fruit,* saith St Paul to the Philippians, *that may abound to your account. But I have all, and abound; I am full, having received of Epaphrodi-*

---

[p] Μία ἀμοιβὴ κυριωτάτη παρὰ ἀνθρώπων, ταῦτα δρᾶν ἅπερ ἀρεστὰ τῷ Θεῷ.—Clem. Alex. Strom. VII. [Opp. Tom. II. p. 840.]

*tus the things which were sent from you, an odour of a sweet smell, a sacrifice acceptable, well pleasing to God.* And, *Inasmuch as ye have done it to* (that is, fed, and clothed, and comforted) *the least of these my brethren, ye have done it unto me,* saith our Saviour; manifestly declaring, that the good we do, and the respect we shew unto good and needy men, God reckons it done unto himself.

And this point I shall conclude with the sayings of the wise Hebrew philosopher Ben-Sirach: *He that keepeth the law, bringeth offerings enough: He that taketh heed to the commandment, offereth a peace-offering. He that requiteth a good turn, offereth fine flour: and he that giveth alms, sacrificeth praise. To depart from wickedness is a thing pleasing to the Lord: and to forsake unrighteousness is a propitiation.* To these I shall only add this one particular;

7 That true gratitude for benefits is always attended with the esteem, veneration, and love of the benefactor. Beneficence is a royal and godlike thing, an argument of eminent goodness and power conspiring; and necessarily therefore, as in them that perceive and duly consider it, it begets respect and reverence; so peculiarly in those that feel its benign influence, it produces love and affection: like the heavenly light, which to all that behold it appears glorious; but more powerfully warms those that are directly subject to its rays, and is by them more vigorously reflected.

And as to those that are immediately concerned therein, it imports more particular regard and goodwill; so, if they be duly sensible thereof, it engages them in mutual correspondence to an extraordinary

SERM. X.

Ps. xviii. 1, 3, 46.

Ps. cxvi. 1.

Luke vii. 47.

esteem and benevolence: such as David upon this account professes to have been in himself toward God, and frequently excites others to. *I will love thee, O Lord, my strength. I will call upon the Lord, who is worthy to be praised. The Lord liveth, and blessed be my rock; and let the God of my salvation be exalted. I love the Lord, because he hath heard my voice and my supplications.* And, (in the gospel,) *Because her sins, being many, were forgiven, therefore she loved much.* So true it is, that sense of favour indulged is naturally productive of love[q].

Thus have I plainly and simply presented you with what my meditations suggested concerning the nature and substance of this duty, with the several branches sprouting from the main stock thereof: I proceed now to that which will exceedingly enlarge the worth, and engage to the performance thereof.

II. The object and term to which it is to be directed; we are to give thanks to God. To God, I say; that is, to him, unto whom we are obliged, not for some small and inconsiderable trifles, but for the most weighty and valuable benefits: from whom we receive, not few or some, but all good things; whatever is necessary for our sustenance, convenient for our use, pleasant for our enjoyment; not only those that come immediately from his hand, but what we obtain from others, who from him receive both the will and the power, the means and the opportunities of doing us good: to whom we owe, not only what we ever did or do at present

[q] Χάρις χάριν γάρ ἐστιν ἡ τίκτουσ' ἀεί.
Soph. [Ajax. 522.]

possess, or can hereafter hope for of good; but that we were, are, or shall ever be in capacity to receive any: to the author, upholder, and preserver of our being; without whose goodness we had never been, and without whose care we cannot subsist one moment.

To him, who is the Lord and true owner of all things we partake of; whose air we breathe, whose ground we tread on, whose food sustains us; whose wholly we are ourselves, both the bodies we carry about us, (which is the work of his hands,) and the soul we think with, which was breathed from his mouth.

To him, who hath created a whole world to serve us, a spacious, a beautiful, a stately world for us to inhabit and to disport in; who hath subjected so fair a territory to our dominion, and consigned to our use so numerous a progeny of goodly creatures, to be managed, to be governed, to be enjoyed by us.

So that wherever we direct our eyes, whether we reflect them inward upon ourselves, we behold his goodness to occupy and penetrate the very root and centre of our beings; or extend them abroad toward the things about us, we may perceive ourselves inclosed wholly and surrounded with his benefits. At home we find a comely body framed by his curious artifice, various organs fitly proportioned, situated, and tempered for strength, ornament, and motion, actuated by a gentle heat, and invigorated with lively spirits, disposed to health, and qualified for a long endurance; subservient to a soul endued with divers senses, faculties, and powers, apt to inquire after, pursue, and perceive various delights and contents. To the satisfaction of which all extrinsical things do minister matter and help; by his kind disposal, who furnishes our palates with variety of delicious fare, entertains our eyes with pleasant spectacles, ravishes our ears with harmonious sounds, perfumes our nostrils with fragrant odours, cheers our spirits with comfortable gales, fills our hearts with food and gladness, supplies our manifold needs, and protects us from innumerable dangers.

To him, who hath inspired us with immortal minds, and impressed upon them perspicuous characters of his own divine essence; hath made us, not in some superficial lineaments, but in our most intimate constitution, to resemble himself, and to partake of his most excellent perfections; an extensive knowledge of truth, a vehement complacency in good, a forward capacity of being completely happy, (according to our degree and within our sphere). To which blessed end by all suitable means (of external ministry and interior assistance) he faithfully conducts us; revealing to us the way, urging us in our process, reclaiming us when we deviate; engaging us by his commands, soliciting us by gentle advices, encouraging us by gracious promises; instructing us by his holy word, and admonishing us by his loving Spirit.

To him, who vouchsafes to grant us a free access unto, a constant intercourse and a familiar acquaintance with himself; to esteem and style us his friends and children; to invite us frequently, and entertain us kindly with those most pleasant delicacies of spiritual repast; yea, to visit us often at our home, and (if we admit) to abide and dwell with us; indulging us the enjoyment of that presence, wherein the life of all joy and comfort consists, and to behold the light of his all-cheering countenance.

Is there any thing more? Yes: To him, who, to redeem us from misery, and to advance our estate, hath infinitely debased himself, and eclipsed the brightness of his glorious majesty; not disdaining to assume us into a near affinity, yea, into a perfect union with himself; to inhabit our frail and mortal nature, to undergo the laws and conditions of humanity, to appear in our shape, and converse, as it were, upon equal terms with us, and at last to taste the bitter cup of a most painful and disgraceful death for us.

Yea, to him, who not only descended from his imperial throne, became a subject, and (which is more) a servant for our sake; but designed thereby to exalt us to a participation of his royal dignity, his divine nature, his eternal glory and bliss; submitting crowns and sceptres to our choice; crowns that cannot fade, and sceptres that can never be extorted from us.

Further yet, To him, the excellent quality, the noble end, the most obliging manner of whose beneficence doth surpass the matter thereof, and hugely augment the benefits; who, not compelled by any necessity, not obliged by any law, (or previous compact,) not induced by any extrinsic arguments, not inclined by our merits, not wearied with our importunities, not instigated by troublesome passions of pity, shame, or fear, (as we are wont to be,) not flattered with promises of recompense, nor bribed with expectation of emolument, thence to accrue unto himself; but being absolute master of his own actions, only both lawgiver and counsellor to himself, all-sufficient, and incapable of admitting any accession to his perfect blissfulness; most willingly and freely, out of pure bounty and good-will, is our Friend and Benefactor; preventing not only our desires, but our knowledge; surpassing not our deserts only, but our wishes, yea, even our conceits, in the dispensation of his inestimable and unrequitable benefits; having no other drift in the collation of them, beside our real good and welfare, our profit and advantage, our pleasure and content.

To him, who not lately began, or suddenly will cease, that is either uncertain or mutable in his intentions, but from everlasting designed, continues daily, and will (if we suffer him) to all eternity persevere unmoveable in his resolutions to do us good.

To him, whom no ingratitude, no undutiful carriage, no rebellious disobedience of ours, could for one minute wholly remove, or divert from his steady purpose of caring for us: who regards us, though we do not attend to him; procures our welfare, though we neglect his concernments; employs his restless thought, extends his watchful eye, exerts his powerful arm, is always mindful, and always busy to do us good; watching over us when we sleep, and remembering us when we forget ourselves: in whom yet 'tis infinite condescension to think of us, who are placed so far beneath his thoughts; to value us, who are but dust and dirt; not to despise and hate us, who are really so despicable and unworthy. For *Though he dwelleth on high,* saith the Psalmist truly and emphatically, *he humbleth himself to behold the things that are done in heaven and earth.*

To him, that is as merciful and gracious, as liberal and munificent toward us; that not only bestows on us more gifts, but pardons us more debts, forgives us more sins, than we live minutes; that with infinite patience endures, not only our manifold infirmities and imperfections, but our petulant follies, our obstinate perversenesses, our treacherous infidelities; overlooks our careless neglects and our wilful miscarriages; puts up the exceedingly many outrageous affronts, injuries, and contumelies continually offered to his supreme Majesty by us base worms, whom he hath always under his feet, and can crush to nothing at his pleasure.

To him yet, who, as St James saith, *Giveth freely, and upbraideth no man;* who calls us neither very frequently nor over strictly to accounts; who exacts of us no impossible, no very difficult, no greatly-burdensome or costly returns; being satisfied with the cheerful acceptance of his favours, the hearty acknowledgments of his goodness, the sincere performance of such duties, to which our own welfare, comfort, and advantage (rightly apprehended) would otherwise abundantly dispose us.

To him, lastly, whose benefits to acknowledge is the greatest benefit of all; to be enabled to thank whom deserves our greatest thanks; to be sensible of whose beneficence, to meditate on whose goodness, to admire whose excellency, to celebrate whose praise, is heaven itself and paradise, the life of angels, the quintessence of joy, the supreme degree of felicity.

*Serm. X.*

James i. 5.

In a word, To him, whose benefits are immensely great, innumerably many, unexpressibly good and precious. For, *Who can utter the mighty acts of the Lord? who can shew forth all his praise?* said he, who had employed often his most active thoughts and his utmost endeavours thereupon, and was incomparably better able to do it.

To this God, to this great, to this only Benefactor of ours, we owe this most natural and easy, this most just and equal, this most sweet and pleasant duty of giving thanks. To whom if we wilfully refuse, if we carelessly neglect to pay it, I shall only say thus much, that we are not only monstrously ingrateful, and horribly wicked; but abominably foolish, and deplorably miserable. I shall repeat this sentence once again, and wish it may have its due effect upon us: To this great, to this only Patron and Benefactor of ours, if we do not in some measure discharge our due debt of gratitude for his inestimable benefits and mercies, we are to be adjudged not only most prodigiously unthankful, most detestably impious, but most wofully stupid also and senseless, most desperately wretched and unhappy.

I should now proceed to consider the circumstance of time determined in the word *Always;* and the extension of the matter, implied in those words, *For all things:* and then to subjoin some further inducements or arguments persuasive to the practice of this duty. But the time (and, I fear, your patience) failing, I shall reserve them to some other opportunity.

# SERMON XI.[a]

## OF THE DUTY OF THANKSGIVING.

EPHES. V. 20.

*Giving thanks always for all things unto God.*

HAVING formerly, in this place, discoursed upon these words, I observed in them four particulars considerable: 1 The substance of a

---

[a] This sermon, preached at St Mary's, July 19, 1663, seems also to have been preached at Gray's Inn, Jan. 10, 1664, with the following introduction.

These words (to omit all matter of needless preface and circumstance) contain three things observable: 1 The substance of a duty to which we are exhorted, *Giving of thanks unto God.* 2 The circumstance of time assigned to the performance of that duty, *Always.* 3 The extent of the matter about which the duty is to be employed, *For all things.* The duty, *Giving thanks*, includes, or implies these things: 1 A diligent attention unto or considerate observation of the Divine benefits. 2 A faithful retention of these benefits in our memory, and frequent reflection upon them. 3 A due esteem and valuation of them. 4 A willing, hearty, and affectionate acceptance and entertainment of them. 5 Fit significations of our notice, declarations of our esteem and acknowledgments of our obligations for the favours received. 6 Competent endeavours of requital and compensation for them. 7 Exhibiting love, respect, and veneration to God our benefactor. These particulars I have largely insisted upon otherwhere in this city; and now proceed to the second particular; which is the circumstance, &c. MS.

duty, to which we are exhorted, to *Give thanks;* 2 The term unto which it is directed, *To God;* 3 The circumstance of time determined in that word *Always;* 4 The extent of the matter about which the duty is employed, *For all things.* Concerning the two former particulars, wherein the duty consisted, and wherefore especially related unto God, I then represented what did occur to my meditation.

III. I proceed now to the third, the circumstance of time allotted to the performance of this duty, expressed by that universal and unlimited term, *Always.*

Which yet is not so to be understood, as if thereby we were obliged in every instant (or singular point of time) actually to remember, to consider, to be affected with, and to acknowledge the divine benefits; for the deliberate operations of our minds being sometimes wholly interrupted by sleep, otherwhile preoccupied by the indispensable care of serving our natural necessities, and with attendance upon other reasonable employments, it were impossible to comply with an obligation to the performance of this duty so interpreted. And those maxims of law, *Impossibilium nulla est obligatio,* and, *Quæ rerum natura prohibentur, nulla lege confirmata sunt,* (that is, *No law or precept can oblige to impossibilities,*) being evidently grounded upon natural equity, seem yet more valid in relation to his laws, who is the Judge of all the world, and in his dispensations most transcendently just and equal.

We may therefore observe, that the Hebrews are wont (in way of synecdoche, or grammatical hyperbole) so to use words of this kind, that their universal importance ought to be restrained by the quality or circumstances of the matter about which they converse. As when our Saviour saith, *Ye shall be hated of all men for my sake;* all is not to be taken of every singular person, (since there were some that loved our Saviour, and embraced the evangelical doctrine,) but for many, or the most. And when David saith, *There is none that doeth good,* he seemeth only to mean, that in the general corruption of his times there were few righteous persons to be found. And so for ever is often used, not for a perpetual and endless, but for a long and lasting duration; and always, not for a continual, unintermitted state of being or action, but for such a perseverance as agrees to the condition of the thing to which it is applied.

SERM. XI.

Matt. x. 22.

Ps. xiv. 1.

'Tis, for instance, prescribed in Exodus, that *Aaron should bear the judgment of the children of Israel* (the Urim and Thummim) *upon his heart before the Lord continually;* that is, (not in absolute and rigorous acceptation continually, but) constantly, ever, when he went into the holy place to discharge the pontifical function, as the context declares. And our Saviour in the gospel saith of himself, Ἐγὼ πάντοτε ἐδίδαξα, *I always taught in the temple;* that is, very often, and ever when fit occasion was presented. And the apostles, immediately after Christ's ascension, Ἦσαν διαπαντὸς ἐν τῷ ἱερῷ, *Were,* as St Luke tells us, *continually in the temple, praising and blessing God;* that is, they resorted thither constantly at the usual times or canonical hours of prayer. In like manner those injunctions (of nearest affinity) of *Praying,* of *Rejoicing,* of

Exod. xxviii. 30.

John xviii. 20.

Luke xxiv. 53.

Luke xviii. 1.

SERM. XI.

1 Thess. v. 16, 17, 18.
Eph. vi. 18.

*Giving thanks always,* are to be taken in a sense so qualified, that the observance of them may be at least morally possible.

Thus far warrantably we may limit the extension and mollify the rigour of this seemingly boundless term; but we can hardly allow any further restriction, without destroying the natural signification, or diminishing the due emphasis thereof. As far therefore as it is possible for us, we must endeavour always to perform this duty of gratitude to Almighty God: and consequently,

1 Hereby is required a frequent performance thereof: that we do often actually meditate upon, be sensible of, confess and celebrate the divine beneficence. For what is done but seldom or never, (as we commonly say,) cannot be understood done always, without a catachresis, or abuse of words too enormous. As therefore no moment of our life wants sufficient matter, and every considerable portion of time ministers notable occasion of blessing God; as he allows himself no spacious intervals or discontinuances of doing us good: so ought we not to suffer any of those many days (vouchsafed by his goodness) to flow beside us, void of the signal expressions of our dutiful thankfulness to him; nor to admit in our course of life any long vacations from this duty. If God incessantly, and through every minute, demonstrates himself gracious unto us; we in all reason are obliged frequently and daily to declare ourselves grateful unto him.

So at least did David, (that most eminent example in this kind, and therefore most apposite to illustrate our doctrine, and to enforce the practice thereof;) for, *Every day*, saith he, *I will bless thee; I will praise thy name for ever and ever. Every day.* The heavenly bodies did not more constantly observe their course, than he his diurnal revolutions of praise: every day in his calendar was as it were festival, and consecrated to thanksgiving. Neither did he adjudge it sufficient to devote some small parcels of each day to this service: for, *My tongue*, saith he, *shall speak of thy righteousness and of thy praise all the day long:* and again, *My mouth shall shew forth thy righteousness and thy salvation all the day; for I know not the numbers thereof.* The benefits of God he apprehended so great and numerous, that no definite space of time would serve to consider and commemorate them. He resolves therefore otherwhere to bestow his whole life upon that employment: *While I live I will praise the Lord: I will sing praises unto my God while I have any being:* and, *I will bless the Lord at all times: his praise shall continually be in my mouth.* No man can reasonably pretend greater impediments, or oftener avocations from the practice of this duty, than he, upon whom the burden of a royal estate, and the care of governing a populous nation, were incumbent: yet could not they thrust out of his memory, nor extinguish in his heart, the lively sense of divine goodness; which (notwithstanding the company of other secular encumbrances) was always present to his mind, and, like a spirit, (excluded from no place by any corporeal resistance,) did mingle with and penetrate all his thoughts and affections and actions. So that he seems to have approached very near to the complete performance of this duty, according to

SERM. XI.

the extremity of a literal interpretation, and to have been always, without any intermission, employed in giving thanks to God. The consideration, methinks, of so noble a pattern, adjoined to the evident reasonableness of the duty, should engage us to the frequent practice thereof[b].

But if the consideration of this excellent example do not, yet certainly that may both provoke us to emulation, and confound us with shame, of Epictetus, a heathen man, whose words to this purpose seem very remarkable: Εἰ γὰρ νοῦν εἴχομεν, (saith he in Arrian's Dissertations[c]) ἄλλο τι ἔδει ἡμᾶς ποιεῖν καὶ κοινῇ καὶ ἰδίᾳ, ἢ ὑμνεῖν τὸ Θεῖον, καὶ εὐφημεῖν, καὶ ἐπεξέρχεσθαι τὰς χάριτας; οὐκ ἔδει καὶ σκάπτοντας, καὶ ἀροῦντας, καὶ ἐσθίοντας, ᾄδειν τὸν ὕμνον τὸν εἰς τὸν Θεόν; Μέγας ὁ Θεός, ὅτι ἡμῖν παρέσχεν ὄργανα τοιαῦτα, δι' ὧν τὴν γῆν ἐργασόμεθα· μέγας ὁ Θεός, ὅτι χεῖρας δέδωκεν, ὅτι κατάποσιν, ὅτι κοιλίαν, ὅτι αὔξεσθαι λεληθότως, ὅτι καθεύδοντας ἀναπνεῖν. Ταῦτα ἐφ' ἑκάστου ἐφυμνεῖν ἔδει, καὶ τὸν μέγιστον καὶ θειότατον ὕμνον ἐφυμνεῖν, ὅτι τὴν δύναμιν ἔδωκε τὴν παρακολουθητικὴν τούτοις, καὶ ὁδῷ χρηστικήν. Τί οὖν; ἐπεὶ οἱ πολλοὶ ἀποτετύφλωσθε, οὐκ ἔδει τινὰ εἶναι τὸν ταύτην ἐκπληροῦντα τὴν χώραν, καὶ ὑπὲρ πάντων ᾄδοντα τὸν ὕμνον τὸν εἰς τὸν Θεόν; τί γὰρ ἄλλο δύναμαι γέρων χωλός, εἰ μὴ ὑμνεῖν τὸν Θεόν; εἰ γοῦν ἀηδὼν ἤμην, ἐποίουν τὰ τῆς ἀηδόνος· εἰ κύκνος, τὰ τοῦ κύκνου. Νῦν δὲ λογικός εἰμι, ὑμνεῖν με δεῖ τὸν Θεόν· τοῦτό μου τὸ ἔργον ἐστί, ποιῶ αὐτό· οὐδ' ἐγκαταλείψω τὴν τάξιν ταύτην,

[b] Εἰ δὲ βασιλεὺς ἀνὴρ μυρίαις βαπτιζόμενος φροντίσι, καὶ πανταχόθεν περιελκόμενος, τοσαυτάκις τῆς ἡμέρας παρεκάλει τὸν Θεόν, τίνα ἂν ἔχοιμεν ἀπολογίαν ἢ συγγνώμην ἡμεῖς, τοσαύτην σχολὴν ἄγοντες, καὶ μὴ συνεχῶς αὐτὸν ἱκετεύοντες, &c.—Chrys. [Orat. XIV. Opp. Tom. V. p. 76.]

[c] Epict. Diss. I. 16. [15—21.]

ἐφ' ὅσον ἂν δίδωται· καὶ ὑμᾶς ἐπὶ τὴν αὐτὴν ταύτην ᾠδὴν παρακαλῶ. That is, in our language, *If we understood ourselves, what other thing should we do, either publicly or privately, than sing hymns to, and speak well of God, and perform thanks unto him? Ought we not, when we were digging, or ploughing, or eating, to sing a (suitable) hymn to him*[d]*? Great is God, in that he hath bestowed on us those instruments wherewith we till the ground: Great is God, because he hath given us hands, a throat, a belly; that we grow insensibly, that sleeping we breathe. Thus should we upon every occurrence celebrate God, and superadd of all the most excellent and most divine hymn, for that he hath given us the faculty of apprehending and using these things orderly. Wherefore since most men are blind and ignorant of this, should there not be some one who should discharge this office, and who should for the rest utter this hymn to God? And what can I, a lame and decrepit old man do else, than celebrate God? Were I indeed a nightingale, I would do what belongs to a nightingale; if a swan, what becomes a swan: but since now I am endued with reason, I ought to praise God. This is my duty and concernment, and so I do; neither will I desert this employment, while it is in my power: and to the same song I exhort you all.* Thus that worthy philosopher, not instructing us only, and exhorting with pathetical discourse, but by his practice inciting us to be continually expressing our gratitude to God.

SERM. XI.

---

[d] Πάντα τοίνυν τὸν βίον ἑορτὴν ἄγοντες, πάντῃ πάντοθεν παρεῖναι τὸν Θεὸν πεπεισμένοι, γεωργοῦμεν αἰνοῦντες, πλέομεν ὑμνοῦντες, κατὰ τὴν ἄλλην πολιτείαν ἐντέχνως ἀναστρεφόμεθα.—Clem. Alex. Strom. VII. [Opp. Tom. II. p. 851.]

And although neither the admonition of prophets, nor precepts of philosophers, nor the examples of both, should prevail; yet the precedents, methinks, of dumb and senseless creatures should animate us thereto; which never cease to obey the law imposed on them by their Maker, and without intermission glorify him. For, *The heavens declare the glory of God, and the firmament sheweth his handywork. Day unto day uttereth speech, and night unto night sheweth knowledge. There is no speech nor language where their voice is not heard.* It is St Chrysostom's argumentation; Καὶ γὰρ αἰσχρὸν ἂν εἴη, saith he, τὸν λογικὸν ἄνθρωπον καὶ τῶν ὁρωμένων ἁπάντων τιμιώτερον, ἔλαττον τῆς κτίσεως φέρειν κατὰ τὸν τῆς εὐφημίας λόγον· οὐκ αἰσχρὸν δὲ μόνον, ἀλλὰ καὶ ἄτοπον. Πῶς δὲ οὐκ ἄτοπον; εἴγε αὐτὴ μὲν καθ' ἑκάστην ἡμέραν καὶ ὥραν ἀναπέμπει τῷ δεσπότῃ δοξολογίαν. *It were an ugly thing, that man, endued with reason, and the most honourable of all things visible, should in rendering thanks and praise be exceeded by other creatures: neither is it only base, but absurd. For how can it be otherwise, since other creatures every day and every hour send up a doxology to their Lord and Maker*[e]? For, *The heavens declare the glory of God,* &c.

If the busy heavens are always at leisure, and the stupid earth is perpetually active in manifesting the wisdom, power, and goodness of their Creator; how shameful is it, that we (the flower of his creation, the most obliged, and most capable of doing it) should commonly be either too busy or too idle to do it; should seldom or never be dis-

---

[e] In Ps. cxliv. [Opp. Tom. I. p. 884.]

## The Duty of Thanksgiving.

posed to contribute our endeavours to the advancement of his glory! But,

2 *Giving thanks always* may import our appointing and punctually observing, certain convenient times of performing this duty; that is, of serious meditation upon, and affectionate acknowledgment of the divine bounty. We know that all persons, who design with advantage to prosecute an orderly course of action, and would not lead a tumultuary life, are wont to distinguish their portions of time, assigning some to the necessary refections of their body, others to the divertisement of their minds, and a great part to the despatch of their ordinary business: otherwise (like St James's double-minded man) they would be unstable in all their ways; they would ever fluctuate in their resolutions, and be uncertain when, and how, and to what they should apply themselves. And so, this main concernment of ours, this most excellent part of our duty, if we do not depute some vacant seasons for it, and observe some periodical recourses thereof, we shall be tempted often to omit it; we shall be listless to do it, apt to defer it, and easily diverted from it by the encroachments of other less behoving affairs.

The Jews, to preserve them in the constant exercise of this duty, had instituted by God a sacrifice called תָּמִיד (*juge*), rendered by the Greek translators, Ἡ διαπαντὸς θυσία, *The continual sacrifice;* to which the divine author of the Epistle to the Hebrews seems to allude, when in these words he exhorts: Δι' αὐτοῦ οὖν ἀναφέρωμεν θυσίαν αἰνέσεως διαπαντὸς τῷ Θεῷ, *By him therefore let us offer the sacrifice of praise to God continually,* (or the con-

SERM. XI.

James i. 8.

Dan. viii. 11.

Heb. xiii. 15.

tinual sacrifice of praise,) *the fruit of our lips, giving thanks to his name.* As that sacrifice therefore, being offered constantly at a set time, was thence denominated continual; so perhaps may we, by constantly observing some fit returns of praise and thanksgiving, be said always to give thanks.

In determining the seasons and proportions of which, what other rule or standard can we better conform to, than that of the royal prophet? I shall not urge his example so much; (according to which we should be obliged to a greater frequency;) for, *Seven times a day,* saith he, *do I praise thee, because of thy righteous judgments:* but rather allege his general direction and opinion, proposed to us in these words of his; *It is a good thing to give thanks unto the Lord, and to sing praises unto thy name, O thou Most High; to shew forth thy lovingkindness every morning, and thy faithfulness every night. It is a good thing;* that is, a seemly, a convenient, a commendable, a due performance: *Every morning;* that is, when our spirits, being recreated with sleep, are become more vigorous, our memories more fresh, our fancies more quick and active: *To shew forth thy lovingkindness;* that is, from a hearty sense of our obligation to acknowledge the free bounty of him, who, in pursuance of his former kindness, hath been pleased to accumulate new favours to us; to guard us by his watchful care, when we were buried, as it were, in a senseless ignorance, and total neglect of our own welfare; to raise us from that temporary death, and to confer a new life upon us, restoring us to our health, to our means of subsistence, to all the necessary supports, and the desirable comforts of life: *Every night* also; that is, when our spirits are exhausted with action, and our minds tired with thoughtfulness; when we are become weary, not of doing only, but almost of being; we should conclude our toils, and wrap up our cares in the sweet sense and grateful memory of his goodness, who hath protected us so many hours from the manifold dangers, and more sins, to which, by our weakness, and our folly, and our bad inclinations, we are through every minute exposed; and withal hath provided us so easy and so delightful a means of recovering our spent activity, of repairing our decayed strength.

Thus if we constantly begin, and thus close up, thus bound and circumscribe our days, dedicating those most remarkable periods of time to blessing God, and *Making*, as the Psalmist speaks, *the outgoings of the morning and evening to rejoice* in him: (since beginning and ending do in a manner comprehend the whole; and the morning and evening, in Moses's computation and style, do constitute a day;) we may (not incongruously) be supposed and said to give thanks always. But yet further, this may import,

3 A vigilant attendance upon this duty, such as men bestow on their employments, whereof though the actual prosecution ceases, yet the design continually proceeds. As we say, such a one is writing a book, building a house, occupying a piece of land, though he be at that present peradventure sleeping, or eating, or satisfying some other desire; because his design never sleeps, and his purpose persists uninterrupted. And thus, it

seems, we are to understand our Saviour and the apostles, when they exhort us Προσκαρτερεῖν, *To continue instant in prayer and thanksgiving*; and, Ἀγρυπνεῖν ἐν πάσῃ προσκαρτερήσει, *To watch with all perseverance*; and Γρηγορεῖν, *To wake in thanksgiving*; and Μὴ παύεσθαι, *Not to give over giving thanks*: and to perform these duties Ἀδιαλείπτως, *Incessantly*, or *without giving off*: Μὴ ἐκκακεῖν, *Not to grow worse, faint*, or *falter*: (which is, in that place, made equivalent to, explicatory of doing duty always). Which expressions denote a most diligent attendance on these duties; that we may make them not a Πάρεργον, a diversion or by-business of our lives, allowing only a perfunctory and desultorious endeavour on them; but esteem them a weighty business, to be pursued with steadfast resolution and unwearied industry.

As our beings and powers did proceed from the goodness, so the results of them naturally tend to the glory of God; and the deliberations of our will ought to conspire with the instincts of our nature; it should be the principal design which our intention should aim at, and our endeavour always drive on, to glorify our Maker. Which doing, we may be reputed to discharge this duty, and in some sense said always to give thanks. But further,

4 This term *Always* doth necessarily imply a ready disposition, or habitual inclination, to give thanks, ever permanent in us: that our hearts, as David's was, be fixed always (that is, fittingly prepared, and steadily resolved) to thank and praise God; that our affections be like tinder, though not always inflamed, yet easily inflammable by the sense of his goodness.

'Tis said of the righteous man, that *He is ever merciful, and lendeth*: not for that he doth ever actually dispense alms, or furnish his poor neighbour with supplies; but because his mind is ever inclinable to do it when need requires. So a grateful man doth always give thanks, by being disposed to do it upon all fit occasions. 'Tis the habit that qualifies and denominates a man such or such in any kind or degree of morality. A good man is in scripture frequently compared to a *Tree bringing forth fruit in due season*; and the root thereof is this habitual disposition, which, being nourished by the dew of heaven, and quickened by the benign influence of divine grace, sprouts forth opportunely, and yields a plentiful increase of good fruit. Though we cannot always sing, our organs may be always rightly tuned for praise; at least, they should never be unstrung, and wholly out of kelter.

We should maintain in ourselves a constant good temper of mind, that no opportunity surprise, and find us unprepared to entertain worthily the effects of divine favour: otherwise we shall as well lose the benefit, as God the thanks and glory due to them. That we be always thus disposed, is not impossible, and therefore requisite. But moreover,

5 Lastly, *Giving thanks always* imports, that we readily embrace every opportunity of actually expressing our thankfulness. For so, what in some places of scripture is enjoined to be done continually, and indesinently, is in others only required to be done upon all opportunities. Which shews, that Πάντοτε is to be expounded, not so

SERM. XI.

Eph. vi. 18.

Luke xxi. 36.

much Ἐν παντὶ χρόνῳ, *At all times*, as Ἐν παντὶ καιρῷ, *In every season*. So Προσευχόμενοι ἐν παντὶ καιρῷ ἐν πνεύματι, *Praying upon every opportunity in your spirit:* and, Ἀγρυπνεῖτε οὖν ἐν παντὶ καιρῷ δεόμενοι, *Be watchful, praying in every season.* And this sense seems probably to be chiefly intended by this apostle, whenever he hath (as he hath often) this expression, Πάντοτε εὐχαριστεῖν, that we embrace every overture or fit occasion of giving thanks.

'Tis true, no time is unseasonable to do it: every moment we receive favours, and therefore every minute we owe thanks: yet there are some especial seasons that do more importunately require them. We should be like those trees that bear fruit (more or less) continually; but then more kindly, and more abundantly, when more powerfully cherished by the heavenly warmth.

When any fresh, any rare, any remarkable benefit happens to us; when prosperous success attends our honest endeavours; when unexpected favours fall as it were of their own accord into our bosoms; (like the grain in the golden age springing up Ἄσπαρτα καὶ ἀνήροτα, without our care or our toil, for our use and enjoyment;) when we are delivered from straits in our apprehension inextricable, surmount difficulties seeming insuperable, escape hazards (as we suspected) inevitable; then is a special season presented us of offering up the sacrifice of praise to the God of mercy, help, and victory.

When we revolve in our minds (as we should often do) the favourable passages of providence, that in the whole course of our lives have befallen us: how in our extreme poverty and distress (when perhaps no help appeared, and all hopes seemed to fail us,) God hath raised us up friends, who have commiserated, comforted, and succoured us; and not only so, but hath changed our sorrowful condition into a state of joy; hath (to use the Psalmist's expressions) *Turned our mourning into dancing;* hath *Put off our sackcloth, and girded us with gladness;* hath *Considered our trouble, and known our soul in adversity;* hath *Set our feet in a large room,* and furnished us with plentiful means of subsistence; how in the various changes and adventures, and travels of our life, upon sea and land, at home and abroad, among friends and strangers and enemies, he hath protected us from wants and dangers; from devouring diseases, and the distemperatures of infectious air; from the assaults of bloody thieves and barbarous pirates; from the rage of fire, and fury of tempests; from disastrous casualties; from treacherous surprises; from open mischiefs, that with a dreadful face approached and threatened our destruction: then most opportunely should we with all thankful exultation of mind admire and celebrate our *Strength and our deliverer;* our faithful *Refuge in trouble,* and *The rock of our salvation.*

SERM. XI.

Ps. xxx. 11.

Ps. xxxi. 7, 8.

Ps. xl. 17; ix. 9; xc. 1.

Also when the ordinary effects of divine providence do, in any advantageous manner, present themselves to our view; when we peruse the volumes of story, and therein observe the various events of human action; especially the seasonable rewards of virtue, the notable protections and deliverances of innocence, and the unexpected punishments of malicious wickedness: then we should with thankful acclamations celebrate the divine goodness and justice; joining in concert with that heavenly choir, and saying, *Hallelujah; salvation, and glory, and honour, and power unto the Lord our God: for true and righteous are his judgments.*

Or when we contemplate the wonderful works of nature, and walking about at our leisure, gaze upon this ample theatre of the world, considering the stately beauty, constant order, and sumptuous furniture thereof; the glorious splendour and uniform motion of the heavens; the pleasant fertility of the earth; the curious figure and fragrant sweetness of plants; the exquisite frame of animals; and all other amazing miracles of nature, wherein the glorious attributes of God (especially his transcendent goodness) are most conspicuously displayed; (so that by them not only large acknowledgments, but even gratulatory hymns, as it were, of praise have been extorted from the mouths of Aristotle, Pliny, Galen, and such like men, never suspected guilty of an excessive devotion;) then should our hearts be affected with thankful sense, and our lips break forth into his praise.

Yea, from every object of sense, from every event of providence, from every common occurrence, we may extract fit matter of thanksgiving: as did our Saviour, when, considering the stupid infidelity of those proud people of Chorazin, Bethsaida, and Capernaum, (who were not at all affected by his miraculous works, nor moved to repentance by his pathetical discourses,) and comparing it with the pious credulity of his meaner disciples, he brake forth into that divine ejaculation; *I thank thee, O Father, Lord of heaven and earth, that thou hast concealed these things from the wise and prudent, and hast revealed them unto babes.* Ἐν ἐκείνῳ τῷ καιρῷ ἀποκριθεὶς Ἰησοῦς εἶπε, saith the evangelical narration; *Upon that occasion Jesus thus spake:* he embraced that convenient opportunity of thankfully acknowledging God's wise and gracious dispensation. And frequent occasion is afforded us daily (were our minds suitably disposed) of doing the like.

SERM. XI.

Matt. xi. 25.

But so much concerning the time of performing this duty.

IV. We proceed to the matter thereof, *For all things.* St Chrysostom (in his Commentary upon the 145th Psalm) having enumerated several particulars for which we are bound to thank God; *Because,* (I recite his words punctually rendered,) *Because, saith he, he hath made us, who before had no being, and made us such as we are; because he upholds us being made, and takes care of us continually, both publicly and privately, secretly and openly, with and without our knowledge; for all visible things created for our sake, the ministry of them afforded to us; the conformation of our bodies, the nobleness of our souls; his daily dispensations by miracles, by laws, by punishments; his various and incomprehensible providence; for the chief of all, that he hath not spared his only-begotten Son for our sake; the benefits conferred on us by baptism, and the other holy mysteries, (or sacraments;) the ineffable good things to be bestowed on us hereafter, the kingdom of heaven, the resurrection, the enjoyment of perfect bliss*[f]; having, I say, in these words com-

---

[f] [Καὶ γὰρ πολλῶν ἐσμεν ὀφειλέται αὐτῷ, ὅτι τε οὐκ ὄντας ἐποίησε,

prised the things for which we are obliged to thank and praise God, he thus despondently concludes: *If any one shall endeavour to recount particularly every one of these things, he will but plunge himself into an unexpressible deep of benefits, and then perceive for how unexpressibly and inconceivably many good things he stands engaged to God*[g]. And to the like *Non plus* doth the devout Psalmist seem to be reduced, when he thus exclaims, *How precious are thy thoughts unto me, O God! how great is the sum of them! If I should count them, they are more in number than the sand.*

I shall not therefore confound myself by launching too far into this immense ocean, nor strive minutely to compute the incomprehensible sum of the divine benefits; but only observe, that in gross, according to our apostle's calculation, all things, which however happen to us, are ingredients thereof. No occurrence (great or small, common or particular, present or past, pleasant or sad, perpetual or transitory) is excluded from being the subject of our thanksgiving: each one may prove beneficial to us; and we are with a cheerful con-

Ps. cxxxix. 17, 18; xxxvi. 5, 6, 7.

καὶ ὅτι τοιούτους εἰργάσατο· ὅτι γενομένους διακρατεῖ, καὶ ὅτι καθ' ἑκάστην προνοεῖ τὴν ἡμέραν, καὶ κοινῇ καὶ ἰδίᾳ, καὶ λάθρα καὶ φανερῶς, καὶ εἰδότων καὶ οὐκ εἰδότων. Τί γὰρ ἄν τις εἴποι τὰ ὁρώμενα ἃ δι' ἡμᾶς ἐποίησε; τὴν διακονίαν αὐτῶν ἣν παρέχεται; τοῦ σώματος τὴν διάπλασιν; τῆς ψυχῆς τὴν εὐγένειαν; τὴν καθ' ἑκάστην ἡμέραν οἰκονομίαν, τὴν διὰ τῶν θαυμάτων, τὴν διὰ τῶν νόμων, τὴν διὰ τῶν τιμωριῶν; τὴν ποικίλην αὐτοῦ πρόνοιαν καὶ ἀκατάληπτον; τὸ κεφάλαιον τῶν ἀγαθῶν, ὅτι οὐδὲ τοῦ μονογενοῦς ἐφείσατο δι' ἡμῶν; τὰ δοθέντα ἤδη διὰ τοῦ βαπτίσματος, διὰ τῶν μυστηρίων; τὰ μέλλοντα δοθήσεσθαι ἀπόρρητα ἐκεῖνα ἀγαθά, τὴν βασιλείαν, τὴν ἀνάστασιν, τὴν λῆξιν τῆς πάσης μακαριότητος γέμουσαν;—In Ps. cxlv. Opp. Tom. I. pp. 884—5.]

[g] [Ἂν γὰρ ἕκαστόν τις τούτων καταλέγῃ, εἰς πέλαγος ἄφατον ἐμπεσεῖται εὐεργεσιῶν, καὶ ὄψεται πόσων ἐστὶν ὑπεύθυνος τῷ Θεῷ.—Id. Ibid.]

tentedness and a grateful resentment to receive them all from God's hand. But to observe some little distinction: I say,

SERM. XI.

1 We are to give thanks, not only for great and notable benefits, but for the least and most ordinary favours of God: though indeed none of God's favours are in themselves small and inconsiderable. Men are wont to bless themselves, if they receive but a transient glance from a prince's eye; a smile from a great personage; any slender intimation of regard from him that is in capacity to do them good. What is it then to receive the least testimony of his good-will, from whom alone every good thing can be expected; upon whose disposal all happy success of our wishes, our hopes, and our endeavours do entirely depend! We repute him unjust who withholds the least part of what is due from the true owner: and is not he ingrateful then, that omits to render thanks for the least of divine mercies?

*There is one glory of the sun, another of the moon, another of the stars,* saith St Paul. Some works of God indeed excel in lustre; yet all are glorious, all are to be discerned, all to be esteemed and thankfully entertained by us. The brightness of the one should not wholly obscure the other; if it do, it argues the weakness of our sense, the dulness of our spiritual faculty. For every beam of light that delights our eye, for every breath of air that cheers our spirits, for every drop of pleasant liquor that cools our thirst, for every minute of comfortable repose, for every step we safely take, for the happy issue of the least undertaking, for escaping the vengeance due to an idle word or

1 Cor. xv. 41.

SERM. XI.

a wanton thought, we owe a hymn of praise to God. But,

2 We are to render thanks, not only for new and present benefits, but for all we have formerly, all that we may hereafter receive. We find David not only frequently acknowledging the gracious dispensations of Providence toward him through the whole course of his life, but looking back in his thankful devotions as far as his very original being, and praising God for favours conferred on him beyond his memory, yea before his life. *I will praise thee,* saith he, *for I am fearfully and wonderfully made: marvellous are thy works, and that my soul knoweth right well. My substance was not hid from thee, when I was made in secret, and curiously wrought in the lower parts of the earth. Thine eyes did see my substance, yet being imperfect; and in thy book all my members were written, which in continuance were fashioned, when as yet there was none of them.* And St Paul, yet further reflecting his grateful consideration, blesses God for his favour commenced before the beginning of things. *Blessed,* saith he, *be the God and Father of our Lord Jesus Christ, who hath blessed us with all spiritual blessings in heavenly places in Christ, according as he hath chosen us before the foundation of the world.*

Ps. cxxxix. 14, 15, 16.

Eph. i. 3, 4.

Neither doth the memory only of former, and the enjoyment of present, but the hope and foresight also of future blessings, worthily claim our thanks. For, saith St Peter, *Blessed be the God and Father of our Lord Jesus Christ, which according to his abundant mercy hath begotten us again unto a lively hope by the resurrection of Jesus Christ from the*

1 Pet. i. 3, 4.

*dead, to an inheritance incorruptible and undefiled, and that fadeth not away, reserved in heaven for you.* Beasts only, and men not much better than they, are affected with present good turns: but men of honest and generous temper resent indifferently the obligations of all times. Sense doth not confine their gratitude, nor absence remove, nor age wear it out. What once is done, is ever done to them; and what of courtesy is proposed, seems to them performed. But having before discoursed somewhat largely concerning the remembrance of benefits, I leave this point. Furthermore,

3 We should bless God, not only for new, rare, extraordinary accidents of providence, but for the common and daily benefits and indulgences thereof[h]. These favours are usually the greatest and most valuable in their own nature. (For what can be imagined of higher consequence to us, than the preservation of our lives and of our estates, by which they are comfortably maintained; than the continuance of our bodies in good health, and our minds in their right wits; than the knowledge of heavenly truth, the encouragements to virtue and piety, the assistances of divine grace, and the promises of eternal bliss continually exhibited to us?) Shall the commonness and continuance of these exceeding favours, that they are not given us once only, and transitorily, but continued, (that is, given us so often as time hath instants,) and with an uninterrupted perseverance renewed unto us; shall

[h] Quem vero astrorum ordines, quem dierum noctiumque vicissitudines, quem mensium temperatio, quemque ea, quæ gignuntur nobis ad fruendum, non gratum esse cogant; hunc hominem omnino numerare qui decet?—Cic. de Leg. II. [7. 16.]

this abate and enervate our gratitude, which in all reason should mainly increase and confirm it? But this point I also touched before, and therefore, forbearing to insist thereon, I proceed.

4 We should give thanks, not only for private and particular, but for public benefits also, and for such as befall others. *I exhort therefore,* saith St Paul, *before all things, that supplications, prayers, intercessions, and thanksgivings be made for all men:* not *Prayers* only, for good things to be bestowed on others; but *Thanksgivings* also, for the benefits received by others. (And Ὑπὲρ πάντων in our text, however otherwise commonly interpreted, may well admit this sense also; and be taken indifferently, *Pro omnibus, For all persons,* and *Propter omnia, For all things.*)

We are all citizens of the world, and concerned in its good constitution; and thence obliged thankfully to adore the mighty Upholder and wise Governor thereof, praising him for all the general benefits liberally poured forth upon mankind[1]. We partake in the commodities of civil society; and therefore should heartily thank him, by whose gracious disposal order is maintained, peace continued, justice administered, plenty provided, our lives made safe and sweet to us therein. We are members of a church, and highly interested in the prosperous estate and well-being thereof: when unity therefore is preserved, and charity abounds; when knowledge is increased, and virtue encouraged; when piety flourishes, and truth triumphs therein; we are bound to render all possible thanks to the gracious bestower of those inestimable blessings.

[1] Vid. Chrys. in 2 Cor. Orat. II. [Opp. Tom. III. p. 553.]

We are much mistaken in our account, if we either determine our own concernments, or measure this duty, by the narrow rule of our private advantage: for subducting either the benefits commonly indulged to mankind, or those which accrue from the welfare of public society, what possibility will remain of subsistence, of safety, of content unto us? what but confusion, want, violence, and disquiet?

As we are concerned with our utmost endeavours to promote, to wish and pray for, to delight and rejoice in, the public good of mankind, the peace of our country, the prosperity of Sion; so we are to bless and thank him, by whose gracious help and furtherance they are attained.

If we consult all history, (sacred and civil,) we shall find it to contain hardly any thing else considerable, but the earnest endeavours of good men for public benefit, and their thankful acknowledgments to the divine goodness for it. Moses, David, Nehemiah, St Paul, all the prophets, and all the apostles, what other things memorable did they do, but serve God in procuring public good, and bless God for conferring it?

Neither only as we are combined with others in common interest, but without selfish respects, purely out of charity, and humanity, and ingenuous pity, are we obliged to thank God for the benefits he is pleased to impart to others. If upon these accounts we are commanded to *Do good to all men;* to *Rejoice with those that rejoice;* to *Love even those that hate us,* and *Bless those that curse us;* 'tis (by fair consequence) surely intended, that we should also

Gal. vi. 10.
Rom. xii. 15.
Matt. v. 44.

SERM. XI.

bless God for the good issue of our honest endeavours, or of our good wishes for them.

And verily could we become endowed with this excellent quality of delighting in others' good, and heartily thanking God for it, we needed not to envy the wealth and splendour of the greatest princes, not the wisdom of the profoundest doctors, not the religion of the devoutest anchorets, no, nor the happiness of the highest angels: for upon this supposition, as the glory of all is God's, so the content in all would be ours. All the fruit they can perceive of their happy condition, of what kind soever, is to rejoice in it themselves, and to praise God for it: and this should we then do as well as they. My neighbour's good success is mine, if I equally triumph therein: his riches are mine, if I delight to see him enjoy them: his health is mine, if it refresh my spirits: his virtue mine, if I by it am bettered, and have hearty complacence therein. By this means a man derives a confluence of joy upon himself, and makes himself, as it were, the centre of all felicity; enriches himself with the plenty, and satiates himself with the pleasure, of the whole world: reserving to God the praise, he enjoys the satisfaction of all good that happens to any.

Thus we see David frequently thanking God, not for his favour only and mercy shewed particularly to himself, but for his common munificence toward all: for (to use his own phrases) *His goodness to all, and his tender mercies over all his works;* for *Executing judgment in behalf of the oppressed;* for *Feeding the hungry;* for *Loosening the prisoners;*

Ps. cxlv. 9; cxlvi. 7, 8, 9.

for *Opening the eyes of the blind*; for *Raising them that are bowed down*; for *Preserving the strangers, and Relieving the fatherless and widow*; for *Lifting up the meek*; for *Loving, and caring for, and defending the righteous*; for *Opening his hand, and satisfying the desire of every living thing*; for *Giving to the beast his food, and to the young ravens when they cry unto him*; in a word, for his goodness to every particular creature, not excluding the most contemptible nor the most savage of all. And how affectionately doth St Paul every where thank God for the growth in grace and spiritual wisdom, for the patience in affliction and perseverance in faith, of those good Christians he writes unto! So should, with an unrestrained exuberance, both our charity to men, and our gratitude to God, abound. But moreover,

SERM. XI.

Ps. cxlvii. 6.
1 Pet. v. 7.
Ps. v. 11;
civ. 28;
cxlv. 16;
cxlvii. 9.

5 We are obliged to give thanks, not only for pleasant and prosperous occurrences of providence, but for those also which are adverse to our desire, and distasteful unto our natural sense; for poverty, sickness, disgrace; for all the sorrows and troubles, the disasters and disappointments, that befall us. We are bound to pay thanks, not for our food only, but for our physic also: (which, though ingrateful to our palate, is profitable for our health:) we are obliged, in the school of providence, not only for the good instructions, but for the seasonable corrections also vouchsafed unto us, (whereby, though our senses are offended, our manners are bettered[k].) Whatever proceeds from good purpose, and tends

[k] Τὸν Θεὸν ὁμοίως ἀνυμνεῖν χρὴ, καὶ κολάζοντα, καὶ ἀνιέντα κολάσεως· ἀμφότερα γὰρ κηδεμονίας, ἀμφότερα ἀγαθότητος, &c.—Chrys. in Ps. cxlviii. [Opp. Tom. I. p. 903.]

to a happy end, that is graciously designed, and effectually conduces to our good, is a fit subject of thanksgiving: and such may all adversities prove unto us. They proceed usually from love and kind intention toward us: for, *Whom God loveth he chasteneth, and scourgeth every son whom he receiveth:* and, *I know, O Lord,* saith David, *that thy judgments are right, and that thou in faithfulness hast afflicted me: in faithfulness,* that is, with a sincere intention of doing me good.

<small>Heb. xii. 6.</small>

<small>Ps. cxix. 75.</small>

God thoroughly knows our constitution, what is noxious to our health, and what may remedy our distempers; and therefore accordingly disposeth to us

<small>Pro jucundis aptissima quæque[1];</small>

instead of pleasant honey, he sometimes prescribes wholesome wormwood for us. We are ourselves greatly ignorant of what is conducible to our real good, and, were the choice of our condition wholly permitted to us, should make very foolish, very disadvantageous elections.

We should (be sure) all of us embrace a rich and plentiful estate; when as, God knows, that would make us slothful and luxurious, swell us with pride and haughty thoughts, encumber us with anxious cares, and expose us to dangerous temptations; would render us forgetful of ourselves and neglectful of him. Therefore he wisely disposeth poverty unto us; poverty, the mother of sobriety, the nurse of industry, the mistress of wisdom; which will make us understand ourselves and our dependance on him, and force us to have recourse unto his help. And is there not reason we should

[1] [Juv. Sat. x. 349.]

*The Duty of Thanksgiving.* 393

be thankful for the means by which we are delivered from those desperate mischiefs, and obtain these excellent advantages?

SERM.
XI.

We should all (certainly) choose the favour and applause of men: but this, God also knows, would corrupt our minds with vain conceit, would intoxicate our fancies with spurious pleasure, would tempt us to ascribe immoderately to ourselves, and sacrilegiously to deprive God of his due honour. Therefore he advisedly suffers us to incur the disgrace and displeasure, the hatred and contempt of men; that so we may place our glory only in the hopes of his favour, and may pursue more earnestly the purer delights of a good conscience. And doth not this part of divine providence highly merit our thanks?

We would all climb into high places, not considering the precipices on which they stand, nor the vertiginousness of our own brains: but God keeps us safe in the humble valleys, allotting to us employments which we are more capable to manage.

We should perhaps insolently abuse power, were it committed to us: we should employ great parts on unwieldy projects, as many do, to the disturbance of others, and their own ruin: vast knowledge would cause us to overvalue ourselves and contemn others: enjoying continual health, we should not perceive the benefit thereof, nor be mindful of him that gave it. A suitable mediocrity therefore of these things the divine goodness allotteth unto us, that we may neither starve for want, nor surfeit with plenty.

In fine, the advantages arising from afflictions are so many, and so great, that (had I time, and were it seasonable to insist largely on this subject) it were easy to demonstrate, that we have great reason, not only to be contented with, but to rejoice in, and to be very thankful for, all the crosses and vexations we meet with: to receive them cheerfully at God's hand, as the medicines of our soul, and the condiments of our fortune; as the arguments of his good-will, and the instruments of virtue; as solid grounds of hope, and comfortable presages of future joy unto us.

6 Lastly, we are obliged to thank God, not only for corporeal and temporal benefits, but also (and that principally) for spiritual and eternal blessings. We are apt, as to desire more vehemently, to rejoice more heartily in the fruition, and more passionately to bewail the loss of temporal good things; so more sincerely and seriously to express our gratitude for the reception of them, than for others relating to our spiritual good, to our everlasting welfare. Wherein we misjudge and misbehave ourselves extremely. For, as much as the reasonable soul (that goodly image of the divine essence, breathed from the mouth of God) doth in dignity of nature, and purity of substance, excel this feculent lump of organized clay, our body; as the blissful ravishments of spirit surpass the dull satisfactions of sense; as the bottomless depth of eternity exceeds that shallow surface of time, which terminates this transitory life; in such proportion should our appetite unto, our complacence in, our gratitude for spiritual blessings transcend the affections (respectively) engaged about these corporeal accommodations.

Consider that injunction of our Saviour to his

disciples: *In this rejoice not, that the spirits are subject unto you; but rather rejoice, because your names are written in heaven. Rejoice not;* that is, Be not at all affected with this (although in itself very rare accomplishment, eminent privilege, glorious power of working that indeed greatest of miracles, subjecting devils; that is, baffling the shrewdest craft, and subduing the strongest force in nature) in comparison of that delight, which the consideration of the divine favour, in order to your eternal felicity, doth afford.

We are, 'tis true, greatly indebted to God for our creation, for that he hath extracted us from nothing, and placed us in so lofty a rank among his creatures; for the excellent faculties of soul and body wherewith he hath endued us; and for many most admirable prerogatives of our outward estate: but much more for our redemption, and the wonderful circumstances of unexpressible love and grace therein declared; for his descending to a conjunction with our nature, and elevating us to a participation of his; for dignifying us with more illustrious titles, and instating us in a sure capacity of a much superior happiness. Our daily food deserves well a grace to be said before and after it: but how much more that constant provision of heavenly manna, the evangelical verity; those savoury delicacies of devotion, whereby our souls are nourished to eternal life? 'Tis a laudable custom, when we are demanded concerning our health, to answer, *Well, I thank God;* but much more reason have we to say so, if our conscience can attest concerning that sound constitution of mind, whereby we are disposed vigorously to perform those virtuous functions, due from reasonable nature, and conformable to the divine law. If for the prosperous success of our worldly attempts; for avoiding dangers that threatened corporal pain and damage to us; for defeating the adversaries of our secular quiet, we make *Te Deum laudamus* our 'Επινίκιον, (our song for victory;) how much more for the happy progress of our spiritual affairs, (affairs of incomparably highest consequence;) for escaping those dreadful hazards of utter ruin, of endless torture; for vanquishing sin and hell, those irreconcileable enemies to our everlasting peace; are we obliged to utter triumphal anthems of joy and thankfulness!

This is the order observed by the Psalmist: inciting his soul to bless God for all his benefits, he begins with the consideration of God's mercy in pardoning his sins; then proceeds to his goodness in bestowing temporal favours. *Who forgiveth all thy sins,* leads the van; *Who satisfieth thy mouth with good things* brings up the rear in the enumeration and acknowledgment of God's benefits. That our minds are illustrated with the knowledge of God and his glorious attributes, of Christ and his blessed gospel, of that straight path which conducteth to true happiness; that by divine assistance we are enabled to elude the allurements, to withstand the violences of temptation, to assuage immoderate desires, to bridle exorbitant passions, to correct vicious inclinations of mind; requires more our hearty thanks, than for that we were able by our natural wit to penetrate the abstrusest mysteries, or to subjugate empires by our bodily strength. The forgiveness of our sins doth more

[marginal: SERM. XI.]
[marginal: Ps. ciii. 1, &c.]

oblige us to a grateful acknowledgment of the divine goodness, than should God enrich us with all the treasures contained in the bowels of the earth, or bottom of the ocean. One glimpse of his favourable countenance should more enflame our affections, than being invested with all the imaginable splendour of wordly glory.

SERM.
XI.

Of these inestimable benefits, and all the advantageous circumstances wherewith they are attended, we ought to maintain in our hearts constant resentments; to excite our thankfulness, to kindle our love, to quicken our obedience, by the frequent contemplation of them.

Thus have I (though, I confess, much more slightly than so worthy a subject did require) prosecuted the several particulars observable in these words. I should conclude with certain inducements persuasive to the practice of this duty; whereof I have in the tenor both of the former and present discourse insinuated divers, and could propound many more: but (in compliance with the time) I shall content myself briefly to consider only these three very obvious ones.

First therefore, we may consider, that there is no disposition whatever more deeply radicated in the original constitution of all souls endued with any kind of perception or passion, than being sensible of benefits received; being kindly affected with love and respect toward them that exhibit them; being ready with suitable expressions to acknowledge them, and to endeavour competent recompenses for them. The worst of men, the most devoid of all, not only piety, but humanity and common ingenuity, the most barbarous and

I.

most wicked, (whom neither sense of equity nor respect to law, no promise of reward or fear of vengeance, can anywise engage to do things just and fitting, or restrain from enormous actions,) retain notwithstanding something of this natural inclination, and are usually sensible of good turns done unto them. Experience teaches us thus much; and so doth that sure oracle of our Saviour: *If,* saith he, *ye do good to those who do good to you, what thanks is it? for even sinners* (that is, men of apparently lewd and dissolute conversation) *do the same.*

Yea even beasts, and those not only the most gentle and sociable of them, (the officious dog, the tractable horse, the docile elephant,) but the wildest also and fiercest of them, (the untameable lion, the cruel tiger, and ravenous bear, as stories tell us[m], and experience attests,) bear some kindness, shew some grateful affection to those that provide for them.

Neither wild beasts only, but even inanimate creatures seem not altogether insensible of benefits, and lively represent unto us a natural abhorrence of ingratitude. The rivers openly discharge into the sea those waters, which by indiscernible conduits they derived thence; the heavens remit in bountiful showers what from the earth they had exhaled in vapour; and the earth by a fruitful increase repays the culture bestowed thereon; if not (as the apostle to the Hebrews doth pronounce,) it deserves cursing and reprobation. So monstrous a thing, and universally abominable to nature, is all ingratitude. And how execrable a

[m] Vid. Aul. Gel. Lib. v. c. 14.

*The Duty of Thanksgiving.*

prodigy is it then toward God, from whom alone we receive whatever we enjoy, whatever we can expect of good?

The second obligation to this duty is most just and equal. For, (as he said well,) *Beneficium dare qui nescit, injuste petit*[n]; *He unjustly requires* (much more unjustly receives) *a benefit, who is not minded to requite it.* In all reason we are indebted for what is freely given, as well as for what is lent unto us. For the freeness of the giver, his not exacting security, nor expressing conditions of return, doth not diminish, but rather increase the debt. He that gives, indeed, according to human (or political) law, (which, in order to preservation of public peace, requires only a punctual performance of contracts,) transfers his right, and alienates his possession: but according to that more noble and perfect rule of ingenuity, (the law which God and angels and good men chiefly observe, and govern themselves by,) what is given is but committed to the faith, deposited in the hand, treasured up in the custody of him that receives it[o]; and what more palpable iniquity is there, than to betray the trust, or to detain the pledge, not of some inconsiderable trifle, but of inestimable goodwill? *Excepta Macedonum gente*, saith Seneca, *non est in ulla data adversus ingratum actio: In no nation (excepting the Macedonians) an action could be preferred against ingrateful persons, as so*[p]. (Though Xenophon, no mean author, reports[q], that

---

[n] [Publ. Syrus. (Poet. Scen. Latin. Vol. vi. p. 228. Ed. Bothe.)]

[o] Καλὸν τὸ θησαύρισμα κειμένη χάρις.
[Menand. Sentent. sing. 295. Ed. Meineke.]

[p] De Benef. [iii. 6. 2.]

[q] [Cyri Discip. i. 2, 7.]

among the Persians also there were judgments assigned, and punishments appointed for ingratitude.) However, in the court of heaven, and at the tribunal of conscience, no offender is more constantly arraigned, none more surely condemned, none more severely punished, than the ingrateful man.

Since therefore we have received all from the divine bounty; if God should in requital exact, that we sacrifice our lives to the testimony of his truth; that we employ our utmost pains, expend our whole estate, adventure our health, and prostitute all our earthly contents to his service; since he did but revoke his own, it were great injustice to refuse compliance with his demands: how much more, when he only expects from us and requires some few acknowledgments of our obligation to him, some little portions of our substance, for the relief of them that need, some easy observances of his most reasonable commands!

III.

Ps. cxxxv. 3.

Ps. cxlvii. 1; ix. 1.

Thirdly, This is a most sweet and delightful duty. *Praise the Lord,* saith the most experienced Psalmist, *for the Lord is good; sing praises to his name, for it is pleasant:* and otherwhere, *Praise the Lord: for it is good to sing praises to our God; for it is pleasant, and praise is comely.* The performance of this duty, as it especially proceeds from good humour, and a cheerful disposition of mind; so it feeds and foments them; both root and fruit thereof are hugely sweet and sapid.

James v. 13.

Whence St James; *If any man be afflicted, let him pray; is any merry, let him sing psalms.* (*Psalms,* the proper matter of which is praise and thanksgiving.)

## The Duty of Thanksgiving. 401

SERM. XI.

Other duties of devotion have something laborious in them, something disgustful to our sense. Prayer minds us of our wants and imperfections; confession induces a sad remembrance of our misdeeds and bad deserts: but thanksgiving includes nothing uneasy or unpleasant; nothing but the memory and sense of exceeding goodness.

All love is sweet; but that especially which arises, not from a bare apprehension only of the object's worth and dignity, but from a feeling of its singular beneficence and usefulness unto us. And what thought can enter into the heart of man more comfortable and delicious than this, that the great Master of all things, the most wise and mighty King of heaven and earth, hath entertained a gracious regard, hath expressed a real kindness toward us? that we are in capacity to honour, to please, to present an acceptable sacrifice to him, who can render us perfectly happy? that we are admitted to the practice of that wherein the supreme joy of paradise, and the perfection of angelical bliss consists? For praise and thanksgiving are the most delectable business of heaven; and God grant they may be our greatest delight, our most frequent employment upon earth.

To these I might add such further considerations: That this duty is of all most acceptable to God, and most profitable to us. That gratitude for benefits procures more, disposing God to bestow, and qualifying us to receive them. That the serious performance of this duty efficaciously promotes and facilitates the practice of other duties; since the more we are sensible of our obligations to God, the more ready we shall be to please him,

Ps. lxix. 30, 31; l. 14, 23.

by obedience to his commandments. What St Chrysostom saith of prayer, *It is impossible that he, who with competent promptitude of mind doth constantly apply himself thereto, should ever sin*[r], is most especially true of this part of devotion: for how can we at the same time be sensible of God's goodness to us, and willingly offend him? That the memory of past benefits, and sense of present, confirms our faith, and nourishes our hope of future. That the circumstances of the divine beneficence mightily strengthen the obligation to this duty; especially his absolute freeness in giving, and our total unworthiness to receive; our very ingratitude itself affording strong inducements to gratitude. That giving thanks hath *de facto* been always the principal part of all religion, (whether instituted by divine command, or prompted by natural reason, or propagated by general tradition;) the Ethnic devotion consisting (as it were totally) in the praise of their gods, and acknowledgment of their benefits; the Jewish more than half in eucharistical oblations, and in solemn commemorations of providential favours; and that of the ancient Christians so far forth, that bystanders could hardly discern any other thing in their religious practice, than that they sang hymns to Christ, and by mutual sacraments obliged themselves to abstain from all villainy[s]. But I will rather wholly omit the

[r] Vid. diviniss. Chrys. locum. Opp. Tom. v. p. 76. [Ἀμήχανον γὰρ, ἀμήχανον ἄνθρωπον μετὰ τῆς προσηκούσης προθυμίας εὐχόμενον, καὶ παρακαλοῦντα τὸν Θεὸν συνεχῶς, ἁμαρτεῖν ποτε.—In Ann. Orat. v.]

[s] Plin. Epist. [x. 97. 7.] [Adfirmabant autem hanc fuisse summam vel culpæ suæ vel erroris, quod essent soliti stato die ante lucem convenire; carmenque Christo, quasi Deo, dicere secum

## The Duty of Thanksgiving.

prosecution of these pregnant arguments, than be further offensive to your patience.

*Now the blessed Fountain of all goodness and mercy inspire our hearts with his heavenly grace, and thereby enable us rightly to apprehend, diligently to consider, faithfully to remember, worthily to esteem, to be heartily affected with, to render all due acknowledgment, praise, love, and thankful obedience for all his (infinitely great and innumerably many) favours, mercies, and benefits freely conferred upon us: and let us say with David,* Ps. lxxii. 18, 19. *Blessed be the Lord God of Israel, who only doeth wondrous things: and blessed be his glorious name for ever; and let the whole earth be filled with his glory. Blessed be the Lord God of Israel from* Ps. cvi. 48. *everlasting to everlasting: and let all the people say, Amen.*

invicem, seque sacramento non in scelus aliquod obstringere, sed ne furta, ne latrocinia, ne adulteria committerent, ne fidem fallerent, ne depositum appellati abnegarent.]

# SERMON XII.

## ON THE KING'S HAPPY RETURN.

1 TIM. II. 1, 2.

*I exhort therefore, that, first of all, supplications, prayers, intercessions, and giving of thanks, be made for all men: for kings, and for all that are in authority.*

SERM. XII.

1 Tim. i. 3, 4.

Ver. 6.

Ver. 5, 19.

ST PAUL in his preceding discourse having insinuated directions to his scholar and spiritual son, Timothy, concerning the discharge of his office, of instructing men in their duty according to the evangelical doctrine; (the main design whereof he teacheth to consist, not (as some men conceited) in fond stories, or vain speculations, but in practice of substantial duties, holding a sincere faith, maintaining a good conscience, performing offices of pure and hearty charity;) in pursuance of such general duty, and as a principal instance thereof, he doth here *First of all exhort*, or, doth *Exhort that first of all* all kinds of devotion should be offered to God, as for *All men* generally, so particularly for *Kings* and magistrates. From whence we may collect two particulars. 1 That the making of prayers for kings is a Christian duty of great importance. (St Paul judging fit to exhort thereto Πρῶτον πάντων, *Before all other things*; or, to *Exhort that before all things* it should be performed.) 2 That it is incumbent on the pastors of the church (such as St Timothy was) to take special care, that this duty should be performed in the church; both publicly in the congregations, and privately in the retirements of each Christian: according to what the apostle, after the proposing divers enforcements of this duty, subsumeth in the eighth verse; *I will therefore, that men pray every where, lifting up holy hands, without wrath or doubting.*

The first of these particulars, That it is a duty of great importance to pray for kings, I shall insist upon: it being indeed now very fit and seasonable to urge the practice of it, when it is perhaps commonly not much considered, or not well observed; and when there is most need of it, in regard to the effects and consequences which may proceed from the conscionable discharge of it.

My endeavour therefore shall be to press it by divers considerations, discovering our obligation thereto, and serving to induce us to its observance: some whereof shall be general, or common to all times; some particular, or suitable to the present circumstances of things.

I. The apostle exhorteth Christians to pray for kings with all sorts of prayer: with Δεήσεις, or *Deprecations,* for averting evils from them; with Προσευχαὶ, or *Petitions,* for obtaining good things to them; with Ἐντεύξεις, or occasional *Intercessions,* for needful gifts and graces to be collated on them: as, after St Austin, interpreters[a], in expounding St Paul's words, commonly distinguish; how accu-

---

[a] Aug [Ep. CXLIX. (ad Paul.) Opp. Tom. II. col. 508 D, E.]
Beza. [in locum. p. 697. Ed. Basil. 1559.]
Grotius [in locum. Opp. Tom. II. p. 961.]

rately, I shall not discuss: it sufficing, that assuredly the apostle meaneth, under this variety of expression, to comprehend all kinds of prayer. And to this I say we are obliged upon divers accounts.

1 Common charity should dispose us to pray for kings. This Christian disposition inclineth to universal benevolence and beneficence; according to that apostolical precept, *As we have opportunity, let us do good unto all men:* it consequently will excite us to pray for all men; seeing this is a way of exerting good-will, and exercising beneficence, which any man at any time, if he hath the will and heart, may have opportunity and ability to pursue.

No man indeed otherwise can benefit all: few men otherwise can benefit many: some men otherwise can benefit none: but in this way any man is able to benefit all, or unconfinedly to oblige mankind, deriving on any somewhat of God's immense beneficence. By performing this good office, at the expense of a few good wishes addressed to the Sovereign Goodness, the poorest may prove benefactors to the richest, the meanest to the highest, the weakest to the mightiest of men: so we may benefit even those who are most remote from us, most strangers and quite unknown to us. Our prayers can reach the utmost ends of the earth; and by them our charity may embrace all the world.

And from them surely kings must not be excluded. For if, because all men are our fellow-creatures, and brethren by the same heavenly Father; because all men are allied to us by cognation and similitude of nature; because all men are the objects of God's particular favour and care: if, because all men are partakers of the common redemption, by the undertakings of him who is the common Mediator and Saviour of all men; and because all men, according to the gracious intent and desire of God, are designed for a consortship in the same blessed inheritance: (which enforcements St Paul in the context doth intimate:) if, in fine, because all men do need prayers, and are capable of benefit from them, we should be charitably disposed to pray for them: then must we also pray for kings, who, even in their personal capacity, as men, do share in all those conditions. Thus may we conceive St Paul here to argue: *For all men*, saith he, *For kings;* that is consequently for kings, or particularly for kings; to pray for whom, at least no less than for other men, universal charity should dispose us.

SERM. XII.

1 Tim. ii. 4, 5, 6.

Indeed, even on this account we may say especially for kings; the law of general charity with peculiar advantage being applicable to them: for that law commonly is expressed with reference to our neighbour, that is, to persons with whom we have to do, who come under our particular notice, who by any intercourse are approximated to us; and such are kings especially. For, whereas the greatest part of men (by reason of their distance from us, from the obscurity of their condition, or for want of opportunity to converse with them) must needs slip beside us, so that we cannot employ any distinct thought or affection toward them: it is not so with kings, who by their eminent and illustrious station become very observable by us; with whom we have frequent transactions and mutual con-

SERM. XII.

cerns; who therefore, in the strictest acception, are our neighbours, whom we are charged to love as ourselves; to whom consequently we must perform this most charitable office of praying for them.

2 To impress which consideration, we may reflect, that commonly we have only this way granted us of exercising our charity toward princes; they being situated aloft above the reach of private beneficence[b]: so that we cannot enrich them, or relieve them by our alms; we cannot help to exalt or prefer them to a better state; we can hardly come to impart good advice, seasonable consolation, or wholesome reproof to them; we cannot profit or please them by familiar conversation. For, as in divers other respects they resemble the Divinity; so in this they are like it, that we may say to them, as the Psalmist to God, *Thou art my Lord; my goodness extendeth not to thee.* Yet this case may be reserved, wherein the poorest soul may benefit the greatest prince, imparting the richest and choicest goods to him: he may be indebted for his safety, for the prosperity of his affairs, for God's mercy and favour toward him, to the prayers of his meanest vassal. And thus to oblige princes, methinks, we should be very desirous; we should be glad to use such an advantage, we should be ambitious of such an honour.

Ps. xvi. 2.

3 We are bound to pray for kings out of charity to the public; because their good is a general good, and the communities of men (both church and

[b] Privatorum ista copia est, inter se esse munificos.—Auson. ad Gratian. Imp. [Opp. p. 699. Ed. Toll. 1671.]

Absit, Auguste, et istud sancta divinitas omen avertat, ut tu a quoquam mortalium expectes vicem beneficii!—Mamert. Grat. Actio Jul. Imp. [cap. xxxii. Paneg. Vet. Tom. II. p. 207.]

state) are greatly concerned in the blessings by prayer derived on them.

SERM. XII.

The safety of a prince is a great part of the common welfare; the commonwealth, as it were, living and breathing in him: his fall, like that of a tall cedar, (to which he is compared,) shaking the earth, and discomposing the state; putting things out of course, and drawing them into new channels; translating the administration of affairs into untried hands, and an uncertain condition. Hence, *Let the king live*, (which our translators render, *God save the king*,) was an usual form of salutation or prayer: and, *O king, live for ever*, was a customary address to princes, whereto the best men did conform, even in application to none of the best princes; as Nehemiah to king Artaxerxes, and Daniel to king Darius. Hence not only good king David is called *The light of Israel;* (*Thou shalt not*, said Abishai, *any more go out with us to battle, that thou quench not the light of Israel;*) but even the wicked and perverse king Zedekiah is by the prophet Jeremy himself (who had been so misused by him) styled *The breath of our nostrils.* (*The breath*, saith he, *of our nostrils, the anointed of the Lord was taken in their pits.*) Hence not only the fall of good king Josiah was so grievously lamented; but a solemn mourning was due to that of Saul; and, *Ye daughters of Jerusalem, weep for Saul*, was a strain becoming the mouth of his great successor king David. Hence the primitive Christians, who could not be constrained to swear by the genius of Cæsar, did not yet, in compliance with the usual practice, scruple to swear by their health or safety[c]:

Isai. ii. 13.

1 Kings i. 25.
2 Kings xi. 12.
2 Chron. xxiii. 11.
1 Kings i. 31.
Dan. ii. 4; iii. 9; v. 10; vi. 6.
Neh. ii. 3.
Dan. vi. 21.
2 Sam. xxi. 17.

Lam. iv. 20.

2 Chron. xxxv. 24.

2 Sam. i. 12, 24.

[c] Sed et juramus, sicut non per genios Cæsarum, ita per salu-

that is, to express their wishing it, with appeal to God's testimony of their sincerity therein; as Joseph may be conceived to have sworn *By the life of Pharaoh.* Hence well might the people tell king David, *Thou art worth ten thousand of us;* seeing the public was so much interested in his safety, and had suffered more in the loss of him, than if a myriad of others had miscarried.

This honour likewise of a prince is the glory of his people; seeing it is founded on qualities or deeds tending to their advantage; seeing it can hardly be supposed, that he should acquire honour without their aid and concurrence, or that he should retain it without their support and their satisfaction. And as the chief grace and beauty of a body is in the head, and the fairest ornaments of the whole are placed there; so is any commonwealth most dignified and beautified by the reputation of its prince.

The wealth and power of a prince are the supports and securities of a state; he thereby being enabled to uphold and defend its safety, its order, its peace; to protect his people from foreign injuries and invasions; to secure them from intestine broils and factions; to repress outrages and oppressions annoying them.

The prosperity of a prince is inseparable from the prosperity of his people; they ever partaking of his fortunes, and thriving or suffering with him. For, as when the sun shineth brightly, there is a clear day and fair weather over the world; so when a prince is not overclouded with adversity or

tem eorum, quæ est augustior omnibus geniis.—Tert. Apol. cap. xxxii. [Opp. p. 28 A.]

disastrous occurrences, the public state must be serene, and a pleasant state of things will appear. Then is the ship in a good condition, when the pilot in open sea, with full sails and a brisk gale, cheerfully steereth on toward his designed port.

Especially the piety and goodness of a prince is of vast consequence, and yieldeth infinite benefit to his country. For, *Vita principis censura est;* the life of a prince is the calling of other men's lives to an account. His example hath an unspeakable influence on the manners of his people, who are apt in all his garb and every fashion to imitate him[d]. His practice is more powerful than his commands, and often doth control them. His authority hath the great stroke in encouraging virtue and checking vice, if it bendeth that way; the dispensation of honours and rewards, with the infliction of ignominies and corrections, being in his hand, and passing from it according to his inclinations. His power is the shield of innocence, the fence of right, the shelter of weakness and simplicity against violences and frauds. His very look (a smile or a frown of his countenance) is sufficient to advance goodness and suppress wickedness; according to that of Solomon, *A king sitting in the throne of judgment scattereth away all evil with his eyes.* His goodness pleasing God procureth his

---

[d] Flexibiles quamcunque in partem ducimur a principe, atque, ut ita dicam, sequaces sumus; huic enim cari, huic probati esse cupimus; quod frustra speraverint dissimiles; eoque obsequii continuatione pervenimus, ut prope omnes homines unius moribus vivamus.—Plin. Paneg. [cap. xlv. 5.]

Vita principis censura est, eaque perpetua; ad hanc dirigimur, ad hanc convertimur; nec tam imperio nobis opus est, quam exemplo.—[Id. Ibid. § 6.]

SERM. XII.

favour, and therewith deduceth from heaven all kinds of blessings on his people. And if those politic aphorisms of the Wise Man be true, that *Righteousness exalteth a nation and establisheth a throne;* that *When it goeth well with the righteous, the city rejoiceth;* and the same *By the blessing of the upright is exalted:* then upon his inclinations to virtue the advancement and stability of public welfare do mainly depend. So, for instance, how did piety flourish in the times of David, who loved, favoured, and practised it! and what abundance of prosperity did attend it! What showers of blessings (what peace, what wealth, what credit and glory) did God then pour down upon Israel! How did the goodness of that prince transmit favours and mercies on his country till a long time after his decease! How often did God profess *For his servant David's sake* to preserve Judah from destruction; so that even in the days of Hezekiah, when the king of Assyria did invade that country, God by the mouth of Isaiah declared, *I will defend this city to save it for mine own sake, and for my servant David's sake.*

Prov. xvi. 12.
2 Sam. vii. 16.
Prov. xi. 10, 11.

2 Sam. vii. 9.
Ps. lxxii. 7.

2 Sam. vii. 16.
1 Kings xi. 13.
Jer. xxxiii. 21.
Ps. lxxxix. 29; cxxxii. 10.
Isai. xxxvii. 35.
1 Kings xi. 32, 34.

We may indeed observe, that, according to the representation of things in holy scripture, there is a kind of moral connection, or a communication of merit and guilt, between prince and people; so that mutually each of them is rewarded for the virtues, each is punished for the vices of the other. As for the iniquities of a people, God withdraweth from their prince the free communications of his grace and of his favour, (suffering him to incur sin, or to fall into misfortune; which was the case of that incomparably good king Josiah, and hath

2 Kings xxiii. 25.

*On the King's happy Return.* 413

been the fate of divers excellent princes, whom God hath snatched away from people unworthy of them, or involved with such a people in common calamities; according to the rule propounded in the Law, of God's dealing with the Israelites in the case of their disobedience; and according to that of Samuel, *If ye shall do wickedly, ye shall be consumed, both ye and your king:*) so reciprocally, for the misdemeanours of princes, (or in them, and by them,) God doth chastise their people. For what confusions in Israel did the offences of Solomon create! What mischiefs did issue thereon from Jeroboam's wicked behaviour! How did the sins of Manasseh stick to his country, since that, even after that notable reformation wrought by Josiah, it is said, *Notwithstanding the Lord turned not from the fierceness of his great wrath wherewith his anger was kindled against Judah, because of all the provocations wherewith Manasseh had provoked him!* And how sorely, by a tedious three years' famine, did God avenge Saul's cruelty toward the Gibeonites!

SERM. XII.

Isai. iii. 1, &c.
Deut. xxviii. 36.
1 Sam. xii. 25.
Prov. xxviii. 2.
1 Kings xi. 33.
1 Kings xv. 30.
2 Kings xvii. 21.

2 Kings xxiii. 26.

2 Sam. xxi. 1.

Nor are only the sins of bad princes affixed to people conspiring with them in impiety; for even of king Hezekiah it is said, *But Hezekiah rendered not again according to the benefit done unto him; for his heart was lifted up: therefore there was wrath upon him, and upon Judah and Jerusalem.* So the pride and ingratitude of an excellent prince were avenged on his subjects. And when good king David (God averting his grace from him) did fall into that arrogant transgression of counting his forces, that, as Joab prudently foretold, became *A cause of trespass to Israel;* and *God,* saith

Jer. xxxii. 32.
2 Chron. xxxii. 25.

1 Chron. xxi. 3, 7.

SERM. XII.

the text, *was displeased with this thing; therefore he smote Israel.*

David indeed seemed to apprehend some iniquity in this proceeding, expostulating thus; *Is it not I that commanded the people to be numbered? even I it is that have sinned and done evil indeed: but as for these sheep, what have they done?* But God had no regard to his plea, nor returned any answer to it; for indeed God's wrath began with the people, and their king's sin was but a judgment executed on them; for *The anger,* it is said, *of the Lord was kindled against Israel,* (by their sin surely, which is the only incentive of divine wrath,) *and he moved David against them to say, Go, number Israel and Judah.*

So indeed it is that princes are bad, that they incur great errors, or commit notable trespasses, is commonly imputable to the fault of subjects; and is a just judgment by divine Providence laid on them, as for other provocations, so especially for their want of devotion, and neglecting duly to pray for them. For if they constantly, with hearty sincerity and earnest fervency, would in their behalf sue to God, who *Fashioneth all the hearts of men,* who especially holdeth the hearts of kings in his hand, and turneth them whithersoever he will; we reasonably might presume, that God by his grace would direct them into the right way, and incline their hearts to goodness; that he would accomplish his own word in the Prophet, *I will make thy officers peace, and thine exactors righteousness:* that we might have occasion to pay thanksgivings like that of Ezra, *Blessed be the Lord God of our fathers, who hath put such things as this in the king's*

1 Chron. xxi. 17.

2 Sam. xxiv. 1.

Ps. xxxiii. 15.
Prov. xxi. 1.

Isai. lx. 17.

Ezra vii. 27.

*heart, to beautify the house of the Lord which is in Jerusalem.*

SERM. XII.

We are apt to impute the ill management of things, and the bad success waiting on it, unto princes, being in appearance the immediate agents and instruments of it: but we commonly do therein mistake, not considering that ourselves are most guilty and blamable for it; that it is an impious people which maketh an unhappy prince; that their offences do pervert his counsels and blast his undertakings; that their profaneness and indevotion do incense God's displeasure, and cause him to desert princes, withdrawing his gracious conduct from them, and permitting them to be misled by temptation, by ill advice, by their own infirmities, lusts, and passions, into courses fit to punish a naughty people. So these were the causes of *Moses's speaking unadvisedly with his lips,* and that *It went ill with him for their sakes;* of Aaron's forming the molten calf; of David's numbering the people; of Josiah's unadvised enterprise against Pharaoh Neco; of Zedekiah's rebellion against the Assyrians, (notwithstanding the strong dissuasions of the prophet Jeremy;) concerning which it is said, *For through the anger of the Lord it came to pass in Jerusalem and Judah, until he had cast them out from his presence, that Zedekiah rebelled against the king of Babylon.*

Ps. cvi. 32, 33.

Exod. xxxii. 7, 8. Deut. ix. 12.

2 Kings xxiv. 20.

Considering which things it is apparent, that prayer for our prince is a great office of charity to the public; and that in praying for his safety, for his honour, for his wealth, for his prosperity, for his virtue, we do in effect pray for the same benefits respectively to our country: that in praying for his welfare, we do in consequence pray for the good of all our neighbours, our friends, our relations, our families; whose good is wrapped in his welfare, doth flow from it, doth hang upon it.

We are bound, and it is a very noble piece of charity, to love our country, sincerely to desire and earnestly to further its happiness, and therefore to pray for it; according to the advice and practice of the Psalmist: *O pray for the peace of Jerusalem; they shall prosper that love thee. Peace be within thy walls, and prosperity within thy palaces.* We are obliged more especially upon the highest accounts, with dearest affection to love the church, (our heavenly commonwealth, the society of our spiritual brethren,) most ardently to tender its good, and seek its advantages; and therefore most urgently to sue for God's favour toward it: being ready to say after David, *Do good, O God, in thy good pleasure to Sion: build thou the walls of Jerusalem. Arise, O Lord, and have mercy upon Sion: for the time to favour her, yea, the set time, is come.*

Now these duties we cannot more easily, more compendiously, or more effectually discharge, than by earnestly praying for our prince; seeing that if we do by our prayers procure God's favour to him, we do certainly draw it on the state and the church. If God, moved by our devout importunities, shall please to guard his person from dangers, and to grant him a long life; to endue his heart with grace, with the love and fear of himself, with a zeal of furthering public good, of favouring piety, of discountenancing sin; if God shall vouchsafe to inspire him with wisdom, and to guide his counsels, to bless his proceedings, and to crown his undertakings with good success: then assuredly we have much promoted the public interest; then infallibly, together with these, all other blessings shall descend on us, all good will flourish in our land. This was the ancient practice of Christians, and directed to this end. For, *We*, saith Lactantius to Constantine, *with daily prayers do supplicate God, that he would first of all keep thee, whom he hath willed to be the keeper of things; then that he would inspire into thee a will, whereby thou mayest ever persevere in the love of God's name; which is salutary to all, both to thee for thy happiness, and to us for our quiet*[e].

4 Wherefore, consequently, our own interest and charity to ourselves should dispose us to pray for our prince. We being nearly concerned in his welfare, as parts of the public, and as enjoying many private advantages thereby; we cannot but partake of his good, we cannot but suffer with him. We cannot live quietly, if our prince is disturbed; we cannot live happily, if he be unfortunate; we can hardly live virtuously, if divine grace do not incline him to favour us therein, or at least restrain him from hindering us[f]. This is St Paul's own consideration: *I exhort you*, saith he, *to make prayers for kings—that we may lead a quiet and peaceable life in all godliness and honesty*. Upon such an account God did command the Jews to pray for

[e] Cui nos quotidianis precibus supplicamus, ut te in primis, quem rerum custodem voluit esse, custodiat; deinde inspiret tibi voluntatem, qua semper in amore divini nominis perseveres. Quod est omnibus salutare, et tibi ad felicitatem, et ceteris ad quietem.—Lact. Instit. VII. 26.

[f] Nescio an plus moribus conferat princeps, qui bonos esse patitur, quam qui cogit.—Plin. Panegyr. [cap. xlv. 4.]

the welfare of that heathen state under which they lived in captivity. *And seek,* said he, *the peace of the city whither I have caused you to be carried away captives, and pray unto the Lord for it: for in the peace thereof shall ye have peace.* And for the like cause the Christians of old deemed themselves bound to pray for the Gentile magistrates; according to that of Tertullian: *We pray for you, because with you the empire is shaken: and the other members of it being shaken, assuredly even we, how far soever we may be thought from troubles, are found in some place of the fall*[g]. Further,

5 Let us consider, that subjects are obliged in gratitude and ingenuity, yea in equity and justice, to pray for their princes. For,

They are most nearly related to us, and allied by the most sacred bands; being constituted by God, in his own room, the parents and guardians of their country; being also avowed and accepted for such by solemn vows, and most holy sacraments of allegiance: whence unto them as such we owe an humble piety, a very respectful affection, a most dutiful observance; the which we cannot better express or exercise, than in our heartiest prayers for their welfare.

[g] Vobiscum enim concutitur imperium, concussis etiam ceteris membris ejus: utique et nos (licet extranei a turbis æstimemur) in aliquo loco casus invenimur.—Tert. Apol. cap. xxxii. [Ed. Pamel. 1617.]

Christianus nullius est hostis, nedum Imperatoris; quem sciens a Deo suo constitui, necesse est, ut et ipsum diligat, et revereatur, et honoret, et salvum velit.—Id. ad Scap. cap. ii. [Opp. p. 69 c.]

Jurant per Deum, et per Christum, et per Spiritum Sanctum et per majestatem Imperatoris, quæ secundum Deum generi humano diligenda est et colenda.—Veget. [de Re Mil. Lib. ii. cap. 5.]

They by God are destined to be the protectors of the church, the patrons of religion, the fosterers and cherishers of truth, of virtue, of piety: for of the church in the evangelical times it was prophesied, *Kings shall be thy nursing fathers; Thou shalt suck the breasts of kings; Kings shall minister to thee:* wherefore to them, not only as men and citizens, but peculiarly as Christians, we owe the highest duty; and consequently we must pay the best devotion for them.

SERM. XII.

Isai. xlix. 23; lx. 16, 10.

To them we stand indebted for the greatest benefits of common life: they necessarily do take much care, they undergo great trouble, they are exposed to many hazards for our advantages; that under their shadow we may enjoy safety and quiet, we may reap the fruits of our industry, we may possess the comforts and conveniences of our life, with security from rapine, from contention, from solicitude, from the continual fears of wrong and outrage.

Lam. iv. 20.

To their industry and vigilancy under God, we owe the fair administration of justice, the protection of right and innocence, the preservation of order and peace, the encouragement of goodness, and correction of wickedness: for *They,* as the apostle telleth us, *are God's ministers, attending continually on these very things.* They indeed so attend as to deny themselves, and so forego much of their own ease, their pleasure, their satisfaction; being frequently perplexed with cares, continually enslaved to business, and subject to various inconveniences, rendering their life to considerate spectators very little desirable.

Rom. xiii. 6.

As therefore, according to our Lord's observation, they are usually styled *Benefactors*, so they really are; even the worst of them (such as Claudius or Nero, of whom our apostles speak) in considerable measure; at least in comparison of anarchy, and considering the mischiefs issuing from want of government. *The matter is not flattery:* (saith St Chrysostom, himself of all men furthest from a flatterer;) *but according to the reason of the case*[h] we must esteem ourselves much obliged to them for the pains they sustain in our behalf, and for the benefits we receive from them. For he indeed must be a very bad governor, to whom that speech of the orator Tertullus may not without glozing be accommodated; *Seeing that by thee we enjoy great quietness, and that very worthy deeds are done unto this nation by thy providence, we accept it always, and in all places, most noble Felix, with all thankfulness.*

However, what Seneca saith of philosophers, that *They of all men are most obliged, and most grateful to kings and magistrates, because from their care they enjoy the leisure, quiet and security of contemplating and practising the best things; upon which account,* saith he, *they could not but reverence the authors of so great a good as parents*[i]; that is, or should be, far more true of Christians.

[h] Οὐ κολακεία ἐστὶ τὸ πρᾶγμα, ἀλλὰ κατὰ τὸν τοῦ δικαίου γίνεται λόγον.—Chrys. in 1 Tim. ii. 1. [Opp. Tom. IV. p. 272.]

[i] Errare mihi videntur, qui existimant, philosophiæ fideliter deditos contumaces esse ac refractarios, et contemtores magistratuum ac regum, eorumve per quos publica administrantur. E contrario enim, nulli adversus illos gratiores sunt; nec immerito, nullis enim plus præstant, quam quibus frui tranquillo otio licet. Itaque hi, quibus aptum ad propositum bene vivendi aditum confert securitas publica, necesse est auctorem hujus boni ut parentem colant.—Sen. Ep. LXXIII.

*That leisure* (to use his words) *which is spent with God, and which rendereth us like to God*[k]; the liberty of studying divine truth, and of serving God with security and quiet; are inestimable benefits, for the which they are indebted to the protection of magistrates: therefore in all reason a grateful retribution of good-will, and of all good offices, particularly of our prayers, is to be paid to them. *Is it not very absurd,* saith St Chrysostom, *that they should labour and venture for us, and we not pray for them*[1]*?*

6 Whereas we are by divine command frequently enjoined to fear and reverence, to honour, to obey kings; we should look on prayer for them as a principal branch, and the neglect thereof as a notable breach of those duties. For,

As to honour and reverence, it is plain that no exterior signification, in ceremonious unveiling or cringing to them, can so demonstrate it, as doth the wishing them well in our hearts, and from thence framing particular addresses to the divine Majesty for their welfare. Than which practice there can be no surer argument, that we hold them in great account and consideration. And how indeed can we much honour them, for whom we do not vouchsafe so much as to offer our good wishes, or to mention them in our intercessions unto him, who requireth us to make them for all men, and particularly for those for whom we are concerned? Doth not this omission evidently place them in the lowest rank, beneath the meanest of our friends

---

[k] Quanti æstimamus hoc otium, quod inter Deos agitur, quod Deos facit?—Ibid.

[1] [Πῶς οὖν οὐκ ἄτοπον αὐτοὺς μὲν ὑπὲρ τούτου στρατεύεσθαι καὶ τὰ ὅπλα τίθεσθαι, ἵν' ἡμεῖς ἐν ἀδείᾳ ὦμην· ἡμᾶς δὲ μηδὲ ὑπὲρ τῶν κινδυνευόντων καὶ στρατευομένων ποιεῖσθαι δεήσεις;—Chrys. ubi supra.]

*Marginal references:* 1 Pet. ii. 13, 17. Rom. xiii. 1. Tit. iii. 1. Prov. xxiv. 21.

SERM. XII.

and relations? doth it not imply a very slender regard had to them?

And as for obedience, prayer for princes is clearly an instance thereof; seeing it may be supposed, that all princes do require it from their subjects. Not only Christian princes, who believe God the sole dispenser of all good things, and the great efficacy of devotion in procuring them from him, may be deemed to exact this beneficial office from us; but even heathens and infidels, from their dim notion of a sovereign Providence, (which hath ever been common in the world,) have made an account of this practice; as we may see by that decree of the Persian king in Ezra, charging his officers to furnish the Jewish elders with sacrifices, *That,* said he, *they may offer sacrifices of sweet savour unto the God of heaven, and pray for the life of the king, and of his sons.* And that such was the practice of the Romans even in their heathenish state, doth appear from those words of Pliny; *We have,* saith he, *been wont to make vows for the eternity of the empire, and for the welfare of the citizens; yea for the welfare of the princes, and in their behalf for the eternity of the empire*[m].

Ezra vi. 10.

Not only pious princes with a serious desire will expect this duty from us; but even profane ones in policy will demand it, as a decent testimony of respect to them, and a proper means of upholding their state; that they may seem to have place in the most serious regards and solemn performances of their subjects. So that to neglect this

[m] Nuncupare vota et pro æternitate imperii, et pro salute civium, imo pro salute principum, ac propter illos pro æternitate imperii, solebamus.—Plin. Paneg. [cap. lxvii. 3.]

duty is ever a violation of our due obedience, and a kind of disloyalty to them. Again,

SERM. XII.

7 The praying for princes is a service peculiarly honourable, and very acceptable to God; which he will interpret as a great respect done to himself: for that thereby we honour his image and character in them, yielding in his presence this special respect to them as his representatives[n]; for that thereby we avow his government of the world by them as his ministers and deputies; for that thereby we acknowledge all power derived from him, and depending on his pleasure; we ascribe to him an authority paramount above all earthly potentates; we imply our persuasion, that he alone is absolute Sovereign of the world, *The King of kings, and Lord of lords*, so that princes are nothing otherwise than in subordination to him, can do nothing without his succour, do owe to him all their power, their safety, their prosperity, and welfare[o]; for that, in fine, thereby disclaiming all other confidences in any son of man, we signify our entire submission to God's will, and sole confidence in his providence. This service therefore is a very grateful kind of adoring our Almighty Lord; and as such St Paul recommendeth it in the words immediately subjoined to our text, *For this*, saith he, *is good and acceptable in the sight of God our Saviour*.

1 Tim. vi. 15.

Ps. cxlvi. 3; cxviii. 8, 9.

1 Tim. ii. 3.

8 Let us consider, that whereas wisdom, guiding our piety and charity, will especially incline

---

[n] Deo vel privatus, vel militans servit, cum fideliter eum diligit, qui Deo regnat auctore.—Veget. [de Re Mil. Lib. II. cap. 5.]

[o] Temperans majestatem Cæsaris infra Deum, magis illum commendo Deo.—Tert. Apol. cap. xxxiii. [Opp. p. 28 B.]

us to place our devotion there where it will be most needful and useful; we therefore chiefly must pray for kings, because they do most need our prayers.

The office is most high, and hard to discharge well or happily: wherefore they need extraordinary supplies of gifts and graces from the divine bounty.

Their affairs are of greatest weight and importance, requiring answerable skill and strength to steer and wield them: wherefore they need from the fountain of wisdom and power special communications of light, of courage, of ability, to conduct, to support, to fortify them in their managements; they need that God should uphold them, Πνεύματι ἡγεμονικῷ[p], with that princely spirit, for which king David prayed.

They often are to deliberate about matters of dark and uncertain consequence; they are to judge in cases of dubious and intricate nature; the which to resolve prudently, or to determine uprightly, no human wisdom sufficiently can enable; wherefore they need *The spirit of counsel*, and *The Spirit of judgment*, from the sole dispenser of them, the great *Counsellor* and most *Righteous Judge*. The wisest and ablest of them hath reason to pray with Solomon, *Give thy servant an understanding heart, to judge thy people, that I may discern between good and bad; for who is able to judge this thy so great a people?* that so, what the Wise Man saith may be verified, *A divine sentence is in the lips of the king, his mouth transgresseth not in judgment:* and that of the wise woman, *As an angel*

---

[p] [Ps. li. 14. LXX.]

*of God, so is my lord the king to discern good* SERM.
*and bad.* XII.

They commonly are engaged in enterprises of greatest difficulty, insuperable by the might or industry of man; in regard to which we may say with Hannah, *By strength shall no man prevail;* 1 Sam. ii. 9.
with the Preacher, *The race is not to the swift, nor* Eccles. ix. 11.
*the battle to the strong;* with the Psalmist, *There is* Ps. xxxiii. 16.
*no king saved by the multitude of an host:* wherefore they need aid and succour from the Almighty, to carry them through, and bless their designs with success.

They are most exposed to dangers and disasters; (standing like high towers, most obnoxious to the winds and tempests of fortune;) having usually many envious ill-willers, many disaffected malecontents, many both open enemies and close insidiators; from whose force or treachery no human providence can sufficiently guard them: they do therefore need the protection of the ever-vigilant *Keeper of Israel* to secure them: for, *Except the* Ps. xxi. 4; xci. 1;
*Lord keep the city, the watchman waketh but in vain;* cxxvii. 1;
except the Lord preserve the king, his guards, his xxxiii. 16.
armies surround him to no purpose.

They have the natural infirmities of other men, and far beyond other men are subject to external temptations. The malicious spirit (as in the case of Job, of David, of Ahab, of Joshua the high Zech. iii. 1.
priest, is expressed) is ever waiting for occasion, ever craving permission of God to seduce and pervert them; success therein being extremely conducible to his villainous designs. The world continually doth assault them with all its advantages, with all its baits of pleasure, with all its enticements to

SERM. XII.

Eccles. viii. 4.

pride and vanity, to oppression and injustice, to sloth, to luxury, to exorbitant self-will and self-conceit, to every sort of vicious practice. Their eminency of state, their affluence of wealth, their uncontrollable power, their exemption from common restraints, their continual distractions and encumbrances by varieties of care and business, their multitude of obsequious followers, and scarcity of faithful friends to advise or reprove them, their having no obstacles before them to check their wills, to cross their humours, to curb their lusts and passions, are so many dangerous snares unto them: wherefore they do need plentiful measures of grace, and mighty assistances from God, to preserve them from the worst errors and sins; into which otherwise it is almost a miracle if they are not plunged.

And being they are so liable to sin, they must consequently stand often in need of God's mercy to bear with them, and to pardon them[q].

They therefore, upon so many accounts needing special help and grace from Heaven, do most need prayers to derive it thence for them.

All princes indeed do need them. Good princes need many prayers for God's help, to uphold and confirm them in their virtue: bad princes need deprecations of God's wrath and judgment toward them, for offending his Majesty; together with supplications for God's grace to convert and reform them: the most desperate and incorrigible need prayers, that God would overrule and restrain them from doing mischief to themselves and others. All

[q] Ὁ πλεῖστα πράσσων, πλεῖσθ' ἁμαρτάνει βροτῶν.
[Eurip. Œnom. Frag. 1.]

princes having many avocations and temptations, hindering them to pray enough for themselves, do need supplemental aids from the devotions of others.

SERM. XII.

Wherefore if we love them, if we love our country, if we love ourselves, if we tender the interests of truth, of piety, of common good, we, considering their case, and manifold need of prayers, will not fail earnestly to sue for them; that God would afford needful assistance to them in the administration of their high office, in the improvement of their great talents, in the conduct and management of their arduous affairs; that he graciously would direct them in their perplexed counsels, would back them in their difficult undertakings, would protect their persons from dangers, would keep their hearts from the prevalency of temptations, would pardon their failings and trespasses. Again,

9 Whereas God hath declared, that he hath special regard to princes, and a more than ordinary care over them, because they have a peculiar relation to him, as his representatives, the *Ministers of his kingdom*, the main instruments of his providence, whereby he conveyeth his favours, and dispenseth his justice to men; because also the good of mankind, which he especially tendereth, is mainly concerned in their welfare; whereas, I say, *It is he that giveth salvation unto kings; That giveth great deliverance to his king, and sheweth mercy to his anointed;* that hath the king's heart, and his breath, and all his ways in his hand: even upon this account our prayers for them are the more required. For it is a method of God, and an esta-

Wisd. vi. 4.

Ps. cxliv. 10; xxi. 1; xviii. 50; lxiii. 11. Prov. xxi. 1. Dan. v. 23.

blished rule of divine providence, not to dispense special blessings without particular conditions, and the concurrence of our duty in observance of what he prescribeth in respect to them. Seeing then he hath enjoined, that, in order to our obtaining those great benefits which issue from his special care over princes, we should pray for it, and seek it from his hands; the omission of this duty will intercept it, or bereave us of its advantages; nor in that case may we expect any blessings of that kind. As without praying for ourselves we must not expect private favours from heaven; so without praying for our prince we cannot well hope for public blessings. For, as a profane person (who in effect disavoweth God, by not regarding to seek his favour and aid) is not qualified to receive any good from him; so a profane nation (which disclaimeth God's government of the world, by not invoking his benediction on those who moderate it under him) is not well capable of common benefits. It is upon all accounts true which Ezra said, *The hand of our God is upon all them for good that seek him: but his power and his wrath is against all them that forsake him.* If therefore we desire, that our prince should not lose God's special regard, if we would not forfeit the benefits thereof to ourselves, we must conspire in hearty prayers for him.

10 To engage and encourage us in which practice, we may further consider, that such prayers, offered duly, (with frequency and constancy, with sincerity and zeal,) do always turn to good account, and never want good effect: the which, if it be not always easily discernible, yet it is certainly

## On the King's happy Return.

real; if it be not perfect, as we may desire, yet it is competent, as expediency requireth, or as the condition of things will bear.

SERM. XII.

There may be impediments to a full success of the best prayers; they may not ever prevail to render princes completely good, or extremely prosperous: for some concurrence of their own will is requisite to produce their virtue, God rarely working with irresistible power, or fatal efficacy; and the state of things, or capacities of persons, are not always fitly suited for prosperity. Yet are not such prayers ever wholly vain or fruitless; for God never prescribeth means unavailable to the end: he never would have commanded us particularly to pray for kings, if he did not mean to bestow a good issue to that practice.

And, surely, he that hath promised to hear all requests, with faith and sincerity and incessant earnestness presented to him, cannot fail to hear those which are of such consequence, which are so agreeable to his will, which do include so much honesty and charity. In this case, surely we may have some confidence, according to that of St John, *This is the confidence we have in him, that, if we ask any thing according to his will, he heareth us.*

1 John v. 14.

As the good bishop, observing St Austin's mother, with what constancy and passionateness she did pray for her son, being then engaged in ways of error and vanity, did encourage her, saying, *It is impossible that a son of those devotions should perish*[r]; so may we hopefully presume, and encourage ourselves, that a prince will not mis-

[r] Fieri non potest, ut filius istarum lacrymarum pereat.—Aug. Conf. III. 12. [Opp. Tom. I. col. 96 F.]

carry, for whose welfare many good people do earnestly solicit: *Fieri non potest, ut princeps istarum lacrymarum pereat.*

You know in general the mighty efficacy of prayer; what pregnant assurances there are, and how wonderful instances thereof occur in holy scripture, both in relation to public and private blessings: how it is often promised, that *All things, whatsoever we shall ask in prayer, believing, we shall receive;* and that, *Whoever asketh receiveth, and he that seeketh findeth, and to him that knocketh it shall be opened:* how the prayer of Abraham did heal Abimelech, and his family of barrenness; how the prayers of Moses did quench the fire, and cure the bitings of the fiery serpents; how the prayer of Joshua did arrest the sun; how the prayer of Hannah did procure Samuel to her, as his name doth import; how Elias's prayers did open and shut the heavens; how the same holy prophet's prayer did reduce a departed soul, and that of Elisha did effect the same, and that of another prophet did restore Jeroboam's withered hand; how the prayers of God's people frequently did raise them up saviours, and *When they cried unto the Lord in their trouble, he delivered them out of their distresses:* how the prayers of Asa discomfited a million of Arabians, and those of Jehoshaphat destroyed a numerous army of his enemies by their own hands, and those of Hezekiah brought down an angel from heaven to cut off the Assyrians, and those of Manasses restored him to his kingdom, and those of Esther saved her people from the brink of ruin, and those of Nehemiah inclined a pagan king's heart to favour his pious design for re-edifying Jerusalem, and those of Daniel obtained strange visions and discoveries. How Noah, Job, Daniel, Moses, and Samuel are represented as powerful intercessors with God; and consequently it is intimated, that the great things achieved by them were chiefly done by the force of their prayers.

SERM. XII.

Ezek. xiv. 14. Jer. xv. 1.

And seeing prayers in so many cases are so effectual, and work such miracles; what may we hope from them in this, wherein God so expressly and particularly directeth us to use them? If our prayers can so much avail to our personal and private advantage, if they may be very helpful to our friends; how much shall the devotions of many good men, all levelled at one mark, and aiming at a public most considerable good, be prevalent with the divine goodness! However, if God be not moved by prayers to convert a prince from all sin, to make him do all the good he might, to bless him in all matters; yet he may thence be induced to restrain him from much evil, to keep him from being worse, or from doing worse than otherwise would be; he may dispose him to do many things well, or better than of himself he would do; he may preserve him from many disasters otherwise incident to him: which will be considerable effects of prayer.

11 I shall add but one general consideration more, which is this, that prayer is the only allowable way of redressing our case, if we do suffer by or for princes.

Are they bad, or do they misdemean themselves in their administration of government and justice? we may not by any violent or rough way attempt to reclaim them; for they are not accountable to us, or liable to our correction. *Where the word of a king is, there is power: and who shall say to him, What doest thou?* was the Preacher's doctrine.

Do they oppress us, or abuse us? do they treat us harshly, or cruelly persecute us? we must not kick against them, nor strive to right ourselves by resistance. For, *Against a king*, saith the Wise Man, *there is no rising up:* and, *Who*, said David, *can stretch out his hand against the Lord's anointed, and be guiltless?* and, *They*, saith St Paul, *that resist, shall receive to themselves damnation.*

We must not so much as ease our stomach, or discharge our passion, by railing or inveighing against them. For, *Thou shalt not speak evil of the ruler of thy people*, is a divine law; and, to *Blaspheme*, or revile, *dignities*, is by St Peter and St Jude reprehended as a notable crime.

We must not be bold or free in taxing their actions. For, *Is it fit*, said Elihu, *to say to a king, Thou art wicked, and to princes, Ye are ungodly?* and, *To reproach the footsteps of God's anointed*, is implied to be an impious practice.

We must forbear even complaining and murmuring against them. For murmurers are condemned as no mean sort of offenders; and the Jews in the wilderness were sorely punished for such behaviour.

We must not (according to the Preacher's advice) so much as curse them in our thoughts; or not entertain ill conceits and ill wishes in our minds toward them.

## On the King's happy Return.

To do these things is not only high presumption in regard to them, (inconsistent with the dutiful affection and respect which we owe to them,) but it is flat impiety toward God, and an invasion of his authority; who alone is *King of kings*, and hath reserved to himself the prerogative of judging, of rebuking, of punishing kings, when he findeth cause.

SERM. XII.

1 Tim. vi. 15.

These were the misdemeanours of those in the late times, who, instead of praying for their sovereign, did clamour and rail at him, did asperse him with foul imputations, did accuse his proceedings, did raise tumults, and levy war against him, pretending by rude force to reduce him to his duty; so usurping on their prince, or rather on God himself; assuming his right, and taking his work out of his hands; discovering also therein great profaneness of mind, and distrust of God's providence; as if God, being implored by prayer, could not, or would not, had it been needful, without such irregular courses, have redressed those evils in church or state, which they pretended to feel or fear.

Nothing therefore in such cases is left to us for our remedy or ease, but having recourse to God himself, and seeking relief from his hand in his good time, by converting our prince, or directing him into a good course; however comforting ourselves in the conscience of submitting to God's will<sup>s</sup>.

This is the only method St Paul did prescribe,

---

<sup>s</sup> Absit enim ut indigne feramus ea nos pati quæ optamus, aut ultionem a nobis aliquam machinemur, quam a Deo expectamus.—Tert. ad Scap. cap. ii. [Opp. p. 69 D.]

SERM. XII.

even when Nero, a most vile, flagitious man, a sorry and naughty governor as could be, a monstrous tyrant, and most bloody persecutor, (the very inventor of persecution,) did sway the empire[t]. He did not advise Christians to stand upon their guard, to contrive plots, to provide arms, to raise mutinies and insurrections against him; but to offer supplications, prayers, and intercessions for him, as the best means of their security and comfort[u]. And this was the course of the primitive Christians, during their hard condition under the domination of heathen princes, impugners of their religion: Prayers and tears were then the only arms of the church; whereby they long defended it from ruin, and at last advanced it to most glorious prosperity[x].

Indeed, if, not assuming the liberty to find fault with princes, we would practise the duty of seeking God for his blessing on their proceedings; if, forbearing to scan and censure acts of state, we would earnestly implore God's direction of them; if, leaving to conceive disgusts, and vent complaints about the state of things, we would assiduously petition God for the settlement of them in good

[t] Qui non dicam regum, sed omnium hominum, et vel immanium bestiarum sordidissimus, dignus exstitit, qui persecutionem in Christianos primus inciperet.—Sulp. Sev. [Hist. Sac. Lib. II. cap. 28. p. 236.]

[u] Ita nos magis oramus pro salute Imperatoris, ab eo eam postulantes, qui præstare potest. Et utique ex disciplina patientiæ divinæ agere nos, satis manifestum esse vobis potest, cum tanta hominum multitudo, pars pene major civitatis cujusque, in silentio et modestia agimus.—Tert. [ubi supra.]

[x] Fundendo sanguinem, et patiendo magis quam faciendo contumelias, Christi fundata est ecclesia. Persecutionibus crevit, martyriis coronata est.—Hieron. [ad Theoph. Ep. XXXIX. Opp. Tom. IV. p. ii. col. 338.]

order; if, instead of being shrewd politicians, or smart judges in such matters, we would be devout orators and humble solicitors at the throne of grace; our endeavours surely would find much better effect toward public advantage: we certainly might do more good in our closets by a few hearty wishes uttered there, than by all our tattling or jangling politics in corners.

There are great contrivances to settle things: every one hath his model of state, or method of policy, to communicate for ordering the state; each is zealous for his own conceit, and apt to be displeased with those who dissent from him: but it is, as the fairest and justest, so the surest and likeliest way of reducing things to a firm composure, (without more ado, letting the world alone to move on its own hinges, and not impertinently troubling ourselves or others with the conduct of it,) simply to request of Almighty God, the sovereign Governor and sole Disposer of things, that he would lead his own vicegerents in the management of the charge by himself committed to them. *Be careful for nothing; but in every thing by prayer and supplication with thanksgiving let your requests be made known to God,* is a rule very applicable to this case.

As God's providence is the only sure ground of our confidence or hope for the preservation of church and state, or for the restitution of things into a stable quiet; so it is only our hearty prayers, joined with a conscientious observance of God's laws, whereby we can incline Providence to favour us. By them alone we may hope to save things from sinking into disorder, we may assuage the factions, we may defeat the machinations against the public welfare.

12 Seeing then we have so many good arguments and motives inducing to pray for kings, it is no wonder that, to back them, we may also allege the practice of the church, continually in all times performing this duty in its most sacred offices, especially in the celebration of the Holy Communion[y].

St Paul indeed, when he saith, *I exhort first of all, that prayers be made*, doth chiefly impose this duty on Timothy, or supposeth it incumbent on the pastors of the church, to take special care, that prayers be made for this purpose, and offered up in the church jointly by all Christians[z]: and accordingly the ancient Christians, as Tertullian doth assure us, did *Always pray for the emperors, that God would grant them a long life, a secure reign, a safe family, valiant armies, a faithful senate, a loyal people, a quiet world, and whatever they, as men or as emperors, could wish*[a]. Thus, addeth he, even for their persecutors, and in the very pangs of their sufferings, they did not fail to practise. Likewise of the church in his time St Chrysostom telleth us, that *All communicants did know*

[y] Constit. Apost. VIII. 13. [Cotel. Pat. Apost. Tom. I. p. 404.] Cf. II. 57. [Ibid. p. 265.]

[z] Polycarp. ad Phil. [cap. xii. (Antiq. Vers.) Cotel. Pat. Apost. Tom. II. p. 189.]

[a] Precantes sumus omnes semper pro omnibus Imperatoribus, vitam illis prolixam, imperium securum, domum tutam, exercitus fortes, senatum fidelem, populum probum, orbem quietum, quæcunque hominis et Cæsaris vota sunt.—Tert. Apol. cap. xxx. [Opp. p. 27 B.]

Hoc agite, boni præsides, extorquete animam Deo supplicantem pro Imperatore.—Ibid. [c.]

*how every day, both at even and morning, they did make supplication for all the world, and for the emperor, and for all that are in authority*[b].

And in the Greek liturgies (the composure whereof is fathered on St Chrysostom) there are divers prayers interspersed for the emperors, couched in terms very pregnant and respectful.

If the offices of the Roman church, and of the churches truckling under it, in latter times, shall seem more defective or sparing in this point of service, the reason may be, for that a superlative regard to the solar or pontifical authority (as pope Innocent III. distinguished) did obscure their devotion for the lunar or regal majesty[c]. But our church hath been abundantly careful, that we should in most ample manner discharge this duty; having in each of her holy offices directed us to pray for our king in expressions most full, hearty, and lively.

She hath indeed been charged as somewhat lavish or over-liberal of her devotions in this case. But it is a good fault, and we little need fear overdoing in observance of a precept so very reasonable, and so important: supposing that we have a

---

[b] Καὶ τοῦτο ἴσασιν οἱ μύσται, πῶς καθ᾿ ἑκάστην ἡμέραν γίνεται, καὶ ἐν ἑσπέρᾳ καὶ ἐν πρωΐᾳ· πῶς ὑπὲρ παντὸς τοῦ κόσμου, καὶ βασιλέων καὶ πάντων τῶν ἐν ὑπεροχῇ ὄντων, ποιούμεθα τὴν δέησιν.—Chrys. in 1 Tim. ii. 1. [Opp. Tom. IV. p. 271.]

[c] [Ad firmamentum igitur cœli, hoc est Universalis Ecclesiæ, fecit Deus duo magna luminaria, id est, duas instituit dignitates, quæ sunt pontificalis auctoritas, et regalis potestas; sed illa quæ præest diebus, id est, spiritualibus, major est; quæ vero carnalibus minor; ut quanta est inter Solem et Lunam, tanta inter Pontifices et Reges differentia cognoscatur.—P. Innoc. III. in Decret. Greg. IX. Lib. I. tit. xxxiii. cap. 6. Corp. Jur. Can. Tom. II. p. 59. Ed. Pith. Paris. 1687.]

SERM. XII.

due care to join our heart with the church's words, and to the frequency of prayers for our prince do confer a suitable fervency. If we be not dead, or merely formal, we can hardly be too copious in this kind of devotion; reiteration of words can do no harm, being accompanied with the renovation of our desires. Our text itself will bear us out in such a practice; the apostle therein by variety of expression appearing solicitous, that abundance of prayers for kings should be offered in the church, and no sort of them omitted.

There are so many general inducements to this duty at all times; and there are beside divers particular reasons enforcing it now, in the present state and posture of things.

Ps. cxlv. 18; xviii. 6; lxxvii. 2; lxxxvi. 7; cxviii. 5; cxlii. 1; cvii. 6. James v. 13.

Times of trouble, of danger, of fear, of darkness and perplexity, of distraction and distress, of guilt and deserved wrath, are most seasonable for recourse to the divine help and mercy in prayer[d].

Ps. lxxxii. 5.

And are not ours such? are they not much like to those of which the Psalmist saith, *They know not, neither will they understand; they walk on in darkness: all the foundations of the earth are out of course?* or like those of which our Lord spake,

Luke xxi. 25, 26. 2 Kings xix. 3.

when there was *Upon the earth distress of nations, with perplexity; men's hearts failing them for fear, and for looking after those things which were coming on the earth?*

Are not the days gloomy, so that no human providence can see far, no wisdom can descry the issue of things?

[d] Inops senatus auxilii humani ad deos populum ac vota vertit.—Liv. III. 7. Cf. v. 16. [Jamque Romani, desperata ope humana, fata et Deos spectabant.]

## On the King's happy Return.

Is it not a very unsettled world, wherein all the public frames are shaken almost off the hinges, and the minds of men extremely discomposed with various passions; with fear, suspicion, anger, discontent, and impatience? How from dissensions in opinion do violent factions and feuds rage; the hearts of men boiling with fierce animosities, and being exasperated against one another, beyond any hopes or visible means of reconcilement!

*SERM. XII.*
*Ps. cvii. 27.*

Are not the fences of discipline cast down? Is there any conscience made of violating laws? Is not the dread of authority exceedingly abated, and all government overborne by unbridled licentiousness?

How many adversaries are there, bearing ill will to our Sion! How many turbulent, malicious, crafty spirits, eagerly bent, and watching for occasion to subvert the church, to disturb the state, to introduce to confusion in all things! How many Edomites, who say of Jerusalem, (both ecclesiastical and civil,) *Down with it, down with it even to the ground!*

*Ps. cxxix. 5; lxxxiii. 5.*

*Ps. cxxxvii. 7.*

Have we not great reason to be fearful of God's just displeasure, and that heavy judgments will be poured on us for our manifold heinous provocations and crying sins; for the prodigious growth of atheism, infidelity, and profaneness; for the rife practice of all impieties, iniquities, and impurities, with most impudent boldness, or rather with outrageous insolence; for the extreme dissoluteness in manners; the gross neglect or contempt of all duties; the great stupidity and coldness of people generally as to all concerns of religion; for the want of religious awe toward God, of charity toward our neighbour, of respect to our superiors, of sobriety in our conversation; for our ingratitude for many great mercies, and incorrigibleness under many sore chastisements, our insensibleness of many plain warnings, loudly calling us to repentance?

Is not all the world about us in combustion, cruel wars raging every where, and Christendom weltering in blood? and although at present, by God's mercy, we are free, who knows but that soon, by God's justice, the neighbouring flames may catch our houses?

In fine, is not our case palpably such, that for any good composure or reinstatement of things in good order, for upholding truth and sound doctrine, for reducing charity and peace, for reviving the spirit of piety, and bringing virtue again into request; for preserving state and church from ruin; we can have no confidence or reasonable hope, but in the good providence and merciful succour of Almighty God; *Beside whom there is no Saviour;* who alone is *The hope of Israel, and Saviour thereof in time of trouble?* we now having great cause to pray with our Lord's disciples in the storm, *Lord, save us, we perish.*

Upon such considerations, and others whereof I suppose you are sufficiently apprehensive, we now especially are obliged earnestly to pray for our king, that God in mercy would preserve his royal person, and inspire his mind with light, and endue his heart with grace, and in all things bless him to us, to be *A repairer of our breaches, and a restorer of paths to dwell in;* so that under him we may lead a quiet life in all godliness and honesty.

I have done with the first duty, (Prayer for kings;) upon which I have the rather so largely insisted, because it is very seasonable to our present condition.

II. The other (Thanksgiving) I shall but touch, and need not perhaps to do more. For,

1 As to general inducements, they are the same, or very like to those which are for prayer; it being plain, that whatever we are concerned to pray for, when we want it, that we are bound to thank God for, when he vouchsafeth to bestow it. And if common charity should dispose us to resent the good of princes with complacence; if their welfare be a public benefit; if ourselves are interested in it, and partake great advantages thereby; if in equity and ingenuity we are bound to seek it; then, surely, we are much engaged to thank God, the bountiful donor of it, for his goodness in conferring it.

2 As for particular motives, suiting the present occasion, I need not by information or impression of them further to stretch your patience; seeing you cannot be ignorant or insensible of the grand benefits by the divine goodness bestowed on our king, and on ourselves, which this day we are bound with all grateful acknowledgment to commemorate. Wherefore, instead of reciting trite stories, and urging obvious reasons, (which a small recollection will suggest to you,) I shall only request you to join with me in the practice of the duty, and in acclamation of praise to God. Even so

Blessed be God, who hath given to us so gracious and benign a prince, (the experiments of 1 Kings i. 48.

whose clemency and goodness no history can parallel,) to sit on the throne of his blessed father and renowned ancestors.

Blessed be God, who hath protected him in so many encounters, hath saved him from so many dangers and snares, hath delivered him from so great troubles.

Blessed be God, who in so wonderful a manner, by such miraculous trains of providence, did reduce him to his country, and reinstate him in the possession of his rights; thereby vindicating his own just providence, *Declaring his salvation, and openly shewing his righteousness in the sight of all people.*

Blessed be God, who in him and with him did restore to us our ancient good constitution of government, our laws and liberties, our peace and quiet; rescuing us from lawless usurpations and tyrannical yokes, from the insultings of error and iniquity, from horrible distractions and confusions.

Ever blessed be God, who hath *Turned the captivity of Sion;* hath raised our church from the dust, and reestablished the sound doctrine, the decent order, the wholesome discipline thereof; hath restored true religion with its supports, advantages, and encouragements.

Blessed be the Lord, who hath granted us to continue these sixteen years in the peaceable fruition of those blessings.

*Praised be God, who hath not cast out our prayer, nor turned his mercy from us.*

Praised be God, *Who hath turned our heaviness into joy, hath put off our sackcloth, and girded us with gladness.*

*Let our mouth speak the praise of the Lord; and let all flesh bless his holy name for ever and ever.* [SERM. XII. Ps. cxlv. 21.]

*The Lord liveth, and blessed be our rock; and let the God of our salvation be exalted.* [Ps. xviii. 46.]

*Blessed be the Lord God of Israel, who only doeth wondrous things; and blessed be his glorious name for ever; and let the whole earth be filled with his glory. Amen, and amen.* [Ps. lxxii. 18, 19.]

*Blessed be the Lord God of Israel, from everlasting to everlasting: and let all the people say, Amen. Praise ye the Lord.* [Ps. cvi. 48; xli. 13; lxxxix. 52; lxviii. 34. 1 Chron. xvi. 8—36.]

# SERMON XIII.[a]

## ON THE GUNPOWDER-TREASON.

PSALM LXIV. 9, 10.

*And all men shall fear, and shall declare the work of God; for they shall wisely consider of his doing. The righteous shall be glad in the Lord, and shall trust in him; and all the upright in heart shall glory.*

SERM. XIII.

IF we should search about for a case parallel to that which we do now commemorate, we should, perhaps, hardly find one more patly such, than is that, which is implied in this Psalm: and if we would know the duties incumbent on us in reference to such an occasion, we could scarce better learn them otherwise than in our text.

With attention perusing the Psalm, we may therein observe, that its great author was apprehensive of a desperate plot by a confederacy of wicked and spiteful enemies, with great craft and secrecy, contrived against his safety. *They,* saith he, *encourage themselves in an evil matter: they commune of laying snares privily; they say, Who shall see them?* That for preventing the blow threatened by this design, (whereof he had some glimpse, or some presumption, grounded upon the knowledge of their implacable and active malice,)

Ver. 5.

[a] Nov. 5, 1673.

he doth implore divine protection: *Hide me*, saith he, *from the secret counsel of the wicked, from the insurrection of the workers of iniquity.* That he did confide in God's mercy and justice for the seasonable defeating, for the fit avenging their machination: *God*, saith he, *shall shoot at them with an arrow; suddenly shall they be wounded.* That they should themselves become the detectors of their crime, and the instruments of the exemplary punishment due thereto: *They*, addeth he, *shall make their own tongue to fall upon themselves: all that see them shall flee away.*

Such was the case; the which, unto what passage in the history it doth relate, or whether it belongeth to any we have recorded, it may not be easy to determine. Expositors commonly do refer it to the designs of Saul upon David's life. But this seeming purely conjecture, not founded upon any express words, or pregnant intimations in the text, I shall leave that inquiry in its own uncertainty. It sufficeth to make good its pertinency, that there was such a mischievous conspiracy, deeply projected, against David; (a very great personage, in whose safety the public state of God's people was principally concerned; he being then king of Israel, at least in designation, and therefore in the precedent Psalm, endited in Saul's time, is so styled;) from the peril whereof he, by the special providence of God, was rescued, with the notable disappointment and grievous confusion of those who managed it. The which case (at least in kind, if not in degree) beareth a plain resemblance to that which lieth before us.

And the duties, which upon that occasion are

signified to concern people then, do no less now sort to us; the which, as they lie couched in our text, are these: 1 Wisely to consider God's doing; 2 To fear; 3 To declare God's work; 4 To be glad in the Lord; 5 To trust in God; 6 To glory. Of which the first three are represented as more generally concerning men; the others as appertaining more peculiarly to righteous and upright persons.

These duties it shall be my endeavour somewhat to explain and press, in a manner applicable to the present case. I call them duties; and to warrant the doing so, it is requisite to consider, that all these particulars may be understood in a double manner; either as declarative of event, or as directive of practice upon such emergencies.

When God doth so interpose his hand, as signally to check and confound mischievous enterprises, it will be apt to stir up in the minds of men an apprehension of God's special providence, to strike into their hearts a dread of his power and justice, to wring from their mouths suitable declarations and acknowledgments; and particularly then good men will be affected with pious joy; they will be encouraged to confide in God, they will be moved to glory, or to express a triumphant satisfaction in God's proceedings. These events naturally do result from such providential occurrences; for production of these events such occurrences are purposely designed; and accordingly (where men are not by profane opinions or affections much indisposed) they do commonly follow.

But yet they are not proposed simply as events, but also as matters of duty: for men are obliged readily to admit such impressions upon their minds, hearts, and lives, from the special works of Providence; they are bound not to cross those natural tendencies, not to frustrate those wise intents of God, aiming at the production of such good dispositions and good practices: whence if those effects do not arise, as often notoriously they do not in some persons, men thereby do incur much guilt and blame.

SERM. XIII.

It is indeed ordinary to represent matter of duty in this way, expressing those practices consequent in effect, which in obligation should follow, according to God's purpose, and the nature of causes ordered by him. As when, for instance, God in the law had prescribed duty, and threatened sore punishment on the disobedient, it is subjoined, *And all the people shall hear, and fear, and do no more presumptuously:* the meaning is, that such exemplary punishment is in its nature apt, and its design tendeth to produce such effects, although not ever, questionless, with due success, so as to prevent all transgression of those laws. So also, *When,* saith the Prophet, *thy judgments are in the land, the inhabitants of the world will learn righteousness:* the sense is, that divine judgments in themselves are instructive of duty, it is their drift to inform men therein, and men ought to learn that lesson from them; although in effect divers there be, whom no judgments can make wiser or better; such as those of whom in the same Prophet it is said, *The people turneth not unto him that smiteth them;* and in another, *In vain have I smitten your children, they received no correction.* As therefore frequently otherwhere, so also

Deut. xvii. 13; xiii. 11; xix. 20.

Isai. xxvi. 9.

Isai. ix. 13.
Jer. ii. 30; v. 3.
Neh. ix. 29.

SERM. XIII.

here, this kind of expression may be taken chiefly to import duty. To begin then with the first of these duties.

1 We are upon such occasions obliged *Wisely to consider,* (or, as the Greek rendereth it, Συνιέναι, *To understand,* or *To perceive,* as our old translation hath it) *God's doing*[b]. This I put in the first place, as previous in nature, and influential upon the rest: whence (although in the Hebrew it be knit to the rest, as they all are to one another, by the conjunctive particle *ve, and,* yet) we do translate it casually, *For they shall wisely consider, for they shall perceive;* because indeed without duly considering and rightly understanding such occurrences to proceed from God, none of the other acts can or will be performed: attentive consideration is needful to beget knowledge and persuasion; these to breed affection and practice.

There are many who, in such cases, are nowise apprehensive of God's special providence, or affected with it; because they do not consider, or do not consider wisely and intelligently.

Some are very inobservant and careless in regard to things of this nature; so drowsy and oscitant, as not to attend to whatever passeth, or to mind what God acteth in the world: such as those of whom the Prophet saith, *The harp, and the viol, the tabret, and pipe, and wine, are in their feasts: but they regard not the work of the Lord, nor the operation of his hands:* that is, their minds are so amused by wanton divertisements, their hearts are so immersed in sensual enjoyments, as nowise

Isai. v. 12.
Ps. xxviii. 5; x. 4.

[b] מַעֲשֵׂהוּ הִשְׂכִּילוּ
Τὰ ποιήματα αὐτοῦ συνῆκαν.—LXX.

to observe the most notable occurrences of Providence.

Others, although they do ken and regard what is done, as matter of news, or story, entertaining curiosity and talk: yet out of sloth or stupidity do little consider it, or study whence it springeth; contenting themselves with none, or with any superficial account which fancy or appearance suggesteth: like beasts they do take in things obvious to their sense, and perhaps stand gazing on them; but do not make any careful reflection, or inquiry into their original causes and reasons; taking (as a dog, when he biteth the stone flung at him, or as a child that is angry with the log he falleth on) whatever appeareth next to be the principal cause: such as the Psalmist again toucheth, when he saith, *A brutish man knoweth not, neither doth a fool understand this:* and as he doth acknowledge himself on one occasion to have been; *So foolish was I, and ignorant; I was as a beast before thee.* Ps. xcii. 6. Ps. lxxiii. 22.

Others pretend to consider much, and seem very inquisitive; yet (being misguided by vain prejudices or foul affections) do not consider wisely, or well understand these matters; the result of their care and study about them being to father them on wrong causes, ascribing them to the mere conduct and agency of visible causes, hurried by a necessary swinge or rolling on by a casual fluctuation of things; not descrying God's hand in them, but profanely discarding and disclaiming it: such as those in the Psalms, who so reflected on Providence as to say, *How doth God know? and is there knowledge in the Most High? The Lord doth not see, neither doth the God of Jacob regard* Ps. lxxiii. 11; xciv. 7; x. 11.

it; such as hath been the brood of *Epicurean* and profane considerers in all times, who have earnestly plodded, and strained their wits, to exclude God from any inspection or influence upon our affairs.

Some indeed there have been so very dull and stupid, or so perverse and profane, as not to discern God's hand, when it was made bare, raised up, and stretched out in the achievement of most prodigious works; not to read Providence, when set forth in the largest and fairest print: such as those of whom it is said in the Psalm, *Our fathers understood not thy wonders in Egypt;* and those of whom it is observed in the Gospel, *Though he had done so many miracles before them, yet they believed not:* such as the mutinous people, who, although they beheld the earth swallowing up Korah with his complices, and a fire from the Lord consuming the men that offered incense; yet presently did fall a charging Moses and Aaron, saying, *Ye have killed the people of the Lord.* No wonder then, if many do not perceive the same hand, when it is wrapped up in a complication with inferior causes; when it is not lifted up so high, or so far extended in miraculous performances.

The special providence of God in events here effected or ordered by him, is indeed commonly not discernible without good judgment and great care; it is not commonly impressed upon events in characters so big and clear, as to be legible to every eye, or to any eye not endued with a sharp perspicacy, not applying an industrious heedfulness: the tracts thereof are too fine and subtle to be descried by a dim sight, with a transient glance, or upon a

## On the Gunpowder-Treason. 451

gross view: it is seldom so very conspicuous, that persons incredulous, or any-wise indisposed to admit it, can easily be convinced thereof, or constrained to acknowledge it: it is often (upon many accounts, from many causes) very obscure, and not easily discernible to the most sagacious, most watchful, most willing observers. For, the instruments of Providence being free agents, acting with unaccountable variety, nothing can happen which may not be imputed to them with some colourable pretence. Divine and human influences are so twisted and knit together, that it is hard to sever them. The manner of divine efficacy is so very soft and gentle, that we cannot easily trace its footsteps. God designeth not commonly to exert his hand in a notorious way, but often purposely doth conceal it. Whereas also it is not fit to charge upon God's special hand of providence any event, wherein special ends of wisdom or goodness do not shine; it is often hard to discover such ends, which usually are wrapped in perplexities: because God acteth variously, (according to circumstances of things, and the disposition, capacity, or state of objects,) so as to do the same thing for different ends, and different things for the same end: because there are different ends, unto which Providence in various order and measure hath regard, which our short and narrow prospect cannot reach: because God, in prosecution of his ends, is not wont to proceed in the most direct and compendious way; but windeth about in a large circuit, enfolding many concurrent and subordinate designs: because the expediency of things to be permitted or performed doth not consist in single acts or events, but in

SERM. XIII.

many conspiring to one common end: because we cannot apprehend the consequences, nor balance the conveniences of things in order to good ends: because we are apt to measure things by their congruity to our opinions, expectations, and affections: because many proceedings of God depend upon grounds inaccessible to our apprehension; such as his own secret decrees, the knowledge of men's thoughts, close purposes, clandestine designs, true qualifications and merits; his prescience of contingent events, and what the result will be from the combination of numberless causes: because sometimes he doth act in methods of wisdom, and by rules of justice, surpassing our capacity to know, either from the finiteness of our nature, or the feebleness of our reason, or the meanness of our state and circumstances here: because all the divine administration of affairs hath no complete determination or final issue here; that being reserved to the great day of reckoning and judgment. It is further also expedient that many occurrences should be puzzling to us, to quash our presumption, to exercise our faith, to quicken our industry, to engage us upon adoring that wisdom which we cannot comprehend. Upon such accounts, for such causes, (which time will not give me leave to explain and exemplify,) the special providence of God is often cloudy, is seldom so clear, that without great heed and consideration we can perceive it. But however to do so is plainly our duty; and therefore possible.

For our reason was not given us to be idle upon so important occasions; or that we should be as brute spectators of what God doeth. He surely in the governance of his noblest creature here discovereth his being, and displayeth his attributes: we therefore carefully should observe it. He thereby (and no otherwise in a public way) doth continually speak, and signify to us his mind: and fit it is, that we his subjects should hear, should attend to the least intimations of his pleasure. To him thence glory should accrue, the which who but we can render? and that we may render it, we must know the grounds of it. In fine, for the support of God's kingdom, for upholding the reverence due to his administration of justice among us, it is requisite, that by apparent dispensation of recompenses duty should be encouraged, and disobedience checked: very foolish therefore we must be, if we regard not such dispensations.

So reason dictateth, and holy scripture more plainly declareth our obligation to consider and perceive God's doings. To do so is recommended to us as a singular point of wisdom: *Whoso is wise, and will observe these things, they shall understand the lovingkindness of the Lord. Let him that glorieth glory in this, that he understandeth and knoweth me, that I am the Lord, which exercise lovingkindness, judgment, and righteousness in the earth. Who is wise? and he shall understand these things; prudent? and he shall know them. For the ways of the Lord are right,* &c. We are vehemently provoked thereto: *Understand, ye brutish among the people; and, ye fools, when will ye be wise?* They are reproved for neglect and defailance, *Who do not regard the work of the Lord, nor the operation of his hand.* The not discerning Providence is reproached as a piece of shameful folly; *A brutish man knoweth* not, *neither doth a fool understand:* and of woful pravity; *O ye hypocrites, ye can discern the face of the sky; but how is it that ye cannot discern this time?* To contemplate and study Providence is the practice of good men. *I will meditate on all thy works,* saith the Psalmist, chiefly respecting works of this kind: and, *The works of the Lord are great, sought out of all them that have pleasure therein.* It is a fit matter of devotion, warranted by the practice of good men, to implore God's manifestation of his justice and power this way. *O Lord God, to whom vengeance belongeth, shew thyself; lift up thyself, thou Judge of the earth.* It is God's manner hereby to notify himself. *The Lord is known by the judgment that he executeth.* He for this very purpose doth interpose his hand; *That men may know it is his hand, and that the Lord hath done it; That,* as it is in Esay, *they may see, and know, and consider, and understand together, that the hand of the Lord hath done this, and the Holy One of Israel hath created it.* He manageth things so that men may be brought to know, may be induced to acknowledge his authority, and his equity in the management thereof[c]; *That they may know that he, whose name is Jehovah, is the Most High over all the earth:* that they may say, *Verily there is a reward for the righteous: verily there is a God that judgeth the earth.* In fine, the knowledge of God's special providence is frequently represented as a mean of nourishing our faith and hope in him, as a ground of thankfulness and praise to him, as an incentive

---

[c] God thereby doth support and encourage good men.
He doth thereby convince and confound ill men.—Ps. ix. 19, 20.
He thereby doth instruct all men.—Isai. xxvi. 9.

of the best affections (of holy joy, and humble fear, and hearty love) toward him: wherefore we ought to seek it, and we may attain it.

There are consequently some distinctive marks or characters, by which we may perceive God's hand: and such may these be which follow, (drawn from the special nature, manner, adjuncts, and consequences of events:) upon which may be grounded rules declarative of special providence, such as commonly will hold, although sometimes they may admit exceptions, and should be warily applied.

1 The wonderful strangeness of events, compared with the ordinary course of things, or the natural influence of causes; when effects are performed by no visible means, or by means disproportionate, unsuitable, repugnant to the effect. Sometimes great exploits are achieved, mighty forces are disconcerted, huge structures are demolished, designs backed with all advantages of wit and strength are confounded, none knows how, by no considerable means that appear; nature rising up in arms against them; panic fear seizing on the abettors of them; dissensions and treacheries springing up among the actors; sudden deaths snatching away the principal instruments of them. As, when *The stars in their course fought against Sisera:* when the wind and skies became auxiliaries to Theodosius[d]: when *The Lord thundered with a great thunder upon the Philistines, and discomfited*

Judg. v. 20.

1 Sam. vii. 10.
2 Sam. xxii. 14, 15.

[d] Aug. de Civ. Dei, v. 26. [Milites nobis qui aderant, retulerunt, extorta sibi esse de manibus quæcunque jaculabantur, cum a Theodosii partibus in adversarios vehemens ventus iret, et non solum quæcunque in eos jaciebantur concitatissime raperet, verum etiam ipsorum tela in eorum corpora retorqueret.—Opp. Tom. VII. col. 140 E.]

SERM. XIII.

*them, and they were smitten before Israel:* when *The Lord made the host of Syrians to hear a noise of chariots, of horses, of a great host;—whence they arose and fled:* when *The children of Ammon and Moab stood up against the inhabitants of mount Seir, utterly to slay and destroy them; and when they had made an end of the inhabitants of Seir, every one helped to destroy another:* when *The angel of the Lord went forth and smote in the camp of the Assyrians* 185,000 *men; and when they arose early in the morning, behold they were all dead corpses:* when the mighty power of Antiochus was, as it is said, to be *Broken without hands:* and when, as it is foretold, *A stone cut out of the mountain without hands should break in pieces the iron, the brass, the clay, the silver, and the gold.* Such events do speak God to be their cause, by his invisible efficacy supplying the defect of apparent means.

2 Kings vii. 6.
2 Chron. xx. 23.
2 Kings xix. 35.
Dan. viii. 25.
Dan. ii. 45.

So likewise, when by weak forces great feats are accomplished, and impotency triumpheth over might[e]; when, as the Prophet saith, *The captives of the mighty are taken away, and the prey of the terrible is delivered:* when *One man,* as is promised, *doth chase a thousand,* and *Two put ten thousand to flight:* when a stripling, furnished only with faith

Isai. xlix. 25.
Josh. xxiii. 10.
Lev. xxvi. 8.
Deut. xxxii. 30.
1 Sam. xvii. 40.

[e] Vid. Artabani Orat. apud Herod. [VII. 10. 5.] ['Ορᾷς τὰ ὑπερέχοντα ζῶα ὡς κεραυνοῖ ὁ Θεός, οὐδὲ ἐᾷ φαντάζεσθαι, τὰ δὲ σμικρὰ οὐδέν μιν κνίζει; ὁρᾷς δὲ ὡς ἐς οἰκήματα τὰ μέγιστα, αἰεὶ καὶ δένδρεα τὰ τοιαῦτα ἀποσκήπτει τὰ βέλεα; φιλέει γὰρ ὁ Θεὸς τὰ ὑπερέχοντα πάντα κολούειν. οὕτω δὴ καὶ στρατὸς πολλὸς ὑπὸ ὀλίγου διαφθείρεται κατὰ τοιόνδε. ἐπεάν σφι ὁ Θεὸς φθονήσας φόβον ἐμβάλῃ, ἢ βροντήν, δι' ὧν ἐφθάρησαν ἀναξίως ἑωυτῶν· οὐ γὰρ ἐᾷ φρονέειν μέγα ὁ Θεὸς ἄλλον ἢ ἑωυτόν.]

Ἀλλ' αἰεί γε Διὸς κρείσσων νόος, ἠέ περ ἀνδρῶν.
Hom. Il. XVI. 688.

and a pebble, shall knock down a monstrous giant, armed with a helmet of brass and a coat of mail, with a huge target, sword, and spear: when successes arrive like those recorded in scripture under the conduct of Joshua, Gideon, Jonathan, Asa, Jehosaphat; wherein very small forces by uncouth means did subdue formidable powers: this doth argue that God doth interpose; with whom, as it is said, it is all one *To save by many, or by few, and those that have no power;* whose *Power is perfected in weakness;* who *Breaketh the arm of the wicked,* and *Weakeneth the strength of the mighty,* and *Delivereth the poor from him that is too strong for him.*

SERM. XIII.

Judg. vii. 7.
1 Sam. xiv. 6.
2 Chron. xiv. 11; xx. 12, 17.
1 Sam. xiv. 6.
2 Cor. xii. 9.
Job xii. 21; xxxviii. 15;
Ps. x. 15; xxxvii. 17; xxxv. 10; lxxvi. 5.

Also, when great policy and craft do effect nothing, but are blasted of themselves, or baffled by simplicity: when cunningly-laid designs are soon thwarted and overturned: when most perspicacious and profound counsellors are so blinded, or so infatuated[f], as to mistake in plain cases, to oversee things most obvious and palpable: when profane, malicious, subtle, treacherous politicians (such as Abimelech, Achitophel, Haman, Sejanus, Stilico, Borgia, with many like occurring in story[g]) are not only supplanted in their wicked contrivances, but dismally chastised for them: the occurrences do more than insinuate divine wisdom to intervene, countermining and confounding such devices. For he it is, *Who,* as the scripture telleth us, *maketh the diviners mad; turneth wise men backward, and maketh their knowledge foolish; Disappointeth the*

2 Sam. xv. 31.

Isai. xliv. 25.

Job v. 12, 13.
Ps. xxxiii. 10.

[f] Μαῖα φίλη, μάργην σε θεοὶ θέσαν.
Hom. Od. XXIII. 11.
[g] Ruffinus, S. Paul, d'Ancre, de Luna, &c.

devices of the crafty[h], so that their hands cannot perform their enterprise; taketh the wise in their own craftiness, and turneth down the counsel of the froward headlong.

Whenever a just cause or honest design, without any support or succour of worldly means, (without authority, power, wit, learning, eloquence,) doth against all opposition of violence and art prevail; this signifieth him to yield a special countenance and aid thereto, who, to depress human pride, and advance his own glory, *Hath chosen the foolish things of the world to confound the wise; and the weak things of the world to confound the things that are mighty; and base things of the world, and things which are despised, and things that are not, to bring to nought things that are:* (that are with us in most request and esteem.)

1 Cor. i. 27, 28.

Again, when plots, with extreme caution and secrecy contrived in darkness are by improbable means, by unaccountable accidents, disclosed and brought to light; *A bird of the air*, as the Wise Man speaketh, *telling the matter; The stones in the wall*, as it is in the Prophet, *crying out* Treason. The king cannot sleep; to divert him the chronicle is called for; Mordecai's service is there pitched on; an inquiry is made concerning his recompense; honour is decreed him; so doth Haman's cruel device come out. Pity seizeth on a pitiless heart toward one among a huge number of innocents devoted to slaughter: that he may be saved, a letter must be sent: in that, words inserted suggesting the manner of execution; that carried to

Eccles. x. 20.
Hab. ii. 11.
Esther vi. 1, &c.

[h] Βουλὴν πολυπλόκων ἐξέστησεν.—LXX.

the wise king, who presently smelleth it out: so this day's plot was discovered. Such events, whence can they well proceed, but from the all-piercing and ever watchful care of him, *Whose eyes,* as Elihu said, *are upon the ways of man, and he seeth all his goings? There is no darkness nor shadow of death, where the workers of iniquity shall hide themselves:* for *Hell is naked before him, and destruction hath no covering.*

SERM. XIII.

Ps. cxxi. 4.
Job xxxiv. 21, 22.

Job xxvi. 6.
Amos ix. 2.
Heb. iv. 13.

Also, when ill men by their perverse wiliness do notably befool and ensnare themselves, laying trains to blow up their own designs, involving themselves in that ruin and mischief into which they studied to draw others; as when Saul, exposing David's life to hazard, increaseth his honour; when the Persian nobles, incensing the king against Daniel, do occasion his growth in favour, with their own destruction; when Haman, by contriving to destroy God's people, doth advance them, and rearing a gallows for Mordecai, doth prepare it for himself: when it happeneth according to those passages in the Psalms, *The wicked are taken in the devices that they imagined; in the net which they hid is their own foot taken: He made a pit and digged it, and is fallen into the ditch which he made: His mischief shall return upon his own head, and his violent dealings shall come upon his own pate:* these are pregnant evidences of God's just and wise providence; for *The Lord is known by the judgment that he executeth; the wicked is snared in the work of his own hand.*

1 Sam. xviii. 25.

Dan. vi. 24.

Esther vii. 10.

Ps. x. 2;
ix. 15;
xxxv. 8;
cxl. 5;
vii. 15;
lvii. 6.

Ps. vii. 16.

Ps. ix. 16.

All such occurrences, containing in them somewhat, if not downrightly miraculous, yet very admirable, in like manner deflecting from the

SERM. XIII.

Ps. lxxii. 18; lxxxvi. 10.

Isai. lxiv. 3.

Ps. cxlii. 4; xliv. 25; cviii. 12. Heb. iv. 16.

Ps. xlvi. 1; ix. 9; xxxvii. 39; xxvii. 5; lxix. 14; xviii. 6. Isai. xxv. 4; xxxiii. 2.
Jer. xiv. 8.
Job xxxiii. 18.
Ps. cvii. 8, 15, 21, 31.

stream of human affairs, as miracles do surmount the course of nature, most reasonably may, most justly should, be ascribed to the special operation of him, *Who only doeth wonderful things.*

2 Another character of special providence is, the seasonableness and suddenness of events. When that, which in itself is not ordinary, nor could well be expected, doth fall out happily, in the nick of an exigency, for the relief of innocence, the encouragement of goodness, the support of a good cause, the furtherance of any good purpose; (so that there is occasion to acknowledge with the Prophet, *Thou didst terrible things, that we looked not for;*) this is a shrewd indication that God's hand is then concerned; not only the event being notable, but the connection thereof with circumstances of need being more admirable.

Thus, in time of distress and despondency, when a man is utterly forlorn, and destitute of all visible relief, when, as the Psalmist speaketh, *Refuge faileth him, and no man careth for his soul:* if then Εὔκαιρος βοήθεια, *An opportune succour* doth arrive; he is then unreasonable and ingrateful, if he doth not avow a special providence, and thankfully ascribe that event unto him who is *Our refuge and strength; a very present help in trouble; A strength to the poor, a strength to the needy in his distress, A refuge from the storm, a shadow from the heat; The hope of Israel, and the Saviour thereof in time of trouble.* This is that, for which, in the 107th Psalm, the divine goodness is so magnificently celebrated; this is the burden of that pathetical rapture, wherein we, by repeated wishes and exhortations, are instigated to bless God; his wonderfully relieving the children of men in their need and distress: this is that, which God himself in the Prophet representeth as a most satisfactory demonstration of his providence. *When the poor and needy seek water, and there is none, and their tongue faileth for thirst, I the Lord will hear them, I the God of Jacob will not forsake them: I will open rivers in high places, and fountains in the midst of the valleys,* &c. *that they may see, and know, and consider, and understand together, that the hand of the Lord hath done this, and the Holy One of Israel hath created it.*

[SERM. XIII.]

[Isai. xli. 17, &c.]

So also, when pestilent enterprises, managed by close fraud or by impetuous violence, are brought to a head and come near to the point of being executed; the sudden detection or seasonable obstruction of them do argue the ever vigilant eye and the all-powerful hand to be engaged: God ever doth see those deceitful workers of iniquity, laying their mischief in the dark; he is always present at their cabals and clandestine meetings, wherein they brood upon it. He often doth suffer it to grow on to a pitch of maturity, till it be thoroughly formed, till it be ready to be hatched, and break forth in its mischievous effects; then in a trice he snappeth and crusheth it to nothing. God beholdeth violent men setting out in their unjust attempts, he letteth them proceed on in a full career, until they reach the edge of their design; then instantly he checketh, putteth in a spoke, he stoppeth, he tumbleth them down, or turneth them backward. Thus was Haman's plot dashed, when he had procured a royal decree, when he had fixed a time, when he had issued forth letters to destroy God's people.

[Esther iii.]

SERM. XIII.

Exod. xiv.

2 Kings xix. 28.

2 Mac. ix. 4, 5.

Isai. lix. 19.

Thus was Pharaoh overwhelmed, when he had just overtaken the children of Israel. Thus were the designs of Abimelech, of Absolom, of Adonijah, of Sanballat nipped. Thus when Sennacherib with an unmatchable host had encamped against Jerusalem, and had to appearance swallowed it, *God did put a hook into his nose, and turned him back into his own land.* Thus when Antiochus was marching on furiously to accomplish his threat of turning Jerusalem into a charnel, a noisome disease did intercept his progress. Thus when the profane Caligula did mean to discharge his bloody rage on the Jews, for refusing to worship him, a domestic sword did presently give vent to his revengeful breath[1]. Thus also, when Julian had by his policy and authority projected to overthrow our religion, his plot soon was quashed, and his life snapped away by an unknown hand[k]. Thus, *Whenever the enemy doth come in like a flood,* (threatening immediately to overflow and overturn all things,) *the Spirit of the Lord doth lift up a standard against him;* that is, God's secret efficacy doth suddenly restrain and repress his outrage. This usually is the method of divine Providence. God could prevent the beginnings of wicked designs; he could supplant them in their first onsets[1]; he could any where sufflaminate and subvert them: but he rather winketh for a time, and suffereth the designers to go on, till they are mounted to the

[1] Joseph. Antiq. Jud. Lib. XVIII. [cap. 8. Opp. Tom. I. p. 905.]

[k] Chrys. in Babyl. Orat. II. [Opp. Tom. v. p. 471.] Greg. Naz. Orat. v. [Opp. Tom. I. p. 162 D.]

[1] Εἰ δὲ μὴ ἐκ προοιμίων, μηδὲ εὐθέως, ἔθος αὐτῷ τοιοῦτον, &c.—Chrys. ad Olymp. [Ep. i. Opp. Tom. VII. p. 52.]

top of confidence[m], and good people are cast on the brink of ruin; then Ἀπὸ μηχανῆς, surprisingly, unexpectedly he striketh in with effectual succour[n]; so declaring how vain the presumption is of impious undertakers; how needful and sure his protection is over innocent people; how much reason the one hath to dread him, and the other to confide in him. Then is God seen, then his care and power will be acknowledged, when he snatcheth us from the jaws of danger, when *Our soul doth escape as a bird out of the snare of the fowler.*

Ps. cxxiv. 7.

3 Another character of special Providence is, the great utility and beneficialness of occurrences, especially in regard to the public state of things, and to great personages, in whose welfare the public is much concerned. To entitle every petty chance that arriveth to special providence may signify lightness; to father on God the mischiefs issuing from our sin and folly may savour of profaneness: but to ascribe every grand and beneficial event unto his good hand hath ever been reputed wisdom and justice[o]. *It hath been,* saith Balbus in Cicero, *a common opinion among the ancients, that whatever did bring great benefit to mankind was never done without divine goodness toward men*[p]. And well might they deem it so, seeing to do so is most agreeable to his nature, and appertaining to

---

[m] Ὅταν κορυφωθῇ, ὅταν αὐξηθῇ, &c.—Id. Ibid.

[n]     Nec Deus intersit, nisi dignus vindice nodus
        Inciderit.—[Hor. Ars Poet. 191.]

[o] Magna dii curant, parva negligunt.—Cic. de Nat. Deor. [II. 66, 167.]

[p] Quicquid enim magnam utilitatem generi adferret humano, id non sine divina bonitate erga homines fieri arbitrabantur.—Ibid. [ii. 23. 60.]

his charge, and may appear to be so by good argumentation *a priori*. For, that God doth govern our affairs may be deduced from his essential attributes; and, consequently, that he doth in especial manner order these things, which are the most proper and worthy objects of his governance. God indeed doth not disregard any thing; he watcheth over the least things by his general and ordinary providence; so that nothing in nature may deviate from its course, or transgress the bounds prescribed to it. *He* thereby *clotheth the grass of the field; He provideth for the raven his food,* and *The young lions seek their meat from him:* without his care *A sparrow doth not fall to the ground;* by it, *All the hairs of our head are numbered.* But his more special hand of providence is chiefly employed in managing affairs of great moment and benefit to mankind; and peculiarly those which concern his people, who do profess to worship and serve him; whose welfare he tendereth with more than ordinary care and affection. He therefore hath a main stroke in all revolutions and changes of state: he presideth in all great counsels and undertakings; in the waging of war, in the settlement of peace; in the dispensation of victory and good success. He is peculiarly interested in the protection of princes, the chief *Ministers of his kingdom;* and in preservation of his people, the choice object of his care, from violent invasions and treacherous surprises; so as to prevent disasters incident, or to deliver from them. *It is he that,* as the Psalmist saith, *doth give salvation unto kings; who delivereth David his servant from the hurtful sword.* It is *He that* continually *keepeth Israel without ever sleeping or slumbering;*

who is *The hope of Israel, and the Saviour thereof; Who is in the midst of her, that she shall not be moved;* who hath declared, that *He will help her, and that right early;* that *He will not cast off his people, nor forsake his inheritance;* that *No weapon formed against* his church *shall prosper;* that *Salvation belongeth to the Lord, and his blessing is upon his people.* When therefore any remarkable event, highly conducing to the public good of church and state, (supporting them in a good condition, or rescuing them from imminent danger,) doth appear, it is most reasonable and most just, to ascribe the accomplishment thereof to God's hand. When any pernicious enterprise, levelled against the safety of prince and people, is disappointed, it is fit we should profess and say, *The righteous Lord hath hewn the snares of the ungodly in pieces.*

SERM. XIII.

Jer. xiv. 8.
Ps. xlvi. 5;
Ps. xciv. 14.
Isai. liv. 17.
Ps. iii. 8.

Ps. cxxix. 4. (O. T.)

4 Another like mark of special providence is, the righteousness of the case, or the advantage springing from events unto the maintenance of right, the vindication of innocence, the defence of truth, the encouragement of piety and virtue. God naturally is the judge of right, the guardian of innocence, the patron of truth, and promoter of goodness. *The Lord is a refuge to the oppressed: He is a father of the fatherless, and a judge of the widow: He will maintain the cause of the afflicted, and the right of the poor: He executeth righteousness and judgment for all that are oppressed: He blesseth the righteous, and compasseth him with favour as with a shield: He preserveth the souls of the righteous, and delivereth them out of the hand of the ungodly: All his paths are mercy and truth, unto such as keep his covenant and his testimonies.*

Ps. ix. 9;
lxviii. 5;
x. 14.
Job xxxvi. 15.
Ps. cxl. 12.
Ps. ciii. 6;
ix. 8.
Ps. v. 12;
xcvii. 10;
xxv. 10;
cxlvi. 6, 7.

SERM. XIII.

Whenever therefore right is oppressed, or perilously invaded; when innocence is grossly abused, or sorely beset; when piety is fiercely opposed, or cunningly undermined; when good men for the profession of truth, or the practice of virtue, are persecuted, or grievously threatened with mischief; then may we presume that God is not unconcerned, nor will prove backward to reach forth his succour. And when accordingly we find, that signal aid or deliverance do then arrive; it is most reasonable to suppose, that God particularly hath engaged himself, and exerted his power in their behalf. For, seeing it is his proper and peculiar work, seeing it most becometh and behoveth him to appear in such cases, affording his helpful countenance; when he doeth it, we should be ready to acknowledge it. In such a case, *The hand of the Lord shall be known toward his servants, and his indignation toward his enemies*, saith the Prophet.

Isai. lxvi. 14.

5   Another character is, the correspondence of events to the prayers and desires of good men. For seeing it is the duty and constant practice of good men in all exigences to implore God's help; seeing such prayers have, as St James telleth us, a mighty energy, it being God's property, by them to be moved to impart his powerful assistance; seeing God most plainly and frequently hath declared, and obliged himself by promise, that he will hear them, so as to perform whatever is expedient in their behalf; seeing we have many notable experiments recorded in scripture (as those of Asa, Jehosaphat, Hezekiah, Elias, Daniel, and the like) of prayers bringing down wonderful effects from heaven, with which the testimonies of all times

Ps. lxix. 13; cii. 1, 2; cxl. 6; lvi. 1.
James v. 16.
Ps. lvi. 9; xxxiv. 15; xci. 15; cxlv. 18.
2 Chron. xiv. 11; xx. 6; xxxii. 20.
1 Kings xvii. 1, &c.
2 Kings xix. 15.

and the daily experience of good men do conspire[q]; seeing the presumption of such efficacy is the main ground and encouragement of devotion: we have great reason, whenever events are answerable to such prayers, to ascribe the performance of them to God's hand: great reason we have in such cases to cry out with David, *Now know I that the Lord saveth his anointed; he will hear him from his holy heaven, with the saving strength of his right hand:* just cause have we, according to his pattern, thankfully to acknowledge God's favour in answering our petitions; *The king,* said he, *shall joy in thy strength, O Lord, and in thy salvation how greatly shall he rejoice! For thou hast given him his heart's desire, and hast not withholden the requests of his lips.*

Ps. xx. 6.

Ps. xxi. 1, 2.

Ps. xxx. 2; lxvi. 17; cxviii. 5.

6 Again, the proceedings of God (especially in way of judgment, or of dispensing rewards and punishments) discover their original by their kind and countenance, which usually do bear a near resemblance, or some significant correspondence, to the actions upon which they are grounded. *Punishments,* saith a father, *are the forced offsprings of willing faults*[r]: and answerably, rewards are the children of good deeds: and God, who formeth both, doth commonly order it so, that the children in their complexion and features shall resemble their parents. So that the deserts of men shall

---

[q] Πόσαι μυριάδες ἀνδρῶν καὶ φάλαγγες, ὅσα ἱκετεύοντες μόνον ἡμεῖς, καὶ Θεὸς βουληθεὶς κατειργάσατο;—Greg. Naz. [Or. v. Opp. Tom. I. p. 168 A.]

*How many myriads and squadrons of men were there, whom we only praying, and God willing, discomfited?* saith Nazianzene in reference to the defeating of Julian's design.

[r] Τῶν γὰρ ἑκουσίων κακῶν τὰ ἀκούσια εἰσὶν ἔκγονα.—Joan. Damas. [De fide Orthod. Lib. IV. cap. 19. Opp. Tom. I. p. 289 E.]

often be legible in the recompenses conferred or inflicted on them[s]: not according to the natural result of their practice, but with a comely reference thereto; apt to raise in them a sense of God's hand, and to wring from them an acknowledgment of his equity in so dealing with them. So when humble modesty is advanced to honour, and ambitious confidence is thrown into disgrace; when liberality is blessed with increase, and avarice is cursed with decay of estate; when craft incurreth disappointment, and simplicity findeth good success; when haughty might is shattered, and helpless innocency is preserved; when the calumnious tongue is blistered, the flattering lips are cut off, the blasphemous throat is torn out; when bloody oppressors have blood given them to drink, and come to welter in their own gore; (an accident which almost continually doth happen;) when treacherous men by their own confidants, or by themselves, are betrayed; when retaliations of vengeance are ministered, extorting confessions like to that of Adoni-bezek, *As I have done, so God hath requited me;* deserving such exprobrations as that of Samuel to Agag, *As thy sword hath made women childless, so shall thy mother be childless among women;* grounding such reflections as that concerning Antiochus, *Thus the murderer and blasphemer having suffered most grievously, as he entreated other men, so died he a miserable death;* by such occurrences the finger of God doth point out and indicate itself; they speak themselves immediately to come from that just God, who doth Ἀνταποδιδό-

[s] Καὶ γὰρ αὐτὸς τῆς κολάσεως ὁ τρόπος τῆς ἁμαρτίας τὸν τρόπον μιμεῖται.—Chrys. Ἀνδρ. ιθ´. [Opp. Tom. VI. p. 591.]

ναι, render to men answerably to their doings; who payeth men their due, sometimes in value, often *in specie*, according to the strictest way of reckoning[t]. *He*, as the Prophet saith, *is great in counsel, and mighty in work: for his eyes are open to all the ways of the sons of men, to give every one according to his ways, and according to the fruits of his doings.* This indeed is a sort of administration most conformable to God's exact justice, and most conducible to his holy designs of instructing and correcting offenders. He therefore hath declared it to be his way. *It is* (saith the Prophet, directing his speech to the instruments of divine vengeance upon Babylon) *the vengeance of the Lord: take vengeance upon her; as she hath done, do unto her.* And, *The day of the Lord* (saith another prophet, concerning the like judgment upon Edom) *is near upon all the heathen: as thou hast done, it shall be done unto thee; thy reward shall return upon thine own head.* Thereby doth God mean to declare himself the Judge and Governor of men: For, *I will*, saith he in Ezekiel, *do unto them after their way, and according to their deserts will I judge them; and they shall know that I am the Lord.* Further,

SERM. XIII.

Jer. xxxii. 19.
Ps. lxii. 12.

Jer. l. 15; li. 49.

Obad. 15.
Ezek. xxxv. 15.

Ezek. vii. 27.
Job xxxiv. 11.

7 Another argument of special providence is, the harmonious conspiracy of various accidents to one end or effect. If that one thing should hit advantageously to the production of some considerable event, it may with some plausibility be attributed to fortune, or common providence: yet that

---

[t] Ἃ κατὰ τῶν τοῦ Θεοῦ μαρτύρων πρῶτος ἐφεῦρε κολαστήρια, ταῦθ' ὑπομείναντα δικαιοτάτῃ ψήφῳ.—Euseb. de Vit. Const. I. [59. Tom. I. p. 531.] (de Maximino.)

Is oculos qui eruerat Christianis, ipse visu orbatus.

SERM. XIII.

divers things, having no dependence or coherence one with the other, in divers places, through several times, should all join their forces to compass it, cannot well otherwise than be ascribed to God's special care wisely directing, to his own hand powerfully wielding, those concurrent instruments to one good purpose. For it is beside the nature, it is beyond the reach of fortune, to range various causes in such order. Blind fortune cannot apprehend or catch the seasons and junctures of things, which arise from the motions of causes in their nature indifferent and arbitrary: to it therefore no such event can reasonably be imputed. So to the bringing about our Lord's passion, (that great event, which is so particularly assigned to God's hand,) we may observe the monstrous treachery of Judas, the strange malignity of the Jewish rulers, the prodigious levity of the people, the wonderful easiness of Pilate, with other notable accidents, to have jumped in order thereto. So also, that a malicious traitor should conceive kindness toward any, that he should be mistaken in the object of his favour, that he should express his mind in a way subject to deliberate examination, in terms apt to breed suspicion where the plot was laid; that the counsellors should despise it, and yet not smother it; that the king instantly, by a light darted into his mind, should descry it: these things so happily meeting, may argue God (who mouldeth the hearts, who guideth the hands, who enlighteneth the minds of men) to have been engaged in the detection of this day's black conspiracy.

Such are some characters of special providence;

each of which, singly appearing in any occurrence, would, in a considerate man, breed an opinion thereof; each of them being very congruous to the supposition of it; no such appearances being otherwise so clearly and cleverly explicable, as by assigning the divine hand for their principal cause. But the connection of them all in one event (when divers odd accidents do befall at a seasonable time[u], according to exigency for the public benefit, the preservation of princes, the security of God's people, the protection of right, the maintenance of truth and piety, according to the wishes and prayers of good men, with proper retribution and vengeance upon the wretched designers of mischief; such a complication, I say, of these marks in one event) may thoroughly suffice to raise a firm persuasion, to force a confident acknowledgment concerning God's providence, in any considerate and ingenuous person: it readily will dispose such persons upon any such occasion to say, *This is the Lord's doing, and it is marvellous in our eyes.*

Ps. cxviii. 23.

Notwithstanding therefore any obscurity or intricacy that sometime may appear in the course of Providence, notwithstanding any general exceptions that may by perverse incredulity be alleged against the conduct of things[x]; there are good marks observable, whereby (if we are not very blockish, drowsy, supine, lazy, or froward; if we will consider wisely, with industrious attention and care, with minds pure from vain prejudices, and

---

[u] Vid. Diod. Sic. Lib. xv. p. 482. [Ed. Steph. 1559.]

[x] Εἰ μὴ σημεῖα καὶ θαύματα, ἀλλ' ἐοικότα σημείοις πράγματα, δείγματα τῆς πολλῆς τοῦ Θεοῦ προνοίας καὶ ἀντιλήψεως ἀφάτου.—Chrys. ad Olymp. Ep. I. [Opp. Tom. VII. p. 55.]

corrupt affections) we may discern and understand God's doing. Which to do is the first duty specified in my text: upon which having insisted so largely, I shall (hoping you will favour me with a little patience) briefly touch the rest.

II. It is the duty of us all, upon such remarkable occurrences of providence, *To fear* God: *All men*, it is said, *shall fear*. It is our duty in such cases to be affected with all sorts of fear; with a fear of awful dread, with a fear of hearty reverence, with a fear of sober caution; yea, sometimes with a fear of dejecting consternation. When God doth appear clad with his robes of vengeance and zeal, denouncing and discharging judgment; when he representeth himself *Fearful in praises, terrible in his doings toward the children of men, working terrible things in righteousness;* it should strike into our hearts a dread of his glorious majesty, of his mighty power, of his severe justice, of *His glorious and fearful name:* it should instil into our minds a reverence of his excellent wisdom, his exceeding goodness, his perfect holiness: it should breed in our souls a solicitous care of displeasing and provoking him: it should cause us in our hearts to shake and tremble before him. Then is that of the Psalmist to be put in practice, *Let all the earth fear the Lord: let all the inhabitants of the world stand in awe of him. Tremble, thou earth, at the presence of the Lord, at the presence of the God of Jacob.* Such dispensations are in their nature declarative of those divine attributes which do require such affections: they are set before our eyes to cast us into a very serious and solemn frame; to abash and deter us from offending, by observing the danger of incurring punishments like to those, which we behold inflicted upon presumptuous transgressors; upon those who do heinously violate right, or furiously impugn truth, or profanely despise piety; who earnestly prosecute wicked enterprises; who persecute the friends of God with outrageous violence, or treacherous subtlety. Upon infliction of such punishments, *All the people shall hear, and fear, and do no more presumptuously,* saith God himself, declaring the nature and drift of them. They do plainly demonstrate, that there is no presuming to escape being detected in our close machinations by God's all-seeing eye; being defeated in our bold attempts by God's almighty hand; being sorely chastised for our iniquity by God's impartial judgment. Extremely blind and stupid therefore must we be, or monstrously sturdy and profane, if such experiments of divine power and justice do not awe us, and fright us from sin. *When the lion roareth, who will not fear? When the trumpet is blown in the city, shall not the people be afraid?* Shall he, *At whom the mountains quake, and the hills melt; Whose indignation the nations are not able to abide; At whose wrath the earth doth shake and tremble; At whose reproof the pillars of heaven are astonished;* shall he visibly frown, shall his wrath flame out, shall he shake his rod of exemplary vengeance over us, and we stand void of sense or fear? If so, then surely a brutish dotage, or a gigantic stoutness doth possess us.

III. We are in such cases obliged *To declare God's work:* that is, openly to acknowledge and avow, to applaud and celebrate the special providence of God, with his adorable perfections displayed in such events; to the glory of God's name, in expression of our reverence and gratitude toward him, for the common edification of men; for which uses they greatly serve, to which purposes they are designed. We should not view such providential occurrences, like dumb beasts, with a dull or careless silence, as if we did not mind them, or were not concerned in them: we should not suppress or stifle the knowledge of them in our breasts, as if they were barely matters of private consideration and use; we should not let our observation and resentment of them be fruitless, so as to yield no honour to God, no benefit to man. But we should propagate and convey them into others: in so loud a tone, in so lively a strain we should vent them, as thereby to excite the notice, to inflame the affections of all men within the reach of our voice; provoking them to conspire with us in acknowledgment of God's power and wisdom, in acclamation to his justice and goodness. This is the due improvement of our *Glory*; that peculiar excellency, wherein chiefly (except in our reason) we do surpass all creatures; that, without which our reason itself is more than half unprofitable; that, whereby we put our best member to its best use. For this we have the devout Psalmist's pious resolutions, his exemplary performances, his zealous wishes, his earnest exhortations to guide and move us. *I will speak of the glorious honour of thy majesty, and of thy wondrous works. Men shall speak of the might of thy terrible acts; and I will declare thy greatness. They shall speak of the glory of thy kingdom, and talk of thy power.* So did he signify his resolution. *I have not hid thy righteousness within my heart; I have declared thy faithfulness and thy salvation: I have not concealed thy loving-kindness and thy truth from the great congregation.* So his conscience testified of his practice. *O that men would praise the Lord for his goodness, and for his wonderful works to the children of men: that they would offer the sacrifice of thanksgiving, and declare his works with gladness.* So doth he pour forth his desire. *O clap your hands, all ye people; shout unto God with the voice of triumph. Sing unto the Lord, bless his name: shew forth his salvation from day to day. Declare his glory among the heathen, his wonders among all people. Come and see the works of God. Sing forth the honour of his name, make his praise glorious. O give thanks unto the Lord; call upon his name; make known his deeds among the people.* So doth he summon, so doth he urge us to this practice; and in his deportment, we may see our duty.

IV. It is peculiarly the duty and practice of good men upon such occasions to feel and to express religious joy. *The righteous shall be glad in the Lord.* Good men indeed then have great matter, and much cause, on many accounts, to be glad.

It becometh them to rejoice, as having an universal complacence in God's proceedings, as gratefully relishing all dispensations of Providence. They, as pious, are disposed to bless and praise God for all things incident, and cannot therefore but rejoice; joy being an inseparable companion of gratitude and praise. Hence, *Light is sown for the righteous, and gladness for the upright in heart.* Hence, *The voice of salvation and rejoicing is in* the tabernacles of the righteous. Hence, *Rejoice in the Lord, O ye righteous: for praise is comely for the upright;* is an exhortation backed with a very good reason.

They cannot but find satisfaction in observing God's providence notably discovered, to the confirmation of their faith, and cherishing their hopes; together with the conviction of infidelity, and confusion of profaneness. *Our heart,* saith the Psalmist, *shall rejoice in him, because we have trusted in his holy name. I have trusted in thy mercy; my heart shall rejoice in thy salvation. The righteous shall see it, and rejoice; and all iniquity shall stop her mouth.*

It is to them no small pleasure to behold God's holy perfections illustriously shining forth; and the glory of him (who is the principal object of their love, their reverence, their hope, and confidence) to be conspicuously advanced. *Rejoice,* saith the Psalmist, *O ye righteous, and give thanks at the remembrance of his holiness. Zion heard, and was glad, and the daughters of Judah rejoiced, because of thy judgments, O Lord. For thou, Lord, art high above all the earth.*

It is to them ground of exceeding comfort to receive so clear pledges of God's love and favour, his truth and fidelity, his bounty and munificence toward them, expressed in such watchful care over them, such protection in dangers, such aid in needs, such deliverance from mischiefs vouchsafed to them. Such benefits they cannot receive from God's hand, without that cheerfulness which always doth adhere to gratitude[y]. *I will,* saith David,

---

[y] Cum accipiendum judicaverimus; hilares accipiamus, profitentes gaudium, &c.—Sen. de Benef. ii. 22. Vid. Ibid. 30.

*sing unto the Lord, because he hath dealt bountifully with me. Because thou hast been my helper, therefore in the shadow of thy wings I will rejoice. My lips shall greatly rejoice in thee; and my soul which thou hast redeemed. I will be glad and rejoice in thy mercy: for thou hast considered my trouble, and hast known my soul in adversities. The Lord hath done great things for us, whereof we are glad. Let all those that put their trust in thee rejoice: let them ever shout for joy, because thou defendest them.*

They are also greatly refreshed with apprehension of the happy fruits sprouting from such dispensations of providence; such as are the benefit of mankind, the peace and prosperity of the civil state, the preservation, settlement, enlargement, advancement of God's church, the support of right, the succour of innocence, the maintenance of truth, the encouragement and furtherance of piety; the restraint of violence, the discountenance of error, the correction of vice and impiety. In these things they, as faithful servants of God, and real friends of goodness, as bearing hearty good-will and compassion to mankind, as true lovers of their country, as living and sensible members of the church, cannot but rejoice. Seeing by these things their own best interest, (which is no other than the advantage of goodness,) their chief honour, (which consists in the promotion of divine glory,) their truest content, (which is placed in the prosperity of Sion,) are highly furthered; how can they look on them springing up, without great delight and complacence? O, saith the Psalmist, *sing unto the Lord—for he hath done marvellous things. He hath remembered his mercy and his truth toward the house of Israel: all the ends of the earth have seen the salvation of our God.* And, *Sing, O heavens,* crieth the Prophet, *and be joyful, O earth, and break forth into singing, O ye mountains: for the Lord hath comforted his people, and will have mercy on his afflicted.* And, *When,* saith he, *ye shall see this,* (the comfort of God's people,) *your heart shall rejoice, and your bones shall flourish like an herb: and the hand of the Lord shall be known toward his servants, and his indignation toward his enemies.*

Even in the frustration of wicked designs, attended with severe execution of vengeance on the contrivers and abetters of them, they may have a pleasant satisfaction; they must then yield a cheerful applause to divine justice. *The righteous,* saith the Psalmist, *shall rejoice when he seeth the vengeance:* and, *Let the wicked,* saith he, *perish at the presence of God; but let the righteous be glad, let them rejoice before God, yea let them exceedingly rejoice.* Whence, at God's infliction of judgment upon Babylon, it is said in Jeremy, *Then the heaven and the earth, and all that is therein, shall sing for Babylon;* and at the fall of mystical Babylon, in the Apocalypse it is likewise said, *Rejoice over her, thou heaven, and ye holy apostles and prophets; for God hath avenged you on her.* Further,

V. The next duty prescribed to good men in such case is, *To trust in God,* that is, to have their affiance in God (upon all semblable occasions, in all urgencies of need) settled, improved, and corroborated thereby. This indeed is the proper end, immediately regarding us, of God's special providence, disclosing itself in any miraculous, or in any remarkable way; to nourish in well-disposed minds that faith in God, which is the root of all piety, and ground of devotion. Such experiments are sound arguments to persuade good men, that God doth govern and order things for their best advantage; they are powerful incentives, driving them in all exigencies to seek God's help; they are most convincing evidences, that God is abundantly able, very willing, and ever ready to succour them. *They*, saith the Psalmist, *that know thy name will put their trust in thee: for thou, Lord, hast not forsaken them that seek thee.* And, *I*, saith he, *will abide in thy tabernacle for ever; I will trust in the covert of thy wings: for thou, O God, hast heard my vows: thou hast been a shelter for me, and a strong tower from the enemy.* It is, indeed, a great aggravation of diffidence in God, that, *Having tasted and seen that the Lord is good;* having felt so manifest experience of divine goodness; having received so notable pledges of God's favourable inclination to help us; we yet will not rely upon him. As a friend, who by signal instances of kindness hath assured his good-will, hath great cause of offence, if he be suspected of unwillingness in a needful season to afford his relief: so may God most justly be displeased, when we, (notwithstanding so palpable demonstrations of his kindness,) by distrusting him, do in effect question the sincerity of his friendship, or the constancy of his goodness toward us.

SERM. XIII.

Ps. lxxviii. 7.

Ps. ix. 10.

Ps. lxi. 4, 5, 3; cxv. 9, &c.; cxxx. 7.

Ps. xxxiv. 8.

Ecclus. ii. 10.

VI. Good men upon such occasions should glory: *All the upright in heart shall glory.* Should glory, that is, in contemplation of such providences, feeling sprightly elevations of mind and transports of affection, they should exhibit triumphant demonstrations of satisfaction and alacrity. It becometh them not in such cases to be dumpish or demure; but jocund and crank in their humour, brisk and gay in their looks, pleasantly flippant and free in their speech, jolly and debonair in their behaviour; every way signifying the extreme complacency they take in God's doing, and the full content they taste in their state. They with solemn exultation should triumph in such events, as in victories achieved by the glorious hand of God in their behalf, in approbation of their cause, in favour toward their persons, for their great benefit and comfort. They may (not as proudly assuming to themselves the glory due to God, but as gratefully sensible of their felicity springing from God's favour) *Se jactare, Se laudibus efferre*, (as the Hebrew word doth signify;) that is, in a sort boast, and commend themselves as very happy in their relation to God, by virtue of his protection and aid. They may (not with a haughty insolence, or wanton arrogance, but with a sober confidence and cheerfulness) insult upon baffled impiety[z], by their expressions and demeanour upbraiding the folly, the baseness, the impotency, and wretchedness thereof, in competition with the wisdom, in opposition to the power of God, their friend and patron. For such carriage in such cases we have the practice and the advice of the Psalmist to warrant and

[z] Ps. lii. 6, 7. *The righteous shall laugh at him*, or, *deride him*, in this manner: *Lo, this is the man that made not God his strength.*

direct us. *In God, saith he, we boast all the day long, and praise thy name for ever. Thou, Lord, hast made me glad through thy work; and I will triumph in the works of thy hands. We will rejoice in thy salvation; and in the name of our God we will set up our banners. Glory ye in his holy name: let the heart of them rejoice that seek the Lord. Sing unto him, sing psalms unto him; talk ye of all his wondrous works. Save us, O Lord our God, and gather us from among the heathen, to give thanks unto thy name, and to triumph in thy praise.* Such should be the result (upon us) of God's merciful dispensations toward his people.

SERM.
XIII.

Ps. xliv. 8; xcii. 4.

Ps. xx. 5.

Ps. cv. 3, 2.

Ps. cvi. 47.

I shall only further remark, that the word here used is by the Greek rendered Ἐπαινεθήσονται, *They shall be praised:* which sense the original will bear, and the reason of the case may admit. For such dispensations ever do adorn integrity, and yield commendation to good men. They declare the wisdom of such persons, in adhering to God, in reposing upon God's help, in embracing such courses which God doth approve and bless: they plainly tell how dear such persons are to God; how incomparably happy in his favour, how impregnably safe under his protection; as having his infallible wisdom and his invincible power engaged on their side. This cannot but render them admirable, and their state glorious in the eyes of all men; inducing them to profess with the Psalmist, *Happy is the people, which is in such a case; yea, happy is that people, whose God is the Lord.* And of such a people, that declaration from the same mouth is verified, *In thy name shall they rejoice all the day long, and in thy righteousness shall they be*

Ps. cxvi. 3; cxxv. 1, &c.; cxxxviii. 1, &c.

Ps. cxliv. 15; xxxiii. 12.

Ps. lxxxix. 16, 17.

*exalted: for thou art the glory of their strength, and in thy favour their horn shall be exalted.*

Such are the duties suggested in our text, as suiting these occasions, when God in a special manner hath vouchsafed to protect his people, or to rescue them from imminent mischiefs, by violent assault or by fraudulent contrivance levelled against them.

I should apply these particulars to the present case solemnized by us: but I shall rather recommend the application to your sagacity, than further infringe your patience, by spending thereon so many words as it would exact. You do well know the story, which by so many years repetition hath been impressed on your minds: and by reflecting thereon:

You will easily discern, how God, in the seasonable discovery of this execrable plot, (the masterpiece of wicked machinations ever conceived in human brain, or devised on this side hell, since the foundation of things,) in the happy deliverance of our nation and church from the desperate mischiefs intended toward them, in the remarkable protection of right and truth, did signalize his providence.

You will be affected with hearty reverence toward the gracious Author of our salvation, and with humble dread toward the just awarder of vengeance upon those miscreant wretches, who digged this pit, and fell into it themselves.

You will be ready with pious acknowledgment and admiration of God's mercy, his justice, his wisdom, to declare and magnify this notable work done by him among us.

You must needs feel devout resentments of joy for the glory arising to God, and the benefits accruing to us, in the preservation of God's anointed, our just sovereign, with his royal posterity: in the freeing our country from civil broils, disorders, and confusions; from the yokes of usurpation and slavery; from grievous extortions and rapines; from bloody persecutions and trials, with the like spawn of disastrous and tragical consequences, by this design threatened upon it: in upholding our church (which was so happily settled, and had so long gloriously flourished) from utter ruin: in securing our profession of God's holy truth, the truly catholic faith of Christ, (refined from those drossy alloys, wherewith the rudeness and sloth of blind times, the fraud of ambition and covetous designers, the pravity of sensual and profane men had embased and corrupted it,) together with a pure worship of God, an edifying administration of God's Word and Sacraments, a comely, wholesome, and moderate discipline, conformable to divine prescription and primitive example; in rescuing us from having impious errors, scandalous practices, and superstitious rites, with merciless violence obtruded upon us: in continuing therefore to us the most desirable comforts and conveniences of our lives.

You further considering this signal testimony of divine goodness, will thereby be moved to hope and confide in God for his gracious preservation from the like pernicious attempts against the safety of our prince and welfare of our country, against our peace, our laws, our religion; especially from Romish zeal and bigotry, (that mint of woful factions and combustions, of treasonable conspiracies, of barbarous massacres, of horrid assassinations, of intestine rebellions, of foreign invasions, of savage tortures and butcheries, of holy leagues and pious frauds, through Christendom, and particularly among us,) which as it without reason damneth, so it would by any means destroy all that will not crouch thereto.

You will, in fine, with joyous festivity, glory and triumph in this illustrious demonstration of God's favour toward us; so as heartily to join in those due acclamations of blessing and praise:

*Blessed be the Lord, who hath not given us as a prey to their teeth. Our soul is escaped as a bird out of the snare of the fowlers: the snare is broken, and we are escaped.* [Ps. cxxiv. 6, 7; lxviii. 32.]

*Alleluiah; Salvation, and glory, and power unto the Lord our God: for true and righteous are his judgments.* [Rev. xix. 1, 2.]

*Great and marvellous are thy works, O Lord God Almighty; just and true are thy ways, O thou King of saints.* [Rev. xv. 3.]

*Blessed be the Lord God of Israel, who only doeth wondrous things. And blessed be his glorious name for ever: and let the whole earth be filled with his glory. Amen, and Amen.* [Ps. lxxii. 18, 19.]

# SERMON XIV.

## A CONSECRATION SERMON[a].

### PSALM CXXXII. 16.

*I will also clothe her priests with salvation.*

THE context runs thus: *The Lord hath sworn in truth unto David; he will not turn from it; Of the fruit of thy body will I set upon thy throne. If thy children will keep my covenant and my testimony that I shall teach them, their children shall also sit upon thy throne for evermore. For the Lord hath chosen Zion; he hath desired it for his habitation. This is my rest for ever: here will I dwell; for I have desired it. I will abundantly bless her provision: I will satisfy her poor with bread.* I WILL ALSO CLOTHE HER PRIESTS WITH SALVATION: *and her saints shall shout aloud for joy. There will I make the horn of David to bud,* &c.

If all, not only inaugurations of persons, but dedications even of inanimate things to some extraordinary use, hath been usually attended with especial significations of joy and festival solemnity; with great reason the consecration of a person to so high and sacred a function, as that of a Christian bishop, (that is, of a prince, or principal pastor

[a] Henry the Seventh's Chapel, July 4, 1663, at the Bishop of Man his consecration.

in God's church,) requires most peculiar testimonies of our gratulation and content: the face of things ought then to be serene and cheerful: the thoughts of men benign and favourable: the words comfortable and auspicious, that are uttered upon such occasion. And that ours at present should be such, the subject, as well as the season, of our discourse doth require; words few, but pregnant, and affording ample matter for our best affections to work upon: and which more particularly will engage us, both to a hearty thankfulness for past benefits, and to a confident expectation of future blessings; while they acquaint us with the ancient exhibition of a gracious promise, remind us of the faithful performance thereof hitherto, and assure us of its certain accomplishment for the future. The occasion whereof was this: King David, moved by a devout inclination to promote God's honour, and benefit the church, had vowed to build a magnificent temple, imploring God's propitious concurrence with, and approbation of, his design. Whereupon Almighty God not only declares his acceptance of that pious resolution, but rewards it with a bountiful promise, consisting of two parts; one conditional, relating to David's children and posterity, that they, in an uninterrupted succession, should for ever enjoy the royal dignity, in case they did constantly persist in observing his covenant, and the testimonies that he should teach them; the other more absolute, that, however, what he chiefly intended concerning God's established worship and the perpetual welfare of the church, God would have an especial care that it should fully and certainly be accomplished: that

*A Consecration Sermon.*

SERM. XIV.

he would for ever fix his residence in Sion; that he would protect and prosper it, and all that did belong thereto; especially those that did most need his favour and assistance, the poor, the priests, and the saints, (or *Gentle ones*[b].) This is briefly the importance of the general promise, wherein is comprehended that particular one whereon we are to treat: and in which we may observe,

1 The Promiser, *I*.

2 The persons who are especially concerned in the promise, *Her priests*.

3 The thing promised, *Clothing with salvation*.

I. I say, the Promiser, *I*: that is, the Lord; the most true, the most constant, the most powerful God; most true and sincere in the declaration of his purpose, most constant and immutable in the prosecution, most powerful and uncontrollable in the perfect execution thereof: *Whose words are right, and all whose works are done in truth: Who will not break his covenant, nor alter the thing that is gone out of his lips: Whose counsel shall stand, and who will do all his pleasure.* These glorious attributes and perfections of his, so often celebrated in holy writ, do ground our reliance upon all God's promises, and do oblige us, notwithstanding the greatest improbabilities or difficulties objected, to believe the infallible performance of this.

Ps. xxxiii. 4; lxxxix. 34.

Isai. xlvi. 10.

II. The persons whom the promise mainly regards, *Her priests*. *Priests*, that is, persons peculiarly devoted to, and employed in, sacred matters; distinguished expressly from the *Poor*,

[b] חֲסִידֵי

SERM. XIV.

*(that is, other meek and humble persons;)* and from the *Saints*, *(that is, all other good and religious men.)* And, *Her* priests; that is, the priests of Sion: of that Sion which *The Lord hath chosen;* which *He hath desired for his* permanent *habitation;* which he hath resolved to *Rest* and *reside in for ever.* Whence it plainly enough follows, that the priests and pastors of the Christian church are hereby, if not solely, yet principally designed. Which interpretation, because it is in a manner the foundation of our subsequent discourse, and by some it may perhaps not be readily admitted, I shall endeavour further to confirm by these few arguments.

Contra 2 Chron. vii. 21.

1 Because the covenant here mentioned is not, as to the main parts thereof, of a conditional or temporary nature, but absolute and perpetual; and must therefore be understood to respect the Christian church: (that of the Jews being long since rejected, their temple demolished, their Sion derelinquished.) For although one particular contained therein, concerning the continual succession of David's posterity in the regal authority over Israel, hath a condition explicitly annexed; (and, consequently, the effects depending upon performance of that condition were contingent and mutable;) yet all the rest of this covenant (or promise) is conceived in terms peremptory, and expressly importing perpetuity. *This is my rest for ever,* עֲדֵי־עַד, that is, as the Greek translators render it, Εἰς αἰῶνα αἰῶνος, *(In seculum seculi,)* that is, to the end of this world; as Εἰς αἰῶνας τῶν αἰώνων denotes the end of all worlds, or the most perfect sempiternity. And that it doth really in this case de-

2 Chron. vii. 16.

## A Consecration Sermon. 489

note a proper and unlimited perpetuity, is also evident by those explications thereof in the eighty-ninth Psalm, where the very same covenant is, as to some parts thereof, more largely recorded. *Once have I sworn by my holiness, that I will not lie unto David: his seed shall endure for ever, and his throne as the sun before me: it shall be established for ever as the moon, and as a faithful witness in heaven.* No words can express more fully a perpetual duration, or at least one coextended with the duration of the world, than those do. And the prophet Jeremy, referring also to this very covenant, and particularly to this very clause thereof, thus expresses the matter: *Thus saith the Lord; If you can break my covenant of the day, and my covenant of the night, and that there should not be day and night in their season; then may also my covenant be broken with David my servant, that he should not have a son to reign upon his throne; and with the Levites the priests, my ministers.* But further,

2 The completion of this individual promise is both by the prophets foretold, and expressed by the evangelists, to appertain to the times of the gospel. Ye heard even now the words of Jeremy, which are by him applied to those times, when God would cause the *Branch of righteousness* (that is, Jesus of Nazareth, our blessed Saviour) *to grow up unto David, who should execute judgment and righteousness in the land. In those days,* saith he further, *shall Judah be saved, and Jerusalem shall dwell safely: and this is the name wherewith she shall be called,* (or rather, *which he shall be called,* as not only the vulgar Latin and the Greek interpreters,

SERM. XIV.

Ps. lxxxix. 35, 36, 37.

Jer. xxxiii. 20, 21.
2 Chron. vii. 16.

Jer. xxxiii. 15.

Ver. 16.

490    *A Consecration Sermon.*

SERM. XIV.

but the Chaldee also read it,) THE LORD OUR RIGHTEOUSNESS. Likewise in the fifty-fifth of Isaiah, God thus invites the Gentiles: *Incline your ear, and come unto me; hear, and your soul shall live: and I will make an everlasting covenant with you, even the sure mercies of David:* that is, I will ratify that everlasting covenant, which, in your behalf, I once made with David, and will confer on you those favours which I faithfully promised him; relating to this very promise also. For both in Solomon's prayer, which in all probability was indited about the same time, and upon the same occasion with this Psalm, and in the eighty-ninth Psalm, the benefits of the same covenant are called *The mercies of David. O Lord God, turn not away the face of thine anointed, remember the mercies of David thy servant*, saith Solomon: and, *My mercy*, saith God, *will I keep with him for evermore, and my covenant shall stand fast with him:* and, *My faithfulness and my mercy shall be with him;* that is, *My faithful (or sure) mercy;* Τὰ ὅσια τὰ πιστά, as the LXX. and St Paul with them in the Acts, render this place of Isaiah. And in the song of Zachary, we have one passage of this promise cited and applied to the times of the gospel: *Blessed be the Lord God of Israel, who hath visited and redeemed his people; and hath raised up a horn of salvation in the house of his servant David; as he spake by the mouth of his holy prophets:* viz. by the mouth of this prophetical Psalmist here, where it is said, *There will I make the horn of David to bud;* and in the parallel Psalm, *In my name shall his horn be exalted.* To omit those many places where our Saviour, in correspondence to this pro-

Isai. lv. 3.

2 Chron. vi. 42.

Ps. lxxxix. 28.

Ver. 24.

Acts xiii. 34.

Luke i. 68, 69, 70.

Ps. lxxxix. 24.

mise, is affirmed to *Possess the throne of his father David*, and to *Rule over the house of Jacob for ever.* Moreover,

SERM. XIV.

Vide Luke i. 32. edit. Curcel.

3 That by the Sion here mentioned is not chiefly meant that material mountain in Judæa, but rather that mystical Rock of divine grace and evangelical truth, upon which the Christian church, the only everlasting temple of God, is unmoveably seated, is very probable, (or rather, manifestly certain,) by the Prophets' constant acception thereof in this sense, when they assign the character of perpetual durability thereto. As in Isaiah, where he thus prophesies of the Christian church: *The sons also of them that afflicted thee shall come bending unto thee, and all they that despised thee shall bow themselves down at the soles of thy feet; and they shall call thee, The city of the Lord, The Sion of the Holy One of Israel. Whereas thou hast been forsaken and hated, so that no man went through thee; I will make thee an eternal excellency, a joy of many generations. Thou shalt also suck the milk of the Gentiles, and shalt suck the breasts of kings,* &c. And the Prophet Micah, speaking of *The last days,* (that is, of the evangelical times, when *The mountain of the house of the Lord should be established in the top of the mountains,*) saith thus: *And I will make her that halted, a remnant; and her that was cast far off, a strong nation: and the Lord shall reign over them in mount Sion from henceforth even for ever.* And the Prophet Joel, speaking of the same times, (when *God would pour out his spirit upon all flesh,*) hath these words: *So shall ye know, that I am the Lord your God, dwelling in Sion, my holy mountain: then shall*

Isai. lx. 14, 15, 16.

Mic. iv. 1.

Ver. 7.

Joel ii. 28; iii. 17.

*Jerusalem be holy, and there shall no strangers pass through her any more.* All which places no man can reasonably doubt, and all Christians do firmly consent to respect the Christian church. To which we may add that passage of the author to the Hebrews, *But ye are come unto mount Sion, and unto the city of the living God, the heavenly Jerusalem;* that is, to the Christian church.

4 The manner of this covenant's delivery, and confirmation by the Divine oath, argues the inconditionate, irreversible, and perpetual constitution thereof: for to God's most absolute and immutable decrees this most august and solemn confirmation doth peculiarly agree. So the Apostle to the Hebrews seems to intimate: *Wherein,* saith he, *God, willing more abundantly to demonstrate the immutability of his counsel,* (Ἐπιδεῖξαι τὸ ἀμετάθετον τῆς βουλῆς αὐτοῦ) *interposed an oath.*

We may therefore, I suppose, upon these grounds, solidly and safely conclude, that this promise doth principally belong, and shall therefore infallibly be made good, to the Christian priesthood; to those who, in the Christian church, by offering spiritual sacrifices of praise and thanksgiving, by directing and instructing the people in the knowledge of the evangelical law, by imploring for and pronouncing upon them the divine benedictions, do bear analogy with, and supply the room of, the Jewish priesthood.

From which discourse we may, by the way, deduce this corollary: That the title of priest, although it did (as most certainly it doth not) properly and primarily signify a Jewish sacrificer, (or slaughterer of beasts,) doth yet nowise deserve that reproach, which is by some, inconsiderately, (not to say profanely,) upon that mistaken ground, commonly cast upon it; since the holy scripture itself, we see, doth here, even in that sense (most obnoxious to exception) ascribe it to the Christian pastors. And so likewise doth the Prophet Isaiah; *And I will also take of them for priests and for Levites, saith the Lord:* speaking (as the context plainly declares) of the Gentiles, which should be converted and aggregated to God's church. And the Prophet Jeremiah: *Neither shall the priests the Levites want a man before me to offer burnt-offerings, and to do sacrifice continually.* Which prophecy also evidently concerns the same time and state of things, of which the prophet Malachi thus foretells: *For, from the rising of the sun to the going down of the same, my name shall be great among the Gentiles; and in every place incense shall be offered to my name, and a pure offering.* It were desirable, therefore, that men would better consider, before they entertain such groundless offences, or pass so uncharitable censures upon either words, or persons, or things. But I proceed to the

III. particular, which is the matter of the promise, *Clothing with salvation.* Where we may observe,

First: that the usual metaphor of being clothed doth in the sacred dialect denote a complete endowment with, a plentiful enjoyment of, or an entire application to, that thing, or quality, with which a person is said to be clothed. So is God himself said to be *Clothed with majesty and strength.* And David prays, that they might be *Clothed with shame and dishonour, that did magnify themselves*

SERM. XIV.

Isai. lxvi. 21.

Jer. xxxiii. 18.

Mal. i. 11.

Ps. xciii. 1.
Ps. xxxv. 26; cix. 29.

*against him.* And in Ezekiel, *The princes of the isles,* being amazed by the ruin of Tyre, are said *to clothe themselves with trembling.* And that bitter adversary of David did *Clothe himself with cursing, as with a garment.* And Job avouched of himself, *I put on righteousness, and it clothed me; my judgment was a robe and a diadem.* And St Peter advises us to *Put on,* or to *be clothed with, humility.* Finally, Isaiah introduces our Saviour speaking thus: *I will greatly rejoice in the Lord, my soul shall be joyful in my God: for he hath clothed me with the garments of salvation, he hath covered me with the robe of righteousness; as a bridegroom decketh himself with ornaments, and as a bride adorneth herself with her jewels.* So that (as by these instances we may discern) to be clothed with salvation is to be perfectly endowed therewith; to be invested with it as with a garment, which wholly encloseth and covereth the body, so that no part is left unguarded and unadorned thereby.

Secondly: But now what is that salvation with which the priests of Sion shall be thus clothed? I answer: Salvation, when it is put absolutely, and not conjoined with any particular object, (or term from which,) doth in the Hebrew language properly signify a deliverance from, or remotion of, all sorts of inconvenience; and, consequently, an affluence of all good things; and, in effect, the same which other languages call felicity and prosperity, or design by terms equivalent to those: the Hebrews having hardly any other word so properly correspondent to those, as this word, salvation. Whence that title of Saviour[c], and the God of sal-

---

[c] Deus Σωτήρ sæpe Platoni.

vation, so often attributed to Almighty God, imports as much as, the Dispenser of all good gifts; the great Benefactor, Assister, and Protector of men: and to save is promiscuously used for, to relieve the needy, to comfort the sorrowful; to restore the sick to his health, the prisoner to his liberty, the captive to his country; to defend the weak from injury, and the humble from contempt; to deliver the distressed from imminent danger, the innocent from unjust condemnation, the slandered from undeserved reproach: in a word, all the effects of God's goodness and power, the whole work of the Divine providence and beneficence, are hereby expressed.

SERM. XIV.

We will recite one or two of those many places which confirm this notion, *Surely his salvation is nigh them that fear him, that glory may dwell in our land.* *His salvation is nigh;* that is, his loving care attends upon them, to assist and preserve them; which is thus otherwise expressed: *He will fulfil the desire of them that fear him; he will hear their cry, and will save them.* And again, *The Lord taketh pleasure in his people; he will beautify the meek with salvation:* that is, he will, by his good providence, dispose them into a convenient and decent condition of life. And again, *It is he that giveth salvation unto kings;* that is, by whose gracious disposal they prosper, and are preserved in dignity, plenty, and safety.

Ps. lxxxv. 9.

Ps. cxlv. 19.

Ps. cxlix. 4.

Ps. cxliv. 10.

I will not, by citation of places, labour to confirm so obvious a notion: it may suffice for that purpose, that the supreme accomplishment of all happiness, the enjoyment of perfect bliss in heaven, is, in agreement with this Jewish acception of the word, most commonly styled salvation. But I must add, that, whereas salvation may relate either to the outward estate of a man's body, life, and fortunes, or to the internal dispositions of the mind; to our present condition in this world, or to our future and eternal estate: it doth seem here (I say not, to exclude the latter altogether, yet) more directly and principally to respect the former, viz. that external and temporal welfare, which is conspicuous and visible in this world. My reason is, because the other parts of this prophetical promise do, in their most natural acception, signify that outward prosperity, wherewith God would vouchsafe to bless his church: that abundant benediction of her store, that satisfying her poor with bread, that joyful exaltation of her saints, that clothing her enemies with shame, being expressions properly denoting a state of external good weal and comfort; and, in consonance to them, require that we thus likewise understand this phrase; the priests being also questionless designed to partake in this glorious felicity of the church. Which is also confirmed by other prophecies of the same tenor and intention: as particularly that in Jeremy concerning the recollection of Israel, and redemption of the spiritual Sion; it is said, *I will satiate the soul of the priests with fatness, and my people shall be satisfied with my goodness, saith the Lord.*

Now, although we may adventure safely to interpret the declarations of the Divine favour according to the most comprehensive sense of which the words are capable, where they are conceived; (it being the manner of the immensely good God, to exceed, rather than to be deficient, in the performance of his word; and to surpass the expectations he hath raised in us, than anywise to disappoint them :) yet, however, the least we can imagine here promised to the priests of Sion will comprehend these three things:

1 A free and safe condition of life: that they be not exposed to continual dangers of ruin, of miserable sufferance, or remediless injury: that the benefits of peace, and law, and public protection shall particularly appertain to them; so that their adversaries (if any they happen to have) shall not be incited, by hope of reward or impunity, to hurt their persons, rifle their goods, disturb their quiet; but that they shall enjoy good degrees of security, liberty, and tranquillity in this world.

2 A provision of competent subsistence for them: that their condition of life be not wholly necessitous, or very penurious, destitute of convenient accommodations, or depending altogether for them upon the arbitrary benevolences of men, which is, at best, but a more plausible kind of beggary; but that they shall be furnished with such reasonable supplies, as are requisite to encourage them in the cheerful performance of their duty.

3 A suitable degree of respect, and so high a station among men, as may commend them to general esteem, and vindicate them from contempt: that they be not reputed among the dregs and refuse of the people; that their persons be not base and despicable, their names made the objects of vulgar obloquy, their functions become prostitute to profane irrision; but that some considerable authority, some more than ordinary regard and

veneration accrue unto them from the high relations which they bear, and from the sacred business which they manage.

All this at east (according to the most moderate interpretation of the phrase) that abundant salvation doth imply, wherewith God hath promised to invest the priests of Sion.

We may therefore presume, or rather not presume, but confidently rely upon, and comfort ourselves in the expectation of, God's faithful continuance to fulfil this promise. We may assure ourselves, that neither the secret envy of them who repine at those encouragements which God's providence hath conferred on priests, nor the open malice of those that furiously oppugn their welfare, shall ever prevail to overwhelm them with extreme misery, penury, or disgrace; since no endeavour of earth or hell can ever be able to reverse this everlasting decree of Heaven, or to defeat that irresistible power which is engaged to its execution. No inferior force can denude them of that salvation, wherewith the Supreme Truth hath promised to clothe them.

Which confidence of ours may be improved, by considering the reasons that might induce Almighty God to resolve, and promise thus favourably in behalf of his priests. (For, though we cannot penetrate the incomprehensible depths of the divine counsel, nor should ever peremptorily conclude concerning the determinate reasons of his actions: yet, when the wisdom of his proceedings doth clearly approve itself to our understandings, we ought readily to acknowledge it, and humbly to praise him for it.) Now the reasons why divine

Providence should undertake to preserve the priesthood in safety, to procure for them liberal maintenance, and to raise them above a state of scorn and infamy, may be especially these three:

1 It concerns God's honour.

2 The good of the church requires so.

3 Equity and the reason of the case exacts it.

In prosecuting which heads of discourse, I shall not seem to you, I hope, to transgress the rules of modesty or decency. There be certain seasons, wherein, confessedly, it is not only excusable, but expedient also, to commend one's self; as when a man is falsely accused, or unjustly afflicted. And with greater reason sometime, men are allowed to praise the country where they were born and bred, the family to which they are allied, the society to which they are more especially related. And if, at this time, I assume the like liberty, the occasion, I hope, will apologize for me. It becomes not me to be an adviser, much less a reprover, in this audience: may I therefore, with your favourable permission, presume to be a commender, or, if you please, a pleader for the welfare of this sacred order, although myself an unworthy and inconsiderable member thereof. I say therefore,

I. God's honour is concerned in the safe, comfortable, and honourable estate of his priests; and that upon account of those manifold relations, whereby they stand allied, appropriated, and devoted to himself.

They are in a peculiar manner his servants. *The servant of the Lord*, saith St Paul, *must not strive, but be gentle unto all men, apt to teach. The servant of the Lord;* who's that? are not all men

2 Tim. ii. 24.

God's servants? is not he Lord of all? Yes; but a Christian priest, such as Timothy was, is by way of excellency so styled. All men owe subjection, obedience, and homage to God: but the priests are (his Ὑπηρέται, his Λειτουργοί) his ministers, his officers, his immediate attendants, his domestics, as it were, and menial servants; that approach his person, that tread the courts of his house, that wear his proper badges, that are employed in his particular business. And is it then for God's honour, to suffer them to be abused, to want convenient sustenance, to live in a mean and disgraceful condition? Would it not redound to the discredit of an earthly prince, to permit, that the attendants on his person, the officers of his court, the executors of his decrees, should have the least injury offered them, should fare scantly or coarsely, should appear in a sordid garb? Are they not therefore, by especial privileges, guarded from such inconveniences? And shall the great King and Lord of all the world be deemed less provident for, less indulgent (not to say less just) unto his servants? servants, I say, and those not of the lowest rank, nor appointed to the vilest drudgeries; but such as are employed in the most honourable charges, and are intrusted with his most especial concernments.

They are his stewards. *A bishop,* saith St Paul, *must be blameless, as the steward of God.* If the church be Οἶκος Θεοῦ, *God's house,* or *family,* as it is called, and the priests the Οἰκονόμοι, the stewards of that house, the comptrollers of that family; it is surely no mean station they obtain therein. The distribution of his bread, (the bread of life, his holy word,) and the dispensation of his most precious goods, (the holy mysteries,) are committed to their care and prudence. *Who then*, saith our Saviour, *is that faithful and wise steward, whom his Lord shall make ruler over his household, to give them their portion of meat in due season?* Who but the priests, who are therefore styled both Προεστῶτες, Ἡγούμενοι, Κυβερνήσεις, (*Presidents, Guides, Rulers,*) and Ποιμένες, (*Feeders*, or *Pastors,*) of the church.

SERM. XIV.

Luke xii. 42.

1 Tim. v. 17. Heb. xiii. 7. 1 Cor. xii. 28. Eph. iv. 11.

Yea, they are Οἰκοδόμοι also, the builders of that house, founding it by initial conversion, rearing it by continued instruction, covering and finishing it by sacramental obsignation of divine grace. *As a wise architect*, saith St Paul, *I have laid the foundation, and another builds upon it.*

1 Cor. iii. 10.

They are Θεοῦ συνεργοί, *Cooperators with God;* that manage his business, and drive on his designs: the solicitors of his affairs, the masters of his requests: his Κήρυκες, *Heralds*, that publish his decrees, denounce his judgments, proclaim his pardons and acts of grace unto his subjects; that blazon his titles, and defend his rightful authority in the world: yea, his ministers of state; the ministers (I say, *absit invidia*) of his most glorious spiritual kingdom; (which is peculiarly denominated the kingdom of God;) the orderly administration of which, its advancement, its preservation, and its enlargement, are especially commended to their diligence and fidelity.

1 Cor. iii. 9.

1 Tim. ii. 7. 2 Tim. i. 11.

They are, lastly, God's ambassadors, delegated by him to treat of peace, and solicit a fair correspondence between heaven and earth. *Now then*, saith St Paul, *we are ambassadors for Christ, as though God did beseech you by us: we pray you in*

Mal. ii. 7.

2 Cor. v. 20.

*Christ's stead, be ye reconciled to God. As though God did beseech you by us*: see, they manage God's concernments, and in a manner represent his person. At least, if the apostles were more properly God's ambassadors, the present ministers of Religion are his agents, and residents here among men, designed to pursue the same negociations commenced by them. Now you know by the Law of Nations, and common consent of all men, all manner of security, good entertainment, and civil respect hath been ever acknowledged due to ambassadors, and public ministers: their employment hath been esteemed honourable, their persons held sacred and inviolable; and whatsoever discourtesy hath been shewed unto, or outrage committed upon them, hath been interpreted done to him from whom they derive their commission, whose person they represent. And so truly the bad usage of God's priests, if not directly and immediately, does yet really and truly, according to moral estimation, terminate on God himself, and reflect on his honour, and prejudice his Religion; a due regard to which cannot be maintained, without proportionable respect to the ministers thereof. The basest of the people may serve to be priests to Jeroboam's calves, but not become the ministry of the God of Israel.

Do we not see the reverence of civil government upheld more by the specious circumstances, than by the real necessity thereof; by the magnificent retinue, and splendid ornaments of princely dignity, than by the eminent benefits of peace and justice springing thence? Shall not (not only the greatest inward worth, but) the highest nobility, if basely attired, badly attended, slenderly accommodated, pass unregarded, yea disregarded by us? men being generally either unable to discern, or unwilling to acknowledge excellency divested of sensible lustre. Religion therefore must be well habited, or it will be ill respected: the priests must wear a comely (if not a costly) livery, or God their master's reputation will be impaired in popular fancy.

Consider David's reasoning; *Lo, I dwell in a house of cedars, but the ark of the covenant of the Lord remaineth under curtains;* and compare such discourse therewith as this; and judge candidly, whether they have not some parity: Lo, my attendants are clad with the finest purple, God's ministers are covered with the coarsest sackcloth; my people surfeit with dainties, his servants pine away for scarcity; my courtiers are respectfully saluted, his priests scornfully derided; no man dare offend mine, every one may trample on his officers.

And lest we should imagine God himself altogether void of such resentments, or such comparisons impertinent, consider that disdainful expression of his; *If ye offer the blind for sacrifice, is it not evil? and if ye offer the lame and sick, is it not evil? Offer it now to thy governor; will he be pleased with thee, or accept thy person? saith the Lord of hosts.* The same testimonies of respect that we shew our governors, God, it seems, expects from us in all kinds, and may reasonably much greater.

Nor is it a matter of slight consideration, how plentiful provision, in the policy devised and constituted by God himself, was made for the priests;

how God assumes the immediate patronage of them, and appropriates the matter of their sustenance unto himself. *The priests, saith the Law, the Levites, and all the tribe of Levi, shall have no part nor inheritance with Israel: they shall eat the offerings of the Lord made by fire, and his inheritance. Therefore shall they have no inheritance among their brethren: the Lord is their inheritance.* So that then, it seems, no man could withhold any part of the priests' maintenance, without sacrilegious encroachment on God's own right, and robbing him of his due: (which is the greatest security of an estate imaginable.) How likewise (next to the prince) the highest dignity and authority was then conferred on the priests: to them the interpretation of law, to them the decision of doubtful cases did appertain; with severe injunctions to comply with their determinations. See how the business is inculcated. *If there arise a matter too hard for thee, between blood and blood, between plea and plea, between stroke and stroke, being matters of controversy within thy gates; then shalt thou arise and get thee up into the place which the Lord thy God shall choose: and thou shalt come unto the priests the Levites, and unto the judge that shall be in those days, and inquire; and they shall shew thee the sentence of judgment. And thou shalt do according to the sentence which they of that place, which the Lord shall choose, shall shew thee; and thou shalt observe to do according to all that they inform thee. According to the sentence of the law which they shall teach thee, and according to the judgment which they shall tell thee, thou shalt do: thou shalt not decline from the sentence, which they shall shew thee, to the right hand, nor to the left. And the man that will do presumptuously, and will not hearken to the priest, that standeth to minister there before the Lord thy God, even that man shall die, and thou shalt put away evil from Israel.* Observe with how eminent a power God then thought fit to endow his priests[d].

And though we are not in all cases obliged punctually to follow those political prescriptions; yet is the reason of them perpetual, and the example venerable: especially since the custom of all times, and the reason of all the world, doth in a sort conspire to back it.

The first priest we meet with in scripture is Melchizedek; a king also; and such a one, as the patriarch Abraham, (a prince also himself, and, what is somewhat more, just then a conqueror,) in the midst of his triumphal heights, was not ashamed to acknowledge his superior, to honour him with a tribute of his spoils, and to receive a benediction from him. The next (if I mistake not) is Potipherah, the priest of On, whose daughter was not thought by the king of Egypt an unequal match for Joseph, his chief favourite, and the next in dignity to himself in that flourishing kingdom. (Though such an alliance would perhaps be thought derogatory to the worships of our days.) The third is Revel, or Jethro, priest of Midian, the father-in-law likewise of the illustrious Moses; a man as of approved wisdom, so doubtless of considerable

---

[d] Καὶ γὰρ ἐπόπται πάντων, καὶ δικασταὶ τῶν ἀμφισβητουμένων, καὶ κολασταὶ τῶν κατεγνωσμένων οἱ ἱερεῖs ἐτάχθησαν, saith Josephus. [Con. Apion. Lib. II. cap. 21. Opp. Tom. II. p. 485.] *The priests were constituted supervisors of all things, and judges of controversies, and punishers of offences.*

dignity too. And the next to him (in order of story) is the venerable Aaron, no meaner a man, than the brother of him who was *King in Jeshurun*. Thus all nations, wise and ignorant, civil and barbarous, were by one common instinct (as it were) of natural reason prompted, by conferring extraordinary privileges of honour and convenience on their priests, to express their reverence of the Deity, and their affection to religion[e].

I will not ransack the closets of antiquity, nor with needless ostentation produce the Egyptian Hierophantæ, the Persian Magi, the Gaulish Druids, the Caliphs, and Muftis of other nations, to shew what pre-eminences of respect they enjoyed, what powerful sway they bore in their respective countries[f]; how the most weighty affairs, both of peace and war, were commonly directed by their oracular dictates. It shall suffice to observe, that the gallant Romans, (whose devout zeal to religion Polybius[g] himself, no especial friend of theirs, could not forbear to admire and applaud,) I say, that the most wise and valiant Romans did set so high a value upon the priestly order, that if their principal magistrates (the Prætors and Consuls themselves) did casually meet with one of Vesta's priests, they caused immediately those dreadful rods, the ensigns of their authority, to submit[h]; and they themselves

---

[e] Οὔτε γὰρ γεωργὸν, οὔτε βάναυσον ἱερέα καταστατέον· ὑπὸ γὰρ τῶν πολιτῶν πρέπει τιμᾶσθαι τοὺς θεούς.—Aristot. Pol. VII. 9. [9.]

[f] Porph. περὶ Ἀποχ. (de Abstin.) Lib. IV. § 16. Cæs. de Bell. Gal. Lib. VI. [cap. 13.]

[g] [Lib. VI. 56, 7.]

Πάντα τὰ πράγματα Ῥωμαίοις εἰς τὸν Θεὸν ἀνήγετο.—Plut. in Marcello. [Opp. Tom. IV. p. 546. Ed. Steph.]

[h] M. A. Sen. Controv. [Lib. I. p. 94. Ed. Var. Amstel. 1672.]

respectfully gave place, as if they meant to confess those priests in a manner their betters. Nor did they among them of the most noble extraction, and of the highest dignity in the commonwealth, (even after many glorious exploits achieved by them,) scornfully disdain, but did rather ambitiously affect to be admitted into the college of priests: insomuch that, after the dissolution of the Republic, the Emperors thought good to assume the Pontifical dignity to themselves, supposing the office too honourable, the title too magnificent for a subject. For they wisely, it seems, and honestly adjudged it no debasement of their quality, no diminution to their personal excellency, to be employed in the service of the immortal gods; whom they acknowledged the patrons of their country, the protectors of their safety: nor that they less deserved of the public, who rightly ordered their religious devotions, than they who prudently advised in the senate, or fought valiantly in the field: for that the good success of public undertakings did as much, or more, depend upon the favourable disposition of divine Providence, as upon the careful endeavour of human industry.

I cannot forbear to allege that so grave and pertinent speech of Cicero, which is the exordium of his oration *ad Pontifices: Cum multa divinitus, pontifices, a majoribus nostris inventa atque instituta sunt; tum nihil præclarius, quam quod vos eosdem et religionibus deorum immortalium, et summæ reipublicæ præesse voluerunt: ut amplissimi et clarissimi cives rempublicam bene gerendo; pontifices religiones sapienter interpretando, rempublicam conservarent.* A wholesome and politic institution he thought it, conducible to the public good and safety, that the civil and sacred authority should be united in the same persons; that it was as well for the interest of the state, as for the credit of Religion, that the priests should be men of honour, or (which is all one) honourable men priests.

All which evinces plainly, that it is in no wise the result of a generous heart, (for what nation ever produced so many brave spirits as that?) but rather proceeds from an inconsiderate delicacy of humour, (or from a profane haughtiness of mind,) to loathe, as now men do, and despise that employment, which in its own nature is of all most noble and most beneficial to mankind. For if to be a courtier in a particular country is of all others the most honourable relation; and to wait upon a mortal king is accounted a most worthy function: to be peculiarly God's servant, and in religious addresses immediately to attend on him, must consequently be the most excellent preferment in the world, which is God's kingdom[1]. And if to supply a man's bodily needs, to restore his liberty, to save his life, be works of generous beneficence; how much more is it so, by good conduct and instruction of men, to adorn their souls with virtue, to free them from the bondage of sin, to rescue them from eternal ruin?

Our magnanimous ancestors, who erected as well trophies of their invincible courage abroad, as

[1] Itane plus decet hominis, quam Dei famulum nominari? ac terreni, quam cœlestis Regis dici Officialem, altioris ducitur dignitatis? Qui clero militiam, forum anteponit Ecclesiæ; divinis profecto humana, cœlestibus præferre terrena convincitur.—Bern. Epist. LXXVIII. [Opp. Tom. I. col. 82 B.]

monuments of their incomparable piety at home, and equally by both did purchase immortal renown to their ingrateful posterity, (for not to imitate good example is the greatest ingratitude,) they, I say, were otherwise disposed; to whose honest devotion we owe those handsome privileges, and those competent revenues, which the priesthood still enjoys; and which are so maligned by this untoward age, not less degenerate in spirit than corrupt in manners: when all wisdom, and virtue, and religion, are almost in most places grown ridiculous: when the serious use of reason is become (in vulgar opinion) the most impertinent and insignificant thing in the world: when innocence is reputed a mere defect of wit and weakness of judgment; integrity, a fond pertinacity of humour; constancy of mind and gravity of demeanour, a kind of sullen morosity or uncouth affectation of singularity; and all strict practice of Christian duty incurs the imputation of some new-found opprobrious name, one or other. No wonder then, when Religion itself hath so much decayed in its love and esteem, if the priests, its professed guardians, do partake in its fortune. Nor is it to be feared, but that, when the predominant vanities of the age are somewhat decocted, and men grow weary of their own inconvenient follies; whenever (not a fierce zeal for some whimsical model, or some paradoxical opinion, but) a sober esteem of, and a cordial affection to virtue and genuine piety do begin to revive in the breasts of men; the love and reverence of the clergy will return. For it will be ever true, what was once said, (though dictated only from the reason and experience of a heathen,) *Qui bona* fide Deos colit, amat et sacerdotes[k]; *He that sincerely worships God, will heartily love his priests.* But not to insist longer on this reason.

II. The good of the church requires, that the priesthood be well protected, well provided for, and well regarded. That men be converted from iniquity, induced to the sincere practice of virtue, is the chief good of the church, that to which the favour of God is annexed, and upon which the salvation of souls doth rely. And this good mainly depends, partly upon the due execution of the priestly office, partly upon the fit disposition of the people to comply therewith: and to both those effects, the comfortable estate of the priesthood is conducible and requisite. The priest must be capable to instruct with advantage, and the people disposed to learn with readiness: he must lead, and they follow cheerfully in the paths of righteousness. Which alacrity how can he be master of, whose mind, care, and grief, the inseparable companions of a needy estate, do continually distract and discompose? whose spirit is dejected with constant regret and frequent disappointments? Can he be free and expedite in the discharge of his duty, who is perplexed with the difficulties, and encumbered with the varieties of secular business, such as the exigences of a narrow condition do necessarily induce? No; few there be that, with Epictetus, can philosophate in slavery; or, like Cleanthes, can draw water all the day, and study most of the night.

The priests are bound, (for the propagation of truth and right, and for the reclaiming of men from error and sin, that is, for the most important

[k] Statius. Epist. Dedic. in v. Lib. Sylvarum.

SERM. XIV.

good of the church,) as the apostles are often related to have done, Παρρησιάζεσθαι, *To speak all out*, (or to use an unconfined liberty of speech;) to exhort to the practice of virtue, as our Saviour did, Μετ' ἐξουσίας, *With license and authority*; to deter from vice, as St Paul enjoins Titus, Μετὰ πάσης ἐπιταγῆς, *With an all-commanding and imperious strain*; and, (as those faithful brethren did, encouraged by St Paul's example,) Τολμᾶν ἀφόβως λαλεῖν τὸν λόγον, *To dare undauntedly to utter the word* of truth: they are obliged to deal impartially with all, to flatter no man: to admonish, yea, and (with prudence, seasonably) to reprove the greatest of men: not to respect the persons of the rich, nor to dread the faces of the most terrible among men. And how shall this necessary courage be engendered, be cherished, be preserved, in the breast of him who grovels upon the ground, and crouches under the depressing loads of want and disgrace[1]? What engines are able to raise the spirits of men above the ordinary fountains from which they spring, their fortunes? What props can sustain them at that due pitch, destitute of solid strength, wealth, and respect? With what face shall a pitiful underling encounter the solemn looks of an oppressing grandee? With what hope of success, in his forlorn habit, shall he adventure to check the

Acts ix. 27;
xiv. 3;
xix. 8.
Ephes. vi. 19, &c.
Luke iv. 32.
Tit. ii. 9.

Phil. i. 14.

[1] Plurima sunt, quæ
Non audent homines pertusa dicere læna.
     Juven. Sat. v. [131.]
Αἰδώς τοι πρὸς ἀνολβίῃ, θάρσος δὲ πρὸς ὄλβῳ.
     Hes. [Op. et Di. 319.]
Πρὸς ἅπαντα δειλόν ἐστιν ὁ πένης πράγματα,
Καὶ πάντας αὐτοῦ καταφρονεῖν ὑπολαμβάνει.
     Menand. [Ἀδελφοι. p. 7. Ed. Meineke.]

vicious extravagances of a ruffling gallant? Will he dare to contradict the opinion, or to disallow the practice, of that wealthy or this powerful neighbour, by whose alms, it may be, he is relieved, and supported by his favour?

But admit it possible a man may be both extremely indigent and sufficiently resolute: (that is, strong without food, and fat by digesting the thin air:) with what regard then, shall his free and faithful advice be entertained? Shall not his moderate confidence be accounted impudence; his open sincerity of speech be styled unmannerly presumption; his minding others of their duty adjudged a forgetfulness of his own condition, or a disorderly transgressing the due limits thereof: if he be not ashamed of the truth, will not the truth be ashamed of him? Shall he not prejudice more by the meanness of his garb, than further by the force of his reason, that good cause which he maintains? Will men respect his words, whose person they despise? Will they be willingly counselled or patiently reproved by him, whom they esteem, yea, whom they plainly see, so much their inferior? No: the same words, which proceed from the mouths of men in eminent dignity, are not the same when they are uttered by those of base degree[m]. Weak and ineffectual are the most eloquent harangues of beggarly orators; obscure, like themselves, and unobserved, the most notable dictates of poor, mercenary pedants. The authority of the

[m] Τὸ δ' ἀξίωμα, κἂν κακῶς λέγῃς τὸ σὸν
Πείσει· λόγος γὰρ ἔκ τ' ἀδοξούντων ἰὼν
Κἀκ τῶν δοκούντων αὐτὸς οὐ ταὐτὸν σθένει.
Eurip. Hec. [293.]

speaker doth usually more incline, than the weight of the matter. It was the observation of the wise son of Sirach: *When a rich man slips, he hath many helpers; he speaketh things not to be spoken, and yet men justify him: the poor man miscarried, and they further rebuked him; he spake discreetly, and yet could have no place. When a rich man speaketh, every man holdeth his tongue; and his words they extol to the clouds*[n]: *but if the poor man speak, they say, Who is this? and if he stumble, they will help to overthrow him.* And Solomon himself notes the same: *The poor man's wisdom is despised, and his words are not heard.* Not only those that swell with pride and swim in plenty, but even the meanest of the people, will be apt to contemn his instructions, whom they perceive in few or no circumstances of life to excel them. If the preacher's condition be not, as well as his pulpit, somewhat elevated above the lowest station, few will hear him, fewer mind his words, very few obey him. Job's case deserves well to be considered. While he flourished in wealth and reputation all men attended to his counsel, and admired his discourse. *The princes,* saith he, *refrained talking, and laid their hand on their mouth: the nobles held their peace, and their tongue cleaved to the roof of their mouth. When the ear heard me, then it blessed me; and when the eye saw me, it gave witness to me. Unto me men gave ear, and waited, and kept silence at my counsel. After my words they spake not again, and my speech dropped upon them.* So officiously attentive were all men

SERM. XIV.

Ecclus. xiii. 22, 23.

Eccles. ix. 16.

Job xxix. 9, 10, 11, 21, 22.

[n] Κάλλιστα Μουσῶν φθέγγεται πλουτῶν ἀνήρ.
[Eurip. Frag. Incert.]

SERM. XIV.

*Job xxx. 1, 9, 10, 11.*

*Job xxx. 25.*

to Job in his prosperity. But when the scale was turned, and he became depressed in estate, no man minded either him or his discourse, except it were to despise and scorn both. *But now,* saith he, *they that are younger than I have me in derision, whose fathers I would have disdained to have set with the dogs of my flock. I am their song, yea, I am their by-word. They abhor me, they fly far from me, and spare not to spit in my face; because he hath loosed my cord, and afflicted me*°. If Job, a person, who so equally and moderately, yea, so humbly, and courteously, and bountifully used his prosperity, as we find he did, was notwithstanding in his adversity so generally slighted and abhorred; what shall their lot be who never enjoyed those advantages? what regard shall their wholesome advice find? what efficacy their most pathetical exhortations obtain? what passion their faint breath raise in men's benumbed hearts? No more, certainly, than their mean condition shall procure among men either of friendship or esteem.

We see therefore, how Almighty God, that he might conciliate credit unto, and infuse a persuasive energy into the words of his prophets and apostles, was pleased to dignify them with extraordinary gifts of foretelling future events and doing miraculous works: their doctrine, it seems, (though of itself most reasonable and plausible,) being not sufficient to convince the hearers, without some remarkable excellency in the teachers, challenging the people's awful regard, and exciting their attention. Otherwise how pitifully scant a draught those

° Prov. xiv. 20. *The poor is hated even of his own neighbour: but the rich hath many friends.*

poor fishers of men had caught by the common allurements only of innocent life and rational discourse, I leave you to imagine. And where such extraordinary commendations are wanting, is it not reasonable that the need of them should be supplied by ordinary and probable expedients?

I might further add, how a necessitous and despicable estate doth commonly not only disturb the minds and deject the spirits of men, but distempereth also their souls, and vitiateth their manners; rendering them not only sad and anxious, slavish and timorous, but greedy also and covetous, peevish and mutinous, rude and ignorant; engages them in sordid company, and tempts them to unworthy courses. From which one cause how scandalous effects, and how prejudicial to the church's both honour and safety, have proceeded, I need not for to say, since woful experience too loudly proclaims it.

I might add, moreover, that the priests do confer to the good of the state; which is secured and advanced by the sincere instruction of men in duties of obedience, justice, and fidelity; and by maintenance of good conscience among men. So that, if things be rightly considered, it will be hard to find a better commonwealth's man, than a good minister.

Seeing therefore the good of the church, upon various accounts, is so much concerned in the priests' encouragement, welfare, and respect, it is very fitting they should have them. Which consideration I conclude with that serious admonition of the Apostle to the Hebrews, wherein the substance of what hath been spoken on this point is contained: *Obey your rulers* (or *guides,*) *and submit to them: for they watch for your souls, as they that are to give an account; that they may do it with joy, and not with complaint,* Μή στενάζοντες: *for this is unprofitable for you,* Ἀλυσιτελὲς γὰρ ὑμῖν τοῦτο: that is, *For this pays no taxes, quits no scores, turns to no account, is nowise advantageous for you;* but rather (for there is a Μείωσις in those words) is hurtful and detrimental to you. But further,

III. Common equity, and the reason of the case exacts, that safety, competent subsistence, and fitting respect be allowed to the priests. If you consider their personal qualities; who, I pray, do, commonly, better deserve those advantages than they? Those qualities, I say, which result from a liberal, a sober, a modest education in the schools of wisdom, and under the influences of good discipline. If birth (that is, at best, an imaginary relation to the gallantry of an ancestor) entitle men to honour; if the cheap favours of fortune be so highly prized and admired; if riches (that is, the happy results of industry in trivial matters) do easily purchase respect: what may not they pretend to, whose constant (and not always unsuccessful) endeavour it hath been to deserve well, to cultivate their minds, and regulate their manners?

True worth, indeed, is not confined to any particular order of men; yet I should wrong none, by saying it is no where more plentifully to be found than in this[p]. What is it that doth advance men's nature, that adorns their minds, that commends their persons to especial regard? Is it knowledge?

[p] Vide Orig. contra Cels. Lib. III. p. 129.

*The priests' lips preserve it;* their discourse doth diffuse it. Is it virtue? Whence have more or greater examples thereof proceeded than from them? Is it piety? It is their proper business: it hath been always, in some measure, their care to promote it. That ignorance and barbarity, dissoluteness and irreligion, have not long since, like a deluge, overspread the face of the world, none, I suppose, will be so unjust as to deny, in greatest part, due to their vigilant endeavours. Even those improvements of wit and eloquence, which are employed to their disgrace and disadvantage, must be acknowledged originally derived from them.

Faults they have had, and will always have; for they are men, and subject to the common imperfections of mortal nature: but that, perhaps, less and fewer than any other distinct sort of men; that as it is their duty, so it hath been their practice, to excel in virtue; and that they have commonly, in effect, made good St Ambrose's words, *Debet præponderare vita sacerdotis, sicut præponderat gratia*[q], were not difficult to demonstrate, if seemly to make comparisons, or to insist upon so invidious a subject. Nor, were they greater than ever really they have been, or than ever malice could misrepresent them, should it be therefore equal, that the miscarriages of some should derogate from the reputation, or prejudice the welfare of the whole order.

But to wave this plea; consider their employment. Is there any office more laborious, more vexatious than theirs; accompanied with more wearisome toil, more solicitous care, more tedious

[q] [Epist. LXIII. Opp. Tom. II. col. 1037 D.]

SERM. XIV.

Heb. xiii. 17.

Ephes. iv. 11.

attendance? They are deservedly called *Watchmen*, being constrained to stand always on the guard, to be always wakeful, attentive, and ready to warn the people of approaching dangers: and *Shepherds* likewise, being forced to endure the various hardships of that uneasy life, the inconveniences of all weathers, the nipping frosts and sweltry heats, and all diversities of irksome travail; they must feed, they must guide, they must defend; they must seek the lost, and reduce the straying sheep. What assiduity of study, what earnest contention of soul are they obliged to use, in the continual instruction, exhortation, and reprehension of the people;, in rectifying their judgments, satisfying their scruples, removing their prejudices, bearing their infirmities, and sympathizing with their afflictions? It is they that are engaged, with all their might, to withstand the prevailing encroachments of iniquity, to stop the progress of pernicious errors, to detect the false pretences of impostors, to confute the fallacies of sophisters, to repel the assaults of all adversaries to the truth; yea, if need be, to expose, not only their dearest contents of life, but even their lives themselves, in the defence thereof.

Eusebius reports thus of Maximinus : Τοὺς τῶν ἐκκλησιῶν ἄρχοντας μόνους, ὡς αἰτίους τῆς κατὰ τὸ εὐαγγέλιον διδασκαλίας, ἀναιρεῖσθαι προστάττει. *He commanded that only the governors of the church (that is, the bishops) should be slaughtered, as the authors of the growth and prevalence of evangelical doctrine*[r]. Neither was it a singular practice of that bloody tyrant; but, as a thing of course, it con-

[r] [Hist. Eccl. vi. 28. Tom. i. p. 293.]

stantly follows, that wherever righteousness and truth are violently impugned, the priests are sure to taste deepest of that bitter cup; that their goods be, in the first place, sequestered and spoiled, their reputation stained, their persons misused, their lives sacrificed to the persecutor's outrageous malice.

SERM. XIV.

Is it not reasonable then, and equal, that they, who, for the service of God and benefit of the church, undergo such difficulties, and are objected to so great hazards, should be sustained, should be refreshed by proportionable encouragements? Is it not barbarous usage, to expect so hard duties from them, to impose such heavy burdens on them, and yet to grudge any suitable comforts, any satisfactory rewards to them? Good king Hezekiah surely was not so minded, of whom it is said, *He commanded the people that dwelt in Jerusalem to give the portion of the priests and Levites, that they might be encouraged in the law of the Lord:* that is, they might be heartened to study, to teach, to perform the duties required of them by the divine law. And St Paul thus rationally expostulates in the priests' behalf: *Who ever goeth to war at his own charges? who planteth a vineyard, and eateth not of the fruit thereof? or who feedeth a flock, and eateth not of the milk of the flock? If we have sown unto you spiritual things, is it a great thing if we shall reap your carnal things? Is it a great thing?* Do you think much of it? If you do, you are unreasonable, you are unjust, you are ingrateful. And otherwhere, he thus very emphatically admonishes: *We beseech you, brethren, to mind them which labour among you, and preside over you*

2 Chron. xxxi. 4.

1 Cor. ix. 7–11. Rom. xv. 27.

1 Thess. v. 12, 13.

(Προϊσταμένους ὑμῶν) *in the Lord, and that admonish you; and to esteem them more than exceedingly* (Ὑπὲρ ἐκ περισσοῦ) *in love, for their work* (or, *for their office*) *sake:* (so Ἔργον frequently signifies in such cases.) And again: *Let the elders* (or *priests,* Οἱ πρεσβύτεροι,) *which rule well, be counted worthy of double honour,* (or *of double recompense:* so Τιμὴ also imports.) Priests, as so, for their office sake, have honour and reward due to them; which, according to the good management of that office, are proportionably to be augmented and multiplied.

But further yet, abstracting from both their personal worth and the merit of their service, consider their condition in this world, and see whether it doth not in equity challenge some reasonable provision to be made for them. Are they not, by the nature of their profession, secluded from all ordinary means of temporal advancement? Be not those usual inlets of wealth, the court, the camp, and the exchange, shut upon them, yea, barred against them, by those insuperable obstacles of law and custom? Can they grow rich by trade, or famous by feats of arms? May they plead for others? It is well if they be allowed to do it for themselves before equal judges. Yet are they not men, endued with human passions and resentments? Are they not citizens, partaking in the common interests of the weal public? Are they not sensible of the inconveniences, and capable of enjoying the benefits of this life? Are they not equally obliged, and would they not be glad, as well as others, to be in a capacity to requite courtesies, to help relations, to gratify friends, to relieve the poor, to express respectively their humanity and their gratitude? Skill they not to use the goods of fortune (or rather the gifts of Providence) with as much discretion, as much sobriety, as much honour, as others? Compare things righteously, and let reason judge; let experience be examined; let those eternal monuments of their piety, their charity, their hospitality, declare and testify. Shall, lastly, the fruits of painful study, the improvement of hopeful parts, the flower of vigorous age and strength spent in the public service, tend only hither, to put a man into a state of struggling with extreme contempt and penury? If this be not, what I pray you, is monstrous iniquity?

SERM. XIV.

Since therefore it appears (upon so many several scores) reasonable, that Almighty God should undertake the protection and assert the honour of his priests, we may not only praise the goodness, but approve also the wisdom of this promise, and by the contemplation thereof strengthen our faith in reliance thereon. To which purpose one consideration more may very much conduce, and withal may provoke our gratitude to celebrate his truth and faithfulness in making good, as well as his goodness and wisdom in making, this promise; viz. the considering how continually hitherto God hath been pleased effectually to clothe his priests with salvation, to provide abundantly for their safety, their accommodation, their respect in this world, and to deliver them from the opposite inconveniences.

If we reflect our thoughts on the first ages of Christianity, (not more dismal for suffering than glorious for piety,) it is admirable to see how sincerely and passionately the Christian people did then love their priests and pastors; how liberally, out of their slender stock and the shipwrecks of their spoiled fortunes, they contributed to their maintenance; what exceeding veneration they bore them; with what incredible alacrity they submitted to the most severe disciplines enjoined by them; how willingly they followed them, though leading into the jaws of death and cruel torture: so that, although it was then necessary for the Christian priests to undergo the greatest hardships, according to the design of Christian religion, (which was to be propagated, not by terror of power, nor by politic artifice, but by the invincible faith, resolution, and patience, of the professors and teachers thereof;) yet never more may they have seemed to thrive and prosper, than in that juncture of time, when they enjoyed the universal good-will and applause of good people, when they unconstrainedly embraced affliction for righteousness' sake, and acquired thereby the certain fruition of a more excellent salvation.

But in the succeeding times, when Christianity, breaking out of the clouds of persecution, began to shine over all with brightest lustre; of the glorious and happy fruits of that illustrious triumph none did partake more fully, than they who had sustained the hardest brunts of the foregoing conflict, and had been the principal causes of the success. Then the joyful acclamations of the faithful people resounded in the praise of their victorious champions: then did the Emperors themselves, with arms outstretched and hearts enlarged, with affection embrace the authors of their happy conversion: then all laws prejudicial to their welfare were rescinded, and new ones were substituted, abundantly providing for their security, honest livelihood, and due reverence; which, in progress of time, not in the Roman empire only, but in all other nations, (that afterwards did entertain Christianity,) were nowise impaired, but were rather ampliated and fortified by the pious favour of princes: the barbarous Goths, and Vandals, and Lombards, being no sooner endued with any tincture of civility, or any sense of Religion, than possessed with a hearty reverence of their bishops and priests.

And ever since, (which is not to be imputed, as some rashly, if not impiously aver, to the prevalence of Antichristian iniquity, but rather to the providence of divine Benignity; ever since, I say,) till the late commotions and alterations in Christendom, they have been the guardians of others' safety, not themselves deprived of protection; have abounded with wealth, rather than wanted sustenance; have been the objects of envy, more than of contempt. Princes have loved and cherished them, have relied upon their advice, and intrusted them with their highest concernments. Nobles have not been ashamed to yield them place. The sacerdotal robe hath been often dyed with purple; and the sons of mighty monarchs have not thought themselves degraded by entering into their order. And if, in some particular places, (before or since those changes) their condition hath not been so high and plentiful, yet hath it been (almost ever) tolerable; the countenance of authority and the respect of the people being in good degree vouchsafed them. Even in those churches, which till this day groan under the oppression of infidel princes, the priests (by the free permission of those princes) retain their jurisdiction in a manner as great as ever; and withal enjoy a maintenance not altogether inconsiderable.

So favourable hitherto hath God been unto his priests, so faithful to his promise: which doth oblige us to thank him; which may encourage us to hope in him; which may arm us with confidence against the present ill-will of those that wish, and against the practices of those that design our ruin.

It is true, this promise is not affixed to all parts of time, to all particularities of place, to all determinate circumstances of things. The priests may, now and then, here and there, in this or that, suffer highly; they may be ejected, be plundered, be degraded, as experience hath shewed us. But they may be also soon restored, repossessed, re-advanced, and (I had almost said) revenged too, as the like experience doth assure us. It is not impossible, I confess, we may relapse into the same, or into a more calamitous estate; the obstinate disaffections of men threaten it, and our own miscarriages more dangerously: yet the most offensive of these (which many honest men dislike, and most men exclaim against) have been in as bitter terms complained of, in almost the first ages. '*Inhiant possessionibus, prædia excolunt, auro incubant, emunt venduntque, quæstui per omnia student,*' said a devout writer of ecclesiastical history[s] about 1300 years ago. And so much no man (without

[s] Sulp. Sev. [Hist. Sacr. Lib. I. cap. 23, p. 24.]

extreme uncharitableness and falsehood) can in so general terms impute to the present clergy: notwithstanding which, God did continue to vouchsafe his protection to them. They were sometimes, (by the inundations of barbarous people,) and we may again, (by national concussions,) be severely chastised for our faults: yet were not they, nor shall we be (at least every where and for ever) utterly rejected. *God may visit our transgressions with the rod, and our iniquity with stripes: nevertheless his lovingkindness will he not utterly take from us, nor suffer his faithfulness to fail. His covenant he will not break, nor alter the thing that is gone out of his lips.* God may for a time hide his face from us; but he will not for ever turn his back upon us: the honour of the priesthood may for a while be overclouded in some part of the world; but shall never totally be eclipsed, nor swallowed up in a perpetual night. While God continues his residence in Sion, and defends his church against *The gates of hell* and powers of darkness; while religion retains any sway in the hearts of men, and truth possesses any room upon earth; the priests shall not be left destitute and naked, but everlastingly be clothed with salvation. Which that it may (to the glory of God and good of his church) more surely come to pass, let us convert this promise into a prayer, and say with Solomon, *Now therefore arise, O Lord God, thou and the ark of thy strength: let thy priests, O Lord God, be clothed with salvation, and let thy saints rejoice in goodness.* Amen.

SERM. XIV.

Ps. lxxxix. 32, 33, 34.

Matt. xvi. 18.

2 Chron. vi. 41.

# SERMON XV.

### NOT TO OFFEND IN WORD AN EVIDENCE OF A HIGH PITCH OF VIRTUE.

---

### JAMES III. 2.

*If any man offend not in word, the same is a perfect man.*

SERM. XV.

THIS sentence stands at the head of a discourse concerning the tongue, (that doubtful engine of good and evil,) wherein how excellent benefits, and how grievous mischiefs, it, as rightly or perversely wielded, is apt to produce, how it is both a sweet instrument of all goodness, and a sharp weapon of all iniquity, is positively laid down, and by fit comparisons illustrated. But secluding all relation to the context, the words may well be considered singly by themselves: and as such they instruct us, asserting a certain truth; they direct us, implying a good duty. They assert that man to be perfect, who offends not in speech; and they consequently imply, that we should strive to avoid offending therein: for to be perfect, and to go on to perfection, are precepts, the observance whereof is incumbent on us. We shall first briefly explain the assertion, and then declare its truth; afterwards we shall press somewhat couched in the duty.

Deut. xviii. 13.
Luke vi. 40.
Matt. v. 48; xix. 21.
2 Cor. xiii. 11.
Heb. vi. 1.

To offend originally signifies to impinge[a], that

---

[a] Εἴ τις ἐν λόγῳ οὐ πταίει.

is, to stumble, or hit dangerously upon somewhat lying cross our way, so as thereby to be cast down, or at least to be disordered in our posture, and stopt in our progress: whence it is well transferred to denote our being, through any incident temptation, brought into sin, whereby a man is thrown down, or bowed from his upright state, and interrupted from prosecuting a steady course of piety and virtue. By an usual and apposite manner of speaking, our tenor of life is called a way, our conversation walking, our actions steps, our observing good laws uprightness, our transgression of them tripping, faltering, falling.

SERM. XV.

Ps. xxxvii. 23, 24.

By not offending in word, we may easily then conceive to be understood such a constant restraint, and such a careful guidance of our tongue, that it doth not transgress the rules prescribed unto it by divine law, or by good reason; that it thwarteth not the natural ends and proper uses for which it was framed, to which it is fitted; such as, chiefly, are promoting God's glory, our neighbour's benefit, and our own true welfare.

By a perfect man is meant a person accomplished and complete in goodness, one of singular worth and integrity, a brave and excellent man, who, as to the continual tenor of his life, is free from all notorious defects and heinous faults; like David, *Fulfilling all God's will*, and *having respect to all God's commandments*; like Zachary and Elizabeth, *Walking in all the commandments and ordinances of the Lord blameless.* Thus was Noah, thus was Abraham, thus was Job perfect. This is the notion of perfection in holy scripture: not an absolute exemption from all blemish of soul, or blame in life; for such a perfection is inconsistent

James i. 4.

Acts xiii. 22.
Ps. cxix. 6.
Luke i. 6.
Gen. vi. 9; xvii. 1.
Job i. 1.

SERM. XV.

Prov. xx. 9.
Job ix. 20.
Eccles. vii. 20.
James iii. 2.

with the nature and state of man here, where none with modesty or with truth can say, *I have made my heart clean, I am pure from my sin;* where every man must confess with Job, *If I justify myself, mine own mouth shall condemn me; if I say, I am perfect, it shall prove me perverse.* For, *There is not,* as the Preacher assures, *a just man upon earth, that doeth good, and sinneth not;* and, *In many things we offend all,* is our Apostle's assertion immediately preceding my text; which words may serve to expound these. *In many things,* saith he, *we offend all;* that is, there is no man absolutely perfect: but *If any man offend not in word,* (that is, if a man constantly govern his tongue well,) *that man is perfect;* perfect in such a kind and degree as human frailty doth admit; he is eminently good; he may be reasonably presumed upright and blameless in all the course of his practice; *Able,* as it follows, *to bridle the whole body,* that is, qualified to order all his actions justly and wisely. So that in effect the words import this; that a constant governance of our speech, according to duty and reason, is a high instance and a special argument of a throughly sincere and solid goodness.

The truth of which aphorism may from several considerations appear.

1 A good governance of speech is a strong evidence of a good mind; of a mind pure from vicious desires, calm from disorderly passions, void of dishonest intentions. For since speech is a child of thought, which the mind always travaileth and teemeth with[b], and which after its birth is

---

[b] *A fool travaileth with a word, as a woman in labour of a child.*—Ecclus. xix. 11.

wont in features to resemble its parent; since every man naturally is ambitious to propagate his conceits, and without a painful force cannot smother his resentments; since, especially, bad affections, like stum or poison, are impetuous and turgid, so agitating all the spirits, and so swelling the heart, that it cannot easily compose or contain them; since a distempered constitution of mind, as of body, is wont to weaken the retentive faculty, and to force an evacuation of bad humours; since he, that wanteth the principal wisdom of well ordering his thoughts and mastering his passions, can hardly be conceived so prudent, as long to refrain, or to regulate their dependence, speech; considering these things, I say, it is scarce possible, that he, which commonly thinks ill, should constantly either be well silent, or speak well. To conceal fire, to check lightning, to confine a whirlwind, may perhaps be no less feasible, than to keep within due compass the exorbitant motions of a soul, wherein reason hath lost its command, so that *Qua data porta*[c], where the next passage occurs, they should not rush forth, and vent themselves. A vain mind naturally will bubble forth or fly out in frothy expressions; wrath burning in the breast will flame out, or at least smoke through the mouth; rancorous imposthumes of spite and malice will at length discharge purulent matter; lust, boiling within, will soon foam out in lewd discourse. If the fountain itself is polluted, or infected, how can the streams be clear or wholesome? *How can ye, being evil, speak good things?* saith our Lord; *for from the abundance of the heart the mouth speaketh.* Matt. xii. 34, 35.

[c] [Virg. Æn. i. 83.]

SERM. XV.

*A good man*, addeth he, *out of the good treasure of the heart bringeth forth good things; and an evil man out of the evil treasure bringeth forth evil things:* Ἐκβάλλει πονηρὰ, *He casteth forth ill things*, as a fountain doth its waters by a natural and necessary ebullition. It is true, that in some particular cases, or at some times, a foul heart may be disguised by fair words, or covered by demure reservedness: shame, or fear, or crafty design, may often repress the declaration of ill thoughts and purposes. But such fits of dissimulation cannot hold; men cannot abide quiet under so violent constraints; the intestine jars, or unkindly truces, between heart and tongue (those natural friends) cannot be perpetual, or very durable: no man can hold his breath long, or live without evaporating through his mouth those steams of passion which arise from flesh and blood. *My heart was hot within me, while I was musing the fire burned; then spake I with my tongue*, saith David, expressing the difficulty of obstructing the eruption of our affections into language. Hence it is, that speech is commonly judged the truest character of the mind[d], and the surest test of inward worth; as that which discloseth *The hidden man of the heart*, which unlocketh the closets of the breast, which draws the soul out of her dark recesses into open light and view, which rendereth our thoughts visible, and our intentions palpable. Hence, *Loquere, ut te videam*, Speak, *that I may see you*, or know what kind of man you are, is a saying which all men, at first meeting, do in their hearts direct

Ps. xxxix. 3.

1 Pet. iii. 4.

[d] Ἀνδρὸς χαρακτὴρ ἐκ λόγου γνωρίζεται.
[Menand. Sentent. Sing. 26. Ed. Meineke.]

one to another: neither commonly doth any man require more to ground a judgment upon, concerning the worth or ability of another, than opportunity of hearing him to discourse for a competent time: yea, often before a man hath spoken ten words, his mind is caught, and a formal sentence is passed upon it. Such a strict affinity and connection do all men suppose between thoughts and words.

2 From hence, that the use of speech is itself a great ingredient into our practice, and hath a very general influence upon whatever we do, may be inferred, that whoever governeth it well, cannot also but well order his whole life. The extent of speech must needs be vast, since it is nearly commensurate to thought itself, which it ever closely traceth, widely ranging through all the immense variety of objects; so that men almost as often speak incogitantly, as they think silently. Speech is indeed the rudder that steereth human affairs, the spring that setteth the wheels of action on going; the hands work, the feet walk, all the members, and all the senses act by its direction and impulse; yea, most thoughts are begotten, and most affections stirred up thereby: it is itself most of our employment, and what we do beside it, is however guided and moved by it. It is the profession and trade of many, it is the practice of all men, to be in a manner continually talking. The chief and most considerable sort of men manage all their concernments merely by words; by them princes rule their subjects, generals command their armies, senators deliberate and debate about the

SERM.
XV.
great matters of state; by them advocates plead causes, and judges decide them; divines perform their offices, and minister their instructions; merchants strike up their bargains, and drive on all their traffick. Whatever almost, great or small, is done in the court or in the hall, in the church or at the exchange, in the school or in the shop, it is the tongue alone that doeth it: it is the force of this little machine that turneth all the human world about. It is indeed the use of this strange organ which rendereth human life, beyond the simple life of other creatures, so exceedingly various and compounded; which creates such a multiplicity of business, and which transacts it; while by it we communicate our secret conceptions, transfusing them into others; while therewith we instruct and advise one another; while we consult about what is to be done, contest about right, dispute about truth; while the whole business of conversation, of commerce, of government, and administration of justice, of learning, and of religion, is managed thereby; yea, while it stoppeth the gaps of time, and filleth up the wide intervals of business, our recreations and divertisements (the which do constitute a great portion of our life) mainly consisting therein, so that, in comparison thereof, the execution of what we determine, and all other action do take up small room: and even all that usually dependeth upon foregoing speech, which persuadeth, or counselleth, or commandeth it. Whence the province of speech being so very large, it being so universally concerned, either immediately as the matter, or by consequence as the

source of our actions, he, that constantly governeth it well, may justly be esteemed to live very excellently.

SERM. XV.

3 To govern the tongue well is a matter of exceeding difficulty, requiring not only hearty goodness, but great judgment and art, together with much vigilance and circumspection; whence the doing it argues a high pitch of virtue. For, since the tongue is a very loose and versatile engine, which the least breath of thought doth stir, and set on going any way, it cannot but need much attention to keep it, either in a steady rest, or in a right motion. Since numberless swarms of things roving in the fancy do thence incessantly obtrude themselves upon the tongue, very much application of mind and great judgment are requisite to select out of them those few which are good and fit, rejecting all that is bad and improper to be spoken. Since continually temptations occur, provoking or alluring to miscarriage in this kind, (for beside internal propensions and commotions of soul, every object we behold, every company we are engaged in, every accident befalling us, doth suggest somewhat inviting thereto; the condition of our neighbour moving us, if high, to flatter, if low, to insult; our own fortune prompting, if prosperous, to boast, if cross, to murmur; any action drawing from us, if it pleaseth us, fond admiration, if it disliketh, harsh censure: since, I say, we are thus at every turn obnoxious to speak amiss,) it must be matter of huge skill and caution, of mighty industry and resolution to decline it. We for that purpose need to imitate that earnest and watchful care of the holy Psalmist, which he thus expresseth; *I have,* Ps. xvii. 3.

saith he, *purposed that my mouth shall not offend:* and, *I said*, saith he again, *I will take heed to my ways, that I sin not with my tongue; I will keep my mouth with a bridle, while the wicked is before me.* And thus to maintain a constant guard over his heart and ways, thus in consequence thereof to curb and rule his speech well, must assuredly be the mark of a very good person. Especially considering, that,

4 Irregular speech hath commonly divers more advantages for it, and fewer checks upon it, than other bad practice hath. A man is apt, I mean, to speak ill with less dissatisfaction and regret from within; he may do it with less control and less hazard from without, than he can act ill. Bad actions are gross and bulky, taking up much time, and having much force spent on them, whence men easily observe and consider them in themselves and others: but ill words are subtile and transient, soon born, and as soon deceased; whence men rashly utter them, without much heed before them, or much reflection after them. Bad actions have also usually visible effects immediately consequent on them: but words operate insensibly and at distance; so that men hardly discern what will follow them, or what they have effected. There are also frequent occasions of speaking ill, upon presumption of secrecy, and thence of indisturbance and impunity; yea, doing so is often entertained with complacence, and encouraged with applause: the vilest abuses of speech (even blasphemy, treason, and slander themselves) may be safely whispered into ears, which will receive them with pleasure and commendation. Bad language also in

most cases is neither strictly prohibited, nor severely chastised by human laws, as bad action is. Whence ordinarily the guilt of this misbehaviour seems little or none; and persons much practising it, both in their own conceit, and in the opinion of others, do often pass for innocent. Men indeed here will hardly discern any rule, or acknowledge any obligation: the tongue they deem is free, and any words may be dispensed with: it is sufficient if they abstain from doing gross wrong or mischief, they have a right and liberty to say any thing: *Our lips are our own; who is Lord over us?* so are men commonly prone to say, with those in the Psalm. Hence whosoever, notwithstanding such encouragements to offend herein, and so few restraints from it, doth yet carefully forbear it, governing his tongue according to rules of duty and reason, may justly be reputed a very good man. Furthermore,

Ps. xii. 4.

5 Whereas most of the enormities, the mischiefs, and the troubles, whereby the souls of men are defiled, their minds discomposed, and their lives disquieted, are the fruits of ill-governed speech; it being that chiefly which perverteth justice, which soweth dissensions, which raiseth all bad passions and animosities, which embroileth the world in seditions and factions, by which men wrong and abuse, deceive and seduce, defame and disgrace one another, whereby consequently innumerable vexations and disturbances are created among men; he that by well governing his speech preserveth himself from the guilt, disengageth his mind and life from the inconveniences of all such evils, (from the discreet and honest management

thereof enjoying both innocence and peace,) **must** necessarily be, as a very wise and happy, so a very good and worthy person.

6 His tongue also, so ruled, cannot but produce very good fruits of honour to God, of benefit to our neighbour, of comfort to himself: it will be sweet and pleasant, it will be wholesome and useful; endearing conversation, cementing peaceful society; breeding and nourishing love, instructing and edifying, or cheering and comforting the hearers. *His tongue is health; His mouth is a well and tree of life; His lips disperse knowledge; He shall be satisfied with good by the fruit of his mouth. Every man shall kiss his lips.* Such, as the Wise Man telleth us, are the effects of innocent, sober, and well-ordered discourse; the which do much commend their author, and declare the excellent virtue of that tree, from which such fruits do grow.

7 Lastly, the observation, how unusual this practice is in any good degree, may strongly assure the excellency thereof. For, the rarer, especially in morals, any good thing is, the more noble and worthy it is; that rarity arguing somewhat of peculiar difficulty in the attainment or the achievement thereof. Nothing is more obvious to common experience, than that persons, who in the rest of their demeanour and dealings appear blameless, yea, who, in regard to other points of duty, would seem nice and precise, are extremely peccant in this kind. We may see divers, otherwise much restraining and much denying themselves, who yet indulge themselves a strange licentiousness in speaking whatever their humour or their passion

dictates. Many, in other respects harmless, (who would not for any thing smite or slay folks,) we may observe with their tongue to commit horrible outrages upon any man that comes in their way. Frequently persons, very punctual in their dealings, are very unjust in their language, cheating and robbing their neighbour of his reputation by envious detraction and hard censure. They, who abhor shedding a man's blood, will yet, without any scruple or remorse, by calumnious tales and virulent reproaches, assassinate his credit, and murder his good name, although to him perhaps far more dear and precious than his life. Commonly such, as are greatly staunch in other enjoyments of pleasure, are enormously intemperate in speaking, and very incontinent of their tongue: men, in all other parts of morality rigorously sober, are often in this very wild and dissolute. Yea, not seldom we may observe, that even mighty pretenders to godliness, and zealous practisers of devotion, cannot forbear speaking things plainly repugnant to God's law, and very prejudicial to his honour. Thus it is observable to be now; and thus we may suppose that it always hath been. So of his time St Hierome, (or rather St Paulinus, in his excellent Epistle to Celantia) testifies: *Such a lust* (saith he, concerning the ill governance of speech) *of this evil hath invaded the minds of men, that even those, who have far receded from other vices, do yet fall into this, as into the last snare of the Devil*[o]. So it appears, that among all sorts of good

SERM. XV.

---

[o] Tanta hujus mali libido mentes hominum invasit, ut etiam qui procul ab aliis vitiis recesserunt, in istud tamen, quasi in ex-

practice, the strict governance of the tongue is least ordinary, and consequently, that it is most admirable and excellent. And this is all I shall say for confirmation of the point asserted.

Now then, as it is our duty to aim at perfection, or to endeavour the attainment of integrity in heart and life, so we should especially labour to govern our tongue, and guard it from offence. To which purpose it is requisite, that we should well understand and consider the nature of those several offences to which speech is liable, together with the special pravity, deformity, and inconvenience of each: for, did we know and weigh them, we should not surely either like or dare to incur them.

The offences of speech are many and various in kind; so many as there be of thought and of action, unto which they do run parallel: accordingly they well may be distinguished from the difference of objects which they do specially respect. Whence, 1 some of them are committed against God, and confront piety; 2 others against our neighbour, and violate justice, or charity, or peace; 3 others against ourselves, infringing sobriety, discretion, or modesty; or, 4 some are of a more general and abstracted nature, rambling through all matters, and crossing all the heads of duty. It is true, that in most, or in all offences of speech, there is a complication of impiety, iniquity, and imprudence; for that by all sorts of ill speaking we sin against God, and break his commandment; we injure our neighbour, at least by contagion

tremum diaboli laqueum, incidant.—[Inter Opp. Hieron. Ep. cix. Tom. IV. p. ii. col. 816.]

and bad example; we abuse ourselves, contracting guilt, and exposing ourselves to punishment: also the general vices of speech (unadvisedness and vanity) do constantly adhere to every bad word: yet commonly each evil speech hath a more direct and immediate aspect upon some one of those objects, (God, our neighbour, or ourselves,) and is peculiarly repugnant to one of those capital virtues (piety, charity, and sobriety) unto which all our duty is reduced. Now, according to this distinction, I should, if time would give leave, describe and dissuade particularly all these sorts of offence: but (since I must be respectful to patience, and careful myself not to offend in speech) I shall confine the rest of my present discourse to the first sort, the offences against piety; and even of them I shall (waving the rest) only touch two or three, insinuating some reasons why we should eschew them. These are,

I. Speaking blasphemously against God, or reproachfully concerning religion, or to the disgrace of piety, with intent to subvert men's faith in God, or to impair their reverence of him. There hath been a race of men (and would to God that race were not even till now continued) concerning whom the Psalmist said, *They speak loftily, they set their mouth against the heavens;* who, like the proud Sennacherib, *Lift up their eyes, and exalt their voice against the Holy One of Israel;* who, with the profane Antiochus, *Speak marvellous things against the God of gods.* This of all impieties is the most prodigiously gigantic, the most signal practice of enmity towards God, and downright waging of war against heaven. Of all weapons formed against God, the tongue most notoriously doth impugn him; for we cannot reach heaven with our hands, or immediately assault God by our actions: other ill practice indeed obliquely, or by consequence dishonoureth God, and defameth goodness; but profane discourse is directly levelled at them, and doth immediately touch them, as its formal objects. Now doing thus argueth an extremity both of folly and naughtiness: for, he that doeth it, either believeth the existence of God, and the truth of religion; or he distrusts them. If he doth believe them, what a desperate madness is it in him, advisedly to invite certain mischief to his home, and pull down heaviest vengeance on his own head, by opposing the irresistible power, and provoking the inflexible justice of God! What an abominable villany and baseness is it thus to abuse God's immense goodness and mercy, offering such despite to the Author of his being, and free Donor of all the good he enjoys! What a monstrous conspiracy is it of stupidity and perverseness in him, thus wilfully to defy his own welfare, to forfeit all capacity of happiness; to precipitate and plunge himself into a double hell, that of bitter remorse here, that of endless pain hereafter! But if he, that reproacheth God and Religion, be supposed distrustful of their being and reality, neither so is he excusable from like degrees of folly and pravity: for, beside the wild extravagance of such disbelief, against legions of cogent arguments and pregnant testimonies, against all the voice of nature and faith of history, against the settled judgment of wise and sober persons who have studied and considered the point, against the current tradition of all ages, and general consent of mankind; all which to withstand, no less demonstrateth high indiscretion than arrogance; beside also the palpable silliness which he displays, in causelessly (or for no other cause than soothing a fantastic humour) drawing upon himself the anger and hatred of all men who are concerned for the interests of their religion, thrusting himself into great dangers and mischiefs thence imminent to him, both from private zeal and public law; beside, I say, these evident follies, there is an unsufferable insolence and horrible malice apparent in this practice; for it is no less than the height of insolence, thus to affront mankind in matters of highest consideration, and deepest resentment with it; not only thwarting its common notions, but vilifying the chief objects of its highest respect and affection, of its main care and concernment; so making the fiercest invasion that can be on its credit, and charging it with greatest fondness. Who can endure that He, whom he apprehends to be his grand Parent, his best Friend and Benefactor, his great Patron and Sovereign, should in downright terms be defamed or disparaged? Who can patiently bear that, wherein he placeth his utmost hopes and supreme felicity, to be expressly slighted or scorned? Who can take the offering to do this, otherwise than for a most injurious reflection upon his judgment and his practice? If he cannot believe in God, he may let them alone who do: if he will not practise Religion, he may forbear to persecute it. He cannot pretend any zeal; it is therefore only pride that moves him to disturb us. So may every man, with all the reason in the world, complain against the

SERM. XV.

profane talker. Seeing also it is most evident, that hearty reverence of God, and a conscientious regard to Religion, do produce great benefits to mankind, being indeed the main supports of common honesty and sobriety, the sole curbs, effectually restraining men from unjust fraud and violence, from brutish lusts and passions; since apparently Religion prescribeth the best rules, and imposeth the strongest engagements to the performance of those actions, whereby not only men's private welfare is promoted, and ordinary conversation is sweetened, and common life is adorned, but also whereby public order and peace are maintained; since, as Cicero with good reason judged, *Piety being removed, it is probable that justice itself* (of all virtues the best guarded and fortified by human power) *could not subsist, no faith could be secured, no society could be preserved among men*[f]; it being manifestly vain to fancy, that assuredly without religious conscience any one will be a good subject, a true friend, or an honest man; or that any other consideration can induce men to prefer duty to their prince, the prosperity of their country, fidelity toward their friends or neighbours, before their own present interests and pleasure: since, I say, the credit of Religion is so very beneficial and useful to mankind, it is plain, that he must be exceedingly spiteful and malicious, who shall, by profane discourse, endeavour to supplant or shake it. He, that speaketh against God's providence, hath assuredly a pique at goodness, and would not have

[f] Haud scio an, pietate adversus Deos sublata, fides etiam, et societas generis humani, et una excellentissima virtus, justitia, tollatur.—Cic. [de Nat. Deor. I. 2, 4.]

it predominant in the hearts of men. He, that disparages Religion, doth certainly take his aim against virtue, and would not have it practised in the world: his meaning plainly is, to effect, if he can, that men should live like beasts in foul impurities, or like fiends in mischievous iniquities. Such an one, therefore, is not to be taken as a simple embracer of error, but as a spiteful designer against common good. For indeed, were any man assured (as none can upon so much as probable grounds think it) that Religion had been only devised by men, as a supplemental aid to reason[g] and force, (drawing them, whom the one could not persuade, nor the other compel, to the practice of things conducible to the public weal;) that it were merely an implement of policy, or a knack to make people loyal to their prince, upright in their dealings, sober in their conversations, moderate in their passions, virtuous in all their doings; it were yet a most barbarous naughtiness and inhumanity in him to assay the overthrow thereof, with the defeating so excellent purposes: he, that should attempt it, justly would deserve to be reputed an enemy to the welfare of mankind, to be treated as a pestilent disturber of the world.

II. Another like offence against piety is, to speak loosely and wantonly about holy things, (things nearly related to God or to Religion,) to make such things the matter of sport and mockery, to play and trifle with them. But of this I shall have occasion to speak in another discourse.

III. Another grand offence against piety is,

[g] Ut quos ratio non posset, eos ad officium religio duceret.—Id.[?]

SERM. XV.

rash and vain swearing in common discourse; an offence which now strangely reigns and rages in the world, passing about in a specious garb and under glorious titles, as a genteel and graceful quality, a mark of fine breeding, and a point of high gallantry. Who, forsooth, now is the brave spark and complete gentleman, but he that hath the skill and confidence (O heavens! how mean a skill! how mad a confidence!) to lard every sentence with an oath or a curse; making bold at every turn to salute God, fetching him down from heaven to avouch any idle prattle, to second any giddy passion, to concern himself in any trivial affair of his; yea, calling and challenging the Almighty to damn and destroy him! But somewhat to repress these fond conceits and vile practices, let us, I pray, consider,

1 That swearing thus is most expressly and strictly prohibited to us. *I say unto you, Swear not at all: but let your conversation be, Yea, yea; Nay, nay; for whatsoever is more than these cometh of evil:* so our Lord forbids it. *But above all things, my brethren, swear not—lest you enter into condemnation:* so doth St James warn against it. And is it not then prodigious, that in Christendom any man should affect to break laws so plain and so severe; that it should pass here, not only for a tolerable, but even for a commendable practice, to violate so manifest and so important a duty; that so directly to thwart our Lord himself should be a thing not in use only, but in credit and request among Christians? What more palpable affront could be offered to our Religion, and to all that is sacred among us? For what respect or force can

Matt. v. 34, 37.

James v. 12.

we imagine reserved to religion, while a practice so indisputably opposite thereto, in a high degree, is so current and prevalent?

2 Again, according to the very nature and reason of things, it is evidently an intolerable profaneness, thus unadvisedly to make addresses and appeals to God, invoking his testimony, and demanding his judgment about trifles; far more such, than it were a high presumption and encroachment upon the majesty of a prince, on every petty occasion to break into his presence, and to assail his ears, dragging him to hear and determine concerning it. Whence the very light of nature condemns this practice, and even heathens have loudly declared against it, as derogatory to the reverence of the Deity, and unsuitable to the gravity of a worthy man.

3 Swearing indeed is, by our holy Oracles, worthily represented to us, as an especial piece of worship and devotion toward God; wherein, duly performed, we piously acknowledge his chief attributes and singular prerogatives: (His being every where present, and conscious of all we say or do; his goodness and fidelity, in favouring truth and protecting right; his justice, in rewarding veracity and equity, in avenging falsehood and iniquity; his being the supreme Lord of all persons, and last Judge in all causes; to signify and avow these things to God's glory, swearing was instituted, and naturally serveth:) wherefore, as all other acts of devotion, so this grand one especially should never be performed without all serious consideration and humble reverence; the cause should be certainly just and true, the matter worthy and weighty, the

manner grave and solemn, the mind framed to earnest attention, and furnished with devout affections. Those conditions are always carefully to be observed, which the prophet intimates when he chargeth thus; *Thou shalt swear, The Lord liveth, in truth, in judgment, and in righteousness.* It is therefore horrible mockery and profanation of a most sacred ordinance, when men presume to use it without any care or consideration, without any respect or awe, upon any slight or vain occasion.

<sub>Jer. iv. 2.</sub>

4 The doing so is also very prejudicial to human society; for the decision of right, the security of government, and the preservation of peace, do much depend upon an awful regard to oaths; and therefore upon their being only used in due manner and season: the same do greatly suffer by the contempt or disregard of them, and consequently by their common and careless use. They are the surest bonds by which the consciences of men are tied to the attestation of truth and observance of faith; the which, as by rare and reverent use they are kept firm and fast, so by frequent and negligent application of them (by their prostitution to every light and toyish matter) they are quite dissolved, or much slackened. Whence the public seems much concerned, that this enormity should be retrenched. For, if oaths generally become cheap and vile, what will that of allegiance signify? If men are wont to dally with swearing every where, can they be expected to be strict and serious therein at the bar, or in the church? Will they regard the testimony of God, or dread his judgment, in one place, or at one time, whenas

every where continually (upon any, upon no occasion) they dare to confront and contemn them?

5 This way of swearing is also a very uncivil and unmannerly practice. It is, not only a gross rudeness toward the main body of men, who justly reverence the name of God, and loathe such abuses thereof; not only an insolent defiance to the common profession and law of our country, which disallows and condemns it; but it is very odious and offensive to any particular society, if at least there be one sober person therein: for, to any such person (who retains a sense of goodness, or is anywise concerned for God's honour) no language or behaviour can be more disgustful; nothing can more grate the ears or fret the heart of such an one, than this kind of talk: to give him the lie were a compliment, to spit in his face were an obligation, in comparison thereto. Wherefore it is a wonder, that any person, having in him a spark of ingenuity, or at all pretending to good manners, should find in his heart or deign to use it.

6 This practice also much derogateth from the credit of him that useth it, rendering the truth of whatever he says, in reason and justice, suspected. For, he that is so void of conscience as to swear vainly, what can engage him to speak truly? He, that is so loose in one such point of obedience to God and reason, what should we conceive him in regard to another?

7 It can be surely no wrong to distrust him, since he implies himself not to be, even in his own opinion, a credible person; since he judges not his own bare affirmation to deserve belief. For why, if he takes his word to be competently good, doth

SERM.
XV.

he back it with such asseverations? Why, unprovoked, calls he God to witness, if he thinks his own honesty sufficient to assure the truth of what he says[h]? An honest man, methinks, should scorn thus to invalidate his own credit, or to detract from the authority of his word, which should stand firm upon itself, and not want an oath to support it.

8  To excuse this, the swearer must be forced to confess another ugly fault in speaking, that is, impertinence, or using of waste and insignificant words; to be charged wherewith, he is indeed however unavoidably liable. For oaths, as they pass commonly, are mere excrescences of speech[i], which do nothing else but encumber and deform it: they embellish discourse, just as a wen or a scab does beautify a face; as a spot or a patch do adorn a garment. For to what purpose, I pray, is God's name haled into our idle talk? Why should we so often mention him, when we never mean any thing about him? Into every sentence to foist a dog, or a horse, would altogether be as proper and pertinent. These superfluous words signify nothing, but that the speaker little skilleth the use of speech, or the rule of conversation, but meaneth to prate any thing without wit or judgment; that his fancy is very beggarly, and craves the aid of any impertinency to relieve it. One would think, that a man of sense should grutch to lend his ears, or incline his attention, to such putid stuff; that, without

[h] Tantus in te sit veri amor, ut quicquid dixeris, juratum putes.—Hier. [(Paulinus) ad Celant. Ep. cix. Opp. Tom. IV. p. ii. col. 817.]

[i] Πρὸς ἀναπλήρωσιν λόγου.—Hierocles. [in Aur. Carm. Com. p. 38.]

nauseating, he should not endure to see men lavish time, and squander breath so frivolously.

SERM. XV.

9 In fine, this offence is particularly most inexcusable, in that it scarce hath any temptation to it, or bringeth with it any advantage; so that it is unaccountable, what (beside mere vanity or perverseness) should dispose men thereto. It gratifieth no sense, it yieldeth no profit, it procureth no honour, for the sound of it is not very melodious, nor, surely, was any man ever preferred for it, or got an estate thereby; it rather, to any good ear, maketh a horrid and jarring noise, it rather produceth displeasure, damage, and disgrace. Wherefore, of all dealers in sin, the swearer is apparently the silliest, and maketh the worst bargains for himself; for he sinneth gratis, and, like those in the Prophet, selleth his soul for nothing. An epicure hath some reason, and an extortioner is a man of wisdom, if compared to him; for they enjoy some pleasure, or acquire some gain here, in lieu of their salvation hereafter. But he offends heaven, and abandons happiness, he knows not why, nor for what; a fond humour possesses him, he inconsiderately follows a herd of fops, he affects to play the ape; that is all he can say for himself. Let me be pardoned, if just indignation against a wickedness so contemptible, so heinous, and so senseless, and withal so notorious, and so rife among us, doth extort from me language somewhat tart and vehement.

Isai. lii. 3.

If men would then but a little consider things, surely this scurvy fashion would be soon discarded, much fitter for the scum of the people, than for the flower of the gentry; yea rather, much below any man endued with a scrap of reason, not to say with a grain of Religion. Could we bethink ourselves, certainly modest, sober, and pertinent discourse, would appear far more generous and manly, than such wild hectoring God Almighty, such rude insulting over the received laws, such ruffianly swaggering against sobriety and goodness. If gentlemen would regard the virtues of their ancestors, (that gallant courage, that solid wisdom, that noble courtesy, which first advanced their families, and severed them from the vulgar,) this degenerate wantonness and dirtiness of speech would return to the dunghill, or rather (which God grant) would be quite banished from the world.

Finally, as to this whole point, about not offending, in our speech, against piety, we should consider, that, as we ourselves, with all our members and powers, were chiefly designed and framed to serve and glorify our Maker; (it being withal the greatest perfection of our nature, and the noblest privilege thereof so to do;) so, especially, our tongue and speaking faculty were given us, to declare our admiration and reverence of him, to express our love and gratitude toward him, to celebrate his praises, to acknowledge his benefits, to promote his honour and service. This, consequently, is the most proper and worthy use thereof; from this it becomes in effect what the Psalmist so often terms it, our *Glory*, and *The best member we have;* as that, whereby we far excel all creatures here below; that, whereby we consort with the blessed angels above, in distinct utterance of praise to our Creator. Wherefore applying it to any impious discourse, (tending anywise to the dishonour of

God, or disparagement of Religion,) is a most unnatural abuse thereof, and a vile ingratitude toward him that gave it to us. From which, and from all other offences, God in his mercy preserve us all, through Jesus Christ our Lord, unto whom for ever, with heart and tongue, let us strive to render all glory and praise. *Amen.*

END OF VOLUME I.

CAMBRIDGE:
PRINTED AT THE UNIVERSITY PRESS.

16 AU 59

Cambridge, February, 1859.

# WORKS
## EDITED FOR THE SYNDICS
### OF THE
## Cambridge University Press.

SOLD AT THE CAMBRIDGE WAREHOUSE,
32 PATERNOSTER ROW, LONDON,

AND BY

DEIGHTON, BELL & CO. CAMBRIDGE.

---

*The Works of* Isaac Barrow, *compared with the* Original MSS. enlarged with Materials hitherto unpublished. A new Edition, by A. NAPIER, M.A. of Trinity College, Vicar of Holkham, Norfolk. 9 Vols. Demy Octavo. *Ready.* £4 14s. 6d.

*A Treatise of the Pope's Supremacy, and a Discourse* concerning the Unity of the Church, by ISAAC BARROW. One Volume, 8vo. *Ready.* 12s.

*Examination of Students who are not members of the* University. Examination Papers, &c. with Lists of Syndics and Examiners, and the Regulations for the Examination held in December 1858. Demy Octavo. 2s. by post 2s. 2d.

Wheatly *on the Common Prayer, edited by* G. E. CORRIE, D.D. Master of Jesus College, Examining Chaplain to the Lord Bishop of Ely. 12s. 6d.

*The Gospel according to Saint Matthew in Anglo-*Saxon and Northumbrian Versions, synoptically arranged: with Collations of the best Manuscripts. By J. M. KEMBLE, M.A. and C. HARDWICK, M.A. Christian Advocate. 10s.

Sancti Irenæi *Episcopi Lugdunensis Libros quinque* adversus Hæreses textu Græco in locis nonnullis locupletato, versione Latina cum Codicibus Claromontano ac Arundeliano denuo collata, præmissa de placitis Gnosticorum prolusione, fragmenta necnon Græce, Syriace, Armeniace, commentatione perpetua et indicibus variis edidit W. WIGAN HARVEY, S.T.B. Collegii Regalis olim socius. 2 Vols. Demy Octavo. *Ready.* 36s.

*Select Discourses, by* John Smith, *late Fellow of* Queens' College, Cambridge. Edited by H. G. WILLIAMS, B.D. Professor of Arabic in the University. *In the Press.*

*Cambridge Greek and English Testament, in Parallel* Columns on the same page. Edited by J. SCHOLEFIELD, M.A. late Regius Professor of Greek in the University. A new Edition printed on Demy 4to. *Writing Paper*, with large margin for MS. notes. 12s.

*Cambridge Greek and English Testament, in Parallel* Columns on the same page. Edited by J. SCHOLEFIELD, M.A. late Regius Professor of Greek in the University. Fourth Edition. Small Octavo. 7s. 6d.

*Cambridge Greek Testament. Ex editione Stephani* tertia, 1550. Small Octavo. 3s. 6d.

*A Catalogue of the Manuscripts preserved in the* Library of the University of Cambridge. Vol. I. Demy Octavo. 30s. Vol. II. 20s. Vol. III. 25s. Vol. IV. *In the Press.*

*Catalogus Bibliothecæ Burckhardtianæ, cum Appen-*dice librorum aliorum Orientalium in Bibliotheca Academiæ Cantabrigiensis asservatorum. Jussu Syndicorum Preli Academici confecit T. PRESTON, A.M. Collegii SS. Trinitatis Socius. Demy 4to. 5s.

M. T. Ciceronis *de Officiis Libri tres, with Marginal* Analysis, an English Commentary, and copious Indices, by H. A. HOLDEN, M.A. Head Master of Ipswich School, late Fellow and Assistant Tutor of Trinity College, Cambridge. Post 8vo. 9s. 6d.

M. T. Ciceronis *Oratio pro Tito Annio Milone*, with a Translation of Asconius' Introduction, Marginal Analysis, and English Notes, by J. S. PURTON, M.A. President and Tutor of St Catharine's College. Post Octavo. 3s. 6d.

M. Minucii Felicis *Octavius. The text newly revised* from the Original MS. with an English Commentary, Analysis, Introduction, and Copious Indices. Edited by H. A. HOLDEN, M.A. Head Master of Ipswich School, late Fellow and Assistant Tutor of Trinity College, Cambridge. Crown Octavo. 9s. 6d.

Cæsar Morgan's *Investigation of the Trinity of Plato,* and of Philo Judæus, and of the effects which an attachment to their writings had upon the principles and reasonings of the Fathers of the Christian Church. A new Edition, revised by H. A. HOLDEN, M.A. Head Master of Ipswich School, late Fellow and Assistant Tutor of Trinity College, Cambridge. Crown Octavo. 4*s*.

Theophili *Episcopi Antiochensis Libri Tres ad Autolycum.* Edidit, Prolegomenis Versione Notulis Indicibus instruxit GULIELMUS GILSON HUMPHRY, S.T.B. Collegii Sanctiss. Trin. apud Cantabrigienses quondam Socius. Post Octavo. 6*s*.

*De Obligatione Conscientiæ Prælectiones Decem* Oxonii in Schola Theologica habitæ a ROBERTO SANDERSON, SS. Theologiæ ibidem Professore Regio. With English Notes, including an abridged Translation, by W. WHEWELL, D.D. Master of Trinity College. Octavo. 9*s*.

Grotius *de Jure Belli et Pacis, with the notes of* Barbeyrac and others; accompanied by an abridged Translation of the Text, by W. WHEWELL, D.D. Master of Trinity College. Three Volumes, 8vo, 42*s*. The translation separate, 14*s*.

*The Homilies, with Various Readings, and the* Quotations from the Fathers given at length in the Original Languages. Edited by G. E. CORRIE, D.D. Master of Jesus College, Examining Chaplain to the Lord Bishop of Ely. Octavo. 10*s*. 6*d*.

*Archbishop* Usher's *Answer to a Jesuit, with other* Tracts on Popery. Edited by J. SCHOLEFIELD, M.A. late Regius Professor of Greek in the University. Octavo. 13*s*. 6*d*.

Wilson's *Illustration of the Method of explaining the* New Testament, by the early opinions of Jews and Christians concerning Christ. Edited by T. TURTON, D.D. Lord Bishop of Ely. Octavo. 8*s*.

*Lectures on Divinity delivered in the University of* Cambridge. By John Hey, D.D. Third Edition, by T. TURTON, D.D. Lord Bishop of Ely. 2 vols. 8vo. 30*s.*

Theophylacti *in Evangelium S. Matthæi Commentarius.* Edited by W. G. HUMPHRY, B.D. Prebendary of St Paul's, and Vicar of St Martin's-in-the-Fields, London, late Fellow of Trinity College. Octavo. 14*s.*

Tertullianus *de Corona Militis, de Spectaculis, de* Idololatria, with Analysis and English Notes, by GEORGE CURREY, B.D. Preacher at the Charter House, late Fellow and Tutor of St John's College. Crown Octavo. 7*s.* 6*d.*

*Astronomical Observations, for the Years* 1849, 1850, and 1851, made at the Observatory of Cambridge, by the Rev. JAMES CHALLIS, M.A. Plumian Professor of Astronomy and Experimental Philosophy in the University of Cambridge, and late Fellow of Trinity College. Royal 4to. *Ready.* 25*s.*

*Astronomical Observations, for the Years* 1846, 1847, and 1848, made at the Observatory of Cambridge, by the Rev. JAMES CHALLIS, M.A. Plumian Professor of Astronomy and Experimental Philosophy in the University of Cambridge, and late Fellow of Trinity College. Royal 4to, 420 pages, 25*s.*

\*\*\* The Publishers are directed to offer a limited number of Copies of the Cambridge Observations of former years at the following reduced prices :—

| For the years | | For the years | |
|---|---|---|---|
| 1828 and 29 | at 4*s.* each | 1839 | at 11*s.* 6*d.* |
| 1830, 31, 82, 33, 34, and 85 | 5*s.* year | 1840 and 1841 | 17*s.* 6*d.* |
| 1836 | 8*s.* 6*d.* | 1842 | 17*s.* |
| 1837 | 10*s.* 6*d.* | 1843 | 15*s.* |
| 1838 | 14*s.* | 1844 and 1845 | 18*s.* |

**London:**
CAMBRIDGE WAREHOUSE, 32 PATERNOSTER ROW.
**Cambridge:** DEIGHTON, BELL AND CO.

www.ingramcontent.com/pod-product-compliance
Lightning Source LLC
Chambersburg PA
CBHW081142230426
43664CB00018B/2773